LITERARY CAPITAL

LITERARY
CAPITAL

A Washington Reader

EDITED BY CHRISTOPHER STEN

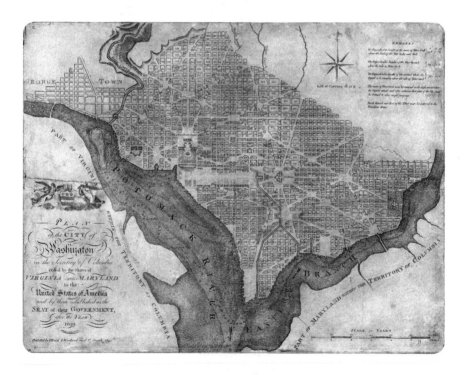

The University of Georgia Press

Athens

Friends Fund publication

Publication of this work was made possible, in part, by a
generous gift from the University of Georgia Friends Fund.

Credits and acknowledgments for previously published
material appear on pages 455–459 and constitute
an extension of this copyright page.

© 2011 by the University of Georgia Press
Athens, Georgia 30602
www.ugapress.org

Designed by April Leidig-Higgins
Set in Garamond by Copperline Book Services, Inc.
Printed and bound by Sheridan Books

The paper in this book meets the guidelines for permanence
and durability of the Committee on Production Guidelines for
Book Longevity of the Council on Library Resources.

Printed in the United States of America

11   12   13   14   15   C   5   4   3   2   1

Library of Congress Cataloging-in-Publication Data
Literary capital : a Washington reader / edited by Christopher Sten.
p.   cm.
Includes bibliographical references and index.
ISBN-13: 978-0-8203-3836-1 (hardcover : alk. paper)
ISBN-10: 0-8203-3836-2 (hardcover : alk. paper)
1. Washington (D.C.) — Literary collections.
I. Sten, Christopher, 1944–
PS548.D6L58   2011
810.8'0358753 — dc22   2011009444

FRONTISPIECE
Plan of the City of Washington, by Pierre L'Enfant, 1793.
Courtesy of the David Rumsey Map Collection,
www.davidrumsey.com

CONTENTS

CHAPTER TWO

Eye of the Storm

Race, Slavery, Civil War (1830–1905)

65

CHAPTER THREE

Vanity Fair

Reconstruction and National Expansion (1865–1910)

117

CHAPTER FOUR

City of Hope and Heartbreak

Minority Reports (1880–2000)

211

CHAPTER SEVEN

Imperial Washington

Power, Corruption, Crisis (1950–2010)

373

ACKNOWLEDGMENTS

Washington is a city that attracts readers as well as writers. It has been my pleasure and good fortune to have received help and encouragement, along with suggestions for additional selections for this collection, from some of the best of them. Among my colleagues (and friends) at George Washington University, I wish to thank G. David Anderson, Antonio Lopez, Jody Bolz, Patricia Chu, John Donaldson, David McAleavey, Robert McRuer, James A. Miller, Faye Moskowitz, and Ann Romines, as well as Constance Kibler, Najiyah Williams, and Rebecca Wood for technical assistance; among colleagues and friends elsewhere, I am especially grateful to Howard Gillette, Robert S. Levine, Sarah Luria, Jessica Matthews, E. Ethelbert Miller, Samuel Otter, and Robert K. Wallace. All of them stretched my original conception of this project or suggested additional material. Among friends, I want to acknowledge especially the contributions of Ben Beach, Paul Carlson, Kathryn Higgins, Jet Lowe, Rodger Schlickeisen, and Jeffrey Seltzer, who showed an abiding interest in this collection and offered suggestions or technical help. Some time ago, I also benefited from a lively discussion with Jeffrey Charis-Carlson, then a doctoral student at the University of Iowa completing a dissertation on the Washington novel, who tracked me down at my office one day to talk about Washington writing.

In recent weeks and months, while this volume has been in production at the University of Georgia Press, I have accumulated additional debts — debts I eagerly acknowledge here with heartfelt gratitude: To Nancy Grayson, executive editor of the press, who believed in this project from the beginning and has supported it in ways large and small; to Assistant Acquisitions Editor Beth Snead, whose energy and skill came to the rescue countless times while securing permission for the many selections covered by copyright; to Dawn McIlvain Stahl, my copy editor, whose prodigious efforts and attention to detail made this a more authoritative collection and saved me from many a misstep; and to Jon Davies, the press's managing editor, who guided me through the intricacies of map making and image selection and provided other technical support. I could not have asked for more expert assistance or more generous-minded support than all of these people were quick to supply; they made production of this project possible, and every step along the way a pleasure for me.

Heartfelt thanks are due also to Peg Barratt, dean of Columbian College of Arts and Sciences, and Gayle Wald, chair of the English Department at George Washington University for generous funding assistance during the late stages of production, when the bills for permission for this volume came due.

Last and most importantly, I wish to thank my wife, Jan, whose love and faith in this project have sustained my efforts over many years. This volume is dedicated to her.

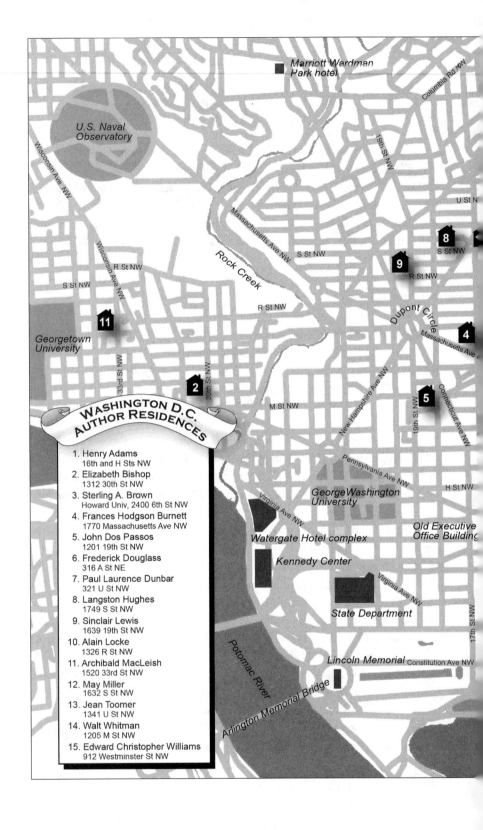

Marriott Wardman
Park hotel

Columbia Rd NW

U.S. Naval
Observatory

19th St NW

U St N

Wisconsin Ave NW

Massachusetts Ave NW

S St NW

8

S St NW

Wisconsin Ave NW

R St NW

9

R St NW

R St NW

S St NW

Rock Creek

R St NW

Dupont Circle

Massachusetts Ave

4

11

Georgetown
University

33rd St NW

30th St NW

2

M St NW

New Hampshire Ave NW

19th St NW

Connecticut Ave NW

5

WASHINGTON D.C.
AUTHOR RESIDENCES

1. Henry Adams
   16th and H Sts NW
2. Elizabeth Bishop
   1312 30th St NW
3. Sterling A. Brown
   Howard Univ, 2400 6th St NW
4. Frances Hodgson Burnett
   1770 Massachusetts Ave NW
5. John Dos Passos
   1201 19th St NW
6. Frederick Douglass
   316 A St NE
7. Paul Laurence Dunbar
   321 U St NW
8. Langston Hughes
   1749 S St NW
9. Sinclair Lewis
   1639 19th St NW
10. Alain Locke
    1326 R St NW
11. Archibald MacLeish
    1520 33rd St NW
12. May Miller
    1632 S St NW
13. Jean Toomer
    1341 U St NW
14. Walt Whitman
    1205 M St NW
15. Edward Christopher Williams
    912 Westminster St NW

Pennsylvania Ave NW

George Washington
University

H St NW

Virginia Ave NW

Old Executive
Office Building

Watergate Hotel complex

Kennedy Center

Virginia Ave NW

State Department

17th St NW

Lincoln Memorial

Constitution Ave NW

Potomac River

Arlington Memorial Bridge

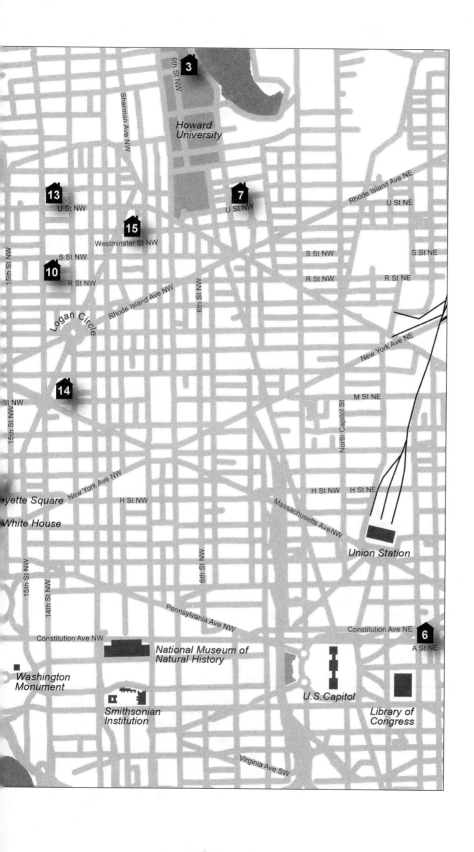

6th St NW

3

Sherman Ave NW

Howard University

Rhode Island Ave NE

U St NE

13
U St NW

7
U St NW

S St NW

S St NE

15
Westminster St NW

15th NW

S St NW

R St NW

R St NE

10
R St NW

Rhode Island Ave NW

Logan Circle

6th St NW

New York Ave NE

14

M St NE

15th St NW

North Capitol St

New York Ave NW

H St NW

H St NE

·yette Square

White House

Massachusetts Ave NW

H St NW

H St NE

15th NW

14th St NW

6th St NW

Union Station

Pennsylvania Ave NW

Constitution Ave NE

6
A St NE

Constitution Ave NW

National Museum of Natural History

Washington Monument

U.S. Capitol

Library of Congress

Smithsonian Institution

Virginia Ave SW

LITERARY CAPITAL

INTRODUCTION

WASHINGTON HAS always been a magnet for writers, a source of interest and fascination for poets, essayists, and novelists no less than for journalists, commentators, and other media figures who report on life in the nation's capital. However, the nature of the writing has changed, becoming more varied and sophisticated over the past two centuries, as the city has evolved from a frontier village to a metropolis with instant, global connections. The first writers were outsiders: visitors, tourists, and short-term residents; and the forms of writing that predominated were letters, travel essays, and autobiographical pieces, with only occasionally a poem, a humorous sketch, or a chapter or two of a novel. After the Civil War, professional writers, such as Mark Twain and Bret Harte, drawn to the city by jobs in politics and journalism, began to see it as a place to work and live — temporarily, if not permanently. African American writers especially — Frederick Douglass, Anna Cooper, and Paul Laurence Dunbar, for example — were attracted to the city by the hope of employment and the promise of equal treatment by the national government that controlled the city, with the important consequence that Washington became host to an African American literary community before any other kind of literary community took hold. These professional and African American authors wrote fiction, memoirs, essays, and poems, sometimes with an eye on the operations of the federal government, but often with an eye on everyday life in the city.

Early in the twentieth century, Washington began to produce native-born writers too, notably Jean Toomer (1894–1967) and Sterling A. Brown (1901–89), the one an avant-garde fiction writer and poet, the other a vernacular poet and professor of African American literature and folk life. However, by far the largest number of "local" authors have been transplants — people who have chosen to make Washington their home for a significant period or a lifetime — teachers, government workers, manual laborers, amateur and professional authors. This mix of local and transplanted writers has grown steadily in strength and diversity over the past hundred years and more, until it exploded in the last several decades, making Washington one of the most active centers of literary production in the United States.

Unlike other U.S. cities, however, Washington is also, as Frederick Douglass once said, "the capital of the whole nation." As such, it is and has been the center of national and international attention, including that of literary artists. From the early days of the Republic, Washington has had a writing scene that is national in scope, created mainly by outsiders with national reputations and an eye for controversy or a big story — authors such as John Greenleaf Whittier, Norman Mailer, or Mary McCarthy. These writers are often personally involved in political debates over nationally contentious issues such as abolition, the Union, the Vietnam War, and the Nixon-Watergate debacle; or they are eager to investigate and write about shadowy government operations or scandals — influence peddling, congressional profiteering, presidential improprieties, and the like — centered in the nation's capital. The two traditions — the one local, the other national — have developed side by side, often with a good deal of interplay between them, making Washington writing an unusually rich and resonant, if sometimes schizoid, body of work, with the national government serving as a backdrop, or foil, to the featured lives of local residents.

Founded as the new nation's capital in 1800, on land chosen by George Washington and located at the confluence of the Potomac and Anacostia rivers, the city is situated in former slave territory on a parallel between North and South, a decision that was of critical importance at the time and has remained so for over two hundred years. Indeed, the long shadow of slavery, race, and sectional rivalry remains in evidence still, in the form of a majority black population; high unemployment among the city's young people; and racial divisions between neighborhoods, such as the social and economic gulf that splits the largely black neighborhood of Anacostia in Southeast D.C. from the white enclaves in Northwest D.C. Adding to these examples is the longstanding distrust on the part of Congress toward "home rule" and statehood for a city with a majority black (and in recent decades, largely Democratic) population.

At first nothing more than a muddy village, surrounded by forests and lacking all but the most basic amenities, Washington became known, in Charles Dickens's somewhat satiric phrase, as the city of "magnificent intentions," thanks to Pierre L'Enfant's ambitious design, with its expansive vistas linking the government's central buildings and wide, European-style boulevards running at diagonals. By the middle of the nineteenth century, the city's development was finally starting to catch up to these early aspirations. With the coming of the Civil War and its aftermath of Reconstruction and the Gilded Age, Washington began to emerge as a full-fledged, modern city, with a large federal workforce, up-to-date transportation and communication systems, a lucrative real estate market, and brisk commercial and tourist trade. By the early 1960s, President John F. Kennedy would capture something of the changing character of Washington when he observed, tongue in cheek, that it was a city of southern efficiency and northern charm.

As the nation's capital, situated near the northern rim of the slave states that made up the old South, Washington has always had a complex, conflicted character, split along several related fault lines — national/local, northern/southern, slave/free, white/black, urban/rural, conservative/liberal. On the one hand, George Washington, Thomas Jefferson, Pierre L'Enfant, and the city's other early planners and builders had great ambitions for the city as the capital of a shining new republic, with national institutions — the Capitol, the executive mansion, the judiciary, a national bank, a university, a mercantile exchange — laid out across a generous and stately landscape. It was to be built on a Roman model, reflecting republican values expressed in architecture worthy of the seat of a large and expanding sovereign nation. On the other hand, the city was being built in what was still the rural South (below the Mason-Dixon Line), using a good deal of slave labor and without the advantages of established commercial trade or transportation systems. Although George Washington had imagined the city as one day becoming a thriving commercial center with close ties to markets and resources beyond the Appalachian Mountains, the men who served in Congress in the early decades were often less interested in providing for the needs of the District of Columbia than in serving the interests of their home districts or their own pockets. Lacking any voting representation in Congress, the city lost out to Baltimore and other urban centers in the race to develop rivers and rail lines to serve the commercial interests of farms, plantations, and towns along the eastern seaboard and into the country's interior.[1] Indeed, the combination of a powerful Congress, with its hands on the purse strings, and a local leadership, with limited fiscal and legislative powers, has tended to limit Washington's economic development throughout its history.

For other reasons, too, the city was destined to remain hardly more than a glorified village — a "company town," as historian James Sterling Young has called it — until well into the last century.[2] Congressional sessions were originally just three months long, so representatives rarely bothered to establish homes in Washington. Living in hotels or rented rooms, they had little incentive to feel invested in the city. Even in more recent times, when sessions ran longer, the city all but closed down for the summer, and members of Congress went home. Finally, the advent of air-conditioning in the 1950s made it possible for the federal workforce to function year-round. That one technological advance made Washington livable throughout the four seasons. It also helped to make it more urban, more cosmopolitan, and more modern, as it is today — an international city and environs with an expanding population of job seekers, refugees, lobbyists, embassy workers, and international trade and finance people eager to make their homes in Washington for a political season of several years' duration, if not permanently.

The first people to write about Washington in the early 1800s were typically travelers — short-term visitors, journalists, petitioners, and occasionally politicians or statesmen. Abigail Adams, wife of the second president, was something of an exception (early novelist and cultural historian Margaret Bayard Smith, who moved to Washington with her journalist husband at the urging of President Jefferson, was another). Even Adams, however, came for only a brief period, at the end of her husband's single term in office. What she found in what she called "this wilderness city" did not make her want to stay: unfinished rooms in the president's house, an absence of firewood for the hearth, no bells to call the servants, and "nothing" by way of shopping, even in the nearby village of George Town. The first writers typically made brief stops in Washington, and their writing about the city was generally limited to first impressions — descriptions of the empty landscape and the impressive, if unfinished, architecture; the wide range of interesting, educated personalities (as Washington Irving had claimed); and the cramped and "shabby" social events, as one early English visitor called them. Many were famous authors — Frances Trollope (or her novelist son, Anthony), Charles Dickens, Alexis de Tocqueville, and America's expatriate son, Henry James — who traveled from abroad to Washington as part of an extended tour of the States. Their accounts appeared in Europe as letters or essays in journals or chapters in travel books, such as Dickens's *American Notes* (1842) and James's *The American Scene* (1907). These accounts provided rich, if subjective, portraits of life in the nation's capital at the time — life as witnessed by educated outsiders and people of privilege. They are valuable as detailed snapshots of the city at particular moments in its history and as points of comparison with other U.S. and foreign urban centers from the same period, as in the case of James's observation of Washington as an unusual "City of Conversation," not the "vulgar vociferous Market" found elsewhere in the United States.

Some early writers went to Washington on personal business, as petitioners of the government, office seekers, or job seekers, and left behind personal accounts of their experiences, in letters or journal entries; others turned their experience into more formal, literary productions. James Fenimore Cooper, for instance, visited in 1822 — the first of at least two such occasions — in an effort to settle some long-standing debts owed him by the navy; Herman Melville, desperate for gainful employment, hoped, on two occasions, to land a job with a consulate abroad. Cooper sent letters home to his wife describing his pleasure at the progress he witnessed in the construction of the Capitol building following a visit he had made years earlier, but he still did not find it grand enough for his taste. Melville, by contrast, turned a brief visit to the Capitol into two late chapters of his fantasy novel *Mardi* (1849), in which he offers a broad satire on the kingly pretensions of members of Congress. Later, both Bret Harte and Paul Laurence Dunbar, job seekers themselves, wrote stories about office seekers — innocent, frustrated figures who lose heart when they discover they lack the powerful connections needed to land a job with the government. A generation or two later, Willa Cather told a somewhat similar tale, one based on observations made while visiting her uncle in the nation's capital, in the "Tom Outland" section of *The Professor's House* (1925), providing a cold-eyed assessment of the careerism of Washington's managerial class and their anxious underlings.

Another kind of Washington writing is represented by John Greenleaf Whittier, who in the 1840s put aside his formal writing and traveled to the capital to work as a journalist. Whittier came to serve as the literary editor of the abolitionist *National Era* but was soon writing in outrage to a newspaper back home about the presence of slave markets in the federal city, within a stone's throw of the Capitol building and other monuments to democratic and republican principles — liberty, equality, and the rule of law. Well-known writers from practically every generation — Nathaniel Hawthorne, Henry James, John Dos Passos, and Mary McCarthy — have ventured to Washington to report on developments or decisions made there, and sometimes to lobby or agitate as well. Black writers in particular have a long history of reporting on the news coming out of Washington; and some, like W. E. B. Du Bois, editor of *The Crisis*, and James Weldon Johnson, went on to assume leadership roles in the fight for reform of the nation's discriminatory laws and judicial decisions in the area of civil rights and social and political equality. Of these, no one better represents the reporter turned activist or lobbyist than Frederick Douglass, the abolitionist orator and newspaper editor who traveled to Washington several times to try to convince President Lincoln to issue executive orders permitting free black Americans to join the Union army and receive pay and treatment equal to that of whites, a story he tells in detail in *The Life and Times of Frederick Douglass* (1881). Douglass finally moved to Washington in 1872 and spent the rest of his life as a resident of the city, holding a number of important public service jobs there and serving as the major spokesman for African Americans, both locally and nationally. By the time he arrived, the population of the city was almost one-third African American; less then a century later, African Americans had become the majority.[3]

In the early days, black slaves were brought to Washington to help build the public buildings and the city's infrastructure. Before long, the city had become an important slave-trading center, at least until the Compromise of 1850, when the portion of the District of Columbia on the west bank of the Potomac River, including the slave-trading city of Alexandria, was retroceded to Virginia in exchange for an end to the slave trade in what remained of Washington, D.C. All the while, free blacks (and poor Irish immigrants) were coming to the city as well, in search of work in construction and domestic service. Although the buying and selling of slaves had been outlawed, the federal government did not make slavery illegal in Washington until April 1862 — a year before Lincoln signed the Emancipation Proclamation eliminating slavery in the Confederate States. Then, since Congress held the purse strings and Radical Republicans were in the ascendancy, there followed a period of relative equality (though little integration), until well after Reconstruction, with blacks and whites earning roughly equal pay for comparable work. This included the job of teaching in the D.C. public schools. This is one reason a good many African Americans writers — Anna Cooper, Mary Church Terrell, and Edward Christopher Williams most prominently — turned to working in the schools, particularly the famous M Street School (later Dunbar High School) in Northwest D.C. Here, despite their status as members of an estranged minority, they could use their education, engage in important work, and be paid a regular wage. (Their students, too, benefited from this arrangement, with large numbers — Sterling A. Brown and Jean Toomer among them — receiving an excellent education, in spite of segregation.)

Equalities achieved in the job market, public accommodations, and the transportation system during Reconstruction, however, were largely overturned in the decades afterward, leading to the sort of powerful complaints voiced by Mary Church Terrell in "What It Means to Be Colored in the United States Capital" (1906). With the 1912 inauguration of Woodrow Wilson, a southerner with a largely southern cabinet, blacks lost further ground, even in the federal workplace. This situation persisted until the early days of the Civil Rights Movement in the 1950s, though even then progress was slow, up to and beyond the assassination of Martin Luther King Jr. in April 1968, an event that sparked fiery riots along the Fourteenth Street corridor in Northwest Washington. Socially, the city remained largely segregated along racial lines through much of the last century, despite notable exceptions early on in otherwise mostly white neighborhoods near Dupont Circle (the educational salon of Anna Cooper at 1706 Seventeenth St. NW, for example) and on U Street in Northwest D.C., where black business owners, artists, writers, and intellectuals came together to build a viable commercial, artistic, and entertainment center, as exemplified by the then-famous Lincoln Theater and Bohemian Caverns.

Southern blacks in particular were attracted to Washington because of its strong public schools and the presence of Howard University, the flagship among historically black colleges. Chartered by Congress just after the Civil War, in 1867, and designated for regular federal funding, Howard was an example of the Radical Republicans' plan to use Washington as a "testing ground," as the historian Constance McLaughlin Green has explained, for Reconstruction measures elsewhere in the South.[4] Admitting both blacks and whites, the university educated a number of teachers and writers who taught in the city's public schools, though the schools themselves remained segregated for decades. Howard has also been the home to several notable writers who have held teaching or research positions at the university, notably Sterling A. Brown, in the early decades of the last century, and Alain Locke, the influential philosophy professor and Rhodes Scholar whose 1925 anthology, *The New Negro*, gave the Harlem Renaissance its initial impetus and definition. In fact, Brown and Locke are just two of the early figures from Howard University who contributed to the Harlem Renaissance. Others are the novelist Zora Neale Hurston and May Miller, a Washington poet who is widely regarded as the most important playwright of the movement. Two additional writers who played a significant role in the Harlem Renaissance — writers with no ties to Howard but strong ties to Washington — are Jean Toomer, who grew up in both black and white neighborhoods in the District of Columbia, and Langston Hughes, who came to Washington as a young man to live with his mother and became famous as the "busboy poet," after Vachel Lindsey discovered him while Hughes was working at the Wardman Park hotel on Connecticut Avenue.

Certainly African Americans constitute the most important constellation of writers in the city's history. But Washington has attracted other groups of writers as well, though their involvement in the city is in some cases more transient if no less intense than that of the above-named minority authors. One such group is made up of active participants, celebrity figures, or leaders in historic, politically charged events — demonstrations, marches, rallies, sit-ins — writers who have reported on their experience afterward, in poems, personal narratives, or novels. Allen Ginsberg, Robert Lowell, Robert Bly, and Denise Levertov, well-known poets in their own right, are now widely identified with the anti–Vietnam War movement of the 1960s and 1970s, a time of great political upheaval in the country when Americans were looking for leaders with moral authority who could articulate their outrage and give vent to their frustration with the country's foreign policy. Several novelists too, most notoriously Norman Mailer and Kurt Vonnegut, took their political passions into the streets during this time. But the energies of the nation's novelists have more often found expression in angry, farcical, or otherwise highly charged narratives — political exposés, satires, and muckraking novels.

William Wells Brown, a former slave, might be said to have started this tradition when he published *Clotel; or, The President's Daughter* (1850), a sensational novel that played off the rumor that Thomas Jefferson had fathered a daughter by one of his slaves (in the novel, the president's mixed-race daughter commits a dramatic act of suicide after escaping from a slave pen in the nation's capital). Henry Adams continued the tradition in *Democracy* (1880), an early classic Washington novel that ridiculed the corruptions of the Grant administration. Other authors, some famous, some not so well known — Mark Twain and Charles Dudley Warner, Gertrude Atherton, John Dos Passos, Gore Vidal, Allen Drury — have written novels that read like exposés, targeting the scandalous practices of thinly disguised political figures during specific moments in U.S. history. The related tradition of muckraking fiction about Washington flourished especially in the early decades of the twentieth century, as seen in David Graham Phillips's *The Fashionable Adventures of Joshua Craig, a Novel* (1909), which treated the growing influence of corporate money in the Senate, and in Samuel Hopkins Adams's *Revelry* (1926), mocking the conspiracy and bribery scandals of the Harding administration. In another form, the dystopian novel, Sinclair Lewis's *It Can't Happen Here* (1935) warns against the growing power of the executive branch, portraying a charismatic, totalitarian-minded leader (or a series of such) who takes over the federal government, suspends the Bill of Rights, and runs the country for his personal profit.

Since the 1960s and the rise of postmodernism, some of America's most popular and acclaimed authors have written novels that go beyond muckraking or exposing corruption and chicanery in the nation's capital, laughing it to scorn in fierce satires, as in Phillip Roth's *Our Gang (Starring Tricky and His Friends)* (1971), Kurt Vonnegut's *Jailbird* (1979), Joseph Heller's *Good as Gold* (1976), Robert Coover's *The Public Burning* (1977), and John Updike's *Memories of the Ford Administration, a Novel* (1992). These authors have typically not resided in Washington, but they are careful observers of American culture, national politics included, and have taken on the responsibility of commenting on contemporary America by exploring certain outrages of Washington's recent political history. It is hardly a coincidence that several of these prominent authors take Richard Nixon and his circle as their chief subject. There was something truly outrageous about the behavior and decision making of this president and his cronies, even by Washington standards, that invited the venomous treatment of some of our most prominent writers of contemporary fiction. Even so, there is a long tradition of political satire in writing about Washington, going back through the generation of Henry Adams and Mark Twain to James Kirke Paulding, who made good fun of the blind ambition and rhetorical excesses of members of Congress in *John Bull in America, or the New Munchausen* (1825).

Several other prominent writers, among them Frederick Douglass, Langston Hughes, and Mary Church Terrell, have written more straightforward, but equally angry assessments of Washington — not novels, but essays and lectures, and not targeting particular political personalities, but the whole racist culture of the city or, in Hughes's case, the hypocrisies of the local black upper classes. These are writers who lived in Washington long enough to develop an informed view of the ruling classes in the capital city and expressed their bitter fury at how difficult and disagreeable it was for minorities to reside in their midst. Douglass stirred up a tempest when the Washington press published reports about the lecture he delivered in Baltimore in the spring of 1877, under the title "Our National Capital" — a lecture the local press had overlooked the year before, when he delivered the same speech in Washington — castigating the city's white population for its persistent racism and failure to root out the attitudes of the old slave system.

Other writers, some of whom lived in Washington at least briefly, wrote less emotionally charged, personal accounts of their time in the capital. Because of the timeliness and acuity of their observations, their narratives offer valuable insights into the character and history of the city in earlier periods. These include Walt Whitman, who came to Washington looking for his wounded brother during the early months of the Civil War and stayed for almost a decade. They include Whitman's contemporary, Louisa May Alcott, who came to serve in the women's nursing corps during the Civil War but contracted typhoid and had to return home after becoming deathly ill from mercury poisoning. They also include the relatively unknown Elizabeth Keckley, a former slave who ventured to the city hoping to support herself as a seamstress and ended up working in the White House as a dressmaker for Mary Todd Lincoln. The feminist Anna Cooper is also among them. She moved to Washington to teach at the M Street School and published a memoir detailing her years of friendship with the celebrated family of Francis Grimké, a former slave who, after 1878, served as minister of the well-known Fifteenth Street Presbyterian Church.

Many authors enjoyed official status as federal employees, either in Washington or abroad as foreign consuls. These included such prominent early writers as Washington Irving (Spain), Nathaniel Hawthorne (England), Bret Harte (Germany), Frederick Douglass (Haiti), Henry Highland Garnet (Liberia), and James Weldon Johnson (Venezuela and Nicaragua). These authors were people of many talents, who worked in one field and made time to write in another. In some cases, their writing related to their government work. For example, in his autobiography, Douglass wrote about his roles as U.S. marshal for the District of Columbia, recorder of deeds for the city, chairman of the (failed) Freedman's Savings Bank in Washington, and consul general in Haiti and then in Santo Domingo. In other cases, their writing and work seemed hardly related:

Archibald MacLeish, for example, held a long series of jobs, sometimes simultaneously, under Franklin Delano Roosevelt before and during World War II
as head of the Library of Congress, head of the Office of Facts and Figures,
assistant director of domestic affairs in the Office of War Information, and assistant secretary of state. Most of MacLeish's writing, beyond the large number
of official reports and memoranda he turned out, was national in scope without
being centered in Washington. No one, perhaps, linked his government work
with his Washington writing more closely than Sterling A. Brown, the Howard
University professor who wrote an important essay, "The Negro in Washington" (1937), while under contract with the federal government as national editor
of "Negro affairs" for the Federal Writers' Project.

In some cases, the connection between a given author's government job and
his or her writing was tenuous but worth mentioning in a brief historical account; it suggests that the federal government has supported many of the nation's writers, even as those writers have often supported the government's various missions. The two have not always been at odds with one another, as they
often were in the years of the Vietnam War and after. The activist and suffragist
Mary Church Terrell came to Washington originally to teach English at the
M Street High School, but she eventually went to work at the government's
War Risk Insurance Bureau, even as she was becoming a well-known writer,
speaker, and activist. The dialect poet Paul Laurence Dunbar, who moved to
the city after marrying Anna Cooper, soon took a government job as a book
runner at the Library of Congress. Conversely, Louis J. Halle came to Washington to work as a policy expert in the State Department but soon discovered
a second calling as a nature writer, specializing in the rich flora and fauna he
encountered on his daily bicycle ride through Rock Creek Park and the surrounding countryside.

Several other writers, all poets, have held at least short-term government positions in Washington, where they have been paid to practice their trade as Poetry
Consultants (renamed, in 1985, Poet Laureate Consultants in Poetry) at the Library of Congress. This is a long list that includes many prominent writers, only
three of whom are represented in this anthology: Allen Tate, Elizabeth Bishop,
and Reed Whittemore. Their work includes occasional poems, meditations on
prominent figures or monuments (like the Lincoln Memorial), and satiric fantasies about the demise of the city. W. E. B. Du Bois deserves mention here as
well, as an author who once worked as a consultant, not in Washington but at
a distance, for the Bureau of Labor Statistics, a federal agency headquartered
in the District of Columbia. Ironically, like several other writers, Du Bois was
investigated during the 1940s and 1950s by the Federal Bureau of Investigation
as a possible subversive, then indicted and tried by the Justice Department as an

unregistered agent of a foreign power, only to be finally acquitted. During this Red Scare, a period of national hysteria and persecution of alleged Communists, other writers, including Langston Hughes, came under investigation by the FBI, the House Un-American Activities Committee, or other federal agencies — often mistakenly, or without legal consequence, as in the case of Hughes.

Although many literary representations of Washington have been the work of visitors or short-term residents, such as the Poetry Consultants and Poets Laureate who come and go every year or two, or longer-term residents whose energies are divided among other tasks, there is a significant group of local Washington writers too. These are people who may or may not have been born and raised in Washington but who have made the city their home for many years and have written extensively on local and national subjects related to Washington. These are the authors (the most prominent ones) who are most clearly deserving, in my view, to be called "Washington writers": Frederick Douglass, abolitionist, journalist, autobiographer; Henry Adams, private secretary, novelist, historian, autobiographer; Jean Toomer, poet, short fiction writer, journalist; John Dos Passos, novelist, journalist, essayist; Sterling A. Brown, educator, linguist, historian, poet; Gore Vidal, novelist, playwright, memoirist, political commentator; Allen Drury, journalist and novelist; Ward Just, reporter, novelist, and short story writer; May Miller, poet and playwright; E. Ethelbert Miller, poet, editor, mentor; Edward P. Jones, short story writer and novelist; Susan Richards Shreve, novelist, essayist, children's writer; Marita Golden, novelist, memoirist, and essayist; George P. Pelecanos, crime fiction writer and producer/screenwriter for the HBO series *The Wire*, which is set in nearby Baltimore. Of these, Toomer, Brown, Golden, Jones, and Pelecanos were born and came of age in the city.

The work of these native or naturalized Washington writers is often less overtly political, less preoccupied with national politics, and more consistently devoted to the local scene — to ordinary people and everyday life in the nation's capital — than is the writing of authors not usually identified with Washington, such as Joseph Heller (*Good as Gold*) or Kurt Vonnegut (*Jailbird*), who play for the big political statement. There are exceptions to this characterization of native Washington writers, of course: Henry Adams and Gore Vidal are two important ones. However, in these more muted, local productions, the government and monumental setting of the city and the public history centered there — slavery, the Civil War, the New Deal, the Red Scare, the Kennedy era, Watergate — are incidental or partial; they may form the backdrop for a story or poem, but in many cases, no more than that. The narratives of Marita Golden and Edward P. Jones, two authors who write about indigenous characters and families, are perhaps the clearest examples of this more intensely local kind of writing. The work of Edward Christopher Williams and Andrew Holleran (also Louis Bayard and Ed Cox) are additional examples of intensely self-conscious local writing, in these instances, writing about the experience of closeted and uncloseted gays. However, sometimes Washington's official setting and history are woven so subtly into the fabric of a work that they risk being overlooked in our estimation of its larger meaning. Consider Toomer's short story "Avey," where the author briefly, quietly hints at an explanation for the title character's life-killing lethargy, when the Capitol building suddenly looms in the early morning distance "like a gray ghost ship drifting in from sea" (49), an ironic, arresting reference to the slave ships of the Middle Passage. These authors are principally devoted to fictional studies of character and generational conflict; the presence of official Washington, though it can sometimes feature in important ways, is muted. While there is no such thing as a "school" of Washington writing, there are three or four generations of homegrown or naturalized authors — extraordinary writers with regional, national, and international reputations — who constitute a tradition of Washington writing. Add to this list the work of gifted authors like Susan Richards Shreve and Ward Just and, more recently, Thomas Mallon and Andrew Holleran, and it is clear that local Washington writing has blossomed into something rich, robust, and remarkable. Beyond this, of course, Washington is currently home to many more writers not included in this anthology — gifted, nationally prominent writers — whose principal work happens not to be set in Washington or connected with its history.

In compiling this collection, I have tried to provide the reader with broad historical exposure to writing on Washington, from the city's founding in 1800 to the present, or nearly so. My aim has been to be generously inclusive but not all-encompassing. At first, I intended to limit the selections to work by Americans, particularly prominent ones, but finally decided I could not exclude examples of the writings of important British and French travelers (Dickens, Trollope, and de Tocqueville), particularly from the first century of Washington's history. What I have sought to create is a collection of representative writings in a wide range of genres — fiction, poetry, essays, letters, chronicles, travel writing — always looking for skillful writing and a telling incident or moment when the author reveals a felt knowledge of the city or a lively connection with its past or present, real or imagined. I began by collecting the Washington writings of the authors I teach, classic American authors like Walt Whitman, Herman Melville, Henry Adams, Jean Toomer, Willa Cather, John Dos Passos, and Gore Vidal, supplemented by the work of local authors I have encountered in many years of living and working in the city. The more I dug, the more I found. Hoping to flesh out the historical and literary record even more, I began to search through local libraries and special collections for works lost to contemporary memory — out-of-print publications, rare early editions, titles unfamiliar even to scholars and specialists. What I found was more than I could have imagined — the work of close to two hundred writers, including some truly marvelous surprises, such as Solomon Northup's *Twelve Years a Slave* (1853) and the early epistolary novel by Edward Christopher Williams, *When Washington Was in Vogue* (originally published serially under a different title in 1925–26 but rediscovered in 1994 and reissued in 2003). In the end, I have tried to convey a sense of the remarkable range of standard authors who have written about Washington, along with a healthy sampling of the large number of local writers the city can claim as its own, almost from the beginning, but particularly in the decades after 1970. My hope is that the general reader and the specialist, the historical-minded tourist as well as the interested native, will find many fresh discoveries here, will feel inspired to read more deeply in the works of the represented authors, and will be on the lookout for other examples of Washington writing, old and new.

NOTES

1. For discussion of Washington's early economic development, see David R. Goldfield, "Antebellum Washington in Context: The Pursuit of Prosperity and Identity," in *Southern City, National Ambition: The Growth of Early Washington, D.C., 1800–1860*, ed. Howard Gillette Jr. (Washington, D.C.: Center for Washington Area Studies, 1995), 1–20. See also Gillette's introduction, iii–viii.

2. James Sterling Young, *The Washington Community, 1800–1828* (New York: Harcourt, Brace & World, 1966), xi.

3. Constance McLaughlin Green, *Washington: A History of the Capital, 1800–1950* (Princeton: Princeton University Press, 1962), 306.

4. Ibid., 308–9, 336–37.

CHAPTER ONE

"THIS WILDERNESS CITY"

Early Impressions

[1800–1860]

THE FIRST GENERATIONS of writers to see Washington witnessed a city in the making. When the nation's capital was moved from Philadelphia in 1800, the new President's House was hardly finished, the roads were a muddy mess, and the commercial ports of George Town and Alexandria were miles away. Abigail Adams vividly recounted her feelings about "this wilderness city," with its "beautiful" setting but lack of comforts and commercial life, in letters to her daughter. Not long after the city's founding, however, Washington Irving and James Fenimore Cooper were praising the levees at the President's House and the "constant round of banqueting, reveling, and dancing," as well as the visible beginnings of a city of grandeur. George Watterston provided an early description of the Capitol and the oratory of the day, while also commenting on the presence of prostitutes and blacks in the gallery; and Margaret Bayard Smith captured the miseries of poor Irish immigrants and free blacks scratching out an existence in the wilds beyond the capital. European diplomats were still complaining in the 1820s and 1830s about the "purgatory" of a winter in Washington and making invidious comparisons with the heady social activities at home, but Frances Trollope was charmed by the public buildings and the lack of commercial hustle so evident in other American cities, though also distressed by the Federal Indian Policy then being debated in Congress. Charles Dickens, on the other hand, considered the city as at best a place of "magnificent intentions" and was genuinely appalled by the debates over slavery and other signs of venality and self-aggrandizement in Congress, a view shared by his contemporary, Herman Melville.

(OVERLEAF) View from the Capitol to the White House along Pennsylvania Avenue, engraving by J. B. Neagle, 1836, after a drawing by J. R. Smith, ca. 1800. From Conrad Malte-Brun, *A System of Universal Geography* (Boston, 1834). Courtesy of George Washington University Special Collections.

ABIGAIL ADAMS

Abigail Adams (1744–1818) is best known today for her loving yet frank letters to her husband, John Adams, the second president of the United States. However, she carried on an extensive correspondence with other family members and friends as well, including her daughter, Mrs. Smith, whom she addressed in late 1800, shortly after arriving in the new capital for the first time. Similar, more-detailed letters containing her initial impressions of Washington City and nearby George Town were addressed to her sister at about the same time. *The Letters of Mrs. Adams, the Wife of John Adams* (1840), originally published by her grandson, Charles Francis Adams, is a valuable collection containing some of the earliest extant descriptions of the federal city, during the time when the President's House, not yet the White House, was located far from the center of government.

From *Letters of Mrs. Adams, the Wife of John Adams*

To Mrs. Smith.
Washington, 21 November, 1800.

My Dear Child,
I arrived here on Sunday last, and without meeting with any accident worth noticing, except losing ourselves when we left Baltimore, and going eight or nine miles on the Frederick road, by which means we were obliged to go the other eight through woods, where we wandered two hours without finding a guide, or the path. Fortunately, a straggling black came up with us, and we engaged him as a guide, to extricate us out of our difficulty; but woods are all you see, from Baltimore until you reach *the city*, which is only so in name. Here and there is a small cot[tage], without a glass window, interspersed amongst the forests, through which you travel miles without seeing any human being. In the city there are buildings enough, if they were compact and finished, to accommodate Congress and those attached to it; but as they are, and scattered as they are, I see no great comfort for them. The river, which runs up to Alexandria, is in full view of my window, and I see the vessels as they pass and repass. The house is upon a grand and superb scale, requiring about thirty servants to attend and keep the apartments in proper order, and perform the ordinary business of the house and stables; an establishment very well proportioned to the President's salary. The lighting the apartments, from the kitchen to parlours and chambers, is a tax indeed; and the fires we are obliged to keep to secure us from daily agues is another very cheering comfort. To assist us in this

great castle, and render less attendance necessary, bells are wholly wanting, not one single one being hung through the whole house, and promises are all you can obtain. This is so great an inconvenience, that I know not what to do, or how to do. The ladies from Georgetown and in the city have many of them visited me. Yesterday I returned fifteen visits, — but such a place as George-town appears — why, our Milton is beautiful. But no comparisons; — if they will put me up some bells, and let me have wood enough to keep fires, I design to be pleased. I could content myself almost anywhere three months; but, sur-rounded with forests, can you believe that wood is not to be had, because people cannot be found to cut and cart it! Briesler entered into a contract with a man to supply him with wood. A small part, a few cords only, has he been able to get. Most of that was expended to dry the walls of the house before we came in, and yesterday the man told him it was impossible for him to procure it to be cut and carted. He has had recourse to coals; but we cannot get grates made and set. We have, indeed, come into *a new country.*

You must keep all this to yourself, and, when asked how I like it, say that I write you the situation is beautiful, which is true. The house is made habitable, but there is not a single apartment finished, and all withinside, except the plas-tering, has been done since Briesler came. We have not the least fence, yard, or other convenience, without, and the great unfinished audience-room I make a drying-room of, to hang up the clothes in. The principal stairs are not up, and will not be this winter. Six chambers are made comfortable; two are occupied by the President and Mr. Shaw; two lower rooms, one for a common parlour, and one for a levee-room. Up stairs there is the oval room, which is designed for the drawing room, and has the crimson furniture in it. It is a very hand-some room now; but, when completed, it will be beautiful. If the twelve years, in which this place has been considered as the future seat of government, had been improved, as they would have been if in New England, very many of the present inconveniences would have been removed. It is a beautiful spot, capable of every improvement, and, the more I view it, the more I am delighted with it.

Since I sat down to write, I have been called down to a servant from Mount Vernon, with a billet from Major Custis, and a haunch of venison, and a kind, congratulatory letter from Mrs. Lewis, upon my arrival in the city, with Mrs. Washington's love, inviting me to Mount Vernon, where, health permitting, I will go, before I leave this place.

The Senate is much behind-hand. No Congress has yet been made. 'Tis said —— is on his way, but travels with so many delicacies in his rear, that he cannot get on fast, lest some of them should suffer.

Thomas comes in and says a House is made; so to-morrow, though Saturday, the President will meet them. Adieu, my dear. Give my love to your brother, and tell him he is ever present upon my mind.

Affectionately your mother,
A. Adams.

To Mrs. Smith.
Washington, 27 November, 1800.

My Dear Child,

I received your letter by Mr. Pintard. Two articles we are much distressed for; the one is bells, but the more important one is wood. Yet you cannot see wood for trees. No arrangement has been made, but by promises never performed, to supply the newcomers with fuel. Of the promises Briesler had received his full share. He had procured nine cords of wood; between six and seven of that was kindly burnt up to dry the walls of the house, which ought to have been done by the commissioners, but which, if left to them, would have remained undone to this day. Congress poured in, but shiver, shiver. No woodcutters nor carters to be had at any rate. We are now indebted to a Pennsylvania wagon to bring us, through the first clerk in the Treasury Office, one cord and a half of wood, which is all we have for this house, where twelve fires are constantly required, and where, we are told, the roads will soon be so bad that it cannot be drawn. Briesler procured two hundred bushels of coals or we must have suffered. This is the situation of almost every person. The public officers have sent to Philadelphia for wood-cutters and wagons.

You will read in the answer to the House to the President's Speech a full and explicit approbation of the Administration; a cooperation with him equal to his utmost expectations; this passed without an amendment of any debate or squabble, and has just now been delivered by the House in a body. The vessel which has my clothes and other matters is not arrived. The ladies are impatient for a drawing room; I have no looking-glasses but dwarfs for this house; nor a twentieth part lamps enough to light it. Many things were stolen, many more broken, by the removal; amongst the number, my tea china is more than half missing. Georgetown affords nothing. My rooms are very pleasant and warm whilst the doors of the hall are closed.

You can scarce believe that here in this wilderness city, I should find my time so occupied as it is. My visitors, some of them, come three and four miles. The return of one of them is the work of one day; most of the ladies reside in Georgetown or in scattered parts of the city at two and three miles distance. Mrs. Otis, my nearest neighbour, is at lodgings almost half a mile from me; Mrs. Senator Otis, two miles.

We have all been very well as yet; if we can by any means get wood, we shall not let our fires go out, but it is at a price indeed; from four dollars it has risen to nine. Some say it will fall, but there must be more industry than is to be found here to bring half enough to the market for the consumption of the inhabitants.

> With kind remembrance to all friends
> I am your truly affectionate mother,
> A. A.

CHRISTIAN HINES

Born in Maryland, Christian Hines (1781–??) was a young boy when his family moved to Washington. His *Recollections of Washington City* (1866) covers the period 1796 to 1814, starting when he was in his early teens, but it wasn't written until 1865 when Hines was eighty-five years old, and it was composed without notes. Some historians have questioned his memory about certain details, but others have found it reliable, particularly when corroborating evidence is available. According to the *Columbia Historical Society Records* (vols. 42–43, p. 108), Hines was "a prominent citizen" and "a member of the Common Council, 1825 & 1826, and at a period well-to-do."

My Early Days
From *Recollections of Washington City*

About this time [1798] business was beginning to be pretty brisk in Washington. Some of the public buildings were nearly finished, and others were in a state of advancement. People began to talk about settling here, and selected such lots as would suit best the business they were engaged in respectively. Some settled at the Navy Yard, a few about the Capitol, and others about the Treasury office as far down F street as St. Patrick's Church. This locality was the most thickly settled at that time. . . .

THE FIRST HOUSE we lived in was an old two-story frame on F Street north, between Twenty-third and Twenty-fourth streets west. This house is standing yet, and is now owned and occupied by a colored man named Foster. At that time Washington might have been truly called the city of magnificent distances. Our neighbors were few and far between, the nearest being William King, Esq., who lived in a brick house near the corner of F and Twentieth streets. . . .

IN THIS YEAR the Government commenced building the Navy Yard wharf, the timber for which was nearly all taken from the white oak slashes in the northern part of the city. A large number of citizens who could handle the axe commenced the work of felling and hewing trees for that purpose. . . . My father, who was a Zimmerman, or coarse carpenter, and could handle the broadaxe pretty well, and my three older brothers, John, Henry, and Daniel, joined in the work with the others. . . .

PENNSYLVANIA AVENUE

I am confident that when I first saw Pennsylvania avenue there was not one house on it. The first house I remember to have seen was Jones' coachmaker shop, a two-story frame a little east of the Old Depot, on the north side of the avenue. This was in the year 1799 or 1800, two or three years after I left Greenleaf's Point. The commons, where now the avenue is, from the foot of Capitol Hill westward, was almost impassable for vehicles of any kind; indeed, it was difficult for a person to walk, in some places, on account of the mud, bushes, thorns, briers, &c., and more particularly on the south side, where the clumps of thorn bushes in some places were so thick that, I believe, they were cut down with scythes so as to enable the workmen to make a footway to Fifteenth street. This they did by carting earth, gravel, chips of freestone, &c., on both sides of the avenue, to the full extent, until a tolerably good footway was made all the way along. On the north side of the street it was not quite so bad, because the road from Georgetown to the Capitol ran pretty much on high ground from about Ninth street, in a southeasterly direction, passing along the foot of the hill below Blodgett's Hotel, (where the Post Office now stands;) thence by McGirk's little jail, and on past the rear of Jackson Hall to Tiber Creek, and thence to the foot of Capitol Hill, where it turned southward and passed along where Breckinridge's church was afterwards erected.

After the footways were completed they commenced filling and levelling the centre of the avenue until a pretty good road had been made of it. Shortly after this (I believe in 1801) the planting of trees was commenced along the avenue. The manner of planting them was rather singular. A row was planted on each side of the street, near where the curbstones were to be set, and in addition to this there were two more rows, of equal distance from the curbstones, and much nearer the centre of the avenue, which left the centre of the avenue quite narrow. The trees were Lombardy poplars, and were planted by an old man named Buntin. I and my younger brothers frequently went down to see old Buntin plant the trees, and I several times saw Mr. Jefferson (the President) there. He was always fond of being where improvements were being made. About this time buildings were being erected on and near the avenue. Among the first houses on the avenue, as well as I can recollect, were the following: A three-story brick house between Eleventh and Twelfth streets, built by William Thompson, Esp., of Georgetown. Here he set up a tinner shop before the house was finished. My brother Jacob, who was then an apprentice, carried on the business for him. This house was, some years since, occupied by Pishey Thompson as a book store. The next house built, I think, was that of Mr. Stettineus, near the Washington Bank; then one by Mr. George Thompson, of Georgetown, followed by one by Mr. Sparrow, and Messrs. John Kennedy, Mr. Morrin, and Mr. Sessford, in the order of their names; then Mr. N. Queen's tavern (sign of the Indian Queen.) This was followed by Davidson's hotel, Bates' auction store, Travers' bake-house, between Eleventh and Twelfth streets, and then a two-story brick house by Mr. Woodward.

One of the first brick yards that I remember was carried on by two brothers named Voss, between the avenue and E and Eleventh and Twelfth streets. The first two lumber yards that I can call to mind were those of Captain Byas, near the bank of the Tiber, (now the canal,) and Mr. Morin, on the Avenue, near Mr. Lepreux's grocery story. Here delegations of the different tribes of Indians would put up when they came to Washington, which was almost every session of Congress, for several years.

WASHINGTON IRVING

Washington Irving (1783–1859), widely regarded as the nation's first professional man of letters, was another early visitor to Washington with friends in high places. Born in New York City into a large patrician family, he planned for a legal career but soon turned to writing satires of New York society, notably *Salmagundi* (1807–8) and the *History of New York* (1809). When he came to Washington in 1811, in an effort to spy out signs of legislation that might prove disastrous to the commercial trading interests of his family, he won friends and influence among a wide range of important Washington figures. Later, he traveled to Europe in search of material and was celebrated there for his writing. That and his earlier politicking paid off in a series of consular appointments over the next two decades: in 1826, he became a diplomatic attaché in Spain; three years later, he was selected to be secretary of the U.S. legation in London. By 1842, he was back in Europe as minister to Spain. His letters to his friend Henry Brevoort and James Kirke Paulding, a member of the Club of Gotham, suggest how quickly Irving came to master the social and political scene in Washington in his early years.

From *Letters of Washington Irving to Henry Brevoort*

City of Washington, Jany. 13th 1811

Dear Brevoort: —

I have been constantly intending to write to you, but you know the hurry and confusion of the life I at present lead, and the distraction of thought which it occasions.... My Journey to Baltimore was terrible and sublime — as full of adventurous matter and direful peril as one of Walter Scott's pantomimic, melodramatic, romantic tales. I was three days on the road, and slept one night in a Log house. Yet somehow or another I lived through it all — and lived merrily into the bargain, for which I thank a large stock of good humour which I put up before my departure from N. York, as traveling stores to last me throughout my expedition. In a word, I left home determined to be pleased with every thing, or if not pleased, to be amused, if I may be allowed the distinction, and I have hitherto kept to my determination....

The ride from Baltimore to Washington was still worse than the former one [between Phila. & Baltimore] — but I had two or three odd geniuses for fellow passengers & made out to amuse myself very well. I arrived at the Inn about dusk and, understanding that Mrs. Madison was to have her levee or drawing room that very evening, I swore by all my gods, I would be there. But how? was the question. I had got away down into Georgetown, & the persons to whom my letters of introduction were directed lived all upon Capitol Hill about three miles off — while the President's house was exactly half way. Here was a nonplus, enough to startle any man of less enterprising spirit — but I had sworn to be there — and I determined to keep my oath, & like Caleb Quotem, to "have a place at the Review." So I mounted with a stout heart to my room, resolved to put on my pease blossoms & silk stockings, gird up my loins — sally forth on my expedition & like a vagabond Knight errant, trust to Providence for success and whole bones. Just as I descended from my attic chamber, full of this valorous spirit, I was met by my landlord, with whom, & the head waiter by the bye, I had held a private cabinet counsel on the subject. Bully Rook informed me that there was a party of gentlemen just going from the house, one of whom, Mr. Fontaine Maury of N. York, had offered his services to introduce me to "the Sublime porte." I cut one of my best opera flourishes, skipped into the dressing room, popped my head into the hands of a sanguinary Jacobinical barber, who carried havoc and desolation into the lower regions of my face, mowed down all the beard on one of my cheeks and laid the other in blood, like a conquered province — and thus like a seconded Banquo, with "Twenty mortal murthers on my head," in a few minutes I emerged from dirt & darkness into the blazing splendour of Mrs. Madison's Drawing room. Here I was most graciously received — found a crowded collection of great and little men, of ugly old women, and beautiful young ones — and in ten minutes was hand and glove with half the people in the assemblage. Mrs. Madison is a fine, portly, buxom dame — who has a smile & pleasant word for every body. Her sisters, Mrs. Cutts & Mrs. Washington are like the two Merry Wives of Windsor — but as to Jemmy Madison — ah! poor Jemmy! he is but a withered little apple-John. But of this no more — perish the thought that would militate against sacred things — Mortals avaunt! touch not the lord's anointed!

Since that memorable evening I have been in a constant round of banqueting, reveling, and dancing — the Congress has been sitting with closed doors, so that I have not seen much of the wisdom of the Nation, but I have had enough matter for observation & entertainment to last me a handful of months. I only want a chosen fellow like yourself to help me wonder, admire, and laugh — as it is I must endeavour to do these things as well as I can by myself.

I am delightfully moored, "head & stern" in the family of John P. Van Ness — Brother of William P. He is an old friend of mine & insisted on my coming to his house the morning after my arrival. The family is very agreeable — Mrs. Van Ness is a pretty & pleasant little woman, & quite gay — then there are two pretty girls likewise — one a Miss Smith, clean from Long Island, her father being Member of Congress; she is a fine blooming country lass, and a great Belle here — you see I am in clover — happy dog! clever Jacob! & all that.

The other evening at the City Assembly I was suddenly introduced to my cousin the congressman from Scaghticoke — and we forthwith became two most loving friends. He is a goodhumoured fellow & with all a very decent country member. He was so overjoyed at the happy coincident of our family compact, that he begged to introduce me to his friend Mr. Simmons. This is a son of old Simmons of N. York of corpulent memory. By dint of steady attention to business — an honest character & a faithful fagging at the heels of Congress he has risen to some post of considerable emolument & respectability. . . .

I received a letter from Mrs. Hoffman the day before yesterday. I would have answered it, but have not time — this letter will do for her as well as yourself. It is now almost one o'clock at night — I must to bed — remember me to all the lads & lassies — Gertrude, Miss Wilkes and the Bonny lasses in Greenwich street, whose fair hands I kiss.

I am my dear fellow
Yours ever
W.I.

Washington, Feb. 7th 1811

Dear Brevoort: —

I am ashamed at not having answered your letter before, but indeed I am too much occupied & indeed distracted here by the multiplicity of objects before me, to write with any degree of coherency.

I wish with all my heart you had come on with me, for my time has passed delightfully. I have become acquainted with almost everybody here, and find the most complete medley of character I ever mingled amongst. As I do not suffer party feelings to bias my mind I have associated with both parties — and have found worthy and intelligent men in both — with honest hearts, enlightened minds, generous feelings and bitter prejudices. A free communication of this kind tends more than anything else to divest a man's mind of party bigotry; to make him regardless of those jaundiced representations of persons & things which he is too apt to have held up to him by party writers, and to beget in him that candid, tolerant, good natured habit of thinking, which I think every man that values his own comfort and utility should strive to cultivate.

You would be amused were you to arrive here just now — to see the odd & heterogeneous circle of acquaintance I have formed. One day I am dining with a knot of honest, furious Federalists, who are damning all their opponents as a set of consummate scoundrels, panders of Bonaparte, &c &c. The next day I dine perhaps with some of the very men I have heard thus anathematized, and find them equally honest, warm, & indignant — and if I take their word for it, I had been dining the day before with some of the greatest knaves in the nation, men absolutely paid & suborned by the British government.

Among my great cronies is General Turreau — who, notwithstanding he is represented abroad as a perfect sanguinary ferocious blood-hound, I have found an exceeding pleasant jocose companion, and a man of shrewdness, information & taste. Latrobe (who is excessively abused here as an extravagant spend-thrift of the public money, &c) is very civil to me. I have been to two or three entertainments at his house, & dine there today with a choice party of intelligent & agreeable men.

To shew you the mode of life I lead, I give you my engagements for this week. On Monday I dined with the mess of Officers at the Barracks — in the evening a Ball at Van Ness's. On Tuesday with my cousin Knickerbocker & several merry Federalists. On Wednesday I dined with General Turreau who had a very pleasant party of Frenchmen & democrats — in the evening at Mrs. Madison's levee, which was brilliant and crowded with interesting men & fine women. On Thursday a dinner at Latrobe's. On Friday a dinner at the Secretary of the Navy's, and in the evening a ball at the Mayor's. Saturday as yet is unengaged — at all these parties you meet with so many intelligent people, that your mind is continually & delightfully exercised.

The Supreme Court has likewise within a day or two brought a crowd of new strangers to the city. Jo. Ingersoll, Clement Biddle, Clymer, Goodloe Harper & several others have arrived — and one of your old flames Miss Keator, with whom Ingersoll is so much in love, as report says. There you see, my good fellow, how much you lost by turning back. This place would suit you to a fraction, as you could find company suitable to every varying mood of mind — and men capable of conversing and giving you information on any subject you wish to be informed. I may compare a place like this to a huge library, where a man may turn to any department of knowledge he pleases, and find an author at hand into which he may dip until his curiosity is satisfied. . . .

> God bless you my dear fellow
> Yours ever
> W. I.

GEORGE WATTERSTON

George Watterston (1783–1854), a lawyer, librarian, novelist, and poet, was appointed by President Madison in 1815 as the young nation's first professional librarian of Congress (a position that had previously been combined with that of clerk of the House of Representatives). The author of more than a dozen titles, many of them published in the federal city, including *The L—— Family at Washington; or, A Winter in the Metropolis* (1822) and *Wanderer in Washington* (1827), Watterston was a satirist whose targets included early versions of blind ambition and the rhetorical excesses of members of Congress.

From *The L—— Family at Washington; or, A Winter in the Metropolis*

Letter XL
City of Washington, ——
From Richard L—— to Moses Y——.

My Dear Moses,
I must take you up where I left you in my last, to preserve the connexion of my narrative. My friend T. and I, after quitting the picture room in the north wing of the capitol, pursued our way through the long wooden passage, where I had met the Cyprian some short time before, and entered a small circular ves-

tibule very handsomely finished. In this we found a young woman dealing out refreshments to the honorable members, with a very smiling and rather *seductive* countenance. We passed on, and ascended a narrow flight of stone steps to the right, till we entered another narrow passage, at the opposite end of which we saw a lady and gentleman, who appeared to be rather more familiar than I thought altogether suited the place. A door on one side of this passage was thrown open by my friend T. and I was suddenly ushered into an apartment, the splendour and magnificence of which really struck me mute with astonishment. I never experienced the effect of architecture before, and did not think it was calculated to produce emotions like those I felt on this occasion. This was the Representatives' Hall, into the gallery of which I had been thus led before I was aware of it. It is built, I understand, according to the plan of Mr. Latrobe, who is allowed to have been a man of fine genius, but who did not receive that encouragement his genius merited. I can give you, my dear Moses, but a very imperfect description of this magnificent Hall — yet, such as it is, be pleased to accept it.

Its form, like the Senate Chamber, is semi-circular, occupying the whole area of the south wing of the Capitol from the second story upwards; twenty-six massive columns of Potomac marble standing on a base of free-stone, support a magnificent dome, painted in a very rich and splendid style, to represent that of the Pantheon at Rome. In the centre of this dome is erected, to admit the light from above, a very handsome cupola, from which is suspended a massy bronze gilt chandelier of immense weight, which reaches within a few feet of the floor of the Chamber. The speaker's chair is elevated and canopied: behind it is a promenade, or *logeum*, for the members, also elevated above the floor, and consisting of columns and pilasters of marble and stone. —Above this, under a sweeping arch near the dome, is placed a colossal figure of Liberty in plaster; and in front of the chair, and immediately over the entrance, stands a beautiful statue in marble, representing History recording the events of the nation. She is placed on a winged car, which seems to roll over the globe, on which is figured in basso relievo, the signs of the Zodiac, and the wheel of the car is the face of the clock of the chamber, finely designated and beautifully executed. Between the columns is suspended fringed drapery of scarlet marines, to retain the sound, and festooned near the gallery, to enable the auditors to see as well as to hear. The difficulty of hearing, however, is one of the greatest objections in this beautiful Chamber, and one which, I think, it will be very difficult to remove — so much for the Representatives' Hall.

We took a seat near the front of the gallery, and were a little surprised to find the whole house in a kind of convulsive titter, and one member, standing on the floor with his mouth open, and his eyes in "a fine frenzy rolling," as if he had lost something he thought he could yet find. We were told, upon inquiring the cause, that the honourable member had been endeavoring to enlighten the body he was addressing, by a *latin quotation*; but unfortunately he could only repeat but a small part of it, and was then striving to recollect the remainder for the especial edification of his coadjutors in legislation, and that, not being successful, they had waited till their patience was exhausted, and had been seized with an irresistible fit of laughter, to the great surprise, as well as amusement, of the orator himself. Finding it impossible to get on, he very quietly took his seat, and was succeeded by the tall saffron complexioned gentlemen [sic] I told you, in one of my former letters, I had met with in the library. My friend informed me it was Mr. R——, of Virginia.

"Is it possible?" said I, "can that be the man of whom I have heard so much, and who has obtained such a reputation for his oratory?"

"The very same," replied T. "there are but few men in this country who have acquired such fame; though I fear it is now a little on the decline, and may, perhaps, in a few years be wholly lost. How miserable it must be to outlive one's reputation, but public applause is transitory and evanescent.

> Thou many headed changeful thing,
> Oh! who would wish to be thy king. . . ."

. . . "Pardon me," said I, "I have not lost a word of what you have been saying, nor have I been inattentive to the speech of the gentleman of whom you have been speaking. But really I have not been able to understand the drift of Mr. R.'s remarks. He is quite too mystical for my comprehension — he seems to be engaged in paraphrasing Sallust, rather than in speaking to the question before the House, which is, as far as I can learn, whether Missouri will be admitted into the Union, with the objectionable constitution she has formed, or not?"

"It is," replied T. "and it must be admitted he has said but little to the purpose, and it is his failing. Old Virginia is his hobby, and Virginia he lugs into almost every speech he makes, without delicacy or mercy." . . .

. . . A COUPLE OF beautiful young women now planted themselves along side of us, and three strapping negro fellows hung over our shoulders. The ladies were dressed in the extreme of fashion, and were very lovely; their cheeks possessing a beautiful *red*, and the rest of the face a most delicate *white*, which I have never noticed before. It was not long before they began to eye me askance, and to be taken, as I thought, with my features and person. I'god, thought I, I have made a conquest already, but I guessed how it would be as soon as I had an opportunity to show out. Conceiving that I was justified in addressing them, I began by asking the one next me some unimportant questions, which she answered without reserve, and with the most bewitching smile imaginable. The honourable members seemed to look up at us with surprise, and I thought, with some jealousy, but that was what I wanted, and so kept up a parley with them for some time to my great gratification as well as theirs. My friend, however, having recovered from a fit of abstraction into which he had fallen, and to which he is subject, noticed my intercourse with the fair ones, with evident astonishment; and touching me on the shoulder, he whispered in my ear, that those damsels with whom I appeared to be so intimate, were *filles de joie*, and that it was not decorous to be seen thus publicly noticing them. This intelligence was like a stroke of thunder, and I instantly started up and left them, mortified to the quick at having been caught publicly conversing with a species of cattle, Daddy has always taught me to abhor. As I passed, I saw the three negroes, who had been hanging over us, grinning like monkeys, at my folly, I suppose; and could have knocked the rascals down, if I dared.

"It appears very strange," said I to T. "that the Speaker should permit these gentry to infest the galleries. It must be very annoying and offensive, I should think, to the decent and virtuous part of the sex who come to hear the debates, to be obliged to be cooped up alongside of a parcel of Meselinas, and must certainly prevent them from attending as often as they might otherwise desire."

"You are right," replied my friend, "but this is a free country, and such things must be tolerated for the sake of freedom. During the whole of this debate, both last Session and this, I have noticed the galleries crowded with blacks who came to listen to discussion, I am sure, they could not understand, and the natural effects of which, if they did, would only tend to make them more dissatisfied with their condition in life. The members from your part of the country in particular, took every opportunity to make them believe that they were as much entitled to freedom as the whites, and to dilate on that part of the Declaration of Independence, which says that all men are born free and equal. This made the blackies in the gallery chuckle amazingly, as you may suppose, and they very naturally concluded that the question before Congress was, whether they should be free or not. One member, yon gentleman with the red wig on, went so far as to undertake to prove man to be, according to Plato, a two legged laughing animal, and that, as the negro had two legs and laughed more than the whites, he was consequently more of a man than his white brother, and of course entitled to greater privileges.

These open discussions tended, as may readily be conceived, to render the blacks very insolent and restless: and to cure this hectic fever which began to spread considerably among that class of our population, so far as it affected his slaves, a certain gentleman took those out, who were in immediate attendance on his person here, and gave them thirty stripes a piece, to keep them cool, as he said, and to teach those at home to know what they were to expect, if they also should be seized with the Missouri fever."

"A devilish cute sort of a remedy," said I, "and I suppose the blackies were entirely cured?"

"Oh, perfectly, sir, and they took care never to go and hear their advocates and friends again in Congress." . . .

Adieu, my dear Moses,
RICHARD L——.

MARGARET BAYARD SMITH

Margaret Bayard Smith (1778–1844), an avid letter writer, novelist, and early chronicler of Washington, moved to the federal city in 1800, after her young husband, Samuel Harrison Smith, was persuaded by Thomas Jefferson to come and start a newspaper, the *National Intelligencer*. She and her husband, who left the business after a decade to become a banker and commissioner of revenue, were popular fixtures in Washington society, especially after they moved near Lafayette Square, across from the White House. In 1824, Smith published her first novel, *A Winter in Washington; or, Memoirs of the Seymour Family*, depicting social and political manners of the city during Jefferson's presidency, but also the lives of poor Irish immigrants and free blacks, whose circumstances she observed firsthand during benevolent work she performed among the lower classes. Smith also published a second novel, *What Is Gentility?* (1828), and an important collection of letters and notebooks, *The First Forty Years of Washington Society* (1906).

From *A Winter in Washington; or, Memoirs of the Seymour Family*

Mrs. Seymour then asked her [the Abbess] if the child appeared to have any recollection of her mother or father, or was able to mention any circumstance that might lead to a discovery of her parents.

"We have frequently questioned her," answered Mrs. Bertrand "about her parents, but all we can gather from her is, that she remembers her mother, or some woman that was like a mother, and that it was in some other place a good way off; that she never saw her father as she can remember till he came one night and carried her in a boat over the water; that he then brought her to Washington, and left her with a family near the Navy Yard; that he afterwards carried her to another house in George Town, where there was a young lady named Miss Ellen; and he used to come there every evening; and that it was the same lady that was in the coach; that one day the gentleman that was also in the coach, came there, and told Miss Ellen that she must go back to her mother in New-York, and that there was a lady in Baltimore who would go with her in the boat; that then Miss Ellen cried very much, and the gentleman told her that her father (Fanny's father) was a bad man; the gentleman, she says, then promised that he would take Fanny along, and put her with some good people that would take care of her, and that he would pay for her board; that the young lady at last agreed to go; and that just at dusk he came with a coach and took the lady and Fanny with him, and came to my door, as I have already told you, ladies; and this is all we can find out from her. She will be home presently, and you can then ask her such questions as you please."

In a few minutes the little girl, whose story had excited much interest in Mrs. Seymour and Louisa, came into the entry in company with one of Mrs. Bertrand's daughters; and Mrs. Bertrand, stepping out of the room, said to her in a tone of eagerness, "Well, Fanny, what luck at the post office?"

"Oh, mother," replied the poor girl, in a sorrowful voice, "the clerk says he is tired of answering us; he says there are no more such letters as we used to get, and we must not trouble him any more about them. — Come, mother, let me go to the poor-house; I know they can't be so kind to me there as you have been, but I dare say they'll treat me well, if I behave myself; and then you know it is not right for me to be a burden any longer to you, who have got so many children of your own to feed, and take care of; and I shall soon be old enough to go out to service."

Mrs. Bertrand then taking her hand, led her into the room, and up to the ladies, saying, "this is the little stranger I was telling you of, ladies."

Mrs. Seymour, who had heard what had just passed in the entry, immediately took her by the hand, and said, "No, my dear little girl, you shall not go to the poor-house; you shall come and live with me and my daughter, if you are willing, and if your mother here has no objection. What say you, are you willing?"

"Oh, yes, madam, if mother is willing; and I am sure you will let me come here sometimes to see her, and Anny, and the others, that I call my brothers and sisters, though I know I am no relation to them; but they have all been so good to me, that I shall feel sorry to leave them."

The appearance of this little girl was, indeed, prepossessing. A fine head of black hair, which fell in ringlets on her neck and shoulders, large blue eyes, with long eye lashes, and a very fair complexion; but both her hair and skin had evidently suffered not a little from the neglect and exposures that are incident to the children of poverty.

Louisa was delighted with the idea of having such a beautiful and intelligent little creature for her pupil; and Mrs. Seymour received additional pleasure from the thought that Louisa would now have so interesting an object to employ her time, and occupy her attention. Mrs. Bertrand very readily consented. Louisa undertook to furnish her with clothes, as well as instruction, and promised to call for her the next morning, and bring with her some medicine, clothes, and other assistance.

As they were walking on —"Here is an instance," said Mrs. Seymour, "of modest merit, shrinking from notice, that might have perished, if, instead of seeking them out, we had waited for them to come to us. These are the poor who most suffer, and who most deserve relief, and yet are most neglected: let this be a lesson to you then, my dear Louisa, to seek out the poor and afflicted."

They had now gone past the President's house, and entered on a bare common that extended down to the mouth of the Tiber, and was bounded on the other side by the Potomac. Here rose the high eminence, which had been proposed as the site of a monument to General Washington. They kept their course round the base of this hill, in search of the dwelling from whence rose the smoke which they saw curling up from the other side. But it was not without difficulty they found the object of their search; they then discovered, in a kind of ravine, or gulley, near the foot of the hill, a shed, for it deserved not even the name of a hovel, from whence the smoke proceeded. After scrambling over broken ground and loose stones, they reached the entrance, for door it had none, and on entering, saw a stout, coarse looking woman, who was splitting up part of a bedstead with an axe, and three children, almost naked, sitting on the floor round the fire. There was no chimney; some broad flat stones were laid on the clay floor, and on these a fire, made of the pieces of bedstead, was burning, filling the shed with a dense and suffocating smoke. Mrs. Seymour and Louisa had to retreat to the entrance, and stood without this miserable dwelling, cold and shivering as they were, while they inquired into the circumstances of these wretched beings.

"Why, what could have brought you to such a place as this, good woman?" said Mrs. Seymour. "Trouble and hard times, belike," answered the woman, carelessly, while she continued splitting up the wood, without taking much notice of her visitors.

"It must be hard times, indeed," said Mrs. Seymour, "since you have to burn up your bedstead."

"Oh, that don't matter much," said the woman, "I have been used to sleep on the floor most of my life, and I sleep just as sound, and sounder too, belike, than the *quality* do on their featherbeds. I burned up my two chairs first ,and my table next; but I don't find but I sit just as easy on the floor, and I'se sure my victuals tastes every morsel as good, eating it out of that there skillet, as if it was in a plate on a table. Indeed, ɪ reckons of a cold day it's better, for it does not get all chilled like, as when ɪ puts it on a cold table."

"But cannot you get wood, that you are obliged to burn up your furniture?"

"Oh, belike I might, if I took the trouble to go up in the city to the overseers of the poor; but I'se as leave wait till the river breaks up, and then, God willing, I means to get a heap, and lay up for a rainy day, as the saying is."

"When the river breaks up!" said Louisa, "how will you get wood then?"

"Law's miss, what a silly question that is; why, now, only to think o' such *quality* as you not to know o' what sights and sights o' wood comes down when there's a freshet in the river, which always there is at the breaking up o' winter; law's *suz*, why people right well off, gets their wood that way; why, now, I'll be bound, if next March like, you walk along the Potomac from up here, down to Greenleaf's-Point, you'll see cords and cords o' drift wood piled up people's yards, and those people too that has no right to the wood, which God sends in his *marcy* a purpose for the poor — and I'se thinks its a sin and a shame for them folks that's well to do in the world, to be robbing the poor at such a rate. The Lord knows, I'se risked my life a many's the time, going paddling in a little canoe out in the middle of the roaring and foaming river to get a good log or two."

"And how do you get victuals to eat?" said Mrs. Seymour; "tell us that, since you have told us how you get wood."

"Law's me," said the woman, laughing, "why you *quality* must be queer folks, not to know nothing of such matters; why, poor folks, to be sartin must work, unless they're all like me, content like, with what they can find, for God sends victuals too, for poor folks."

"Sends victuals? and of what kind, pray?"

"Right good, I'se assure you; as nice fish as ever you bought with the best gold in your pocket. Law's me, if you were to come down along the shore here, when they are drawing o' the seines, you would be 'mazed for sartin. Why, thousands and thousands of herrings, and shad too, for the matter o' that, may be had for the picking up; and then helping to draw the seine, or helping to clean fish for other folks, we get salt to pickle as many as will sarve the family the year thro'. Yes," continued she, smacking her lips, "and a good dram o' whiskey in the bargain."

"But do you not get tired of fish all the year round?"

"Why, as to that, I never had the trial yet; when I have a notion for some meat, I'se just goes out a washing, and I'se gets my half a dollar a day, and a good turn of broken victuals in the bargain; and, as for washing, I just thinks no more of such a day's work than a frolic. Folks, taking all in all, are main kind, here in Washington, and when I washes a few times in a place, some how or other the folks take a liking to me, and gives me old clothes, and old shoes, and bread and meat, and the like; and then God sends a heap of strawberries, and blackberries, and huckleberries, (whortle-berries,) and wild sallad, and yarbs o' one sort or t'other, that poor folks picks and carries to market all summer long, and it turns a pretty penny, I 'sure you."

"Wild sallad!" said Louisa, "what kind of sallad is that?"

"Law's suz, didn't you never eat wild sallad? why its a heap better than garden stuff; let's see, there's *varus* kinds; there's shepherd's-purse, that's the earliest in the spring, then there's wildmustard, and lamb's-quarters, and dandeline, and purseley, and water cresses, and — oh, I don't know how many more ; but to my mind *poke-sallad* is worth them all."

"Is not poke poison?" asked Louisa.

"Laws, no to be sure; why some folks likes it better than sparrow-grass, and it fetches from five to eight cents a bunch in market; why, last spring I made the matter of four dollars from *poke*, and such like truck."

"And how much have you made by strawberries?"

"Laws, there's hardly any reckoning, I made such a sight; I makes no doubt but last spring I got near a twenty dollars."

"Are they so plenty?"

"Plenty! why the hills over there are kivered with them, and in the old fields they stand so thick you can't walk without your feet looking as red as blood ; and my customers always give me as high as six cents a quart, 'cause I pick 'em so clean and nice; and then in the fall, God sends a plenty of mushrooms, though, to be sartin, poor as I am, I never could bring *myself* to eat such trash ; but I guess as how the *quality* has stronger stomachs than poor folks, for they buys as many as they can get; it's my notion they'd eat nothing else if they could get enough of them. It's well they have such a notion, or the mushrooms might rot where they grow; for the trades-people, let alone the poor people, can't stomach them; though, as for wild-sallad and strawberries, they's be our best customers."

"If you make so much money, I wonder you do not dress your children better."

"Why, what would be the use o' that? The stomach craves more than the back, I reckon. It's all use; if you smother yourself with ever so many clothes, it don't hinder you from taking cold. I'se sure all the *quality* as ever I know'd, had a sight more o' aches and pains than poor folks, tho' they have such warm clothes and grand houses, and rides in carriages for fear o' getting the tip o' their toes wet. Now, here's me, and my brats there, if we're out all day long in the rain and snow with our bare feet, or drabbling days together in the river o' the fish season, we're not a whit the worse for it than them canvass-back-ducks be, that lives in the water, as a body may say."

"Truly," said Mrs. Seymour to Louisa, "God tempers the wind to the shorn lamb."

"But do you not wish your children should have some education?" asked Louisa.

"Edication, indeed! why, what service would that be of? they need'nt larn out o' books how to pick up fish, or gather strawberries; or, the worst come to the worst, they could wash a good day's washing, from one week's end to the other, without book-larning. Edication, indeed! — much good it would do the likes o' them!"

"Then you do not stand in need of our assistance?"

"No, God be thanked, without you had two or three cents; I should not object to a dram, this cold day."

Mrs. Seymour and Louisa turned away, quite disgusted with the rudeness and hardness of this woman; and, as they walked homewards, moralized on what they had seen and heard. They really would have admired her contented disposition, had it proceeded from resignation to the evils of her condition; but arising from utter insensibility, they could deem her little better than a savage, and could imagine no means of improving her situation. — Some flakes of snow began to fall; they had got completely chilled at the cabin of the *wild-woman*, as they called her, and determined to hasten home. But, as they came near the bridge that crosses the Tiber, they saw a poor little mulatto-child, carrying a handkerchief with something tied in it, who was crying piteously with the cold: they could not hear the sound of distress, and pass it unheeded. On inquiring, the child said he had been out to buy a loaf of bread; that he lived in that house the other side of the Tiber, and that his feet and hands were almost frozen. The poor thing had sat down, and was so benumbed Mrs. Seymour could scarcely force it to get up and walk. She and Louisa each took a hand; Louisa carried the handkerchief, and they resolved to take the child home.

It blew piercingly cold, as they crossed the bridge, and the snow now fell fast, and soon covered the ground, so that they could not discern the foot path that led to the cabin. At last, almost blinded by the wind and snow, which was driving full in their faces, they reached a little log dwelling, not much bigger than a pig-pen; the child ran forward and pushed open the door. There, huddled round a smouldering fire made of *grubs*, (the roots of trees,) sat a tall, brawny, athletic looking mulatto man, a pale, thin white woman, and three or four mulatto children. The man sprang on his feet, when he saw the ladies enter, and, bowing and scraping a dozen times, begged they would come into his poor bit of a cabin, and wished he had a chair to offer them, but as he had none, begged they would sit on the old chest.

This they willingly did; for they were completely tired.

"Why, you little rascal," said the woman, catching hold of the child, and shaking it violently, "where ha' ye been, ye baggage ye? If as how you'r been at your old tricks a begging o' white folks, I'll shake the very soul out o'ye, so I will;" and she seemed as if she would fulfill her threats, for she shook it almost limb from limb.

"Come, now," said the man, taking the child from her, "that's enough for this time. I don't see what great harm there is, if he did civilly ask a white person for something; there's more white people in the world besides you, Mrs. Jenny, let me tell you."

"Hold your tongue, Joseph; do you think because I bemean'd myself to marry such a neger as you, I'll be beholden to them white trash, that with their hard hearted ways forced me to do the like? No, indeed; if they could turn their own colour out to perish, no child of mine shall be beholden to them."

She darted a revengeful look at Mrs. Seymour and Louisa, and then, turning her back to them, sat down on the block of wood from which she had risen, and leaning her face on her hands, while she supported her elbows on her knees, she sat grumbling to herself.

"You must excuse poor Jenny, ladies; she has been very misfortunate. She met with an accident like, when she was young, and her father turned her and her child out a doors, and the poor thing wandered about without house or home, and must a perished in the streets, had'nt she a consented to ha' married me. Not that I looked then as I do now, ladies — no, no; I was a smart young fellow, then; had a good place in a gentleman's family, and made my ten dollars a month. But so be, after we were married, I built this here cabin, and for all it looks so poorly and lonesome in winter, its a right pleasant place in summer. A pretty bit of a garden — plenty of fowls and eggs, and a cow and four or five pigs, make us very comfortable, if it were not for my poor wife's queer temper; — one bitter drop often spoils a whole bowl of cream. She despised to work; and said, the least I could do was to maintain her like a lady, and as a white woman should be maintained. But, dear's heart, children come so fast on a body, it was unpossible for one man to find bread for so many mouths, and clothes for so many backs — why, mistress, I have at this present moment ten stout children to feed and clothe."

"But why do you not put them out to service?"

"Put them out to service!" exclaimed Jenny, turning her head, and glaring her angry eyes on them; "put them out to service, indeed! do you suppose they are slaves?"

"They might better be slaves, than be kept at home to starve," said Mrs. Seymour.

"They had better be in their graves," muttered the woman.

"Fie, fie, Jenny, to say the like o' that; but they shan't starve while this old arm can saw a stick of wood."

Mrs. Seymour had been trying for some time to catch a view of some object she saw in the chimney corner, or rather sitting crouched up in the chimney itself, but which the mulatto man seemed desirous to conceal. At last Mrs. Seymour asked him to move; but she could not tell whether it was a man or woman, so completely was the figure wrapped up in a large dirty blanket.

"Who have you got there?" asked Mrs. Seymour.

"Another of the victims of the proud, hardhearted whites!" muttered Jenny.

"What does she say?" asked Mrs. Seymour.

"Oh, it don't matter, mistress, what she says; that there poor creature in the corner, is only a street-walker, that got frozen to death like in the road last night; the poor soul was in liquor, and laid down in the mud; and it froze in the night so hard round her, that this morning when she came to herself, finding she could'nt stir, she began a screaming, and two or three of us went to her assistance; and you know, mistress, it would not do to let a fellow creature perish like a beast in the streets; and as nobody would let her come in their houses, why, you know, I could'nt help bringing her home; but you must not think the worse of me, mistress, for having such a body in the house; but indeed I could'nt find it in the heart o' me to let her die o' cold and hunger."

"I think the worse of you! no, my honest fellow, and I hope you will be rewarded better for your kindness to her, than for the compassion which induced you to take a wife."

"Oh, don't say that, mistress; for after all, Jenny's a main good wife, and she loves me, as much as she hates her own colour, and that's not a little, as yon see."

"Will you hold your foolish tongue?" said Jenny.

"Ah, mistress, the best of us have our faults; and my wife, it must be owned, has hers; and yet I shall always think it an honour that she took me for her husband; and she shall never do a turn o' work, as long as I can crawl to do it for her."

"You are a kind hearted creature," said Mrs. Seymour, "and, giving so much to others, it is a pity you should ever want. Come to me for work or assistance. If you can persuade your wife to put your children out to service, do; if not, I will try to get one or two bound out to some trade. Meanwhile, I will procure you an order to send that poor creature to the poorhouse; and here is something for your present necessity."

"Thank you, thank you, mistress, a thousand and a thousand times," said the grateful fellow, as Mrs. Seymour went out.

"I how much more dreadful is vice, than mere physical evils," said Mrs. Seymour; "and though it is our duty to endeavour to reclaim the vicious, as well as relieve the suffering, we feel a repugnance to the task, which makes us too often negligent of this duty."

"I felt more pity for that poor outcast," said Louisa, "than for that vindictive, degraded woman. There is something so disgusting, so revolting, in the idea of her having married a black man, that it totally destroyed every feeling of compassion; it is the first time in my life I ever heard of such a connexion. It is because Jenny is sensible of the irremediable disgrace and degradation of her situation, that she is so jealous and vindictive. Poor wretch!"

JAMES FENIMORE COOPER

The son of a wealthy landowner and congressman from central New York, James Fenimore Cooper (1789–1851) came to Washington for the first time in 1822 to settle some debts with the secretary of the navy for back pay as a naval officer and out-of-pocket expenses from his time as a recruiting officer during the War of 1812. A few years later, he published, anonymously, a series of letters under the title, *Notions of the Americans: Picked Up by a Travelling Bachelor* (1828), the second volume of which is datelined "Washington." These fictional letters were written to counteract some of the critical views of British travellers in America at the time, but in fact, Cooper objected to a good deal about the city, particularly its layout and construction. A decade later, he published *The American Democrat* (1838), spelling out his aristocratic conception of the national government in Washington; that same year, he wrote a letter home that revealed his delight at the new magnificence of the city. In addition to his many historical romances, Cooper wrote a scholarly *History of the Navy* (1839).

From *Notions of the Americans: Picked Up by a Travelling Bachelor*

To the Count Jules de Bethizy,
Colonel en Retraite of the Imperial Guard.
Washington, ——

I write you from the little capital of this great republic. After lingering at Baltimore until reasons for all further delay were exhausted, we reluctantly turned our faces westward. Cadwallader had pointed out to me sundry busy-looking travellers, who were strolling through the streets of the town, with more gravity of mien (assumed or natural) than is common to meet in a city, and whispered in my ears that they were members of Congress, on their way to the seat of government. This was a hint not to be disregarded. Tearing ourselves from the attraction of bright eyes and soft voices, we gallantly entered a coach, and broke the chain of attraction which, like the fabled magnet of Mahomet's coffin, had so long kept me suspended between heaven and earth. . . .

PLAN OF THE CITY

As we approached the capital, we saw before us an extent of open country that did not appear to be used for any agricultural purposes. It lay, without fences, neglected, and waste. This appearance is common just here, and is owing to the circumstance that tobacco exhausts the soil so much, that, in a country where land and its products are still so cheap, it is not worth the cost of restoring it. We soon got a view of the dome of the Capitol, and the whole of the facade of that noble edifice came into view, as we mounted a slight eminence which had partly concealed it. As my eye first wandered eagerly around, at this point, to gather together the scattered particles of the city, I will take the present occasion to convey a general impression of its appearance.

The seat of government was removed from Philadelphia to this place, in order that it might be more central. So far as a line drawn north and south is in question, this object is sufficiently answered. But Washington stands so very far east of a central meridian as to render it probable that other considerations influenced the change. I have never heard it so said, but nothing is more probable than that the slave-holding States required some such concession to their physical inferiority. At all events, every body appears perfectly satisfied with the present position of the capital. Perhaps, notwithstanding the difference on the map, the place is practically nearer the centre than if it stood farther west. The member from Alabama, or Louisiana, or Missouri, arrives by sea, or by means of the great rivers of the west, with about the same expense of money and of labour as the member from Vermont, Maine, or New Hampshire. Some one must always have the benefit of being nearest the political centre, and it is of no great moment whether he be a Virginian or an Ohiese. As the capital is now placed, it is more convenient for quick communication with Europe than if farther inland, and it is certainly nearer the centre of interests where it stands, than it would be in almost any other spot in the confederation.

Had the plan of the city been as well conceived as its locality, there would be less ground of complaint. The perspective of American character was certainly exhibited to great advantage in the conceptions of the individual who laid out the site of this town. It is scarcely possible to imagine a more unfortunate theory than the one he assumed for the occasion. He appears to have egregiously mistaken the relative connexion between streets and houses, since it is fair to infer he would not have been so lavish of the one without the aid of the other, did he not believe the latter to be made use of as accessories to the former, instead of the reverse, as is every where else found to be the case. And, yet I think, both nature and art had united to point out the true plan for this city, as I shall endeavour to convince you without delay.

The ground occupied by the city of Washington, may be described as forming a tolerably regular triangle. Two of its sides are washed by the two branches of the Potomac, which diverge towards the north-east and north-west, while on its third, there are no limits to its extent, the land being a somewhat gentle acclivity, gradual on the whole, though undulating, and often broken in its minute parts. The river below the point is a noble stream, stretching for many miles to the southward, in full view of the town. Both of its branches are navigable for near a league. At the distance of about two miles from the point, the main river (west branch), which had hitherto washed a champaign country, enters a range of low mountains, and makes a still more decided inclination to the west. Here is the head of tide and of navigation. The latter circumstance had early pointed out the place for the site of a town, and accordingly a little city grew on the spot, whence tobacco and lumber were shipped for other ports, long before the neighbourhood was thought of, as the capital of a great nation. This place is called Georgetown. It is rather well built than otherwise, and the heights, in its rear, for it lies against an acclivity, are not only beautiful in themselves, but they are occupied by many pretty villas. It contains in itself, perhaps 9000 inhabitants. It has a college and five churches, two of which are Episcopal.

Georgetown is divided from what is termed Washington City, by a rapid little stream called Rock Creek.* The land, for a considerable distance after the creek is crossed, is well adapted for a town. It is sufficiently unequal to carry off the water, and yet sufficiently level for convenient streets. Here is the spot, I think, where the buildings should have been collected for the new city. But at the distance of about a mile and a quarter from the bridge, a vast square is laid out. On one of its sides is the President's House, flanked by the public offices. A few houses and a church are on two more of its sides, though the one opposite to the 'White House' is as yet entirely naked. From this square, sundry great avenues diverge, as do others from another centre, distant a mile and a half still further east. The latter square is adorned by the Capitol. Across all these avenues, which are parallel to nothing, there is a sort of net-work of streets, running at right angles with each other. Such is Washington on the map. . . .

. . . In consequence of the gigantic scale on which Washington is planned, and the different interests which influence the population, its inhabitants (including Georgetown) are separated into four distinct little towns, distant from each other about a mile. Thus we have Georgetown in the west, containing 9000 souls; the town immediately around the President's House, (extending towards the Capitol,) with perhaps 10,000; that around the Capitol, of some two or three thousand souls; and the buildings at the Navy-Yard, which lies on the east branch, still a mile further. The whole *city* including its three divisions, with here and there a few scattered buildings, may now contain about 16,000 souls.

When the people of the United States determined to have a more central capital, it was thought best to give the general government absolute jurisdiction over it. In order to effect this object, it was necessary to extinguish the State rights. This was done by Virginia and Maryland ceding sufficient territory to make a district of ten miles square at the point I have described. In this little territory the President exercises the authority which a governor commonly exercises in a State, or rather, there is no intermediate or concurrent executive authority between him and the people, as in the several States; and Congress, though in fact elected by the citizens of the States, does all the legislation. Thus the inhabitants of this territory have no representation whatever; neither voting for members of Congress, nor for members of any State legislature. But their voices are often heard in the way of petitions and demands. It is probable that when they shall become as numerous as the smallest State, they will receive the right of electing representatives.

I think you must be enabled to understand the anomaly of the district of Columbia. It has been necessarily fostered by the nation, for as it has been entirely called into existence, as a separate community, for their use, it owes most of all it possesses to the public grants and to the presence of the ministers of the government. With a view to *force a town*, establishments have been formed which will probably linger in a doubtful state of existence for a long time to come, if, indeed, they ever prosper. . . .

Mr. Monroe and Mr. Adams
to the Comte Jules de Bethizy,
Washington,

I have just witnessed one of the most imposing ceremonies of this government; I allude to the inauguration of the President of the United States. It took place about noon, on the 4th of March, when the power of the late incumbent ceased, and that of his successor commenced. It was simple in its forms, but it may possess sufficient interest to amuse a few leisure minutes.

Every body was in the Capitol by the appointed hour. As it is altogether a ceremony of convention (with the exception of the oath of office) such persons were admitted to be spectators, as the officers who controlled the proceedings chose. But in a country like this, exclusion must proceed on a principle, and on such a principle, too, as shall satisfy the reason of the community. In the first place, the galleries of the hall of the House of Representatives were thrown open to every body; a measure that in itself served to commence with a system of equality. The floor of the house was next occupied, as a matter of course, by the Senators and Representatives. The foreign ministers and their suites, the officers of the government, including those of the army and navy, ex-members of Congress, and citizens of eminence from distant States, and finally strangers, who were deemed worthy of attention, composed the rest of the assembly.

The officers of the army and navy appeared in uniforms; and as there were a great many handsome and well-dressed women present, the scene was sufficiently gay. But here all attempts at display ceased. There were no guards, no processions, no wands, no robes, nor any of the usual accompaniments of an European ceremony.

At the proper time, the President (Mr. Monroe) and the President elect (Mr. Quincy Adams) entered the hall, accompanied by the great officers of state, the judges of the supreme court, &c. &c. The two former took their seats on the sofa of the Speaker, while the others occupied chairs that had been reserved for them. After a short pause, the chief justice of the United States arose, and ascended to the little elevation on which the sofa stands. He held in his hand the sacred volume. Mr. Adams then took the oath, in the presence of the assembly, with solemnity and distinctness. The form was as follows: "I do solemnly swear (or affirm) that I will faithfully execute the office of President of the United States, and will, to the best of my ability, preserve, protect, and defend, the constitution of the United States."

With this brief but impressive office, a change in the executive power of this vast republic was effected. The moment Mr. Adams had pronounced the words just quoted, he was the chief magistrate of a great nation, and his predecessor retired to the station of a private citizen.

After a momentary delay, the new President commenced what is called his "inaugural address." It was long, and it was delivered with earnestness and apparent sincerity. It is customary to recognise, on this occasion, the leading principles of the constitution, and for the new functionary to make some manifestation of the particular course of policy by which he intends to be governed. Such professions are, however, rather general than minute, and seldom go farther than a confession of political faith, that depends much more on received axioms than on any private opinions. Still, there was a simplicity in the air of the President, and in the forms of the ceremony, which irresistibly led to the belief you were listening to professions that were entitled to more credit than those which similar scenes elsewhere are wont to create. When the address was ended, the assembly intermingled; and after the congratulations and compliments proper to such an event, the multitude quietly dispersed. Immediately after, the Senators proceeded to their chamber, where the oath was administered to Mr. Calhoun, who then took the chair of that body, in virtue of his office of Vice-President of the United States. He made a short and pertinent address, and the Senate soon after adjourned. During the course of that, or the succeeding day, Mr. Adams nominated Mr. Clay, the late Speaker of the House of Representatives, to fill the vacancy (Secretary of State) occasioned by his own election to the chair of the chief magistrate. Mr. Crawford, the Secretary of the Treasury, also retired; and Mr. Rush, who had recently been minister in England, was selected to fill the situation. The place of Mr. Calhoun was supplied by a gentleman from Virginia (Mr. Barbour.) With these changes the new cabinet was complete, the other incumbents retaining office. I understand it is a practice for every member of the cabinet to tender his resignation on the election of a new President, which gives the latter an opportunity of making such alterations as he may deem expedient, in the most delicate manner possible. Two of the vacancies, in the present instance, were the results of promotions; and it is understood that Mr. Adams would have gladly retained Mr. Crawford, had that gentleman been disposed to serve.

I confess I have been struck with the imposing simplicity of such a quiet transfer of power. The office of President of the United States is one of great dignity and high trust, and its duties have always been discharged with singular moderation and zeal. The present incumbent is a prudent and zealous patriot, and there is no reason to distrust his intelligence or intentions.

Letter to His Wife

From *The Letters and Journals of James Fenimore Cooper*

Gadsby's Washington. March 11th [1838]

Dearest,

. . . I came here yesterday, where every thing is tranquil. The better opinion seems to be against the duelists, and the inquiry is going on.

The Capitol appears to me, now, more magnificent than it did four years ago — and I walked about it, and through it, yesterday, with a pleasure I have not experienced since quitting Europe, a love of grand architecture being a passion with me you know. Still the building is not half large enough, is mean in many respects, and has a bad style. The grounds are improved and enlarged since 1833, and the effect is positively good. Indeed this was wanted in every

sense, for it now ennobles the whole edifice. I think there must now be quite
forty acres in the area — I have not yet been as far as the President's House, but
am to dine with Commodore [Isaac] Chauncey, who lives near it.

I have not yet seen More, but do not anticipate much, by what I can learn.

Gregory has left the explorers, and Aulick will probably be offered the squadron, if it goes at all, which is very doubtful. Shubrick will command the coast
squadron, though [Thomas Ap Catesby] Jones is recovered, and is applying
for it. The Secretary is dissatisfied with Shubrick on account of his obtaining a
promise from the President, through the secretary of war, but the probability is
that the secretary at war will become Secretary of the Navy, and then the orders
will at once be given. The delay I am told, proceeds from Mr. Dickerson, of
whose imbecility, every body speaks openly.

Messrs Clay and Calhoun had a intellectual duello yesterday; one of those
pitiful personal wranglings, in which a day was lost in humoring the vanity and
self consequence of two men. I heard a part of it, and thought it very miserable.

Washington has certainly an air of more magnificence than any other American town. It is mean in detail, but the outline has a certain grandeur about it.
The women dress a good deal, and many a village belle, who is not even receiv-
able in her own county, passes here, for a prodigy, in consequence of political
rank. It is amazing how politics colours every thing — Vulgarity is made genteel, dullness, clever, and infamy honest, by means of its magic. Even Mr. Webb
has a party, in his favor, though it be but an indifferent one. . . .

Kiss all our babes, and bless them too, and rest assured of my tenderest
love. . . .

                                                                J.F.C —

FRANCES TROLLOPE

Frances Trollope (1780–1863), the mother of famed British novelist Anthony
Trollope, turned to novel writing as a young woman to support her family.
Today, she is best known as the author of *Domestic Manners of the Americans*
(1832), based on her sojourn through the United States. Like Margaret Hall's
contemporaneous account, *The Aristocratic Journey* (1827–28), it was offensive
to Americans at the time it appeared and much reviled for its negative portrayal
of manners in the young country. It is a more thoughtful and balanced account,
however, and often more illuminating about life in the nation's capital at the
end of the Federal Period, than Mrs. Hall's.

From *Domestic Manners of the Americans*

By far the shortest route to Washington, both as to distance and time, is by land; but I much wished to see the celebrated Chesapeake bay, and it was therefore decided that we should take our passage in the steamboat. It is indeed a beautiful little voyage, and well worth the time it costs; but as to the beauty of the bay, it must, I think, be felt only by sailors. It is, I doubt not, a fine shelter for ships from the storms of the Atlantic, but its very vastness prevents its striking the eye as beautiful: it is, in fact, only a fine sea-view. But the entrance from it into the Potomac river is very noble, and is one of the points at which one feels conscious of the gigantic proportions of the country, without having recourse to a graduated pencil-case.

The passage up this river to Washington is interesting, from many objects that it passes, but beyond all else, by the view it affords of Mount Vernon, the seat of General Washington. It is there that this truly great man passed the last years of his virtuous life, and it is there that he lies buried: it was easy to distinguish, as we passed, the cypress that waves over his grave.

I was delighted with the whole aspect of Washington; light, cheerful, and airy, it reminded me of our fashionable watering-places. It has been laughed at by foreigners, and even by natives, because the original plan of the city was upon an enormous scale, and but a very small part of it has been as yet executed. But I confess I see nothing in the least degree ridiculous about it; the original design, which was as beautiful as it was extensive, has been in no way departed from, and all that has been done has been done well. From the base of the hill on which the capitol stands extends a street of most magnificent width, planted on each side with trees, and ornamented by many splendid shops. This street, which is called Pennsylvania avenue, is above a mile in length, and at the end of it is the handsome mansion of the President; conveniently near to his residence are the various public offices, all handsome, simple, and commodious; ample areas are left round each, where grass and shrubs refresh the eye. In another of the principal streets is the general post-office, and not far from it a very noble town-hall. Towards the quarter of the president's house are several handsome dwellings, which are chiefly occupied by the foreign ministers. The houses in the other parts of the city are scattered, but without ever losing sight of the regularity of the original plan; and to a person who has been travelling much through the country, and marked the immense quantity of new manufactories, new canals, new rail-roads, new towns, and new cities, which are springing, as it were, from the earth in every part of it, appearance of the metropolis rising gradually into life and splendour, is a spectacle of high historic interest.

Commerce had already produced large and handsome cities in America be-

fore she had attained to an individual political existence, and Washington may
be scorned as a metropolis, where such cities as Philadelphia and New York
exist; but I considered it as the growing metropolis of the growing population
of the Union, and it already possesses features noble enough to sustain its dignity as such.

The residence of the foreign legations and their families gives a tone to the
society of this city which distinguishes it greatly from all others. It is also, for
a great part of the year the residence of the senators and representatives, who
must be presumed to be the *elite* of the entire body of citizens, both in respect
to talent and education. This cannot fail to make Washington a more agreeable
abode than any other city in the Union.

The total absence of all sights, sounds, or smells of commerce, adds greatly to
the charm. Instead of drays you see handsome carriages; and instead of the busy
bustling hustle of men, shuffling on to a sale of "dry goods" or "prime bread
stuffs," you see very well-dressed personages lounging leisurely up and down
Pennsylvania avenue.

Mr. Pishey Thompson, the English bookseller, with his pretty collection of
all sorts of pretty literature, fresh from London, and Mr. Somebody, the jewel-
ler, with his brilliant shop full of trinkets, are the principal points of attraction
and business. What a contrast to all other American cities! The members, who
pass several months every year in this lounging, easy way, with no labour but
a little-talking, and with the *douceur* of eight dollars a day to pay them for it,
must feel the change sadly when their term of public service is over.

There is another circumstance which renders the evening parties at Washington extremely unlike those of other places in the Union; this is the great
majority of gentlemen. The expense, the trouble, or the necessity of a ruling
eye at home, one or all of these reasons prevents the members' ladies from ac-
companying them to Washington; at least, I heard of very few who had their
wives with them. The female society is chiefly to be found among the families
of the foreign ministers, those of the officers of state, and of the few members,
the wealthiest and most aristocratic of the land, who bring their families with
them. Some few independent persons reside in or near the city, but this is a class
so thinly scattered that they can hardly be accounted a part of the population.

But, strange to say, even here a theatre cannot be supported for more than
a few weeks at a time. I was told that gambling is the favourite recreation of
the gentlemen, and that it is carried to a very considerable extent; but here, as
elsewhere within the country, it is kept extremely well out of sight. I do not
think I was present with a pack of cards a dozen times during more than three
years that I remained in the country. Billiards are much played, though in most

places the amusement is illegal. It often appeared to me that the old women of a state made the laws, and the young men broke them.

Notwithstanding the diminutive size of the city, we found much to see and to amuse us.

The patent-office is a curious record of the fertility of the mind of man when left to its own resources; but it gives ample proof also that it is not under such circumstances it is most usefully employed. This patent-office contains models of all the mechanical inventions that have been produced in the Union, and the number is enormous. I asked the man who showed these what proportion of them had been brought into use; he said about one in a thousand; he told me also, that they chiefly proceeded from mechanics and agriculturists settled in remote parts of the country, who had begun by endeavouring to hit upon some contrivance to enable them to *get along* without sending some thousand and odd miles for the thing they wanted. If the contrivance succeeded, they generally became so fond of this offspring of their ingenuity, that they brought it to Washington for a patent.

At the secretary of state's office we were shown autographs of all the potentates with whom the Union were in alliance; which, I believe, pretty well includes all. To the parchments bearing these royal signs manual were appended, of course, the official seals of each, enclosed in gold or silver boxes of handsome workmanship: I was amused by the manner in which one of their own, just prepared for the court of Russia, was displayed to us, and the superiority of their decorations pointed out. They were superior, and in much better taste than the rest; and I only wish that the feeling that induced this display would spread to every corner of the Union, and mix itself with every act and with every sentiment. Let America give a fair portion of her attention to the arts and the graces that embellish life, and I will make her another visit, and write another book as unlike this as possible. . . .

The bureau for Indian affairs contains a room of great interest; the walls are entirely covered with original portraits of all the chiefs who, from time to time, have come to negotiate with their great father, as they call the president. These portraits are by Mr. [Charles Bird] King, and, it cannot be doubted, are excellent likenesses, as are all the portraits I have ever seen from the hands of that gentleman. The countenances are full of expression, but the expression in most of them is extremely similar; or rather, I should say that they have but two sorts of expression; the one is that of very noble and warlike daring, the other of a gentle and *naive* simplicity, that has no mixture of folly in it, but which is inexpressibly engaging, and the more touching, perhaps, because at the moment we were looking at them, those very hearts which lent the eyes such meek and friendly softness, were wrung by a base, cruel and most oppressive act of their *great father.*

We were at Washington at the time that the measure for chasing the last of several tribes of Indians from their forest homes, was canvassed in Congress, and finally decided upon by the *fiat* of the president. If the American character may be judged by their conduct in this matter, they are most lamentably deficient in every feeling of honour and integrity. It is among themselves, and from themselves, that I have heard the statements which represent them as treacherous and false almost beyond belief, in their intercourse with the unhappy Indians. Had I, during my residence in the United States, observed any single feature in their national character that could justify their eternal boast of liberality and the love of freedom, I might have respected them, however much my taste might have been offended by what was peculiar in their manners and customs. But it is impossible for any mind of common honesty not to be revolted by the contradictions in their principles and practice. They inveigh against the governments of Europe, because, as they say, they favour the powerful and oppress the weak. You may hear this declaimed upon in Congress, roared out in taverns, discussed in every drawing-room, satirized upon the stage, nay, even anathematized from the pulpit: listen to it, and then look at them at home; you will see them with one hand hoisting the cap of liberty, and with the other flogging their slaves. You will see them one hour lecturing their mob on the indefeasible rights of man, and the next driving from their homes the children of the soil, whom they have bound themselves to protect by the most solemn treaties.

In justice to those who approve not this treacherous policy, I will quote a paragraph from a New-York paper, which shows that there are some among them who look with detestation on the bold bad measure decided upon at Washington in the year 1830.

"We know of no subject, at the present moment, of more importance to the character of our country for justice and integrity than that which relates to the Indian tribes in Georgia and Alabama, and particularly the Cherokees in the former state. The act passed by Congress, just at the end of the session, co-operating with the tyrannical and iniquitous statute of Georgia, strikes a formidable blow at the reputation of the United States, in respect to their faith, pledged in almost innumerable instances, in the most solemn treaties and compacts."

There were many objects of much interest shown us at this Indian bureau; but, from the peculiar circumstances of this most unhappy and ill-used people, it was a very painful interest.

The dresses worn by the chiefs when their portraits were taken, are many of them splendid, from the embroidery of beads and other ornaments; and the room contains many specimens of their ingenuity, and even of their taste. There is a glass case in the room, wherein are arranged specimens of worked muslin and other needlework, some very excellent handwriting, and many other little productions of male and female Indians, all proving clearly that they are perfectly capable of civilization. Indeed, the circumstance which renders their expulsion from their own, their native lands, so peculiarly lamentable is, that they were yielding rapidly to the force of example; their lives were no longer those of wandering hunters, but they were becoming agriculturists, and the tyrannical arm of brutal power has not now driven them, as formerly, only from their hunting-grounds, their favourite springs, and the sacred bones of their fathers, but it has chased them from the dwellings their advancing knowledge had taught them to make comfortable; from the newly-ploughed fields of their pride; and from the crops their sweat had watered. And for what? To add some thousand acres of territory to the half-peopled wilderness which borders them....

... THE THEATRE WAS NOT open while we were in Washington, but we afterward took advantage of our vicinity to the city to visit it. The house is very small, and most astonishingly dirty and void of decoration, considering that it is the only place of public amusement that the city affords. I have before mentioned the want of decorum at the Cincinnati theatre, but certainly that of the capital at least rivalled it in the freedom of action and attitude; a freedom which seems to disdain the restraints of civilized manners. One man in the pit was seized with a violent fit of vomiting, which appeared not in the least to annoy or surprise his neighbours; and the happy coincidence of a physician being at that moment personated on the stage, was hailed by many of the audience as an excellent joke, of which the actor took advantage, and elicited shouts of applause by saying, "I expect my services are wanted elsewhere."

The spitting was incessant; and not one in ten of the male part of the illustrious legislative audience sat according to the usual custom of human beings; the legs were thrown sometimes over the front of the box, sometimes over the side of it; here and there a senator stretched his entire length along a bench, and in many instances the front rail was preferred as a seat.

I remarked one young man, whose handsome person, and most elaborate toilet, led me to conclude he was a first-rate personage, and so I doubt not he was; nevertheless, I saw him take from the pocket of his silk waistcoat a lump of tobacco, and daintily deposit it within his cheek.

I am inclined to think this most vile and universal habit of chewing tobacco is the cause of a remarkable peculiarity in the male physiognomy of Americans; their lips are almost uniformly thin and compressed. At first I accounted for this upon Lavater's theory, and attributed it to the arid temperament of the people; but it is too universal to be so explained; whereas the habit above mentioned, which pervades all classes (except the literary) well accounts for it, as the act of expressing the juices of this loathsome herb, enforces exactly that position of the lips which gives this remarkable peculiarity to the American countenance.

ALEXIS DE TOCQUEVILLE

Alexis de Tocqueville (1805–59) was a political scientist, sociologist, and politician who originally traveled to the United States in 1831 to observe and report on prison reform. A member of an aristocratic Norman family with ties to the French monarch, he came to believe democracy was the political system of the future and undertook his study of "democracy in America" with the hope that France might learn from its New World counterpart and avoid some of its mistakes and problems. De Tocqueville's brief visit to Washington, while on his American tour, led to the chapter "Of Parliamentary Eloquence in the United States," wherein he observed that because the views of the people in a democracy are constantly changing, their representatives must constantly seek to court their constituents and call attention to themselves by rhetorical excess. In aristocracies, however, representatives are free to maintain a certain distance and independence from their constituents, while keeping a lower rhetorical profile. In 1839, de Tocqueville was elected to the Chamber of Deputies in France and, after the Revolution of 1848, served briefly as foreign minister under Louis Napoleon.

Of Parliamentary Eloquence in the United States
From *Democracy in America*

Among aristocratic nations all the members of the community are connected with, and dependent upon, each other; the graduated scale of different ranks acts as a tie, which keeps every one in his proper place, and the whole body in subordination. Something of the same kind always occurs in the political assemblies of these nations. Parties naturally range themselves under certain leaders, whom they obey by a sort of instinct, which is only the result of habits contracted elsewhere. They carry the manners of general society into the lesser assemblage.

   In democratic countries it often happens that a great number of citizens are tending to the same point; but each one only moves thither, or at least flatters himself that he moves, of his own accord. Accustomed to regulate his doings by personal impulse alone, he does not willingly submit to dictation from without. This taste and habit of independence accompany him into the councils of the nation. If he consents to connect himself with other men in the prosecution of the same purpose, at least he chooses to remain free to contribute to the common success after his own fashion. Hence it is that in democratic countries parties are so impatient of control, and are never manageable except in moments of great public danger. Even then, the authority of leaders, which under such circumstances may be able to make men act or speak, hardly ever reaches the extent of making them keep silence.

Among aristocratic nations the members of political assemblies are at the same time members of the aristocracy. Each of them enjoys high established rank in his own right, and the position which he occupies in the assembly is often less important in his eyes than that which he fills in the country. This consoles him for playing no part in the discussion of public affairs, and restrains him from too eagerly attempting to play an insignificant one.

In America, it generally happens that a representative only becomes somebody from his position in the assembly. He is therefore perpetually haunted by a craving to acquire importance there, and he feels a petulant desire to be constantly obtruding his opinions upon the House. His own vanity is not the only stimulant which urges him on in this course, but that of his constituents, and the continual necessity of propitiating them. Among aristocratic nations, a member of the legislature is rarely in strict dependence upon his constituents: he is frequently to them a sort of unavoidable representative; sometimes they are themselves strictly dependent upon him; and if, at length, they reject him, he may easily get elected elsewhere, or, retiring from public life, he may still enjoy the pleasures of splendid idleness. In a democratic country, like the United States, a representative has hardly ever a lasting hold on the minds of his constituents. However small an electoral body may be, the fluctuations of democracy are constantly changing its aspect: it must therefore be courted unceasingly. He is never sure of his supporters, and, if they forsake him, he is left without a resource; for his natural position is not sufficiently elevated for him to be easily known to those not close to him; and, with the complete state of independence prevailing among the people, he cannot hope that his friends or the government will send him down to be returned by an electoral body unacquainted with him. The seeds of his fortune are, therefore, sown in his own neighbourhood: from that nook of earth he must start, to raise himself to the command of a people and to influence the destinies of the world. Thus it is natural, that in democratic countries, the members of political assemblies think more of their constituents than of their party, while in aristocracies they think more of their party than of their constituents.

But what ought to be said to gratify constituents is not always what ought to be said in order to serve the party to which representatives profess to belong. The general interest of a party frequently demands that members belonging to it should not speak on great questions which they understand imperfectly; that they should speak but little on those minor questions which impede the greater ones; lastly, and for the most part, that they should not speak at all. To keep silence is the most useful service that an indifferent spokesman can render to the commonwealth.

Constituents, however, do not think so. The population of a district sends a representative to take a part in the government of a country, because they entertain a very lofty notion of his merits. As men appear greater in proportion to the littleness of the objects by which they are surrounded, it may be assumed, that the opinion entertained of the delegate will be so much the higher as talents are more rare among his constituents. It will therefore frequently happen, that the less constituents have to expect from their representative, the more will they anticipate from him; and, however incompetent he may be, they will not fail to call upon him for signal exertions, corresponding to the rank they have conferred upon him.

Independently of his position as a legislator of the state, electors also regard their representative as the natural patron of the constituency in the legislature; they almost consider him as the proxy of each of his supporters, and they flatter themselves that he will not be less zealous in defence of their private interests than of those of the country. Thus electors are well assured beforehand that the representative of their choice will be an orator; that he will speak often if he can, and that in case he is forced to refrain, he will strive at any rate to compress into his less frequent orations an inquiry into all the great questions of state, combined with a statement of all the petty grievances they have themselves to complain of; so that, though he be not able to come forward frequently, he should on each occasion prove what he is capable of doing; and that, instead of perpetually lavishing his powers, he should occasionally condense them in a small compass, so as to furnish a sort of complete and brilliant epitome of his constituents and of himself. On these terms they will vote for him at the next election.

These conditions drive worthy men of humble abilities to despair; who, knowing their own powers, would never voluntarily have come forward. But thus urged on, the representative begins to speak, to the great alarm of his friends; and rushing imprudently into the midst of the most celebrated orators, he perplexes the debate and wearies the House.

All laws which tend to make the representative more dependent on the elector, not only affect the conduct of the legislators, as I have remarked elsewhere, but also their language. They exercise a simultaneous influence on affairs themselves, and on the manner in which affairs are discussed.

There is hardly a member of Congress who can make up his mind to go home without having dispatched at least one speech to his constituents; nor who will endure any interruption until he has introduced into his harangue whatever useful suggestions may be made touching the six-and-twenty States of which the Union is composed, and especially the district which he represents. He therefore presents to the mind of his auditors a succession of great general truths (which he himself only comprehends, and expresses, confusedly,) and of petty minutia, which he is but too able to discover and to point out. The consequence is that the debates of that great assembly are frequently vague and perplexed, and that they seem rather to drag their slow length along, than to advance toward a distinct object. Some such state of things will, I believe, always arise in the public assemblies of democracies.

Propitious circumstances and good laws might succeed in drawing to the legislature of a democratic people men very superior to those who are returned by the Americans to Congress; but nothing will ever prevent the men of slender abilities who sit there from obtruding themselves with complacency, and in all ways, upon the public. The evil does not appear to me to be susceptible of entire cure, because it not only originates in the tactics of that Assembly, but in its constitution and in that of the country. The inhabitants of the United States seem themselves to consider the matter in this light; and they show their long experience of parliamentary life, not by abstaining from making bad speeches, but by courageously submitting to hear them made. They are resigned to it, as to an evil which they know to be inevitable.

We have shown the petty side of political debates in democratic assemblies — let us now exhibit the more imposing one. The proceedings within the Parliament of England for the last one hundred and fifty years have never occasioned any great sensation out of that country; the opinions and feelings expressed by the speakers have never awakened much sympathy, even among the nations placed nearest to the great arena of British liberty; whereas Europe was excited by the very first debates which took place in the small colonial assemblies of America, at the time of the revolution.

This was attributable not only to particular and fortuitous circumstances, but to general and lasting causes. I can conceive nothing more admirable or more powerful than a great orator debating on great questions of state in a democratic assembly. As no particular class is ever represented there by men commissioned to defend its own interests, it is always to the whole nation, and in the name of the whole nation, that the orator speaks. This expands his thoughts, and heightens his power of language. As precedents have there but little weight — as there are no longer any privileges attached to certain property, nor any rights inherent in certain bodies or in certain individuals, the mind must have recourse to general truths derived from human nature to resolve the particular question under discussion. Hence the political debates of a democratic people, however small it may be, have a degree of breadth which frequently renders them attractive to mankind. All men are interested by them, because they treat of *man*, who is everywhere the same.

Among the greatest aristocratic nations, on the contrary, the most general questions are almost always argued on some special grounds derived from the practice of a particular time, or the rights of a particular class; which interest that class alone, or at most the people among whom that class happens to exist.

It is owing to this, as much as to the greatness of the French people, and the favourable disposition of the nations who listen to them, that the great effect which the French political debates sometimes produce in the world, must be attributed. The orators of France frequently speak to mankind, even when they are addressing their countrymen only.

CHARLES DICKENS

Charles Dickens (1812–70) got his start reporting on the debates in the British Commons and then turned to fiction, beginning with *The Pickwick Papers*. When he came to the United States in 1842 for a tour, he upset many Americans by his remarks favoring the protections of international copyright and the abolition of slavery. He responded to his critics in *American Notes for General Circulation* (1842) and in the novel *Martin Chuzzlewit* (1843–44). In *American Notes*, he also reported on the typical tourist highlights of his tour of Washington City — visits to the Capitol to hear various senators and congressmen perform, the Patent Office, the Post Office, the President's mansion, and Georgetown ("George Town").

From *American Notes for General Circulation*

WASHINGTON. THE LEGISLATURE.
AND THE PRESIDENT'S HOUSE

We left Philadelphia by steamboat at six o'clock one very cold morning, and turned our faces towards Washington. . . .

We reached Washington at about half-past six that evening, and had upon the way a beautiful view of the Capitol, which is a fine building of the Corinthian order, placed upon a noble and commanding eminence. Arrived at the hotel, I saw no more of the place that night, being very tired, and glad to get to bed.

Breakfast over next morning, I walk about the streets for an hour or two, and, coming home, throw up the window in the front and back, and look out. Here is Washington, fresh in my mind and under my eye.

Take the worst parts of the City Road and Pentonville, or the straggling outskirts of Paris, where the houses are smallest, preserving all their oddities, but especially the small shops and dwellings, occupied in Pentonville (but not in Washington) by furniture-brokers, keepers of poor eating-houses, and fanciers of birds. Burn the whole down; build it up again in wood and plaster; widen it a little; throw in part of St. John's Wood; put green blinds outside all the private houses, with a red curtain and a white one in every window; plough up all the roads; plant a great deal of coarse turf in every place where it ought *not* to be; erect three handsome buildings in stone and marble anywhere, but the more entirely out of everybody's way the better; call one the Post Office, one the Patent Office, and one the Treasury; make it scorching hot in the morning, and freezing cold in the afternoon, with an occasional tornado of wind and dust; leave a brick-field without the bricks, in all central places where a street may naturally be expected: and that's Washington.

The hotel in which we live is a long row of small houses fronting on the street, and opening at the back upon a common yard, in which hangs a great triangle. Whenever a servant is wanted, somebody beats on this triangle from one stroke up to seven, according to the number of the house in which his presence is required; and as all the servants are always being wanted, and none of them ever come, this enlivening engine is in full performance the whole day through. Clothes are drying in this same yard; female slaves, with cotton handkerchiefs twisted round their heads, are running to and fro on the hotel business; black waiters cross and recross with dishes in their hands; two great dogs are playing upon a mound of loose bricks in the centre of the little square; a pig is turning up his stomach to the sun, and grunting, "That's comfortable!"; and neither the men nor the women nor the dogs nor the pig nor any created creature takes the smallest notice of the triangle, which is tingling madly all the time.

I walk to the front window, and look across the road upon a long, straggling row of houses, one story high, terminating nearly opposite, but a little to the left, in a melancholy piece of waste ground with frowzy grass, which looks like a small piece of country that has taken to drinking, and has quite lost itself. Standing anyhow and all wrong, upon this open space, like something meteoric that has fallen down from the moon, is an odd, lop-sided, one-eyed kind of wooden building, that looks like a church, with a flagstaff as long as itself sticking out of a steeple something larger than a tea-chest. Under the window is a small stand of coaches, whose slave-drivers are sunning themselves on the steps of our door, and talking idly together. The three most obtrusive houses near at hand are the three meanest. On one — a shop, which never has anything in the window, and never has the door open — is painted, in large characters, "THE CITY LUNCH," At another, which looks like the back way to somewhere else, but is an independent building in itself, oysters are procurable in every style. At the third, which is a very, very little tailor's shop, pants are fixed to order; or, in other words, pantaloons are made to measure. And that is our street in Washington.

It is sometimes called the City of Magnificent Distances, but it might with greater propriety be termed the City of Magnificent Intentions; for it is only on taking a bird's-eye view of it from the top of the Capitol, that one can at all comprehend the vast designs of its projector, an aspiring Frenchman. Spacious avenues, that begin in nothing and lead nowhere; streets, mile long, that only want houses, roads, and inhabitants; public buildings that need but a public to be complete; and ornaments of great thoroughfares which only lack great thoroughfares to ornament, — are its leading features. One might fancy the season over, and most of the houses gone out of town forever with their masters. To the admirers of cities it is a Barmecide Feast; a pleasant field for the imagination to rove in; a monument raised to a deceased project, with not even a legible inscription to record its departed greatness.

Such as it is it is likely to remain. It was originally chosen for the seat of government as a means of averting the conflicting jealousies and interests of the different States; and very probably, too, as being remote from mobs, — a consideration not to be slighted, even in America. It has no trade or commerce of its own; having little or no population beyond the President and his establishment, the members of the legislature who reside there during the session, the government clerks and officers employed in the various departments, the keepers of the hotels and boarding-houses, and the tradesmen who supply their tables. It is very unhealthy. Few people would live in Washington, I take it, who were not obliged to reside there; and the tides of emigration and speculation, those rapid and regardless currents, are little likely to flow at any time towards such dull and sluggish water.

The principal features of the Capitol are, of course, the two Houses of Assembly. But there is, besides, in the centre of the building, a fine rotunda, ninety-six feet in diameter, and ninety-six high, whose circular wall is divided into compartments, ornamented by historical pictures. Four of these have for their subjects prominent events in the Revolutionary struggle. They were painted by Colonel Trumbull, himself a member of Washington's staff at the time of their occurrence; from which circumstance they derive a peculiar interest of their own. In this same hall Mr. Greenough's large statue of Washington has been lately placed. It has great merits, of course, but it struck me as being rather strained and violent for its subject. I could wish, however, to have seen it in a better light than it can ever be viewed in where it stands.

There is a very pleasant and commodious library in the Capitol; and from a balcony in front, the bird's-eye view of which I have just spoken, may be had, together with a beautiful prospect of the adjacent country. In one of the ornamental portions of the building there is a figure of Justice; whereunto, the Guide Book says, "the artist at first contemplated giving more of nudity, but he was warned that the public sentiment in this country would not admit of it, and in his caution he has gone, perhaps, into the opposite extreme." Poor Justice! she has been made to wear much stranger garments in America than those she pines in, in the Capitol. Let us hope that she has changed her dress-maker since they were fashioned, and that the public sentiment of the country did not cut out the clothes she hides her lovely figure in just now. . . .

. . . Did I see in this public body an assemblage of men bound together in the sacred names of Liberty and Freedom, and so asserting the chaste dignity of those twin goddesses, in all their discussions, as to exalt at once the Eternal Principles to which their names are given, and their own character, and the character of their countrymen, in the admiring eyes of the whole world?

It was but a week since an aged, gray-haired man, a lasting honor to the land that gave him birth, who has done good service to his country, as his forefathers did, and who will he remembered scores upon scores of years after the worms bred in its corruption are but so many grains of dust — it was but a week since this old man had stood for days upon his trial before this very body, charged with having dared to assert the infamy of that traffic which has for its accursed merchandise men and women and their unborn children. Yes. And publicly exhibited in the same city all the while, gilded, framed, and glazed, hung up for general admiration, shown to strangers not with shame, but pride, its face not turned towards the wall, itself not taken down and burned, is the Unanimous Declaration of The Thirteen United States of America, which solemnly declares that All Men are created Equal, and are endowed by their Creator with the Inalienable rights of Life, Liberty, and the Pursuit of Happiness!

It was not a month since this same body had sat calmly by, and heard a man, one of themselves, with oaths which beggars in their drink reject, threaten to cut another's throat from ear to ear. There he sat among them; not crushed by the general feeling of the assembly, but as good a man as any.

There was but a week to come, and another of that body, for doing his duty to those who sent him there; for claiming in a Republic the Liberty and Freedom of expressing their sentiments, and making known their prayer; would

be tried, found guilty, and have strong censure passed upon him by the rest.
His was a grave offence indeed; for, years before, he had risen up and said, "A
gang of male and female slaves for sale, warranted to breed like cattle, linked
to each other by iron fetters, are passing now along the open street beneath the
windows of your Temple of Equality! Look!" But there are many kinds of hunters engaged in the Pursuit of Happiness, and they go variously armed. It is the
Inalienable Right of some among them, to take the field after *their* Happiness,
equipped with cat and cartwhip, stocks and iron collar, and to shout their view
halloa! (always in praise of Liberty) to the music of clanking chains and bloody
stripes.

Where sat the many legislators of coarse threats, of words and blows such as
coal-heavers deal upon each other, when they forget their breeding? On every
side. Every session had its anecdotes of that kind, and the actors were all there.

Did I recognize in this assembly a body of men who, applying themselves in
a new world to correct some of the falsehoods and vice of the old, purified the
avenues to Public Life, paved the dirty ways to Place and Power, debated and
made laws for the Common Good, and had no party but their Country?

I saw in them the wheels that move the merest perversion of virtuous Political Machinery that the worst tools ever wrought. Despicable trickery at elections; underhanded tamperings with public officers; cowardly attacks upon
opponents, with scurrilous newspapers for shields, and hired pens for daggers;
shameful trucklings to mercenary knaves, whose claim to be considered is, that
every day and week they sow new crops of ruin with their venal types, which are
the dragon's teeth of yore, in everything but sharpness; aidings and abettings
of every bad inclination in the popular mind, and artful suppressions of all its
good influences: such things as these, and, in a word, Dishonest Faction in its
most depraved and most unblushing form, stared out from every corner of the
crowded hull.

Did I see among them the intelligence and refinement, the true, honest,
patriotic heart of America? Here and there were drops of its blood and life,
but they scarcely colored the stream of desperate adventurers which sets that
way for profit and for pay. It is the game of these men, and of their profligate
organs, to make the strife of politics so fierce and brutal, and so destructive of
all self-respect in worthy men, that sensitive and delicate-minded persons shall
be kept aloof, and they, and such as they, be left to battle out their selfish views
unchecked. And thus this lowest of all scrambling fights goes on, and they who
in other countries would, from their intelligence and station, most aspire to
make the laws, do here recoil the furthest from that degradation.

That there are among the representatives of the people in both Houses, and
among all parties some men of high character and great abilities, I need not say.

The foremost among those politicians who are known in Europe have been already described, and I see no reason to depart from the rule I have laid down for my guidance, of abstaining from all mention of individuals. It will be sufficient to add, that to the most favorable accounts that have been written of them I more than fully and most heartily subscribe; and that personal intercourse and free communication have bred within me, not the result predicted in the very doubtful proverb, but increased admiration and respect. They are striking men to look at, hard to deceive, prompt to act, lions in energy, Crichtons in varied accomplishments, Indians in fire of eye and gesture, Americans in strong and generous impulse; and they as well represent the honor and wisdom of their country at home as the distinguished gentleman who is now its minister at the British Court sustains its highest character abroad. . . .

. . . The Senate is a dignified and decorous body, and its proceedings are conducted with much gravity and order. Both houses are handsomely carpeted; but the state to which these carpets are reduced by the universal disregard of the spittoon with which every honorable member is accommodated, and the extraordinary improvements on the pattern which are squirted and dabbled upon it in every direction, do not admit of being described. I will merely observe, that I strongly recommend all strangers not to look at the floor; and if they happen to drop anything, though it be their purse, not to pick it up with an ungloved hand on any account.

It is somewhat remarkable too, at first, to say the least, to see so many honorable members with swelled faces; and it is scarcely less remarkable to discover that this appearance is caused by the quantity of tobacco they contrive to stow within the hollow of the check. It is strange enough, too, to see an honorable gentleman leaning back in his tilted chair, with his legs on the desk before him, shaping a convenient "plug" with his penknife, and when it is quite ready for use, shooting the old one from his mouth, as from a popgun, and clapping the new one in its place.

I was surprised to observe that even steady old chewers of great experience are not always good marksmen, which has rather inclined me to doubt that general proficiency with the rifle of which we have heard so much in England. Several gentlemen called upon me who, in the course of conversation, frequently missed the spittoon at five paces, and one (but he was certainly short-sighted) mistook the closed sash for the open window, at three. On another occasion, when I dined out, and was sitting with two ladies and some gentlemen round a fire before dinner, one of the company fell short of the fireplace, six distinct times. I am disposed to think, however, that this was occasioned by his not aiming at that object, as there was a white marble hearth before the fender, which was more convenient, and may have suited his purpose better.

HERMAN MELVILLE

New York–born Herman Melville (1819–91) made three visits to Washington: the first two, in 1847 and 1861, seeking political appointment, and the third, in 1864, to see the war firsthand, in the nearby Virginia countryside, while composing his volume of Civil War poems, *Battle-Pieces and Aspects of the War* (1866). During his first visit, he attended sessions of the Twenty-ninth Congress, an experience that found its way into two satirical chapters in *Mardi, and a Voyage Thither* (1849), his early imaginary voyage novel, and he met the famous Commodore Thomas ap Catesby Jones, an event that surfaced again in his man-of-war narrative, *White-Jacket* (1850).

They Visit the Great Central Temple of Vivenza
From *Mardi, and a Voyage Thither*

The throng that greeted us upon landing were exceedingly boisterous.

"Whence came ye?" they cried. "Whither bound? Saw ye ever such a land as this? Is it not a great and extensive republic? Pray, observe how tall we are; just feel of our thighs; are we not a glorious people? Here, feel of our beards. Look round; look round; be not afraid; behold those palms; swear now, that this land surpasses all others. Old Bello's [England's] mountains are mole-hills to ours; his rivers, rills; his empires, villages; his palm-trees, shrubs."

"True," said Babbalanja. "But great Oro must have had some hand in making your mountains and streams. — Would ye have been as great in a desert?"

"Where is your king?" asked Media, drawing himself up in his robe, and cocking his crown.

"Ha, ha, my fine fellow! We are all kings here; royalty breathes in the common air. But come on, come on. Let us show you our great Temple of Freedom."

And so saying, irreverently grasping his sacred arm, they conducted us toward a lofty structure, planted upon a bold hill, and supported by thirty pillars of palm; four quite green; as if recently added; and beyond these, an almost interminable vacancy, as if all the palms in Mardi, were at some future time, to aid in upholding that fabric.

Upon the summit of the temple was a staff; and as we drew nigh, a man with a collar round his neck, and the red marks of stripes upon his back, was just in the act of hoisting a tappa standard — correspondingly striped. Other collared menials were going in and out of the temple.

Near the porch, stood an image like that on the top of the arch we had seen. Upon its pedestal, were pasted certain hieroglyphical notices; according to Mohi, offering rewards for missing men, so many hands high.

Entering the temple, we beheld an amphitheatrical space, in the middle of which, a great fire was burning. Around it, were many chiefs, robed in long togas, and presenting strange contrasts in their style of tattooing.

Some were sociably laughing, and chatting; others diligently making excavations between their teeth with slivers of bamboo; or turning their heads into mills, were grinding up leaves and ejecting their juices. Some were busily inserting the down of a thistle into their ears. Several stood erect, intent upon maintaining striking attitudes; their javelins tragically crossed upon their chests. They would have looked very imposing, were it not, that in rear their vesture was sadly disordered. Others, with swelling fronts, seemed chiefly indebted to their dinners for their dignity. Many were nodding and napping. And, here and there, were sundry indefatigable worthies, making a great show of imperious and indispensable business; sedulously folding banana leaves into scrolls, and recklessly placing them into the hands of little boys, in gay turbans and trim little girdles, who thereupon fled as if with salvation for the dying.

It was a crowded scene; the dusky chiefs, here and there, grouped together, and their fantastic tattooings showing like the carved work on quaint old chimney-stacks, seen from afar. But one of their number overtopped all the rest. As when, drawing nigh unto old Rome, amid the crowd of sculptured columns and gables, St. Peter's grand dome soars far aloft, serene in the upper air; so, showed one calm grand forehead among those of this mob of chieftains. That head was Saturnina's. Gall and Spurzheim! saw you ever such a brow! — poised like an avalanche, and under the shadow of a forest! woe betide the devoted valleys below! Lavater! behold those lips, — like mystic scrolls! Those eyes, — like panthers' caves at the base of Popocatepetl!

"By my right hand, Saturnina," cried Babbalanja, "but thou were made in the image of thy Maker! Yet, have I beheld men, to the eye as commanding as thou; and surmounted by heads globe-like as thine, who never had thy caliber. We must measure brains, not heads, my lord; else, the sperm-whale, with his tun of an occiput, would transcend us all."

Near by, were arched ways, leading to subterranean places, whence issued a savory steam, and an extraordinary clattering of calabashes, and smacking of lips, as if something were being eaten down there by the fattest of fat fellows, with the heartiest of appetites, and the most irresistible of relishes. It was a quaffing, guzzling, gobbling noise. . . . we were told that those worthies below, were a club in secret conclave; very busy in settling certain weighty state affairs upon a solid basis. They were all chiefs of immense capacity: — how many gallons, there was no finding out.

Be sure, now, a most riotous noise came up from those catacombs, which seemed full of the ghosts of fat Lamberts; and this uproar it was, that heightened the din above-ground.

But heedless of all, in the midst of the amphitheater, stood a tall, gaunt warrior, ferociously tattooed, with a beak like a buzzard; long dusty locks; and his hands full of headless arrows. He was laboring under violent paroxysms; three benevolent individuals essaying to hold him. But repeatedly breaking loose, he burst anew into his delirium; while with an absence of sympathy, distressing to behold, the rest of the assembly seemed wholly engrossed with themselves; nor did they appear to care how soon the unfortunate lunatic might demolish himself by his frantic proceedings.

Toward one side of the amphitheatrical space, perched high upon an elevated dais, sat a white-headed old man with a tomahawk in his hand: earnestly engaged in overseeing the tumult; though not a word did he say. Occasionally, however, he was regarded by those present with a mysterious sort of deference; and when they chanced to pass between him and the crazy man, they invariably did so in a stooping position; probably to elude the atmospheric grape and canister, continually flying from the mouth of the lunatic.

"What mob is this?" cried Media.

"'Tis the grand council of Vivenza [the U.S. Senate]," cried a bystander. "Hear ye not Alanno? [Senator William Allen of Ohio]" and he pointed to the lunatic.

Now coming close to Alanno, we found that with incredible volubility, he was addressing the assembly upon some all-absorbing subject connected with King Bello, and his presumed encroachments toward the northwest of Vivenza.

One hand smiting his hip, and the other his head, the lunatic thus proceeded; roaring like a wild beast, and beating the air like a windmill: —

"I have said it! the thunder is flashing, the lightning is crashing! already there's an earthquake in Dominora [Europe]! Full soon will old Bello discover that his diabolical machinations against this ineffable land must soon come to naught. Who dare not declare, that we are not invincible? I repeat it, we are. Ha! ha! Audacious Bellow must bite the dust! Hair by hair, we will trail his gory gray beard at the end of our spears! Ha, ha! I grow hoarse; but would mine were a voice like the wild bulls of Bullorom, that I might be heard from one end of this great and gorgeous land to its farthest zenith; ay, to the uttermost diameter of its circumference. Awake! oh Vivenza. The signs of the times are portentous; nay, extraordinary; I hesitate not to add, peculiar! Up! up! Let us not descend to the bathos, when we should soar to the climax! Does not all Mardi wink and look on? Is the great sun itself a frigid spectator? Then let us double up our mandibles to the deadly encounter. Methinks I see it now. Old Bello is crafty, and his oath is recorded to obliterate us! Across this wide lagoon he casts his serpent eyes; whets his insatiate bill; mumbles his barbarous tusks; licks his forked tongues; and who knows when we shall have the shark in our midst? Yet be not deceived; for though as yet, Bello has forborne molesting us openly, his emissaries are at work; his infernal sappers, and miners, and wet-nurses, and midwives, and grave-diggers are busy! His canoe-yards are all in commotion! In navies his forests are being launched upon the wave; and ere long typhoons, zephyrs, white-squalls, balmy breezes, hurricanes, and besoms will be raging round us!"

His philippic concluded, Alanno was conducted from the place; and being now quite exhausted, cold cobble-stones were applied to his temples, and he was treated to a bath in a stream.

This chieftain, it seems, was from a distant western valley, called Hio-Hio, one of the largest and most fertile in Vivenza, though but recently settled. Its inhabitants, and those of the vales adjoining, — a right sturdy set of fellows, — were accounted the most dogmatically democratic and ultra of all the tribes in Vivenza; ever seeking to push on their brethren to the uttermost; and especially were they bitter against Bello. But they were a fine young tribe, nevertheless. Like strong new wine they worked violently in becoming clear. Time, perhaps, would make them all right.

An interval of greater uproar than ever now ensued; during which, with his tomahawk, the white-headed old man repeatedly thumped and pounded the seat where he sat, apparently to augment the din, though he looked anxious to suppress it.

At last, tiring of his posture, he whispered in the ear of a chief, his friend; who, approaching a portly warrior present, prevailed upon him to rise and address the assembly. And no sooner did this one do so, than the whole convocation dispersed, as if to their yams; and with a grin, the little old man leaped from his seat, and stretched his legs on a mat.

The fire was now extinguished, and the temple deserted.

EYE OF THE STORM

Race, Slavery, Civil War

[1830–1905]

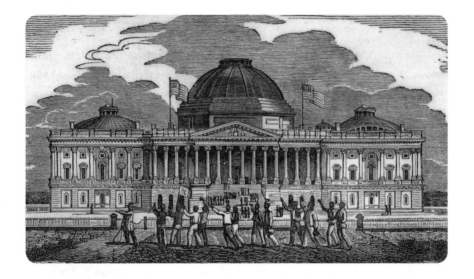

EGINNING IN THE middle decades of the nineteenth century, writing on Washington centered on the volatile matters of race and slavery, and after 1861, the War between the States. For Ralph Waldo Emerson, the political decisions and legal compromises over slavery coming out of Washington City revealed the nation's elected officials to be shameless —"as wicked as they dare." For John Greenleaf Whittier, William Wells Brown, and Solomon Northup (a free African American who was illegally captured and sold into slavery) the presence of slave prisons and slave markets in the District of Columbia, in plain sight of the Capitol, was a national outrage. Once the war started, travelers such as Nathaniel Hawthorne reported on what a melancholy and forbidding place the city had become: the center of the North's military effort, removed from the culture of the South. Louisa May Alcott and Walt Whitman recorded wartime impressions of the city gathered during their rounds as hospital nurses, ministering to the needs of hundreds, even thousands, of wounded soldiers. Several authors from this period, including Hawthorne, Whitman, and Elizabeth Hobbs Keckley (a former slave who became a dressmaker for Mary Todd Lincoln) also provide vivid but sensitive portraits of the most dominant political figure of the nineteenth century, Abraham Lincoln.

(OVERLEAF) "The Home of the Oppressed," detail from "Slave Market of America . . . District of Columbia" broadside, 1836, showing slaves being driven in a chain gang in front of the nation's Capitol. Courtesy of the Library of Congress.

BLACK HAWK

Black Hawk (1767–1838) led the Sac (Sauk) and Fox resistance to the U.S. treaty of 1804 that required Native Americans to move west of the Mississippi. In 1831, after years of skirmishing in present-day Illinois, the whites imposed a new treaty that forced Native Americans from their lands. Again, Black Hawk led a resistance: the Black Hawk War (1832). His *Autobiography* (1833) offers a defense of his reading of the treaty and his response. The portion excerpted here describes being called from prison to Washington to meet with the Great Father, President Andrew Jackson, to explain why he warred against Jackson's "white children." It also reveals Black Hawk's quiet faith that the president already knew the answer. Many chiefs and warriors were called to Washington under similar circumstances over many decades. Such missions were usually designed to impress Native American leaders with the power of the federal government and the futility of resisting white efforts to establish settlements across the North American continent.

From *Autobiography*

We passed away the time making pipes, until spring, when we were visited by the agent, trader, and interpreter, from Rock Island, Ke-o-kuck, and several chiefs and braves of our nation, and my wife and daughter. I was rejoiced to see the two latter, and spent my time very agreeably with them and my people, as long as they remained.

The trader presented me with some dried venison, which had been killed and cured by some of my friends. This was a valuable present; and although he had given me many before, none ever pleased me so much. This was the first meat I had eaten for a long time, that reminded me of the former pleasures of my own wigwam, which had always been stored with plenty.

Ke-o-kuck and his chiefs, during their stay at the barracks, petitioned our Great Father, the President, to release us; and pledged themselves for our good conduct. I now began to hope that I would soon be restored to liberty, and the enjoyment of my family and friends; having heard that Ke-o-kuck stood high in the estimation of our Great Father, because he did not join me in the war. But I was soon disappointed in my hopes. An order came from our Great Father to the White Beaver, to send us on to Washington.

In a little while all were ready, and left Jefferson barracks on board of a steam boat, under charge of a young war chief, whom the White Beaver sent along as a guide to Washington. He carried with him an interpreter and one soldier. On our way up the Ohio, we passed several large villages, the names of which were explained to me [including Louisville, Cincinnati, Wheeling, and finally Hagerstown]. . . .

Here we came to another road, much more wonderful than that through the mountains. They call it a *rail road*! I examined it carefully, but need not describe it, as the whites know all about it. It is the most astonishing sight I ever saw. . . .

On our arrival at Washington, we called to see our Great Father, the President [Andrew Jackson]. He looks as if he had seen as many winters as I have, and seems to be a *great brave*! I had very little talk with him, as he appeared to be busy, and did not seem much disposed to talk. I think he is a good man; and although he talked but little, he treated us very well. His wigwam is well furnished with every thing good and pretty, and is very strongly built.

He said he wished to know the *cause* of my going to war against his white children. I thought he ought to have known this before; and, consequently, said but little to him about it — as I expected he knew as well as I could tell him.

He said he wanted us to go to fortress Monroe [i.e., the prison at Hampton, Virginia], and stay awhile with the war chief who commanded it. But, having been so long from my people, I told him that I would rather return to my nation — that Ke-o-kuck had come here once on a visit to see him, as we had done, and he let him return again, as soon as he wished; and that I expected to be treated in the same way. He insisted, however, on our going to fortress Monroe; and as our interpreter could not understand enough of our language to interpret a speech, I concluded it was best to obey our Great Father, and say nothing contrary to his wishes.

During our stay at the city, we were called upon by many of the people, who treated us well, particularly the squaws! We visited the great *council house* of the Americans — the place where they keep their *big guns* — and all the public buildings, and then started to fortress Monroe. . . .

JOHN GREENLEAF WHITTIER

One of the popular "Fireside Poets," John Greenleaf Whittier (1807–92) was a militant Quaker who published poetry in William Lloyd Garrison's abolitionist newspaper and wrote on issues of social justice in the 1830s. He joined the abolitionist cause as a speaker and editor and was elected to the Massachusetts legislature in 1834–35. After a break with Garrison, he founded the Liberty Party, ran for Congress as a Liberty candidate, and edited its newspaper. He also helped found the Republican Party. Like his friend Grace Greenwood, he wrote for the abolitionist *National Era* in Washington and served as a corresponding editor (1847–59) there. Though he never lived in Washington, he visited several times and was well acquainted with the city. The piece reprinted here is a long letter, written in fall 1843 to the *Essex Transcript*, in Whittier's native Massachusetts. It addresses the horrors of the "Great Slave Market" in Washington, expressing Whittier's outrage that such a thing should exist in the shadow of the Capitol.

Letter to the *Essex Transcript*
From *The Letters of John Greenleaf Whittier*

Amesbury, October 30, 1843

THE GREAT SLAVE MARKET

I find in a late number of the Albany Patriot a letter from a gentleman in the city of Washington addressed to the Editor from which I take the following paragraph:

"This year, over 5,000 have already been sold in our dens of diabolism, and many more heart strings will be broken before the winter sets in, by sundering all the ties of life to meet the demand for human victims in the Louisiana market. In Florida, also, the demand has been greatly increased by the diabolical law, to 'encourage the armed settlement' of that slavery-cursed territory, and thus increase the political weight of the slave system in the councils of our country.

"Scenes have taken place in Washington this summer that would make the devil blush through the darkness of the pit, if he had been caught in them. A fortnight ago last Tuesday, no less than Sixty Human-Beings were carried right by the Capitol yard to a slave ship! The *men* were *chained* in couples and fastened to a log chain as it is common in this region. The women walked by their side. The little children were carried along in wagons."

In the summer of 1840 when in Washington I took occasion in company with two friends to visit the principal slave trading establishments of the District. In Alexandria at the great Slave-Prison formerly known as Franklin and Armfield's, there were about fifty slaves. — They were enclosed by high strong walls, with grated iron doors. Among them was a poor woman who had escaped twelve years before from slavery and who had married a free man. She had been hunted out by some of those human bloodhounds, who are in the detestable occupation of slave catchers, separated from her husband, and with her child had been sold to the speculators for the New Orleans market. Another woman whose looks and manner were expressive of deep anguish had, with her nine children been sold away from her husband — an everlasting separation!

But, her sorrows had but just begun. Long ere this she and her children have probably been re-sold, scattered and divided and are now toiling in hopeless bereavement, or buried like brutes, without a tear or Christian rite, on the banks of the Mississippi! . . .

We visited the next day a slave dealer's establishment in the city of Washington. It stood somewhat apart from the dense part of the city, yet in full view of the Capitol. Its dark strong walls rose in grim contrast with the green beauty of early Summer, — a horror and an abomination — a blot upon the fair and pleasant landscape. We looked in upon a group of human beings herded together like cattle for the market. The young man in attendance informed us that there were five or six other regular slave-dealers in the city, who have no prisons of their own, kept their slaves in this establishment or in the City Prison. The following advertisement of this infernal market house I have copied from the Washington Globe and the Intelligencer.

"Cash for Negroes"

"The subscriber wishes to purchase a number of negroes for the Louisiana and Mississippi markets. He will pay the highest price which the market will justify. Himself or an agent at all times can be found at his Jail on 7th street, the first house south of the market bridge on the West side. Letters addressed to him, will receive the earliest attention.

Wm. H. Williams."

In the same papers, four other regular dealers in human beings advertised themselves. In addition, Geo. Kephart of Alexandria advertised "the copper fastened brig 'Isaac Franklin,' was nearly ready to sail with slaves for New Orleans." So much for National newspaper organs of the Whig and Democratic parties! What must be the state of parties which acknowledge such papers as their mouth pieces?

On the walls of the slave-dealer's office were suspended some low and disgraceful pictures and caricatures in which abolitionists and blacks were represented and in which Daniel O'Connell and John Quincy Adams, held a prominent position, as objects for the obscene jokes and witticisms of the scoundrel traffickers. . . .

Known to God only is the dreadful amount of human agony and suffering which from this slave-jail has sent its cry, unheard or unheeded of man up to His ear. — The mother weeping for her children — the wife separated from her husband, breaking the night silence with the shriek of broken hearts. Now and then an appalling fact sheds light upon the secret horrors of the prison-house. In the winter of 1838, a poor colored man, overcome with the horror at being sold South, put an end to his life by cutting his throat.

From the private establishment we next proceeded to the old city-prison — built by the people of the United States — the common property of the nation. It is a damp dark loathsome building. We passed between two ranges of stone cells filled with blacks. — We noticed five or six in a single cell which seemed scarcely large enough for a solitary tenant. The heat was suffocating. In rainy weather the keeper told us that the prison was uncomfortably wet. In the winter there could be no fire in these cells. The keeper with some reluctance admitted that he received slaves from traders, and kept them until they were sold at 34 cents per day. Men of the North! it was your money which helped pile the granite of these cells, and forge the massy iron doors, for the benefit of slave traders! — It is your property which is thus perverted! . . .

Scarcely an hour before my visit to this prison I had been in the Senate Chamber of the U. States. I had seen the firm lip, the broad full brow, and beaming eye of Calhoun, — the stern repose of a face written over with thought, and irradiated with the deep still fires of genius. I had conversed with Henry Clay, once the object of my boyish enthusiasm, and encountered the fascination of his smile, and winning voice as he playfully reproached me for deserting an old friend. I had there, in spite of my knowledge of its gross perversion to the support of wrong, felt something of that respect and reverence which is always extorted by intellectual power. For the moment I half forgot in my appreciation of the gifts of genius with which these men have been so wonderfully endowed the fact that they have employed their talents in upholding a system which crushes and kills the mind of millions. But here in the loathsome slave-prison, I saw them in another light. — The fascination of genius which, like the silver veil of the Eastern Prophet, had covered them, fell off, and left only the deformity of tyranny. I looked upon the one as the High Priest of Slavery, ministering at its altar, and scowling defiance to the religion and the philanthropy of Christendom — the fitting champion of that Southern Democracy whose appropriate emblem is the Slave-Whip, with a negro at one end and an overseer at the other. As I looked down that range of dungeons, filled with God's immortal children converted into merchandise, I thought of Henry Clay's declaration "that *is* property which makes law property," and that "two hundred years of legislation had sanctioned and sanctified Slavery." I thought of Van Buren's Veto Pledge — and its reiteration in Gen. Harrison's Inaugural Message — and of the two great parties thus pledged by their chiefs to the support of the system whose bitter fruits were now visible before me. I saw the intimate and complete connexion between the planter who raises the slave for market, the dealer who buys him, the legislator who sustains and legalizes the traffic, and *the Northern freeman who by his vote places that legislator in power*. In the silence of my soul, I pledged myself anew to Liberty; and felt at that moment the baptism of a new life-long consecration to the cause. — God helping me, the resolution which I then formed shall be fulfilled to the uttermost!

I left that prison with mingled feelings of shame, sorrow, indignation. Before me was the great dome of the Capitol — our national representatives were passing and re-passing the marble stairs — over the stripes and stars fluttered in the breeze which swept down the Potomac. I was thus compelled to realize the fact that the abominations I had looked upon were in the District of Columbia — the chosen home of our republic — the hearth-stone of the national honor — that the representatives of the nations of Europe here looked at one and the same glance upon the capitol and the slave-jail. Not long before a friend had placed in my hand a letter from Seidensticker, one of the leaders of the patriotic movement in behalf of German liberty in 1831. It was written from the prison of Celle, where he has been for eight years a living martyr to the cause of Freedom. In this letter the noble German expresses his indignant astonishment at the speeches of Calhoun and others in Congress on the subject of slavery, and deplores the sad influence which our slave system is exerting upon the freedom of Europe. I could thus estimate, in some degree, the blighting effects of our union of liberty and slavery, upon the cause of political reform in the old world, strengthening the hands of the Peels and Meternichs, and deepening around the martyrs and confessors of European freedom, the cold shadow of their prisons. All that I have said or done for the cause of Emancipation heretofore seemed cold and trifling at that moment, and even now, when I am disposed to blame the ardor and enthusiasm of some of my friends, and censure their harsh denunciations of Slavery and its abettors, I think of the slave jails of the District of Columbia and am constrained to exclaim with Jonathan Edwards, when in his day, he was accused of fanaticism: —"If these things be enthusiasm and the fruits of a distempered imagination let me still ever more possess them." It is a very easy thing at our comfortable northern fire-sides to condemn and deplore the zeal and extravagance of the abolitionists, and to come to the conclusion that Slavery is a trifling matter in comparison with the grave questions of Banks and sub-Treasuries, but he who can visit the Slave-Markets of the District, without feeling his whole nature aroused in sorrow and indignation, must be more or less than a man.

John G. Whittier

RALPH WALDO EMERSON

Ralph Waldo Emerson (1803–82) was a poet, essayist, lecturer, and onetime Unitarian minister. Never much of a political activist, he observed events in Washington with interest and, at times, despair. Both are evident in the journal entry for 1847 excerpted here, concerning the debates in Congress leading up to the war with Mexico. After Congress passed the Fugitive Slave Law of 1850, however, Emerson vowed to become more active, exclaiming: "The last year has forced us all into politics." Still, it wasn't until 1862, after the start of the Civil War, that he made his first visit to the federal city. Ostensibly, the visit was in response to an invitation to address the Smithsonian Association, but he also saw the occasion as an opportunity to meet with President Lincoln to convince him to issue an emancipation proclamation as a strategy for defeating the South.

From *The Journals of Ralph Waldo Emerson, 1820–1872*

MARCH–APRIL 1847   The name of Washington City in the newspapers is every day of blacker shade. All the news from that quarter being of a sadder type, more malignant. It seems to be settled that no act of honour or benevolence or justice is to be expected from the American government, but only this, that they will be as wicked as they dare. No man now can have any sort of success in politics without a streak of infamy crossing his name.

Things have another order in these men's eyes. Heavy is hollow, and good is evil. A Western man in Congress the other day spoke of the opponents of the Texan and Mexican plunder as "every light character in the House," and our good friend in State Street speaks of "the solid portion of the community," meaning, of course, the sharpers. I feel, meantime, that those who succeed in life, in civilized society, are beasts of prey. It has always been so. The Demostheneses, the Phocions, the Aristideses, the Washingtons even, must bear that deduction, that they were not pure souls, or they would not have been fishers and gunners. They had large infusions of virtue, and hence their calamities and the mischievous dignity they have lent to the rogues that belong in those piratical employments.

We live in Lilliput. The Americans are freewillers, fussy, self-asserting, buzzing all round creation. But the Asiatics believe it is writ on the iron leaf, and will not turn on their heel to save them from famine, plague, or sword. That is great, gives a great air to the people.

We live in Lilliput. Men are unfit to live, from their obvious inequality to their own necessities, . . . the only path of escape is Virtue. Cause and Effect are the gamesters who win, and it will beget a resignation to Fate that even the Americans will be exalted.

The question recurs whether we should descend into the ring. My own very small experience instructs me that the people are to be taken in very small doses. Vestry meetings and primary assemblies do not edify me. And I caution philosophers and scholars to use lenses and media.

Alcott said, the rest of the man will follow his head. His head is not his contemporary, but his ancestor and predecessor. Let him be a Cause.

JANUARY 31, 1862   At Washington, 31 January, 1 Feb, 2d, & 3rd, saw Sumner, who on the 2d, carried me to Mr Chase, Mr Bates, Mr Stanton, Mr Welles, Mr Seward, Lord Lyons, and President Lincoln. The President impressed me more favorably than I had hoped. A frank, sincere, well-meaning man, with a lawyer's habit of mind, good clear statement of his fact, correct enough, not vulgar, as described; but with a sort of boyish cheerfulness, or that kind of sincerity & jolly good meaning that our class meetings on Commencement Days show, in telling our old stories over. When he has made his remark, he looks up at you with great satisfaction, & shows all his white teeth, & laughs. He argued to Sumner the whole case of Gordon, the slave-trader, point by point, and added that he was not quite satisfied yet, & meant to refresh his memory by looking again at the evidence.

All this showed a fidelity & conscientiousness very honorable to him.

When I was introduced to him, he said, "O Mr Emerson, I once heard you say in a lecture, that a Kentuckian seems to say by his air & manners, *'Here am I; if you don't like me, the worse for you.'*"...

Mr Seward received us in his dingy State Department.... He began, "Yes I know Mr Emerson. The President said yesterday, when I was going to tell him a story, 'Well, Seward, don't let it be smutty.'"...

The next morning, at 10¼, I visited Mr Seward, in his library, who was writing, surrounded by his secretary & some stock brokers....

We went to Church. I told him "I hoped he would not demoralize me; I was not much accustomed to churches, but trusted he would carry me to a safe place." He said, he attended Rev. Dr Pyne's Church. On the way, we met Gov. Fish, who was also to go with him. Miss Seward, to whom I had been presented, accompanied us. I was a little aukward in finding my place in the Common Prayer Book, & Mr Seward was obliging in guiding me, from time to time. But I had the old wonder come over me at the Egyptian stationariness of the English church. The hopeless blind antiquity of life & thought — indicated alike by prayers & creed & sermon — was wonderful to see, & amid worshippers & in times like these. There was something exceptional too in the Doctor's sermon. His church was all made up of secessionists; he had remained loyal, they had all left him, & abused him in the papers: And in the sermon he presented his griefs,

& preached Jacobitish passive obedience to powers that be, as his defence. In going out, Mr S. praised the sermon. I said that the Doctor did not seem to have read the Gospel according to San Francisco, or the Epistle to the Californians; he had not got quite down into these noisy times.

Mr S. said, "Will you go & call on the President? I usually call on him at this hour." Of course, I was glad to go.

We found in the President's chamber his two little sons — boys of 7 & 8 years perhaps — whom the barber was dressing & "whiskeying their hair," as he said, not much to the apparent contentment of the boys, when the cologne got into their eyes. The eldest boy immediately told Mr Seward, "he could not guess what they had got." Mr Seward "bet a quarter of a dollar that he could. — Was it a rabbit? was it a bird? was it a pig?" he guessed always wrong, & paid his quarter to the youngest, before the eldest declared it was a rabbit. But he sent away the mulatto to find the President, & the boys disappeared. The President came, and Mr Seward said, "You have not been to Church today." "No," he said, "and, if he must make a frank confession, he had been reading for the first time Mr Sumner's speech (on the Trent affair)."

. . . Mr Seward told the President somewhat of Dr Pyne's sermon, & the President said, he intended to show his respect for him some time by going to hear him.

. . . In the Congressional Library I found Spofford Assistant Librarian. He told me, that, for the last twelve (?) years, it had been under Southern domination, & as under dead men. Thus the Medical department was very large, and the Theological very large, whilst of modern literature very imperfect.

There was no copy of the "Atlantic Monthly," or of the "Knickerbocker," none of the "Tribune," or "Times," or any N.Y. Journal. There was no copy of the "London Saturday Review" taken, or any other live journal, but the "London Court Journal," in a hundred volumes, duly bound. Nor was it possible now to mend matters, because no money could they get from Congress, though an appropriation had been voted.

WILLIAM WELLS BROWN

The son of a white man and a slave woman, William Wells Brown (1814–84) was born on a Kentucky plantation, became a fugitive slave at twenty, and began lecturing for the Western New York Anti-Slavery Society in 1843. A natural writer who worked in many genres, including fiction, drama, poetry, travel writing, and history, he composed the first version of his personal narrative in 1847. The work went through several British and American editions and is included as an introduction to his recently recovered novel *Clotel; or, The President's Daughter: A Narrative of Slave Life in the United States* (1853), a portion of which is set in the slave prisons of Washington City. *Clotel* is generally regarded as the first full-length novel written by an African American. The poem that concludes this excerpt was originally written by Grace Greenwood, a popular author and abolitionist, and published in her *Poems* (1851). It was the genesis of Clotel's leap from the long bridge crossing the Potomac. Brown appropriated the poem almost in its entirety (along with other works, such as newspaper stories), but added a final stanza of his own.

Death Is Freedom
From *Clotel; or, The President's Daughter:*
A Narrative of Slave Life in the United States

> "I asked but freedom, and ye gave
> Chains, and the freedom of the grave."
> — *Snelling.*

There are, in the District of Columbia, several slave prisons, or "negro pens," as they are termed. These prisons are mostly occupied by persons to keep their slaves in, when collecting their gangs together for the New Orleans market. Some of them belong to the government, and one, in particular, is noted for having been the place where a number of free coloured persons have been incarcerated from time to time. In this district is situated the capitol of the United States. Any free coloured persons visiting Washington, if not provided with papers asserting and proving their right to be free, may be arrested and placed in one of these dens. If they succeed in showing that they are free, they are set at liberty, provided they are able to pay the expenses of their arrest and imprisonment; if they cannot pay these expenses, they are sold out. Through this unjust and oppressive law, many persons born in the Free States have been consigned to a life of slavery on the cotton, sugar, or rice plantations of the Southern States. By order of her master, Clotel was removed from Richmond and placed in one of these prisons, to await the sailing of a vessel for New Orleans. The prison in which she was put stands midway between the capitol at Washington and the president's house. Here the fugitive saw nothing but slaves brought in and taken out, to be placed in ships and sent away to the same part of the country to which she herself would soon be compelled to go. She had seen or heard nothing of her daughter while in Richmond, and all hope of seeing her now had fled. If she was carried back to New Orleans, she could expect no mercy from her master.

At the dusk of the evening previous to the day when she was to be sent off, as the old prison was being closed for the night, she suddenly darted past her keeper, and ran for her life. It is not a great distance from the prison to the Long Bridge, which passes from the lower part of the city across the Potomac, to the extensive forests and woodlands of the celebrated Arlington Place, occupied by that distinguished relative and descendant of the immortal Washington, Mr. George W. Curtis. Thither the poor fugitive directed her flight. So unexpected was her escape, that she had quite a number of rods the start before the keeper had secured the other prisoners, and rallied his assistants in pursuit. It was at an hour when, and in a part of the city where, horses could not be readily obtained for the chase; no bloodhounds were at hand to run down the flying woman; and for once it seemed as though there was to be a fair trial of speed and endurance between, the slave and the slave-catchers. The keeper and his forces raised the hue and cry on her pathway close behind; but so rapid was the flight along the wide avenue, that the astonished citizens, as they poured forth from their dwellings to learn the cause of alarm, were only able to comprehend the nature of the case in time to fall in with the motley mass in pursuit, (as many a one did that night,) to raise an anxious prayer to heaven, as they refused to join in the pursuit, that the panting fugitive might escape, and the merciless soul dealer for once be disappointed of his prey. And now with the speed of an arrow — having passed the avenue — with the distance between her and her pursuers constantly increasing, this poor hunted female gained the *"Long Bridge"* as it is called, where interruption seemed improbable, and already did her heart begin to beat high with the hope of success. She had only to pass three-fourths of a mile across the bridge, and she could bury herself in a vast forest, just at the time when the curtain of night would close around her, and protect her from the pursuit of her enemies.

But God by his Providence had otherwise determined. He had determined that an appalling tragedy should be enacted that night, within plain sight of the President's house and the capital of the Union, which should be an evidence wherever it should be known, of the unconquerable love of liberty the heart may inherit; as well as a fresh admonition to the slave dealer, of the cruelty and enormity of his crimes. Just as the pursuers crossed the high draw for the passage of sloops, soon after entering upon the bridge, they beheld three men slowly approaching from the Virginia side. They immediately called to them to arrest the fugitive, whom they proclaimed a runaway slave. True to their Virginian instincts as she came near, they formed in line across the narrow bridge, and prepared to seize her. Seeing escape impossible in that quarter, she stopped suddenly, and turned upon her pursuers. On came the profane and ribald crew, faster than ever, already exulting in her capture, and threatening punishment for her flight. For a moment she looked wildly and anxiously around to see if there was no hope of escape. On either hand, far down below, rolled the deep foamy waters of the Potomac, and before and behind the rapidly approaching step and noisy voices of pursuers, showing how vain would be any further effort for freedom. Her resolution was taken. She clasped her *hands* convulsively, and raised *them*, as she at the same time raised her *eyes* towards heaven, and begged for that mercy and compassion *there*, which had been denied her on earth; and then, with a single bound, she vaulted over the railings of the bridge, and sunk for ever beneath the waves of the river!

Thus died Clotel, the daughter of Thomas Jefferson, a president of the United States; a man distinguished as the author of the Declaration of American Independence, and one of the first statesmen of that country.

Had Clotel escaped from oppression in any other land, in the disguise in which she fled from the Mississippi to Richmond, and reached the United States, no honour within the gift of the American people would have been too good to have been heaped upon the heroic woman. But she was a slave, and therefore out of the pale of their sympathy. They have tears to shed over Greece and Poland; they have an abundance of sympathy for "poor Ireland;" they can furnish a ship of war to convey the Hungarian refugees from a Turkish prison to the "land of the free and home of the brave." They boast that America is the "cradle of liberty;" if it is, I fear they have rocked the child to death. The body of Clotel was picked up from the bank of the river, where it had been washed by the strong current, a hole dug in the sand, and there deposited, without either inquest being held over it, or religious service being performed. Such was the life and such the death of a woman whose virtues and goodness of heart would have done honour to one in a higher station of life, and who, if she had been born in any other land but that of slavery, would have been honoured and loved. A few days after the death of Clotel, the following poem appeared in one of the newspapers:

"Now, rest for the wretched! the long day is past,
And night on yon prison descendeth at last.
Now lock up and bolt! Ha, jailor, look there!
Who flies like a wild bird escaped from the snare?
A woman, a slave — up, out in pursuit,
While linger some gleams of day!
Let thy call ring out! — now a rabble rout
Is at thy heels — speed away!

"A bold race for freedom! — On, fugitive, on!
Heaven help but the right, and thy freedom is won.
How eager she drinks the free air of the plains;
Every limb, every nerve, every fibre she strains;

From Columbia's glorious capitol,
Columbia's daughter flees
To the sanctuary God has given —
The sheltering forest trees.

"Now she treads the Long Bridge — joy lighteth her eye —
Beyond her the dense wood and darkening sky —
Wild hopes thrill her heart as she neareth the shore:
O, despair! there are *men* fast advancing before!
Shame, shame on their manhood! they hear, they heed
The cry, her flight to stay,
And like demon forms with their outstretched arms,
They wait to seize their prey!

"She pauses, she turns! Ah, will she flee back?
Like wolves, her pursuers howl loud on their track;
She lifteth to Heaven one look of despair —
Her anguish breaks forth in one hurried prayer —
Hark! her jailor's yell! like a bloodhound's bay
On the low night wind it sweeps!
Now, death or the chain! to the stream she turns,
And she leaps! O God, she leaps!

"The dark and the cold, yet merciful wave,
Receives to its bosom the form of the slave:
She rises — earth's scenes on her dim vision gleam,
Yet she struggleth not with the strong rushing stream:
And low are the death-cries her woman's heart gives,
As she floats adown the river,
Faint and more faint grows the drowning voice,
And her cries have ceased for ever!

"Now back, jailor, back to thy dungeons, again,
To swing the red lash and rivet the chain!
The form thou would'st fetter — returned to its God;
The universe holdeth no realm of night
More drear than her slavery —
More merciless fiends than here stayed her flight —
Joy! the hunted slave is free!

"That bond-woman's corse — let Potomac's proud wave
Go bear it along *by our Washington's grave*,
And heave it high up on that hallowed strand,

> *To tell of the freedom he won for our land.*
> A weak woman's corse, by freemen chased down;
> Hurrah for our country! hurrah!
> To freedom she leaped, through drowning and death —
> Hurrah for our country! hurrah!"

SOLOMON NORTHUP

Solomon Northup (1808–63?) was a freeborn black from upstate New York who lived a quiet life as a farmer, laborer, and family man before being kidnapped, in 1841, and sold into slavery. Tricked into joining a traveling circus, he was sold to slave traders and imprisoned in Washington, D.C., before being sold again and shipped to the Deep South, where he was forced into slavery on a series of plantations. When he finally regained his freedom, he returned to New York and almost immediately published his story under the title *Twelve Years a Slave* (1853). His narrative sold over 30,000 copies and was cited by Harriet Beecher Stowe in her *Key to Uncle Tom's Cabin* (1853) with the hope of bolstering her famous novel's claims concerning the evils of slavery.

From *Twelve Years a Slave*

Some three hours elapsed, during which time I remained seated on the low bench, absorbed in painful meditations. At length I heard the crowing of a cock, and soon a distant rumbling sound, as of carriages hurrying through the streets, came to my ears, and I knew that it was day. No ray of light, however, penetrated my prison. Finally, I heard footsteps immediately overhead, as of some one walking to and fro. It occurred to me then that I must be in an underground apartment, and the damp, mouldy odors of the place confirmed the supposition. The noise above continued for at least an hour, when, at last, I heard footsteps approaching from without. A key rattled in the lock — a strong door swung back upon its hinges, admitting a flood of light, and two men entered and stood before me. One of them was a large, powerful man, forty years of age, perhaps, with dark, chestnut-colored hair, slightly interspersed with gray. His face was full, his complexion flush, his features grossly coarse, expressive of nothing but cruelty and cunning. He was about five feet ten inches high, of full habit, and, without prejudice, I must be allowed to say, was a man whose whole appearance was sinister and repugnant. His name was James H. Burch, as I learned afterwards — a well-known slave-dealer in Washington; and then, or lately, connected in business, as a partner, with Theophilus Freeman, of

New-Orleans. The person who accompanied him was a simple lackey, named Ebenezer Radburn, who acted merely in the capacity of turnkey. Both of these men still live in Washington, or did, at the time of my return through that city from slavery in January last.

The light admitted through the open door enabled me to observe the room in which I was confined. It was about twelve feet square — the walls of solid masonry. The floor was of heavy plank. There was one small window, crossed with great iron bars, with an outside shutter, securely fastened.

An iron-bound door led into an adjoining cell, or vault, wholly destitute of windows, or any means of admitting light. The furniture of the room in which I was, consisted of the wooden bench on which I sat, an old-fashioned, dirty box stove, and besides these, in either cell, there was neither bed, nor blanket, nor any other thing whatever. The door, through which Burch and Radburn entered, led through a small passage, up a flight of steps into a yard, surrounded by a brick wall ten or twelve feet high, immediately in rear of a building of the same width as itself. The yard extended rearward from the house about thirty feet. In one part of the wall there was a strongly ironed door, opening into a narrow, covered passage, leading along one side of the house into the street. The doom of the colored man, upon whom the door leading out of that narrow passage closed, was sealed. The top of the wall supported one end of a roof, which ascended inwards, forming a kind of open shed. Underneath the roof there was a crazy loft all round, where slaves, if so disposed, might sleep at night, or in inclement weather seek shelter from the storm. It was like a farmer's barnyard in most respects, save it was so constructed that the outside world could never see the human cattle that were herded there.

The building to which the yard was attached, was two stories high, fronting on one of the public streets of Washington. Its outside presented only the appearance of a quiet private residence. A stranger looking at it, would never have dreamed of its execrable uses. Strange as it may seem, within plain sight of this same house, looking down from its commanding height upon it, was the Capitol. The voices of patriotic representatives boasting of freedom and equality, and the rattling of the poor slave's chains, almost commingled. A slave pen within the very shadow of the Capitol!

Such is a correct description as it was in 1841, of Williams' slave pen in Washington, in one of the cellars of which I found myself so unaccountably confined.

"Well, my boy, how do you feel now?" said Burch, as he entered through the open door. I replied that I was sick, and inquired the cause of my imprisonment. He answered that I was his slave — that he had bought me, and that he was about to send me to New-Orleans. I asserted, aloud and boldly, that I

was a free man — a resident of Saratoga, where I had a wife and children, who
were also free, and that my name was Northup. I complained bitterly of the
strange treatment I had received, and threatened, upon my liberation, to have
satisfaction for the wrong. He denied that I was free, and with an emphatic
oath, declared that I came from Georgia. Again and again I asserted I was no
man's slave, and insisted upon his taking off my chains at once. He endeavored
to hush me, as if he feared my voice would be overheard. But I would not be
silent, and denounced the authors of my imprisonment, whoever they might be,
as unmitigated villains. Finding he could not quiet me, he flew into a towering
passion. With blasphemous oaths, he called me a black liar, a runaway from
Georgia, and every other profane and vulgar epithet that the most indecent
fancy could conceive.

During this time Radburn was standing silently by. His business was, to
oversee this human, or rather inhuman stable, receiving slaves, feeding and
whipping them, at the rate of two shillings a head per day. Turning to him,
Burch ordered the paddle and cat-o'-ninetails to be brought in. He disappeared,
and in a few moments returned with these instruments of torture. The paddle,
as it is termed in slave-beating parlance, or at least the one with which I first
became acquainted, and of which I now speak, was a piece of hard-wood board,
eighteen or twenty inches long, moulded to the shape of an old-fashioned pudding stick, or ordinary oar. The flattened portion, which was about the size in
circumference of two open hands, was bored with a small auger in numerous
places. The cat was a large rope of many strands — the strands unraveled, and a
knot tied at the extremity of each.

As soon as these formidable whips appeared, I was seized by both of them,
and roughly divested of my clothing. My feet, as has been stated, were fastened
to the floor. Drawing me over the bench, face downwards, Radburn placed his
heavy foot upon the fetters, between my wrists, holding them painfully to the
floor. With the paddle, Burch commenced beating me. Blow after blow was inflicted upon my naked body. When his unrelenting arm grew tired, he stopped
and asked if I still insisted I *was* a free man. I did insist upon it, and then the
blows were renewed, faster and more energetically, if possible, than before.
When again tired, he would repeat the same question, and receiving the same
answer, continue his cruel labor. All this time, the incarnate devil was uttering
most fiendish oaths. At length the paddle broke, leaving the useless handle in
his hand. Still I would not yield. All his brutal blows could not force from my
lips the foul lie that I was a slave. Casting madly on the floor the handle of the
broken paddle, he seized the rope. This was far more painful than the other.
I struggled with all my power, but it was in vain. I prayed for mercy, but my
prayer was only answered with imprecations and with stripes. I thought I must

die beneath the lashes of the accursed brute. Even now the flesh crawls upon my bones, as I recall the scene. I was all on fire. My sufferings I can compare to nothing else than the burning agonies of hell!

At last I became silent to his repeated questions. I would make no reply. In fact, I was becoming almost unable to speak. Still he plied the lash without stint upon my poor body, until it seemed that the lacerated flesh was stripped from my bones at every stroke. A man with a particle of mercy in his soul would not have beaten even a dog so cruelly. At length Radburn said that it was useless to whip me any more — that I would be sore enough. Thereupon, Burch desisted, saying, with an admonitory shake of his fist in my face, and hissing the words through his firm-set teeth, that if ever I dared to utter again that I was entitled to my freedom, that I had been kidnapped, or any thing whatever of the kind, the castigation I had just received was nothing in comparison with what would follow. He swore that he would either conquer or kill me. With these consolatory words, the fetters were taken from my wrists, my feet still remaining fastened to the ring; the shutter of the little barred window, which had been opened, was again closed, and going out, locking the great door behind them, I was left in darkness as before.

In an hour, perhaps two, my heart leaped to my throat, as the key rattled in the door again. I, who had been so lonely, and who had longed so ardently to see some one, I cared not who, now shuddered at the thought of man's approach. A human face was fearful to me, especially a white one. Radburn entered, bringing with him, on a tin plate, a piece of shriveled fried pork, a slice of bread and a cup of water. He asked me how I felt, and remarked that I had received a pretty severe flogging. He remonstrated with me against the propriety of asserting my freedom. In rather a patronizing and confidential manner, he gave it to me as his advice, that the less I said on that subject the better it would be for me. The man evidently endeavored to appear kind — whether touched at the sight of my sad condition, or with the view of silencing, on my part, any further expression of my rights, it is not necessary now to conjecture. He unlocked the fetters from my ankles, opened the shutters of the little window, and departed, leaving me again alone.

By this time I had become stiff and sore; my body was covered with blisters, and it was with great pain and difficulty that I could move. From the window I could observe nothing but the roof resting on the adjacent wall. At night I laid down upon the damp, hard floor, without any pillow or covering whatever. Punctually, twice a day, Radburn came in, with his pork, and bread, and water. I had but little appetite, though I was tormented with continual thirst. My wounds would not permit me to remain but a few minutes in any one position; so, sitting, or standing, or moving slowly round, I passed the days and nights.

I was heart sick and discouraged. Thoughts of my family, of my wife and children, continually occupied my mind. When sleep overpowered me I dreamed of them — dreamed I was again in Saratoga — that I could see their faces, and hear their voices calling me. Awakening from the pleasant phantasms of sleep to the bitter realities around me, I could but groan and weep. Still my spirit was not broken. I indulged the anticipation of escape, and that speedily. It was impossible, I reasoned, that men could be so unjust as to detain me as a slave, when the truth of my case was known. Burch, ascertaining I was no runaway from Georgia, would certainly let me go. Though suspicions of Brown and Hamilton were not unfrequent, I could not reconcile myself to the idea that they were instrumental to my imprisonment. Surely they would seek me out — they would deliver me from thraldom. Alas! I had not then learned the measure of "man's inhumanity to man," nor to what limitless extent of wickedness he will go for the love of gain.

In the course of several days the outer door was thrown open, allowing me the liberty of the yard. There I found three slaves — one of them a lad of ten years, the others young men of about twenty and twenty-five. I was not long in forming an acquaintance, and learning their names and the particulars of their history.

The eldest was a colored man named Clemens Ray. He had lived in Washington; had driven a hack, and worked in a livery stable there for a long time. He was very intelligent, and fully comprehended his situation. The thought of going south overwhelmed him with grief. Burch had purchased him a few days before, and had placed him there until such time as he was ready to send him to the New-Orleans market. From him I learned for the first time that I was in William's Slave Pen, a place I had never heard of previously. He described to me the uses for which it was designed. I repeated to him the particulars of my unhappy story, but he could only give me the consolation of his sympathy. He also advised me to be silent henceforth on the subject of my freedom, for, knowing the character of Burch, he assured me that it would only be attended with renewed whipping. The next eldest was named John Williams. He was raised in Virginia, not far from Washington. Burch had taken him in payment of a debt, and he constantly entertained the hope that his master would redeem him — a hope that was subsequently realized. The lad was a sprightly child, that answered to the name of Randall. Most of the time he was playing about the yard, but occasionally would cry, calling for his mother, and wondering when she would come. His mother's absence seemed to be the great and only grief in his little heart. He was too young to realize his condition, and when the memory of his mother was not in his mind, he amused us with his pleasant pranks.

At night, Ray, Williams, and the boy, slept in the left of the shed, while I was locked in the cell. Finally we were each provided with blankets, such as are used upon horses — the only bedding I was allowed to have for twelve years afterwards. Ray and Williams asked me many questions about New-York — how colored people were treated there; how they could have homes and families of their own, with none to disturb and oppress them; and Ray, especially, sighed continually for freedom. Such conversations, however, were not in the hearing of Burch, or the keeper Radburn. Aspirations such as these would have brought down the lash upon our backs.

NATHANIEL HAWTHORNE

A famous author of allegorical tales and historical romances, Nathaniel Hawthorne (1804–64) served in the Boston Custom House for a time and then as surveyor of the port at Salem. A classmate of Franklin Pierce at Bowdoin College, he published a campaign biography of the future president in 1852; in return, he was made consul in Liverpool, a post he held throughout Pierce's term in office, and then repaired to Italy. The Civil War began shortly after he returned from Europe. Wishing to do something for his country, Hawthorne made a trip to Washington and vicinity to report on his findings at the front. The result was *Chiefly About War-Matters. By a Peaceable Man* (originally published in *Atlantic Monthly*, 1862), a sardonic travelogue that takes into view Secretary Seward; the "essential representative of all Yankees," President Lincoln; the nearby port of Alexandria; and contrabands out of the South or "Secessia."

From "Chiefly About War-Matters. By a Peaceable Man"

There is no remoteness of life and thought, no hermetically sealed seclusion, except, possibly, that of the grave, into which the disturbing influences of this war do not penetrate. Of course, the general heart-quake of the country long ago knocked at my cottage-door, and compelled me, reluctantly, to suspend the contemplation of certain fantasies, to which, according to my harmless custom, I was endeavoring to give a sufficiently life-like aspect to admit of their figuring in a romance. As I make no pretensions to state-craft or soldiership, and could promote the common weal neither by valor nor counsel, it seemed, at first, a pity that I should be debarred from such unsubstantial business as I had contrived for myself, since nothing more genuine was to be substituted for it. But I magnanimously considered that there is a kind of treason in insulating one's self from the universal fear and sorrow, and thinking one's idle thoughts in the dread time of civil war; and could a man be so cold and hard-hearted, he would better deserve to be sent to Fort Warren than many who have found their way thither on the score of violent, but misdirected sympathies. . . . So I gave myself up to reading newspapers and listening to the click of the telegraph, like other people; until, after a great many months of such pastime, it grew so abominably irksome that I determined to look a little more closely at matters with my own eyes.

Accordingly we set out — a friend and myself — towards Washington, while it was still the long, dreary January of our Northern year, though March in name; nor were we unwilling to clip a little margin off the five months' winter, during which there is nothing genial in New England save the fireside. It was a clear, frosty morning, when we started. . . .

. . . We were not in time to see Washington as a camp. On the very day of our arrival sixty thousand men had crossed the Potomac on their march towards Manassas; and almost with their first step into the Virginia mud, the phantas-magory of a countless host and impregnable ramparts, before which they had so long remained quiescent, dissolved quite away. It was as if General McClellan had thrust his sword into a gigantic enemy, and, beholding him suddenly col-lapse, had discovered to himself and the world that he had merely punctured an enormously swollen bladder. . . .

. . . Everybody seems to be at Washington, and yet there is a singular dearth of imperatively noticeable people there. I question whether there are half a dozen individuals, in all kinds of eminence, at whom a stranger, wearied with the contact of a hundred moderate celebrities, would turn round to snatch a second glance. Secretary Seward, to be sure, — a pale, largenosed, elderly man, of moderate stature, with a decided originality of gait and aspect, and a cigar in his mouth, — etc., etc.

Of course, there was one other personage, in the class of statesmen, whom I should have been truly mortified to leave Washington without seeing; since (temporarily, at least, and by force of circumstances) he was the man of men. But a private grief had built up a barrier about him, impeding the customary free intercourse of Americans with their chief magistrate; so that I might have come away without a glimpse of his very remarkable physiognomy, save for a semi-official opportunity of which I was glad to take advantage. The fact is, we were invited to annex ourselves, as supernumeraries, to a deputation that was about to wait upon the President, from a Massachusetts whip-factory, with a present of a splendid whip.

Our immediate party consisted only of four or five (including Major Ben Perley Poore, with his notebook and pencil), but we were joined by several other persons, who seemed to have been lounging about the precincts of the White

House, under the spacious porch, or within the hall, and who swarmed in with us to take the chances of a presentation. Nine o'clock had been appointed as the time for receiving the deputation, and we were punctual to the moment; but not so the President, who sent us word that he was eating his breakfast, and would come as soon as he could. His appetite, we were glad to think, must have been a pretty fair one; for we waited about half an hour in one of the antechambers, and then were ushered into a reception-room, in one corner of which sat the Secretaries of War and of the Treasury, expecting, like ourselves, the termination of the Presidential breakfast. During this interval there were several new additions to our group, one or two of whom were in a working-garb, so that we formed a very miscellaneous collection of people, mostly unknown to each other, and without any common sponsor, but all with an equal right to look our head-servant in the face. By and by there was a little stir on the stair-case and in the passage-way, and in lounged a tall, loosejointed figure, of an exaggerated Yankee port and demeanor, whom (as being about the homeliest man I ever saw, yet by no means repulsive or disagreeable) it was impossible not to recognize as Uncle Abe.

Unquestionably, Western man though he be, and Kentuckian by birth, President Lincoln is the essential representative of all Yankees, and the veritable specimen, physically, of what the world seems determined to regard as our characteristic qualities. It is the strangest and yet the fittest thing in the jumble of human vicissitudes, that he, out of so many millions, unlooked for, unselected by any intelligible process that could be based upon his genuine qualities, unknown to those who chose him, and unsuspected of what endowments may adapt him for his tremendous responsibility, should have found the way open for him to fling his lank personality into the chair of state, — where, I presume, it was his first impulse to throw his legs on the council-table, and tell the Cabinet Ministers a story. There is no describing his lengthy awkwardness, nor the uncouthness of his movement; and yet it seemed as if I had been in the habit of seeing him daily, and had shaken hands with him a thousand times in some village street; so true was he to the aspect of the pattern American, though with a certain extravagance which, possibly, I exaggerated still further by the delighted eagerness with which I took it in. If put to guess his calling and livelihood, I should have taken him for a country schoolmaster as soon as anything else. He was dressed in a rusty black frockcoat and pantaloons, unbrushed, and worn so faithfully that the suit had adapted itself to the curves and angularities of his figure, and had grown to be an outer skin of the man. He had shabby slippers on his feet. His hair was black, still unmixed with gray, stiff, somewhat bushy, and had apparently been acquainted with neither brush nor comb that morning, after the disarrangement of the pillow; and as to a night-cap, Uncle Abe probably knows nothing of such effeminacies. His complexion is dark and sallow, betokening, I fear, an insalubrious atmosphere around the White House; he has thick black eyebrows and an impending brow; his nose is large, and the lines about his mouth are very strongly defined.

The whole physiognomy is as coarse a one as you would meet anywhere in the length and breadth of the States; but, withal, it is redeemed, illuminated, softened, and brightened by a kindly though serious look out of his eyes, and an expression of homely sagacity, that seems weighted with rich results of village experience. A great deal of native sense; no bookish cultivation, no refinement; honest at heart, and thoroughly so, and yet, in some sort, sly, — at least, endowed with a sort of tact and wisdom that are akin to craft, and would impel him, I think, to take an antagonist in flank, rather than to make a bull-run at him right in front. But, on the whole, I like this sallow, queer, sagacious visage, with the homely human sympathies that warmed it; and, for my small share in the matter, would as lief have Uncle Abe for a ruler as any man whom it would have been practicable to put in his place.

Immediately on his entrance the President accosted our member of Congress, who had us in charge, and, with a comical twist of his face, made some jocular remark about the length of his breakfast. He then greeted us all round, not waiting for an introduction, but shaking and squeezing everybody's hand with the utmost cordiality, whether the individual's name was announced to him or not. His manner towards us was wholly without pretence, but yet had a kind of natural dignity, quite sufficient to keep the forwardest of us from clapping him on the shoulder and asking him for a story. A mutual acquaintance being established, our leader took the whip out of its case, and began to read the address of presentation. The whip was an exceedingly long one, its handle wrought in ivory (by some artist in the Massachusetts State Prison, I believe), and ornamented with a medallion of the President, and other equally beautiful devices; and along its whole length there was a succession of golden bands and ferrules. The address was shorter than the whip, but equally well made, consisting chiefly of an explanatory description of these artistic designs, and closing with a hint that the gift was a suggestive and emblematic one, and that the President would recognize the use to which such an instrument should be put.

This suggestion gave Uncle Abe rather a delicate task in his reply, because, slight as the matter seemed, it apparently called for some declaration, or intimation, or faint foreshadowing of policy in reference to the conduct of the war, and the final treatment of the Rebels. But the President's Yankee aptness and not-to-be-caughtness stood him in good stead, and he jerked or wiggled himself out of the dilemma with an uncouth dexterity that was entirely in character; although, without his gesticulation of eye and mouth, — and especially the flourish of the whip, with which he imagined himself touching up a pair of fat horses, — I doubt whether his words would be worth recording, even if I could remember them. The gist of the reply was, that he accepted the whip as an emblem of peace, not punishment; and, this great affair over, we retired out of the presence in high good-humor, only regretting that we could not have seen the President sit down and fold up his legs (which is said to be a most extraordinary spectacle), or have heard him tell one of those delectable stories for which he is so celebrated. A good many of them are afloat upon the common talk of Washington, and are certainly the aptest, pithiest, and funniest little things imaginable; though, to be sure, they smack of the frontier freedom, and would not always bear repetition in a drawing-room, or on the immaculate page of the Atlantic.

Good Heavens! what liberties have I been taking with one of the potentates of the earth, and the man on whose conduct more important consequences depend than on that of any other historical personage of the century! But with whom is an American citizen entitled to take a liberty, if not with his own chief magistrate? However, lest the above allusions to President Lincoln's little peculiarities (already well known to the country and to the world) should be misinterpreted, I deem it proper to say a word or two in regard to him, of unfeigned respect and measurable confidence. He is evidently a man of keen faculties, and, what is still more to the purpose, of powerful character. As to his integrity, the people have that intuition of it which is never deceived. Before he actually entered upon his great office, and for a considerable time afterwards, there is no reason to suppose that he adequately estimated the gigantic task about to be imposed on him, or, at least, had any distinct idea how it was to be managed; and I presume there may have been more than one veteran politician who proposed to himself to take the power out of President Lincoln's hands into his own, leaving our honest friend only the public responsibility for the good or ill success of the career. The extremely imperfect development of his statesmanly qualities, at that period, may have justified such designs. But the President is teachable by events, and has now spent a year in a very arduous course of education; he has a flexible mind, capable of much expansion, and convertible towards far loftier studies and activities than those of his early life; and if he came to Washington a backwoods humorist, he has already transformed himself into as good a statesman (to speak moderately) as his prime-minister. . . .

. . . EVEN IN AN aesthetic point of view, however, the war has done a great deal of enduring mischief, by causing the devastation of great tracts of woodland scenery, in which this part of Virginia would appear to have been very rich.

Around all the encampments, and everywhere along the road, we saw the bare sites of what had evidently been tracts of hard-wood forest, indicated by the unsightly stumps of well-grown trees, not smoothly felled by regular axe-men, but hacked, haggled, and unevenly amputated, as by a sword, or other miserable tool, in an unskilful hand. Fifty years will not repair this desolation. An army destroys everything before and around it, even to the very grass; for the sites of the encampments are converted into barren esplanades, like those of the squares in French cities, where not a blade of grass is allowed to grow. As to the other symptoms of devastation and obstruction, such as deserted houses, unfenced fields, and a general aspect of nakedness and ruin, I know not how much may be due to a normal lack of neatness in the rural life of Virginia, which puts a squalid face even upon a prosperous state of things; but undoubtedly the war must have spoilt what was good, and made the bad a great deal worse. The carcasses of horses were scattered along the wayside. One very pregnant token of a social system thoroughly disturbed was presented by a party of contrabands, escaping out of the mysterious depths of Secessia; and its strangeness consisted in the leisurely delay with which they trudged forward, as dreading no pursuer, and encountering nobody to turn them back.

They were unlike the specimens of their race whom we are accustomed to see at the North, and, in my judgment, were far more agreeable. So rudely were they attired, — as if their garb had grown upon them spontaneously, — so picturesquely natural in manners, and wearing such a crust of primeval simplicity (which is quite polished away from the northern black man), that they seemed a kind of creature by themselves, not altogether human, but perhaps quite as good, and akin to the fauns and rustic deities of olden times. I wonder whether I shall excite anybody's wrath by saying this. It is no great matter. At all events, I felt most kindly towards these poor fugitives, but knew not precisely what to wish in their behalf, nor in the least how to help them. For the sake of the manhood which is latent in them, I would not have turned them back; but I should have felt almost as reluctant, on their own account, to hasten them forward to the stranger's land; and I think my prevalent idea was, that, whoever may be benefited by the results of this war, it will not be the present generation of negroes, the childhood of whose race is now gone forever, and who must henceforth fight a hard battle with the world, on very unequal terms. On behalf of my own race, I am glad and can only hope that an inscrutable Providence means good to both parties. . . .

. . . FROM THESE VARIOUS excursions, and a good many others (including one to Manassas), we gained a pretty lively idea of what was going on; but, after all, if compelled to pass a rainy day in the hall and parlors of Willard's Hotel, it proved about as profitably spent as if we had floundered through miles of Virginia mud, in quest of interesting matter. This hotel, in fact, may be much more justly called the centre of Washington and the Union than either the Capitol, the White House, or the State Department. Everybody may be seen there. It is the meeting-place of the true representatives of the country, — not such as are chosen blindly and amiss by electors who take a folded ballot from the hand of a local politician, and thrust it into the ballot-box unread, but men who gravitate or are attracted hither by real business, or a native impulse to breathe the intensest atmosphere of the nation's life, or a genuine anxiety to see how this life-and-death struggle is going to deal with us. Nor these only, but all manner of loafers. Never, in any other spot, was there such a miscellany of people. You exchange nods with governors of sovereign States; you elbow illustrious men, and tread on the toes of generals; you hear statesmen and orators speaking in their familiar tones. You are mixed up with officeseekers, wire-pullers, inventors, artists, poets, prosers (including editors, army-correspondents, *attachés* of foreign journals, and long-winded talkers), clerks, diplomatists, mail-contractors, railway-directors, until your own identity is lost among them. Occasionally you talk with a man whom you have never before heard of, and are struck by the brightness of a thought, and fancy that there is more wisdom hidden among the obscure than is anywhere revealed among the famous. You adopt the universal habit of the place, and call for a mint-julep, a whiskey-skin, a gin cocktail, a brandy-smash, or a glass of pure Old Rye; for the conviviality of Washington sets in at an early hour, and, so far as I had an opportunity of observing, never terminates at any hour, and all these drinks are continually in request by almost all these people. A constant atmosphere of cigar-smoke, too, envelops the motley crowd, and forms a sympathetic medium, in which men meet more closely and talk more frankly than in any other kind of air. If legislators would smoke in session, they might speak truer words, and fewer of them, and bring about more valuable results.

It is curious to observe what antiquated figures and costumes sometimes make their appearance at Willard's. You meet elderly men with frilled shirt-fronts, for example, the fashion of which adornment passed away from among the people of this world half a century ago. It is as if one of Stuart's portraits were walking abroad. I see no way of accounting for this, except that the trouble of the times, the impiety of traitors, and the peril of our sacred Union and Constitution have disturbed, in their honored graves, some of the venerable fathers of the country, and summoned them forth to protest against the meditated and half-accomplished sacrilege. If it be so, their wonted fires are not altogether extinguished in their ashes, — in their throats, I might rather say, — for I beheld one of these excellent old men quaffing such a horn of Bourbon whiskey as a toper of the present century would be loath to venture upon. But, really, one would be glad to know where these strange figures come from. It shows, at any rate, how many remote, decaying villages and country-neighborhoods of the North, and forest-nooks of the West, and old mansion-houses in cities, are shaken by the tremor of our native soil, so that men long hidden in retirement put on the garments of their youth and hurry out to inquire what is the matter. The old men whom we see here have generally more marked faces than the young ones, and naturally enough; since it must be an extraordinary vigor and renewability of life that can overcome the rusty sloth of age, and keep the senior flexible enough to take an interest in new things; whereas hundreds of commonplace young men come hither to stare with eyes of vacant wonder, and with vague hopes of finding out what they are fit for. And this war (we may say so much in its favor) has been the means of discovering that important secret to not a few.

We saw at Willard's many who had thus found out for themselves, that, when Nature gives a young man no other utilizable faculty, she must be understood as intending him for a soldier. The bulk of the army had moved out of Washington before we reached the city; yet it seemed to me that at least two thirds of the guests and idlers at the hotel wore one or another token of the military profession. Many of them, no doubt, were self-commissioned officers, and had put on the buttons and the shoulder-straps, and booted themselves to the knees, merely because captain, in these days, is so good a travelling-name. The majority, however, had been duly appointed by the President, but might be none the better warriors for that. It was pleasant, occasionally, to distinguish a grizzly veteran among this crowd of carpet-knights, — the trained soldier of a lifetime, long ago from West Point, who had spent his prime upon the frontier, and very likely could show an Indian bullet-mark on his breast, — if such decorations, won in an obscure warfare, were worth the showing now.

The question often occurred to me, — and, to say the truth, it added an indefinable piquancy to the scene, — what proportion of all these people, whether soldiers or civilians, were true at heart to the Union, and what part were tainted, more or less, with treasonable sympathies and wishes, even if such had never blossomed into purpose. Traitors there were among them, — no doubt of that, — civil servants of the public, very reputable persons, who yet deserved to dangle from a cord; or men who buttoned military coats over their breasts, hiding perilous secrets there, which might bring the gallant officer to stand pale-faced before a file of musketeers, with his open grave behind him. But, without insisting upon such picturesque criminality and punishment as this, an observer, who kept both his eyes and heart open, would find it by no means difficult to discern that many residents and visitors of Washington so far sided with the South as to desire nothing more nor better than to see everything re-established a little worse than its former basis. If the cabinet of Richmond were transferred to the Federal city, and the North awfully snubbed, at least, and driven back within its old political limits, they would deem it a happy day. It is no wonder, and, if we look at the matter generously, no unpardonable crime. Very excellent people hereabouts remember the many dynasties in which the Southern character has been predominant, and contrast the genial courtesy, the warm and graceful freedom of that region, with what they call (though I utterly disagree with them) the frigidity of our Northern manners, and the Western plainness of the President. They have a conscientious, though mistaken belief, that the South was driven out of the Union by intolerable wrong on our part, and that we are responsible for having compelled true patriots to love only half their country instead of the whole, and brave soldiers to draw their swords against the Constitution which they would once have died for, — to draw them, too, with a bitterness of animosity which is the only symptom of brotherhood (since brothers hate each other best) that any longer exists. They whisper these things with tears in their eyes, and shake their heads, and stoop their poor old shoulders, at the tidings of another and another Northern victory, which, in their opinion, puts farther off the remote, the already impossible, chance of a reunion.

I am sorry for them, though it is by no means a sorrow without hope. Since the matter has gone so far, there seems to be no way but to go on winning victories, and establishing peace and a truer union in another generation, at the expense, probably, of greater trouble, in the present one, than any other people ever voluntarily suffered. We woo the South "as the Lion woos his bride"; it is a rough courtship, but perhaps love and a quiet household may come of it at last. Or, if we stop short of that blessed consummation, heaven was heaven still, as Milton sings, after Lucifer and a third part of the angels had seceded from its golden palaces, — and perhaps all the more heavenly, because so many gloomy brows, and soured, vindictive hearts, had gone to plot ineffectual schemes of mischief elsewhere.

LOUISA MAY ALCOTT

The author of well-known novels *Little Women* (1868–69) and *Little Men* (1871), Louisa May Alcott (1832–88) went to Washington early in the Civil War to work as a nurse in a Union hospital, which she named "the Hurly burly Hotel" because of its "disorder, discomfort, bad management, and no visible head." *Hospital Sketches* (1863) — part satire, part travelogue, part autobiography

— is the record of her experience attending to the sick, wounded, and dying. It was an experience cut short by a serious illness brought on by mercury poisoning (mercury was thought to be an antidote to typhoid) that plagued her for the rest of her life. Brought up in Boston and Concord during a time when a "women's rights woman" like herself had few outlets for her energies, Alcott came to nursing out of boredom and a desire to do "the right thing" — on the chance suggestion of a friend. A shrewd observer of character, with a deft comic writer's touch, she could also be deadly serious about a wide range of subjects, including race prejudice, slavery, the draft riots, Victorian mourning practices, male bodies, and class conflict.

From *Hospital Sketches*

Very soon after leaving the care of my ward, I discovered that I had no appetite, and cut the bread and butter interests almost entirely, trying the exercise and sun cure instead. Flattering myself that I had plenty of time, and could see all that was to be seen, so far as a lone lorn female could venture in a city, one-half of whose male population seemed to be taking the other half to the guard-house, — every morning I took a brisk run in one direction or another; for the January days were as mild as Spring. A rollicking north wind and occasional snow storm would have been more to my taste, for the one would have braced and refreshed tired body and soul, the other have purified the air, and spread a clean coverlid over the bed, wherein the capital of these United States appeared to be dozing pretty soundly just then.

One of these trips was to the Armory Hospital, the neatness, comfort, and convenience of which makes it an honor to its presiding genius, and arouses all the covetous propensities of such nurses as came from other hospitals to visit it.

The long, clean, warm, and airy wards, built barrack-fashion, with the nurse's room at the end, were fully appreciated by Nurse Periwinkle, whose ward and private bower were cold, dirty, inconvenient, up stairs and down stairs, and in everybody's chamber. At the Armory, in ward K, I found a cheery, bright-eyed, white-aproned little lady, reading at her post near the stove; matting under her feet; a draft of fresh air flowing in above her head; a table full of trays, glasses, and such matters, on one side, a large, well-stocked medicine chest on the other; and all her duty seemed to be going about now and then to give doses, issue orders, which well-trained attendants executed, and pet, advise, or comfort Tom, Dick, or Harry, as she found best. As I watched the proceedings, I recalled my own tribulations, and contrasted the two hospitals in a way that would have caused my summary dismissal, could it have been reported at headquarters. Here, order, method, common sense and liberality seemed to rule in a style that did one's heart good to see; at the Hurly burly Hotel, disorder, discomfort, bad management, and no visible head, reduced things to a condition which I despair of describing. The circumlocution fashion prevailed, forms and fusses tormented our souls, and unnecessary strictness in one place was counterbalanced by unpardonable laxity in another. Here is a sample: I am dressing Sam Dammer's shoulder; and, having cleansed the wound, look about for some strips of adhesive plaster to hold on the little square of wet linen which is to cover the gunshot wound; the case is not in the tray; Frank, the sleepy, half-sick attendant, knows nothing of it; we rummage high and low; Sam is tired, and fumes; Frank dawdles and yawns; the men advise and laugh at the flurry; I feel like a boiling tea-kettle, with the lid ready to fly off and damage somebody.

"Go and borrow some from the next ward, and spend the rest of the day in finding ours," I finally command. A pause; then Frank scuffles back with the message: "Miss Peppercorn ain't got none, and says you ain't no business to lose your own duds and go borrowin' other folkses." I say nothing, for fear of saying too much, but fly to the surgery. Mr. Toddypestle informs me that I can't have anything without an order from the surgeon of my ward. Great heavens! where is he? and away I rush, up and down, here and there, till at last I find him, in a state of bliss over a complicated amputation, in the fourth story. I make my demand; he answers: "In five minutes," and works away, with his head upside down, as he ties an artery, saws a bone, or does a little needle-work, with a visible relish and very sanguinary pair of hands. The five minutes grow to fifteen, and Frank appears, with the remark that, "Dammer wants to know what in thunder you are keeping him there with his finger on a wet rag for?" Dr. P. tears himself away long enough to scribble the order, with which I plunge downward to the surgery again, find the door looked, and, while hammering away on it, am told that two friends are waiting to see me in the hall. The matron being away, her parlor is locked, and there is no where to see my guests but in my own room, and no time to enjoy them till the plaster is found. I settle this matter, and circulate through the house to find Toddypestle, who has no right to leave the surgery till night. He is discovered in the dead house, smoking a cigar, and very much the worse for his researches among the spirituous preparations that fill the surgery shelves. He is inclined to be gallant, and puts the finishing blow to the fire of my wrath; for the tea-kettle lid flies off, and driving him before me to his post, I fling down the order, take what I choose; and, leaving the absurd incapable kissing his hand to me, depart, feeling as Grandma Riglesty is reported to have done, when she vainly sought for chips, in Bimleck Jackwood's "shifless paster."

I find Dammer a well acted charade of his own name, and, just as I get him done, struggling the while with a burning desire to clap an adhesive strip across his mouth, full of heaven defying oaths, Frank takes up his boot to put it on, and exclaims:

"I'm blest ef here ain't that case now! I recollect seeing it fall in this mornin', but forgot all about it, till my heel went smash inter it. Here, ma'am, ketch hold on it, and give the boys a sheet on't all round, 'gainst it tumbles inter t'other boot next time yer want it."

If a look could annihilate, Francis Saucebox would have ceased to exist; but it couldn't; therefore, he yet lives, to aggravate some unhappy woman's soul, and wax fat in some equally congenial situation.

Now, while I'm freeing my mind, I should like to enter my protest against employing convalescents as attendants, instead of strong, properly trained, and cheerful men. How it may be in other places I cannot say; but here it was a source of constant trouble and confusion, these feeble, ignorant men trying to sweep, scrub, lift, and wait upon their sicker comrades. One, with a diseased heart, was expected to run up and down stairs, carry heavy trays, and move helpless men; he tried it, and grew rapidly worse than when be first came: and, when be was ordered out to march away to the convalescent hospital, fell, in a sort of fit, before he turned the corner, and was brought back to die. Another, hurt by a fall from his horse, endeavored to do his duty, but failed entirely, and the wrath of the ward master fell upon the nurse, who must either scrub the rooms herself, or take the lecture; for the boy looked stout and well, and the master never happened to see him turn white with pain, or hear him groan in his sleep when an involuntary motion strained his poor back. Constant complaints were being made of incompetent attendants, and some dozen women did double duty, and then were blamed for breaking down. If any hospital director fancies this a good and economical arrangement, allow one used up nurse to tell him it isn't, and beg him to spare the sisterhood, who sometimes, in their sympathy, forget that they are mortal, and run the risk of being made immortal, sooner than is agreeable to their partial friends.

Another of my few rambles took me to the Senate Chamber, hoping to hear and see if this large machine was run any better than some small ones I knew of. I was too late, and found the Speaker's chair occupied by a colored gentleman of ten; while two others were on their legs, having a hot debate on the cornball question, as they gathered the waste paper strewn about the floor into bags; and several white members played leap-frog over the desks, a much wholesomer relaxation than some of the older Senators indulge in, I fancy. Finding the coast clear, I likewise gambolled up and down, from gallery to gallery; sat in Sumner's chair, and cudgelled an imaginary Brooks within an inch of his life; examined Wilson's books in the coolest possible manner; warmed my feet at one of the national registers; read people's names on scattered envelopes, and pocketed a castaway autograph or two; watched the somewhat unparliamentary proceedings going on about me, and wondered who in the world all the sedate gentlemen were, who kept popping out of odd doors here and there, like respectable Jacks-in-the-box. Then I wandered over the palatial residence of Mrs. Columbia, and examined its many beauties, though I can't say I thought her a tidy housekeeper, and didn't admire her taste in pictures, for the eye of this humble individual soon wearied of expiring patriots, who all appeared to be quitting their earthly tabernacles in convulsions, ruffled shirts, and a whirl of torn banners, bomb shells, and buff and blue arms and legs.

The statuary also was massive and concrete, but rather wearying to examine; for the colossal ladies and gentlemen carried no cards of introduction in face or figure; so whether the meditative party in a kilt, with well-developed legs, shoes like army slippers, and a ponderous nose, was Columbus, Cato, or Cockelorum Tibby the tragedian, was more than I could tell. Several robust ladies attracted me; but which was America and which Pocahontas was a mystery; for all affected much looseness of costume, dishevelment of hair, swords, arrows, lances, scales, and other ornaments quite *passé* with damsels of our day, whose effigies should go down to posterity armed with fans, crochet needles, riding whips, and parasols, with here and there one holding pen or pencil, rolling-pin or broom. The statue of Liberty I recognized at once, for it had no pedestal as yet, but stood flat in the mud, with Young America most symbolically making dirt pies, and chip forts, in its shadow. But high above the squabbling little throng and their petty plans, the sun shone full on Liberty's broad forehead, and, in her hand, some summer bird had built its nest. I accepted the good omen then, and, on the first of January, the Emancipation Act gave the statue a nobler and more enduring pedestal than any marble or granite ever carved and quarried by human hands.

One trip to Georgetown Heights, where cedars sighed overhead, dead leaves rustled underfoot, pleasant paths led up and down, and a brook wound like a silver snake by the blackened ruins of some French Minister's house, through the poor gardens of the black washerwomen who congregated there, and, passing the cemetery with a murmurous lullaby, rolled away to pay its little tribute to the river. This breezy run was the last I took; for, on the morrow, came rain and wind: and confinement soon proved a powerful reinforcement to the enemy, who was quietly preparing to spring a mine, and blow me five hundred miles from the position I had taken in what I called my Chickahominy Swamp.

Shut up in my room, with no voice, spirits, or books, that week was not a holiday, by any means. Finding meals a humbug, I stopped away altogether, trusting that if this sparrow was of any worth, the Lord would not let it fall to the ground. Like a flock of friendly ravens, my sister nurses fed me, not only

with food for the body, but kind words for the mind; and soon, from being half
starved, I found myself so beteaed and betoasted, petted and served, that I was
nearly killed with kindness, in spite of cough, headache, a painful consciousness of my pleura, and a realizing sense of bones in the human frame. From
the pleasant house on the hill, the home in the heart of Washington, and the
Willard caravansary, came friends new and old, with bottles, baskets, carriages
and invitations for the invalid; and daily our Florence Nightingale climbed the
steep stairs, stealing a moment from her busy life, to watch over the stranger,
of whom she was as thoughtfully tender as any mother. Long may she wave!
Whatever others may think or say, Nurse Periwinkle is forever grateful; and
among her relics of that Washington defeat, none is more valued than the little
book which appeared on her pillow, one dreary day; for the D D. written in it
means to her far more than Doctor of Divinity.

Being forbidden to meddle with fleshly arms and legs, I solaced myself by
mending cotton ones, and, as I sat sewing at my window, watched the moving
panorama that passed below; amusing myself with taking notes of the most
striking figures in it. Long trains of army wagons kept up a perpetual rumble
from morning till night; ambulances rattled to and fro with busy surgeons,
nurses taking an airing, or convalescents going in parties to be fitted to artificial
limbs. Strings of sorry looking horses passed, saying as plainly as dumb creatures could, "Why, in a city full of them, is there no *horse*pital for us?" Often
a cart came by, with several rough coffins in it and no mourners following;
barouches, with invalid officers, rolled round the corner, and carriage loads of
pretty children, with black coachmen, footmen, and maids. The women who
took their walks abroad, were so extinguished in three story bonnets, with
overhanging balconies of flowers, that their charms were obscured; and all I
can say of them is, that they dressed in the worst possible taste, and walked like
ducks.

The men did the picturesque, and did it so well that Washington looked like
a mammoth masquerade. Spanish hats, scarlet lined riding cloaks, swords and
sashes, high boots and bright spurs, beards and mustaches, which made plain
faces comely, and comely faces heroic; these vanities of the flesh transformed
our butchers, bakers, and candlestick makers into gallant riders of gaily capari-
soned horses, much handsomer than themselves; and dozens of such figures
were constantly prancing by, with private prickings of spurs, for the benefit of
the perambulating flower-bed. Some of these gentlemen affected painfully tight
uniforms, and little caps, kept on by some new law of gravitation, as they covered only the bridge of the nose, yet never fell off; the men looked like stuffed
fowls, and rode as if the safety of the nation depended on their speed alone. The
fattest, greyest officers dressed most, and ambled statelily along, with orderlies

behind, trying to look as if they didn't know the stout party in front, and doing much caracoling on their own account.

The mules were my especial delight; and an hour's study of a constant succession of them introduced me to many of their characteristics; for six of these odd little beasts drew each army wagon, and went hopping like frogs through the stream of mud that gently rolled along the street. The coquettish mule had small feet, a nicely trimmed tassel of a tail, perked up ears, and seemed much given to little tosses of the head, affected skips and prances; and, if he wore the bells, or were bedizzened with a bit of finery, put on as many airs as any belle. The moral mule was a stout, hard-working creature, always tugging with all his might; often pulling away after the rest had stopped, laboring under the conscientious delusion that food for the entire army depended upon his private exertions. I respected this style of mule; and, had I possessed a juicy cabbage, would have pressed it upon him, with thanks for his excellent example. The historical mule was a melodramatic quadruped, prone to startling humanity by erratic leaps, and wild plunges, much shaking of his stubborn head, and lashing out of his vicious heels; now and then falling flat, and apparently dying *a la* Forrest: a gasp — a squirm — a flop, and so on, till the street was well blocked up, the drivers all swearing like demons in bad hats, and the chief actor's circulation decidedly quickened by every variety of kick, cuff, jerk and haul. When the last breath seemed to have left his body, and "Doctors were in vain," a sudden resurrection took place; and if ever a mule laughed with scornful triumph, that was the beast, as he leisurely rose, gave a comfortable shake; and, calmly regarding the excited crowd seemed to say —"A hit! a decided hit! for the stupidest of animals has bamboozled a dozen men. Now, then! what are *you* stopping the way for?" . . .

. . . PIGS ALSO POSSESSED attractions for me, never having had an opportunity of observing their graces of mind and manner, till I came to Washington, whose porcine citizens appeared to enjoy a larger liberty than many of its human ones. Stout, sedate looking pigs, hurried by each morning to their places of business, with a preoccupied air, and sonorous greeting to their friends. Genteel pigs, with an extra curl to their tails, promenaded in pairs, lunching here and there, like gentlemen of leisure. Rowdy pigs pushed the passers by off the side walk; tipsy pigs hiccoughed their version of "We wont go home till morning," from the gutter; and delicate young pigs tripped daintily through the mud, as if they plumed themselves upon their ankles, and kept themselves particularly neat in point of stockings. Maternal pigs, with their interesting families, strolled by in the sun; and often the pink, baby-like squealers lay down for a nap, with a trust in Providence worthy of human imitation.

But more interesting than officers, ladies, mules, or pigs, were my colored brothers and sisters, because so unlike the respectable members of society I'd known in moral Boston. Here was the genuine article — no, not the genuine article at all, we must go to Africa for that — but the sort of creatures generations of slavery have made them: obsequious, trickish, lazy and ignorant, yet kind-hearted, merry-tempered, quick to feel and accept the least token of the brotherly love which is slowly teaching the white hand to grasp the black, in this great struggle for the liberty of both the races.

Having been warned not to be too rampant on the subject of slavery, as secesh principles flourished even under the shadow of Father Abraham, I had endeavored to walk discreetly, and curb my unruly member; looking about me with all my eyes the while, and saving up the result of my observations for future use. I had not been there a week before the neglected, devil-may care expression in many of the faces about me, seemed an urgent appeal to leave nursing white bodies, and take some care for these black souls. Much as the lazy boys and saucy girls tormented me, I liked them, and found that any show of interest or friendliness brought out the better traits which live in the most degraded and forsaken of us all. I liked their cheerfulness, for the dreariest old hag, who scrubbed all day in that pestilential steam, gossipped and grinned all the way out, when night set her free from drudgery. The girls romped with their dusky sweethearts, or tossed their babies, with the tender pride that makes mother-love a beautifier to the homeliest face. The men and boys sang and whistled all day long; and often, as I held my watch, the silence of the night was sweetly broken by some chorus from the street, full of real melody, whether the song was of heaven, or of hoe-cakes; and, as I listened, I felt that we never should doubt nor despair concerning a race which, through such griefs and wrongs, still clings to this good gift, and seems to solace with it the patient hearts that wait and watch and hope until the end.

I expected to have to defend myself from accusations of a prejudice against color; but was surprised to find things just the other way, and daily shocked some neighbor by treating the blacks as I did the whites. The men *would* swear at the "darkies," would put two *gs* into negro, and scoff at the idea of any good coming from such trash. The nurses were willing to be served by the colored people, but seldom thanked them, never praised, and scarcely recognized them in the streets; whereas the blood of two generations of abolitionists waxed hot in my veins, and, at the first opportunity, proclaimed itself, and asserted the right of free speech as doggedly as the irrepressible Folsom herself.

Happening to catch up a funny little black baby, who was toddling about the nurses' kitchen, one day, when I went down to make a mess for some of my men, a Virginia woman standing by elevated her most prominent feature, with a sniff of disapprobation, exclaiming:

"Gracious, Miss P.! how can you? I've been here six months, and never so much as touched the little toad with a poker."

"More shame for you, ma'am," responded Miss P.; and, with the natural perversity of a Yankee, followed up the blow by kissing "the toad," with ardor. His face was providentially as clean and shiny as if his mamma had just polished it up with a corner of her apron and a drop from the tea-kettle spout, like old Aunt Chloe. This rash act, and the anti-slavery lecture that followed, while one hand stirred gruel for sick America, and the other hugged baby Africa, did not produce the cheering result which I fondly expected; for my comrade henceforth regarded me as a dangerous fanatic, and my protégé nearly came to his death by insisting on swarming up stairs to my room, on all occasions, and being walked on like a little black spider.

I waited for New Year's day with more eagerness than I had ever known before; and, though it brought me no gift, I felt rich in the act of justice so tardily performed toward some of those about me. As the bells rung midnight, I electrified my room-mate by dancing out of bed, throwing up the window, and flapping my handkerchief, with a feeble cheer, in answer to the shout of a group of colored men in the street below. All night they tooted and tramped, fired crackers, sung "Glory, Hallelujah," and took comfort, poor souls! in their own way. The sky was clear, the moon shone benignly, a mild wind blew across the river, and all good omens seemed to usher in the dawn of the day whose noontide cannot now be long in coming. If the colored people had taken hands and danced around the White House, with a few cheers for the much abused gentleman who has immortalized himself by one just act, no President could have had a finer levee, or one to be prouder of.

WALT WHITMAN

Walt Whitman (1819–92) started his career as a teacher, journalist, and editor on Long Island and in Brooklyn, but lost his job at the *Brooklyn Daily Eagle* because of his outspoken abolitionism and "free soil" politics. He flourished as a poet in the late 1850s, but when the Civil War broke and his brother was reported wounded near Fredericksburg, Virginia, he traveled to Washington and soon volunteered to work as a hospital nurse, a job he performed from 1862 to 1865. At this time, reverting to his journalistic training, he kept an informal record of his observations, *Memoranda During the War* (1875–76), but contin-

ued to write poetry, including poetry situated in and around Washington, for
Drum-Taps (1865) and *Memories of President Lincoln* (1865). In his Civil War
poems, and even in the poems written well before the war, as seen in the am-
bitiously panoramic "Song of Myself" (1855), Whitman was deeply concerned
with preserving the Union, like the president he so loved and admired. After
the war he worked as a clerk in the Department of the Interior but was fired by
Secretary James Harlan when it was reported he had written an immoral book;
Whitman then went to work in the office of the attorney general. He lived in
Washington for nearly a decade.

From *Memoranda During the War*

*During the Union War I commenced at the close of 1862, and continued steadily
through '63, '64, and '65, to visit the sick and wounded of the Army, both on the
field and in the Hospitals in and around Washington city. From the first I kept
little note-books for impromptu jottings in pencil to refresh my memory of names
and circumstances, and what was specially wanted, &c. In these I brief'd cases,
persons, sights, occurrences in camp, by the bedside, and not seldom by the corpses
of the dead.... I have perhaps forty such little note-books left, forming a special
history of those years, for myself alone, full of associations never to be possibly said
or sung....*

    Washington, January, '63. — ... I am now remaining in and around Wash-
ington, daily visiting the hospitals. Am much in Patent Office, Eighth street,
H street, Armory Square and others. Am now able to do a little good, having
money, (as almoner of others home,) and getting experience.... To-day, Sunday
afternoon and till nine in the evening, visited Campbell Hospital; attended
specially to one case in Ward 1; very sick with pleurisy and typhoid fever; young
man, farmer's son, D. F. Russell, Company E, Sixtieth New York; downhearted
and feeble; a long time before he would take any interest; wrote a letter home to
his mother, in Malone, Franklin County, N.Y., at his request; gave him some
fruit and one or two other gifts; envelop'd and directed his letter, &c. Then
went thoroughly through Ward 6; observ'd every case in the Ward, without, I
think, missing one; gave perhaps from twenty to thirty persons, each one some
little gift, such as oranges, apples, sweet crackers, figs, &c.

    Thursday, Jan. 21. — Devoted the main part of the day to Armory Square
Hospital; went pretty thoroughly through Wards F, G, H, and I; some fifty
cases in each Ward. In Ward F supplied the men throughout with writing paper
and stamp'd envelope each; distributed in small portions, to proper subjects,
a large jar of first-rate preserv'd berries, which had been donated to me by a
lady — her own cooking. Found several cases I thought good subjects for small

sums of money, which I furnish'd. (The wounded men often come up broke, and it helps their spirits to have even the small sum I give them.) My paper and envelopes all gone, but distributed a good lot of amusing reading matter; also, as I thought judicious, tobacco, oranges, apples, &c. Interesting cases in Ward I; Charles Miller, bed No. 19, Company D, Fifty-third Pennsylvania, is only sixteen years of age, very bright, courageous boy, left leg amputated below the knee; next bed to him, another young lad very sick; gave each appropriate gifts. In the bed above, also, amputation of the left leg; gave him a little jar of raspberries; bed No. 1, this Ward, gave a small sum; also to a soldier on crutches, sitting on his bed near.... (I am more and more surprised at the very great proportion of youngsters from fifteen to twenty-one in the army. I afterwards found a still greater proportion among the Southerners.)

Evening, same day, went to see D. F. R., before alluded to; found him remarkably changed for the better; up and dress'd — quite a triumph; he afterwards got well, and went back to his regiment.... Distributed in the Wards a quantity of notepaper, and forty or fifty stamp'd envelopes, of which I had recruited my stock, and the men were much in need....

Feb. 23. — I must not let the great Hospital at the Patent Office pass away without some mention. A few weeks ago the vast area of the second story of that noblest of Washington buildings, was crowded close with rows of sick, badly wounded and dying soldiers. They were placed in three very large apartments. I went there many times. It was a strange, solemn and with all its features of suffering and death, a sort of fascinating sight. I go sometimes at night to soothe and relieve particular cases. Two of the immense apartments are fill'd with high and ponderous glass cases, crowded with models in miniature of every kind of utensil, machine or invention, it ever enter'd into the mind of man to conceive; and with curiosities and foreign presents. Between these cases are lateral openings, perhaps eight feet wide, and quite deep, and in these were placed the sick; besides a great long double row of them up and down through the middle of the hall. Many of them were very bad cases, wounds and amputations. Then there was a gallery running above the hall, in which there were beds also. It was, indeed, a curious scene at night, when lit up. The glass cases, the beds, the forms lying there, the gallery above, and the marble pavement under foot — the suffering, and the fortitude to bear it in various degrees — occasionally, from some, the groan that could not be repress'd — sometimes a poor fellow dying, with emaciated face and glassy eye, the nurse by his side, the doctor also there, but not friend, no relative — such were the sights but lately in the Patent Office....

Aug. 12. — I see the President almost every day, as I happen to live where he passes to or from his lodgings out of town. He never sleeps at the White House during the hot season, but has quarters at a healthy location, some three miles north of the city, the Soldiers' Home, a United States military establishment. I saw him this morning about 8½ coming into business, riding on Vermont avenue, near L street. The sight is a significant one.... He always has company of twenty-five or thirty cavalry, with sabers drawn, and held upright over their shoulders. The party makes no great show in uniforms or horses. Mr. Lincoln, on the saddle, generally rides a good-sized easy-going gray horse, is dress'd in plain black, somewhat rusty and dusty; wears a black stiff hat, and looks about as ordinary in attire, &c., as the commonest man. A Lieutenant, with yellow straps, rides at his left, and following behind, two by two, come the cavalry men in their yellow-striped jackets. They are generally going at a slow trot, as that is the pace set them by the One they wait upon. The sabers and accoutrements clank, and the entirely unornamental *cortege* as it trots towards Lafayette square, arouses no sensation, only some curious stranger stops and gazes. I see very plainly Abraham Lincoln's dark brown face, with the deep cut lines, the eyes, &c., always to me with a deep latent sadness in the expression. We have got so that we always exchange bows, and very cordial ones....

Heated term. — There has lately been much suffering here from heat. We have had it upon us now eleven days. I go around with an umbrella and a fan. I saw two cases of sun-stroke yesterday, one in Pennsylvania avenue, and another in Seventh street. The City Railroad Company loses some horses every day. Yet Washington is having a livelier August, and is probably putting in a more energetic and satisfactory summer, than ever before during its existence. There is probably more human electricity, more population to make it, more business, more light-heartedness, than ever before. The armies that swiftly circumambiated from Fredericksburgh, march'd, struggled, fought, had out their mighty clinch and hurl at Gettysburgh, wheel'd, have circumambiated again, return'd to their ways, touching us not, either at their going or coming. And Washington feels that she has pass'd the worst; perhaps feels that she is henceforth mistress. So here she sits with her surrounding hills and shores spotted with guns; and is conscious of a character and identity different from what it was five or six short weeks ago, and very considerably pleasanter and prouder....

March 1st. — Plenty more butternut or clay-color'd escapees every day. About 160 came in to-day, a large portion South Carolinians. They generally take the oath of allegiance, and are sent north, west, or extreme south-west if they wish. Several of them told me that the desertions in their army, of men going home, leave or no leave, are far more numerous than their desertions to our side. I saw a very forlorn looking squad of about a hundred, late this afternoon, on their way to the Baltimore depot.

To-night I have been wandering awhile in the Capitol, which is all lit up. The illuminated Rotunda looks fine. I like to stand aside and look a long, long while, up at the dome; it comforts me somehow. The House and Senate were both in session till very late. I look'd in upon them, but only a few moments; they were hard at work on tax and appropriation bills. I wander'd through the long and rich corridors and apartments under the Senate; an old habit of mine, former winters, and now more satisfaction than ever. Not many persons down there, occasionally a flitting figure in the distance. . . .

Murder of President Lincoln. — The day, April 14, 1865, seems to have been a pleasant one throughout the whole land — the moral atmosphere pleasant too — the long storm, so dark, so fratricidal, full of blood and doubt and gloom, over and ended at last by the sun-rise of such an absolute National victory, and utter breaking-down of Secessionism — we almost doubted our own senses! . . .

. . . THE POPULAR afternoon paper of Washington, the little Evening Star, had spatter'd all over its third page, divided among the advertisements in a sensational manner in a hundred different places, *The President and his Lady will be at the Theatre this evening. . . .*

On this occasion the theatre was crowded, many ladies in rich and gay costumes, officers in their uniforms, many well known citizens, young folks, the usual clusters of gas-lights, the usual magnetism of so many people, cheerful, with perfumes, music of violins and flutes — (and over all, and saturating all, that vast vague wonder, *Victory*, the Nations' [sic] Victory, the triumph of the Union, filling the air, the thought, the sense, with exhilaration more than all perfumes.)

The President came betimes, and, with his wife, witness'd the play, from the large stage-boxes of the second tier, two thrown into one, and profusely draped with the National flag. The acts and scenes of the piece — one of those singularly written compositions which have at least the merit of giving entire relief to an audience engaged in mental action or business excitements and cares during the day, as it makes not the slightest call on either the moral, emotional, esthetic, or spiritual nature — a piece, ('Our American Cousin,') in which, among other characters, so call'd, a Yankee, certainly such a one as was never seen, or the least like it ever seen, in North America, is introduced in England, with a varied fol-de-rol of talk, plot, scenery, and such phantasmagoria as goes to make up a modern popular drama — had progress'd through perhaps a couple of its acts, when in the midst of this comedy, or tragedy, or non-such, or whatever it is to be call'd, and to off-set it or finish it out, as if in Nature's and the Great Muse's mockery of those poor mimes, comes interpolated that Scene, not really or exactly to be described at all, (for on the many hundreds who were there it seems to this hour to have left little but a passing blur, a dream, a blotch) — and yet partially to be described as I now proceed to give it. . . . There is a scene in the play representing a modern parlor, in which two unprecedented English ladies are inform'd by the unprecedented and impossible Yankee that he is not a man of fortune, and therefore undesirable for marriage-catching purposes; after which, the comments being finish'd, the dramatic trio make exit, leaving the stage clear for a moment. There was a pause, a hush as it were. At this period came the murder of Abraham Lincoln. Great as that was, with all its manifold train, circling round it, and stretching into the future for many a century, in politics, history, art, &c., of the New World, in point of fact the main thing, the actual murder, transpired with the quiet and simplicity of any commonest occurrence — the bursting of a bud or pod in the growth of vegetation, for instance. Through the general hum following the stage pause, with the change of position, &c., came the muffled sound of a pistol shot, which not one hundredth part of the audience heard at the time — and yet a moment's hush — somehow, surely a vague startled thrill — and then, through the ornamented, draperies, star'd and striped space-way of the President's box, a sudden figure, a man raises himself with hands and feet, stands a moment on the railing, leaps below to the stage, (a distance of perhaps fourteen or fifteen feet,) falls out of position, catching his boot-heal in the copious draper, (the American flag,) falls on one knee, quickly recovers himself, rises as if nothing had happen'd, (he really sprains his ankle, but unfelt then,) — and so the figure, Booth, the murderer, dress'd in plain black broad-cloth, bare-headed, with a full head of glossy, raven hair, and his eyes like some mad animal's flashing with light and resolution, yet with a certain strange calmness, holds aloft in one hand a large knife — walks along not much back from the foot-lights — turns fully toward the audience his face of statuesque beauty, lit by those basilisk eyes, flashing with desperation, perhaps insanity — launches out in a firm and steady voice the words, *Sic semper tyrannis* — and then walks with neither slow nor very rapid pace diagonally across to the back of the stage, and disappears . . . (had not all this terrible scene — making the mimic ones preposterous — had it not all been rehears'd, in blank, by Booth, beforehand?)

A moment's hush, incredulous — a scream — the cry of *Murder* — Mrs. Lincoln leaning out of the box, with ashy cheeks and lips, with involuntary cry, pointing to the retreating figure, *He has kill'd the President.* . . . And still a moment's strange, incredulous suspense — and then the deluge! — then that mixture of horror, noises, uncertainty — (the sound, somewhere back, of a horse's hoofs clattering with speed) — the people burst through chairs and railings, and break them up — that noise adds to the queerness of the scene — there is inextricable confusion and terror — women faint — quite feeble persons fall, and are trampled on — many cries of agony are heard — the broad stage suddenly fills to suffocation with a dense and motley crowd, like some horrible carnival — the audience rush general upon it — at least the strong men do — the actors and actresses are all there in their play-costumes and painted faces, with mortal fright showing through the rouge, some trembling — some in tears — the screams and calls, confused talk — redoubled, trebled — two or three manage to pass up water from the stage to the President's box — others try to clamber up — &c., &c., &c.

In the midst of all this, the soldiers of the President's Guard, with others, suddenly drawn to the scene, burst in — (some two hundred altogether) — they storm the house, through all the tiers, especially the upper ones, inflamed with fury, literally charging the audience with fix'd bayonets, muskets and pistols, shouting *Clear out! clear out! you sons of* ——. . . . Such the wild scene, or a suggestion of it rather, inside the playhouse that night.

Outside, too, in the atmosphere of shock and craze, crowds of people, fill'd with frenzy, ready to seize any outlet for it, come near committing murder several times on innocent individuals. One such case was especially exciting. The infuriated crowd, through some chance, got started against one man, either for words he utter'd, or perhaps without any cause at all, and were proceeding at once to actually hang him on a neighboring lamp post, when he was rescued by a few heroic policemen, who placed him in their midst and fought their way slowly and amid great peril toward the Station House. . . . It was a fitting episode of the whole affair. The crowd rushing and eddying to and fro — the night, the yells, the pale faces, many frighten'd people trying in vain to extricate themselves — the attack'd man, not yet freed from the jaws of death, looking like a corpse — the silent resolute half-dozen policemen, with no weapons but their little clubs, yet stern and steady through all those eddying swarms — make indeed a fitting side-scene to the grand tragedy of the murder. . . . They gain'd the Station House with the protected man, whom they placed in security for the night and discharged him in the morning.

And in the midst of that night-pandemonium of senseless hate, infuriated soldiers, the audience and the crowd — the stage, and all its actors and actresses, its paint-pots, spangles, and gas-lights — the life-blood from those veins, the best and sweetest of the land, drips slowly down, and death's ooze already begins its little bubbles on the lips. . . . Such, hurriedly sketch'd, were the accompaniments of the death of President Lincoln. So suddenly and in murder and horror unsurpass'd he was taken from us. But his death was painless.

ELIZABETH HOBBS KECKLEY

Born a slave in rural Virginia and sold to a new owner in St. Louis, Elizabeth Hobbs Keckley (c. 1818–1907) purchased her freedom, and that of her mulatto son, by working as a seamstress and saving her earnings. On the eve of the Civil War, in 1860, she moved to Washington, where she worked as a dressmaker, first for the wife of Senator Jefferson Davis and then for Mary Todd Lincoln. *Behind the Scenes: Thirty Years a Slave and Four Years in the White House* (1868) was a controversial book that was eventually removed from sale. Depicting her close friendship with a prominent white woman, the book also revealed more of White House life than people were accustomed to know, including details about the death of the Lincolns' young son and the aftermath of the assassination of the president. Keckley was founder and president of the Contraband Relief Association, an aid society providing relief for escaped slaves who had been declared "contraband" during the war. She later taught sewing at Wilberforce University in Ohio. She retired to Washington and lived at the Home for Destitute Women and Children, an institution she helped found.

My Introduction to Mrs. Lincoln
From *Behind the Scenes: Thirty Years a Slave
and Four Years in the White House*

Ever since arriving in Washington I had a great desire to work for the ladies of the White House, and to accomplish this end I was ready to make almost any sacrifice consistent with propriety. Work came in slowly, and I was beginning to feel very much embarrassed, for I did not know how I was to meet the bills staring me in the face. It is true, the bills were small, but then they were formidable to me, who had little or nothing to pay them with. While in this situation I called at the Ringolds, where I met Mrs. Captain Lee. Mrs. L. was in a state bordering on excitement, as the great event of the season, the dinner-party given in honor of the Prince of Wales, was soon to come off, and she must have a dress suitable for the occasion. The silk had been purchased, but a dressmaker had not yet been found. Miss Ringold recommended me, and I received the order to make the dress. When I called on Mrs. Lee the next day, her husband was in the room, and handing me a roll of bank bills, amounting to one hundred dollars, he requested me to purchase the trimmings, and to spare no expense in making a selection. With the money in my pocket I went out in the street, entered the store of Harper & Mitchell, and asked to look at their laces. Mr. Harper waited on me himself, and was polite and kind. When I asked permission to carry the laces to Mrs. Lee, in order to learn whether she could approve my selection or not, he gave a ready assent. When I reminded him that I was a stranger, and that the goods were valuable, he remarked that he was not afraid to trust me — that he believed my face was the index to an honest heart. It was pleasant to be spoken to thus, and I shall never forget the kind words of Mr. Harper. I often recall them, for they are associated with the dawn of a brighter period in my dark life. I purchased the trimmings, and Mr. Harper allowed me a commission of twenty-five dollars on the purchase. The dress was done in time, and it gave complete satisfaction. Mrs. Lee attracted great attention at the dinner-party, and her elegant dress proved a good card for me. I received numerous orders, and was relieved from all pecuniary embarrassments. One of my patrons was Mrs. Gen. McClean, a daughter of Gen. Sumner. One day when I was very busy, Mrs. McC. drove up to my apartments, came in where I was engaged with my needle, and in her emphatic way said:

"Lizzie, I am invited to dine at Willard's on next Sunday, and positively I have not a dress fit to wear on the occasion. I have just purchased material, and you must commence work on it right away."

"But Mrs. McClean," I replied, "I have more work now promised than I can do. It is impossible for me to make a dress for you to wear on Sunday next."

"Pshaw! Nothing is impossible. I must have the dress made by Sunday;" and she spoke with some impatience.

"I am sorry," I began, but she interrupted me.

"Now don't say no again. I tell you that you must make the dress. I have often heard you say that you would like to work for the ladies of the White House. Well, I have it in my power to obtain you this privilege. I know Mrs. Lincoln well, and you shall make a dress for her provided you finish mine in time to wear at dinner on Sunday."

The inducement was the best that could have been offered. I would undertake the dress if I should have to sit up all night — every night, to make my pledge good. I sent out and employed assistants, and, after much worry and trouble, the dress was completed to the satisfaction of Mrs. McClean. It appears that Mrs. Lincoln had upset a cup of coffee on the dress she designed wearing on the evening of the reception after the inauguration of Abraham Lincoln as President of the United States, which rendered it necessary that she should have a new one for the occasion. On asking Mrs. McClean who her dress-maker was, that lady promptly informed her,

"Lizzie Keckley."

"Lizzie Keckley? The name is familiar to me. She used to work for some of my lady friends in St. Louis, and they spoke well of her. Can you recommend her to me?"

"With confidence. Shall I send her to you?"

"If you please. I shall feel under many obligations for your kindness."

The next Sunday Mrs. McClean sent me a message to call at her house at four o'clock p.m., that day. As she did not state why I was to call, I determined to wait till Monday morning. Monday morning came, and nine o'clock found me at Mrs. McC.'s house. The streets of the capital were thronged with people, for this was Inauguration day. A new President, a man of the people from the broad prairies of the West, was to accept the solemn oath of office, was to assume the responsibilities attached to the high position of Chief Magistrate of the United States. Never was such deep interest felt in the inauguration proceedings as was felt to-day; for threats of assassination had been made, and every breeze from the South came heavily laden with the rumors of war. Around Willard's hotel swayed an excited crowd, and it was with the utmost difficulty that I worked my way to the house on the opposite side of the street, occupied by the McCleans. Mrs. McClean was out, but presently an aide on General McClean's staff called, and informed me that I was wanted at Willard's. I crossed the street, and on entering the hotel was met by Mrs. McClean, who greeted me:

"Lizzie, why did you not come yesterday, as I requested? Mrs. Lincoln wanted to see you, but I fear that now you are too late."

"I am sorry, Mrs. McClean. You did not say what you wanted with me yesterday, so I judged that this morning would do as well."

"You should have come yesterday," she insisted. "Go up to Mrs. Lincoln's room" — giving me the number — "she may find use for you yet."

With a nervous step I passed on, and knocked at Mrs. Lincoln's door. A cheery voice bade me come in, and a lady, inclined to stoutness, about forty years of age, stood before me.

"You are Lizzie Keckley, I believe."

I bowed assent.

"The dress-maker that Mrs. McClean recommended?"

"Yes, madam."

"Very well; I have not time to talk to you now, but would like to have you call at the White House, at eight o'clock to-morrow morning, where I shall then be."

I bowed myself out of the room, and returned to my apartments. The day passed slowly, for I could not help but speculate in relation to the appointed interview for the morrow. My long-cherished hope was about to be realized, and I could not rest.

Tuesday morning, at eight o'clock, I crossed the threshold of the White House for the first time. I was shown into a waiting-room, and informed that Mrs. Lincoln was at breakfast. In the waiting-room I found no less than three mantua-makers waiting for an interview with the wife of the new President. It seems that Mrs. Lincoln had told several of her lady friends that she had urgent need for a dress-maker, and that each of these friends had sent her mantua-maker to the White House. Hope fell at once. With so many rivals for the position sought after, I regarded my chances for success as extremely doubtful. I was the last one summoned to Mrs. Lincoln's presence. All the others had a hearing, and were dismissed. I went up-stairs timidly, and entering the room with nervous step, discovered the wife of the President standing by a window, looking out, and engaged in lively conversation with a lady, Mrs. Grimsly, as I afterwards learned. Mrs. L. came forward, and greeted me warmly.

"You have come at last. Mrs. Keckley, who have you worked for in the city?"

"Among others, Mrs. Senator Davis has been one of my best patrons," was my reply.

"Mrs. Davis! So you have worked for her, have you? Of course you gave satisfaction; so far, good. Can you do my work?"

"Yes, Mrs. Lincoln. Will you have much work for me to do?"

"That, Mrs. Keckley, will depend altogether upon your prices. I trust that your terms are reasonable. I cannot afford to be extravagant. We are just from the West, and are poor. If you do not charge too much, I shall be able to give you all my work."

"I do not think there will be any difficulty about charges, Mrs. Lincoln; my terms are reasonable."

"Well, if you will work cheap, you shall have plenty to do. I can't afford to pay big prices, so I frankly tell you so in the beginning."

The terms were satisfactorily arranged, and I measured Mrs. Lincoln, took the dress with me, a bright rose-colored moire-antique, and returned the next day to fit it on her. A number of ladies were in the room, all making preparations for the levee to come off on Friday night. These ladies, I learned, were relatives of Mrs. L.'s, — Mrs. Edwards and Mrs. Kellogg, her own sisters, and Elizabeth Edwards and Julia Baker, her nieces. Mrs. Lincoln this morning was dressed in a cashmere wrapper, quilted down the front; and she wore a simple head-dress. The other ladies wore morning robes.

I was hard at work on the dress, when I was informed that the levee had been postponed from Friday night till Tuesday night. This, of course, gave me more time to complete my task. Mrs. Lincoln sent for me, and suggested some alteration in style, which was made. She also requested that I make a waist of blue watered silk for Mrs. Grimsly, as work on the dress would not require all my time.

Tuesday evening came, and I had taken the last stitches on the dress. I folded it and carried it to the White House, with the waist for Mrs. Grimsly. When I went up-stairs, I found the ladies in a terrible state of excitement. Mrs. Lincoln was protesting that she could not go down, for the reason that she had nothing to wear.

"Mrs. Keckley, you have disappointed me — deceived me. Why do you bring my dress at this late hour?"

"Because I have just finished it, and I thought I should be in time."

"But you are not in time, Mrs. Keckley; you have bitterly disappointed me. I have no time now to dress, and, what is more, I will not dress, and go down-stairs."

"I am sorry if I have disappointed you, Mrs. Lincoln, for I intended to be in time. Will you let me dress you? I can have you ready in a few minutes."

"*No*, I won't be dressed. I will stay in my room. Mr. Lincoln can go down with the other ladies."

"But there is plenty of time for you to dress, Mary," joined in Mrs. Grimsly and Mrs. Edwards. "Let Mrs. Keckley assist you, and she will soon have you ready."

Thus urged, she consented. I dressed her hair, and arranged the dress on her. It fitted nicely, and she was pleased. Mr. Lincoln came in, threw himself on the sofa, laughed with Willie and little Tad, and then commenced pulling on his gloves, quoting poetry all the while.

"You seem to be in a poetical mood to-night," said his wife.

"Yes, mother, these are poetical times," was his pleasant reply. "I declare, you look charming in that dress. Mrs. Keckley has met with great success." And then he proceeded to compliment the other ladies.

Mrs. Lincoln looked elegant in her rose-colored moire-antique. She wore a pearl necklace, pearl ear-rings, pearl bracelets, and red roses in her hair. Mrs. Baker was dressed in lemon-colored silk; Mrs. Kellogg in a drab silk, ashes of rose; Mrs. Edwards in a brown and black silk; Miss Edwards in crimson, and Mrs. Grimsly in blue watered silk. Just before starting down-stairs, Mrs. Lincoln's lace handkerchief was the object of search. It had been displaced by Tad, who was mischievous, and hard to restrain. The handkerchief found, all became serene. Mrs. Lincoln took the President's arm, and with smiling face led the train below. I was surprised at her grace and composure. I had heard so much, in current and malicious report, of her low life, of her ignorance and vulgarity, that I expected to see her embarrassed on this occasion. Report, I soon saw, was wrong. No queen, accustomed to the usages of royalty all her life, could have comported herself with more calmness and dignity than did the wife of the President. She was confident and self-possessed, and confidence always gives grace.

This levee was a brilliant one, and the only one of the season. I became the regular modiste of Mrs. Lincoln. I made fifteen or sixteen dresses for her during the spring and early part of the summer, when she left Washington; spending the hot weather at Saratoga, Long Branch, and other places. In the mean time I was employed by Mrs. Senator Douglas, one of the loveliest ladies that I ever met, Mrs. Secretary Wells, Mrs. Secretary Stanton, and others. Mrs. Douglas always dressed in deep mourning, with excellent taste, and several of the leading ladies of Washington society were extremely jealous of her superior attractions.

UPTON SINCLAIR

Upton Sinclair (1878–1968) wrote *Manassas: A Novel of the War* (1904), a Civil War–era novel set near Washington, to help pay for his expenses as a graduate student in New York. The next year he was commissioned by a Socialist magazine to write a novel about immigrants working in the Chicago meatpacking industry. After reading that novel, *The Jungle* (1906), President Theodore Roosevelt ordered an investigation into the industry, but when he met Sinclair, he reproved him for his Socialism. Still, the novel inspired passage of the Pure Food and Drug and the Meat Inspection acts (both 1906) and made Sinclair an instant celebrity. That same year, he accepted a draft from the Socialist Party to run for a seat in Congress from New Jersey; he lost but ran again in 1920 from California, and then for the Senate in 1922, also from California. In 1927, he published *Oil!* concerning the oil scandals, particularly the Teapot Dome Scandal of the Harding administration. Sinclair is buried in Rock Creek Cemetery in Washington, D.C.

From *Manassas: A Novel of the War*

It was the afternoon of the eighteenth of that momentous month of April that Allan found himself at last in Washington. It lacked but a few hours of a week from the time when he had seen the first shell burst over Sumter; and in all that time he had had no news from home, save the few facts which the Southern papers chose to give him. When he stepped out upon the dock he felt, in his joy, as if he could have clasped the whole city in his arms. He went on, half running, his eyes and ears upon the alert.

Everything in Washington was a-quiver with feverish excitement. Flags were fluttering from all the buildings, public and private — how suddenly beautiful the flag had come to be! Patrols of the district militia were marching through the streets — officers were galloping here and there — people who passed one were walking more swiftly than usual, talking more excitedly.

Allan had not believed the tales he had heard, and he had hopes that his fears for the capital would vanish when he reached it; but he found now that

Washington was a very whirlpool of rumors, shaken every hour with a new
alarm. Virginia was moving on Harper's Ferry, and McCullough's raiders were
to strike that night. Ex-Governor Wise was leaving Richmond with troops —
uprisings were occurring in Maryland — mobs were sacking Baltimore — bridges
were burning, telegraph wires were down. Everywhere one turned he heard a
fresh story; and always one terrible chorus, "No troops yet from the North!"
It had been three days since the call, and still they did not come! Allan went
into Willard's Hotel, which was packed; he could see that nearly all the people
there were Southerners, and they talked to each other apart, and in whispers.
It was said that General Scott was dreading the outbreak of a conspiracy that
night, and had turned the Capitol building into an arsenal for the defence of
the President and his cabinet.

The young man bought newspapers, and then for the first time the wonderful light burst in upon him in its fulness. He went down the street, racing
through them, darting from column to column, his cheeks flushed, his hands
trembling, — in the end he was laughing, singing to himself, shaking the tears
out of his eyes. The country was up! There was never anything like it — it could
hardly be grasped, it could hardly be believed. There were public meetings in
every city, flags from every house, a universal holiday throughout sixteen States.
Companies were offering from every town, banks lending funds, business
houses and public councils subscribing for the support of soldiers. Accounts of
such things filled columns of each day's paper; and also there were speeches and
sermons, letters and poems and editorials. The fervor of the country was like a
forest-fire — it had seized upon everything, swept everything away. There was
no longer a disloyal voice, scarcely a voice of hesitation; Douglas was out for the
war, Buchanan was out for the war — even the mayor of New York, who had
wanted to secede himself, had issued an address blazing with patriotic ardor.
There were no longer any parties, no longer any classes; clergymen and college professors were enlisting by the side of day-laborers and clerks. They were
coming, the student from his desk and the workman from his bench, "leaving
all things to save the Republic." The very newspapers in which one read these
reports were changed — the meanest reporter or correspondent was suddenly
become a seer of visions, a man with a duty and a faith, speaking invocations
and prophecies. The whole face of the land seemed altered — Allan stared at it,
unable to realize that it was the same country he had left two weeks before. All
the selfishness in it was gone, all the cowardice in it, the dulness, the blindness,
the baseness — the very thugs and blacklegs of the Bowery were organizing a
regiment, and being presented with Bibles!

Allan recognized in it all the counterpart of his own experience as he stood
upon the Battery in Charleston. The shot that had so shaken him — it had

shaken the country from Maine to Kansas, had roused it like a sleeping lion; it had sprung up, gigantic, terrible in its fury. The nation was coming forth like a young giant — girding its armor about it, calling for the combat; and fear and doubt fled before it, victory and salvation came in its train. Well might men, North as well as South, stand dismayed; it was more than any dreamer in his wildest hour had dreamed. It was something superhuman, beyond thought; something colossal, cosmic, seizing the mind like the sweep of the planets, the upheavals of the ages and the crashing of the skies. Was it any word spoken upon earth that had lifted these twenty millions of men in one swift surge of wrath and resolution? Allan's soul took fire as he read of it, it lifted him out of himself, it lent him wings; his step grew light, and there was singing within him, like the singing of the storm-wind on the mountains. Ah, how wonderful it was — how beyond all words it was! How little he had understood his country: so patient, so long-suffering and slow to anger! And he so blind and poor, so full of doubts and hatreds, so little wise! He did penance upon his knees before his country, he pledged his vows anew. Let it nevermore be his way — let it be her way! The voice of his grandfather spoke to him again — those lessons which as a child he had not understood, how terribly he understood them now! That his country was humanity — that its hope was the hope of man, and its purpose the purpose of God! The songs that the old man had sung came back to him, the prayers he had whispered, the consecrations of which he had never spoken without a trembling at the lips; the statesmen who had toiled for her, the soldiers who had died for her, the agonies, the heroisms that had been poured into her lap — the memories of them rushed over Allan, shaking his soul. He saw it now — that faith which had been the old man's religion, in America, in freedom, in democracy — in the people! In the people, that moved towards righteousness; so slowly, and yet so irresistibly, with a movement like the movement of time!

— And now they were coming! From the cities and the farms, from the mountains and the prairies, from the East and the West they were coming, to redeem the heritage of their fathers, to save the land of their love. To do the work which all men had said was impossible — and yet which must be done! Allan, laughing aloud in his excitement, read the news of one State after another — it was like a sight of the floods in the springtime, turbulent, uproarious, all-compelling!

And Massachusetts, glorious old Massachusetts, was leading them all! They had asked her for two regiments — she was sending five. The banks of Boston had offered the money, and the same night that the call had come they had begun to gather. They were pouring into Boston from every county in the State, and their towns were voting them money, and flags, and clothing, and whatever else they could think of. They were quartered in Faneuil Hall — the "Cradle of Liberty" — where Hancock and Otis watched over their slumber!

Allan looked for the Fifth Regiment — it was in the Fifth that he meant to enlist himself, with his cousin and his friends. He saw no mention of it; but the Sixth had left the afternoon before, and was due in Washington the next morning; the Eighth had left the same evening, and the rest were close behind. On the morrow would start the New York "Seventh," the "dandy" regiment of that city; the journalists of the metropolis had lost their sense of humor in this crisis, and one of them told of a fond mother who had taken her young militiaman into a store, and, after purchasing him a new uniform and rifle, with all accessories, had flung her arms about him, weeping, and said, while the spectators cheered, "Go, my son; I have done for you all that I can do!"

Allan sent a telegram home, inquiring about the regiment; and then he started up the street again, gazing about him. He was on Pennsylvania Avenue; galloping along it he saw a group of officers, and some artillerymen with a small field-gun. They were going toward the Capitol, and he watched them go by in a cloud of dust, and then set out to follow. Before long, however, he halted, seeing some one on the other side of the avenue. Surely he could not be mistaken — that long, lanky figure, striding swiftly, staring straight ahead! He darted across, calling out; and the man turned — yes, he was right — it was Edward Lovejoy!

Lovejoy, turning, rushed toward him, and seized his hand in a paralyzing grip. "You got my message?" he cried.

"Message!" gasped the other. "No! What do you mean?"

"I wired you ten days ago," said Lovejoy, "telling you there'd be war, and to come."

"I didn't get it," Allan answered. "But I'm here!"

CHAPTER THREE

VANITY FAIR

Reconstruction and National Expansion

[1865–1910]

B ETWEEN THE CIVIL WAR and the U.S. entry into World War I, much of the writing set in Washington was satiric or simply critical, focusing on matters of political corruption and outlandish spending in the nation's capital. Not coincidentally, the Washington novel emerged during this time. It was an era identified in the early years by Mark Twain and Charles Dudley Warner as "The Gilded Age" and later given a satirist's treatment by John William DeForest in *Honest John Vane*, Bret Harte in "The Office-Seeker," Henry Adams in *Democracy*, and David Graham Phillips in *The Fashionable Adventures of Joshua Craig*. Some authors, such as Booker T. Washington and Frances Hodgson Burnett, expressed open anxiety about the corrupting influences of Washington or wrote with a controlled rage, as did Frederick Douglass. A notable exception during this period was the expatriate Henry James. In his *The American Scene*, he related how he found Washington an attractive, socially dynamic "City of Conversation," unlike the other, business-oriented cities he encountered on his American tour.

(OVERLEAF) Executive Office Building (originally Departments of State, War, and Navy Building), Pennsylvania Avenue and 17th Street, NW, completed in 1888; an example of French Imperial architecture expressing America's emergence as a world power. Courtesy of the Historic American Buildings Survey, Ronald Comedy, photographer, 1969.

MARK TWAIN

Mark Twain, pen name of Samuel Clemens (1835–1910), came to Washington for the first time in 1867, ostensibly to serve as the private secretary of Senator William M. "Bill" Stewart and otherwise to solidify his career as a newspaper correspondent. Apparently he did little work during his few months in the senator's employ, but his humorous accounts in "My Late Senatorial Secretaryship" and "The Facts Concerning the Recent Resignation" are perhaps not to be trusted for factual accuracy. He found the city "dead" or "in a trance" and had choice words for the politicians he encountered there, at one point calling congressmen the only "distinctly native American criminal class." Clearly not a company-town man, he returned to California on a matter of urgent business with his old publishers.

The Facts Concerning the Recent Resignation

WASHINGTON, *Dec. 2*, 1867.

I have resigned. The Government appears to go on much the same, but there is a spoke out of its wheel, nevertheless. I was clerk of the Senate Committee on Conchology, and I have thrown up the position. I could see the plainest disposition on the part of the other members of the Government to debar me from having any voice in the counsels of the nation, and so I could no longer hold office and retain my self-respect. If I were to detail all the outrages that were heaped upon me during the six days that I was connected with the Government in an official capacity, the narrative would fill a volume. They appointed me clerk of that Committee on Conchology, and then allowed me no amanuensis to play billiards with. I would have borne that, lonesome as it was, if I had met with that courtesy from the other members of the Cabinet which was my due. But I did not. Whenever I observed that the head of a department was pursuing a wrong course, I laid down everything and went and tried to set him right, as it was my duty to do; and I never was thanked for it in a single instance. I went, with the best intentions in the world, to the Secretary of the Navy, and said:

"Sir, I cannot see that Admiral Farragut is doing anything but skirmishing around there in Europe, having a sort of picnic. Now, that may be all very well, but it does not exhibit itself to me in that light. If there is no fighting for him to do, let him come home. There is no use in a man having a whole fleet for a pleasure excursion. It is too expensive. Mind, I do not object to pleasure excursions for the naval officers — pleasure excursions that are in reason — pleasure excursions that are economical. Now they might go down the Mississippi on a raft —"

You ought to have heard him storm! One would have supposed I had committed a crime of some kind. But I didn't mind. I said it was cheap, and full of republican simplicity, and perfectly safe. I said that, for a tranquil pleasure excursion, there was nothing equal to a raft.

Then the Secretary of the Navy asked me who I was; and when I told him I was connected with the Government, he wanted to know in what capacity. I said that, without remarking upon the singularity of such a question, coming, as it did, from a member of that same Government, I would inform him that I was clerk of the Senate Committee on Conchology. Then there was a fine storm! He finished by ordering me to leave the premises, and give my attention strictly to my own business in future. My first impulse was to get him removed. However, that would harm others beside himself, and do me no real good, and so I let him stay.

I went next to the Secretary of War, who was not inclined to see me at all until he learned that I was connected with the Government. If I had not been on important business, I suppose I could not have got in. I asked him for a light (he was smoking at the time), and then I told him I had no fault to find with his defending the parole stipulations of General Lee and his comrades in arms, but that I could not approve of his method of fighting the Indians on the Plains. I said he fought too scattering. He ought to get the Indians more together — get them together in some convenient place, where he could have provisions enough for both parties, and then have a general massacre. I said there was nothing so convincing to an Indian as a general massacre. If he could not approve of the massacre, I said the next surest thing for an Indian was soap and education. Soap and education are not as sudden as a massacre, but they are more deadly in the long run; because a half-massacred Indian may recover, but if you educate him and wash him, it is bound to finish him some time or other. It undermines his constitution; it strikes at the foundation of his being. "Sir," I said, "the time has come when blood-curdling cruelty has become necessary. Inflict soap and a spelling-book on every Indian that ravages the Plains, and let them die!"

The Secretary of War asked me if I was a member of the Cabinet, and I said I was. He inquired what position I held, and I said I was clerk of the Senate Committee on Conchology. I was then ordered under arrest for contempt of court, and restrained of my liberty for the best part of the day.

I almost resolved to be silent thenceforward, and let the Government get along the best way it could. But duty called, and I obeyed. I called on the Secretary of the Treasury. He said:

"What will *you* have?"

The question threw me off my guard. I said, "Rum punch."

He said: "If you have got any business here, sir, state it — and in as few words as possible."

I then said that I was sorry he had seen fit to change the subject so abruptly, because such conduct was very offensive to me; but under the circumstances I would overlook the matter and come to the point. I now went into an earnest expostulation with him upon the extravagant length of his report. I said it was expensive, unnecessary, and awkwardly constructed; there were no descriptive passages in it, no poetry, no sentiment — no heroes, no plot, no pictures — not even woodcuts. Nobody would read it, that was a clear case. I urged him not to ruin his reputation by getting out a thing like that. If he ever hoped to succeed in literature, he must throw more variety into his writings. He must beware of dry detail. I said that the main popularity of the almanac was derived from its poetry and conundrums, and that a few conundrums distributed around through his Treasury report would help the sale of it more than all the internal revenue he could put into it. I said these things in the kindest spirit, and yet the Secretary of the Treasury fell into a violent passion. He even said I was an ass. He abused me in the most vindictive manner, and said that if I came there again meddling with his business, he would throw me out of the window. I said I would take my hat and go, if I could not be treated with the respect due to my office, and I did go. It was just like a new author. They always think they know more than anybody else when they are getting out their first book. Nobody can tell *them* anything.

During the whole time that I was connected with the Government it seemed as if I could not do anything in an official capacity without getting myself into trouble. And yet I did nothing, attempted nothing, but what I conceived to be for the good of my country. The sting of my wrongs may have driven me to un-just and harmful conclusions, but it surely seemed to me that the Secretary of State, the Secretary of War, the Secretary of the Treasury, and others of my *con-freres*, had conspired from the very beginning to drive me from the Administra-tion. I never attended but one Cabinet meeting while I was connected with the Government. That was sufficient for me. The servant at the White House door did not seem disposed to make way for me until I asked if the other members of the Cabinet had arrived. He said they had, and I entered. They were all there; but nobody offered me a seat. They stared at me as if I had been an intruder. The President said:

"Well, sir, who are *you?*"

I handed him my card, and he read: "The HON. MARK TWAIN, Clerk of the Senate Committee on Conchology." Then he looked at me from head to foot, as if he had never heard of me before. The Secretary of the Treasury said:

"This is the meddlesome ass that came to recommend me to put poetry and conundrums in my report, as if it were an almanac."

The Secretary of War said: "It is the same visionary that came to me yesterday with a scheme to educate a portion of the Indians to death, and massacre the balance."

The Secretary of the Navy said: "I recognize this youth as the person who has been interfering with my business time and again during the week. He is distressed about Admiral Farragut's using a whole fleet for a pleasure excursion, as he terms it. His proposition about some insane pleasure excursion on a raft is too absurd to repeat."

I said: "Gentlemen, I perceive here a disposition to throw discredit upon every act of my official career; I perceive, also, a disposition to debar me from all voice in the counsels of the nation. No notice whatever was sent to me to-day. It was only by the merest chance that I learned that there was going to be a Cabinet meeting. But let these things pass. All I wish to know is, is this a Cabinet meeting or is it not?"

The President said it was.

"Then," I said, "let us proceed to business at once, and not fritter away valuable time in unbecoming fault-findings with each other's official conduct."

The Secretary of State now spoke up, in his benignant way, and said, "Young man, you are laboring under a mistake. The clerks of the Congressional committees are not members of the Cabinet. Neither are the doorkeepers of the Capitol, strange as it may seem. Therefore, much as we could desire your more than human wisdom in our deliberations, we cannot lawfully avail ourselves of it. The counsels of the nation must proceed without you; if disaster follows, as follow full well it may, be it balm to your sorrowing spirit, that by deed and voice you did what in you lay to avert it. You have my blessing. Farewell."

These gentle words soothed my troubled breast, and I went away. But the servants of a nation can know no peace. I had hardly reached my den in the Capitol, and disposed my feet on the table like a representative, when one of the Senators on the Conchological Committee came in in a passion and said:

"Where have you been all day?"

I observed that, if that was anybody's affair but my own, I had been to a Cabinet meeting.

"To a Cabinet meeting? I would like to know what business you had at a Cabinet meeting?"

I said I went there to consult — allowing for the sake of argument that he was in anywise concerned in the matter. He grew insolent then, and ended by saying he had wanted me for three days past to copy a report on bomb-shells, egg-shells, clamshells, and I don't know what all, connected with conchology, and nobody had been able to find me.

This was too much. This was the feather that broke the clerical camel's back. I said, "Sir, do you suppose that I am going to *work* for six dollars a day? If that is the idea, let me recommend the Senate Committee on Conchology to hire somebody else. I am the slave of *no* faction! Take back your degrading commission. Give me liberty, or give me death!"

From that hour I was no longer connected with the Government. Snubbed by the department, snubbed by the Cabinet, snubbed at last by the chairman of a committee I was endeavoring to adorn, I yielded to persecution, cast far from me the perils and seductions of my great office, and forsook my bleeding country in the hour of her peril.

But I had done the State some service, and I sent in my bill:

The United States of America in account with the
Hon. Clerk of the Senate Committee on Conchology, Dr.

To consultation with Secretary of War,	$50
To consultation with Secretary of Navy,	50
To consultation with Secretary of the Treasury,	50
Cabinet consultation,	No charge.
To mileage to and from Jerusalem,* *via* Egypt, Algiers, Gibraltar, and Cadiz, 14,000 miles, at 20c. a mile,	2800
To salary as Clerk of Senate Committee on Conchology, six days, at $6 per day,	36
Total,	$2986

Not an item of this bill has been paid, except that trifle of thirty-six dollars for clerkship salary. The Secretary of the Treasury, pursuing me to the last, drew his pen through all the other items, and simply marked in the margin "Not allowed." So, the dread alternative is embraced at last. Repudiation has begun! The nation is lost.

I am done with official life for the present. Let those clerks who are willing to be imposed on remain. I know numbers of them in the departments who are never informed when there is to be a Cabinet meeting, whose advice is never asked about war, or finance, or commerce, by the heads of the nation, any more than if they were not connected with the Government, and who actually stay in their offices day after day and work! They know their importance to the nation, and they unconsciously show it in their bearing, and the way they order their

---

*Territorial delegates charge mileage both ways, although they never go back when they get here once. Why my mileage is denied me is more than I can understand.

sustenance at the restaurant — but they work. I know one who has to paste all sorts of little scraps from the newspaper into a scrapbook — sometimes as many as eight or ten scraps a day. He doesn't do it well, but he does it as well as he can. It is very fatiguing. It is exhausting to the intellect. Yet he only gets eighteen hundred dollars a year. With a brain like his, that young man could amass thousands and thousands of dollars in some other pursuit, if he chose to do it. But no — his heart is with his country, and he will serve her as long as she has got a scrapbook left. And I know clerks that don't know how to write very well, but such knowledge as they possess they nobly lay at the feet of their country, and toil on and suffer for 2500 dollars a year. What they write has to be written over again by other clerks sometimes; but when a man has done his best for his country, should his country complain? Then there are clerks that have no clerkships, and are waiting, and waiting, and waiting, for a vacancy — waiting patiently for a chance to help their country out — and while they are waiting, they only get barely two thousand dollars a year for it. It is sad — it is very, very sad. When a member of Congress has a friend who is gifted, but has no employment wherein his great powers may be brought to bear, he confers him upon his country, and gives him a clerkship in a department. And there that man has to slave his life out, fighting documents for the benefit of a nation that never thinks of him, never sympathizes with him — and all for two thousand or three thousand dollars a year. When I shall have completed my list of all the clerks in the several departments, with my statement of what they have to do, and what they get for it, you will see that there are not half enough clerks, and that what there are do not get half enough pay.

MARK TWAIN AND CHARLES DUDLEY WARNER

The Gilded Age, a Tale of Today (1873), Mark Twain's popular novel cowritten with Charles Dudley Warner (1829–1900), captures the unscrupulous political profiteering and influence peddling of the boom time after the Civil War. Twain revisited Washington several times in his later years, often at the invitation of President Cleveland and his wife, and a final time in 1906, when he led the successful effort to lobby Congress to revise the country's copyright laws.

From *The Gilded Age, a Tale of Today*

"*Cante-teca.* Iapi-Waxte otonwe kin he cajeyatapi nawahon;
   otonwe wijice hinca keyape se wacanmi.
Toketu-kaxta. Han, hecetu; takuwicawaye wijicapi ota hen tipi."
  — *Mahp. Ekta Oicim. ya.*

The capital of the Great Republic was a new world to country-bred Washington Hawkins. St. Louis was a greater city, but its floating population did not hail from great distances, and so it had the general family aspect of the permanent population: but Washington gathered its people from the four winds of heaven, and so the manners, the faces and the fashions there, presented a variety that was infinite. Washington had never been in "society" in St. Louis, and he knew nothing of the ways of its wealthier citizens, and had never inspected one of their dwellings. Consequently, everything in the nature of modern fashion and grandeur was a new and wonderful revelation to him.

Washington is an interesting city to any of us. It seems to become more and more interesting the oftener we visit it. Perhaps the reader has never been there? Very well. You arrive either at night, rather too late to do anything or see anything until morning, or you arrive so early in the morning that you consider it best to go to your hotel and sleep an hour or two while the sun bothers along over the Atlantic. You cannot well arrive at a pleasant intermediate hour, because the railway corporation that keeps the keys of the only door that leads into the town or out of it take care of that. You arrive in tolerably good spirits, because it is only thirty-eight miles from Baltimore to the capital, and so you have only been insulted three times (provided you are not in a sleeping car — the average is higher, there): once when you renewed your ticket after stopping over in Baltimore, once when you were about to enter the "ladies' car" without knowing it *was* a lady's car, and once when you asked the conductor at what hour you would reach Washington.

You are assailed by a long rank of hackmen, who shake their whips in your face as you step out upon the sidewalk; you enter what they regard as a "carriage" in the capital, and you wonder why they do not take it out of service and put it in the museum; we have few enough antiquities, and it is little to our credit that we make scarcely any effort to preserve the few we have. You reach your hotel, presently — and here let us draw the curtain of charity — because of course you have gone to the wrong one. You being a stranger, how could you do otherwise? There are a hundred and eighteen bad hotels, and only one good one. The most renowned and popular hotel of them all is perhaps the worst one known to history. It is winter, and night. When you arrived it was snowing. When you reached the hotel, it was sleeting. When you went to bed, it was raining. During the night it froze hard, and the wind blew some chimneys down. When you got up in the morning, it was foggy. When you finished your breakfast at ten o'clock and went out, the sunshine was brilliant, the weather balmy and delicious, and the mud and slush deep and all-pervading. You will like the climate — when you get used to it.

You naturally wish to view the city: so you take an umbrella, an overcoat, and a fan, and go forth. The prominent features you soon locate and get familiar with; first you glimpse the ornamental upper works of a long, snowy palace projecting above a grove of trees, and a tall, graceful white dome with a statue on it surmounting the palace and pleasantly contrasting with the background of blue sky. That building is the capitol; gossips will tell you that by the original estimates it was to cost $12,000,000, and that the government did come within $27,200,000 of building it for that sum.

You stand at the back of the capitol to treat yourself to a view, and it is a very noble one. You understand, the capitol stands upon the verge of a high piece of table land, a fine commanding position, and its front looks out over this noble situation for a city — but it don't see it, for the reason that when the capitol extension was decided upon, the property owners at once advanced their prices to such inhuman figures that the people went down and built the city in the muddy low marsh *behind* the temple of liberty; so now the lordly front of the building, with its imposing colonnades, its projecting, graceful wings, its picturesque groups of statuary, and its long terraced ranges of steps, flowing down in white marble waves to the ground, merely looks out upon a sorrowful little desert of cheap boarding-houses.

So you observe, that you take your view from the back of the capitol. And yet not from the airy outlooks of the dome, by the way, because to get there you must pass through the great rotunda; and to do that, you would have to see the marvellous Historical Paintings that hang there, and the bas-reliefs — and what have you done that you should suffer thus? And besides, you might have to pass through the old part of the building, and you could not help seeing Mr. Lincoln, as petrified by a young lady artist for $10,000 — and you might take his marble emancipation proclamation, which he holds out in his hand and contemplates, for a folded napkin; and you might conceive from his expression and his attitude, that he is finding fault with the washing. Which is not the case. Nobody knows what *is* the matter with him; but everybody feels for him. Well, you ought not to go into the dome anyhow, because it would be utterly impossible to go up there without seeing the frescoes in it — and why should you be interested in the delirium tremens of art.

The capitol is a very noble and a very beautiful building, both within and without, but you need not examine it now. Still, if you greatly prefer going into the dome, go. Now your general glance gives you picturesque stretches of gleaming water, on your left, with a sail here and there and a lunatic asylum on shore: over beyond the water, on a distant elevation, you see a squat yellow temple which your eye dwells upon lovingly through a blur of unmanly moisture, for it recalls your lost boyhood and the Parthenons done in molasses candy which made it blest and beautiful. Still in the distance, but on this side of the water and close to its edge, the Monument to the Father of his Country towers out of the mud — sacred soil is the customary term. It has the aspect of a factory chimney with the top broken off. The skeleton of a decaying scaffolding lingers about its summit, and tradition says that the spirit of Washington often comes down and sits on those rafters to enjoy this tribute of respect which the nation has reared as the symbol of its unappeasable gratitude. The Monument is to be finished, some day, and at that time our Washington will have risen still higher in the nation's veneration, and will be known as the Great-Great-Grandfather of his Country. The memorial Chimney stands in a quiet pastoral locality that is full of reposeful expression. With a glass you can see the cow-sheds about its base, and the contented sheep nibbling pebbles in the desert solitudes that surround it, and the tired pigs dozing in the holy calm of its protecting shadow.

Now you wrench your gaze loose and you look down in front of you and see the broad Pennsylvania Avenue stretching straight ahead for a mile or more till it brings up against the iron fence in front of a pillared granite pile, the Treasury building — an edifice that would command respect in any capital. The stores and hotels that wall in this broad avenue are mean, and cheap, and dingy, and are better left without comment. Beyond the Treasury is a fine large white barn, with wide unhandsome grounds about it. The President lives there. It is ugly enough outside, but that is nothing to what it is inside. Dreariness, flimsiness, bad taste reduced to mathematical completeness, is what the inside offers to the eye, if it remains yet what it always has been.

The front and right-hand views give you the city at large. It is a wide stretch of cheap little brick houses, with here and there a noble architectural pile lifting itself out of the midst — government buildings, these. If the thaw is still going on when you come down and go about town, you will wonder at the short-sightedness of the city fathers, when you come to inspect the streets, in that they do not dilute the mud a little more and use them for canals.

If you inquire around a little, you will find that there are more boarding-houses to the square acre in Washington than there are in any other city in the land, perhaps. If you apply for a home in one of them, it will seem odd to you to have the landlady inspect you with a severe eye, and then ask you if you are a member of Congress. Perhaps, just as a pleasantry, you will say yes. And then she will tell you that she is "full." Then you show her her advertisement in the morning paper, and there she stands, convicted and ashamed. She will try to blush, and it will be only polite in you to take the effort for the deed. She shows you her rooms, now, and lets you take one — but she makes you pay in advance for it. That is what you will get for pretending to be a member of Congress. If you had been content to be merely a private citizen, your trunk would have been sufficient security for your board. If you are curious and inquire into this thing, the chances are that your landlady will be ill-natured enough to say that the person and property of a Congressman are exempt from arrest or detention, and that with the tears in her eyes she has seen several of the people's representatives walk off to their several States and Territories carrying her unreceipted board bills in their pockets for keepsakes. And before you have been in Washington many weeks you will be mean enough to believe her, too.

Of course you contrive to see everything and find out everything. And one of the first and most startling things you find out is, that every individual you encounter in the City of Washington almost — and certainly every separate and distinct individual in the public employment, from the highest bureau chief, clear down to the maid who scrubs Department halls, the night watchmen of the public buildings and the darkey boy who purifies the Department spittoons — represents Political Influence. Unless you can get the ear of a Senator, or a Congressman, or a Chief of a Bureau or Department, and persuade him to use his "influence" in your behalf, you cannot get an employment of the most trivial nature in Washington. Mere merit, fitness, and capability are useless baggage to you without "influence." The population of Washington consists pretty much entirely of government employés and the people who board them. There are thousands of these employés, and they have gathered there from every corner of the Union and got their berths through the intercession (command is nearer the word) of the Senators and Representatives of their respective States. It would be an odd circumstance to see a girl get employment at three or four dollars a week in one of the great public cribs without any political grandee to back her, but merely because she was worthy, and competent, and a good citizen of a free country that "treats all persons alike." Washington would be mildly thunderstruck at such a thing as that. If you are a member of Congress (no offence), and one of your constituents who doesn't know anything, and does not want to go into the bother of learning something, and has no money, and no employment, and can't earn a living, comes besieging you for help, do you say, "Come, my friend, if your services were valuable you could get employment elsewhere — don't want you here?" Oh, no. You take him to a Department and say, "Here, give this person something to pass away the time at — and a salary" — and the thing is done. You throw him on his country. He is his country's child, let his country support him. There is something good and motherly about Washington, the grand old benevolent National Asylum for the Helpless.

The wages received by this great hive of employés are placed at the liberal figure meet and just for skilled and competent labour. Such of them as are imme-

diately employed about the two Houses of Congress are not only liberally paid
also, but are remembered in the customary Extra Compensation bill which
slides neatly through, annually, with the general grab that signalizes the last
night of a session, and thus twenty per cent. is added to their wages, for — for
fun, no doubt.

Washington Hawkins' new life was an unceasing delight to him. Senator
Dilworthy lived sumptuously, and Washington's quarters were charming — gas:
running water, hot and cold; bath-room, coal fires, rich carpets, beautiful pictures on the walls; books on religion, temperance, public charities and financial
schemes; trim coloured servants, dainty food, — everything a body could wish
for. And as for stationery, there was no end to it; the government furnished it;
postage stamps were not needed — the Senator's frank could convey a horse
through the mails, if necessary.

And then he saw such dazzling company. Renowned generals and admirals who had seemed but colossal myths when he was in the far west, went in
and out before him, or sat at the Senator's table, solidified into palpable flesh
and blood; famous statesmen crossed his path daily; that once rare and awe-
inspiring being, a Congressman, was become a common spectacle — a spectacle so common, indeed, that he could contemplate it without excitement,
even without embarrassment; foreign ministers were visible to the naked eye at
happy intervals; he had looked upon the President himself and lived. And more,
this world of enchantment teemed with speculation — the whole atmosphere
was thick with it — and that indeed was Washington Hawkins' native air; none
other refreshed his lungs so gratefully. He had found paradise at last.

The more he saw of his chief, the Senator, the more he honoured him, and
the more conspicuously the moral grandeur of his character appeared to stand
out. To possess the friendship and the kindly interest of such a man, Washington said in a letter to Louise, was a happy fortune for a young man whose career
had been so impeded and so clouded as his.

The weeks drifted by; Harry Brierly flirted, danced, added lustre to the brilliant Senatorial receptions, and diligently "buzzed" and "button-holed" Congressmen in the interest of the Columbus River scheme; meantime Senator Dilworthy laboured hard in the same interest — and in others of equal national
importance. Harry wrote frequently to Sellers, and always encouragingly; and
from these letters it was easy to see that Harry was a pet with all Washington,
and was likely to carry the thing through; that the assistance rendered him by
"old Dilworthy" was pretty fair — pretty fair; "and every little helps, you know,"
said Harry.

Washington wrote Sellers officially, now and then. In one of his letters, it appcarcd that whereas no member of the House Committee favoured the scheme at first, there was now needed but one more vote to compass a majority report. Closing sentence:

> "Providence seems to further our efforts."
> (Signed,) "ABNER DILWORTHY, U. S. S.
> per WASHINGTON HAWKINS, P. S."

At the end of a week, Washington was able to send the happy news, — officially, as usual, — that the needed vote had been added, and the bill favourably reported from the Committee. Other letters recorded its perils in Committee of the whole, and by-and-by its victory, by just the skin of its teeth, on third reading and final passage. Then came letters telling of Mr. Dilworthy's struggles with a stubborn majority in his own Committee in the Senate; of how these gentlemen succumbed, one by one, till a majority was secured.

Then there was a hiatus. Washington watched every move on the board, and he was in a good position to do this, for he was clerk of this committee, and also one other. He received no salary as private secretary, but these two clerkships, procured for him by his benefactor, paid him at the rate of twelve dollars a day, without counting the twenty per cent, extra compensation which would of course be voted to him on the last night of the session.

He saw the bill go into Committee of the whole and struggle for its life again, and finally worry through. In the fullness of time he noted its second reading, and by-and-by the day arrived when the grand ordeal came, and it was put upon its final passage. Washington listened with bated breath to the "Aye!" "No!" "No!" "Aye!" of the voters, for a few dread minutes, and then could bear the suspense no longer. He ran down from the gallery and hurried home to wait.

At the end of two or three hours the Senator arrived in the bosom of his family, and dinner was waiting. Washington sprang forward, with the eager question on his lips, and the Senator said:

> "We may rejoice freely now, my son — Providence has crowned our efforts with success."

JOHN WILLIAM DEFOREST

Born in Connecticut, John William DeForest (1826–1906) is best known for his realistic portrayal of soldiers in battle and of a southern woman at the time of the Civil War in his *Miss Ravenel's Conversion from Secession to Loyalty* (1867). A captain during the war, DeForest fought in New Orleans and elsewhere. For a time, he was stationed in Washington and later served as a district commander of the Freedmen's Bureau in South Carolina. A prolific author of fiction, travel narratives, poetry, and letters, he wrote two novels set in the corrupt Washington of the Grant era, *Playing the Mischief* and *Honest John Vane, a Story* (both 1875). The latter, excerpted here, is an amusing if serious, allegorical meditation on the amateurism of American politics. Unsuccessful and humiliated by Washington bureaucrats in a later bid to secure a diplomatic post for himself, DeForest turned the experience into a third Washington novel, *Justine's Lovers* (1878).

From *Honest John Vane, a Story*

"Special legislation is the great field for what I call Congressional *usefulness*," pursued Mr. Sharp, again bringing down a violent emphasis on the word, as if he were trying to drive it into his listener's head.

"Ah! is it?" stared John Vane. "That's news to me. I thought general legislation was the big thing, — reform, foreign relations, sectional questions, constitutional points, and so on; I thought those were the diggings to get a reputation out of."

"All exploded, my dear sir!" answered Mr. Sharp. "All gone out with Calhoun and Webster, or at the latest, with Lincoln and Stanton. All dead issues, as dead as the war. Special legislation — or, as some people prefer to call it, finance — is the sum and substance of Congressional business in our day. It is the great field, and it pays for the working. It pays every way. Your vote helps people, and they are grateful and help *you*. Your vote brings something to pass, and the public sees that it does, and respects you. Work into finance, Mr. Vane," exhorted Mr. Sharp, gently moving his hand in a spiral, as if to signify the insinuation of a corkscrew, "work slow - ly into — finance — so to call it. Take up some great national enterprise, and engineer it through. Get your name associated with a navigation scheme, or a railroad scheme, to advance commerce, you understand, or to move the crops." And as he alluded to these noble purposes, his voice became little less than reverential. "The millions yet unborn — you understand," here he seemed to be suggesting hints for a speech in advocacy of said scheme, —"millions yet unborn will have reason to remember you. Capital will become your friend. And capital — ah, Mr. Vane, there's a word! My very blood curdles when I think of the power and majesty of *capital*. This land, sir, this whole gigantic Republic, with its population of forty millions, its incomparably productive and energetic industry, and its vast network of continental communications, is the servant, and I had almost said the creature, of *capital*. Capital guides it by its wisdom and sustains it by its beneficence. Capital is to be, and already is, its ruler. Make capital your friend. Do something for it, and secure its gratitude. Link your fortunes and your name with some gigantic financial enterprise. Then, when you have won the reputation of advancing the industrial interests of the country, and gathered around you hosts of admirers and friends, you can return to your pet measure. Now, there is my advice — the advice of an old hand. Doesn't it strike you as worth considering? My maxim, as you see, is slow and sure. I also have my little reform at heart, but I keep it waiting until I can get strong enough to push it, and meantime I strengthen myself by helping other people. Never mind now what that reform is," he added, noting a gleam of inquiry in Vane's eye; "you will hear of it some day. Let us come to the immediate and the practical. While I make my humble little project bide its time, I am busy with a scheme which combines capital and industry, a scheme of national importance and magnitude. I don't mind mentioning it to you. It is the great Subfluvial Tunnel Road, meant to run through our country from north to south, under the Mississippi River, uniting Lake Superior with the Gulf of Mexico. It is a gigantic idea: you must admit it. Of course, the business minutiae and prospects of it are beyond me," he conceded, with an air of innocence and simplicity which seemed to relieve him of all responsibility as to those points. "There I have to trust to the judgment of business men. But where my information fails, Mr. Dorman here can fill the gap. Dorman, suppose you let our friend into this if he wants to come in."

John Vane, being quite beyond his honest depth by this time, had nothing to say to the Great Subfluvial either in condemnation or praise, but merely stared in expectant silence.

"It is the job I gave you a hint about in Slowburgh," began Darius Dorman, turning upon his member a pair of sombre, lurid, smoky eyes, which were at once utterly unearthly and utterly worldly. "We have just got it well under way."

"What! stock taken?" exclaimed Vane, amazed that he had not heard of such a huge financial success.

Darius smiled, as a slave-trader might smile upon a stalwart, unsuspicious negro who should express a curiosity to see the interior of his schooner.

"The subscription is to be started by the government," he proceeded. "That is, the government will loan the capital necessary to build the tunnel, and then secure itself by a mortgage on the same. No particular risk, you see, to capitalists, especially as they will get the first issue of stock cheap, and won't be called on to pay in a heavy percentage. What they don't want to keep they can sell to the outside public, — the raft of small investors. Now, bankers and financiers won't neglect such a chance as that; they will pile in as fast and as plenty as need be. With a government loan to start on, the stock is sure to be floated and the thing finished; and after that is done, why, it will go on pretty much as railroads do, — gradually increase its business, and in the end pay well, like railroads."

Just here there was a malicious twinkle in his charcoal-pits of eyes, as though he were thinking of the numberless widows and orphans and other unprotected creatures whose little all had gone into railroads without ever bringing out a dividend. At the same, time, he glanced suddenly at his grimy hands and rubbed them uneasily against each other, as if he would have been glad to get them clean for once in his existence, or as if the maculations on them itched and scalded quite intolerably.

"O, there's nothing unusual or extra smart about the enterprise!" he resumed, perhaps detecting in honest John Vane's countenance a gleam of suspicion. "It's about the way railroads in general are got up, except the one notion of a government loan to start the thing. That is new and patented. Don't mention that for the Devil's sake!" he implored, with an outburst of his characteristically eccentric profanity. "Keep as dark as hell about the whole thing. All we want of you is to bear the job in mind, and when the House comes to the question of the loan, give us your voice and vote."

"It will be a grand thing for the country," put in Mr. Sharp, seeing that Vane pondered.

"O, magnificent!" exclaimed Dorman. "Give us another New York at New Orleans. Double the value of land in the Mississippi Valley."

"Unite the North and South," continued Sharp. "Close up the bloody chasm. Bind together the national unity in chains of cast-iron."

"Pour the wild rice of Green Bay upon the dinner-tables of our working-men," responded Dorman.

"Bring the Menomonie Indians within easy reach of Christian missionaries," was Sharp's next word in this litany.

"Providing the whole tribe hasn't already got to the happy hunting-grounds," suggested Dorman.

The Whetstone statesman glanced at the business man, and the business man glanced at the Whetstone statesman. Apparently (only John Vane did not perceive it) the two came very near laughing in each other's faces.

"Besides, it will pay well, at least to first investors," resumed Dorman.

"Yes, I should think it might pay *them* well," answered John Vane, with just a suspicion of satire in his tone.

"If you should ever care to invest, by the way," suggested the business man, as though that were a thing which he had just thought of, and which would of course not influence his representative's decision, "if you should ever fancy putting something of your own in, we can promise you a sure return for it. You shall have your pick, — stock at the opening figure,   corner lots cheap around the stations, — something paying and safe, you know, something salable if you don't want it."

"Well, I'll think of it," nodded Vane, who had already made up his honest mind to have nothing to do with the Great Subfluvial, judging it to be a scheme for swindling the government and the general public.

"Do so," begged Mr. Simon Sharp, his broad array of yellow teeth showing in a manner which vaguely reminded one of the phrase, "dead men's bones and all uncleanness." The member from the old Whetstone State seemed at the moment to be as full of teeth as ever a freshly opened tomb was of skeletons. It was an error in him to make exhibition of those ravening tushes and grinders; they neutralized abominably the expression of integrity and piety which gleamed from the Puritanic lacker of his venerable mug. "Do, Mr. Vane," he continued, "give the project your intelligent consideration, and see if it is not worthy of your highly reputable and valuable support. And now, sir, I am compelled, very much against my wishes, to bid you a good morning. Delighted to have made your acquaintance, and to welcome you as a brother Congressman. Don't go to the door with me, don't! You are altogether too urbane. I thank you kindly."

FREDERICK DOUGLASS

Frederick Douglass (c.1818–95) escaped from slavery in Talbot County, Maryland, in 1838 and soon after went to work as a speaker for the Massachusetts Anti-Slavery Society, the first stop in a career that included being a powerful newspaper editor and one of the most important African American leaders in the nineteenth century. During the Civil War, he made several visits to Washington to meet with President Lincoln and his staff — to promote the idea of permitting freedmen to enlist in the Union Army, to lobby for equal pay for black soldiers, and to consult about saving freedmen and -women once the war was over. He later met with Lincoln's successors as well. In 1872, he moved to the city to assume the job of editor of the *New National Era*, a reformist weekly. In later years he was awarded a series of federal appointments — as marshal of the United States for the District of Columbia, as recorder of deeds for D.C., as minister and consul general to Haiti, and as chargé d'affaires for Santo Domingo. Douglass created a furor when the Washington press published reports about the scathing lecture he presented in Baltimore, "Our National Capital" (1877), and he had to survive a petition drive to remove him from his new office as D.C. marshal. Oddly, there had been no furor when he delivered the same lecture earlier in Washington. (One of Douglass's Washington homes, Cedar Hill in Anacostia, is now a popular visitors' site, maintained by the National Park Service.)

From "Our National Capital: An Address Delivered in Baltimore, Maryland, on 8 May 1877"

Ladies and Gentlemen: — It is not from any sense of my superior knowledge of men and things at the National Capital, or from any decided impression of your special destitution of such knowledge, that I venture to lecture upon the subject announced for this evening; on the contrary, the selection may be best explained upon the principle that large bodies attract small ones, and, in the comparison between the large and the small, you are the large and I am the small. You may know much, and I may know little. Nevertheless, having spent in Washington, several of the most eventful, stormy and perilous years of the Republic; having seen it both during and since the late tremendous war; having been a deeply interested spectator and student of passing events; and being compelled by my position and antecedents to view men and things from a peculiar point of observation, and knowing too, that truth is a very large and many sided matter, and that it requires a very large variety of men and women to tell it, I have naturally enough thought it might be well for me to tell my story about our National Capital. . . .

. . . Thus far I have given you thoughts concerning Washington, and have told in what regard the national metropolis should be held by the American people. I have to speak now more particularly of the fact of Washington; of its character and composition; of its past, present, and future. It will be easily seen that the contemplation of the city is one thing, and the city itself is quite another thing; and that there may be a wide difference between what it ought to be, and what it may be in reality, and what it may be in the reforming hand of the future.

In regard to the character and influence of Washington we have to deal with some broad and striking contradictions. . . . Justice is not always found on the bench, nor purity in the pulpit, nor saints at the altar. It will not do to assume for Washington, either moral or material preeminence over other cities of the union; on the contrary, Washington, as compared with many other parts of the country, has been, and still is, a most disgraceful and scandalous contradiction to the march of civilization. . . .

Looking to the influence exerted by simple local surroundings, I have no hesitation in saying that the selection of Washington as the National Capital

was one of the greatest mistakes made by the fathers of the Republic. The seat
of government ought never to have been planted there. This, however, is not to
be spoken so much in censure, as in sorrow.

Beautiful and charming as are the shores of the Potomac, they were not
selected as the national seat of government as a matter of absolutely free and
deliberate choice. . . . That the capital rested at last upon the shores of the Potomac was due largely to two causes: First, to the bad manners and brutality of
a Pennsylvania Militia Mob, and secondly, to the potent influence of George
Washington. By the first it was insulted and driven from Philadelphia; by the
second it was invited and lured to its present location. . . .

Seemingly a small matter in itself at the time, experience has shown that it
contained the seeds of civil war and disunion.

Sandwiched between two of the oldest slave states, each of which was a nurs-
ery and a hot-bed of slavery; surrounded by a people accustomed to look upon
the youthful members of a colored man's family as a part of the annual crop
for the market; pervaded by the manners, morals, politics, and religion peculiar to a slaveholding community, the inhabitants of the national capital were,
from first to last, frantically and fanatically sectional. Until the war, it neither
tolerated freedom of speech, nor of the press. Slavery was its idol, and, like all
idol worshippers, its people howled with rage, when this ugly idol was called in
question.

Like most slaveholding communities, Washington was tolerant of drinking, gambling, sensuality, indolence, and many other forms of vice, common
to an idle and lounging people. It was the home of the bully and the duelist. A
member of Congress, or an editor, who went there from the more industrious
and civilized parts of the country, found himself at an immense disadvantage
and of small account. He was in an enemy's land, a victim of insult and intimidation, and found that he must either submit to the lash and sting of the most
insolent of human tongues, or accept a challenge to Bladensburg and be shot at
by a trained duelist.

If, for any reason, however noble, he refused to submit to the barbarous code
of honor, he was branded as a coward, and regarded with contempt and scorn
by the elite of Washington society.

The place as it was before the war, might, without an unpardonable freedom
of fancy, be painted as a garden worthy of the best productions, but mainly
choked with poisonous weeds and infested by twisting serpents.

The wealth of Washington was tainted with corruption. Its moral life was
a miserable sham. Its industry was the wielding of the lash; its politeness, polished iniquity; its respect for the rights of man was bounded by the white line;
its courage was to ship a negro with his hands tied; its religion was, like all the

rest, a soft raiment, fair without, but foul within, worn to cover the festering sores of a diseased and leprous body.

Like any other moral monster, there was contamination in its touch, poison in its breath, and death in its embrace. There was something more than a wild and witty exaggeration in the saying of senator [William Gannaway] Brownlow when he remarked to a fellow passenger that he must be getting near Washington, for he began to feel as if he wanted to steal something.

In fostering and fomenting the late slaveholders rebellion, Washington performed its full share. It sustained Buchanan when he trifled with treason. It applauded Breckenridge when he served the rebellion better in the senate with his tongue than he could possibly serve it in the field with his sword. It stood between President Johnson and deserved impeachment, and cheered him on in his ministry of disorganization. It smiled upon the cowardly and murderous assault of Brooks upon Senator Sumner. It hatched out in its heat and moral debasement, the horrible brood of assassins who murdered the noble Lincoln and attempted the murder of Seward. Its people would at any time during the great war for union and liberty, have preferred Davis to Lincoln, and Lee to Grant. . . .

. . . THIS NEIGHBORHOOD power of Washington, as already indicated, has played a high hand in directing public affairs heretofore, and may be safely depended upon to secure for the people here, ample protection of person and property without the ballot. But who are the people of Washington and of the District of Columbia, the people who have given to the place its peculiar tone and character? The answer is, as already intimated, that they are mainly of the old slave holding stock of Virginia and Maryland. They were on the ground when the District of Columbia was ceded to the Federal Government and have been largely increased by additions from the same states. They were in part persons of wealth, culture, and refinement. They had undisputed possession of Washington during the entire existence of the national capital up to the war to suppress rebellion. They lived in fine houses, rode in fine carriages, had fine old wines in their cellars, and knew how to give fine and sparkling champaign [sic] suppers. Judging from the social influence, they were a charming community of gentlemen and ladies. Association with them easily produced an intermediate class, known as northern men with southern principles. The sources of their revenue were, slavery and the Government. Of Uncle Sam's good things, Virginia and Maryland always got the lion's share.

All this is now considerably changed, and the change has come none too soon. With the suppression of the rebellion and the abolition of slavery, the prestige of Virginia has vanished and her glory has departed. She is no longer the old dominion; no longer the mother of living statesmen, and her sons are not preferred above all others. They still deport themselves with an air of dignity; but dignity without station, masters without slaves, lords without lands, Honorables without honors, idols without worshippers, shock and repel by reason of contradiction. . . .

. . . But Washington has among its old inhabitants of the old Virginia class, another variety, not less typical of southern civilization than those already described.

They are what are commonly called, by way of extreme contempt, "Poor white trash." They never held an office, never owned a slave, and never called a piece of land their own. They have never aspired to wealth, education or respectability. In the days of slavery, they touched the master class only at the lowest point of moral and social degradation. They were the slave drivers, the overseers, the slavehunters, the spies, the patrol men, the informers, the watch dogs of the plantation. They were generally on hand when a refractory negro was to be beaten with many stripes. . . .

. . . But I would do injustice in the matter of the population of Washington if I failed to say a word of another element in the social composition of the capital, in no degree more agreeable and commendable than those already referred to.

They are the spoilsmen of every grade and description. They are the office holders, office seekers, contract buyers, pension agents, lobbyists, commissioners, and runbetweens in general. Men are here with all sorts of schemes and enterprises; some with claims valid and just, and some with claims neither valid nor just. Some have to secure the extension of a patent which ought to be extended, and some are here to prevent such extension. Some are here to contest the seat of a sitting member, and some are here to assist him.

Some are here to use their influence for friends at a distance who are too modest or too timid to come themselves; some are here with heads full of brains, pockets full of money, and faces full of brass, to lobby through Congress a great patriotic measure with millions in it, and all are here to get, if possible, something for nothing. . . .

. . . No where will you find a greater show of insincere politeness. The very air is vexed with clumsy compliments and obsequious hat lifting.

Everybody wants favor; everybody expects favor; everybody is looking for favor; everybody is afraid of losing favor; hence everybody smiles, bows, and fawns toward everybody else, and everybody knows the full value and quality of this general self abasement. You will seldom hear an honest, square, upright and downright no, in all this eager and hungry crowd. All look yes, say yes, and smile yes, even when they mean anything else than yes. . . .

. . . I now turn from the past with its gloom to the present with its promise, and to the future with its glory.

I have already spoken of the great change which has taken place in the physical condition of Washington. The change in its moral condition is equally vast and wonderful.

Men breathe freer here than ever they did before. Northern men with northern principles may now speak and write without the liability of being knocked down by street bullies and hired assassins, as in the time of slavery. The Senate is no longer a theatre of threats and brutal intimidation.

The colored people of Washington constitute one third of its population, and the change in their condition is truly marvelous. Some of the school buildings erected for the education of their children would do no discredit to the finest towns and cities of the north, and the freedom from annoyance with which these children are allowed to go and come from school, with their books and slates in their hands, is one of the most encouraging features of the times.

Washington, from being one of the most oppressive and illiberal cities of the Union, toward the colored race, has now become one of the most enlightened and liberal to that race. The colored man may now go to market, or attend church, or funeral, without a written permit from master or mayor. He is no longer arrested for being a stranger, and sold out of prison to pay his jail fees.

The moral tone of Washington has likewise been improved in many other respects.

Under the old dispensation, when slavery ruled and ruined, Washington was not a desirable place of residence for the wives and daughters of members of Congress and others whose business or pleasure took them thither. Gentlemen came here alone and lived here alone.

In the absence of good women and the family, man sinks rapidly to barbarism. In the olden times Members of Congress came here and left behind them all the restraints and endearments of home. Their manners and morals were shaped by those of the restaurant, the hotel and the gambling hall, and other resorts of men of the world.

But now, thanks to the abolition of slavery, thanks to the increasing influence and power of the North, thanks to the spirit of improvement, thanks to the increase of cheap and easy modes of travel, Members of Congress and others who have business at the Capital can bring their families with them and surround themselves with all the restraints and endearments of home.

I do not pretend to say that Washington is at all perfect. There is of course within her borders a full share of vice and crime of every conceivable kind and quality, but I do mean to say that there is now much less of these, in proportion to the numbers, than under the old regimen, and that this is especially true in respect of the influential classes.

Washington is still, and, in the nature of things, must continue to be, a city of boarding houses and hotels; but it is also rapidly becoming a city of sweet and beautiful homes. All signs indicate that the national capital will ultimately become one of the most desirable cities for residence, in the world. . . .

. . . In its grandeur and significance, it may be a sign and a bond of the American Union, a pledge of the righteousness that exalts a nation, a place where the best men and the best women from all sections of our widely extended country shall delight to meet and bury their differences, renew their covenants of patriotism, and shake hands, not over a bloody chasm, but over a free, prosperous, happy and progressive REPUBLIC.

BRET HARTE

Born in Albany, New York, Bret Harte (1836–1902) rose to fame in the 1860s and 1870s writing tales of Spanish California and the mother lode. He returned to the East to capitalize on his recent success by contracting with various magazines to publish his work. He ventured to Washington in 1877 with the expectation of editing a new publication to be called "The Capitol." As he said, innocently, in a letter to his wife: "Washington is the place for a literary man to make money." A few months later, the magazine failed, its assets — including the fee Harte was to receive for a story he had been working on — seized by creditors. His "The Office-Seeker," originally published in the *New York Sun* in 1877, provides an ironic prediction of the author's own disappointment regarding the elusive promise of the federal city. His influential friends, however, soon came to his rescue by helping to secure an appointment as U.S. consul at Crefield in Germany and, later, as consul in Scotland.

The Office-Seeker

He asked me if I had ever seen the "Remus Sentinel." I replied that I had not, and would have added that I did not even know where Remus was, when he continued by saying it was strange the hotel proprietor did not keep the "Sentinel" on his files, and that he himself should write to the editor about it. He would not have spoken about it, but he himself had been a humble member of the profession to which I belonged, and had often written for its columns. Some friends of his — partial, no doubt — had said that his style somewhat resembled Junius's; but of course, you know — well, what he could say was that in the last campaign his articles were widely sought for. He did not know but he had a copy of one. Here his hand dived into the breast-pocket of his coat, with a certain deftness that indicated long habit, and after depositing on his lap a bundle of well-worn documents, every one of which was glaringly suggestive of certificates and signatures, he concluded he had left it in his trunk.

I breathed more freely. We were sitting in the rotunda of a famous Washington hotel, and only a few moments before had the speaker, an utter stranger to me, moved his chair beside mine and opened a conversation. I noticed that he had that timid, lonely, helpless air which invests the bucolic traveler who, for the first time, finds himself among strangers, and his identity lost, in a world so much larger, so much colder, so much more indifferent to him than he ever imagined. Indeed, I think that what we often attribute to the impertinent familiarity of countrymen and rustic travelers on railways or in cities is largely due to their awful loneliness and nostalgia. I remember to have once met in a smoking-car on a Kansas railway one of these lonely ones, who, after plying me with a thousand useless questions, finally elicited the fact that I knew slightly a man who had once dwelt in his native town in Illinois. During the rest of our journey the conversation turned chiefly upon this fellow-townsman, whom it afterwards appeared that my Illinois friend knew no better than I did. But he had established a link between himself and his far-off home through me, and was happy.

While this was passing through my mind I took a fair look at him. He was a spare young fellow, not more than thirty, with sandy hair and eyebrows, and eyelashes so white as to be almost imperceptible. He was dressed in black, somewhat to the "rearward o' the fashion," and I had an odd idea that it had been his wedding suit, and it afterwards appeared I was right. His manner had the precision and much of the dogmatism of the country schoolmaster, accustomed to wrestle with the feeblest intellects. From his history, which he presently gave me, it appeared I was right here also.

He was born and bred in a Western State, and, as schoolmaster of Remus and clerk of supervisors, had married one of his scholars, the daughter of a clergyman, and a man of some little property. He had attracted some attention by his powers of declamation, and was one of the principal members of the Remus Debating Society. The various questions then agitating Remus — "Is the doctrine of immortality consistent with an agricultural life?" and, "Are round dances morally wrong?" — afforded him an opportunity of bringing himself prominently before the country people. Perhaps I might have seen an extract copied from the "Remus Sentinel" in the "Christian Recorder" of May 7, 1875? No? He would get it for me. He had taken an active part in the last campaign. He did not like to say it, but it had been universally acknowledged that he had elected Gashwiler.

Who?

Gen. Pratt C. Gashwiler, member of Congress from our deestrict.

Oh!

A powerful man, sir, — a very powerful man; a man whose influence will presently be felt here, sir, — *here*! Well, he had come on with Gashwiler, and — well, he did not know why — Gashwiler did not know why he should not, you know (a feeble, half-apologetic laugh here), receive that reward, you know, for these services which, etc., etc.

I asked him if he had any particular or definite office in view.

Well, no. He had left that to Gashwiler. Gashwiler had said — he remembered his very words: "Leave it all to me; I'll look through the different departments, and see what can be done for a man of your talents."

And —

He's looking. I'm expecting him back here every minute. He's gone over to the Department of Tape to see what can be done there. Ah! here he comes.

A large man approached us. He was very heavy, very unwieldy, very unctuous and oppressive. He affected the "honest farmer," but so badly that the poorest husbandman would have resented it. There was a suggestion of a cheap lawyer about him that would have justified any self-respecting judge in throwing him over the bar at once. There was a military suspicion about him that would have entitled him to a court-martial on the spot. There was an introduction, from which I learned that my office-seeking friend's name was Expectant Dobbs. And then Gashwiler addressed me: —

"Our young friend here is waiting, waiting. Waiting, I may say, on the affairs of state. Youth," continued the Hon. Mr. Gashwiler, addressing an imaginary constituency, "is nothing but a season of waiting — of preparation — ha, ha!"

As he laid his hand in a fatherly manner — a fatherly manner that was as much of a sham as anything else about him — on Mr. Dobbs's shoulder, I don't know whether I was more incensed at him or his victim, who received it with evident pride and satisfaction. Nevertheless he ventured to falter out: —

"Has anything been done yet?"

"Well, no; I can't say that anything — that is, that anything has been *completed*; but I may say we are in excellent position for an advance — ha, ha! But we must wait, my young friend, wait. What is it the Latin philosopher says? 'Let us by all means hasten slowly' — ha, ha!" and he turned to me as if saying confidentially, "Observe the impatience of these boys!" "I met, a moment ago, my old friend and boyhood's companion, Jim McGlasher, chief of the Bureau for the Dissemination of Useless Information, and," lowering his voice to a mysterious but audible whisper, "I shall see him again tomorrow."

The "All aboard!" of the railway omnibus at this moment tore me from the presence of this gifted legislator and his protégé; but as we drove away I saw through the open window the powerful mind of Gashwiler operating, so to speak, upon the susceptibilities of Mr. Dobbs.

I did not meet him again for a week. The morning of my return I saw the two conversing together in the hall, but with the palpable distinction between this and their former interviews, that the gifted Gashwiler seemed to be anxious to get away from his friend. I heard him say something about "committees" and "to-morrow," and when Dobbs turned his freckled face toward me I saw that he had got at last some expression into it, — disappointment. I asked him pleasantly how he was getting on. He had not lost his pride yet. He was doing well, although such was the value set upon his friend Gashwiler's abilities by his brother members that he was almost always occupied with committee business. I noticed that his clothes were not in as good case as before, and he told me that he had left the hotel, and taken lodgings in a bystreet, where it was less expensive. Temporarily, of course. A few days after this I had business in one of the great departments. From the various signs over the doors of its various offices and bureaus it always oddly reminded me of Stewart's or Arnold & Constable's. You could get pensions, patents, and plants. You could get land and the seeds to put in it, and the Indians to prowl round it, and what not. There was a perpetual clanging of office desk bells, and a running hither and thither of messengers strongly suggestive of "Cash 47."

As my business was with the manager of this Great National Fancy Shop, I managed to push by the sad-eyed, eager-faced crowd of men and women in the anteroom, and entered the secretary's room, conscious of having left behind me a great deal of envy and uncharitableness of spirit. As I opened the door I heard a monotonous flow of Western speech which I thought I recognized. There was no mistaking it. It was the voice of Gashwiler.

"The appointment of this man, Mr. Secretary, would be most acceptable to the people in my deestrict. His family are wealthy and influential, and it's just as well in the fall elections to have the supervisors and county judge pledged to support the administration. Our delegates to the State Central Committee are to a man" — but here, perceiving from the wandering eye of Mr. Secretary that there was another man in the room, he whispered the rest with a familiarity that must have required all the politician in the official's breast to keep from resenting.

"You have some papers, I suppose?" asked the secretary wearily.

Gashwiler was provided with a pocketful, and produced them. The secretary threw them on the table among the other papers, where they seemed instantly to lose their identity, and looked as if they were ready to recommend anybody but the person they belonged to. Indeed, in one corner the entire Massachusetts delegation, with the Supreme Bench at their head, appeared to be earnestly advocating the manuring of Iowa waste lands; and to the inexperienced eye, a noted female reformer had apparently appended her signature to a request for a pension for wounds received in battle.

"By the way," said the secretary, "I think I have a letter here from somebody in your district asking an appointment, and referring to you? Do you withdraw it?"

"If anybody has been presuming to speculate upon my patronage," said the Hon. Mr. Gashwiler with rising rage.

"I've got the letter somewhere here," said the secretary, looking dazedly at his table. He made a feeble movement among the papers, and then sank back hopelessly in his chair, and gazed out of the window as if he thought and rather hoped it might have flown away. "It was from a Mr. Globbs, or Gobbs, or Dobbs, of Remus," he said finally, after a superhuman effort of memory.

"Oh, that's nothing, — a foolish fellow who has been boring me for the last month."

"Then I am to understand that this application is withdrawn?"

"As far as my patronage is concerned, certainly. In fact, such an appointment would not express the sentiments — indeed, I may say, would be calculated to raise active opposition in the deestrict."

The secretary uttered a sigh of relief, and the gifted Gashwiler passed out. I tried to get a good look at the honorable scamp's eye, but he evidently did not recognize me.

It was a question in my mind whether I ought not to expose the treachery of Dobbs's friend, but the next time I met Dobbs he was in such good spirits that I forebore. It appeared that his wife had written to him that she had discovered a second cousin in the person of the Assistant Superintendent of the Envelope Flap Moistening Bureau of the Department of Tape, and had asked his assistance; and Dobbs had seen him, and he had promised it. "You see," said Dobbs, "in the performance of his duties he is often very near the person of the secretary, frequently in the next room, and he is a powerful man, sir, — a powerful man to know, sir, — a very powerful man."

How long this continued I do not remember. Long enough, however, for Dobbs to become quite seedy, for the giving up of wrist-cuffs, for the neglect of shoes and beard, and for great hollows to form round his eyes, and a slight flush on his cheek-bones. I remember meeting him in all the departments, writing letters or waiting patiently in ante-rooms from morning till night. He had lost all his old dogmatism, but not his pride. "I might as well be here as anywhere, while I'm waiting," he said, "and then I'm getting some knowledge of the details of official life."

In the face of this mystery I was surprised at finding a note from him one day, inviting me to dine with him at a certain famous restaurant. I had scarce got over my amazement, when the writer himself overtook me at my hotel. For a moment I scarcely recognized him. A new suit of fashionably-cut clothes had changed him, without, however, entirely concealing his rustic angularity of figure and outline. He even affected a fashionable dilettante air, but so mildly and so innocently that it was not offensive.

"You see," he began, explanatory-wise, "I've just found out the way to do it. None of these big fellows, these cabinet officers, know me except as an applicant. Now, the way to do this thing is to meet 'em fust sociably; wine 'em and dine 'em. Why, sir" — he dropped into the schoolmaster again here — "I had two cabinet ministers, two judges, and a general at my table last night."

"On *your* invitation?"

"Dear, no! all I did was to pay for it. Tom Soufflet gave the dinner and invited the people. Everybody knows Tom. You see, a friend of mine put me up to it, and said that Soufflet had fixed up no end of appointments and jobs in that way. You see, when these gentlemen get sociable over their wine, he says, carelessly, "By the way, there's So-and-so — a good fellow — wants something; give it to him." And the first thing you know, or they know, he gets a promise from them. They get a dinner — and a good one — and he gets an appointment."

"But where did you get the money?"

"Oh" — he hesitated — "I wrote home, and Fanny's father raised fifteen hundred dollars some way, and sent it to me. I put it down to political expenses." He laughed a weak foolish laugh here, and added, "As the old man don't drink nor smoke, he'd lift his eyebrows to know how the money goes. But I'll make it all right when the office comes — and she's coming, sure pop."

His slang fitted as poorly on him as his clothes, and his familiarity was worse than his former awkward shyness. But I could not help asking him what had been the result of this expenditure.

"Nothing just yet. But the Secretary of Tape and the man at the head of the Inferior Department, both spoke to me, and one of them said he thought he'd heard my name before. He might," he added with a forced laugh, "for I've written him fifteen letters."

Three months passed. A heavy snowstorm stayed my chariot wheels on a Western railroad, ten miles from a nervous lecture committee and a waiting audience; there was nothing to do but to make the attempt to reach them in a sleigh. But the way was long and the drifts deep; and when at last four miles out we reached a little village, the driver declared his cattle could hold out no longer, and we must stop there. Bribes and threats were equally of no avail. I had to accept the fact.

"What place is this?"

"Remus."

"Remus, Remus," — where had I heard that name before? But while I was reflecting he drove up before the door of the tavern. It was a dismal, sleep-forbidding place, and only nine o'clock, and here was the long winter's night before me. Failing to get the landlord to give me a team to go farther, I resigned myself to my fate and a cigar, behind the red-hot stove.

In a few moments one of the loungers approached me, calling me by name, and in a rough but hearty fashion condoled me for my mishap, advising me to stay at Remus all night, and added: —

"The quarters ain't the best in the world yer at this hotel. But thar's an old man yer — the preacher that was — that for twenty years hez taken in such fellers as you and lodged 'em free gratis for nothing, and hez been proud to do it. The old man used to be rich; he ain't so now; sold his big house on the cross-roads, and lives in a little cottage with his darter right over yan. But ye could n't do him a better turn than to go over thar and stay, and if he thought I'd let ye go out o' Remus without axing ye, he'd give me h — ll. Stop, I'll go with ye."

I might at least call on the old man, and I accompanied my guide through the still falling snow until we reached a little cottage. The door opened to my guide's knock, and with the brief and discomposing introduction, "Yer, ole man, I've brought you one of them snowbound lecturers," he left me on the threshold, as my host, a kindly-faced, white-haired man of seventy, came forward to greet me.

His frankness and simple courtesy overcame the embarrassment left by my guide's introduction, and I followed him passively as he entered the neat but plainly furnished sitting-room. At the same moment a pretty but faded young woman arose from the sofa and was introduced to me as his daughter. "Fanny and I live here quite alone, and if you knew how good it was to see somebody from the great outside world now and then, you would not apologize for what you call your intrusion."

During this speech I was vaguely trying to recall where and when and under what circumstances I had ever before seen the village, the house, the old man, or his daughter. Was it in a dream, or in one of those dim reveries of some previous existence to which the spirit of mankind is subject? I looked at them again. In the careworn lines around the once pretty girlish mouth of the young woman, in the furrowed seams over the forehead of the old man, in the ticking of the old-fashioned clock on the shelf, in the faint whisper of the falling snow outside, I read the legend "Patience, Patience; Wait and Hope."

The old man filled a pipe, and offering me one, continued, "Although I seldom drink myself, it was my custom to always keep some nourishing liquor in my house for passing guests, but to-night I find myself without any." I hastened to offer him my flask, which, after a moment's coyness, he accepted, and presently under its benign influence at least ten years dropped from his shoulders, and he sat up in his chair erect and loquacious.

"And how are affairs at the national capital, sir?" he began.

Now, if there was any subject of which I was profoundly ignorant, it was this. But the old man was evidently bent on having a good political talk. So I said vaguely, yet with a certain sense of security, that I guessed there wasn't much being done.

"I see," said the old man, "in the matters of resumption of the sovereign rights of States and federal interference, you would imply that a certain conservative policy is not to be promulgated until after the electoral committee have given their verdict." I looked for help towards the lady, and observed feebly that he had very clearly expressed my views.

The old man, observing my looks, said, "Although my daughter's husband holds a federal position in Washington, the pressure of his business is so great that he has little time to give us mere gossip — I beg your pardon, did you speak?"

I had unconsciously uttered an exclamation. This, then, was Remus, — the home of Expectant Dobbs, — and these his wife and father; and the Washington banquet-table, ah me! had sparkled with the yearning heart's blood of this poor wife, and had been upheld by this tottering Caryatid of a father.

"Do you know what position he has?"

The old man did not know positively, but thought it was some general supervising position. He had been assured by Mr. Gashwiler that it was a first-class clerkship; yes, a *first*-class.

I did not tell him that in this, as in many other official regulations in Washington, they reckoned backward, but said: —

"I suppose that your M. C., Mr. — Mr. Gashwiler" —

"Don't mention his name," said the little woman, rising to her feet hastily; "he never brought Expectant anything but disappointment and sorrow. I hate, I despise, the man."

"Dear Fanny," expostulated the old man gently, "this is unchristian and unjust. Mr. Gashwiler is a powerful, a very powerful man! His work is a great one; his time is preoccupied with weightier matters."

"His time was not so preoccupied but he could make use of poor Expectant," said this wounded dove a little spitefully.

Nevertheless it was some satisfaction to know that Dobbs had at last got a place, no matter how unimportant, or who had given it to him; and when I went to bed that night in the room that had been evidently prepared for their conjugal chamber, I felt that Dobbs's worst trials were over. The walls were hung with souvenirs of their ante nuptial days. There was a portrait of Dobbs, ætat. 25; there was a faded bouquet in a glass case, presented by Dobbs to Fanny on examination-day; there was a framed resolution of thanks to Dobbs from the Remus Debating Society; there was a certificate of Dobbs's election as President of the Remus Philomathean Society; there was his commission as captain in the Remus Independent Contingent of Home Guards; there was a Freemason's chart, in which Dobbs was addressed in epithets more fulsome and extravagant than any living monarch. And yet all these cheap glories of a narrow life and narrower brain were upheld and made sacred by the love of the devoted priestess who worshiped at this homely shrine, and kept the light burning through gloom and doubt and despair. The storm tore round the house, and shook its white fists in the windows. A dried wreath of laurel that Fanny had placed on Dobbs's head after his celebrated centennial address at the schoolhouse, July 4, 1876, swayed in the gusts, and sent a few of its dead leaves down on the floor, and I lay in Dobbs's bed and wondered what a first-class clerkship was.

I found out early the next summer. I was strolling through the long corridors of a certain great department, when I came upon a man accurately yoked across the shoulders, and supporting two huge pails of ice on either side, from which he was replenishing the pitchers in the various offices. As I passed I turned to look at him again. It was Dobbs!

He did not set down his burden; it was against the rules, he said. But he gossiped cheerily, said he was beginning at the foot of the ladder, but expected soon to climb up. That it was Civil Service Reform, and of course he would be promoted soon.

Had Gashwiler procured the appointment?

No. He believed it was *me*. *I* had told his story to Assistant-Secretary Blank, who had in turn related it to Bureau-Director Dash — both good fellows — but this was all they could do. Yes, it was a foothold. But he must go now.

Nevertheless I followed him up and down, and cheered him with a rose-colored picture of his wife and family, and my visit there, and promising to come and see him the next time I came to Washington, I left him with his self-imposed yoke.

With a new administration Civil Service Reform came in, crude and ill-digested, as all sudden and sweeping reforms must be; cruel to the individual, as all crude reforms will ever be; and among the list of helpless men and women, incapaciated for other work by long service in the dull routine of federal office who were decapitated, the weak, foolish, emaciated head of Expectant Dobbs went to the block. It afterwards appeared that the gifted Gashwiler was responsible for the appointment of twenty clerks, and that the letter of poor Dobbs, in which he dared to refer to the now powerless Gashwiler, had sealed his fate. The country made an example of Gashwiler and — Dobbs.

From that moment he disappeared. I looked for him in vain in anterooms, lobbies, and hotel corridors, and finally came to the conclusion that he had gone home.

How beautiful was that July Sabbath, when the morning train from Baltimore rolled into the Washington depot! How tenderly and chastely the morning sunlight lay on the east front of the Capitol until the whole building was hushed in a grand and awful repose! How difficult it was to think of a Gashwiler creeping in and out of those milling columns, or crawling beneath that portico, without wondering that yon majestic figure came not down with flat of sword to smite the fat rotundity of the intruder! How difficult to think that parricidal hands have ever been lifted against the Great Mother, typified here in the graceful white chastity of her garments, in the noble tranquillity of her face, in the gathering up her white-robed children within her shadow!

This led me to think of Dobbs, when, suddenly, a face flashed by my carriage window. I called to the driver to stop, and, looking again, saw that it was a woman standing bewildered and irresolute on the street corner. As she turned her anxious face toward me I saw that it was Mrs. Dobbs.

What was she doing here, and where was Expectant?

She began an incoherent apology, and then burst into explanatory tears. When I had got her in the carriage she said, between her sobs, that Expectant had not returned; that she had received a letter from a friend here saying he was sick, — oh, very, very sick, — and father could not come with her, so she came alone. She was so frightened, so lonely, so miserable.

Had she his address?

Yes, just here! It was on the outskirts of Washington, near Georgetown. Then I would take her there, if I could, for she knew nobody.

On our way I tried to cheer her up by pointing out some of the children of the Great Mother before alluded to, but she only shut her eyes as we rolled down the long avenues, and murmured, "Oh, these cruel, cruel distances!"

At last we reached the locality, a negro quarter, yet clean and neat in appearance. I saw the poor girl shudder slightly as we stopped at the door of a low, two-story frame house, from which the unwonted spectacle of a carriage brought a crowd of half-naked children and a comely, cleanly, kind-faced mulatto woman.

Yes, this was the house. He was upstairs, rather poorly, but asleep, she thought.

We went upstairs. In the first chamber, clean, though poorly furnished, lay Dobbs. On a pine table near his bed were letters and memorials to the various departments, and on the bed-quilt, unfinished, but just as the weary fingers had relaxed their grasp upon it, lay a letter to the Tape Department.

As we entered the room he lifted himself on his elbow. "Fanny!" he said quickly, and a shade of disappointment crossed his face. "I thought it was a message from the secretary," he added apologetically.

The poor woman had suffered too much already to shrink from this last crushing blow. But she walked quietly to his side without a word or cry, knelt, placed her loving arms around him, and I left them so together.

When I called again in the evening he was better; so much better that, against the doctor's orders, he had talked to her quite cheerfully and hopefully for an hour, until suddenly raising her bowed head in his two hands, he said, "Do you know, dear, that in looking for help and influence there was One, dear, I had forgotten; One who is very potent with kings and councilors; and I think, love, I shall ask Him to interest Himself in my behalf. It is not too late yet, darling, and I shall seek him tomorrow."

And before the morrow came he had sought and found Him, and I doubt not got a good place.

HENRY ADAMS

Henry Adams (1838–1918) was the quintessential Washington writer. Born in Quincy, Massachusetts, the grandson of one president and the great-grandson of another, he first went to the federal city as a twelve-year-old. He returned several years later as his congressman father's private secretary, and then again as a journalist and editor, finally settling in the city for good on Lafayette Square in 1877. His decision to make Washington his home marks an important turning point in the city's development, socially and materially, in the years following the Civil War — reflecting the fact that Washington had finally come of age. Adams wrote one Washington novel, *Democracy, an American Novel* (1880), which explores the romance of power and the conflicts between politics and statecraft, while at the same time excoriating the corruptions of the Grant administration. He also wrote a masterful nine-volume *History of the United States during the Administrations of Jefferson and Madison* (1889–91). His most memorable writing about Washington, however, is found in his eccentric autobiographical account, *The Education of Henry Adams* (1907). When Adams died in 1918, he was buried next to his wife, Marian (Clover) Hooper Adams, in Rock Creek Cemetery. At the site of the famous memorial, stands a bronze sculpture of a hooded figure, known unofficially as "Grief," created by his friend, Augustus Saint-Gaudens.

From *Democracy, an American Novel*

To tie a prominent statesman to her train and to lead him about like a tame bear, is for a young and vivacious woman a more certain amusement than to tie herself to him and to be dragged about like an Indian squaw. This fact was Madeleine Lee's first great political discovery in Washington, and it was worth to her all the German philosophy she had ever read, with even a complete edition of Herbert Spencer's works into the bargain. There could be no doubt that the honours and dignities of a public career were no fair consideration for its pains. She made a little daily task for herself of reading in succession the lives and letters of the American Presidents, and of their wives, when she could find that there was a trace of the latter's existence. What a melancholy spectacle it was, from George Washington down to the last incumbent; what vexations, what disappointments, what grievous mistakes, what very objectionable manners! Not one of them, who had aimed at high purpose, but had been thwarted, beaten, and habitually insulted! What a gloom lay on the features of those famous chieftains, Calhoun, Clay, and Webster; what varied expression of defeat and unsatisfied desire; what a sense of self-importance and senatorial magniloquence; what a craving for flattery; what despair at the sentence of fate! And what did they amount to, after all?

They were practical men, these! they had no great problems of thought to settle, no questions that rose above the ordinary rules of common morals and homely duty. How they had managed to befog the subject! What elaborate show-structures they had built up, with no result but to obscure the horizon! Would not the country have done better without them? Could it have done worse? What deeper abyss could have opened under the nation's feet, than that to whose verge they brought it?

Madeleine's mind wearied with the monotony of the story. She discussed the subject with Ratcliffe, who told her frankly that the pleasure of politics lay in the possession of power. He agreed that the country would do very well without him. "But here I am," said he, "and here I mean to stay." He had very little sympathy for thin moralising, and a statesmanlike contempt for philosophical politics. He loved power, and he meant to be President. That was enough.

Sometimes the tragic and sometimes the comic side was uppermost in her mind, and sometimes she did not herself know whether to cry or to laugh. Washington more than any other city in the world swarms with simpleminded exhibitions of human nature; men and women curiously out of place, whom it would be cruel to ridicule and ridiculous to weep over. The sadder exhibitions are fortunately seldom seen by respectable people; only the little social accidents come under their eyes. One evening Mrs. Lee went to the President's first evening reception. As Sybil flatly refused to face the crowd, and Carrington mildly said that he feared he was not sufficiently reconstructed to appear at home in that august presence, Mrs. Lee accepted Mr. French for an escort, and walked across the Square with him to join the throng that was pouring into the doors of the White House. They took their places in the line of citizens and were at last able to enter the reception-room. There Madeleine found herself before two seemingly mechanical figures, which might be wood or wax, for any sign they showed of life. These two figures were the President and his wife; they stood stiff and awkward by the door, both their faces stripped of every sign of intelligence, while the right hands of both extended themselves to the column of visitors with the mechanical action of toy dolls. Mrs. Lee for a moment began to laugh, but the laugh died on her lips. To the President and his wife this was clearly no laughing matter. There they stood, automata, representatives of the society which streamed past them. Madeleine seized Mr. French by the arm.

"Take me somewhere at once," said she, "where I can look at it. Here! in the corner, I had no conception how shocking it was!"

Mr. French supposed she was thinking of the queer-looking men and women who were swarming through the rooms, and he made, after his own delicate notion of humour, some uncouth jests on those who passed by. Mrs. Lee, however, was in no humour to explain or even to listen. She stopped him short: —

"There, Mr. French! Now go away and leave me. I want to be alone for half an hour. Please come for me then." And there she stood, with her eyes fixed on the President and his wife, while the endless stream of humanity passed them, shaking hands.

What a strange and solemn spectacle it was, and how the deadly fascination of it burned the image in upon her mind! What a horrid warning to ambition! And in all that crowd there was no one besides herself who felt the mockery of this exhibition. To all the others this task was a regular part of the President's duty, and there was nothing ridiculous about it. They thought it a democratic institution, this droll aping of monarchical forms. To them the deadly dulness of the show was as natural and proper as ever to the courtiers of the Philips and Charleses seemed the ceremonies of the Escurial. To her it had the effect of a nightmare, or of an opium-eater's vision. She felt a sudden conviction that this was to be the end of American society; its realisation and dream at once. She groaned in spirit.

"Yes! at last I have reached the end! We shall grow to be wax images, and our talk will be like the squeaking of toy dolls. We shall all wander round and round the earth and shake hands. No one will have any object in this world, and there will be no other. It is worse than anything in the 'Inferno.' What an awful vision of eternity!"

Suddenly, as through a mist, she saw the melancholy face of Lord Skye approaching. He came to her side, and his voice recalled her to reality.

"Does it amuse you, this sort of thing?" he asked in a vague way.

"We take our amusement sadly, after the manner of our people," she replied; "but it certainly interests me."

They stood for a time in silence, watching the slowly eddying dance of Democracy, until he resumed:

"Whom do you take that man to be — the long, lean one, with a long woman on each arm?"

"That man," she replied, "I take to be a Washington department-clerk, or perhaps a member of Congress from Iowa, with a wife and wife's sister. Do they shock your nobility?"

He looked at her with comical resignation. "You mean to tell me that they are quite as good as dowager-countesses. I grant it. My aristocratic spirit is broken, Mrs. Lee. I will even ask them to dinner if you bid me, and if you will come to meet them. But the last time I asked a member of Congress to dine, he sent me back a note in pencil on my own envelope that he would bring two of his friends with him, very respectable constituents from Yahoo city, or some such place; nature's noblemen, he said."

"You should have welcomed them."

"I did. I wanted to see two of nature's noblemen, and I knew they would probably be pleasanter company than their representative. They came; very respectable persons, one with a blue necktie, the other with a red one: both had diamond pins in their shirts, and were carefully brushed in respect to their hair. They said nothing, ate little, drank less, and were much better behaved than I am. When they went away, they unanimously asked me to stay with them when I visited Yahoo city."

"You will not want guests if you always do that."

"I don't know. I think it was pure ignorance on their part. They knew no better, and they seemed modest enough. My only complaint was that I could get nothing out of them. I wonder whether their wives would have been more amusing."

"Would they be so in England, Lord Skye?"

He looked down at her with half-shut eyes, and drawled: "You know my countrywomen?"

"Hardly at all."

"Then let us discuss some less serious subject."

"Willingly. I have waited for you to explain to me why you have to-night an expression of such melancholy."

"Is that quite friendly, Mrs. Lee? Do I really look melancholy?"

"Unutterably, as I feel, I am consumed with curiosity to know the reason."

The British minister coolly took a complete survey of the whole room, ending with a prolonged stare at the President and his wife, who were still mechanically shaking hands; then he looked back into her face, and said never a word.

She insisted: "I must have this riddle answered. It suffocates me. I should not be sad at seeing these same people at work or at play, if they ever do play; or in a church or a lecture-room. Why do they weigh on me like a horrid phantom here?"

"I see no riddle, Mrs. Lee. You have answered your own question; they are neither at work nor at play."

"Then please take me home at once. I shall have hysterics. The sight of those two suffering images at the door is too mournful to be borne. I am dizzy with looking at these stalking figures. I don't believe they're real. I wish the house would take fire. I want an earthquake. I wish some one would pinch the President, or pull his wife's hair."

Mrs. Lee did not repeat the experiment of visiting the White House, and indeed for some time afterwards she spoke with little enthusiasm of the presidential office. To Senator Ratcliffe she expressed her opinions strongly. The Senator tried in vain to argue that the people had a right to call upon their chief magistrate, and that he was bound to receive them; this being so, there was no less objectionable way of proceeding than the one which had been chosen. "Who gave the people any such right?" asked Mrs. Lee. "Where does it come from? What do they want it for? You know better, Mr. Ratcliffe! Our chief magistrate is a citizen like any one else. What puts it into his foolish head to cease being a citizen and to ape royalty? Our governors never make themselves ridiculous. Why cannot the wretched being content himself with living like the rest of us, and minding his own business? Does he know what a figure of fun he is?" And Mrs. Lee went so far as to declare that she would like to be the President's wife only to put an end to this folly; nothing should ever induce *her* to go through such a performance; and if the public did not approve of this, Congress might impeach her, and remove her from office; all she demanded was the right to be heard before the Senate in her own defence.

Nevertheless, there was a very general impression in Washington that Mrs. Lee would like nothing better than to be in the White House. Known to comparatively few people, and rarely discussing even with them the subjects which deeply interested her, Madeleine passed for a clever, intriguing woman who had her own objects to gain. True it is, beyond peradventure, that all residents of Washington may be assumed to be in office or candidates for office; unless they avow their object, they are guilty of an attempt — and a stupid one — to deceive; yet there is a small class of apparent exceptions destined at last to fall within the rule. Mrs. Lee was properly assumed to be a candidate for office. To the Washingtonians it was a matter of course that Mrs. Lee should marry Silas P. Ratcliffe. That he should be glad to get a fashionable and intelligent wife, with twenty or thirty thousand dollars a year, was not surprising. That she should accept the first public man of the day, with a flattering chance for the Presidency — a man still comparatively young and not without good looks — was perfectly natural, and in her undertaking she had the sympathy of all well-regulated Washington women who were not possible rivals; for to them the President's wife is of more consequence than the President; and, indeed, if America only knew it, they are not very far from the truth.

Some there were, however, who did not assent to this good-natured though worldly view of the proposed match. These ladies were severe in their comments upon Mrs. Lee's conduct, and did not hesitate to declare their opinion that she was the calmest and most ambitious minx who had ever come within their observation. Unfortunately it happened that the respectable and proper Mrs. Schuyler Clinton took this view of the case, and made little attempt to conceal her opinion. She was justly indignant at her cousin's gross worldliness, and possible promotion in rank.

"If Madeleine Ross marries that coarse, horrid old Illinois politician," said she to her husband, "I never will forgive her so long as I live."

Mr. Clinton tried to excuse Madeleine, and even went so far as to suggest that the difference of age was no greater than in their own case; but his wife trampled ruthlessly on his argument.

"At any rate," said she, "I never came to Washington as a widow on purpose to set my cap for the first candidate for the Presidency, and I never made a public spectacle of my indecent eagerness in the very galleries of the Senate; and Mrs. Lee ought to be ashamed of herself. She is a cold-blooded, heartless, unfeminine cat."

Little Victoria Dare, who babbled like the winds and streams, with utter indifference as to what she said or whom she addressed, used to bring choice bits of this gossip to Mrs. Lee. She always affected a little stammer when she said anything uncommonly impudent, and put on a manner of languid simplicity. She felt keenly the satisfaction of seeing Madeleine charged with her own besetting sins. For years all Washington had agreed that Victoria was little better than one of the wicked; she had done nothing but violate every rule of propriety and scandalise every well-regulated family in the city, and there was no good in her. Yet it could not be denied that Victoria was amusing, and had a sort of irregular fascination; consequently she was universally tolerated. To see Mrs. Lee thrust down to her own level was an unmixed pleasure to her, and she carefully repeated to Madeleine the choice bits of dialogue which she picked up in her wanderings.

"Your cousin, Mrs. Clinton, says you are a ca-ca-cat, Mrs. Lee."

"I don't believe it, Victoria. Mrs. Clinton never said anything of the sort."

"Mrs. Marston says it is because you have caught a ra-ra-rat, and Senator Clinton was only a m-m-mouse!"

Naturally all this unexpected publicity irritated Mrs. Lee not a little, especially when short and vague paragraphs, soon followed by longer and more positive ones, in regard to Senator Ratcliffe's matrimonial prospects, began to appear in newspapers, along with descriptions of herself from the pens of enterprising female correspondents for the press, who had never so much as seen her. At the first sight of one of these newspaper articles, Madeleine fairly cried with mortification and anger. She wanted to leave Washington the next day, and she hated the very thought of Ratcliffe. There was something in the newspaper style so inscrutably vulgar, something so inexplicably revolting to the sense of feminine decency, that she shrank under it as though it were a poisonous spider. But after the first acute shame had passed, her temper was roused, and she vowed that she would pursue her own path just as she had begun, without regard to all the malignity and vulgarity in the wide United States. She did not care to marry Senator Ratcliffe; she liked his society and was flattered by his confidence; she rather hoped to prevent him from ever making a formal offer, and if not, she would at least push it off to the last possible moment; but she was not to be frightened from marrying him by any amount of spitefulness or gossip, and she did not mean to refuse him except for stronger reasons than these. She even went so far in her desperate courage as to laugh at her cousin, Mrs. Clinton, whose venerable husband she allowed and even encouraged to pay her such public attention and to express sentiments of such youthful ardour as she well knew would inflame and exasperate the excellent lady his wife.

Carrington was the person most unpleasantly affected by the course which this affair had taken. He could no longer conceal from himself the fact that he was as much in love as a dignified Virginian could be. With him, at all events, she had shown no coquetry, nor had she ever either flattered or encouraged him. But Carrington, in his solitary struggle against fate, had found her a warm friend; always ready to assist where assistance was needed, generous with her money in any cause which he was willing to vouch for, full of sympathy where sympathy was more than money, and full of resource and suggestion where money and sympathy failed. Carrington knew her better than she knew herself. He selected her books; he brought the last speech or the last report from the Capitol or the departments; he knew her doubts and her vagaries, and as far as he understood them at all, helped her to solve them. Carrington was too modest, and perhaps too shy, to act the part of a declared lover, and he was too proud to let it be thought that he wanted to exchange his poverty for her wealth. But he was all the more anxious when he saw the evident attraction which Ratcliffe's strong will and unscrupulous energy exercised over her. He saw that Ratcliffe was steadily pushing his advances; that he flattered all Mrs. Lee's weaknesses by the confidence and deference with which he treated her; and that in a very short time, Madeleine must either marry him or find herself looked upon as a heartless coquette. He had his own reasons for thinking ill of Senator Ratcliffe, and he meant to prevent a marriage; but he had an enemy to deal with not easily driven from the path, and quite capable of routing any number of rivals.

Ratcliffe was afraid of no one. He had not fought his own way in life for nothing, and he knew all the value of a cold head and dogged self-assurance. Nothing but this robust Americanism and his strong will carried him safely through the snares and pitfalls of Mrs. Lee's society, where rivals and enemies beset him on every hand. He was little better than a schoolboy, when he ventured on their ground, but when he could draw them over upon his own territory of practical life he rarely failed to trample on his assailants. It was this practical sense and cool will that won over Mrs. Lee, who was woman enough to assume that all the graces were well enough employed in decorating her, and it was enough if the other sex felt her superiority. Men were valuable only in proportion to their strength and their appreciation of women. If the senator had only been strong enough always to control his temper, he would have done very well, but his temper was under a great strain in these times, and his incessant effort to control it in politics made him less watchful in private life. Mrs. Lee's tacit assumption of superior refinement irritated him, and sometimes made him show his teeth like a bull-dog, at the cost of receiving from Mrs. Lee a quick stroke in return such as a well-bred tortoiseshell cat administers to check over-familiarity; innocent to the eye, but drawing blood. One evening when he was more than commonly out of sorts, after sitting some time in moody silence, be roused himself, and, taking up a book that lay on her table, he glanced at its title and turned over the leaves. It happened by ill luck to be a volume of Darwin that Mrs. Lee had just borrowed from the Library of Congress.

"Do you understand this sort of thing?" asked the Senator abruptly, in a tone that suggested a sneer.

"Not very well," replied Mrs. Lee, rather curtly.

"Why do you want to understand it?" persisted the Senator. "What good will it do you?"

"Perhaps it will teach us to be modest," answered Madeleine, quite equal to the occasion. "Because it says we descend from monkeys?" rejoined the Senator, roughly. "Do you think you are descended from monkeys?" "Why not?" said Madeleine. "Why not?" repeated Ratcliffe, laughing harshly. "I don't like the connection. Do you mean to introduce your distant relations into society?"

"They would bring more amusement into it than most of its present members," rejoined Mrs. Lee, with a gentle smile that threatened mischief.

But Ratcliffe would not be warned; on the contrary, the only effect of Mrs. Lee's defiance was to exasperate his ill-temper, and whenever he lost his temper he became senatorial and Websterian. "Such books," he began, "disgrace our civilization; they degrade and stultify our divine nature; they are only suited for Asiatic despotisms where men are reduced to the level of brutes; that they should be accepted by a man like Baron Jacobi, I can understand; he and his masters have nothing to do in the world but to trample on human rights. Mr. Carrington, of course, would approve those ideas; he believes in the divine doctrine of flogging negroes; but that you, who profess philanthropy and free principles, should go with them, is astonishing; it is incredible; it is unworthy of you."

"You are very hard on the monkeys," replied Madeleine, rather sternly, when the Senator's oration was ended. "The monkeys never did you any harm; they are not in public life; they are not even voters; if they were, you would be enthusiastic about their intelligence and virtue. After all, we ought to be grateful to them, for what would men do in this melancholy world if they had not inherited gaiety from the monkeys — as well as oratory."

Ratcliffe, to do him justice, took punishment well, at least when it came from Mrs. Lee's hands, and his occasional outbursts of insubordination were sure to be followed by improved discipline; but if he allowed Mrs. Lee to correct his faults, he had no notion of letting himself be instructed by her friends, and he lost no chance of telling them so. But to do this was not always enough. Whether it were that he had few ideas outside of his own experience, or that he would not trust himself on doubtful ground, he seemed compelled to bring every discussion down to his own level. Madeleine puzzled herself in vain to find out whether he did this because he knew no better, or because he meant to cover his own ignorance.

"The Baron has amused me very much with his account of Bucharest society," Mrs. Lee would say: "I had no idea it was so gay."

"I would like to show him our society in Peoria," was Ratcliffe's reply; "he would find a very brilliant circle there of nature's true noblemen."

"The Baron says their politicians are precious sharp chaps," added Mr. French.

"Oh, there are politicians in Bulgaria, are there?" asked the Senator, whose ideas of the Roumanian and Bulgarian neighbourhood were vague, and who had a general notion that all such people lived in tents, wore sheepskins with the wool inside, and ate curds: "Oh, they have politicians there! I would like to see them try their sharpness in the west."

"Really!" said Mrs. Lee. "Think of Attila and his hordes running an Indiana caucus?"

"Anyhow," cried French with a loud laugh, "the Baron said that a set of bigger political scoundrels than his friends couldn't be found in all Illinois."

"Did he say that?" exclaimed Ratcliffe angrily.

"Didn't he, Mrs. Lee? but I don't believe it; do you? What's your candid opinion, Ratcliffe? What you don't know about Illinois politics isn't worth knowing; do you really think those Bulgrascals couldn't run an Illinois state convention?"

Ratcliffe did not like to be chaffed, especially on this subject, but he could not resent French's liberty which was only a moderate return for the wooden nutmeg. To get the conversation away from Europe, from literature, from art, was his great object, and chaff was a way of escape.

Carrington was very well aware that the weak side of the Senator lay in his blind ignorance of morals. He flattered himself that Mrs. Lee must see this and be shocked by it sooner or later, so that nothing more was necessary than to let Ratcliffe expose himself. Without talking very much, Carrington always aimed at drawing him out. He soon found, however, that Ratcliffe understood such tactics perfectly, and instead of injuring, he rather improved his position. At times the man's audacity was startling, and even when Carrington thought him hopelessly entangled, he would sweep away all the hunter's nets with a sheer effort of strength, and walk off bolder and more dangerous than ever.

When Mrs. Lee pressed him too closely, he frankly admitted her charges. "What you say is in great part true. There is much in politics that disgusts and disheartens; much that is coarse and bad. I grant you there is dishonesty and corruption. We must try to make the amount as small as possible."

"You should be able to tell Mrs. Lee how she must go to work," said Carrington; "you have had experience. I have heard, it seems to me, that you were once driven to very hard measures against corruption."

Ratcliffe looked ill-pleased at this compliment, and gave Carrington one of his cold glances that meant mischief. But he took up the challenge on the spot: —

"Yes, I was, and am very sorry for it. The story is this, Mrs. Lee; and it is well-known to every man, woman, and child in the State of Illinois, so that I have no reason for softening it. In the worst days of the war there was almost a certainty that my State would be carried by the peace party, by fraud, as we thought, although, fraud or not, we were bound to save it. Had Illinois been lost then, we should certainly have lost the Presidential election, and with it probably the Union. At any rate, I believed the fate of the war to depend on the result. I was then Governor, and upon me the responsibility rested. We had entire control of the northern counties and of their returns. We ordered the returning officers in a certain number of counties to make no returns until they heard from us, and when we had received the votes of all the southern counties and learned the precise number of votes we needed to give us a majority, we telegraphed to our northern returning officers to make the vote of their districts such and such, thereby overbalancing the adverse returns and giving the State to us. This was done, and as I am now senator I have a right to suppose that what I did was approved. I am not proud of the transaction, but I would do it again, and worse than that, if I thought it would save this country from disunion. But of course I did not expect Mr. Carrington to approve it. I believe he was then carrying out his reform principles by bearing arms against the government."

"Yes!" said Carrington drily; "you got the better of me, too. Like the old Scotchman, you didn't care who made the people's wars provided you made its ballots."

Carrington had missed his point. The man who has committed a murder for his country, is a patriot and not an assassin, even when he receives a seat in the Senate as his share of the plunder. Women cannot be expected to go behind the motives of that patriot who saves his country and his election in times of revolution.

From "Washington (1850–1854)"
In *The Education of Henry Adams*

One lived in the atmosphere of the Stamp Act, the Tea Tax, and the Boston Massacre. Within Boston, a boy was first an eighteenth-century politician, and afterwards only a possibility; beyond Boston the first step led only further into politics. After February, 1848, but one slight tie remained of all those that, since 1776, had connected Quincy with the outer world. The Madam stayed in Washington, after her husband's death, and in her turn was struck by paralysis and bedridden. From time to time her son Charles, whose affection and sympathy for his mother in her many tribulations were always pronounced, went on to see her, and in May, 1850, he took with him his twelve-year-old son. The journey was meant as education, and as education it served the purpose of fixing in memory the stage of a boy's thought in 1850. He could not remember taking special interest in the railroad journey or in New York; with railways and cities he was familiar enough. His first impression was the novelty of crossing New York Bay and finding an English railway carriage on the Camden and Amboy Railroad. This was a new world; a suggestion of corruption in the simple habits of American life; a step to exclusiveness never approached in Boston; but it was amusing. The boy rather liked it. At Trenton the train set him on board a steamer which took him to Philadelphia where he smelt other varieties of town life; then again by boat to Chester, and by train to Havre de Grace; by boat to

Baltimore and thence by rail to Washington. This was the journey he remembered. The actual journey may have been quite different, but the actual journey
has no interest for education. The memory was all that mattered; and what
struck him most, to remain fresh in his mind all his lifetime, was the sudden
change that came over the world on entering a slave State. He took education
politically. The mere raggedness of outline could not have seemed wholly new,
for even Boston had its ragged edges, and the town of Quincy was far from
being a vision of neatness or good-repair; in truth, he had never seen a finished
landscape; but Maryland was raggedness of a new kind.

The railway, about the size and character of a modern tram, rambled through
unfenced fields and woods, or through village streets, among a haphazard variety of pigs, cows, and negro babies, who might all have used the cabins for pens
and styes, had the Southern pig required styes, but who never showed a sign of
care. This was the boy's impression of what slavery caused, and, for him, was all
it taught. Coming down in the early morning from his bedroom in his grandmother's house — still called the Adams Building — in F Street and venturing
outside into the air reeking with the thick odor of the catalpa trees, he found
himself on an earth-road, or village street, with wheel-tracks meandering from
the colonnade of the Treasury hard by, to the white marble columns and fronts
of the Post Office and Patent Office which faced each other in the distance,
like white Greek temples in the abandoned gravel-pits of a deserted Syrian city.
Here and there low wooden houses were scattered along the streets, as in other
Southern villages, but he was chiefly attracted by an unfinished square marble
shaft, half-a-mile below, and he walked down to inspect it before breakfast. His
aunt drily remarked that, at this rate, he would soon get through all the sights;
but she could not guess — having lived always in Washington — how little the
sights of Washington had to do with its interest.

The boy could not have told her; he was nowhere near an understanding of
himself. The more he was educated, the less he understood. Slavery struck him
in the face; it was a nightmare; a horror; a crime; the sum of all wickedness!
Contact made it only more repulsive. He wanted to escape, like the negroes, to
free soil. Slave States were dirty, unkempt, poverty-stricken, ignorant, vicious!
He had not a thought but repulsion for it; and yet the picture had another side.
The May sunshine and shadow had something to do with it; the thickness of
foliage and the heavy smells had more; the sense of atmosphere, almost new,
had perhaps as much again; and the brooding indolence of a warm climate
and a negro population hung in the atmosphere heavier than the catalpas. The
impression was not simple, but the boy liked it: distinctly it remained on his
mind as an attraction, almost obscuring Quincy itself. The want of barriers, of
pavements, of forms; the looseness, the laziness; the indolent Southern drawl;

the pigs in the streets; the negro babies and their mothers with bandanas; the
freedom, openness, swagger, of nature and man, soothed his Johnson blood.
Most boys would have felt it in the same way, but with him the feeling caught
on to an inheritance. The softness of his gentle old grandmother as she lay in
bed and chatted with him, did not come from Boston. His aunt was anything
rather than Bostonian. He did not wholly come from Boston himself. Though
Washington belonged to a different world, and the two worlds could not live
together, he was not sure that he enjoyed the Boston world most. Even at twelve
years old he could see his own nature no more clearly than he would at twelve
hundred, if by accident he should happen to live so long.

His father took him to the Capitol and on the floor of the Senate, which
then, and long afterwards, until the era of tourists, was freely open to visitors.
The old Senate Chamber resembled a pleasant political club. Standing behind
the Vice-President's chair, which is now the Chief Justice's, the boy was presented to some of the men whose names were great in their day, and as familiar
to him as his own. Clay and Webster and Calhoun were there still, but with
them a Free Soil candidate for the Vice-Presidency had little to do; what struck
boys most was their type. Senators were a species; they all wore an air, as they
wore a blue dress coat or brass buttons; they were Roman. The type of Senator
in 1850 was rather charming at its best, and the Senate, when in good temper,
was an agreeable body, numbering only some sixty members, and affecting the
airs of courtesy. Its vice was not so much a vice of manners or temper as of attitude. The statesman of all periods was apt to be pompous, but even pomposity
was less offensive than familiarity — on the platform as in the pulpit — and
Southern pomposity, when not arrogant, was genial and sympathetic, almost
quaint and childlike in its simplemindedness; quite a different thing from the
Websterian or Conklinian pomposity of the North. The boy felt at ease there,
more at home than he had ever felt in Boston State House, though his acquaintance with the codfish in the House of Representatives went back beyond distinct recollection. Senators spoke kindly to him, and seemed to feel so, for they
had known his family socially; and, in spite of slavery, even J. Q. Adams in
his later years, after he ceased to stand in the way of rivals, had few personal
enemies. Decidedly the Senate, pro-slavery though it were, seemed a friendly
world.

This first step in national politics was a little like the walk before breakfast;
an easy, careless, genial, enlarging stride into a fresh and amusing world, where
nothing was finished, but where even the weeds grew rank. The second step
was like the first, except that it led to the White House. He was taken to see
President Taylor. Outside, in a paddock in front, "Old Whitey," the President's
charger, was grazing, as they entered; and inside, the President was receiving

callers as simply as if he were in the paddock too. The President was friendly, and the boy felt no sense of strangeness that he could ever recall. In fact, what strangeness should he feel? The families were intimate; so intimate that their friendliness outlived generations, civil war, and all sorts of rupture. President Taylor owed his election to Martin Van Buren and the Free Soil Party. To him, the Adamses might still be of use. As for the White House, all the boy's family had lived there, and, barring the eight years of Andrew Jackson's reign, had been more or less at home there ever since it was built. The boy half thought he owned it, and took for granted that he should some day live in it. He felt no sensation whatever before Presidents. A President was a matter of course in every respectable family; he had two in his own; three, if he counted old Nathaniel Gorham, who was the oldest and first in distinction. Revolutionary patriots, or perhaps a Colonial Governor, might be worth talking about, but any one could be President, and some very shady characters were likely to be. Presidents, Senators, Congressmen, and such things were swarming in every street.

Every one thought alike whether they had ancestors or not. No sort of glory hedged Presidents as such, and, in the whole-country, one could hardly have met with an admission of respect for any office or name, unless it were George Washington. That was — to all appearance sincerely — respected. People made pilgrimages to Mount Vernon and made even an effort to build Washington a monument. The effort had failed, but one still went to Mount Vernon, although it was no easy trip. Mr. Adams took the boy there in a carriage and pair, over a road that gave him a complete Virginia education for use ten years afterwards. To the New England mind, roads, schools, clothes, and a clean face were connected as part of the law of order or divine system. Bad roads meant bad morals. The moral of this Virginia road was clear, and the boy fully learned it. Slavery was wicked, and slavery was the cause of this road's badness which amounted to social crime — and yet, at the end of the road and product of the crime stood Mount Vernon and George Washington.

Luckily boys accept contradictions as readily as their elders do, or this boy might have become prematurely wise. He had only to repeat what he was told — that George Washington stood alone. Otherwise this third step in his Washington education would have been his last. On that line, the problem of progress was not soluble, whatever the optimists and orators might say — or, for that matter, whatever they might think. George Washington could not be reached on Boston lines. George Washington was a primary, or, if Virginians liked it better, an ultimate relation, like the Pole Star, and amid the endless restless motion of every other visible point in space, he alone remained steady, in the mind of Henry Adams, to the end. All the other points shifted their bearings; John Adams, Jefferson, Madison, Franklin, even John Marshall, took varied lights, and assumed new relations, but Mount Vernon always remained where it was, with no practicable road to reach it; and yet, when he got there, Mount Vernon was only Quincy in a Southern setting. No doubt it was much more charming, but it was the same eighteenth-century, the same old furniture, the same old patriot, and the same old President.

The boy took to it instinctively. The broad Potomac and the coons in the trees, the bandanas and the box-hedges, the bedrooms upstairs and the porch outside, even Martha Washington herself in memory, were as natural as the tides and the May sunshine; he had only enlarged his horizon a little; but he never thought to ask himself or his father how to deal with the moral problem that deduced George Washington from the sum of all wickedness. In practice, such trifles as contradictions in principle are easily set aside; the faculty of ignoring them makes the practical man; but any attempt to deal with them seriously as education is fatal. Luckily Charles Francis Adams never preached and was singularly free from cant. He may have had views of his own, but he let his son Henry satisfy himself with the simple elementary fact that George Washington stood alone.

Life was not yet complicated. Every problem had a solution, even the negro. The boy went back to Boston more political than ever, and his politics were no longer so modern as the eighteenth century, but took a strong tone of the seventeenth. Slavery drove the whole Puritan community back on its Puritanism. The boy thought as dogmatically as though he were one of his own ancestors. The Slave power took the place of Stuart kings and Roman popes. Education could go no further in that course, and ran off into emotion; but, as the boy gradually found his surroundings change, and felt himself no longer an isolated atom in a hostile universe, but a sort of herring-fry in a shoal of moving fish, he began to learn the first and easier lessons of practical politics. Thus far he had seen nothing but eighteenth-century statesmanship. America and he began, at the same time, to become aware of a new force under the innocent surface of party machinery.

FRANCES HODGSON BURNETT

Born in England, Frances Hodgson Burnett (1849–1924) emigrated to the United States in her teens and began publishing romantic fiction before she was thirty. Well known in her own time as the author of *Little Lord Fauntleroy* (1886), she is famous today also for her children's story *The Secret Garden* (1911). After her husband moved to Washington to open an eye practice, she soon joined him (1877), dividing her time between writing novels and raising her sons. *Through One Administration* (serialized in 1881), her lone Washington novel, focuses on the unhappy marriage of a woman whose husband is a lobbyist and on the social and political maneuvering that compromise the legislative process as well as individual lives. The novel is based on Burnett's firsthand experience, but it is not strictly autobiographical. Burnett and her husband were popular figures in the city's social world, though their marriage was unhappy.

From *Through One Administration*

Mrs. Amory did not receive on New Year's day. The season had well set in before she arrived in Washington. One morning in January Mrs. Sylvestre, sitting alone, reading, caught sight of the little *coupe* as it drew up before the carriage-step, and, laying aside her book, reached the parlor door in time to meet Bertha as she entered it. She took both her hands and drew her toward the fire, still holding them.

"Why did I not know you had returned?" she said. "When did you arrive?"

"Last night," Bertha answered. "You see I come to you early."

It was a cold day and she was muffled in velvet and furs. She sat down, loosened her wrap and let it slip backward, and as its sumptuous fulness left her figure it revealed it slender to fragility, and showed that the outline of her cheek had lost all its roundness. She smiled faintly, meeting Agnes' anxious eyes.

"Don't look at me," she said. "I am not pretty. I have been ill. You heard I was not well in Newport? It was a sort of low fever, and I am not entirely well yet. Malaria, you know, is always troublesome. But you are very well?"

"Yes, I am well," Agnes replied.

"And you begin to like Washington again?"

"I began last winter."

"How did you enjoy the spring? You were here until the end of June."

"It was lovely."

"And now you are here once more, and how pretty everything about you is!" Bertha said, glancing around the room. "And you are ready to be happy all winter until June again. Do you know, you look happy. Not excitably happy, but gently, calmly happy, as if the present were enough for you."

"It is," said Agnes, "I don't think I want any future."

"It would be as well to abolish it if one could," Bertha answered; "but it comes — *it comes*!"

She sat and looked at the fire a few seconds under the soft shadow of her lashes, and then spoke again.

"As for me," she said, "I am going to give dinner-parties to Senator Plane-field's friends."

"Bertha!" exclaimed Agnes.

"Yes," said Bertha, nodding gently. "It appears somehow that Richard belongs to Senator Planefield, and, as I belong to Richard, why, you see" —

She ended with a dramatic little gesture, and looked at Agnes once more.

"It took me some time to understand it," she said. "I am not quite sure that I understand it quite thoroughly even now. It is a little puzzling, or, perhaps, I am dull of comprehension. At all events, Richard has talked to me a great deal. It is plainly my duty to be agreeable and hospitable to the people he wishes to please and bring in contact with each other."

"And those people?" asked Agnes.

"They are political men: they are members of committees, members of the House, members of the Senate; and their only claim to existence in our eyes is that they are either in favor of or opposed to a certain bill not indirectly connected with the welfare of the owners of Westoria lands."

"Bertha," said Agnes, quickly, "you are not yourself."

"Thank you," was the response, "that is always satisfactory, but the compliment would be more definite if you told me who I happened to be. But I can tell you that I am that glittering being, the female lobbyist. I used to wonder last winter if I was not on the verge of it; but now I know. I wonder if they all begin as innocently as I did, and find the descent — isn't it a descent? — as easy and natural. I feel queer, but not exactly disreputable. It is merely a matter of being a dutiful wife and smiling upon one set of men instead of another. Still, I am slightly uncertain as to just how disreputable I am. I was beginning to be quite reconciled to my atmosphere until I saw Colonel Tredennis, and I confess he unsettled my mind and embarrassed me a little in my decision."

"You have seen him already?"

"Accidentally, yes. He did not know I had returned, and came to see Richard. He is quite intimate with Richard now. He entered the parlor and found me there. I do not think he was glad to see me. I left him very soon."

She drew off her glove, and smoothed it out upon her knee, with a thin and fragile little hand upon which the rings hung loosely. Agnes bent forward and involuntarily laid her own hand upon it.

"Dear," she said.

Bertha hurriedly lifted her eyes.

"What I wish to say," she said, "was that the week after next we give a little dinner to Senator Blundel, and I wanted to be sure I might count on you. If you are there — and Colonel Tredennis — you will give it an unprofessional aspect, which is what we want. But perhaps you will refuse to come?"

"Bertha," said Mrs. Sylvestre, "I will be with you at any time — at all times — you wish for or need me."

"Yes," said Bertha, reflecting upon her a moment, "I think you would."

She got up and kissed her lightly and without effusion, and then Agnes rose, too, and they stood together.

"You were always good," Bertha said. "I think life has made you better instead of worse. It is not so always. Things are so different — everything seems to depend upon circumstances. What is good in me would be far enough from your standards to be called wickedness."

She paused abruptly, and Agnes felt that she did so to place a check upon herself; she had seen her do it before. When she spoke again it was in an entirely different tone, and the remaining half-hour of her visit was spent in the discussion of every-day subjects. Agnes listened, and replied to her with a sense of actual anguish. She could have borne better to have seen her less self-controlled; or she fancied so, at least. The summer had made an alteration in her, which it was almost impossible to describe. Every moment revealed some new, sad change in her, and yet she sat and talked commonplaces, and was bright, and witty, and epigrammatic until the last.

"When we get our bill through," she said, with a little smile, just before her departure, "I am to go abroad for a year, — for two, for three, if I wish. I think that is the bribe which has been offered me. One must always be bribed, you know."

As she stood at the window watching the carriage drive away, Agnes was conscious of a depression which was very hard to bear. The brightness of her own atmosphere seemed to have become heavy, — the sun hid itself behind the drifting, wintry clouds, — she glanced around her room with a sense of dreariness. Something carried her back to the memories which were the one burden of her present life.

"Such grief cannot enter a room and not leave its shadow behind it," she said. And she put her hand against the window-side, and leaned her brow upon it sadly. It was curious, she thought, the moment after, that the mere sight of a familiar figure should bring such a sense of comfort with it as did the sight of the one she saw approaching. It was that of Laurence Arbuthnot, who came with a business communication for Mrs. Merriam, having been enabled, by chance, to leave his work for an hour. He held a roll of music in one hand and a bunch of violets in the other, and when he entered the room was accompanied by the fresh fragrance of the latter offering.

Agnes made a swift involuntary movement toward him.

"Ah!" she said, "I could scarcely believe that it was you."

He detected the emotion in her manner and tone at once.

"Something has disturbed you," he said. "What is it?"

"I have seen Bertha," she answered, and the words had a sound of appeal in them, which she herself no more realized or understood than she comprehended the impulse which impelled her to speak.

"She has been here! She looks so ill — so worn. Everything is so sad! I" —
She stopped and stood looking at him.

"Must I go away?" he said, quietly. "Perhaps you would prefer to be alone. I understand what you mean, I think."

"Oh, no!" she said, impulsively, putting out her hand. "Don't go. I am unhappy. It was — it was a relief to see you."

And when she sank on the sofa, he took a seat near her and laid the violets on her lap, and there was a faint flush on his face.

GERTRUDE ATHERTON

A California author of prodigious output, Gertrude Atherton (1857–1948) published more than twenty volumes of fiction, including one Washington novel, *Senator North* (1900), which is set at the time of Senate debates leading up to the Spanish-American War. Atherton, a contemporary of Henry James and Edith Wharton, is known for promoting the "new American woman" in her fiction. In *Senator North*, her heroine is an independent-minded young woman from the South who sets her mind to learning about the "dreadful" class of American politicians after an English lord shames her for her ignorance of the subject. The book was controversial because Atherton's title character mirrored the life of a senator from Maine, Eugene Hale, and also contained tabooed racial themes. Atherton also wrote a fictionalized biography of Alexander Hamilton, *The Conqueror* (1902), and an autobiography, *The Adventures of a Novelist* (1932).

From *Senator North*

"If we receive this Lady Mary Montgomery, we shall also have to receive her dreadful husband."

"He is said to be quite charming."

"He is a Representative!"

"Of course they are all wild animals to you, but one or two have been pointed out to me that looked quite like ordinary gentlemen — really."

"Possibly. But no person in official life has ever entered my house. I do not feel inclined to break the rule merely because the wife of one of the most objectionable class is an Englishwoman with a title. I think it very inconsiderate of Lady Barnstaple to have given her a letter to us."

"Lee, never having lived in Washington, doubtless fancies, like the rest of the benighted world, that its officials are its aristocracy. The Senate of the United States is regarded abroad as a sort of House of Peers. One has to come and live in Washington to hear of the 'Old Washingtonians,' the 'cave-dwellers,' as Sally calls us; I expected to see a coat of blue mould on each of them when I returned."

"Really, Betty, I do not understand you this morning."

Mrs. Madison moved uneasily and took out her handkerchief. When her daughter's rich Southern voice hardened itself to sarcasm, and her brilliant hazel eyes expressed the brain in a state of cold analysis, Mrs. Madison braced herself for a contest in which she inevitably must surrender with what slow dignity she could command. Betty had called her Molly since she was fourteen months old, and, sweet and gracious in small matters, invariably pursued her own way when sufficiently roused by the strength of a desire. Mrs. Madison, however, kept up the fiction of an authority which she thought was due to herself and her ancestors. She continued impatiently, —

"You have been standing before that fireplace for ten minutes with your shoulders thrown back as if you were going to make a speech. It is not a nice attitude for a girl at all, and I wish you would sit down. I hope you don't think that because Sally Carter crosses her knees and cultivates a brutal frankness of expression you must do the same now that you have dropped all your friends of your own age and become intimate with her. I suppose she is old enough to do as she chooses, and she always was eccentric."

"She is only eight years older than I. You forget that I shall be twenty-seven in three months."

"Well, that is no reason why you should stand before the fireplace like a man. Do sit down."

"I'd rather stand here till I've said what is necessary — if you don't mind. I am sorry to be obliged to say it, and I can assure you that I have not made up my mind in a moment."

"What is it, for heaven's sake?"

Mrs. Madison drew a short breath and readjusted her cushions. In spite of her wealth and exalted position she had known much trouble and grief. Her first six children had died in their early youth. Her husband, brilliant and charming, had possessed a set of affections too restless and ardent to confine themselves within the domestic limits. His wife had buried him with sorrow, but with a deep sigh of relief that for the future she could mourn him without torment. He had belonged to a collateral branch of a family of which her father had been the heir; consequently the old Madison house in Washington was hers, as well as a large fortune. Harold Madison had been free to spend his own inheritance

as he listed, and he had left but a fragment. Mrs. Madison's nerves, never strong,
had long since given way to trouble and ill-health, and when her active strong-
willed daughter entered her twentieth year, she gladly permitted her to become
the mistress of the household and to think for both. Betty had been educated by
private tutors, then taken abroad for two years, to France, Germany, and Italy,
in order, as she subsequently observed, to make the foreign attache feel more
at ease when he proposed. Her winters thereafter until the last two had been
spent in Washington, where she had been a belle and ranked as a beauty. In the
fashionable set it was believed that every attaché in the city had proposed to her,
as well as a large proportion of the old beaux and of the youths who pursue the
business of Society. Her summers she spent at her place in the Adirondacks, at
Northern watering-places, or in Europe; and the last two years had been passed,
with brief intervals of Paris and Vienna, in England, where she had been presented with distinction and seen much of country life. She had returned with
her mother to Washington but a month ago, and since then had spent most of
her time in her room or on horseback, breaking all her engagements after the
first ten days. Mrs. Madison had awaited the explanation with deep uneasiness.
Did her daughter, despite the health manifest in her splendid young figure, feel
the first chill of some mortal disease? She had not been her gay self for months,
and although her complexion was of that magnolia tint which never harbors
color, it seemed to the anxious maternal eye, looking back to six young graves, a
shade whiter than it should. Or had she fallen in love with an Englishman, and
hesitated to speak, knowing her mother's love for Washington and bare tolerance of the British Isles? She looked askance at Betty, who stood tapping the
front of her habit with her crop and evidently waiting for her mother to express
some interest. Mrs. Madison closed her eyes. Betty therefore continued, —

"I see you are afraid I am going to marry an Oriental minister or something.
I hear that one is looking for an American with a million. Well, I am going to
do something you will think even worse. I am going in for politics."

"You are going to do what?" Mrs. Madison's voice was nearly inaudible between relief and horrified surprise, but her eyes flew open. "Do you mean that
you are going to vote? — or run for Congress? — but women don't sit in Congress, do they?"

"Of course not. Do you know I think it quite shocking that we have lived
here in the very brain of the United States all our lives and know less of politics than if we were Indians in Alaska? I was ashamed of myself, I can assure
you, when Lord Barnstaple asked me so many questions the first time I visited
Maundrell Abbey. He took for granted, as I lived in Washington, I must be
thoroughly well up in politics, and I was obliged to tell him that although I had
occasionally been in the room with one or two Senators and Cabinet Ministers,

who happened to be in Society first and politics afterward, I did n't know the others by name, had never put my foot in the White House or the Capitol, and that no one I knew ever thought of talking politics. He asked me what I had done with myself during all the winters I had spent in Washington, and I told him that I had had the usual girls'-goodtime, — teas, theatre, germans, dinners, luncheons, calls, calls, calls! I was glad to add that I belonged to several charities and had read a great deal; but that did not seem to interest him. Well, I met a good many men like Lord Barnstaple, men who were in public life. Some of them were dull enough, judged by the feminine standard, but even they occasionally said something to remember, and others were delightful. This is the whole point — I can't and won't go back to what I left here two years ago. My day for platitudes and pouring tea for men who are contemptible enough to make Society their profession, is over. I am going to know the real men of my country. It is incredible that there are not men in that Senate as well worth talking to as any I met in England. The other day I picked up a bound copy of the Congressional Record in a book-shop. It was frantically interesting."

"It must have been! But, my dear — of course I understand, darling, your desire for a new intellectual occupation; you always were so clever — but you can't, you really can't know these men. They are — they are — politicians. We never have known politicians. They are dreadful people, who have come from low origins and would probably call me 'marm.'"

"You are all wrong, Molly. I bought a copy of the Congressional Directory a day or two ago, and have read the biography of every Senator. Nine-tenths of them are educated men; if only a few attended the big Universities, the rest went to the colleges of their State. That is enough for an American of brains. And most of them are lawyers; others served in the war, and several have distinguished records. They cannot be boors, whether they have blue blood in them or not. I'm sick of blue blood, anyway. Vienna was the deadliest place I ever visited. What makes London interesting is its red streak of plebeianism; — well, I repeat, I think it really dreadful that we should not know even by name the men who make our laws, who are making history, who may be called upon at any moment to decide our fate among nations. I feel a silly little fool."

"I suppose you mean that I am one too. But it always has been my boast, Betty, that I never have had a politician in my house. Your father knew some, but he never brought them here; he knew the fastidious manner in which I had been brought up; and although I am afraid he kept late hours with a good many of them at Chamberlin's and other dreadful places, he always spared me. I suppose this is heredity working out in you."

"Possibly. But you will admit, will you not, that I am old enough to choose my own life?"

"You always have done every single thing you wanted, so I don't see why you talk like that. But if you are going to bring a lot of men to this house who will spit on my carpets and use toothpicks, I beg you will not ask me to receive with you."

"Of course you will receive with me, Molly dear — when I know anybody worth receiving. Unfortunately I am not the wife of the President and cannot send out a royal summons. I am hoping that Lady Mary Montgomery will help me. But my first step shall be to pay a daily visit to the Senate Gallery."

"What!" Mrs. Madison's weary voice flew to its upper register. "I *do* know something about politics — I remember now — the only women who go to the Capitol are lobbyists — dreadful creatures who — who — do all sorts of things. You can't go there, you'll be taken for one."

"We none of us are taken very long for what we are not. I shall take Leontine with me, and those interested enough to notice me will soon learn what I go for."

Mrs. Madison burst into tears. "You are your father all over again! I've seen it developing for at least three years. At first you were just a hard student, and then the loveliest young girl, only caring to have a good time, and coquetting more bewitchingly than any girl I ever saw. I don't see why you had to change."

"Time develops all of us, one way or another. I suppose you would like me to be a charming girl flirting bewitchingly when I am forty-five. I am finished with the meaningless things of life. I want to live now, and I intend to."

"It will be wildly exciting — the Senate Gallery every day, and knowing a lot of lank raw-boned Yankees with political beards."

"I am not expecting to fall in love with any of them. I merely discovered some time since that I had a brain, and they happen to be the impulse that possesses it. You always have prided yourself that I am intellectual, and so I am in the flabby 'well-read' fashion. I feel as if my brain had been a mausoleum for skeletons and mummies; it felt alive for the first time when I began to read the newspapers in England. I want no more memoirs and letters and biographies, nor even of the history that is shut up in calf-skin. I want the life of to-day. I want to feel in the midst of current history. All these men here in Washington must be alive to their finger-tips. Sally Carter admires Senator North and Senator Maxwell immensely."

"What does she say about politicians in general?" Mrs. Madison looked almost distraught. "Of course the Norths and the Maxwells come of good New England families — I never did look down on the North as much as some of us did; after all, nearly three hundred years are very respectable indeed — and if these two men had not been in politics I should have been delighted to receive them. I met Senator North once — at Bar Harbor, while you were with the Carters at Homburg — and thought him charming; and I had some most interesting chats with his wife, who is much the same sort of invalid that I am. But when I establish a standard I am consistent enough to want to keep to it. I asked you what Sally Carter says of the others."

"Oh, she admits that there may be others as *convenable* as Senator North and Senator Maxwell, and that there is no doubt about there being many bright men in the Senate; but she 'does not care to know any more people.' Being a good cave-dweller, she is true to her traditions."

"People will say you are *passée*," exclaimed Mrs. Madison, hopefully. "They will be sure to."

Her daughter laughed, showing teeth as brilliant as her eyes. Then she snatched off her riding-hat and shook down her mane of warm brown hair. Her black brows and lashes, like her eyes and mouth, were vivid, but her hair and complexion were soft, without lustre, but very warm. She looked like a flower set on so strongly sapped a stem that her fullness would outlast many women's decline. She had inherited the beauty of her father's branch of the family. Mrs. Madison was very small and thin; but she carried herself erectly and her delicately cut face was little wrinkled. Her eyes were blue, and her hair, which was always carefully rolled, was as white as sea foam. Betty would not permit her to wear black, but dressed her in delicate colors, and she looked somewhat like an animated miniature. She dabbed impatiently at her tears.

"Everybody will cut you — if you go into that dreadful political set."

"I am on the verge of cutting everybody myself, so it does n't matter. Positively — I shall not accept an invitation of the old sort this winter. The sooner they drop me the better."

Mrs. Madison wept bitterly. "You will become a notorious woman," she sobbed. "People will talk terribly about you. They will say — all sorts of things I have heard come back to me — these politicians make love to every pretty woman they meet. They are so tired of their old frumps from Oshkosh and Kalamazoo."

"They do not all come from Oshkosh and Kalamazoo. There are six New England States whose three centuries you have just admitted lift them into the mists of antiquity. There are fourteen Southern States, and I need make no defence — "

"Their gentlemen don't go into politics any more."

"You have admitted that Senator North and Senator Maxwell are gentlemen. There is no reason why there should not be many more."

"Count de Bellairs told me that there was a spittoon at every desk in the Senate and that he counted eight toothpicks in one hour."

"Well, I'll reform them. That will be my holy mission. As for spittoons and toothpicks, they are conspicuous in every hotel in the United States. They should be on our coat-of-arms, and the Great American Novel will be called 'The Great American Toothpick.' Statesmen have cut their teeth on it, and it has been their solace in the great crises of the nation's history. As for spittoons, they were invented for our own Southern aristocrats who loved tobacco then as now. They decorate our Capitol as a mere matter of form. I don't pretend to hope that ninety representative Americans are Beau Brummels, but there must be a respectable minority of gentlemen — whether selfmade or not I don't care. I am going to make a deliberate attempt to know that minority, and shall call on Lady Mary Montgomery this afternoon as the first step. So you are resigned, are you not, Molly dear?"

"No, I am not! But what can I do? I have spoiled you, and you would be just the same if I had n't. You are more like the men of the family than the women — they always would have their own way. Are they all married?" she added anxiously.

"Do you mean the ninety Senators and the three hundred and fifty-six Representatives? I am sure I do not know. Don't let that worry you. It is my mind that is on the *qui vive*, not my heart."

"You'll hear some old fool make a Websterian speech full of periods and rhetoric, and you'll straightway imagine yourself in love with him. Your head will be your worst enemy when you do fall in love."

"Webster is the greatest master of style this country has produced. I should hate a man who used either 'periods' or rhetoric. I am the concentrated essence of modernism and have no use for 'oratory' or 'eloquence.' Some of the little speeches in the Record are masterpieces of brevity and pure English, particularly Senator North's."

"You *are* modern. If we had a Clay, I could understand you — I am too exhausted to discuss the matter further; you *must* drop it for the present. What will Jack Emory say?"

"I have never given him the least right to say anything."

"I almost wish you were safely married to him. He has not made a great success of his life, but he is your equal and his manners are perfect. I shall live in constant fear now of your marrying a horror with a twang and a toothpick."

"I promise you I won't do that — and that I never will marry Jack Emory."

II

Betty Madison had exercised a great deal of self-control in resisting the natural impulse to cultivate a fad and grapple with a problem. Only her keen sense of humor saved her. On the Sunday following her return, while sauntering home after a long restless tramp about the city, she passed a church which many colored people were entering. Her newly awakened curiosity in all things pertaining to the political life of her country prompted her to follow them and sit through the service. The clergyman was light in color, and prayed and preached in simpler and better English than she had heard in more pretentious pulpits, but there was nothing noteworthy in his remarks beyond a supplication to the Almighty to deliver the negro from the oppression of the "Southern tyrant," followed by an admonition to the negro to improve himself in mind and character if he would hope to compete with the Whites; bitter words and violence but weakened his cause.

This was sound common-sense, but the reverse of the sensational entertainment Betty had half expected, and her eyes wandered from the preacher to his congregation. There were all shades of Afro-American color and all degrees of prosperity represented. Coal-black women were there, attired in deep and expensive mourning. "Yellow girls" wore smart little tailor costumes. Three young girls, evidently of the lower middle class of colored society, for they were cheaply dressed, had all the little airs and graces and mannerisms of the typical American girl. In one corner a sleek mulatto with a Semitic profile sat in the recognized attitude of the banker in church; filling his corner comfortably and setting a worthy example to the less favored of Mammon.

But Betty's attention suddenly was arrested and held by two men who sat on the opposite side of the aisle, although not together, and apparently were unrelated. There were no others quite like them in the church, but the conviction slowly forced itself into her mind, magnetic for new impressions, that there were many elsewhere. They were men who were descending the fifties, tall, with straight gray hair. One was very slender, and all but distinguished of carriage; the other was heavier, and would have been imposing but for the listless droop of his shoulders. The features of both were finely cut, and their complexions far removed from the reproach of "yellow." They looked like sunburned gentlemen.

For nearly ten minutes Betty stared, fascinated, while her mind grappled with the deep significance of all those two sad and patient men expressed. They inherited the shell and the intellect, the aspirations and the possibilities of the gay young planters whose tragic folly had called into being a race of outcasts with all their own capacity for shame and suffering.

Betty went home and for twenty-four hours fought the desire to champion the cause of the negro and make him her life-work. But not only did she abominate women with missions, she looked at the subject upon each of its many sides and asked a number of indirect questions of her cousin, Jack Emory. Sincere reflection brought with it the conclusion that her energies in behalf of the negro would be superfluous. The careless planters were dead; she could not harangue their dust. The Southerners of the present generation despised and feared the colored race in its enfranchised state too actively to have more to do with it than they could help; if it was a legal offence for Whites and Blacks to marry, there was an equally stringent social law which protected the colored girl from the lust of the white man. Therefore, as she could not undo the harm already done, and as a crusade in behalf of the next generation would be meaningless, not to say indelicate, she dismissed the "problem" from her mind. But the image of those two sad and stately reflections of the old school sank indelibly into her memory, and rose to their part in one of the most momentous decisions of her life.

BOOKER T. WASHINGTON

In *My Larger Education* (1911), Booker T. Washington (1856–1915) admitted, "I never liked the atmosphere of Washington." He said he didn't like politics and thought a person's time could be better spent than trying to land a job with the government or getting elected to public office. In 1878, Washington attended the Wayland Theological Seminary in D.C., an experience he describes in *Up from Slavery, an Autobiography*. After his success as the head of Tuskegee Institute, he visited Washington several more times on business, twice at the invitation of Theodore Roosevelt, who after McKinley's assassination wanted to talk with the black leader about new appointments in the government and new policies in the South regarding race relations. On the second visit, Roosevelt also invited him to join him for dinner in the White House; the event caused a huge public outcry, particularly among southerners. Washington had as much influence with Roosevelt's successor, William H. Taft, especially on the matter of political appointments.

From "The Reconstruction Period"
In *Up from Slavery, an Autobiography*

The years from 1867 to 1878 I think may be called the period of Reconstruction. This included the time that I spent as a student at Hampton and as a teacher in West Virginia. During the whole of the Reconstruction period two ideas were constantly agitating the minds of the coloured people, or, at least, the minds of a large part of the race. One of these was the craze for Greek and Latin learning, and the other was a desire to hold office.

It could not have been expected that a people who had spent generations in slavery, and before that generations in the darkest heathenism, could at first form any proper conception of what an education meant. In every part of the South, during the Reconstruction period, schools, both day and night, were filled to overflowing with people of all ages and conditions, some being as far along in age as sixty and seventy years. The ambition to secure an education was most praiseworthy and encouraging. The idea, however, was too prevalent that, as soon as one secured a little education, in some unexplainable way he would be free from most of the hardships of the world, and, at any rate, could live without manual labour. There was a further feeling that a knowledge, however little, of the Greek and Latin languages would make one a very superior human being, something bordering almost on the supernatural. I remember that the first coloured man whom I saw who knew something about foreign languages impressed me at that time as being a man of all others to be envied. . . .

IN THE FALL OF 1878, after having taught school in Malden for two years, and after I had succeeded in preparing several of the young men and women, besides my two brothers, to enter the Hampton Institute, I decided to spend some months in study at Washington, D.C. I remained there for eight months. I derived a great deal of benefit from the studies which I pursued, and I came into contact with some strong men and women. At the institution I attended there was no industrial training given to the students, and I had an opportunity of comparing the influence of an institution with no industrial training with that of one like the Hampton Institute, that emphasized the industries. At this school I found the students, in most cases, had more money, were better dressed, wore the latest style of all manner of clothing, and in some cases were more brilliant mentally. At Hampton it was a standing rule that, while the institution would be responsible for securing some one to pay the tuition for the students, the men and women themselves must provide for their own board, books, clothing, and room wholly by work, or partly by work and partly in cash. At the institution at which I now was, I found that a large proportion of the students by some means had their personal expenses paid for them. At Hampton the student was constantly making the effort through the industries to help himself, and that very effort was of immense value in character-building. The students at the other school seemed to be less self-dependent. They seemed to give more attention to mere outward appearances. In a word, they did not appear to me to be beginning at the bottom, on a real, solid foundation, to the extent that they were at Hampton. They knew more about Latin and Greek when they left school, but they seemed to know less about life and its conditions as they would meet it at their homes. Having lived for a number of years in the midst of comfortable surroundings, they were not as much inclined as the Hampton students to go into the country districts of the South, where there was little of comfort, to take up work for our people, and they were more inclined to yield to the temptation to become hotel waiters and Pullman-car porters as their life-work.

During the time I was a student in Washington the city was crowded with coloured people, many of whom had recently come from the South. A large proportion of these people had been drawn to Washington because they felt that they could lead a life of ease there. Others had secured minor government positions, and still another large class was there in the hope of securing Federal positions. A number of coloured men — some of them very strong and brilliant — were in the House of Representatives at that time, and one, the Hon. B. K. Bruce, was in the Senate. All this tended to make Washington an attractive place for members of the coloured race. Then, too, they knew that at all times they could have the protection of the law in the District of Columbia. The public schools in Washington for coloured people were better then than they were elsewhere. I took great interest in studying the life of our people there closely at that time. I found that while among them there was a large element of substantial, worthy citizens, there was also a superficiality about the life of a large class that greatly alarmed me. I saw young coloured men who were not earning more than four dollars a week spend two dollars or more for a buggy on Sunday to ride up and down Pennsylvania Avenue in, in order that they might try to convince the world that they were worth thousands. I saw other young men who received seventy-five or one hundred dollars per month from the Government, who were in debt at the end of every month. I saw men who but a few months previous were members of Congress, then without employment and in poverty. Among a large class there seemed to be a dependence upon the Government for every conceivable thing. The members of this class had little ambition to create a position for themselves, but wanted the Federal officials to create one for them. How many times I wished then, and have often wished since, that by some power of magic I might remove the great bulk of these people into the country districts and plant them upon the soil, upon the solid and never deceptive foundation of Mother Nature, where all nations and races that have ever succeeded have gotten their start, — a start that at first may be slow and toilsome, but one that nevertheless is real.

In Washington I saw girls whose mothers were earning their living by laundrying. These girls were taught by their mothers, in rather a crude way it is true, the industry of laundrying. Later, these girls entered the public schools and remained there perhaps six or eight years. When the public school course was finally finished, they wanted more costly dresses, more costly hats and shoes. In a word, while their wants had been increased, their ability to supply their wants had not been increased in the same degree. On the other hand, their six or eight years of book education had weaned them away from the occupation of their mothers. The result of this was in too many cases that the girls went to the bad. I often thought how much wiser it would have been to give these girls the same amount of mental training — and I favour any kind of training, whether in the languages or mathematics, that gives strength and culture to the mind — but at the same time to give them the most thorough training in the latest and best methods of laundrying and other kindred occupations.

From "Colonel Roosevelt and What I Have Learned from Him"
In *My Larger Education*

Some years ago — and not so very many, either — I think that I should have been perfectly safe in saying that the highest ambition of the average Negro in America was to hold some sort of office, or to have some sort of job that connected him with the Government. Just to be able to live in the capital city was a sort of distinction, and the man who ran an elevator or merely washed windows in Washington (particularly if the windows or the elevator belonged to the United States Government) felt that he was in some way superior to a man who cleaned windows or ran an elevator in any other part of the country. He felt that he was an office-holder!

There has been a great change in this respect in recent years. Many members of my race have learned that, in the long run, they can earn more money and be of more service to the community in almost any other position than that of an employé or office-holder under the Government. I know of a number of recent cases in which Negro business men have refused positions of honour and trust in the Government service because they did not care to give up their business interests. Notwithstanding, the city of Washington still has a peculiar attraction and even fascination for the average Negro.

I do not think that I ever shared that feeling of so many others of my race. I never liked the atmosphere of Washington. I early saw that it was impossible to build up a race of which the leaders were spending most of their time, thought, and energy in trying to get into office, or in trying to stay there after they were in. So, for the greater part of my life, I have avoided Washington; and even now I rarely spend a day in that city which I do not look upon as a day practically thrown away.

I do not like politics, and yet, in recent years, I have had some experience in political matters. However, no man who is in the least interested in public questions can escape some sort of connection with politics, I suppose, even if he does not want a political position. As a matter of fact, it was just, because it was well known that I sought no political office of any kind and would accept no position with the Government, unless it were an honorary one, that brought my connection with politics about.

One thing that has taught me to dislike politics is the observation that, as soon as any person or thing becomes the subject of political discussion, he or it at once assumes in the public mind an importance out of all proportion to his or its real merits. Time and time again I have seen a whole community (sometimes a whole county or state) wrought up to the highest pitch of excitement over the appointment of some person to a political position paying perhaps not more than $25 or $50 a month. At the same time I have seen individuals secure important positions at the head of a manufacturing house or receive an appointment to some important educational position that paid three or four times as much money (or perhaps purchase a farm), where just as much executive ability was required, without arousing public attention or causing comment in the newspapers. I have also seen white men and coloured men resign important positions in private life where they were earning much more than they could get under the Government, simply because of the false and mistaken ideas of the importance which they attached to a political position. All this has given me a distaste for political life.

In Mississippi, for example, a coloured man and his wife had charge, a few years ago, of a post-office. In some way or other a great discussion was started in regard to this case, and before long the whole community was in a state of excitement because coloured people held that position. A little later the post-office was given up and the coloured man, Mr. W. W. Cox, started a bank in the same town. At the present time he is the president of the bank and his wife assists him. As bankers they receive three or four times as much pay as they received from the post-office. The bank is patronized by both white and coloured people, and, when last I heard of it, was in a flourishing condition. As president of a Negro bank, Mr. Cox is performing a much greater service to the community than he could possibly render as postmaster. There are, no doubt, a great many people in his town who would be able to fill the position of postmaster, but there are very few who could start and successfully carry on an institution that would so benefit the community as a Negro bank. While he was postmaster, merely because his office was a political one, Mr. Cox occupied for some time the attention of the whole state of Mississippi; in fact, he (or rather his wife) was for a brief space almost a national figure. Now he is occupying a much more remunerative and important position in private life, but I do not think that he has attracted attention to amount to anything outside of the community in which he lives.

The effect of the excitement about this case has been greatly to exaggerate the importance of holding a Government position. The average Negro naturally feels that there must be some special value to him as an individual, as well as to his race, in holding a position which white people don't want him to hold, simply because he is a Negro. It leads him to believe that it is in some way more honourable or respectable to work for the Government as an official than for the community and himself as a private citizen.

Because of these facts, as well as for other reasons, I have never sought nor accepted a political position. During President Roosevelt's administration I was asked to go as a Commissioner of the United States to Liberia. In considering whether I should accept this position, it was urged that, because of the work that I had already done in this country for my own people and because my name was already known to some extent to the people of Liberia, I was the person best fitted to undertake the work that the Government wanted done. While I did not like the job and could ill spare the time from the work which I was trying to do for the people of my own race in America, I finally decided to accept the position. I was very happy, however, when President Taft kindly decided to relieve me from the necessity of making the trip and allowed my secretary, Mr. Emmett J. Scott, to go to Africa in my stead. This was as near as I ever came to holding a Government job. But there are other ways of getting into politics than by holding office.

In the case of the average man, it has seemed to me that as soon as he gets into office he becomes an entirely different man. Some men change for the better under the weight of responsibility; others change for the worse. I never could understand what there is in American politics that so fatally alters the character of a man. I have known men who, in their private life and in their business, were scrupulously careful to keep their word — men who would never, directly or indirectly, deceive any one with whom they were associated. When they took political office all this changed.

I once asked a coloured hack-driver in Washington how a certain coloured man whom I had known in private life (but who was holding a prominent office) was getting on. The old driver had little education but he was a judge of men, and he summed up the case in this way:

"Dere is one thing about Mr.; you can always depend on him." The old fellow shook his head and laughed. Then he added: "If he tells you he's gwine to do anything, you can always depend upon it that he's *not* gwine to do it."

This sort of change that comes over people after they get office is not confined, however, to the Negro race. Other races seem to suffer in the same way. I have seen men who, in the ordinary affairs of life, were cool and level headed, grow suspicious and jealous, give up interest in everything, neglect their busi ness, sometimes even neglect their families; in short, lose entirely their mental and moral balance as soon as they started out in quest of an office.

I have watched these men after the political microbe attacked them, and I know all the symptoms of the disease that follows. They usually begin by carefully studying the daily newspapers. They attach great importance to the slightest thing that is said (or not said) by persons who they believe have politi- cal influence or authority. These men (the men who dispense the offices) soon come to assume an enormous importance in the minds of office-seekers. They watch all the movements of the political leaders with the greatest anxiety, and study every chance word that they let drop, as if it had some dark and awful significance. Then, when they get a little farther along, the office-seekers will, perhaps, be found tramping the streets, getting signatures of Tom, Dick, and Harry as a guarantee that they are best qualified to fill some office that they have in view.

I remember the case of a white man who lived in Alabama when President McKinley was first elected. This man gave up his business and went to Wash- ington with a full determination to secure a place in the President's cabinet. He wrote me regularly concerning his prospects. After President McKinley had filled all the places in his cabinet, the same individual applied for a foreign am- bassadorship; failing in that, he applied for an auditorship in one of the depart- ments; failing in that, he tried to get a clerkship in Washington; failing in that, he finally wrote to me (and to a number of other acquaintances in Alabama) and asked me to lend him enough money to defray his travelling expenses back to Alabama.

Of course, not all men who go into politics are affected in the way that I have described. Let me add that I have known many public men and have studied them carefully, but the best and highest example of a man that was the same in political office that he was in private life is Col. Theodore Roosevelt. He is not the only example, but he is the most conspicuous one in this respect that I have ever known.

I was thrown, comparatively early in my career, in contact with Colonel Roosevelt. He was just the sort of man to whom any one who was trying to do work of any kind for the improvement of any race or type of humanity would naturally go to for advice and help. I have seen him and been in close contact with him under many varying circumstances and I confess that I have learned much from studying his career, both while he was in office and since he has been in private life. One thing that impresses me about Mr. Roosevelt is that I have never known him, having given a promise, to overlook or forget it; in fact, he seems to forget nothing, not even the most trivial incidents. I found him the same when he was President that he was as a private citizen, or as Governor of New York, or as Vice-President of the United States. In fact, I have no hesitation in saying that I consider him the highest type of all-round man that I have ever met.

One of the most striking things about Mr. Roosevelt, both in private and public life, is his frankness. I have been often amazed at the absolute directness and candour of his speech. He does not seem to know how to hide anything. In fact, he seems to think aloud. Many people have referred to him as being impulsive and as acting without due consideration. From what I have seen of Mr. Roosevelt in this regard, I have reached the conclusion that what people describe as impulsiveness in him is nothing else but quickness of thought. While other people are thinking around a question, he thinks through it. He reaches his conclusions while other people are considering the preliminaries. He cuts across the field, as it were, in his methods of thinking. It is true that in doing so he often takes great chances and risks much. But Colonel Roosevelt is a man who never shrinks from taking chances when it is necessary to take them. I remember that, on one occasion, when it seemed to me that he had risked a great deal in pursuing a certain line of action, I suggested to him that it seemed to me that he had taken a great chance.

"One never wins a battle," he replied, "unless he takes some risks."

Another characteristic of Colonel Roosevelt, as compared with many other prominent men in public life, is that he rarely forgets or forsakes a friend. If a man once wins his confidence, he stands by that man. One always knows where to find him — and that, in my opinion, accounts to a large degree for his immense popularity. His friend, particularly if he happens to be holding a public position, may become very unpopular with the public, but unless that friend has disgraced himself, Mr. Roosevelt will always stand by him, and is not afraid or ashamed to do so. In the long run the world respects a man who has the courage to stand by his friends, whether in public or private life, and Mr. Roosevelt has frequently gained popularity by doing things that more discreet politicians would have been afraid to do.

I first became acquainted with Mr. Roosevelt through correspondence. Later, in one of my talks with him — and this was at a time when there seemed little chance of his ever becoming President, for it was before he had even been mentioned for that position — he stated to me in the frankest manner that some day he would like to be President of the United States. The average man, under such circumstances, would not have thought aloud. If he believed that there was a remote opportunity of gaining the Presidency, he would have said that he was not seeking the office; that his friends were thrusting it on him; that he did not have the ability to be President, and so forth. Not so with Colonel Roosevelt.

He spoke out, as is his custom, that which was in his mind. Even then, many years before he attained his ambition, he began to outline to me how he wanted to help not only the Negro, but the whole South, should he ever become President. I question whether any man ever went into the Presidency with a more sincere desire to be of real service to the South than Mr. Roosevelt did.

That incident will indicate one of the reasons why Mr. Roosevelt succeeds. He not only thinks quickly, but he plans and thinks a long distance ahead. If he had an important state paper to write, or an important magazine article or speech to prepare, I have known him to prepare it six or eight months ahead. The result is that he is at all times master of himself and of his surroundings. He does not let his work push him; he pushes his work.

Practically everything that he tried to do for the South while he was President was outlined in conversations to me many years before it became known to most people that he had the slightest chance of becoming President. What he did was not a matter of impulse but the result of carefully matured plans.

An incident which occurred immediately after he became President will illustrate the way in which Mr. Roosevelt's mind works upon a public problem. After the death of President McKinley I received a letter from him, written in his own hand, on the very day that he took the oath of office at Buffalo as President — or was it the day following? — in which he asked me to meet him in Washington. He wanted to talk over with me the plans for helping the South that we had discussed years before. This plan had lain matured in his mind for months and years and, as soon as the opportunity came, he acted upon it.

When I received this letter from Mr. Roosevelt, asking me to meet him in Washington, I confess that it caused me some grave misgivings. I felt that I must consider seriously the question whether I should allow myself to be drawn into a kind of activity that I had definitely determined to keep away from. But here was a letter which, it seemed to me, I could not lightly put aside, no matter what my personal wishes or feelings might be. Shortly after Mr. Roosevelt became established in the White House I went there to see him and we spent the greater part of an evening in talk concerning the South. In this conversation he emphasized two points in particular: First, he said that wherever he appointed a white man to office in the South he wished him to be the very highest type of native Southern white man — one in whom the whole country had faith. He repeated and emphasized his determination to appoint such a type of man regardless of political influences or political consequences.

Then he stated to me, quite frankly, that he did not propose to appoint a large number of coloured people to office in any part of the South, but that he did propose to do two things which had not been done before that time — at least not to the extent and with the definite purpose that he had in mind.

Wherever he did appoint a coloured man to office in the South, he said that he wanted him to be not only a man of ability, but of character — a man who had the confidence of his white and coloured neighbours. He did not propose to appoint a coloured man to office simply for the purpose of temporary political expediency. He added that, while he proposed to appoint fewer coloured men to office in the South, he proposed to put a certain number of coloured men of high character and ability in office in the Northern states. He said that he had never been able to see any good reason why coloured men should be put in office in the Southern states and not in the North as well.

As a matter of fact, before Mr. Roosevelt became President, not a single coloured man had ever been appointed, so far as I know, to a Federal office in any Northern state. Mr. Roosevelt determined to set the example by placing a coloured man in a high office in his own home city, so that the country might see that he did not want other parts of the country to accept that which he himself was not willing to receive. Some months afterward, as a result of this policy, the Hon. Charles W. Anderson was made collector of internal revenues for the second district of New York. This is the district in which Wall Street is located and the district that receives, perhaps, more revenue than any other in the United States. Later on, Mr. Roosevelt appointed other coloured men to high office in the North and West, but I think that any one who examines into the individual qualifications of the coloured men appointed to office by Mr. Roosevelt will find, in each case, that they were what he insisted that they should be — men of superior ability and of superior character.

President Taft happily has followed the same policy. He has appointed Whitefield McKinlay, of Washington, to the collectorship of the port of Georgetown, a position which has never heretofore been held by a black man. He had designated J. C. Napier, cashier of the One-Cent Savings Bank of Nashville, Tenn., to serve as register of the United States treasury; and he has recently announced the appointment of William H. Lewis, assistant United States district attorney, Boston, Mass., to the highest appointive position ever held by a black man under the Federal Government, namely, to a place as assistant attorney general of the United States.

Back of their desire to improve the public service, Mr. Roosevelt and Mr. Taft have had another purpose in appointing to office the kind of coloured people that I have named. They have said that they desire the persons appointed by them to be men of the highest character in order that the younger generation of coloured people might see that men of conspicuous ability and conspicuous purity of character are recognized in politics as in other walks of life. They have hoped that such recognition might lead other coloured people to strive to attain a high reputation.

Mr. Roosevelt did not apply this rule to the appointments of coloured people alone. He believed that he could not only greatly improve the public service, but to some extent could change the tone of politics in the South and improve the relations of the races by the appointment of men who stood high in their professions and who were not only friendly to the coloured people but had the confidence of the white people as well. These men, he hoped, would be to the South a sort of model of what the Federal Government desired and expected of its officials in their relations with all parties.

During the first conference with Mr. Roosevelt in the White House, after discussing many matters, he finally agreed to appoint a certain white man, whose name had been discussed, to an important judicial position. Within a few days the appointment was made and accepted. I question whether any appointment made in the South has ever attracted more attention or created more favourable comment from people of all classes than was true of this one.

During the fall of 1901, while I was making a tour of Mississippi, I received word to the effect that the President would like to have a conference with me, as soon as it was convenient, concerning some important matters. With a friend, who was travelling with me, I discussed very seriously the question whether, with the responsibilities I already had, I should take on others. After considering the matter carefully, we decided that the only policy to pursue was to face the new responsibilities as they arose, because new responsibilities bring new opportunities for usefulness of which I ought to take advantage in the interest of my race. I was the more disposed to feel that this was a duty because Mr. Roosevelt was proposing to carry out the very policies which I had advocated ever since I began work in Alabama. Immediately after finishing my work in Mississippi I went to Washington. I arrived there in the afternoon and went to the house of a friend, Mr. Whitefield McKinlay, with whom I was expected to stop during my stay in Washington.

This trip to Washington brings me to a matter which I have hitherto constantly refused to discuss in print or in public, though I have had a great many requests to do so. At the time, I did not care to add fuel to the controversy which it aroused, and I speak of it now only because it seems to me that an explanation will show the incident in its true light and in its proper proportions.

When I reached Mr. McKinlay's house I found an invitation from President Roosevelt asking me to dine with him at the White House that evening at eight o'clock. At the hour appointed I went to the White House and dined with the President and members of his family and a gentleman from Colorado. After dinner we talked at considerable length concerning plans about the South which the President had in mind. I left the White House almost immediately and took a train the same night for New York. When I reached New York the next morning I noticed that the New York *Tribune* had about two lines stating that I had dined with the President the previous night. That was the only New York paper, so far as I saw, that mentioned the matter. Within a few hours the whole incident completely passed from my mind. I mentioned the matter casually, during the day, to a friend — Mr. William H. Baldwin, Jr., then president of the Long Island Railroad — but spoke of it to no one else and had no intention of doing so. There was, in fact, no reason why I should discuss it or mention it to any one.

My surprise can be imagined when, two or three days afterward, the whole press, North and South, was filled with despatches and editorials relating to my dinner with the President. For days and weeks I was pursued by reporters in quest of interviews. I was deluged with telegrams and letters asking for some expression of opinion or an explanation; but during the whole of this period of agitation and excitement I did not give out a single interview and did not discuss the matter in any way.

Some newspapers attempted to weave into this incident a deliberate and well-planned scheme on the part of President Roosevelt to lead the way in bringing about the social intermingling of the two races. I am sure that nothing was farther from the President's mind than this; certainly it was not in my mind. Mr. Roosevelt simply found that he could spare the time best during and after the dinner hour for the discussion of the matters which both of us were interested in.

The public interest aroused by this dinner seemed all the more extraordinary and uncalled for because, on previous occasions, I had taken tea with Queen Victoria at Windsor Castle; I had dined with the governors of nearly every state in the North; I had dined in the same room with President McKinley at Chicago at the Peace-jubilee dinner; and I had dined with ex-President Harrison in Paris, and with many other prominent public men.

Some weeks after the incident I was making a trip through Florida. In some way it became pretty generally known along the railroad that I was on the train, and the result was that at nearly every station a group of people would get aboard and shake hands with me. At a little station near Gainesville, Fla., a white man got aboard the train whose dress and manner indicated that he was from the class of small farmers in that part of the country. He shook hands with me very cordially, and said:

"I am mighty glad to see you. I have heard about you and I have been wanting to meet you for a long while."

I was naturally pleased at this cordial reception, but I was surprised when, after looking me over, he remarked: "Say, you are a great man. You are the greatest man in this country!"

I protested mildly, but he insisted, shaking his head and repeating, "Yes, sir, the greatest man in this country." Finally I asked him what he had against President Roosevelt, telling him at the same time that, in my opinion, the President of the United States was the greatest man in the country.

"Huh! Roosevelt?" he replied with considerable emphasis in his voice. "I used to think that Roosevelt was a great man until he ate dinner with you. That settled him for me."

This remark of a Florida farmer is but one of the many experiences which have taught me something of the curious nature of this thing that we call prejudice — social prejudice, race prejudice, and all the rest. I have come to the conclusion that these prejudices are something that it does not pay to disturb. It is best to "let sleeping dogs lie." All sections of the United States, like all other parts of the world, have their own peculiar customs and prejudices. For that reason it is the part of common-sense to respect them. When one goes to European countries or into the Far West, or into India or China, he meets certain customs and certain prejudices which he is bound to respect and, to a certain extent, comply with. The same holds good regarding conditions in the North and in the South. In the South it is not the custom for coloured and white people to be entertained at the same hotel; it is not the custom for black and white children to attend the same school. In most parts of the North a different custom prevails. I have never stopped to question or quarrel with the customs of the people in the part of the country in which I found myself.

Thus, in dining with President Roosevelt, there was no disposition on my part — and I am sure there was no disposition on Mr. Roosevelt's part — to attack any custom of the South. There is, therefore, absolutely no ground or excuse for the assertion sometimes made that our dining together was part of a preconcerted and well-thought-out plan. It was merely an incident that had no thought or motive behind it except the convenience of the President.

I was born in the South and I understand thoroughly the prejudices, the customs, the traditions of the South — and, strange as it may seem to those who do not wholly understand the situation, I love the South. There is no Southern white man who cherishes a deeper interest than I in everything that promotes the progress and the glory of the South. For that reason, if for no other, I will never willingly and knowingly do anything that, in my opinion, will provoke bitterness between the races or misunderstanding between the North and the South.

Now that the excitement in regard to it is all over, it may not be out of place, perhaps, for me to recall the famous order disbanding a certain portion of the Twenty-fifth Infantry (a Negro regiment) because of the outbreak at Brownsville, Texas, particularly since this is an illustration of the trait in Mr. Roosevelt to which I have referred. I do not mind stating here that I did not agree with

Mr. Roosevelt's method of punishing the Negro soldiers, even supposing that they were guilty. In his usual frank way, he told me several days prior to issuing that order what he was going to do. I urged that he find some other method of punishing the soldiers. While, in some matters, I was perhaps instrumental in getting him to change an opinion that he had formed, in this case he told me that his mind was perfectly clear and that he had reached a definite decision which he would not change, because he was certain that he was right.

At the time this famous order was issued there was no man in the world who was so beloved by the ten millions of Negroes in America as Colonel Roosevelt. His praises were sung by them on every possible occasion. He was their idol. Within a few days — I might almost say hours — as a consequence of this order, the songs of praise of ten millions of people were turned into a chorus of criticism and censure.

Mr. Roosevelt was over and over again urged and besought by many of his best friends, both white and coloured, to modify or change this order. Even President Taft, who was at that time Secretary of War, urged him to withdraw the order or modify it. I urged him to do the same thing. He stood his ground and refused. He said that he was convinced that he was right and that events would justify his course.

Notwithstanding the fact that I was deeply concerned in the outcome of this order, I confess that I could not but admire the patience with which Mr. Roosevelt waited for the storm to blow over. I do not think that the criticisms and denunciation which he received had the effect of swerving him in the least from the general course that he had determined to pursue with regard to the coloured people of the country. He was just as friendly in his attitude to them after the Brownsville affair as before.

Months have passed since the issuing of the order; the agitation has subsided and the bitterness has disappeared. I think that I am safe in saying that, while the majority of coloured people still feel that Colonel Roosevelt made a mistake in issuing the order, there is no individual who is more popular and more loved by the ten millions of Negroes in America than he.

HENRY JAMES

Henry James (1843–1916) made one visit to Washington before leaving the United States to take up residence in England and another twenty years later on the tour that resulted in the collection of essays titled *The American Scene* (1907). In the chapter devoted to Washington, he gushed over the beauty and grandeur of the federal city — the Capitol, the Library of Congress (completed, after his first visit, in 1897), and the White House — but was most struck by the new social advances that made Washington the "City of Conversation." Weary of the type of American "business man" found in abundance in other American cities, James expressed his hope that Washington might serve as an example of the city of the future, one based on social relations.

From "Washington"
In *The American Scene*

I was twice in Washington, the first time for a winter visit, the second to meet the wonderful advance of summer, to which, in that climate of many charms, the first days of May open wide the gates. This latter impression was perforce much the more briefly taken; yet, though I had gathered also from other past occasions, far-away years now, something of the sense of the place at the earlier season, I find everything washed over, at the mention of the name, by the rare light, half green, half golden, of the lovely leafy moment. I see all the rest, till I make the effort to break the spell, through that voluminous veil; which operates, for memory, quite as the explosion of spring works, even to the near vision, in respect to the American scene at large — dressing it up as if for company, preparing it for social, for human intercourse, making it in fine publicly presentable, with an energy of renewal and an effect of redemption not often to be noted, I imagine, on other continents. . . .

I must ask myself, I meanwhile recognize, none the less, why I should have found Mount Vernon exquisite, the first of May, if the interest had all to be accounted for in the light of nature. The light of nature was there, splendid and serene; the Potomac opened out in its grandest manner; the bluff above the river, before the sweep of its horizon, raised its head for the historic crown. But it was not for a moment to be said that this was the whole story; the human interest and the human charm lay in wait and held one fast — so that, if one had been making light, elsewhere, of their suggestion and office, one had at least this case seriously to reckon with. I speak straightway, thus, of Mount Vernon, though it be but an outlying feature of Washington, and at the best a minor impression; the image of the particular occasion is seated so softly in my path. There was a glamour, in fine, for the excursion — that of an extraordinarily gracious hospitality; and the glamour would still have been great even if I had not, on my return to the shadow of the Capitol, found the whole place transfigured. The season was over, the President away, the two Houses up, the shutters closed, the visitor rare; and one lost one's way in the great green vistas of the avenues quite as one might have lost it in a "sylvan solitude" — that is in the empty alleys of a park. The emptiness was qualified at the most, here and there, by some encounter with a stray diplomatic agent, wreathed for the most part in sincerer smiles than we are wont to attribute to his class. "This" — it was the meaning of these inflections —"was the *real* Washington, a place of enchantment; so that if the enchantment were never less who could ever bring himself to go away?" The enchantment had been so much less in January — one could easily understand; yet the recognition seemed truly the voice of the hour, and one picked it up with a patriotic flutter not diminished by the fact that the speaker would probably be going away, and with delight, on the morrow.

The memory of some of the smiles and inflections comes back in that light; Washington being the one place in America, I think, where those qualities are the values and vehicles, the medium of exchange. No small part of the interest of the social scene there consists, inevitably, for any restless analyst, in wonder about the "real" sentiments of appointed foreign participants, the delegates of Powers and pledged alike to penetration and to discretion, before phenomena which, whatever they may be, differ more from the phenomena of other capitals and other societies than they resemble them. This interest is susceptible, on occasion, of becoming intense; all the more that curiosity must, for the most part, pursue its object (that of truly looking over the alien shoulder and of see-ing, judging, building, fearing, reporting with the alien sense) by subtle and tortuous ways. This represents, first and last, even for a watcher abjectly irre-sponsible, a good deal of speculative tension; so that one's case is refreshing in presence of the clear candor of such a proposition as that the national capital *is* charming in proportion as you don't see it. For that is what it came to, in the bowery condition; the as yet unsurmounted bourgeois character of the whole was screened and disguised; the dressing-up, in other words, was complete, and the great park-aspect gained, and became nobly artificial, by the very complex-ity of the plan of the place — the perpetual perspectives, the converging, radiat-ing avenues, the frequent circles and crossways, where all that was wanted for full illusion was that the bronze generals and admirals, on their named ped-estals, should have been great garden-gods, mossy mythological marble. This would have been the perfect note; the long vistas yearned for it, and the golden chequers scattered through the gaps of the high arches waited for some bend-ing nymph or some armless Hermes to pick them up. The power of the scene to evoke such visions sufficiently shows, I think, what had become, under the mercy of nature, of the hard facts, as one must everywhere call them; and yet though I could, diplomatically, patriotically pretend, at the right moment, that such a Washington *was* the "real" one, my assent had all the while a still finer meaning for myself. . . .

. . . WASHINGTON ITSELF meanwhile — the Washington always, I premise, of the rank outsider — had struck me from the first as presenting two distinct faces; the more obvious of which was the public and official, the monumental, with features all more or less majestically playing the great administrative, or, as we nowadays put it, Imperial part. This clustered, yet at the same time oddly scattered, city, a general impression of high granite steps, of light gray corniced colonnades, rather harmoniously low, contending for effect with slaty mansard roofs and masses of iron excrescence, a general impression of somewhat vague, empty, sketchy, fundamentals, however expectant, however spacious, overweighted by a single Dome and overaccented by a single Shaft — this loose congregation of values seemed, strangely, a matter disconnected and remote, though remaining in its way portentous and bristling all incoherently at the back of the scene. The back of the scene, indeed, to one's quite primary sense, might have been but an immense painted, yet unfinished cloth, hung there to a confessedly provisional end and marked with the queerness, among many queernesses, of looking always the same; painted once for all in clear, bright, fresh tones, but never emerging from its flatness, after the fashion of other capitals, into the truly, the variously, modelled and rounded state. (It appeared provisional therefore because looking as if it might have been unhooked and removed as a whole; because any one object in it so treated would have made the rest also come off.) The foreground was a different thing, a thing that, ever so quaintly, seemed to represent the force really in possession; though consisting but of a small company of people engaged perpetually in conversation and (always, I repeat, for the rank outsider) singularly destitute of conspicuous marks or badges. This little society easily became, for the detached visitor, the city itself, *the* national capital and the greater part of the story; and that, ever, in spite of the comparatively scant intensity of its political permeation. The political echo was of course to be heard in it, and the public character, in its higher forms, to be encountered — though only in "single spies," not in battalions; but there was something that made it much more individual than any mere predominance of political or administrative color would have made it; leaving it in that case to do no more than resemble the best society in London, or that in best possession of the field in Paris.

Two sharp signs my remoter remembrance had shown me the then Washington world, and the first met, as putting forth; one of these the fact of its being extraordinarily easy and pleasant, and the other that of one's appearing to make out in it not more than half a dozen members of the Lower House and not more than a dozen of the Upper. This kept down the political permeation, and was bewildering, if one was able to compare, in the light of the different London condition, the fact of the social ubiquity there of the acceptable M.P. and that of the social frequency even of his more equivocal hereditary colleague. A London nestling under the towers of Westminster, yet practically void of members of the House of Commons, and with the note of official life far from exclusively sounding, that might have been in those days the odd image of Washington, had not the picture been stamped with other variations still. These were a whole cluster, not instantly to be made out, but constituting the unity of the place as soon as perceived; representing that finer extract or essence which the self-respecting observer is never easy till he be able to shake up and down in bottled form. The charming company of the foreground then, which referred itself so little to the sketchy back-scene, the monstrous Dome and Shaft, figments of the upper air, the pale colonnades and mere myriad-windowed Buildings, was the second of the two faces, and the more one lived with it the more, up to a certain point, one lived away from the first. In time, and after perceiving *how* it was what it so agreeably was, came the recognition of common ground; the recognition that, in spite of strange passages of the national life, liable possibly to recur, during which the President himself was scarce thought to be in society, the particular precious character that one had apprehended could never have ripened without a general consensus. One had put one's finger on it when one had seen disengage itself from many anomalies, from not a few drolleries, the superior, the quite majestic fact of the City of Conversation pure and simple, and positively of the only specimen, of any such intensity, in the world.

That had remained for me, from the other time, the properest name of Washington, and nothing could so interest me, on a renewal of acquaintance, too long postponed and then too woefully brief, as to find my description wholly justified. If the emphasis added by "pure and simple" be invariably retained, the description will continue, I think, to embrace and exhaust the spectacle, while yet leaving it every inch of its value. Clearly quite immeasurable, on American ground, the value of such an assertion of a town-type directly opposed to the unvarying American, and quite unique, on any ground, so organized a social indifference to the vulgar vociferous Market. Washington may of course *know* more than she confesses — no community could perhaps really be as ignorant as Washington used at any rate to look, and to like to look, of this particular thing, of "goods" and shares and rises and falls and all such sordidities; but she knows assuredly still the very least she can get off with, and nothing even yet pleases her more than to forget what she does know. She unlearns, she turns her back, while London, Paris, Berlin, Rome, in their character of political centres, strike us as, on the contrary, feverishly learning, trying more and more to do the exact opposite. (I speak, naturally, as to Washington, of knowing actively and interestedly, in the spirit of gain — not merely of the enjoyed lights of political and administrative science, doubtless as abundant there as anywhere else). It might fairly have been, I used to think, that the charming place — charming in the particular connection I speak of — had on its conscience to make one forget for an hour the colossal greed of New York. Nothing, in fact, added more to

its charm than its appearing virtually to invite one to impute to it some such
vicarious compunction.

If I be reminded, indeed, that the distinction I here glance at is negative,
and be asked what then (if she knew nothing of the great American interest)
Washington did socially know, my answer, I recognize, has at once to narrow
itself, and becomes perhaps truly the least bit difficult to utter. It none the less
remains distinct enough that, the City of Conversation being only in question, and a general subject of all the conversation having thereby to be predi-
cated, our responsibility is met as soon as we are able to say what Washington
mainly talks, and appears always to go mainly talking, about. Washington talks
about herself, and about almost nothing else; falling superficially indeed, on
that ground, but into line with the other capitals. London, Paris, Berlin, Rome,
goodness knows, talk about themselves: that is each member of this sisterhood
talks, sufficiently or inordinately, of the great number of divided and differing
selves that form together her controlling identity. London, for instance, talks
of everything in the world without thereby for a moment, as it were, ceasing to
be egotistical. It has taken everything in the world to make London up, so that
she is in consequence simply doomed never to get away from herself. Her conversation is largely, I think, the very effort to do that; but she inevitably figures
in it but as some big buzzing insect which keeps bumping against a treacherous
mirror. It is in positive quest of an identity of some sort, much rather — an identity other than merely functional and technical — that Washington goes forth,
encumbered with no ideal of avoidance or escape: it is about herself *as* the City
of Conversation precisely that she incessantly converses; adorning the topic,
moreover, with endless ingenuity and humor. But that, absolutely, remains the
case; which thus becomes one of the most thorough, even if probably one of
the most natural and of the happiest, cases of collective self-consciousness that
one knows. The spectacle, as it at first met my senses, was that of a numerous
community in ardent pursuit of some workable conception of its social self, and
trying meanwhile intelligently to talk itself, and even this very embarrassment,
into a *subject* for conversation. Such a picture might not seem purely pleasing,
on the side of variety of appeal, and I admit one may have had one's reserves
about it; reserves sometimes reflected, for example, in dim inward speculation
— one of the effects of the Washington air I have already glanced at — as to the
amount of response it might evoke in the diplomatic body. It may have been on
my part a morbid obsession, but the diplomatic body was liable to strike one
there as more characteristically "abysmal" than elsewhere, more impenetrably
bland and inscrutably blank; and it was obvious, certainly, that their concern to
help the place intellectually to find itself was not to be expected to approach in
intensity the concern even of a repatriated absentee. You were concerned only

if you had, by your sensibility, a stake in the game; which was the last thing a foreign representative would wish to confess to, this being directly opposed to all his enjoined duties. It is no part of the office of such personages to assist the societies to which they are accredited to find themselves — it is much more their mission to leave all such vaguely and, so far as may be, grotesquely groping: so apt are societies, in finding themselves, to find other things too. This detachment from the whole mild convulsion of effort, the considerate pretence of not being too aware of it, combined with latent probabilities of alarm about it no less than of amusement, represented, to the unquiet fancy, much more the spirit of the old-time Legations.

What *was*, at all events, better fun, of the finer sort, than having one's self a stake in the outcome? — what helped the time (so much of it as there was!) more to pass than just to join in the so fresh experiment of constitutive, creative talk? The boon, it should always be mentioned, meanwhile went on not in the least in the tone of solemnity. That would have been fatal, because probably irritating, and it was where the good star of Washington intervened. The tone was, so to speak, of *conscious* self-consciousness, and the highest genius for conversation doubtless dwelt in the fact that the ironic spirit was ready always to give its very self away, fifty times over, for the love, or for any quickening, of the theme. The foundation for the whole happy predicament remained, moreover, of the firmest, and the essence of the case was to be as easily stated as the great social fact is, in America, whether through exceptions or aggravations, everywhere to be stated. Nobody was in "business" — that was the sum and substance of it; and for the one large human assemblage on the continent of which this was true the difference made was huge. Nothing could strike one more than that it was the only way in which, over the land, a difference *could* be made, and than how, in our vast commercial democracy, almost any difference — by which I mean almost any exception — promptly acquires prodigious relief. The value here was at once that the place could offer to view a society, the only one in the country, in which Men existed, and that that rich little fact became the key to everything. Superficially taken, I recognize, the circumstance fails to look portentous; but it looms large immediately, gains the widest bearing, in the light of any direct or extended acquaintance with American conditions. From the moment it is adequately borne in mind that the business-man, in the United States, may, with no matter what dim struggles, gropings, yearnings, never hope to be anything *but* a business-man, the size of the field he so abdicates is measured, as well as the fact of the other care to which his abdication hands it over. It lies there waiting, pleading from all its pores, to be occupied — the lonely waste, the boundless gaping void of "society"; which is but a rough name for all the *other* so numerous relations with the world he lives in that are imputable to the civilized being. Here it is then that the world he lives in accepts its doom and becomes, by his default, subject and plastic to his mate; his default having made, all around him, the unexampled opportunity of the woman — which she would have been an incredible fool not to pounce upon. It needs little contact with American life to perceive how she *has* pounced, and how, outside business, she has made it over in her image. She has been, up to now, on the vast residual tract, in peerless possession, and is occupied in developing and extending her wonderful conquest, which she appreciates to the last inch of its extent.

She has meanwhile probably her hours of amazement at the size of her windfall; she cannot quite live without wonder at the oddity of her so "sleeping" partner, the strange creature, by her side, with his values and his voids, but who is best known to her as having yielded what she would have clutched to the death. Yet these are mere mystic, inscrutable possibilities — dreams, for us, of her hushed, shrouded hours: the face she shows, on all the facts, is that of mere unwinking tribute to the matter of course. The effect of these high signs of assurance in her has been — and it is really her masterstroke — to represent the situation as perfectly normal. Her companion's attitude, totally destitute of high signs, does everything it can to further this feat; so that, as disposed together in the American picture, they testify, extraordinarily, to the *successful* rupture of a universal law, the sight is at first, for observation, most mystifying. Then the impunity of the whole thing gains upon us; the equilibrium strikes us, however strangely, as at least provisionally stable; we see that a society in many respects workable would seem to have been arrived at, and that we shall in any case have time to study it. The phenomenon may easily become, for a spectator, the sentence written largest in the American sky: when he is in search of the characteristic, what else so plays the part? The woman is two-thirds of the apparent life — which means that she is absolutely all of the social; and, as this is nowhere else the case, the occasion is unique for seeing what such a situation may make of her. The result elsewhere, in Europe generally, of conditions in which men have actively participated and to which, throughout, they personally contribute, she has only the old story to tell, and keeps telling it after her fashion. The woman produced by a women-made society alone has obviously quite a new story — to which it is not for a moment to be gainsaid that the world at large has, for the last thirty years in particular, found itself lending an attentive, at times even a charmed, ear. The extent and variety of this attention have been the specious measure of the personal success of the type in question, and are always referred to when its value happens to be challenged. "The American woman? — why, she has beguiled, she has conquered, the globe: look at her fortune everywhere and fail to accept her if you can." ...

... One might have been sure in advance that the character of a democracy would nowhere more sharply mark itself than in the democratic substitute for a court city, and Washington is cast in the mould that expresses most the absence of salient social landmarks and constituted features. Here it is that conversation, as the only invoked presence, betrays a little its inadequacy to the furnishing forth, all by itself, of an outward view. It tells us it must be there, since in all the wide empty vistas nothing else is, and the general elimination *can* but have left it. A pleading, touching effect, indeed, lurks in this sense of it as seated, at receipt of custom, by any decent door of any decent domicile and watching the vacancy for reminder and appeal. It is left to conversation alone to people the scene with accents; putting aside two or three objects to be specified, there is *never* an accent in it, up and down, far and wide, save such as fall rather on the ear of the mind: those projected by the social spirit starved for the sense of an occasional emphasis. The White House is an accent — one of the lightest, sharpest possible; and the Capitol, of course, immensely, another; though the latter falls on the exclusively political page, as to which I have been waiting to say a word. It should meanwhile be mentioned that we are promised these enhancements, these illustrations, of the great general text, on the most magnificent scale; a splendid projected and announced Washington of the future, with approaches even now grandly outlined and massively marked; in face of which one should perhaps confess to the futility of any current estimate. If I speak thus of the Capitol, however, let me not merely brush past the White House to get to it — any more than feel free to pass into it without some preliminary stare at that wondrous Library of Congress which glitters in fresh and almost unmannerly emulation, almost frivolous irrelevance of form, in the neighborhood of the greater building. About the ingenuities and splendors of this last costly structure, a riot of rare material and rich ornament, there would doubtless be much to say — did not one everywhere, on all such ground, meet the open eye of criticism simply to establish with it a private intelligence, simply to respond to it by a deprecating wink. The guardian of that altar, I think, is but too willing, on such a hint, to let one pass without the sacrifice.

It is a case again here, as on fifty other occasions, of the tribute instantly paid by the revisiting spirit; but paid, all without question, to the general *kind* of presence for which the noisy air, over the land, feels so sensibly an inward ache — the presence that corresponds there, no matter how loosely, to that of the housing and harboring European Church in the ages of great disorder. The Universities and the greater Libraries (the smaller, for a hundred good democratic reasons, are another question), repeat, in their manner, to the imagination, East and West, the note of the old thick-walled convents and quiet cloisters: they are large and charitable, they are sturdy, often proud and often rich, and they have the incalculable value that they represent the only intermission to inordinate rapacious traffic that the scene offers to view. With this suggestion of sacred ground they play even upon the most restless of analysts as they will, making him face about, with ecstasy, any way they seem to point; so that he feels it his business much less to count over their shortcomings than to proclaim them places of enchantment. They are better at their worst than anything else at its best, and the comparatively sweet sounds that stir their theoretic stillness are for him as echoes of the lyre of Apollo. The Congressional Library is magnificent, and would become thus a supreme sanctuary even were it ten times more so: there would seem to be nothing then but to pronounce it a delight and have done with it — or let the appalled imagination, in other words, slink into it and stay there. But here is pressed precisely, with particular force, the spring of the question that takes but a touch to sound: is the case of this remarkable creation, by exception, a case in which the violent waving of the pecuniary wand *has* incontinently produced interest? The answer can only be, I feel, a shy assent — though shy indeed only till the logic of the matter is apparent. This logic is that, though money alone can gather in on such a scale the treasures of knowledge, these treasures, in the form of books and documents, themselves organize and furnish their world. They appoint and settle the proportions, they thicken the air, they people the space, they create and consecrate all their relations, and no one shall say that, where they scatter life, which they themselves in fact *are*, history does not promptly attend. Emphatically yes, therefore, the great domed and tiered, galleried and statued central hall of the Congressional, the last word of current constructional science and artistic resource, already crowns itself with that grace.

The graceful thing in Washington beyond any other, none the less, is the so happily placed and featured White House, the late excellent extensions and embellishments of which have of course represented expenditure — but only of the refined sort imposed by some mature portionless gentlewoman on relatives who have accepted the principle of making her, at a time of life, more honorably comfortable. The whole ample precinct and margin formed by the virtual continuity of its grounds with those expanses in which the effect of the fine Washington Obelisk rather spends or wastes itself (not a little as if some loud monosyllable had been uttered, in a preoccupied company, without a due production of sympathy or sense) — the fortunate isolation of the White House, I say, intensifies its power to appeal to that musing and mooning visitor whose perceptions alone, in all the conditions, I hold worthy of account. Hereabouts, beyond doubt, history had from of old seemed to me insistently seated, and I remember a short spring-time of years ago when Lafayette Square itself, contiguous to the Executive Mansion, could create a rich sense of the past by the use of scarce other witchcraft than its command of that pleasant perspective and its possession of the most prodigious of all Presidential effigies, Andrew Jackson, as archaic as a Ninevite king, prancing and rocking through the ages. If that atmosphere, moreover, in the fragrance of the Washington April, was even a quarter of a century since as a liquor of bitter-sweet taste, overflowing its cup, what was the ineffable mixture now, with all the elements further distilled, all the life further sacrificed, to make it potent? One circled about the place as for meeting the ghosts, and one paused, under the same impulse, before the high palings of the White House drive, as if wondering at haunted ground. There the ghosts stood in their public array, spectral enough and clarified; yet scarce making it easier to "place" the strange, incongruous blood-drops, looked through the rails, on that revised and freshened page. But one fortunately has one's choice, in all these connections, as one turns away; the mixture, as I have called it, is really here so fine. General Jackson, in the centre of the Square, still rocks his hobby and the earth; but the fruit of the interval, to my actual eyes, hangs nowhere brighter than in the brilliant memorials lately erected to Lafayette and to Rochambeau. Artful, genial, expressive, the tribute of French talent, these happy images supply, on the spot, the note without which even the most fantasticating sense of our national past would feel itself rub forever against mere brown homespun. Everything else gives way, for me, I confess, as I again stand before them; everything, whether as historic fact, or present *agrément*, or future possibility, yields to this one high luxury of our old friendship with France.

The "artistic" Federal city already announced spreads itself then before us, in plans elaborated even to the finer details, a city of palaces and monuments and gardens, symmetries and circles and far radiations, with the big Potomac for water-power and water-effect and the recurrent Maryland spring, so prompt and so full-handed, for a perpetual benediction. This imagery has, above all, the value, for the considering mind, that it presents itself as under the wide-spread wings of the general Government, which fairly make it figure to the rapt vision as the object caught up in eagle claws and lifted into fields of air that even the high brows of the municipal boss fail to sweep. The wide-spread wings affect us, in the prospect, as great fans that, by their mere tremor, will blow the work, at all steps and stages, clean and clear, disinfect it quite ideally of any germ of the job, and prepare thereby for the American voter, on the spot and in the pride of possession, quite a new kind of civic consciousness. The scheme looms largest, surely, as a demonstration of the possibilities of that service to him, and nothing about it will be more interesting than to measure — though this may take time — the nature and degree of his alleviation. Will the new pride I speak of sufficiently inflame him? Will the taste of the new consciousness, finding him so fresh to it, prove the right medicine? One can only regret that we must still rather indefinitely wait to see — and regret it all the more that there is always, in America, yet another lively source of interest involved in the execution of such designs, and closely involved just in proportion as the high intention, the formal majesty, of the thing seems assured. It comes back to what we constantly feel, throughout the country, to what the American scene everywhere depends on for half its appeal or its effect; to the fact that the social conditions, the material, pressing and pervasive, make the particular experiment or demonstration, whatever it may pretend to, practically a new and incalculable thing. This general Americanism is often the one tag of character attaching to the case after every other appears to have abandoned it. The thing is happening, or will have to happen, in the American way — that American way which is more different from all other native ways, taking country with country, than any of these latter are different from each other; and the question is of how, each time, the American way will see it through. . . .

. . . I WAS AGAIN TO FIND the Capitol, whenever I approached, and above all whenever I entered it, a vast and many-voiced creation. The thing depends of course somewhat on the visitor, who will be the more responsive, I think, the further back into the "origins" of the whole American spectacle his personal vision shall carry him; but this hugest, as I suppose it, of all the homes of debate only asks to put forth, on opportunity, an incongruous, a various, an inexhaustible charm. I may as well say at once that I had found myself from the first adoring the Capitol, though I may not pretend here to dot all the i's of all my reasons — since some of these might appear below the dignity of the subject and others alien to its simplicity. The ark of the American covenant may strike one thus, at any rate, as a compendium of all the national ideals, a museum, crammed full, even to overflowing, of all the national terms and standards, weights and measures and emblems of greatness and glory, and indeed as a builded record of half the collective vibrations of a people; their conscious spirit, their public faith, their bewildered taste, their ceaseless curiosity, their arduous and interrupted education. Such were to my vision at least some of its aspects, but the place had a hundred sides, and if I had had time to look for others still I felt I should have found them. What it comes to — whereby the "pull," in America, is of the greatest — is that association really reigns there, and in the richest, and even again and again in the drollest, forms; it is thick and vivid and almost gross, it assaults the wondering mind. The labyrinthine pile becomes thus inordinately *amusing* — taking the term in its finer modern sense. The analogy may seem forced, but it affected me as playing in Washington life very much the part that St. Peter's, of old, had seemed to me to play in

Roman: it offered afternoon entertainment, at the end of a longish walk, to any spirit in the humor for the uplifted and flattered vision — and this without suggesting that the sublimities in the two cases, even as measured by the profanest mind, tend at all to be equal. The Washington dome is indeed capable, in the Washington air, of admirable, of sublime, effects; and there are cases in which, seen at a distance above its yellow Potomac, it varies but by a shade from the sense — yes, absolutely the divine campagna-sense — of St. Peter's and the like-colored Tiber.

But the question is positively of the impressiveness of the great terraced Capitol hill, with its stages and slopes, staircases and fountains, its general presentation of its charge. And if the whole mass and prospect "amuse," as I say, from the moment they are embraced, the visitor curious of the *democratic assimilation* of the greater dignities and majesties will least miss the general logic. That is the light in which the whole thing is supremely interesting; the light of the fact, illustrated at every turn, that the populations maintaining it deal with it so directly and intimately, so sociably and humorously. We promptly take in that, if ever we are to commune in a concentrated way with the sovereign people, and see their exercised power raise a side-wind of irony for forms and arrangements other than theirs, the occasion here will amply serve. Indubitably, moreover, at a hundred points, the irony operates, and all the more markedly under such possible interference; the interference of the monumental spittoons, that of the immense amount of vulgar, of barbaric, decoration, that of the terrible artistic tributes from, and scarce less to, the different States — the unassorted marble mannikins in particular, each a portrayal by one of the commonwealths of her highest Worthy, which make the great Rotunda, the intended Valhalla, resemble a stone-cutter's collection of priced sorts and sizes. Discretion exists, throughout, only as a flower of the very first or of these very latest years; the large middle time, corresponding, and even that unequally, with the English Victorian, of sinister memory, was unacquainted with the name, and waits there now, in its fruits, but for a huge sacrificial fire, some far-flaring act-of-faith of the future: a tribute to the aesthetic law which one already feels stirring the air, so that it may arrive, I think, with an unexampled stride. Nothing will have been more interesting, surely, than so public a wiping-over of the aesthetic slate, with all the involved collective compunctions and repudiations, the general exhibition of a colossal conscience, a conscience proportionate to the size and wealth of the country. To such grand gestures does the American scene lend itself! . . .

DAVID GRAHAM PHILLIPS

A native of Indiana, David Graham Phillips (1867–1911) moved to New York and became a well-known muckraker and prolific novelist who focused on social problems of the day. In 1906, he published a series of articles, "The Treason of the Senate," in *Cosmopolitan* magazine revealing that politicians from both parties were being paid sizable sums to promote the interests of corporations to the Senate. His novel *The Plum Tree* (1905) explores the corrupting influences of money and political patronage (the "plum tree"). *The Fashionable Adventures of Joshua Craig, a Novel* (1909) also treats the corruption and Machiavellianism of official Washington at the turn of the century. Two years after it was published, Phillips was murdered by a deranged man who thought the narrative libeled his family.

From "A Memorable Meeting"
In *The Fashionable Adventures of Joshua Craig, a Novel*

In that administration the man "next" the President was his Secretary of the Treasury, John Branch, cold and smooth and able, secreting, in his pale-gray soul, an icy passion for power more relentless than heat ever bred. To speak of him as unscrupulous would be like attributing moral quality to a reptile. For him principle did not exist, except as an eccentricity of some strangely-constructed men which might be used to keep them down. Life presented itself to him as a series of mathematical problems, as an examination in mathematics. To pass it meant a diploma as a success; to fail to pass meant the abysmal disgrace of obscurity. Cheating was permissible, but not to get caught at it. Otherwise Branch was the most amiable of men; and why should he not have been, his digestion being good, his income sufficient, his domestic relations admirable, and his reputation for ability growing apace? No one respected him, no one liked him; but every one admired him as an intellect moving quite unhampered of the restraints of conscience. In person he was rather handsome, the weasel type of his face being well concealed by fat and by judicious arrangements of mustache and side-whiskers. By profession he was a lawyer, and had been most successful as adviser to wholesale thieves on depredations bent or in search of immunity for depredations done. It was incomprehensible to him why he was unpopular with the masses. It irritated him that they could not appreciate his purely abstract point of view on life; it irritated him because his unpopularity with them meant that there were limits, and very narrow ones, to his ambition.

It was to John Branch that Madam Bowker applied when she decided that Joshua Craig must be driven from Washington. She sent for him, and he came promptly. He liked to talk to her because she was one of the few who thoroughly appreciated and sympathized with his ideas of success in life. Also, he respected her as a personage in Washington, and had it in mind to marry his daughter, as soon as she should be old enough, to one of her grandnephews.

"Branch," said the old lady, with an emphatic wave of the ebony staff, "I want that Craig man sent away from Washington."

"Josh, the joke?" said Branch with a slow, sneering smile that had an acidity in it interesting in one so even as he.

"That's the man. I want you to rid us of him. He has been paying attention to Margaret, and she is encouraging him."

"Impossible!" declared Branch. "Margaret is a sensible girl and Josh has nothing — never will have anything."

"A mere politician!" declared Madam Bowker. "Like hundreds of others that wink in with each administration and wink out with it. He will not succeed even at his own miserable political game — and, if he did, he would still be poor as poverty."

"I don't think you need worry about him and Margaret. I repeat, she is sensible — an admirable girl — admirably brought up. She has distinction. She has the right instincts."

Madam Bowker punctuated each of these compliments with a nod of her haughty head. "But," said she, "Craig has convinced her that he will amount to something."

"Ridiculous!" scoffed Branch, with an airy wave of the hand. But there was in his tone a concealment that set the shrewd old lady furtively to watching him.

"What do they think of him among the public men?" inquired she.

"He's laughed at there as everywhere." Her vigilance was rewarded; as Branch said that, malignance hissed, ever so softly, in his suave voice, and the snake peered furtively from his calm, cold eyes. Old Madam Bowker had not lived at Washington's great green tables for the gamblers of ambition all those years without learning the significance of eyes and tone. For one politician to speak thus venomously of another was sure sign that that other was of consequence; for John Branch, a very Machiavelli at self-concealment and usually too egotistic to be jealous, thus to speak, and that, without being able to conceal his venom —"Can it be possible," thought the old lady, "that this Craig is about to be a somebody?" Aloud she said: "He is a preposterous creature. The vilest manners I've seen in three generations of Washington life. And what vanity, what assumptions! The first time I met him he lectured me as if I were a schoolgirl — lectured me about the idle, worthless life he said I lead. I decided not to recognize him next time I saw him. Up he came, and without noticing that I did not speak he poured out such insults that I was answering him before I realized it."

"He certainly is a most exasperating person."

"So Western! The very worst the West ever sent us. I don't understand how he happened to get about among decent people. Oh, I remember, it was Grant Arkwright who did it. Grant picked him up on one of his shooting trips."

"He is insufferable," said Branch.

"You must see that the President gets rid of him. I want it done at once. I assure you, John, my alarm is not imaginary. Margaret is very young, has a streak of sentimentality in her. Besides, you know how weak the strongest women are before a determined assault. If the other sex wasn't brought up to have a purely imaginary fear of them I don't know what would become of the world."

Branch smiled appreciatively but absently. "The same is true of men," said he. "The few who amount to anything — at least in active life — base their calculations on the timidity and folly of their fellows rather than upon their own abilities. About Craig — I'd like to oblige you, but — well, you see, there is — there are certain political exigencies — "

"Nonsense!" interrupted the old lady. "I know the relative importance of officials. A mere understrapper like Craig is of no importance."

"The fact is," said Branch with great reluctance, "the President has taken a fancy to Craig."

Branch said it as if he hardly expected to be believed — and he wasn't. "To be perfectly frank," he went on, "you know the President, how easily alarmed he is. He's afraid Craig may, by some crazy turn of this crazy game of politics, develop into a Presidential possibility. Of course, it's quite absurd, but — "

"The more reason for getting rid of him."

"The contrary. The President probably reasons that, if Craig has any element of danger in him the nearer he keeps him to himself the better. Craig, back in the West, would be free to grow. Here the President can keep him down if necessary. And I think our friend Stillwater will succeed in entangling him disastrously in some case sooner or later." There Branch laughed pleasantly, as at the finding of the correct solution to a puzzling problem in analytics or calculus.

"What a cowardly, shadow-fighting, shadow-dodging set you men are!" commented Madam Bowker. Though she did not show it, as a man certainly would, her brain was busy with a wholly different phase of the matter they were discussing.

"Isn't Stillwater going to retire?" she asked presently.

Branch startled. "Where did you hear that?" he demanded.

The old lady smiled. "There are no secrets in Washington," said she. "Who will be his successor?"

Branch's cold face showed annoyance. "You mustn't speak of it," replied he, "but the President is actually thinking of appointing Craig—in case the vacancy should occur. Of course, I am trying to make him see the folly of such a proceeding, but— You are right. Men are cowards. That insufferable upstart is actually bullying the President into a state of terror. Already he has compelled him to prosecute some of our best friends out in the Western country, and if the Courts weren't with us—" Branch checked himself abruptly. It was not the first time he had caught himself yielding to Washington's insidious custom of rank gossip about everything and everybody; but it was about his worst offense in that direction. "I'm getting to be as leaky as Josh Craig is—as he *seems* to be," he muttered, so low, however, that not even her sharp ears caught it.

"So it is to be Attorney-General Craig," said the old lady, apparently abstracted but in reality catlike in watchfulness, and noting with secret pleasure Branch's anger at this explicit statement of the triumph of his hated rival.

"Isn't it frightful?" said Branch. "What is the country coming to?"

But she had lost interest in the conversation. She rid herself of Branch as speedily as the circumstances permitted. She wished to be alone, to revolve the situation slowly from the new viewpoint which Branch, half-unconsciously and wholly reluctantly, had opened up. She had lived a long time, had occupied a front bench overlooking one of the world's chief arenas of action. And, as she had an acute if narrow mind, she had learned to judge intelligently and to note those little signs that are, to the intelligent, the essentials, full of significance. She had concealed her amazement from Branch, but amazed she was, less at his news of Craig as a personage full of potentiality than at her own failure, through the inexcusable, manlike stupidity of personal pique, to discern the real man behind his mannerisms. "No wonder he has pushed so far, so fast," reflected she; for she appreciated that in a man of action manners should always be a cloak behind which his real campaign forms. It must be a fitting cloak, it should be a becoming one; but always a cloak. "He fools everybody, apparently," thought she. "The results of his secret work alarm them; then, along he comes, with his braggart, offensive manners, his childish posings, his peacock vanity, and they are lulled into false security. They think what he did was an accident that will not happen again. Why, he fooled even *me!*"

That is always, with every human being, the supreme test, necessarily. Usually it means nothing. In this case of Cornelia Bowker it meant a great deal; for Cornelia Bowker was not easily fooled. The few who appear in the arena of ambition with no game to play, with only sentiment and principle to further, the few who could easily have fooled her cynical, worldly wisdom could safely be disregarded. She felt it was the part of good sense to look the young man over again, to make sure that the new light upon him was not false light. "He may be a mere accident in spite of his remarkable successes," thought she. "The same number sometimes comes a dozen times in succession at roulette." She sent her handy man, secretary, social manager and organizer, *maître d'hôtel*, companion, scout, gossip, purveyor of comfort, J. Worthington Whitesides, to seek out Craig and to bring him before her forthwith.

As Mr. Whitesides was a tremendous swell, in dress, in manner and in accent, Craig was much impressed when he came into his office in the Department of Justice. Whitesides' manner, the result of Madam Bowker's personal teaching, was one of his chief assets in maintaining and extending her social power. It gave the greatest solemnity and dignity to a summons from her, filled the recipient with pleasure and with awe, prepared him or her to be duly impressed and in a frame of mind suitable to Madam Bowker's purposes.

"I come from Madam Bowker," he explained to Craig, humbly conscious of his own disarray and toiler's unkemptness. "She would be greatly obliged if you will give her a few minutes of your time. She begs you to excuse the informality. She has sent me in her carriage, and it will be a great satisfaction to her if you will accompany me."

Craig's first impulse of snobbish satisfaction was immediately followed by misgivings. Perhaps this was not the formal acceptance of the situation by the terrible old woman as he had, on the spur, fancied. Perhaps she had sent for him to read him the riot act. Then he remembered that he was himself in doubt as to whether he wished to marry the young woman. All his doubts came flooding back, and his terrors — for, in some of its aspects, the idea of being married to this delicate flower of conventionality and gentle breeding was literally a terror to him. If he went he would be still further committing himself; all Washington would soon know of the journey in the carriage of Madam Bowker, the most imposing car of state that appeared in the streets of the Capital, a vast, lofty affair, drawn by magnificent horses, the coachman and footman in costly, quiet livery, high ensconced.

"No, thanks," said Josh, in his most bustlingly-bounderish manner. "Tell the old lady I'm up to my neck in work."

Mr. Whitesides was taken aback, but he was far too polished a gentleman to show it. "Perhaps later?" he suggested.

"I've promised Margaret to go out there later. If I get through here in time I'll look in on Mrs. Bowker on the way. But tell her not to wait at home for me."

Mr. Whitesides bowed, and was glad when the outer air was blowing off him the odor of this vulgar incident. "For," said he to himself, "there are some manners so bad that they have a distinct bad smell. He is 'the limit!' The little Severence must be infernally hard-pressed to think of taking him on. Poor child!

She's devilish interesting. A really handsome bit, and smart, too — excellent ideas about dress. Yet somehow she's been marooned, overlooked, while far worse have been married well. Strange, that sort of thing. Somewhat my own case. I ought to have been able to get some girl with a bunch, yet I somehow always just failed to connect — until I got beyond the marrying age. Devilish lucky for me, too. I'm no end better off." And Mr. Whitesides, sitting correctly upon Madam Bowker's gray silk cushions, reflected complacently upon his ample salary, his carefully built-up and most lucrative commissions, his prospects for a "smashing-good legacy when her majesty deigns to pass away."

At four Madam Bowker, angry yet compelled to a certain respect, heard with satisfaction that Craig had come. "Leave me, Whitesides," said she. "I wish to be quite alone with him throughout."

Thus Craig, entering the great, dim drawing-room, with its panel paintings and its lofty, beautifully-frescoed ceiling, found himself alone with her. She was throned upon a large, antique gold chair, ebony scepter in one hand, the other hand white and young-looking and in fine relief against the black silk of her skirt; she bent upon him a keen, gracious look. Her hazel eyes were bright as a bird's; they had the advantage over a bird's that they saw — saw everything in addition to seeming to see.

Looking at him she saw a figure whose surfaces were, indeed, not extraordinarily impressive. Craig's frame was good; that was apparent despite his clothes. He had powerful shoulders, not narrow, yet neither were they of the broad kind that suggest power to the inexpert and weakness and a tendency to lung trouble to the expert. His body was a trifle long for his arms and legs, which were thick and strong, like a lion's or a tiger's. He had a fine head, haughtily set; his eyes emphasized the impression of arrogance and force. He had the leader's beak-like nose, a handsome form of it, like Alexander's, not like Attila's. The mouth was the orator's — wide, full and flexible of lips, fluent. It was distinctly not an aristocratic mouth. It suggested common speech and common tastes — ruddy tastes — tastes for quantity rather than for quality. His skin, his flesh were also plainly not aristocratic; they lacked that fineness of grain, that finish of surface which are got only by eating the costly, rare, best and best-prepared food. His hair, a partially disordered mop overhanging his brow at the middle, gave him fierceness of aspect. The old lady had more than a suspicion that the ferocity of that lock of hair and somewhat exaggerated forward thrust of the jaw were pose — in part, at least, an effort to look the valiant and relentless master of men — perhaps concealing a certain amount of irresolution. Certainly those eyes met hers boldly rather than fearlessly.

She extended her hand. He took it, and with an effort gave it the politician's

squeeze — the squeeze that makes Hiram Hanks and Bill Butts grin delightedly and say to each other: "B'gosh, he ain't lost his axe-handle grip yet, by a
durn sight, has he? — dog-gone him!"

Madam Bowker did not wince, though she felt like it. Instead she smiled — a
faint, derisive smile that made Craig color uncomfortably.

"You young man," said she in her cool, high-bred tones, "you wish to marry
my granddaughter."

Craig was never more afraid nor so impressed in his life. But there was no
upflaming of physical passion, here to betray him into yielding before her as he
had before her granddaughter. "I do not," replied he arrogantly. "Your granddaughter wants to marry me."

Madam Bowker winced in spite of herself. A very sturdy-appearing specimen
of manhood was this before her; she could understand how her granddaughter
might be physically attracted. But that rude accent, that common mouth, those
uncouth clothes, hand-me-downs or near it, that cheap look about the collar,
about the wrists, about the ankles —

"We are absolutely unsuited to each other — in every way," continued Craig.
"I tell her so. But she won't listen to me. The only reason I've come here is to
ask you to take a hand at trying to bring her to her senses." The old lady, recovered from her first shock, gazed at him admiringly. He had completely turned
her flank, and by a movement as swift as it was unexpected. If she opposed the
engagement he could hail her as an ally, could compel her to contribute to her
own granddaughter's public humiliation. On the other hand, if she accepted
the engagement he would have her and Margaret and all the proud Severence
family in the position of humbly seeking alliance with him. Admirable! No
wonder Branch was jealous and the President alarmed. "Your game," said she
pleasantly, "is extremely unkempt, but effective. I congratulate you. I owe you
an apology for having misjudged you."

He gave her a shrewd look. "I know little Latin and less Greek," said he, "but,
'timeo Danaos dona ferentes.' And I've got no game. I'm telling you the straight
truth, and I want you to help save me from Margaret and from myself. I love
the girl. I honestly don't want to make her wretched. I need a sock-darner, a
wash-counter, a pram-pusher, for a wife, as Grant would say, not a dainty piece
of lace embroidery. It would soon be covered with spots and full of holes from
the rough wear I'd give it."

Madam Bowker laughed heartily. "You are — delicious," said she. "You state
the exact situation. Only I don't think Rita is quite so fragile as you fancy. Like
all persons of common origin, Mr. Craig, you exaggerate human differences.
They are not differences of kind, but of degree."

Craig quivered and reddened at "common origin," as Madam Bowker expected and hoped. She had not felt that she was taking a risk in thus hardily ignoring her own origin; Lard had become to her, as to all Washington, an unreality like a shadowy reminiscence of a possible former sojourn on earth. "I see," pursued she, "that I hurt your vanity, by my frankness — "

"Not at all! Not at all!" blustered Joshua, still angrier — as Madam Bowker had calculated.

"Don't misunderstand me," pursued she tranquilly. "I was simply stating a fact without aspersion. It is the more to your credit that you have been able to raise yourself up among us — and so very young! You are not more than forty, are you?"

"Thirty-four," said Craig surlily. He began to feel like a cur that is getting a beating from a hand beyond the reach of its fangs. "I've had a hard life — "

"So I should judge," thrust the old lady with gentle sympathy. It is not necessary to jab violently with a red-hot iron in order to make a deep burn.

"But I am the better for it," continued Craig, eyes flashing and orator lips in action. "And you and your kind — your granddaughter Margaret — would be the better for having faced — for having to face — the realities of life instead of being pampered in luxury and uselessness."

"Then why be resentful?" inquired she. "Why not merely pity us? Why this heat and seeming jealousy?"

"Because I love your granddaughter," replied Craig, the adroit at debate. "It pains, it angers me to see a girl who might have been a useful wife, a good mother, trained and set to such base uses."

The old lady admired his skillful parry. "Let us not discuss that," said she. "We look at life from different points of view. No human being can see beyond his own point of view. Only God sees life as a whole, sees how its seeming inconsistencies and injustices blend into a harmony. Your mistake — pardon an old woman's criticism of experience upon inexperience — your mistake is that you arrogate to yourself divine wisdom and set up a personal opinion as eternal truth."

"That is very well said, admirably said," cried Craig. Madam Bowker would have been better pleased with the compliment had the tone been less gracious and less condescending.

"To return to the main subject," continued she. "Your hesitation about my granddaughter does credit to your manliness and to your sense. I have known marriages between people of different station and rank to turn out well — again — "

"That's the second or third time you've made that insinuation," burst out Craig. "I must protest against it, in the name of my father and mother, in the name of my country, Mrs. Bowker. It is too ridiculous! Who are you that you talk about rank and station? What is Margaret but the daughter of a plain human being of a father, a little richer than mine and so a little nearer opportunities for education? The claims to superiority of some of the titled people on the other side are silly enough when one examines them — the records of knavery and thievery and illegitimacy and insanity. But similar claims over here are laughable at a glance. The reason I hesitate to marry your daughter is not to her credit, or to her parents' credit — or to yours."

Madam Bowker was beside herself with rage at these candid insults, flung at her with all Craig's young energy and in his most effective manner; for his crudeness disappeared when he spoke thus, as the blackness and roughness of the coal vanish in the furnace heat, transforming it into beauty and grace of flames.

"Do I make myself clear?" demanded Craig, his eyes flashing superbly upon her.

"You certainly do," snapped the old lady, her dignity tottering and a very vulgar kind of human wrath showing uglily in her blazing eyes and twitching nose and mouth and fingers.

"Then let us have no more of this caste nonsense," said the young man. "Forbid your granddaughter to marry or to see me. Send or take her away. She will thank you a year from now. My thanks will begin from the moment of release."

"Yes, you have made yourself extremely clear," said Madam Bowker in a suffocating voice. To be thus defied, insulted, outraged, in her own magnificent salon, in her own magnificent presence! "You may be sure you will have no further opportunity to exploit your upstart insolence in my family. Any chance you may have had for the alliance you have so cunningly sought is at an end." And she waved her ebony scepter in dismissal, ringing the bell at the same time.

Craig drew himself up, bowed coldly and haughtily, made his exit in excellent style; no prince of the blood, bred to throne rooms, no teacher of etiquette in a fashionable boarding-school could have done better.

AFTER EMANCIPATION and the end of the Civil War, Washington remained a beacon of hope, particularly for African Americans. During and after the war, Congress initiated legislation that benefited African Americans living in Washington — in education, jobs and salaries, and even transportation. Such social experiments, however, were short-lived. Even before the end of the nineteenth century, the capital was proving to be not a haven for African Americans but, as Paul Laurence Dunbar later wrote, "a hard, white liar." As Mary Church Terrell and others have written, restrictive Jim Crow practices were soon in place and more subtle forms of racial prejudice limited the freedoms and opportunities of black people in Washington. A few African Americans reported social and economic advances and experienced something like the "good life" in Washington (a life Langston Hughes criticized as "bourgeois" and imitative of white culture), but their numbers were limited and restricted to certain areas of the city. Anna Cooper, in her "Reminiscences," recalls the salon life that centered on the Grimké sisters' Dupont Circle home around the turn of the last century. A thriving artistic and commercial center on U Street in Northwest Washington helped bring about the "New Negro" movement and the Harlem Renaissance. Local expression of this movement included short stories, novels, and poetry about the life of African Americans — work by Dunbar, Pauline Elizabeth Hopkins, W. E. B. Du Bois, and Jean Toomer.

(OVERLEAF) M Street School (later known as Dunbar High School), 128 M Street, NW, the first public high school for African Americans in the United States. Reprinted from Allan B. Slauson, *A History of the City of Washington: Its Men and Institutions* (Washington, D.C.: Washington Post, 1903), 140.

ANNA COOPER

Anna Cooper (1858–1964) was born in North Carolina, educated at Oberlin College, taught at the M Street High School in Washington (later Paul Laurence Dunbar High School), and served as its principal before being forced out by supporters of Booker T. Washington. After earning a PhD at the Paris-Sorbonne University, at the age of 67, she served as president of Frelinghuysen University, a night school in the federal city. In 1951, she privately published the autobiographical essay "The Early Years in Washington: Reminiscences of Life with the Grimkés." Beginning with 1887, the essay detailed an era of friendship and salon activities in her home at 1706 Seventeenth St. in Northwest D.C. and around the corner at the Corcoran Street home of her good friends Charlotte Forten Grimké and Francis Grimké, a former slave who, in 1878, became minister at the famous Fifteenth Street Presbyterian Church in Washington. Cooper is best known for her Victorian-era feminist writings, collected in *A Voice from the South* (1892). She also wrote *Legislative Measures Concerning Slavery in the United States: 1787–1850* (1942).

From "The Early Years in Washington: Reminiscences of Life with the Grimkés"

In 1887 I received, unsought, thro the kindly offices of my Alma Mater, an appointment to teach in a Washington High School. About the same time the Grimké Family returned to Washington, after a temporary sojourn in Florida, to resume [the] pastorate of the Fifteenth Street Presbyterian Church here. On the Branch, so to speak, for a year they had quarters in transit on Eleventh street in what was then facetiously called "Quality Row," while I made my home with Dr. and Mrs. Alexander Crummell, who were deep in the anxieties of constructing St. Luke's Church at Fifteenth and Church streets, northwest. In spite of absorbing cares and worries of house hunting and home prospecting for permanent anchorage on both sides, even in that first year we met we knew the meeting to be no chance acquaintanceship. Each saw and realized the "grappling hoops of steel" which clinched and finally stamped with the sacred seal of a permanent friendship the unspoken pledge: *Toute ma vie et au delá*. The very next year I had planted my little North Carolina colony on Seventeenth street where I immediately began, like the proverbial beaver to build a home, not merely a house to shelter the body, but a home to sustain and refresh the mind, a home where friends foregather for interchange of ideas and agreeable association of sympathetic spirits. The Grimkés also soon had their *Lares and Penates* comfortably ensconced on Corcoran street, their books and their pictures, their statues and flowering plants, the things they loved and would enjoy all the more by sharing with others of harmonious tastes and congenial minds. From that day till death began his inroads into that circle of kindred spirits, I can safely say not a week passed for thirty years or more that did not mark the blending of those two homes in planned, systematic and enlightening but pleasurable and progressive intercourse of a cultural and highly stimulating kind. The weekends were something to look forward to, Friday evenings on Corcoran street, Sunday evenings at 1706 Seventeenth street; and I think if there had been some "She-that-must-be-obeyed" to say to me, "If you don't watch your step you can't go to the Grimkés this week," I would have fallen into line pronto.

As may be supposed, it took a pretty stiff course of study to hold us so long. The Friday meets we called the Art Club. We never organized, had no officials, no constitution, no dues. Besides our two families and whoever chanced to be visiting either of them, Dr. Blyden, when on this side of the Atlantic, Richard T. Greener, Mrs. Frederick Douglass (we were too dilettante for the Honorable Frederick), Mrs. John R. Francis, Mrs. John H. Smyth, (known locally as "Smythe-Smith"), wife of the Ex-Minister to Liberia, and a few others met there. We drew no color line, in fact I believe were not conscious of any. Visitors in my home such as Miss Alice M. Bacon of Hampton, Mary Churchill ("David Churchill" the author), when stopping over Sunday were pleased to meet my friends, the Grimkés, who were always in for music on that evening; likewise the denizens of "1706" had the pleasant privilege of meeting many choice New England spirits at Corcoran street on Fridays.

An amusing incident occurred in connection with the presence of Coleridge-Taylor to conduct his "wedding of Hiawatha" given by the Coleridge-Taylor Choral Society at Washington. Naturally and as a matter of course, when not busy with rehearsals, he made himself very much at home both with the Corcoran street coterie and with our circle on Seventeenth street. In fact, in a way, I may say I was responsible for his making the trip to Washington, and had to put forth no lion-hunting wiles to have him meet my friends when he came.

It happened this way. In the summer of 1900 I was on the program to speak in Westminster Hall at a Conference in London. Coleridge-Taylor furnished the music for that program, and afterwards he and his wife invited me to attend as their guest a presentation of "Hiawatha" in Alexandra Palace, at which time he received the greatest ovation my small-town "colored" experience had ever read or dreamed of. Mrs. Coleridge-Taylor took me at once right to her heart, and immediately began planning to come to "the States." I saw that she was just at the stage of love's lunacy, when you yearn for the sacrificial altar to prove by dying the undying attachment of conjugal devotion. I approved Mr. Taylor's coming but strongly opposed her making the trip with him. She argued. She knew all about the prejudice "over there." She "wouldn't mind it a'tall." She was sure that where Mr. Taylor went she would be only too happy to go. I argued that, however becoming the martyr's crown might be upon her pretty head, her friends should not be subjected to the pain of seeing it there; that what she knew about prejudice on the other side of hearsay, to moil through it was quite another thing. My argument finally prevailed, and Mr. Taylor came alone to "shed his sweetness" quite generously on "colored" America. Some whites bravely attended the concert given in a "colored" church. The Marine Band rehearsed faithfully under his baton and took orders quite meekly from the little brown Englishman. Not a ripple on the surface. The last goodbyes were said; colored Washington and neighboring boroughs were gloating over the triumph "for the Race." But Mr. White Man rarely gets left for long — that is, if he can get near enough to bribe the conductor and maul the engineer. As a few of us learned afterwards, a committee of "Bokkras" quietly boarded the train at Union Station, rode with Mr. Taylor as far as Philadelphia, brought him back as their guest, and banqueted him at the Shoreham! We were not invited. It was never noted in the papers, and we were left to imagine our friend at the time already en route to his native heath in Bonnie England. When we learned the truth, we had no regrets. Short'nin' bread fills the hungry soul more completely than caviar and champagne, and what is more to the point it leaves no hangover for the morning after.

I wish I could find in the English language a word to express the rest, the stimulating, eager sense of pleasurable growth of those days — eight to ten p.m. Fridays regularly at Corcoran street, Sundays at "1706" the same hours. The word study (Latin: *studere*) connotes zealous striving, suggests a teacher, competition, percentage marks, school, and inevitably some sort of promotion or reward of merit card at the end; and there is always an end to that sort of thing. You want it, and work for it, and hope for it. But here was just growth with the sheer joy of growing, — conscious, satisfying, complete, each hour of energized happiness sufficient unto itself, expecting no end and desiring none. Like the Tree that looks at God all day and lifts its leafy arms to pray, or the lowly cabbage that roots its way in the luscious bosom of mother earth and does no more than "head up," reveling all the time in the process. Here was activity, planned and purposeful, strenuous but joyous, not hunger-driven animal action to appease wants, rather spirit-driven by the inner spur and need for life — the more abundant life. Perhaps, in the way we went at it we may catch a figure from the war horse, quivering for the fray, with the smell of battle dilating his nostrils, the certainty of conflict sending quickening thrills into his hoofbeats. Or better still, perhaps, the Atlantean swimmer buffeting angry billows with affectionate strokes of leg and arm, rejoicing in the strength of the Universe as he feels it surge thro his tingling veins with every impact of the salt sea waves. . . .

PAUL LAURENCE DUNBAR

A well-known dialect poet and lyricist, Paul Laurence Dunbar (1872–1906) won praise for his command of the language and folk culture of African Americans but was sometimes faulted for continuing the old stereotypes of the "happy Negro." The only black graduate in his high school class in Dayton, Ohio, he was a precocious, prolific writer who published a dozen volumes of poetry and several more of fiction, including *The Strength of Gideon and Other Stories* (1900) during his short lifetime. "Mr. Cornelius Johnson, Office-Seeker," which portrays Washington as a Vanity Fair, is taken from this volume. (Another story from this collection, "A Council of State," concerns political infighting and deal making.) In 1898, Dunbar married Alice Ruth Moore, the future Alice Dunbar Nelson, a young teacher, writer, and activist, and moved to Washington, where he worked at the Library of Congress until tuberculosis forced him to quit.

Mr. Cornelius Johnson, Office-Seeker

It was a beautiful day in balmy May and the sun shone pleasantly on Mr. Cornelius Johnson's very spruce Prince Albert suit of gray as he alighted from the train in Washington. He cast his eyes about him, and then gave a sigh of relief and satisfaction as he took his bag from the porter and started for the gate. As he went along, he looked with splendid complacency upon the less fortunate mortals who were streaming out of the day coaches. It was a Pullman sleeper on which he had come in. Out on the pavement he hailed a cab, and giving the driver the address of a hotel, stepped in and was rolled away. Be it said that he had cautiously inquired about the hotel first and found that he could be accommodated there.

As he leaned back in the vehicle and allowed his eyes to roam over the streets, there was an air of distinct prosperity about him. It was in evidence from the tips of his ample patent-leather shoes to the crown of the soft felt hat that sat rakishly upon his head. His entrance into Washington had been long premeditated, and he had got himself up accordingly.

It was not such an imposing structure as he had fondly imagined, before which the cab stopped and set Mr. Johnson down. But then he reflected that it was about the only house where he could find accommodation at all, and he was content. In Alabama one learns to be philosophical. It is good to be philosophical when the proprietor of a cafe fumbles vaguely around in the region of his hip pocket and insinuates that he doesn't want one's custom. But the visitor's ardor was not cooled for all that. He signed the register with a flourish, and bestowed a liberal fee upon the shabby boy who carried his bag to his room.

"Look here, boy," he said, "I am expecting some callers soon. If they come, just send them right up to my room. You take good care of me and look sharp when I ring and you'll not lose anything."

Mr. Cornelius Johnson always spoke in a large and important tone. He said the simplest thing with an air so impressive as to give it the character of a pronouncement. Indeed, his voice naturally was round, mellifluous and persuasive. He carried himself always as if he were passing under his own triumphal arch. Perhaps, more than anything else, it was these qualities of speech and bearing that had made him invaluable on the stump in the recent campaign in Alabama. Whatever it was that held the secret of his power, the man and principles for which he had labored triumphed, and he had come to Washington to reap his reward. He had been assured that his services would not be forgotten, and it was no intention of his that they should be.

After a while he left his room and went out, returning later with several gentlemen from the South and a Washington man. There is some freemasonry among these office-seekers in Washington that throws them inevitably together. The men with whom he returned were such characters as the press would designate as "old wheelhorses" or "pillars of the party." They all adjourned to the bar, where they had something at their host's expense. Then they repaired to his room, whence for the ensuing two hours the bell and the bellboy were kept briskly going.

The gentleman from Alabama was in his glory. His gestures as he held forth were those of a gracious and condescending prince. It was his first visit to the city, and he said to the Washington man: "I tell you, sir, you've got a mighty fine town here. Of course, there's no opportunity for anything like local pride, because it's the outsiders, or the whole country, rather, that makes it what it is, but that's nothing. It's a fine town, and I'm right sorry that I can't stay longer."

"How long do you expect to be with us, Professor?" inquired Mr. Toliver, the horse who had bent his force to the party wheel in the Georgia ruts.

"Oh, about ten days, I reckon, at the furthest. I want to spend some time sightseeing. I'll drop in on the Congressman from my district to-morrow, and call a little later on the President."

"Uh, huh!" said Mr. Toliver. He had been in the city for some time.

"Yes, sir, I want to get through with my little matter and get back home.

I'm not asking for much, and I don't anticipate any trouble in securing what I desire. You see, it's just like this, there's no way for them to refuse us. And if any one deserves the good things at the hands of the administration, who more than we old campaigners who have been helping the party through its fights from the time that we had our first votes?"

"Who, indeed?" said the Washington man.

"I tell you, gentlemen, the administration is no fool. It knows that we hold the colored vote down there in our vest pockets and it ain't going to turn us down."

"No, of course not, but sometimes there are delays — "

"Delays, to be sure, where a man doesn't know how to go about the matter. The thing to do is to go right to the center of authority at once. Don't you see?"

"Certainly, certainly," chorused the other gentlemen.

Before going, the Washington man suggested that the new-comer join them that evening and see something of society at the capital. "You know," he said, "that outside of New Orleans, Washington is the only town in the country that has any colored society to speak of, and I feel that you distinguished men from different sections of the country owe it to our people that they should be allowed to see you. It would be an inspiration to them."

So the matter was settled, and promptly at 8:30 o'clock Mr. Cornelius Johnson joined his friends at the door of his hotel. The gray Prince Albert was scrupulously buttoned about his form, and a shiny top hat replaced the felt of the afternoon. Thus clad, he went forth into society, where he need be followed only long enough to note the magnificence of his manners and the enthusiasm of his reception when he was introduced as Prof. Cornelius Johnson, of Alabama, in a tone which insinuated that he was the only really great man his state had produced.

It might also be stated as an effect of this excursion into Vanity Fair, that when he woke the next morning he was in some doubt as to whether he should visit his Congressman or send for that individual to call upon him. He had felt the subtle flattery of attention from that section of colored society which imitates — only imitates, it is true, but better than any other, copies — the kindnesses and cruelties, the niceties and deceits, of its white prototype. And for the time, like a man in a fog, he had lost his sense of proportion and perspective. But habit finally triumphed and he called upon the Congressman, only to be met by an under-secretary who told him that his superior was too busy to see him that morning.

"But — "

"Too busy," repeated the secretary.

Mr. Johnson drew himself up and said: "Tell Congressman Barker that

Mr. Johnson, Mr. Cornelius Johnson, of Alabama, desires to see him. I think he will see me."

"Well, I can take your message," said the clerk, doggedly, "but I tell you now it won't do you any good. He won't see any one."

But, in a few moments an inner door opened and the young man came out followed by the desired one. Mr. Johnson couldn't resist the temptation to let his eyes rest on the underling in a momentary glance of triumph as Congressman Barker hurried up to him, saying: "Why, why, Cornelius, how'do? how'do? Ah, you came about that little matter, didn't you? Well, well, I haven't forgotten you; I haven't forgotten you."

The colored man opened his mouth to speak, but the other checked him and went on: "I'm sorry, but I'm in a great hurry now. I'm compelled to leave town to-day, much against my will, but I shall be back in a week; come around and see me then. Always glad to see you, you know. Sorry I'm so busy now; good-morning, good-morning."

Mr. Johnson allowed himself to be politely, but decidedly, guided to the door. The triumph died out of his face as the reluctant good-morning fell from his lips. As he walked away, he tried to look upon the matter philosophically. He tried to reason with himself — to prove to his own consciousness that the Congressman was very busy and could not give the time that morning. He wanted to make himself believe that he had not been slighted or treated with scant ceremony. But, try as he would, he continued to feel an obstinate, nasty sting that would not let him rest, nor forget his reception. His pride was hurt. The thought came to him to go at once to the President, but he had experience enough to know that such a visit would be vain until he had seen the dispenser of patronage for his district. Thus, there was nothing for him to do but to wait the necessary week. A whole week! His brow knitted as he thought of it.

In the course of these cogitations, his walk brought him to his hotel, where he found his friends of the night before awaiting him. He tried to put on a cheerful face. But his disappointment and humiliation showed through his smile, as the hollows and bones through the skin of a cadaver.

"Well, what luck?" asked Mr. Toliver, cheerfully.

"Are we to congratulate you?" put in Mr. Perry.

"Not yet, not yet, gentlemen. I have not seen the President yet. The fact is — ahem — my Congressman is out of town."

He was not used to evasions of this kind, and he stammered slightly and his yellow face turned brick-red with shame.

"It is most annoying," he went on, "most annoying. Mr. Barker won't be back for a week, and I don't want to call on the President until I have had a talk with him."

"Certainly not," said Mr. Toliver, blandly. "There will be delays." This was not his first pilgrimage to Mecca.

Mr. Johnson looked at him gratefully. "Oh, yes; of course, delays," he assented; "most natural. Have something."

At the end of the appointed time, the office-seeker went again to see the Congressman. This time he was admitted without question, and got the chance to state his wants. But somehow there seemed to be innumerable obstacles in the way. There were certain other men whose wishes had to be consulted; the leader of one of the party factions, who, for the sake of harmony, had to be appeased. Of course, Mr. Johnson's worth was fully recognized, and he would be rewarded according to his deserts. His interests would be looked after. He should drop in again in a day or two. It took time, of course, it took time.

Mr. Johnson left the office unnerved by his disappointment. He had thought it would be easy to come up to Washington, claim and get what he wanted, and, after a glance at the town, hurry back to his home and his honors. It had all seemed so easy — before election; but now —

A vague doubt began to creep into his mind that turned him sick at heart. He knew how they had cheated Davis, of Louisiana. He had heard how they had once kept Brotherton, of Texas — a man who had spent all his life in the service of his party — waiting clear through a whole administration, at the end of which the opposite party had come into power. All the stories of disappointment and disaster that he had ever heard came back to him, and he began to wonder if some one of these things was going to happen to him.

Every other day for the next two weeks he called upon Barker, but always with the same result. Nothing was clear yet, until one day the bland legislator told him that considerations of expediency had compelled them to give the place he was asking for to another man.

"But what am I to do?" asked the helpless man.

"Oh, you just bide your time. I'll look out for you. Never fear."

Until now, Johnson had ignored the gentle hints of his friend, Mr. Toliver, about a boarding-house being more convenient than a hotel. Now he asked him if there was a room vacant where he was staying, and finding that there was, he had his things moved thither at once. He felt the change keenly, and although no one really paid any attention to it, he believed that all Washington must have seen it, and hailed it as the first step in his degradation.

For a while the two together made occasional excursions to a glittering palace down the street, but when the money had grown lower and lower Mr. Toliver had the knack of bringing "a little something" to their rooms without a loss of dignity. In fact, it was in these hours with the old man, over a pipe and a bit of something, that Johnson was most nearly cheerful. Hitch after hitch had occurred in his plans, and day after day he had come home unsuccessful and discouraged. The crowning disappointment, though, came when, after a long session that lasted even up into the hot days of summer, Congress adjourned and his one hope went away. Johnson saw him just before his departure, and listened ruefully as he said: "I tell you, Cornelius, now, you'd better go on home, get back to your business and come again next year. The clouds of battle will be somewhat dispelled by then and we can see clearer what to do. It was too early this year. We were too near the fight still, and there were party wounds to be bound up and little factional sores that had to be healed. But next year, Cornelius, next year we'll see what we can do for you."

His constituent did not tell him that even if his pride would let him go back home a disappointed applicant, he had not the means wherewith to go. He did not tell him that he was trying to keep up appearances and hide the truth from his wife, who, with their two children, waited and hoped for him at home.

When he went home that night, Mr. Toliver saw instantly that things had gone wrong with him. But here the tact and delicacy of the old politician came uppermost and, without trying to draw his story from him — for he already divined the situation too well — he sat for a long time telling the young man stories of the ups and downs of men whom he had known in his long and active life.

They were stories of hardship, deprivation and discouragement. But the old man told them ever with the touch of cheeriness and the note of humor that took away the ghastly hopelessness of some of the pictures. He told them with such feeling and sympathy that Johnson was moved to frankness and told him his own pitiful tale.

Now that he had some one to whom he could open his heart, Johnson himself was no less willing to look the matter in the face, and even during the long summer days, when he had begun to live upon his wardrobe, piece by piece, he still kept up; although some of his pomposity went, along with the Prince Albert coat and the shiny hat. He now wore a shiny coat, and less showy headgear. For a couple of weeks, too, he disappeared, and as he returned with some money, it was fair to presume that he had been at work somewhere, but he could not stay away from the city long.

It was nearing the middle of autumn when Mr. Toliver came home to their rooms one day to find his colleague more disheartened and depressed than he had ever seen him before. He was lying with his head upon his folded arm, and when he looked up there were traces of tears upon his face.

"Why, why, what's the matter now?" asked the old man. "No bad news, I hope."

"Nothing worse than I should have expected," was the choking answer. "It's a letter from my wife. She's sick and one of the babies is down, but"   his voice broke —"she tells me to stay and fight it out. My God, Toliver, I could stand it if she whined or accused me or begged me to come home, but her patient, long-suffering bravery breaks me all up."

Mr. Toliver stood up and folded his arms across his big chest. "She's a brave little woman," he said, gravely. "I wish her husband was as brave a man." Johnson raised his head and arms from the table where they were sprawled, as the old man went on: "The hard conditions of life in our race have taught our women a patience and fortitude which the women of no other race have ever displayed. They have taught the men less, and I am sorry, very sorry. The thing that as much as anything else made the blacks such excellent soldiers in the civil war was their patient endurance of hardship. The softer education of more prosperous days seems to have weakened this quality. The man who quails or weakens in this fight of ours against adverse circumstances would have quailed before — no, he would have run from, an enemy on the field."

"Why, Toliver, your mood inspires me. I feel as I could go forth to battle cheerfully." For the moment, Johnson's old pomposity had returned to him, but in the next, a wave of despondency bore it down. "But that's just it; a body feels as if he could fight if he only had something to fight. But here you strike out and hit — nothing. It's only a contest with time. It's waiting — waiting — waiting!"

"In this case, waiting is fighting."

"Well, even that granted, it matters not how grand his cause, the soldier needs his rations."

"Forage," shot forth the answer like a command.

"Ah, Toliver, that's well enough in good country, but the army of office-seekers has devastated Washington. It has left a track as bare as lay behind Sherman's troopers." Johnson rose more cheerfully. "I'm going to the telegraph office," he said as he went out.

A few days after this, he was again in the best of spirits, for there was money in his pocket.

"What have you been doing?" asked Mr. Toliver.

His friend laughed like a boy. "Something very imprudent, I'm sure you will say. I've mortgaged my little place down home. It did not bring much, but I had to have money for the wife and the children, and to keep me until Congress assembles; then I believe that everything will be all right."

Mr. Toliver's brow clouded and he sighed.

On the reassembling of the two Houses, Congressman Barker was one of the first men in his seat. Mr. Cornelius Johnson went to see him soon.

"What, you here already, Cornelius?" asked the legislator.

"I haven't been away," was the answer.

"Well, you've got the hang-on, and that's what an office-seeker needs. Well, I'll attend to your matter among the very first. I'll visit the President in a day or two."

The listener's heart throbbed hard. After all his waiting; triumph was his at last.

He went home walking on air, and Mr. Toliver rejoiced with him. In a few days came word from Barker: "Your appointment was sent in to-day. I'll rush it through on the other side. Come up to-morrow afternoon."

Cornelius and Mr. Toliver hugged each other.

"It came just in time," said the younger man; "the last of my money was about gone, and I should have had to begin paying off that mortgage with no prospect of ever doing it."

The two had suffered together, and it was fitting that they should be together to receive the news of the long-desired happiness, so arm in arm they sauntered down to the Congressman's office about five o'clock the next afternoon. In honor of the occasion, Mr. Johnson had spent his last dollar in redeeming the gray Prince Albert and the shiny hat. A smile flashed across Barker's face as he noted the change.

"Well, Cornelius," he said, "I'm glad to see you still prosperous-looking, for there were some alleged irregularities in your methods down in Alabama, and the Senate has refused to confirm you. I did all I could for you, but — "

The rest of the sentence was lost, as Mr. Toliver's arms received his friend's fainting form.

"Poor devil!" said the Congressman. "I should have broken it more gently."

Somehow Mr. Toliver got him home and to bed, where for nine weeks he lay wasting under a complete nervous give-down. The little wife and the children came up to nurse him, and the woman's ready industry helped him to such creature comforts as his sickness demanded. Never once did she murmur; never once did her faith in him waver. And when he was well enough to be moved back, it was money that she had earned, increased by what Mr. Toliver, in his generosity of spirit, took from his own narrow means, that paid their second-class fare back to the South.

During the fever-fits of his illness, the wasted politician first begged piteously that they would not send him home unplaced, and then he would break out in the most extravagant and pompous boasts about his position, his Congressman and his influence. When he came to himself, he was silent, morose and bitter. Only once did he melt. It was when he held Mr. Toliver's hand and bade him good-bye. Then the tears came into his eyes, and what he would have said was lost among his broken words.

As he stood upon the platform of the car as it moved out, and gazed at the white dome and feathery spires of the city, growing into gray indefiniteness, he ground his teeth, and raising his spent hand, shook it at the receding view. "Damn you! damn you!" he cried. "Damn your deceit, your fair cruelties; damn you, you hard, white liar!"

PAULINE ELIZABETH HOPKINS

Pauline Elizabeth Hopkins (1859–1930) is best known for her magazine fiction and turn-of-the-century novels of black female protest, particularly *Contending Forces: A Romance Illustrative of Negro Life North and South* (1900) and *Hagar's Daughter: A Story of Southern Caste Prejudice* (1901). Educated in Boston, she performed on the stage, worked as a stenographer, and was editor of *Colored American Magazine* until it was taken over in 1904 by proponents of Booker T. Washington. Hopkins's "General Washington: A Christmas Story" (1900) tells the tale of a homeless African American child who experiences raw prejudice but also the timeless miracle of the holiday season.

General Washington: A Christmas Story

I

General Washington did any odd jobs he could find around the Washington market, but his specialty was selling chitlins.

General Washington lived in the very shady atmosphere of Murderer's Bay in the capital city. All that he could remember of father or mother in his ten years of miserable babyhood was that they were frequently absent from the little shanty where they were supposed to live, generally after a protracted spell of drunkenness and bloody quarrels when the police were forced to interfere for the peace of the community. During these absences, the child would drift from one squalid home to another wherever a woman — God save the mark! — would take pity upon the poor waif and throw him a few scraps of food for his starved stomach, or a rag of a shawl, apron or skirt, in winter, to wrap about his attenuated little body.

One night the General's daddy being on a short vacation in the city, came home to supper; and because there was no supper to eat, he occupied himself in beating his wife. After that time, when the officers took him, the General's daddy never returned to his home. The General's mammy? Oh, she died!

General Washington's resources developed rapidly after this. Said resources consisted of a pair of nimble feet dancing the hoe-down, shuffles intricate and dazzling, and the Juba; a strong pair of lungs, a wardrobe limited to a pair of pants originally made for a man, and tied about the ankles with strings, a shirt with one gallows, a vast amount of "brass," and a very, very small amount of nickel. His education was practical: "Ef a corn-dodger costs two cents, an' a fellar hain't got de two cents, how's he gwine ter git do corn-dodger?"

General Washington ranked first among the knights of the pavement. He could shout louder and hit harder than any among them; that was the reason they called him "Buster" and "the General." The General could swear, too; I am sorry to admit it, but the truth must be told.

He uttered an oath when he caught a crowd of small white aristocrats tormenting a kitten. The General landed among them in quick time and commenced knocking heads at a lively rate. Presently he was master of the situation, and marched away triumphantly with the kitten in his arms, followed by stones and other missiles which whirled about him through space from behind the safe shelter of back yards and street corners.

The General took the kitten home. Home was a dry-goods box turned on end and filled with straw for winter. The General was as happy as a lord in summer, but the winter was a trial. The last winter had been a hard one, and Buster called a meeting of the leading members of the gang to consider the advisability of moving farther south for the hard weather.

"'Pears lak to me, fellers, Wash'nton's heap colder'n it uster be, an' I'se mighty onscruplus 'bout stoppin' hyar."

"Bisness am mighty peart," said Teenie, the smallest member of the gang, "s'pose we put off menderin' tell after Chris'mas; Jeemes Henry, fellers, it hain't no Chris'mas fer me outside ob Wash'nton."

"Dat's so, Teenie," came from various members as they sat on the curbing playing an interesting game of craps.

"Den hyar we is tell after Chris'mas, fellers; then dis sonny's gwine ter move, sho, hyar me?"

"De gang's wid yer, Buster; move it is."

It was about a week before Chris'mas, and the weather had been unusually severe.

Probably because misery loves company — nothing could be more miserable than his cat — Buster grew very fond of Tommy. He would cuddle him in his arms every night and listen to his soft purring while he confided all his own hopes and fears to the willing ears of his four-footed companion, occasionally poking his ribs if he showed any signs of sleepiness.

But one night poor Tommy froze to death. Buster didn't — more's the wonder — only his ears and his two big toes. Poor Tommy was thrown off the dock into the Potomac the next morning, while a stream of salt water trickled down his master's dirty face, making visible, for the first time in a year, the yellow hue of his complexion. After that the General hated all flesh and grew morose and cynical.

Just about a week before Tommy's death, Buster met the fairy. Once, before his mammy died, in a spasm of reform she had forced him to go to school, against his better judgment, promising the teacher to go up and "wallop" the General every day if he thought Buster needed it. This gracious offer was declined with thanks. At the end of the week the General left school for his own good and the good of the school. But in that week he learned something about fairies; and so, after she threw him the pinks that she carried in her hand, he called her to himself "the fairy."

Being Christmas week, the General was pretty busy. It was a great sight to see the crowds of people coming and going all day long about the busy market; wagon loads of men, women and children, some carts drawn by horses, but more by mules. Some of the people well-dressed, some scantily clad, but all intent on getting enjoyment out of this their leisure season. This was the season for selling crops and settling the year's account. The store-keepers, too, had prepared their most tempting wares, and the thoroughfares were crowded.

"I 'clare to de Lord, I'se done busted my ol' man, shure," said one woman to another as they paused to exchange greetings outside a store door.

"N'em min'," returned the other, "he'll work fer mo'. Dis is Chris'mas, honey."

"To be sure," answered the first speaker, with a flounce of her ample skirts.

Meanwhile her husband pondered the advisability of purchasing a mule, feeling in his pockets for the price demanded, but finding them nearly empty. The money had been spent on the annual festival.

"Ole mule, I want yer mighty bad, but you'll have to slide dis time; it's Chris'mas, mule."

The wise old mule actually seemed to laugh as he whisked his tail against his bony sides and steadied himself on his three sound legs.

The venders were very busy, and their cries were wonderful for ingenuity of invention to attract trade:

"Hellow, dar, in de cellar, I'se got fresh aggs fer de 'casion; now's yer time fer agg-nogg wid new aggs in it."

There were the stalls, too, kept by venerable aunties and filled with specimens of old-time southern cheer: Coon, corn-pone, possum fat and hominy; there was piles of gingerbread and boiled chestnuts, heaps of walnuts and roasting apples. There were great barrels of cider, not to speak of something stronger. There were terrapin and the persimmon and the chinquapin in close proximity to the succulent viands — chine and spare-rib, sausage and crackling, savory

souvenirs of the fine art of hog-killing. And everywhere were faces of dusky
hue; Washington's great negro population bubbled over in every direction.

The General was peddling chitlins. He had a tub upon his head and was
singing in his strong childish tones:

> "Here's yer chitlins, fresh an' sweet,
> Young hog's chitlins hard to beat,
> Methodis chitlins, jes' been biled,
> Right fresh chitlins, dey ain't spiled,
> Baptis' chitlins by de pound,
> As nice chitlins as ever was foun."

"Hyar, boy, duz yer mean ter say dey is real Baptis' chitlins, sho nuff?"

"Yas, mum."

"How duz you make dat out?"

"De hog raised by Mr. Robberson, a hard-shell Baptis', mum."

"Well, lem-me have two poun's."

"Now," said a solid-looking man as General finished waiting on a crowd
of women and men, "I want some o' de Methodess chitlins you's bin hollerin'
'bout."

"Hyar dey is, ser."

"Take 'em all out o' same tub?"

"Yas, ser. Only dair leetle mo' water on de Baptis' chitlins, an' dey's whiter."

"How you tell 'em?"

"Well, ser, two hog's chitlins in dis tub an one ob de hogs raised by Unc.
Bemis, an' he's a Methodes,' ef dat don't make him a Methodes hog nuthin'
will."

"Weigh me out four pounds, ser."

In an hour's time the General had sold out. Suddenly at his elbow he heard
a voice:

"Boy, I want to talk to you."

The fairy stood beside him. She was a little girl about his own age, well
wrapped in costly velvet and furs; her long, fair hair fell about her like an aure-
ole of glory; a pair of gentle blue eyes set in a sweet, serious face glanced at him
from beneath a jaunty hat with a long curling white feather that rested light
as thistle-down upon the beautiful curly locks. The General could not move
for gazing, and as his wonderment grew his mouth was extended in a grin that
revealed the pearly whiteness of two rows of ivory.

"Boy, shake hands."

The General did not move; how could he?

"Don't you hear me?" asked the fairy, imperiously.

"Yas'm," replied the General meekly. "'Deed, missy, I'se 'tirely too dirty to tech dem clos o' yourn."

Nevertheless he put forth timidly and slowly a small paw begrimed with the dirt of the street. He looked at the hand and then at her; she looked at the hand and then at him. Then their eyes meeting, they laughed the sweet laugh of the free-masonry of childhood.

"I'll excuse you this time, boy," said the fairy, graciously, "but you must remember that I wish you to wash your face and hands when you are to talk with me; and," she added, as though inspired by an afterthought, "it would be well for you to keep them clean at other times, too."

"Yas'm," replied the General.

"What's your name, boy?"

"Gen'r'l Wash'nton," answered Buster, standing at attention as he had seen the police do in the courtroom.

"Well, General, don't you know you've told a story about the chitlins you've just sold?"

"Tol' er story?" queried the General with a knowing look. "Course I got to sell my chitlins ahead ob de oder fellars, or lose my trade."

"Don't you know it's wicked to tell stories?"

"How come so?" asked the General, twisting his bare toes about in his rubbers, and feeling very uncomfortable.

"Because, God says we musn't."

"Who's he?"

The fairy gasped in astonishment. "Don't you know who God is?"

"No'pe; never seed him. Do he live in Wash'nton?"

"Why, God is your Heavenly Father, and Christ was His son. He was born on Christmas Day a long time ago. When He grew a man, wicked men nailed Him to the cross and killed Him. Then He went to heaven, and we'll all live with Him some day if we are good before we die. O I love Him; and you must love Him, too, General."

"Now look hyar, missy, you kayn't make this chile b'lieve nufin lak dat."

The fairy went a step nearer the boy in her eagerness:

"It's true; just as true as you live."

"Whar'd you say He lived?"

"In heaven," replied the child, softly.

"What kin' o' place is heaven?"

"Oh, beautiful!"

The General stared at the fairy. He worked his toes faster and faster.

"Say, kin yer hab plenty to eat up dar?"

"O, yes; you'll never be hungry there."

"An' a fire, an' clos?" he queried in suppressed, excited tones.

"Yes, it's all love and plenty when we get to heaven, if we are good here."

"Well, missy, dat's a pow'ful good story, but I'm blamed ef I b'lieve it." The General forgot his politeness in his excitement.

"An' ef it's true, tain't only fer white fo'ks; you won't fin' nary nigger dar."

"But you will; and all I've told you is true. Promise me to come to my house on Christmas morning and see my mother. She'll help you, and she will teach you more about God. Will you come?" she asked eagerly, naming a street and number in the most aristocratic quarter of Washington. "Ask for Fairy, that's me. Say quick; here is my nurse."

The General promised.

"Law, Miss Fairy, honey; come right hyar. I'll tell yer mawmaw how you's done run 'way from me to talk to dis dirty little monkey. Pickin' up sech trash fer ter talk to."

The General stood in a trance of happiness. He did not mind the slurring remarks of the nurse, and refrained from throwing a brick at the buxom lady, which was a sacrifice on his part. All he saw was the glint of golden curls in the winter sunshine, and the tiny hand waving him good-bye.

"An' her name is Fairy! Jes' ter think how I hit it all by my lonesome."

Many times that week the General thought and puzzled over Fairy's words. Then he would sigh:

"Heaven's where God lives. Plenty to eat, warm fire all de time in winter; plenty o' clos', too, but I'se got to be good. 'Spose dat means keepin' my face an' han's clean an' stop swearin' an lyin'. It kayn't be did."

The gang wondered what had come over Buster.

II

The day before Christmas dawned clear and cold. There was snow on the ground. Trade was good, and the General, mindful of the visit next day, had bought a pair of second-hand shoes and a new calico shirt.

"Git onter de dude!" sang one of the gang as he emerged from the privacy of the dry-goods box early Christmas Eve.

The General was a dancer and no mistake. Down at Dutch Dan's place they kept the old-time Southern Christmas moving along in hot time until the dawn of Christmas Day stole softly through the murky atmosphere. Dutch Dan's was the meeting place of the worst characters, white and black, in the capital city. From that vile den issued the twin spirits murder and rapine as the early winter shadows fell, there the criminal entered in the early dawn and was lost to the accusing eye of justice. There was a dance at Dutch Dan's Christmas Eve, and the General was sent for to help amuse the company.

The shed-like room was lighted by oil lamps and flaring pine torches. The center of the apartment was reserved for dancing. At one end the inevitable bar stretched its yawning mouth like a monster awaiting his victims. A long wooden table was built against one side of the room, where the game could be played to suit the taste of the most expert devotee of the fickle goddess.

The room was well filled, early as it was, and the General's entrance was the signal for a shout of welcome. Old Unc' Jasper was tuning his fiddle and blind Remus was drawing sweet chords from an old banjo. They glided softly into the music of the Mobile shuffle. The General began to dance. He was master of the accomplishment. The pigeon-wing, the old buck, the hoe-down and the Juba followed each other in rapid succession. The crowd shouted and cheered and joined in the sport. There was hand-clapping and a rhythmic accompaniment of patting the knees and stamping the feet. The General danced faster and faster:

> "Juba up and juba down,
> Juba all aroun' de town;
> Can't you hyar de juba pat?
> Juba!"

sang the crowd. The General gave fresh graces and new embellishments. Occasionally he added to the interest by yelling, "Ain't dis fin'e!" "Oh, my!" "Now I'm gittin' loose!" "Hol' me, hol' me!"

The crowd went wild with delight.

The child danced until he fell exhausted to the floor. Someone in the crowd "passed the hat." When all had been waited upon the bar-keeper counted up the receipts and divided fair — half to the house and half to the dancer. The fun went on, and the room grew more crowded. General Wash'nton crept under the table and curled himself up like a ball. He was lucky, he told himself sleepily, to have so warm a berth that cold night; and then his heart glowed as he thought of the morrow and Fairy, and wondered if what she had said were true. Heaven must be a fine place if it could beat the floor under the table for comfort and warmth. He slept. The fiddle creaked, the dancers shuffled. Rum went down their throats and wits were befogged. Suddenly the General was wide awake with a start. What was that?

"The family are all away to-night at a dance, and the servants gone home. There's no one there but an old man and a kid. We can be well out of the way before the alarm is given. 'Leven sharp, Doc. And, look here, what's the number agin?"

Buster knew in a moment that mischief was brewing, and he turned over softly on his side, listening mechanically to catch the reply. It came. Buster sat up. He was wide awake then. They had given the street and number where Fairy's home was situated.

III

Senator Tallman was from Maryland. He had owned slaves, fought in the Civil War on the Confederate side, and at its end had been returned to a seat in Congress after reconstruction, with feelings of deeply rooted hatred for the Negro. He openly declared his purpose to oppose their progress in every possible way. His favorite argument was disbelief in God's handiwork as shown in the Negro.

"You argue, suh, that God made 'em. I have my doubts, suh. God made man in His own image, suh, and that being the case, suh, it is clear that he had no hand in creating niggers. A nigger, suh, is the image of nothing but the devil." He also declared in his imperious, haughty, Southern way: "The South is in the saddle, suh, and she will never submit to the degradation of Negro domination; never, suh."

The Senator was a picture of honored age and solid comfort seated in his velvet armchair before the fire of blazing logs in his warm, well-lighted study. His lounging coat was thrown open, revealing its soft silken lining, his feet were thrust into gaily embroidered fur-lined slippers. Upon the baize covered table beside him a silver salver sat holding a decanter, glasses and fragrant mint, for the Senator loved the beguiling sweetness of a mint julep at bedtime. He was writing a speech which in his opinion would bury the blacks too deep for resurrection and settle the Negro question forever. Just now he was idle; the evening paper was folded across his knees; a smile was on his face. He was alone in the grand mansion, for the festivities of the season had begun and the family were gone to enjoy a merry-making at the house of a friend. There was a picture in his mind of Christmas in his old Maryland home in the good old days "befo' de wah," the great ball-room where giggling girls and matrons fair glided in the stately minuet. It was in such a gathering he had met his wife, the beautiful Kate Channing. Ah, the happy time of youth and love! The house was very still; how loud the ticking of the clock sounded. Just then a voice spoke beside his chair:

"Please, sah, I'se Gen'r'l Wash'nton."

The Senator bounded to his feet with an exclamation:

"Eh! Bless my soul, suh; where did you come from?"

"Ef yer please, boss, froo de winder."

The Senator rubbed his eyes and stared hard at the extraordinary figure before him. The Gen'r'l closed the window and then walked up to the fire, warmed himself in front, then turned around and stood with his legs wide apart and his shrewd little gray eyes fixed upon the man before him.

The Senator was speechless for a moment; then he advanced upon the intruder with a roar warranted to make a six-foot man quake in his boots:

"Through the window, you black rascal! Well, I reckon you'll go out through the door, and that in quick time, you little thief."

"Please, boss, it hain't me; it's Jim the crook and de gang from Dutch Dan's."

"Eh!" said the Senator again.

"What's yer cronumter say now, boss? 'Leven is de time fer de perfahmance ter begin. I reckon'd I'd git hyar time nuff fer yer ter call de perlice."

"Boy, do you mean for me to understand that burglars are about to raid my house?" demanded the Senator, a light beginning to dawn upon him.

The General nodded his head: "Dat's it, boss, ef by 'buglers' you means Jim de crook and Dutch Dan."

It was ten minutes of the hour by the Senator's watch. He went to the telephone, rang up the captain of the nearest station, and told him the situation. He took a revolver from a drawer of his desk and advanced toward the waiting figure before the fire.

"Come with me. Keep right straight ahead through that door; if you attempt to run I'll shoot you."

They walked through the silent house to the great entrance doors and there awaited the coming of the police. Silently the officers surrounded the house. Silently they crept up the stairs into the now darkened study. "Eleven" chimed the little silver clock on the mantel. There was the stealthy tread of feet a moment after, whispers, the flash of a dark lantern, — a rush by the officers and a stream of electricity flooded the room.

"It's the nigger did it!" shouted Jim the crook, followed instantly by the sharp crack of a revolver. General Washington felt a burning pain shoot through his breast as he fell unconscious to the floor. It was all over in a moment. The officers congratulated themselves on the capture they had made — a brace of daring criminals badly wanted by the courts.

When the General regained consciousness, he lay upon a soft, white bed in Senator Tallman's house. Christmas morning had dawned, clear, cold and sparkling; upon the air the joy-bells sounded sweet and strong: "Rejoice, your Lord is born." Faintly from the streets came the sound of merry voices: "Chris'mas gift, Chris'mas gift."

The child's eyes wandered aimlessly about the unfamiliar room as if seeking and questioning. They passed the Senator and Fairy, who sat beside him and rested on a copy of Titian's matchless Christ which hung over the mantel. A glorious stream of yellow sunshine fell upon the thorn-crowned Christ.

> "God of Nazareth, see!
> Before a trembling soul
> Unfoldeth like a scroll
> Thy wondrous destiny!"

The General struggled to a sitting position with arms outstretched, then fell back with a joyous, awesome cry:

"It's Him! It's Him!"

"O General," sobbed Fairy, "don't you die, you're going to be happy all the rest of your life. Grandpa says so."

"I was in time, little Missy; I tried mighty hard after I knowed what' dem debbils was a-comin' to."

Fairy sobbed; the Senator wiped his eyeglasses and coughed. The General lay quite still a moment, then turned himself again on his pillow to gaze at the pictured Christ.

"I'm a-gittin sleepy, missy, it's so warm an' comfurtable here. 'Pears lak I feel right happy sence I'se seed Him." The morning light grew brighter. The face of the Messiah looked down as it must have looked when He was transfigured on Tabor's heights. The ugly face of the child wore a strange, sweet beauty. The Senator bent over the quiet figure with a gesture of surprise.

The General had obeyed the call of One whom the winds and waves of stormy human life obey. Buster's Christmas Day was spent in heaven.

For some reason, Senator Tallman never made his great speech against the Negro.

MARY CHURCH TERRELL

Mary Church Terrell (1863–1954) had a long career — much of it in Washington — as an activist, suffragist, speaker, and essayist. Like Anna Cooper, she was educated at Oberlin College and moved to Washington to teach at the famed M Street High School. In 1895, she was appointed to the D.C. Board of Education, the first African American woman in the United States to serve in such a position. Later, she worked as a clerk in the federal War Risk Insurance Bureau. An accomplished speaker, Terrell gave a famous 1906 talk before the United Women's Club of Washington, "What It Means to Be Colored in the Capital of the United States," refuting the popular notion that Washington had become "the Colored Man's Paradise." Integration advances she had seen as a child during Reconstruction had long disappeared by the early twentieth century. A nationally prominent figure, Terrell was a founder of the National Association of Colored Women and a charter member of the National Association for the Advancement of Colored People (NAACP). In 1953, at nearly ninety years of age, she organized and led demonstrations that resulted in the Supreme Court decision ending segregation in Washington, D.C., restaurants. Her autobiography, *A Colored Woman in a White World*, was published in 1940.

From "What It Means to Be Colored in the Capital of the United States"

Washington, D.C., has been called "The Colored Man's Paradise." Whether this sobriquet was given to the national capital in bitter irony by a member of the handicapped race, as he reviewed some of his own persecutions and rebuffs, or whether it was given immediately after the war by an ex-slaveholder who for the first time in his life saw colored people walking about like free men, minus the overseer and his whip, history saith not. It is certain that it would be difficult to find a worse misnomer for Washington than "The Colored Man's Paradise" if so prosaic a consideration as veracity is to determine the appropriateness of a name.

For fifteen years I have resided in Washington, and while it was far from being a paradise for colored people when I first touched these shores, it has been doing its level best ever since to make conditions for us intolerable. As a colored woman I might enter Washington any night, a stranger in a strange land, and walk miles without finding a place to lay my head. Unless I happened to know colored people who live here or ran across a chance acquaintance who could recommend a colored boarding-house to me, I should be obliged to spend the entire night wandering about. Indians, Chinamen, Filipinos, Japanese and representatives of any other dark race can find hotel accommodations, if they can pay for them. The colored man alone is thrust out of the hotels of the national capital like a leper. . . .

As a colored woman I may walk from the Capitol to the White House, ravenously hungry and abundantly supplied with money with which to purchase a meal, without finding a single restaurant in which I would be permitted to take a morsel of food, if it was patronized by white people, unless I were willing to sit behind a screen. As a colored woman I cannot visit the tomb of the Father of this Country, which owes its very existence to the love of freedom in the human heart and which stands for equal opportunity to all, without being forced to sit in the Jim Crow section of an electric car which starts from the very heart of the city — midway between the Capitol and the White House. If I refuse thus to be humiliated, I am cast into jail and forced to pay a fine for violating the Virginia laws....

As a colored woman I may enter more than one white church in Washington without receiving that welcome which as a human being I have a right to expect in the sanctuary of God....

Unless I am willing to engage in a few menial occupations, in which the pay for my services would be very poor, there is no way for me to earn an honest living, if I am not a trained nurse or a dressmaker or can secure a position as a teacher in the public schools, which is exceedingly difficult to do. It matters not what my intellectual attainments may be or how great is the need of the services of a competent person, if I try to enter many of the numerous vocations in which my white sisters are allowed to engage, the door is shut in my face.

From one Washington theater I am excluded altogether. In the remainder certain seats are set aside for colored people, and it is almost impossible to secure others....

With the exception of the Catholic University, there is not a single white college in the national capital to which colored people are admitted.... A few years ago the Columbian Law School admitted colored students, but in deference to the Southern white students the authorities have decided to exclude them altogether.

Some time ago a young woman who had already attracted some attention in the literary world by her volume of short-stories answered an advertisement which appeared in a Washington newspaper, which called for the services of a skilled stenographer and expert typewriter.... The applicants were requested to send specimens of their work and answer certain questions concerning their experience and their speed before they called in person. In reply to her application the young colored woman ... received a letter from the firm stating that her references and experience were the most satisfactory that had been sent and requesting her to call. When she presented herself there was some doubt in the mind of the man to whom she was directed concerning her racial pedigree, so he asked her point-blank whether she was colored or white. When she confessed the truth the merchant expressed ... deep regret that he could not avail himself of the services of so competent a person, but frankly admitted that employing a colored woman in his establishment in any except a menial position was simply out of the question....

Not only can colored women secure no employment in the Washington stores, department and otherwise, except as menials, and such positions, of course, are few, but even as customers they are not infrequently treated with discourtesy both by the clerks and the proprietor himself....

Although white and colored teachers are under the same Board of Education, and the system for the children of both races is said to be uniform, prejudice against the colored teachers in the public schools is manifested in a variety of ways. From 1870 to 1900 there was a colored superintendent at the head of the colored schools. During all that time the directors of the cooking, sewing, physical culture, manual training, music and art departments were colored people. Six years ago a change was inaugurated. The colored superintendent was legislated out of office and the directorships, without a single exception, were taken from colored teachers and given to the whites. . . . Now, no matter how competent or superior the colored teachers in our public schools may be, they know that they can never rise to the height of a directorship, can never hope to be more than an assistant and receive the meager salary therefore, unless the present regime is radically changed. . . .

Strenuous efforts are being made to run Jim Crow cars in the national capital. . . . Representative [James T.] Heflin, of Alabama, who introduced a bill providing for Jim Crow street cars in the District of Columbia last winter, has just received a letter from the president of the East Brookland Citizens Association "indorsing the movement for separate street cars and sincerely hoping that you will be successful in getting this enacted into a law as soon as possible." Brookland is a suburb of Washington.

The colored laborer's path to a decent livelihood is by no means smooth. Into some of the trades unions here he is admitted, while from others he is excluded altogether. By the union men this is denied, although I am personally acquainted with skilled workmen who tell me they are not admitted into the unions because they are colored. But even when they are allowed to join the unions they frequently derive little benefit, owing to certain tricks of the trade. When the word passes round that help is needed and colored laborers apply, they are often told by the union officials that they have secured all the men they needed, because the places are reserved for white men, until they have been provided with jobs, and colored men must remain idle, unless the supply of white men is too small. . . .

And so I might go on citing instance after instance to show the variety of ways in which our people are sacrificed on the altar of prejudice in the capital of the United States and how almost insurmountable are the obstacles which block our paths to success. . . .

It is impossible for any white person in the United States, no matter how sympathetic and broadminded, to realize what life would mean to him if his incentive to effort were suddenly snatched away. To the lack of incentive to effort, which is the awful shadow under which we live, may be traced the wreck and ruin of scores of colored youth. And surely nowhere in the world do oppression and persecution based solely on the color of the skin appear more hateful and hideous than in the capital of the United States, because the chasm between the principles upon which this Government was founded, in which it still professes to believe, and those which are daily practiced under the protection of the flag, yawns so wide and deep.

W. E. B. DU BOIS

William Edward Burghardt Du Bois (1868–1963) never lived in Washington but visited often on business, worked as a consultant for the Bureau of Labor Statistics and other federal agencies, and wrote on a wide range of national policy issues of interest to people in all three branches of government. By the 1930s he had lost faith in the government as the solution to the "problem of the color line" and saw it instead as the source of the problem, nationally and internationally. In 1951, as a result of his work with the Peace Information Center, he was indicted and tried by the Justice Department (the judge later dismissed the charges) as an unregistered agent of a foreign power (i.e., a Communist), an experience he recounted in his autobiographical *In Battle for Peace* (1952). His first novel, *The Quest of the Silver Fleece* (1911), excerpted here, is an economic study that moves between Alabama and Washington, D.C. A late novel and the first volume in *The Black Flame* trilogy, *The Ordeal of Mansart* (1957) focuses on African American migration within the South. It includes a fictionalized account of a White House visit by Du Bois's earlier antagonist, Booker T. Washington, with President Teddy Roosevelt.

From "Miss Caroline Wynn"
In *The Quest of the Silver Fleece*

Bles Alwyn was seated in the anteroom of Senator Smith's office in Washington. The Senator had not come in yet, and there were others waiting, too.

The young man sat in a corner, dreaming. Washington was his first great city, and it seemed a never-ending delight — the streets, the buildings, the crowds; the shops, and lights, and noise; the kaleidoscopic panorama of a world's doing, the myriad forms and faces, the talk and laughter of men. It was all wonderful magic to the country boy, and he stretched his arms and filled his lungs and cried: "Here I shall live!"

Especially was he attracted by his own people. They seemed transformed, revivified, changed. Some might be mistaken for field hands on a holiday — but not many. Others he did not recognize — they seemed strange and alien — sharper, quicker, and at once more overbearing and more unscrupulous.

There were yet others — and at the sight of these Bles stood straighter and breathed like a man. They were well dressed, and well appearing men and women, who walked upright and looked one in the eye, and seemed like persons of affairs and money. They had arrived — they were men — they filled his mind's ideal — he felt like going up to them and grasping their hands and saying, "At last, brother!" Ah, it was good to find one's dreams, walking in the light, in flesh and blood. Continually such thoughts were surging through his brain, and they were rioting through it again as he sat waiting in Senator Smith's office.

The Senator was late this morning; when he came in he glanced at the morning paper before looking over his mail and the list of his callers. "Do fools like the American people deserve salvation?" he sneered, holding off the headlines and glancing at them.

"'League Beats Trust.' . . . 'Farmers of South Smash Effort to Bear Market . . . Send Cotton to Twelve Cents . . . Common People Triumph.'

"A man is induced to bite off his own nose and then to sing a paean of victory. It's nauseating — senseless. There is no earthly use striving for such blockheads; they'd crucify any Saviour." Thus half consciously Senator Smith salved his conscience, while he extracted a certificate of deposit for fifty thousand dollars from his New York mail. He thrust it aside from his secretary's view and looked at his list as he rang the bell: there was Representative Todd, and somebody named Alwyn — nobody of importance. Easterly was due in a half-hour. He would get rid of Todd meantime.

"Poor Todd," he mused; "a lamb for the slaughter."

But he patiently listened to him plead for party support and influence for his bill to prohibit gambling in futures.

"I was warned that it was useless to see you, Senator Smith, but I would come. I believe in you. Frankly, there is a strong group of your old friends and followers forming against you; they met only last night, but I did not go. Won't you take a stand on some of these progressive matters — this bill, or the Child Labor movement, or Low Tariff legislation?"

Mr. Smith listened but shook his head.

"When the time comes," he announced deliberately, "I shall have something to say on several of these matters. At present I can only say that I cannot support this bill," and Mr. Todd was ushered out. He met Mr. Easterly coming in and greeted him effusively. He knew him only as a rich philanthropist, who had helped the Neighborhood Guild in Washington — one of Todd's hobbies.

Easterly greeted Smith quietly.

"Got my letter?"

"Yes."

"Here are the three bills. You will go on the Finance Committee to-morrow; Sumdrich is chairman by courtesy, but you'll have the real power. Put the Child Labor Bill first, and we'll work the press. The Tariff will take most of the session, of course. We'll put the cotton inspection bill through in the last days of the session — see? I'm manoeuvring to get the Southern Congressmen into line. . . . Oh, one thing. Thompson says he's a little worried about the Negroes; says there's something more than froth in the talk of a bolt in the Northern Negro vote. We may have to give them a little extra money and a few more minor offices than usual. Talk with Thompson; the Negroes are sweet on you and he's going to be the new chairman of the campaign, you know. Ever met him?"

"Yes."

"Well — so long."

"Just a moment," the statesman stayed the financier.

"Todd just let fall something of a combination against us in Congress — know anything of it?"

"Not definitely; I heard some rumors. Better see if you can run it down. Well, I must hurry — good day."

While Bles Alwyn in the outer office was waiting and musing, a lady came in. Out of the corner of his eye he caught the curve of her gown, and as she seated herself beside him, the suggestion of a faint perfume. A vague resentment rose in him. Colored women would look as well as that, he argued, with the clothes and wealth and training. He paused, however, in his thought: he did not want them like the whites — so cold and formal and precise, without heart or marrow. He started up, for the secretary was speaking to him.

"Are you the — er — the man who had a letter to the Senator?"

"Yes, sir."

"Let me see it. Oh, yes — he will see you in a moment."

Bles was returning the letter to his pocket when he heard a voice almost at his ear.

"I beg your pardon — "

He turned and started. It was the lady next to him, and she was colored! Not extremely colored, but undoubtedly colored, with waving black hair, light brown skin, and the fuller facial curving of the darker world. And yet Bles was surprised, for everything else about her — her voice, her bearing, the set of her gown, her gloves and shoes, the whole impression was — Bles hesitated for a word — well, "white."

"Yes — yes, ma'am," he stammered, becoming suddenly conscious that the

lady had now a second time asked him if he was acquainted with Senator Smith.
"That is, ma'am," — why was he saying " ma'am," like a child or a servant? —
"I know his sister and have a letter for him."

"Do you live in Washington?" she inquired.

"No — but I want to. I've been trying to get in as a clerk, and I have n't
succeeded yet. That's what I'm going to see Senator Smith about."

"Have you had the civil-service examinations?"

"Yes. I made ninety-three in the examination for a treasury clerkship."

"And no appointment? I see — they are not partial to us there."
Bles was glad to hear her say "us."

She continued after a pause:

"May I venture to ask a favor of you?"

"Certainly," he responded.

"My name is Wynn," lowering her voice slightly and leaning toward him.
"There are so many ahead of me and I am in a hurry to get to my school; but I
must see the Senator — could n't I go in with you? I think I might be of service
in this matter of the examination, and then perhaps I'd get a chance to say a
word for myself."

"I'd be very glad to have you come," said Bles, cordially.

The secretary hesitated a little when the two started in, but Miss Wynn's air
was so quietly assured that he yielded.

Senator Smith looked at the tall, straight black man with his smooth skin
and frank eyes. And for a second time that morning a vision of his own youth
dimmed his eyes. But he spoke coldly:

"Mr. Alwyn, I believe."

"Yes, sir."

"And — "

"My friend, Miss Wynn."

The Senator glanced at Miss Wynn and she bowed demurely. Then he
turned to Alwyn.

"Well, Mr. Alwyn, Washington is a bad place to start in the world."

Bles looked surprised and incredulous. He could conceive of no finer starting-
place, but he said nothing.

"It is a grave," continued the Senator, "of ambitions and ideals. You would
far better go back to Alabama"— pausing and looking at the young man keenly
—"but you won't — you won't — not yet, at any rate." And Bles shook his head
slowly.

"No — well, what can I do for you?"

"I want work — I'll do anything."

"No, you'll do one thing— be a clerk, and then if you have the right stuff in
you you will throw up that job in a year and start again."

"I'd like at least to try it, sir."

"Well, I can't help you much there; that's in civil-service, and you must take the examination."

"I have, sir."

"So? Where, and what mark? "

"In the Treasury Department; I got a mark of ninety-three."

"What! — and no appointment?" The Senator was incredulous.

"No, sir; not yet."

Here Miss Wynn interposed.

"You see, Senator," she said, "civil-service rules are not always impervious to race prejudice."

The Senator frowned.

"Do you mean to intimate that Mr. Alwyn's appointment is held up because he is colored?"

"I do."

"Well — well!" The Senator rang for a clerk.

"Get me the Treasury on the telephone."

In a moment the bell rang.

"I want Mr. Cole. Is that you, Mr. Cole? Good-morning. Have you a young man named Alwyn on your eligible list? What? Yes?" A pause. "Indeed? Well, why has he no appointment? Of course, I know, he's a Negro. Yes, I desire it very much — thank you."

"You'll get an appointment to-morrow morning," and the Senator rose. "How is my sister?" he asked absently.

"She was looking worried, but hopeful of the new endowment when I left." The Senator held out his hand; Bles took it and then remembered.

"Oh, I beg pardon, but Miss Wynn wanted a word on another matter."

The Senator turned to Miss Wynn.

"I am a school-teacher, Senator Smith, and like all the rest of us I am deeply interested in the appointment of the new school-board."

"But you know the district committee attends to those things," said the Senator hastily. "And then, too, I believe there is talk of abolishing the school-board and concentrating power in the hands of the superintendent."

"Precisely," said Miss Wynn. "And I came to tell you, Senator Smith, that the interests which are back of this attack upon the schools are no friends of yours." Miss Wynn extracted from her reticule a typewritten paper.

He took the paper and read it intently. Then he keenly scrutinized the young woman, and she steadily returned his regard.

"How am I to know this is true?"

"Follow it up and see."

He mused.

"Where did you get these facts?" he asked suddenly.

She smiled.

"It is hardly necessary to say."

"And yet," he persisted, "if I were sure of its source I would know my ground better and — my obligation to you would be greater."

She laughed and glanced toward Alwyn. He had moved out of ear-shot and was waiting by the window.

"I am a teacher in the M Street High School," she said, "and we have some intelligent boys there who work their way through."

"Yes," said the Senator.

"Some," continued Miss Wynn, tapping her boot on the carpet, "some — wait on table."

The Senator slowly put the paper in his pocket.

"And now," he said, "Miss Wynn, what can I do for you?"

She looked at him.

"If Judge Haynes is reappointed to the school-board I shall probably continue to teach in the M Street High School," she said slowly.

The Senator made a memorandum and said:

"I shall not forget Miss Wynn — nor her friends." And he bowed, glancing at Alwyn.

The woman contemplated Bles in momentary perplexity, then bowing in turn, left. Bles followed, debating just what he ought to say, how far he might venture to accompany her, what — but she easily settled it all.

"I thank you — good-bye," she said briefly at the door, and was gone. Bles did not know whether to feel relieved or provoked, or disappointed, and by way of compromise felt something of all three.

The next morning he received notice of his appointment to a clerkship in the Treasury Department, at a salary of nine hundred dollars. The sum seemed fabulous and he was in the seventh heaven. For many days the consciousness of wealth, the new duties, the street scenes, and the city life kept him more than busy. He planned to study, and arranged with a professor at Howard University to guide him. He bought an armful of books and a desk, and plunged desperately to work.

Gradually as he became used to the office routine, and in the hours when he was weary of study, he began to find time hanging a little heavily on his hands; indeed — although he would not acknowledge it — he was getting lonesome, homesick, amid the myriad men of a busy city. He argued to himself that this was absurd, and yet he knew that he was longing for human companionship. When he looked about him for fellowship he found himself in a strange dilemma: those black folk in whom he recognized the old sweet-tempered Negro traits, had also looser, uglier manners than he was accustomed to, from which he shrank. The upper classes of Negroes, on the other hand, he still observed from afar; they were strangers not only in acquaintance but because of a curious coldness and aloofness that made them cease to seem his own kind; they seemed almost at times like black white people — strangers in way and thought.

He tried to shake off this feeling but it clung, and at last in sheer desperation, he promised to go out of a night with a fellow clerk who rather boasted of the "people" he knew. He was soon tired of the strange company, and had turned to go home, when he met a newcomer in the doorway.

"Why, hello, Sam! Sam Stillings!" he exclaimed delightedly, and was soon grasping the hand of a slim, well-dressed man of perhaps thirty, with yellow face, curling hair, and shifting eyes.

"Well, of all things, Bles — er — ah — Mr. Alwyn! Thought you were hoeing cotton."

Bles laughed and continued shaking his hand. He was foolishly glad to see the former Cresswell butler, whom he had known but slightly. His face brought back unuttered things that made his heart beat faster and a yearning surge within him.

"I thought you went to Chicago," cried Bles.

"I did, but goin' into politics — having entered the political field, I came here. And you graduated, I suppose, and all that?"

"No," Bles admitted a little sadly, as he told of his coming north, and of Senator Smith's influence. "But — but how are — all?"

Abruptly Sam hooked his arm into Alwyn's and pulled him with him down the street. Stillings was a type. Up from servility and menial service he was struggling to climb to money and power. He was shrewd, willing to stoop to anything in order to win. The very slights and humiliations of prejudice he turned to his advantage. When he learned all the particulars of Alwyn's visit to Senator Smith and his cordial reception he judged it best to keep in touch with this young man, and he forthwith invited Bles to accompany him the next night to the Fifteenth Street Presbyterian Church.

"You'll find the best people there," he said; "the aristocracy. The Treble Clef gives a concert, and everybody that's anybody will be there."

They met again the following evening and proceeded to the church. It was a simple but pleasant auditorium, nearly filled with well-dressed people. During the programme Bles applauded vociferously every number that pleased him, which is to say, every one — and stamped his feet, until he realized that he was attracting considerable attention to himself. Then the entertainment straightway lost all its charm; he grew painfully embarrassed, and for the remainder of the evening was awkwardly self-conscious. When all was over, the audience rose leisurely and stood in little knots and eddies, laughing and talking; many moved forward to say a word to the singers and players. Stillings stepped aside to a group of men, and Bles was left miserably alone. A man came to him, a white-faced man, with slightly curling close gray hair, and high-bred ascetic countenance.

"You are a stranger?" he asked pleasantly, and Bles liked him.

"Yes, sir," he answered, and they fell to talking. He discovered that this was the pastor of the church.

"Do you know no one in town?"

"One or two of my fellow clerks and Mr. Stillings. Oh, yes, I've met Miss Wynn."

"Why, here is Miss Wynn now."

Bles turned. She was right behind him, the centre of a group. She turned, slowly, and smiled.

"Oh!" she uttered twice, but with difference cadence. Then something like amusement lurked a moment in her eye, and she quietly presented Bles to her friends, while Stillings hovered unnoticed in the offing:

"Miss Jones — Mr. Alwyn of — " she paused a second — "Alabama. Miss Taylor — Mr. Alwyn — and," with a backward curving of her neck, "Mr. Teerswell," and so on. Mr. Teerswell was handsome and indolent, with indecision in his face and a cynical voice. In a moment Bles felt the subtle antagonism of the group. He was an intruder. Mr. Teerswell nodded easily and turned away, continuing his conversation with the ladies.

But Miss Wynn was perverse and interrupted. "I saw you enjoyed the concert, Mr. Alwyn," she said, and one of the young ladies rippled audibly. Bles darkened painfully, realizing that these people must have been just behind him. But he answered frankly:

"Yes, I did immensely — I hope I did n't disturb you; you see, I'm not used to hearing such singing."

Mr. Teerswell, compelled to listen, laughed drily.

"Plantation melodies, I suppose, are more your specialty," he said with a slight cadence.

"Yes," said Bles simply. A slight pause ensued.

Then came the surprise of the evening for Bles Alwyn. Even his inexperienced eye could discern that Miss Wynn was very popular, and that most of the men were rivals for her attentions.

"Mr. Alwyn," she said graciously, rising, "I'm going to trouble you to see me to my door; it's only a block. Good-night, all!" she called, but she bowed to Mr. Teerswell.

Miss Wynn placed her hand lightly on Bles's arm, and for a moment he paused. A thrill ran through him as he felt again the weight of a little hand and saw beside him the dark beautiful eyes of a girl. He felt again the warm quiver of her body. Then he awoke to the lighted church and the moving, well-dressed throng. The hand on his arm was not so small; but it was well-gloved, and somehow the fancy struck him that it was a cold hand and not always sympathetic in its touch.

EDWARD CHRISTOPHER WILLIAMS

Edward Christopher Williams (1871–1929) was born in Cleveland to a black father and a white (Irish) mother. He graduated from Case Western Reserve University, where he soon after worked as a librarian. Married to the daughter of author Charles W. Chesnutt, he moved to Washington in 1909 to become the principal of the M Street High School; several years later he was hired by Howard University to teach library science and foreign language. While at Howard, Williams wrote and published plays, short stories, and an anonymous epistolary novel, *When Washington Was in Vogue: A Love Story* (2003). His novel was originally serialized in *The Messenger* in 1925–26, under the title *The Letters of Davy Carr: A True Story of Colored Vanity Fair*. Lost for more than half a century, it was rediscovered in 1994 by a doctoral student, Adam McKible. *When Washington Was in Vogue* tells the story of Davy Carr, a vaguely autobiographical, conservative, older man from the South who takes a room in a bustling middle-class black household in Washington and carries on a budding romance with the young flapper daughter of the house.

From *When Washington Was in Vogue: A Love Story*

Sunday, a.m., October 29, 1922

Dear Bob,

I am happy to note that you survived my last letter. You must be a glutton for punishment to come back for more. While I am not sure I agree with your "diagnosis" concerning my friends, and especially your estimate of Miss Barton, still I am glad that I have succeeded in making you see them somewhat vividly, even if a trifle out of focus. I don't remember all that I wrote about Miss Barton, and, though I admit that one or two of my experiences with her might suggest the flirt, you would have to *see* her for yourself to get a *total* effect which would be reasonably just.

So you like Caroline best? I guess that's because I have written more about her, and I have written more because she is always around, and because she has a rather aggressive — I was about to say "obtrusive" — personality. But, my dearest friend, if you should at any one time see Caroline, and Lillian Barton, and Mary Hale, and Tommie Dawson — not to mention Genevieve and a half dozen others I have met — I'll wager you would have a brainstorm such as you have never experienced. I should give quite a tidy sum to see you in such a pickle.

Last Tuesday I spent the early part of the evening with Don Verney and I tried to get his ideas regarding the present phase of our social life in cities like Washington and New York. His views are certainly interesting, though I am not quite prepared to say that I agree with him completely.

According to Don, we are suffering — and especially those of us who call ourselves the "best people" — with a dreadful "inferiority complex," to use the phrase of the celebrated Dr. Freud. We imitate the white American in everything, except the few points in which he really excels. Indeed, we have a gift for picking the wrong things to imitate. For example, we (our so-called "best people," I mean) have run wild on lavish spending and frivolous pleasures, in the modern American fashion, but we have not learned the art of hard work which underlies these things in the typically American life. Socially we are beginning to imitate the rather "sporty" classes of Americans, such as infest the ordinary summer resorts and are obtrusively present in all places of public entertainment, under the erroneous impression that these people are typical Americans, whereas in fact they are only the parasites who live on the great body of the American social organism. They spend from their superfluity, which has been piled up often through the efforts of generations of toilers, of which this present generation is but the last bitter dregs. Our women spend as much for a gown as a white woman with many times as great resources, and the wives of men with limited salaries feel constrained to make the conspicuous display which in the case of white Americans would be made only by the very rich or by irresponsible women of the underworld, who live but for the hour. Pretty dresses are all very well, and most of us realize their aesthetic and social value, but no middle-class group seems to be justified in any great amount of *display for its own sake*, and quite apart from real needs. For example, during the festivities attendant upon the last inauguration, when there were many elaborate functions given within the space of a few days, one local lady wore five *different* costumes, each one expensive, to five successive dress affairs, and yet her husband is a man living on a salary which, to a white American of the business world, would be moderate indeed. We have the lavishness of Jews, without their acquisitive ability, and the love of pleasure of the tropical races, while trying to compete with the hardest-headed and most energetic people in the world, the Yankee Anglo-Saxon. Since the law does not permit Sunday dances, one hall on You Street advertises dances to begin at midnight Sunday, and last until dawn on Monday, as if an eighteen-hour day is not long enough to satisfy our lust for pleasure. In no *similar* middle-class community among any other race in the world could such performances be made to pay, but the midnight show is a regular institution in colored Washington and New York.

As we talked, I noted Shand's *White and Black* lying on the table. I opened it at the passage in which the author makes one of his characters, an educated colored preacher, rebuke his brethren for wanting to be white, and for wanting only the fairest mulatto or quadroon women for wives.

"What do you think of that statement?" I asked, handing him the open book.

"I guess it's true of too many men in Washington as well as in Texas. There are circles here in which one rarely sees a woman of brown complexion, and the men choose the women, you know. Of course, the reasons and motives back of such a selection are complex. It isn't a mere color prejudice in probably most of the cases, though it is in some, no doubt. In a country with such a hellish system of discrimination, not only in social life, but in employment, in places of public entertainment and service, on railways, ships, in schools, in stores, in courts of law, in the army and navy — in every possible relation of life, in fact — the possibility of approximation to the white type becomes a very practical ideal. Who can blame a man if he wants his children to be as nearly white in appearance as possible, or, at any rate, perhaps more nearly white than he is himself?"

"From a practical viewpoint, certainly no one!" I said. "But what of those who, while living *socially* as colored people, in their desire to be treated as white in public places 'cut' their too palpably colored friends? Do you uphold them?"

"No, I don't!" he answered. "But if I don't uphold them, and if I could not find it in my heart to imitate them, I at least understand. Some of these people are holding government jobs which they would lose if they were known to be colored, so they have to protect themselves. They are, therefore, white downtown and colored uptown, which is a most regrettable situation, whatever the extenuating circumstances. But it is not only those who are dependent on their apparent whiteness for their chance to make a living who do this sort of dodging. There are those who do it merely because they want to be able to pass as white in restaurants, theaters, and stores. Their reason is not quite so good, but after all, they would say, and with some justice, that it is a reason. There is no doubt that, especially in the upper strata of society, and particularly among the women, a very fair skin is regarded as a distinct and indisputable evidence of superiority. Just as the Germans tried — and almost succeeded — in making the French believe that they were a degenerate people, so has white America for the moment succeeded in making some of us feel our inferiority, even though we refuse to admit it. yes, we have — many of us — a distinct inferiority complex!"

"What would you say should be the attitude of those fair enough to 'pass'? Should they never go anywhere where their whiteness will procure them better treatment than would be accorded them if they were known to be colored?"

"No, I should not take such an extreme position. If that were the case, there would be very few places left for us in Washington. My rule is not so far to seek, after all. I go where I please, when the notion strikes me, and in all places where one must pay for what one gets, I accept gladly the best treatment my appearance procures for me. But if by chance any friend or acquaintance comes in whose color clearly indicates his race connection, I make it a point to treat him just as cordially as our previous intimacy would warrant."

When you think it over, that's a pretty good rule. Many more things Don said and many were the illustrations he gave, but I shall not overload this one letter with them. Too much solid food in one meal is a bad thing.

I believe I said in my last that I had not seen Jeffreys for several days. Well, he turned up the other evening a trifle haggard, perhaps, but more dapper and prosperous looking than ever. As Caroline would say, if it's a question of mere clothes, he surely is "the class"! I was in the lower hall talking to Mrs. Rhodes and Caroline when he dropped out of a taxi in front of the door. To the questions as to where he had been, he gave serene and untroubled responses.

"To tell the exact truth," he said, with his widest smile, "I have been to a tailor in Philadelphia. I was getting positively shabby, you know."

If that were the case, he surely brought home clothes enough. He had on a new fur-lined overcoat whose cost would dress an ordinary young fellow for a whole year, and then some, and a diamond ring such as only a champion pugilist or a circus owner might wear. It was easily worth the price of an ordinary automobile. I have noticed before that Jeffreys is very much given to wearing expensive jewelry, especially rings, of which he seems to have a great variety.

Well, he laughed and joked for a few minutes, fished from his bag a five-pound box of Huyler's most expensive candy for Caroline, and ran upstairs where he spent the time before dinner getting straight. I happened to be looking at Caroline as she followed him with her eyes — a steady, half-puzzled, reflective look. She caught me watching her, and blushed, I thought, just a trifle.

Caroline, as I said, is taking evening work at the University in order to make up some needed credits on her college record. She goes to classes every evening but Saturday, all of which does not prevent her from having company after eight-thirty or nine o'clock several nights a week. Very often she comes in with some young chap who has brought her home in his car. She is indeed a popular young lady. But I should hate to have a sister of mine pawed over as she is by these modern youngsters. I heard one of the older men refer to them as cubs, and it's a good name, when one sees them maul the girls around. The whole arrangement between girls and fellows seems to have changed since I came up in a little provincial Southern city. The girls do all the leading, a good deal of the inviting, and more than their share of the wooing, and the boys seem to expect it. When you speak to them, they laugh and say, "Oh, well, this is 1922!" That answer seems to fit almost any situation. While Caroline seems rather independent in most ways, she does let the fellows maul her about too much. I never like to see it. I am not used to it. In my early days a fellow who tried it would get called down pretty fast and pretty hard.

Caroline is taking French and history in her classes, and she often asked my help on some point or other. In fact, she has the habit of coming up to my room to study or write when I am out in the evening, for if she is in her room on the floor below, she is more likely to be disturbed. On the night of Jeffreys's arrival, she came up about nine o'clock, having sent away her escort as soon as she reached home.

"I didn't know you were in," she said. "Would I bother you if I curled up here to study? Genevieve has two or three teacher friends downstairs, and if I am in sight, I can have no peace."

I was busy writing, but I assured her that she was welcome. Before settling herself down, she looked inquiringly at Jeffreys's door.

"Did he look as if he were going out for the evening?" she asked.

When I assured her he did, she stretched out with her book under the wall electric as if relieved, and said no more for some time. After a long while she came over and sat on the arm of my chair, which seems to be her favorite post, and asked me to translate a troublesome passage from her French text. While we looked on the book together, she leaned against me, and put her right arm over my shoulder. It was very sweet and very intimate, but I could give Saint Anthony a few pointers about temptations. When the difficulties had been satisfactorily smoothed out, and she had gone back to her place on the couch, I said, in a teasing mood, "Don't you ever read and study in Mr. Jeffreys's room?"

"No," she answered quickly, looking up at me.

"Why not?" I persisted.

"Because he would not understand."

"Understand what?"

"Well, because he might *misunderstand.*"

"And you think *I won't?*" I continued, taking a sort of malicious satisfaction in cornering her — or rather, trying to corner her.

"No, I *know* you won't."

"But — *why?*"

She smiled at me serenely, and was it indulgently?

"Because Old Grouchy, *you* are *you*."

I checked for a moment. Then I returned to the attack.

"You have only known me a few days, let us say, and yet do you assume that you know me so precisely? Am I so transparent, so shallow as all that? May I not be, for example, a monument of deceit and duplicity? How do you know I am not? I am afraid your conclusions are not entirely flattering to me."

She laughed a merry little laugh, and turned on her elbow to look at me.

"Old Grouchy, I thought you were old and wise. Or are you just trying to draw me out? Well, I have seen transparent water that was not shallow as far as that goes, so your analogy does not hold exactly. More than that, I am by way of being complimentary, but you, like most weak mortals, would rather be thought inscrutably wicked than naively good. And yet you have the nerve to preach to *me!*"

"You're wrong there, little lady. I never *preach* to you!"

"You may call it by another name, but I choose to call it preaching! Of course it is not always expressed orally. You have very eloquent eyes, Old Grouchy, did anyone ever tell you that? You surely can *look* disapproval!"

She laughed, and I laughed, and I dropped the subject as being too personal.

Everyone here is talking about the Thanksgiving Day game between Howard and Lincoln. I suppose you recall how our New York friends tried to persuade us to go to Philadelphia last year. Well, this year's game will be in Washington, and the University folks and the society folks are getting ready for "big doings." The Rhodeses expect a house full of company to judge from the talk downstairs. Caroline is having new dresses made, and I have recently heard her complaining that her fur coat is not "fit to wear to a dogfight," to quote her exact words. If Genevieve is making any preparations, she makes no outward display, but "little sister" is not so reticent. Mrs. Rhodes, usually so cheerful, was complaining today of the high cost of living, which in this particular case means the high cost of clothing. It seems the boy, who, as you may remember is a medical student, must have a new outfit, for his "frat" is turning on some great stunts during Thanksgiving recess. I sympathized with her as one who knew what trouble and expense it is to bring up a boy. Well, have you not given me lots of trouble, old fellow, not to say expense? So using you as my particular burden, I listened to the good lady with the most sympathetic consideration, and thus, I hope, advanced myself several grades in her good graces. And we both know, don't we, Buddie, that it pays — yea, even a thousandfold — to try to please one's landlady!

Just to prove how very right I am in this last assertion, as the upshot of our conversation, I was invited to partake of some very special extra fritters, with "gobs" of butter and some heavenly syrup. Let me tell you, my friend, the Rhodes house is completely appointed for living, from the outermost part of the kitchen porch to the attic door. (As I have never been in the attic, I can't say as to that.) Don't you envy me from the very bottom of your soul? You know you do! I know that third-floor front in Harlem which you inhabit — one could hardly say you *live* there!

But before I forget it — can't you come down to the game? I know I ought not tempt you from the hard path of virtue and devotion to learning which you are now following, but this once won't hurt. We had about decided, had we not, that you were to come Christmas anyway, but I am wondering if you might not enjoy the Thanksgiving festivities more. From what I hear, there will be college folks from everywhere and we are sure to meet many old friends. Think it over, and write me in your next, so that I can have time to make plans.

ALAIN LOCKE

A Harvard graduate and Rhodes Scholar, Alain Locke (1885–1954) went to Washington as a young man to teach philosophy at Howard University and enjoyed a long career there. A prolific scholar, critic, and editor of important collections of African American poetry, plays, art, and music, he was also a centrally important figure in the Harlem Renaissance — Langston Hughes called him one of its "midwives." He nurtured black talent and served as editor of *The New Negro* (1925), a collection containing the work of more than thirty African American writers, all eager to bear witness to a new attitude of racial pride and self-determination. Interestingly, as he explains in his essay, "Beauty and the Provinces," Locke felt that Washington was too provincial and too tied to an outworn form of politics and political change for the revolutionary cultural dynamic he and his collaborators had imagined; whereas New York — with Harlem at its heart — was not. Locke thought it was time for a new paradigm, one where art and human creativity, not politics, would initiate social change.

Beauty and the Provinces

Of the many ways of defining the provinces, after all there is none more reliable than this — capitals are always creative centers, and where living beauty is the provinces are not. Not that capitals are always beautiful, but they are always, at the least, the meccas of the beauty seekers and the workshops of the beauty-makers. Between capital and province, many draw the distinction merely of pomp and power; for them it is where the king lives, where the money barons

thrive, where the beau-monde struts. While this is superficially true, after all
a capital that is not a center of culture is no capital at all, and must look to its
laurels if it cannot buy or borrow sufficient talent to become so. One of the missions of a new metropolis is the quest for genius; it is as inevitable as the passion
of sudden wealth for jewels. In a country like ours that still lives primarily on
borrowed culture, the metropolis becomes the market-place for genius and its
wares, and with its tentacles of trade and traffic captures and holds the prize.

It was those same forces that have made New York the culture-capital of
America, which made Harlem the mecca of the New Negro and the first creative center of the Negro Renaissance. Older centers of what was thought to
be culture resented the parvenu glory of careless, congested, hectic Harlem.
But though many a home-town ached to be robbed of the credit for its village Homer, it was inevitable. It was also just. For oftener than not genius was
starved, despised and even crucified in the home-town, but by the more discern-
ing judgment and quickened sensibilities of the capital was recognized, stimu-
lated, imitated, even though still perhaps half starved. In this way more than
one Negro community has been forced to pay its quota of talent as tribute, and
then smart under the slur of being lumped with the provinces. There has been
only one way out — and that, to compete for creative talent and light a candle
from the central torch. Even the hill towns of Italy, veritable nests of genius, had
to yield first to Florence and then to Rome.

The current cultural development of Negro life has been no exception. But
now as the movement spreads and beauty invades the provinces, it can be told —
at least without offense. Chicago, Philadelphia, Boston, Washington, Nashville,
Atlanta — is this the order, or shall we leave it to the historian? — have in turn
had their awakening after nightmares of envy and self-delusion. For culture, in
last analysis, is a matter not of consumption but of production. It is not a matter
of degrees and diplomas, or even of ability to follow and appreciate. It is the capacity to discover and to create. Thereby came the illusion which has duped so many
who cannot distinguish between dead and living culture, between appreciation
and creativeness, between borrowed spiritual clothes and living beauty — even if
living beauty be a bit more naked.

For the moment, we are all concerned with Washington — that capital of the
nation's body which is not the capital of its mind or soul. That conglomeration
of negro folk which basks in the borrowed satisfactions of white Washington
must some day awake to realize in how limited a degree Washington is the
capital of the nation. A double tragedy, this of the city of magnificent distances,
tragically holding to its bosom the illusion that it is not provincial. In spite of
its title, its coteries, its avenues, it is only a candidate for metropolitan life, a

magnificent body awaiting a soul. And but for the stultification of borrowed illusions, Negro Washington would have realized that it contains more of the elements of an intellectual race capital proportionately than the Washington of political fame and power. It is in its way a greater and more representative aggregation of intellectual and cultural talent. Had this possibility been fully realized by the Washington Negro intelligentsia a decade or so ago, and constructively striven after, Washington would have out-distanced Harlem and won the palm of pioneering instead of having merely yielded a small exodus of genius that went out of the smug city with passports of persecution and returned with visas of metropolitan acclaim.

One may pardonably point with pride — with collective pride and not too ironic satisfaction — to certain exceptions, among them the pioneer work of Howard University in the development of the drama of Negro life and the Negro Theater. Close beside it should be bracketed the faith of which this little magazine is a renewed offshoot — the pioneer foundation at Howard University in 1913 of THE STYLUS, a group for creative writing, with the explicit aim at that comparative early date of building literature and art on the foundation of the folk-roots and the race tradition. Since then over a score of such drama and writing groups have sprung up — the Writers' Guild of New York, Krigwa of New York and elsewhere, the Scribblers of Baltimore, the Gilpins of Cleveland, the Quill Club of Boston, the Philadelphia group that so creditably publishes *Black Opals*, the several Chicago groups from the Ethiopian Folk Theater to the most promising drama group of the present "Cube Theater," the Writers' Guild of Fisk, the Dixwell Group of New Haven, the Ethiopian Guild of Indianapolis, the recently organized Negro company of the Dallas players in far Texas. The very enumeration indicates what has been accomplished in little more than a decade. The provinces are waking up, and a new cult of beauty stirs throughout the land.

But it is not enough merely to have been a pioneer. THE STYLUS and the Howard Players must carry on — vitally, creatively. The University, at least, can be — should be — a living center of culture; both of that culture which is the common academic heritage and of that which alone can vitalize it, the constant conversion of our individual and group experiences in creative thought, and the active distillation of our hearts and minds in beauty and art. The path of progress passes through a series of vital centers whose succession is the most significant line of human advance. A province conscious of its provinciality has its face turned in the right direction, and if it follows through with effort can swerve the line of progress to its very heart.

As he tells in *The Big Sea* (1940), Langston Hughes (1902–1967) traveled to Washington in 1924 to live with his mother, who had recently moved from New York. He viewed Washington, unlike Paris, where he had spent the previous year, as uninviting and socially divided along racial and class lines, a position he spelled out in his bitter indictment of the city's black middle class "Our Wonderful Society: Washington," which appeared in *Opportunity* magazine in 1927. After a series of jobs, he and his mother moved to 1749 S Street in Northwest Washington; in late 1925, he took a job as a busboy in the Wardman Park hotel, where he had a famous breakthrough encounter with the poet Vachel Lindsay, the publicity from which launched his career.

Washington Society
From *The Big Sea*

My mother and kid brother were in Washington. This time, she wrote, she and my step-father had separated for good, and she had decided to come to Washington to live with our cousins there, who belonged to the more intellectual and high-class branch of our family, being direct descendants of Congressman John M. Langston. She asked me to join her. It all sounded risky to me, but I decided to try it. My cousins extended a cordial invitation to come and share their life with them. They were proud of my poems, they said, and would be pleased to have a writer in the house.

By now, I wanted to go back to college, anyhow. And I thought that Howard, in Washington, would be a good place to start, if I could manage to get together the tuition. So I bought a ticket to Washington. The twenty dollars from the *Crisis* would not cover both a ticket and an overcoat, which I needed, so I arrived in Washington with only a sailor's peajacket protecting me from the winter winds. All my shirts were ragged and my trousers frayed. I am sure I did not look like a distinguished poet, when I walked up to my cousin's porch in Washington's Negro society section, LeDroit Park, next door to the famous colored surgeon and heart specialist, Dr. Carson.

Listen, everybody! Never go to live with relatives if you're broke! That is an error. My cousins introduced me as just back from Europe, but they didn't say I came by chipping decks on a freight ship — which seemed to me an essential explanation.

The nice, cultured colored people I met in Washington seemed to think that by just being a poet I could get a dignified job, such as a page boy in the Library of Congress. I thought such a job would be nice, too, so they sent me to see

Mary Church Terrell and some other famous Negro leaders who had political influence. But to be a page boy in the Library of Congress seems to require a tremendous list of qualifications and influential connections, and a great capacity for calling on politicians and race leaders, as well as a vast patience for waiting and waiting. So, being broke, I finally got a job in a wet wash laundry instead.

I had to help unload the wagons, and open the big bags of dirty clothes people send to wet wash laundries. Then I had to sort out and pin the clothes together with numbered pins so that, once washed, they could be reassembled again. I never dreamed human beings sent such dirty clothes to a laundry. But I knew that, as a rule, only very poor people use wet wash laundries. And very poor people cannot afford to be changing clothes every day. Nor every week, either, I guess, from the look of those I handled.

Cultured Washington, I mean cultured colored Washington, who read my poems in the *Crisis*, did not find it fitting and proper that a poet should work in a wet wash laundry. Still, they did nothing much about it. And since none of them had any better jobs to offer me, I stayed there. The laundry at least paid twelve dollars a week.

I spoke with Dean Kelly Miller at Howard University about the possibility of trying for a scholarship at the college. And he spoke grandiloquently about my grand-uncle, who had been the first Dean of the Howard Law School, and what a fine man he was. But it seems that there were no scholarships forthcoming. I spoke with Dr. Alain Locke, who said my poems were about to appear in the New Negro Issue of the *Survey Graphic*, and who declared I was the most racial of the New Negro poets. But he didn't have any scholarships up his sleeve, either.

So I began to try to save a dollar a week toward entering college. But if you ever started out with nothing, maybe you know how hard it is to work up even to an overcoat.

I wanted to return to college mostly in order to get a better background for writing and for understanding the world. I wanted to study sociology and history and psychology, and find out why countries and people were the kind of countries and people they are. . . .

One day my mother came to the laundry, crying. She said she couldn't stay at our cousin's house a minute longer, not one minute! It seems that in some way they had hurt both her pride and her feelings. So I took my lunch hour off to help her find a new place to stay. We located two small rooms on the second floor in an old brick house not far from where I worked. The rooms were furnished, but they had no heat in them, so we bought a second-hand oil stove, which we had to take turns using, carrying it back and forth between my room and my mother's room, since we couldn't afford two oil stoves that winter. . . .

I felt very bad in Washington that winter, so I wrote a great many poems. (I wrote only a few poems in Paris, because I had had such a good time there.) But in Washington I didn't have a good time. I didn't like my job, and I didn't know what was going to happen to me, and I was cold and half-hungry, so I wrote a great many poems. I began to write poems in the manner of the Negro blues and the spirituals.

Seventh Street in Washington was the nearest thing I had known to the South up to that time, never having been in Dixie proper. But Washington is like the South. It has all the prejudices and Jim Crow customs of any Southern town, except that there are no Jim Crow sections on the street cars.

Negro life in Washington is definitely a ghetto life and only in the Negro sections of the city may colored people attend theaters, eat a meal, or drink a Coca-Cola. Strangely undemocratic doings take place in the shadow of "the word's greatest democracy."

In Europe and in Mexico I have lived with white people, worked and eaten and slept with white people, and no one seemed any the worse for it. In New York I have sat beside white people in theaters and movie houses and neither they nor I appeared to suffer. But in Washington I could not see a legitimate stage show, because the theaters would not sell Negroes a ticket. I could not get a cup of coffee on a cold day anywhere within sight of the Capitol, because no "white" restaurant would serve a Negro. I could not see the new motion pictures, because they did not play in the Negro houses.

I asked some of the leading Washington Negroes about this, and they loftily said that they had their own society and their own culture — so I looked around to see what that was like.

To me it did not seem good, for the "better class" Washington colored people, as they called themselves, drew rigid class and color lines within the race against Negroes who worked with their hands, or who were dark in complexion and had no degrees from colleges. These upper class colored people consisted largely of government workers, professors and teachers, doctors, lawyers, and resident politicians. They were on the whole as unbearable and snobbish a group of people as I have ever come in contact with anywhere. They lived in comfortable homes, had fine cars, played bridge, drank Scotch, gave exclusive "formal" parties, and dressed well, but seemed to be altogether lacking in real culture, kindness, or good common sense.

Lots of them held degrees from colleges like Harvard and Dartmouth and Columbia and Radcliffe and Smith, but God knows what they had learned there. They all had the manners and airs of reactionary, ill-bred *nouveaux riches* — except that they were not really rich. Just middle class. And many of them had less fortunate brothers or cousins working as red-caps and porters —

so near was their society standing to that of the poorest Negro. (Their snob-bishness was so precarious, that I suppose for that very reason it had to be dou-bly reinforced.)

To seem people of culture, they performed in an amazing fashion. Perhaps, because I was very young and easily hurt, I remember so well some of the things that happened to me. When Dr. Locke's fine collection of articles, stories, pic-tures, and poems by and about Negroes was published, *The New Negro*, Wash-ington's leading colored literary club decided to honor the "new Negro" writers by inviting them to their annual dinner, a very "formal" event in the city. To represent the younger poets, they invited Countee Cullen and me. Mr. Cullen wrote from New York that he accepted the invitation.

I dropped them a note saying that I could not come, because, among other reasons, I had no dinner clothes to wear to a formal dinner. They assured me that in such a case I could attend their dinner without dinner clothes — just so I would read some of my poems. They also stated that their invitation included my mother, who, they knew, would be proud to see me so honored.

I did not want to go to the dinner, but finally I agreed. On the evening of the dinner, however, I came home from work to find my mother in tears. She had left her job early to get ready to go with me. But about five o'clock, one of the ladies of the committee had telephoned her to say that, after all, she didn't feel it wise for her to come — since it was to be a formal dinner, and perhaps my mother did not possess an evening gown.

We didn't go.

Again, some months later, at the home of a prominent hostess, at a supper for Roland Hayes after his first big Washington concert, I was placed near the end of the table. The lady next to me kept her back turned all the time, talking up the table in the direction of Mr. Hayes. A few days later, however (amusingly enough), I got a note from this lady, saying she was extremely sorry she hadn't known she was sitting next to *Langston* Hughes, the poet, because we could have talked together!

One of the things that amused me in Washington, though, was that with all their conventional-mindedness, a number of the families in the best colored so-ciety made proud boast of being directly descended from the leading Southern white families, "on the colored side" — which, of course, meant the *illegitimate* side. One prominent Negro family tree went straight back to George Washing-ton and his various slave mistresses.

From all this pretentiousness Seventh Street was a sweet relief. Seventh Street is the long, old, dirty street, where the ordinary Negroes hang out, folks with practically no family tree at all, folks who draw no color line between mulattoes and deep dark-browns, folks who work hard for a living with their hands. On

Seventh Street in 1924 they played the blues, ate watermelon, barbecue, and fish sandwiches, shot pool, told tall tales, looked at the dome of the Capitol and laughed out loud. I listened to their blues:

> Did you ever dream lucky —
> Wake up cold in hand?

And I went to their churches and heard the tambourines play and the little tinkling bells of the triangles adorn the gay shouting tunes that sent sisters dancing down the aisles for joy.

I tried to write poems like the songs they sang on Seventh Street — gay songs, because you had to be gay or die; sad songs, because you couldn't help being sad sometimes. But gay or sad, you kept on living and you kept on going. Their songs — those of Seventh Street — had the pulse beat of the people who keep on going.

Like the waves of the sea coming one after another, always one after another, like the earth moving around the sun, night, day — night, day — night, day — forever, so is the undertow of black music with its rhythm that never betrays you, its strength like the beat of the human heart, its humor, and its rooted power.

> I'm goin' down to de railroad, baby,
> Lay ma head on de track.
> I'm goin' down to de railroad, baby,
> Lay ma head on de track —
> But if I see de train a-comin',
> I'm gonna jerk it back.

I liked the barrel houses of Seventh Street, the shouting churches, and the songs. They were warm and kind and didn't care whether you had an overcoat or not.

In one of the little churches one night I saw something that reminded me of my own unfortunate "conversion." A revival had been going full swing since early evening. It was now nearing one o'clock. A sinner, overcome by his guilt, had passed out in front of the mourners' bench and was lying prone on the floor. All the other sinners by now had been brought to Jesus, but this fellow looked distinctly as if he had fallen asleep.

It was a Sanctified Church, so the Saints came and gathered around the prostrate soul in prayer. They prayed and prayed and they sang and sang. But some of the less devout, as the hour grew late, had to get up and go home, leaving the unsaved soul for another day. Others prayed on. Still the man did not rise. He was resting easy. Neither prayer nor song moved him until, finally, one old lady bent down, shook him, and said sternly: "Brother! You get up — 'cause de Saints is getting' tired!"

WORKING IN THE steam of the wet wash laundry that winter, I caught a bad cold, stayed home from work a week — and found my job gone when I went back. So I went to work for a colored newspaper. But I only made eighty cents in two weeks, so I quit the newspaper game. Then an old school friend of my mother's, Amanda Grey Hilyer, who once owned a drug store, spoke to Dr. Carter G. Woodson about me, and Dr. Woodson gave me a job in the offices of the Association for the Study of Negro Life and History as his personal assistant.

My new job paid several dollars more a week than the wet wash laundry. It was what they call in Washington "a position." But it was much harder work than the laundry....

... Although I realized what a fine contribution Dr. Woodson was making to the Negro people and to America, publishing his histories, his studies, and his *Journal of Negro History*, I personally did not like the work I had to do. Besides, it hurt my eyes. So when I got through the proofs, I decided I didn't care to have "a position" any longer, I preferred a job, so I went to work at the Wardman Park Hotel as a bus boy, where meals were thrown in and it was less hard on the sight, although the pay was not quite the same and there was no dignity attached to bus boy work in the eyes of upper class Washingtonians, who kept insisting that a colored poet should be a credit to his race.

But I am glad I went to work at the Wardman Park Hotel, because there I met Vachel Lindsay. Diplomats and cabinet members in the dining room did not excite me much, but I was thrilled the day Vachel Lindsay came. I knew him, because I'd seen his picture in the papers that morning. He was to give a reading of his poems in the little theater of the hotel that night. I wanted very much to hear him read his poems, but I knew they did not admit colored people in the auditorium.

That afternoon I wrote out three of my poems, "Jazzonia," "Negro Dancers," and "The Weary Blues," on some pieces of paper and put them in the pocket of my white bus boy's coat. In the evening when Mr. Lindsay came down to dinner, quickly I laid them beside his plate and went away, afraid to say anything to so famous a poet, except to tell him I liked his poems and that these were poems of mine. I looked back once and saw Mr. Lindsay reading the poems, as I picked up a tray of dirty dishes from a side table and started for the dumb-waiter.

The next morning on the way to work, as usual I bought a paper — and there I read that Vachel Lindsay had discovered a Negro bus boy poet! At the hotel the reporters were already waiting for me. They interviewed me. And they took my picture, holding up a tray of dirty dishes in the middle of the dining room. The picture, copyrighted by Underwood and Underwood, appeared in lots of newspapers throughout the country. It was my first publicity break.

RALPH ELLISON

Ralph Ellison (1914–94) made various trips to Washington, first as a journalist for *New Masses* and *Negro Quarterly*, and then, in his later years, as a trustee or board member for such organizations as the Kennedy Center for the Performing Arts and the National Council on the Arts. From 1940 to the late 1960s, he published several pieces on Washington, D.C. — a report on the third National Negro Congress; a dream-vision about southern congressmen defying the Supreme Court on segregation; and an appreciative account of President Lyndon B. Johnson, "The Myth of the Flawed White Southerner." His *Invisible Man* (1952) is widely considered one of the great novels of the twentieth century. When Ellison died in 1994, he was still working on a long-awaited second novel begun in 1954–55, the posthumously published *Juneteenth* (1999). Set mainly in Washington, *Juneteenth* tells the story of the assassination of a senator, a white man raised as an African American.

From *Juneteenth*

Two days before the shooting a chartered planeload of Southern Negroes swooped down upon the District of Columbia and attempted to see the Senator. They were all quite elderly: old ladies dressed in little white caps and white uniforms made of surplus nylon parachute material, and men dressed in neat but old-fashioned black suits, wearing wide-brimmed, deep-crowned panama hats which, in the Senator's walnut-paneled reception room now, they held with a grave ceremonial air. Solemn, uncommunicative and quietly insistent, they were led by a huge, distinguished-looking old fellow who on the day of the chaotic event was to prove himself, his age notwithstanding, an extraordinarily powerful man. Tall and broad and of an easy dignity, this was the Reverend A. Z. Hickman — better known, as one of the old ladies proudly informed the Senator's secretary, as "God's Trombone."

This, however, was about all they were willing to explain. Forty-four in number, the women with their fans and satchels and picnic baskets, and the men carrying new blue airline take-on bags, they listened intently while Reverend Hickman did their talking.

"Ma'am," Hickman said his voice deep and resonant as he nodded toward the door of the Senator's private office, "you just tell the Senator that Hickman has arrived. When he hears who's out here he'll know that it's important and want to see us."

"But I've told you that the Senator isn't available," the secretary said. "Just what is your business? Who are you, anyway? Are you his constituents?"

"Constituents?" Suddenly the old man smiled. "No, miss," he said, "the Senator doesn't even have anybody like us in *his* state. We're from down where we're among the counted but not among the heard."

"Then why are you coming here?" she said. "What is your business?"

"He'll tell you, ma'am," Hickman said. "He'll know who we are; all you have to do is tell him that we have arrived. . . ."

The secretary, a young Mississippian, sighed. Obviously these were Southern Negroes of a type she had known all her life — and old ones; yet instead of being already in herdlike movement toward the door they were calmly waiting, as though she hadn't said a word. And now she had a suspicion that, for all their staring eyes, she actually didn't exist for them. They just stood there, now looking oddly like a delegation of Asians who had lost their interpreter along the way, and were trying to tell her something which she had no interest in hearing, through this old man who himself did not know the language. Suddenly they no longer seemed familiar, and a feeling of dreamlike incongruity came over her. They were so many that she could no longer see the large abstract paintings hung along the paneled wall, nor the framed facsimiles of State Documents which hung above a bust of Vice-President Calhoun. Some of the old women were calmly plying their palm-leaf fans, as though in serene defiance of the droning air conditioner. Yet she could see no trace of impertinence in their eyes, nor any of the anger which the Senator usually aroused in members of their group. Instead, they seemed resigned, like people embarked upon a difficult journey who were already far beyond the point of no return. Her uneasiness grew; then she blotted out the others by focusing her eyes narrowly upon their leader. And when she spoke again her voice took on a nervous edge.

"I've told you that the Senator isn't here," she said, "and you must realize that he is a busy man who can only see people by appointment. . . ."

"We know, ma'am," Hickman said, "but . . ."

"You don't just walk in here and expect to see him on a minute's notice."

"We understand that, ma'am," Hickman said, looking mildly into her eyes, his close-cut white-head tilted to one side, "but this is something that developed of a sudden. Couldn't you reach him by long distance? We'd pay the charges. And I don't even have to talk, miss; you can do the talking. All you have to say is that we have arrived."

"I'm afraid this is impossible," she said.

The very evenness of the old man's voice made her feel uncomfortably young, and now, deciding that she had exhausted all the tried-and-true techniques her region had worked out (short of violence) for getting quickly rid of Negroes, the secretary lost her patience and telephoned for a guard.

They left as quietly as they had appeared, the old minister waiting behind until the last had stepped into the hall, then turned, and she saw his full height, framed by the doorway, as the others arranged themselves beyond him in the hall. "You're really making a mistake, miss," he said. "The Senator knows us and—"

"*Knows* you," she said indignantly. "I've heard Senator Sunraider state that the only colored he knows is the boy who shines shoes at his golf club."

"Oh?" Hickman shook his head as the others exchanged knowing glances. "Very well, ma'am. We're sorry to have caused you this trouble. It's just that it's very important that the Senator know we're on the scene. So I hope you won't forget to tell him that we have arrived, because soon it might be too late."

There was no threat in it; indeed, his voice echoed the odd sadness which she thought she detected in the faces of the others just before the door blotted them from view.

In the hall they exchanged no words, moving silently behind the guard who accompanied them down to the lobby. They were about to move into the street when the security-minded chief guard observed their number, stepped up, and ordered them searched.

They submitted patiently, amused that anyone should consider them capable of harm, and for the first time an emotion broke the immobility of their faces. They chuckled and winked and smiled, fully aware of the comic aspect of the situation. Here they were, quiet, old, and obviously religious black folk who, because they had attempted to see the man who was considered the most vehement enemy of their people in either house of Congress, were being energetically searched by uniformed security police, and they knew what the absurd outcome would be. They were found to be armed with nothing more dangerous than pieces of fried chicken and ham sandwiches, chocolate cake and sweet-potato fried pies. Some obeyed the guards' commands with exaggerated sprightliness, the old ladies giving their skirts a whirl as they turned in their flat-heeled shoes. When ordered to remove his wide-brimmed hat, one old man held it for the guard to look inside; then, flipping out the sweatband, he gave the crown a tap, causing something to fall to the floor, then waited with a callused palm extended as the guard bent to retrieve it. Straightening and unfolding the object, the guard saw a worn but neatly creased fifty-dollar bill, which he dropped upon the outstretched palm as though it were hot. They watched silently as he looked at the old man and gave a dry, harsh laugh; then as he continued laughing the humor slowly receded behind their eyes. Not until they were allowed to file into the street did they give further voice to their amusement.

"These here folks don't understand nothing," one of the old ladies said. "If we had been the kind to depend on the sword instead of on the Lord, we'd been in our graves long ago — ain't that right, Sis' Arter?"

"You said it," Sister Arter said. "In the grave and done long finished mold'ing!"

"Let them worry, our conscience is clear on that. . . ."

"Amen!"

On the sidewalk now, they stood around Reverend Hickman, holding a hushed conference; then in a few minutes they disappeared in a string of taxis and the incident was thought closed.

Shortly afterwards, however, they appeared mysteriously at a hotel where the Senator leased a private suite, and tried to see him. How they knew of this secret suite they would not explain.

Next they appeared at the editorial offices of the newspaper which was most critical of the Senator's methods, but here too they were turned away. They were taken for a protest group, just one more lot of disgruntled Negroes crying for justice as though theirs were the only grievances in the world. Indeed, they received less of a hearing here than elsewhere. They weren't even questioned as to why they wished to see the Senator — which was poor newspaper work, to say the least; a failure of technical alertness, and, as events were soon to prove, a gross violation of press responsibility.

So once more they moved away.

Although the Senator returned to Washington the following day, his secretary failed to report his strange visitors. There were important interviews scheduled and she had understandably classified the old people as just another annoyance. Once the reception room was cleared of their disquieting presence they seemed no more significant than the heavy mail received from white liberals and Negroes, liberal and reactionary alike, whenever the Senator made one of his taunting remarks. She forgot them. Then at about eleven a.m. Reverend Hickman reappeared without the others and started into the building. This time, however, he was not to reach the secretary. One of the guards, the same who had picked up the fifty-dollar bill, recognized him and pushed him bodily from the building.

Indeed, the old man was handled quite roughly, his sheer weight and bulk and the slow rhythm of his normal movements infuriating the guard to that quick, heated fury which springs up in one when dealing with the unexpected recalcitrance of some inanimate object — the huge stone that resists the bulldozer's power, or the chest of drawers that refuses to budge from its spot on the floor. Nor did the old man's composure help matters. Nor did his passive resistance hide his distaste at having strange hands placed upon his person. As he was being pushed about, old Hickman looked at the guard with a kind of tolerance, an understanding which seemed to remove his personal emotions to some far, cool place where the guard's strength could never reach them. He even managed to pick up his hat from the sidewalk where it had been thrown after him with no great show of breath or hurry, and arose to regard the guard with a serene dignity.

"Son," he said, flicking a spot of dirt from the soft old panama with a white handkerchief, "I'm sorry that this had to happen to you. Here you've worked up a sweat on this hot morning and not a thing has been changed — except that you've interfered with something that doesn't concern you. After all, you're only a guard, you're not a mind-reader. Because if you were, you'd be trying to get me *in* there as fast as you could instead of trying to keep me out. You're probably not even a good guard, and I wonder what on earth you'd do if I came here prepared to make some trouble."

Fortunately, there were too many spectators present for the guard to risk giving the old fellow a demonstration. He was compelled to stand silent, his thumbs hooked over his cartridge belt, while old Hickman strolled — or more accurately, *floated* — up the walk and disappeared around the corner.

Except for two attempts by telephone, once to the Senator's office and later to his home, the group made no further effort until that afternoon, when Hickman sent a telegram asking Senator Sunraider to phone him at a T Street hotel. A message which, thanks again to the secretary, the Senator did not see. Following this attempt there was silence.

During the late afternoon the group of closed-mouthed old folk were seen praying quietly within the Lincoln Memorial. An amateur photographer, a high-school boy from the Bronx, was there at the time and it was his chance photograph of the group, standing facing the great sculpture with bowed heads beneath old Hickman's outspread arms, that was flashed over the wires following the shooting. Asked why he had photographed that particular group, the boy replied that he had seen them as a "good composition. . . . I thought their faces would make a good scale of grays between the whiteness of the marble and the blackness of the shadows." And for the rest of the day the group appears to have faded into those same peaceful shadows, to remain there until the next morning — when they materialized shortly before chaos erupted.

MARIO BENCASTRO

Born in 1949, Mario Bencastro began his professional life as a painter but turned to writing when his home country of El Salvador was plunged into civil war in the late 1970s. His first novel, *A Shot in the Cathedral* (1990), and his first short story collection, *The Tree of Life: Stories of Civil War* (1993), were originally published in Spanish and have since been translated into English. Bencastro also writes for the stage, and since the late 1980s, several of his plays and short stories have been performed locally in Virginia and Washington. *Odyssey to the North* (1998), excerpted here, uses a collage technique to tell an alternating story of Central American immigrants escaping political repression and violence at home, only to encounter other dangerous and difficult conditions in transit across the Mexico-U.S. border and then in the Mount Pleasant section of Washington and elsewhere — racism, street crime, joblessness, and overcrowding. Mario Bencastro currently lives in suburban Virginia; his latest book, *A Promise to Keep*, appeared in 2005.

From *Odyssey to the North*
Translated by Susan Giersbach Rascón

I

"It's going to be a beautiful day here in Washington!" exclaimed the voice on the radio. "Clear blue skies, seventy degrees, sunny with no threat of rain. A perfect spring day!"

Two policemen were making their rounds in the Adams Morgan district, the windows of their patrol car open to receive the cool breeze which caressed the groves of trees in Rock Creek Park, carrying the perfume of the multicolored flowers outlined against the delicate blue sky.

The metallic voice coming over the transmitter from headquarters shook them out of their deep thoughts, ordering them to proceed immediately to a building on Harvard Street, across from the zoo, just a few minutes away.

When they arrived on the scene, they had to fight their way through the crowd of residents who had come running in response to the desperate shouts of a woman.

They ordered the people to move aside and then they saw the cause of the commotion: a smashed body stuck to the hot cement. The cranium was demolished. The facial features were disfigured by the grimace of pain. The eyes were still open, with an enigmatic gaze. The arms and legs were arranged incoherently, not at all in the normal symmetry of the human body. One leg was bent with the foot up by the neck. One shoulder was completely separated from the body, as if it had been chopped off.

"Spiderman!" someone exclaimed.

One of the policemen approached the man who had shouted and said to him, "Hey, show some respect; this is no joke!"

The man turned around and walked away, hanging his head. But as soon as he was out of the officer's reach, he turned around and screamed, "Spiderman! Spiderman!" and took off running toward the zoo, where he hid among some bushes.

The policeman started to chase him, but settled for insulting the man silently, biting his lip to keep the words from escaping.

"Is there anyone here who knows the victim?" asked the other officer, scrutinizing the group of curious onlookers with an indecisive expression.

No one dared to say a word.

"You?" he asked a brown-skinned man. "Do you know him?"

"I don't speak English," the man answered fearfully.

"¿Tú, conocer, muerto?" insisted the officer, stammering in thickly accented Spanish.

"I don't speak Spanish either," said the man in broken English. "I'm from Afghanistan."

The policeman appeared utterly disconcerted at the people's silence. The loud sound of a lion's roar came from the zoo.

Finally, a woman approached the men in uniform and, in an anxious voice, stated, "I was coming home from the store and when I was climbing the stairs to go into the building I heard a scream . . . Then I saw the shape of a man in the sky . . . With his arms stretched out like he was flying . . . But he came crashing down headfirst on the cement . . . He was just a ball of flesh and blood . . . He didn't move anymore . . ."

The people listened openmouthed as the terrified woman described what had happened. One of the officers took down all the details in a small notebook. A reporter took countless photographs per second, as if unable to satisfy his camera.

The shouts of "Spiderman! Spiderman!" were heard again, but this time they were completely ignored.

Calixto was among the spectators, stunned, terrified, and livid, unable to say a word about the tragedy, incapable of testifying that as they were washing the windows outside the eighth floor, the rope tied around his companion's waist broke. Calixto feared they would blame him for the death and he would end up in jail, if not deported for being undocumented. "And then," he thought, "who would support my family?"

The superintendent of the building was observing the scene from the lobby. He was not willing to talk either. He feared he would lose his job for permitting windows at that height to be washed without proper equipment for such a dangerous task. It would come out that he employed undocumented workers and paid them only a third of what cleaning companies usually charged.

The ambulance siren sounded in the neighborhood with such shrillness that it frightened the animals in the zoo. The lion roared as if protesting all the commotion.

The paramedics made their way through the crowd and laid a stretcher on the ground near the body. After a brief examination, one of them said dryly, "He's dead," confirming what everyone already knew.

"Who is he?" one of the paramedics asked the police. "What's his name?"

"No one knows," responded the officer. "Nobody seems to recognize him."

"He looks Hispanic," stated the other paramedic, observing the body closely.

"Maybe he's from Central America," said a woman, clutching her purse to her chest. "A lot of them live in this neighborhood . . . You know, they come here fleeing the wars in their countries . . ."

"If he's not from El Salvador, he must be from Guatemala," agreed one of the paramedics. "Although now they're coming from all over: Bolivia, Peru, Colombia. We used to be the ones who invaded their countries; now they invade ours. Soon Washington will look like Latin America."

"Poor devils," said the other paramedic. "They die far from home, like strangers."

Meanwhile, in the zoo, the lion's loud roar was answered by that of the lioness. The pair of felines, oblivious to the conflicts going on around them, were consummating the reproduction of their species, part of the ancient rites of spring.

The paramedics put the body into the ambulance. The Policemen left. The crowd dispersed. A strange red stain remained on the cement.

Calixto entered the zoo and began to walk absent-mindedly among the cages, thinking about his co-worker who just half an hour ago had been telling him that he had already bought his ticket to return to his country, where he planned to open a grocery store with the money he had saved from five years of hard work in the United States.

Suddenly Calixto realized that in a matter of minutes he had become unemployed. Despair seized him as he remembered that it had taken him a month and a half of constant searching to get the window washing job.

He spent the entire day at the zoo and, as he agonized over whether to return to his country or stay in Washington, he walked from one end of the zoo to the other several times. When they closed the park, he began to walk down long

streets with strange names, until finally night fell and he had no choice but to
return to the place where he lived, a tiny one-bedroom apartment occupied by
twenty people.

"At least I'm alive," he said to himself. "That's good enough for me."

2

Calixto got up early and, without eating breakfast, left the apartment to look
for work. He stopped at several businesses along Columbia Road where, according to the comments he had heard at the apartment, Spanish was spoken.
But they gave him no hope of a job because he did not have a Social Security
card or a green card. Nevertheless, he did not give up; he knew he would find
something. "Even if it's cleaning bathrooms, it doesn't matter; in this country
people aren't ashamed to do anything."

To alleviate his desperation a little, he paused in front of the window of a
clothing store. His gaze fell on the tiny alligator that adorned one of the shirts,
and the price of the shirt startled him. He remembered that in his country they
made clothing like that. In his neighborhood, in fact, everyone went around
with that little figure on their chests. It made no difference that the crocodile
faded with the first washing, came loose with the second, and that after the
third washing nothing was left of the reptile but a hole in the shirt. Calixto
realized it was pointless to dream about new things when he did not even have
a job, and he continued walking along Columbia Road. When he reached the
corner of 18th Street, he decided to go into McDonald's. A fellow country-
man from Intipuca whom Calixto had met at the apartment had heard that
there were job opportunities there. He noticed a dark-skinned man who looked
Latin American picking up papers from the floor and wiping off tables. He approached him, and asked in Spanish, "Do you know if they're hiring here?"

The man responded with a smile and strange gestures.

"Work," repeated Calixto. "Washing dishes or anything."

But the man did not understand him because he was Indian and did not
speak Spanish.

"Go to Hell!" said Calixto, frustrated because the man did nothing but smile
at him.

He left McDonald's in despair and stood for a moment on the corner, unable to decide whether to walk down 18th Street or continue on Columbia
Road. The memory of his home in El Salvador suddenly flooded his mind, the
memory of the life of hunger and misery he led there, and he realized that little
or nothing had changed for him. He was suffering in this country too; and he
wasn't sure if it was better to be here or there. What he did know was that he
was out of work, and that he did not even have enough money in his pocket to

buy a beer to drown the sorrow of feeling lonely and abandoned in a strange land.

He continued wandering down Columbia Road, then took Connecticut Avenue and walked to Dupont Circle Park. He sat down on a bench to watch the transients and elderly people who were sitting in the sun and throwing bread crumbs to the pigeons. He noticed several beggars dragging large bundles which apparently represented their belongings but to him looked like garbage. They reminded him of Old Rag, one of the many beggars in his neighborhood, who also dragged big bags of garbage through the streets, and Calixto concluded that misery was everywhere. He consoled himself with the thought that at least he was healthy and had a family, even though they were now far away.

He returned to the apartment after dark and was pleasantly surprised to find his cousin Juancho there.

"Tomorrow I'm starting work in a hotel," said Juancho. "Come with me. I've been told they need a lot of people because a few days ago the *migra* raided the place and arrested a lot of the employees."

"Well let's go!" said Calixto. "Maybe I'll get a job too."

"I'll meet you tomorrow at the corner of 18th and Columbia Road, at 8 a.m. sharp," said Juancho.

"I'll be there," said Calixto. "For sure."

He said goodbye to his cousin and went to bed with his stomach empty but his soul full of hope.

The next day when they went to the hotel, a manager told them they did need people urgently, and they could start work that very moment.

"The misfortune of some is the good fortune of others," Calixto said to himself.

They immediately put on their uniforms and went into the kitchen.

"We look like nurses," said Calixto. "I've never dressed in white before."

"Never say never," laughed Juancho. "In this country the strangest things happen."

Used to surviving in difficult situations, Calixto was an extremely optimistic person. This had given him the courage necessary to leave his homeland and come to a strange country. As they said back home, he "didn't turn up his nose at anything," because Calixto was a capable man.

CHAPTER FIVE

A CAPITAL TOWN

Private Lives and Public Views

[1920–2010]

THOUGH KNOWN AS A city of politicians who come and go with each new administration, Washington is also a place where generations of private citizens, authors included, have grown up and put down roots or lived for extended periods, enough to become well-acquainted with the local landscape. Several native writers, such as Jean Toomer, Marita Golden, Edward P. Jones, and George Pelecanos, have thrived in Washington, often without paying more than passing attention to politics and, instead, providing intimate, insider views of the city, through the creation of local scenes and characters who are native-born or longtime residents — adolescents, working-class men and women, office workers, the unemployed, senior citizens. Other writers, including such nationally prominent figures as Sinclair Lewis and Willa Cather, have made extended stays in the city and have written memorably about the struggles of ordinary or marginalized characters — people like Carol Kennicott from Lewis's *Main Street* or the anxious young government clerk and his wife in Cather's *The Professor's House* — who fill out the panorama of life in Washington, D.C. With the growing presence of both types of writers over the last century, along with the ongoing generations who write exclusively about the Washington political scene — authors of political fiction, essays, and such — the city has come of age as a "literary capital."

(OVERLEAF) Boulder Bridge, Rock Creek Park. Courtesy of the Historic American Engineering Record, Jet T. Lowe, photographer, 1988.

SINCLAIR LEWIS

In 1910, Sinclair Lewis (1885–1951) moved to Washington for the first time to do hackwork and serve as the editorial assistant to his Yale classmate Kinny Noyes on Alexander Graham Bell's *Volta Review*. When he returned in 1919, it was to free himself from the distractions and expense of New York so that he could rewrite the novel *Main Street: The Story of Carol Kennicott* (1920). Washington features prominently in the concluding chapters of *Main Street*, as Carol Kennicott tries to make a new life for herself far from Gopher Prairie. During this time, Lewis and his wife rented a house at 1814 Sixteenth St., and he joined the Cosmos Club, where he resided while his wife and son traveled. In *It Can't Happen Here: A Novel* (1935), Lewis imagines the unthinkable: a small-town politician who becomes president, turns dictator, gains control over the legislature and judiciary, rides roughshod over the Bill of Rights, and suppresses all opposition and dissent through totalitarian means, only to be deposed in a seemingly endless cycle.

From *Main Street: The Story of Carol Kennicott*

I

She found employment in the Bureau of War Risk Insurance. Though the armistice with Germany was signed a few weeks after her coming to Washington, the work of the bureau continued. She filed correspondence all day; then she dictated answers to letters of inquiry. It was an endurance of monotonous details, yet she asserted that she had found "real work."

Disillusions she did have. She discovered that in the afternoon, office routine stretches to the grave. She discovered that an office is as full of cliques and scandals as a Gopher Prairie. She discovered that most of the women in the government bureaus lived unhealthfully, dining on snatches in their crammed apartments. But she also discovered that business women may have friendships and enmities as frankly as men, and may revel in a bliss which no housewife attains — a free Sunday. It did not appear that the Great World needed her inspiration, but she felt that her letters, her contact with the anxieties of men and women all over the country, were a part of vast affairs, not confined to Main Street and a kitchen, but linked with Paris, Bangkok, Madrid.

She perceived that she could do office work without losing any of the putative feminine virtue of domesticity; that cooking and cleaning, when divested of the fussing of an Aunt Bessie, take but a tenth of the time which, in a Gopher Prairie, it is but decent to devote to them.

Not to have to apologize for her thoughts to the Jolly Seventeen, not to have to report to Kennicott at the end of the day all that she had done or might do, was a relief which made up for the office weariness. She felt that she was no longer one-half of a marriage but the whole of a human being.

II

Washington gave her all the graciousness in which she had had faith: white columns seen across leafy parks, spacious avenues, twisty alleys. Daily she passed a dark square house with a hint of magnolias and a courtyard behind it, and a tall curtained second-story window through which a woman was always peering. The woman was mystery, romance, a story which told itself differently every day; now she was a murderess, now the neglected wife of an ambassador. It was mystery which Carol had most lacked in Gopher Prairie, where every house was open to view, where every person was but too easy to meet, where there were no secret gates opening upon moors over which one might walk by moss-deadened paths to strange high adventures in an ancient garden.

As she flitted up Sixteenth Street after a Kreisler recital, given late in the afternoon for the government clerks, as the lamps kindled in spheres of soft fire, as the breeze flowed into the street, fresh as prairie winds and kindlier, as she glanced up the elm alley of Massachusetts Avenue, as she was rested by the integrity of the Scottish Rite Temple, she loved the city as she loved no one save Hugh. She encountered negro shanties turned into studios, with orange curtains and pots of mignonette; marble houses on New Hampshire Avenue, with butlers and limousines; and men who looked like fictional explorers and aviators. Her days were swift, and she knew that in her folly of running away she had found the courage to be wise.

She had a dispiriting first month of hunting lodgings in the crowded city. She had to roost in a hall-room in a moldy mansion conducted by an indignant decayed gentlewoman, and leave Hugh to the care of a doubtful nurse. But later she made a home.

III

Her first acquaintances were the members of the Tincomb Methodist Church, a vast red-brick tabernacle. Vida Sherwin had given her a letter to an earnest woman with eye-glasses, plaid silk waist, and a belief in Bible Classes, who introduced her to the Pastor and the Nicer Members of Tincomb. Carol recognized in Washington as she had in California a transplanted and guarded Main Street. Two-thirds of the church-members had come from Gopher Prairies. The church was their society and their standard; they went to Sunday service, Sunday School, Epworth League, missionary lectures, church suppers, precisely as they had at home; they agreed that ambassadors and flippant newspapermen and infidel scientists of the bureaus were equally wicked and to be avoided; and by cleaving to Tincomb Church they kept their ideals from all contamination.

They welcomed Carol, asked about her husband, gave her advice regarding colic in babies, passed her the gingerbread and scalloped potatoes at church suppers, and in general made her very unhappy and lonely, so that she wondered if she might not enlist in the militant suffrage organization and be allowed to go to jail.

Always she was to perceive in Washington (as doubtless she would have perceived in New York or London) a thick streak of Main Street. The cautious dullness of a Gopher Prairie appeared in boarding-houses where ladylike bureau-clerks gossiped to polite young army officers about the movies; a thousand Sam Clarks and a few Widow Bogarts were to be identified in the Sunday motor procession, in theater parties, and at the dinners of State Societies, to which the emigres from Texas or Michigan surged that they might confirm themselves in the faith that their several Gopher Prairies were notoriously "a whole lot peppier and chummier than this stuck-up East."

But she found a Washington which did not cleave to Main Street.

Guy Pollock wrote to a cousin, a temporary army captain, a confiding and buoyant lad who took Carol to tea-dances, and laughed, as she had always wanted some one to laugh, about nothing in particular. The captain introduced her to the secretary of a congressman, a cynical young widow with many acquaintances in the navy. Through her Carol met commanders and majors, newspapermen, chemists and geographers and fiscal experts from the bureaus, and a teacher who was a familiar of the militant suffrage headquarters. The teacher took her to headquarters. Carol never became a prominent suffragist. Indeed her only recognized position was as an able addresser of envelopes. But she was casually adopted by this family of friendly women who, when they were not being mobbed or arrested, took dancing lessons or went picnicking up the Chesapeake Canal or talked about the politics of the American Federation of Labor.

With the congressman's secretary and the teacher Carol leased a small flat. Here she found home, her own place and her own people. She had, though it absorbed most of her salary, an excellent nurse for Hugh. She herself put him to bed and played with him on holidays. There were walks with him, there were motionless evenings of reading, but chiefly Washington was associated with people, scores of them, sitting about the flat, talking, talking, talking, not always wisely but always excitedly. It was not at all the "artist's studio" of which, because of its persistence in fiction, she had dreamed. Most of them were in offices all day, and thought more in card-catalogues or statistics than in mass and color. But they played, very simply, and they saw no reason why anything which exists cannot also be acknowledged.

She was sometimes shocked quite as she had shocked Gopher Prairie by these girls with their cigarettes and elfish knowledge. When they were most eager about Soviets or canoeing, she listened, longed to have some special learning which would distinguish her, and sighed that her adventure had come so late. Kennicott and Main Street had drained her self-reliance; the presence of Hugh made her feel temporary. Some day — oh, she'd have to take him back to open fields and the right to climb about hay-lofts.

But the fact that she could never be eminent among these scoffing enthusiasts did not keep her from being proud of them, from defending them in imaginary conversations with Kennicott, who grunted (she could hear his voice), "They're simply a bunch of wild impractical theorists sittin' round chewing the rag," and "I haven't got the time to chase after a lot of these fool fads; I'm too busy putting aside a stake for our old age."

Most of the men who came to the flat, whether they were army officers or radicals who hated the army, had the easy gentleness, the acceptance of women without embarrassed banter, for which she had longed in Gopher Prairie. Yet they seemed to be as efficient as the Sam Clarks. She concluded that it was because they were of secure reputation, not hemmed in by the fire of provincial jealousies. Kennicott had asserted that the villager's lack of courtesy is due to his poverty. "We're no millionaire dudes," he boasted. Yet these army and navy men, these bureau experts, and organizers of multitudinous leagues, were cheerful on three or four thousand a year, while Kennicott had, outside of his land speculations, six thousand or more, and Sam had eight.

Nor could she upon inquiry learn that many of this reckless race died in the poorhouse. That institution is reserved for men like Kennicott who, after devoting fifty years to "putting aside a stake," incontinently invest the stake in spurious oil-stocks.

IV

She was encouraged to believe that she had not been abnormal in viewing Gopher Prairie as unduly tedious and slatternly. She found the same faith not only in girls escaped from domesticity but also in demure old ladies who, tragically deprived of esteemed husbands and huge old houses, yet managed to make a very comfortable thing of it by living in small flats and having time to read.

But she also learned that by comparison Gopher Prairie was a model of daring color, clever planning, and frenzied intellectuality. From her teacher-housemate she had a sardonic description of a Middlewestern railroad-division town, of the same size as Gopher Prairie but devoid of lawns and trees, a town where the tracks sprawled along the cinder-scabbed Main Street, and the railroad shops, dripping soot from eaves and doorway, rolled out smoke in greasy coils.

Other towns she came to know by anecdote: a prairie village where the wind blew all day long, and the mud was two feet thick in spring, and in summer the flying sand scarred new-painted houses and dust covered the few flowers set out in pots. New England mill-towns with the hands living in rows of cottages like blocks of lava. A rich farming-center in New Jersey, off the railroad, furiously pious, ruled by old men, unbelievably ignorant old men, sitting about the grocery talking of James G. Blaine. A Southern town, full of the magnolias and white columns which Carol had accepted as proof of romance, but hating the negroes, obsequious to the Old Families. A Western mining-settlement like a tumor. A booming semi-city with parks and clever architects, visited by famous pianists and unctuous lecturers, but irritable from a struggle between union labor and the manufacturers' association, so that in even the gayest of the new houses there was a ceaseless and intimidating heresy-hunt.

v

The chart which plots Carol's progress is not easy to read. The lines are broken and uncertain of direction; often instead of rising they sink in wavering scrawls; and the colors are watery blue and pink and the dim gray of rubbed pencil marks. A few lines are traceable.

Unhappy women are given to protecting their sensitiveness by cynical gossip, by whining, by high-church and new-thought religions, or by a fog of vagueness. Carol had hidden in none of these refuges from reality, but she, who was tender and merry, had been made timorous by Gopher Prairie. Even her flight had been but the temporary courage of panic. The thing she gained in Washington was not information about office-systems and labor unions but renewed courage, that amiable contempt called poise. Her glimpse of tasks involving millions of people and a score of nations reduced Main Street from bloated importance to its actual pettiness. She could never again be quite so awed by the power with which she herself had endowed the Vidas and Blaussers and Bogarts.

From her work and from her association with women who had organized suffrage associations in hostile cities, or had defended political prisoners, she caught something of an impersonal attitude; saw that she had been as touchily personal as Maud Dyer.

And why, she began to ask, did she rage at individuals? Not individuals but institutions are the enemies, and they most afflict the disciples who the most generously serve them. They insinuate their tyranny under a hundred guises and pompous names, such as Polite Society, the Family, the Church, Sound Business, the Party, the Country, the Superior White Race; and the only defense against them, Carol beheld, is unembittered laughter.

From *It Can't Happen Here: A Novel*

The followers of President Windrip trumpeted that it was significant that he should be the first president inaugurated not on March fourth, but on January twentieth, according to the provision of the new Twentieth Amendment to the Constitution. It was a sign straight from Heaven (though, actually, Heaven had not been the author of the amendment, but Senator George W. Norris of Nebraska), and proved that Windrip was starting a new paradise on earth.

The inauguration was turbulent. President Roosevelt declined to be present — he politely suggested that he was about half ill unto death, but that same noon he was seen in a New York shop, buying books on gardening and looking abnormally cheerful.

More than a thousand reporters, photographers, and radio men covered the inauguration. Twenty-seven constituents of Senator Porkwood, of all sexes, had to sleep on the floor of the Senator's office, and a hall-bedroom in the suburb of Bladensburg rented for thirty dollars for two nights. The presidents of Brazil, the Argentine, and Chile flew to the inauguration in a Pan-American aeroplane, and Japan sent seven hundred students on a special train from Seattle.

A motor company in Detroit had presented to Windrip a limousine with armor plate, bulletproof glass, a hidden nickel-steel safe for papers, a concealed private bar, and upholstery made from the Troissant tapestries of 1670. But Buzz chose to drive from his home to the Capitol in his old Hupmobile sedan, and his driver was a youngster from his home town whose notion of a uniform for state occasions was a blue-serge suit, red tie, and derby hat. Windrip himself did wear a topper, but he saw to it that Lee Sarason saw to it that the one hundred and thirty million plain citizens learned, by radio, even while the inaugural parade was going on, that he had borrowed the topper for this one sole occasion from a New York Republican Representative who had ancestors.

But following Windrip was an un-Jacksonian escort of soldiers: the American Legion and, immensely grander than the others, the Minute Men, wearing trench helmets of polished silver and led by Colonel Dewey Haik in scarlet tunic and yellow riding-breeches and helmet with golden plumes.

Solemnly, for once looking a little awed, a little like a small-town boy on Broadway, Windrip took the oath, administered by the Chief Justice (who disliked him very much indeed) and, edging even closer to the microphone, squawked, "My fellow citizens, as the President of the United States of America, I want to inform you that the *real* New Deal has started right this minute, and we're all going to enjoy the manifold liberties to which our history entitles us — and have a whale of a good time doing it! I thank you!"

That was his first act as President. His second was to take up residence in the White House, where he sat down in the East Room in his stocking feet and shouted at Lee Sarason, "This is what I've been planning to do now for six years! I bet this is what Lincoln used to do! Now let 'em assassinate me!"

His third, in his role as Commander-in-Chief of the Army, was to order that the Minute Men be recognized as an unpaid but official auxiliary of the Regular Army, subject only to their own officers, to Buzz, and to High Marshal Sarason; and that rifles, bayonets, automatic pistols, and machine guns be instantly issued to them by government arsenals. That was at 4 p.m. Since 3 p.m., all over the country, bands of M.M.'s had been sitting gloating over pistols and guns, twitching with desire to seize them.

Fourth coup was a special message, next morning, to Congress (in session since January fourth, the third having been a Sunday), demanding the instant passage of a bill embodying Point Fifteen of his election platform — that he should have complete control of legislation and execution, and the Supreme Court be rendered incapable of blocking anything that it might amuse him to do.

By Joint Resolution, with less than half an hour of debate, both houses of Congress rejected that demand before 3 p.m., on January twenty-first. Before six, the President had proclaimed that a state of martial law existed during the "present crisis," and more than a hundred Congressmen had been arrested by Minute Men, on direct orders from the President. The Congressmen who were hot-headed enough to resist were cynically charged with "inciting to riot"; they who went quietly were not charged at all. It was blandly explained to the agitated press by Lee Sarason that these latter quiet lads had been so threatened by "irresponsible and seditious elements" that they were merely being safeguarded. Sarason did not use the phrase "protective arrest," which might have suggested things.

To the veteran reporters it was strange to see the titular Secretary of State, theoretically a person of such dignity and consequence that he could deal with the representatives of foreign powers, acting as press-agent and yes-man for even the President.

There were riots, instantly, all over Washington, all over America.

The recalcitrant Congressmen had been penned in the District Jail. Toward it, in the winter evening, marched a mob that was noisily mutinous toward the Windrip for whom so many of them had voted. Among the mob buzzed hundreds of Negroes, armed with knives and old pistols, for one of the kidnapped Congressmen was a Negro from Georgia, the first colored Georgian to hold high office since carpetbagger days.

Surrounding the jail, behind machine guns, the rebels found a few Regulars, many police, and a horde of Minute Men, but at these last they jeered, calling them "Minnie Mouses" and "tin soldiers" and "mama's boys." The M.M.'s looked nervously at their officers and at the Regulars who were making so professional a pretense of not being scared. The mob heaved bottles and dead fish. Half-a-dozen policemen with guns and night sticks, trying to push back the van of the mob, were buried under a human surf and came up grotesquely battered and ununiformed — those who ever did come up again. There were two shots; and one Minute Man slumped to the jail steps, another stood ludicrously holding a wrist that spurted blood.

The Minute Men — why, they said to themselves, they'd never meant to be soldiers anyway — just wanted to have some fun marching! They began to sneak into the edges of the mob, hiding their uniform caps. That instant, from a powerful loudspeaker in a lower window of the jail brayed the voice of President Berzelius Windrip:

"I am addressing my own boys, the Minute Men, everywhere in America! To you and you only I look for help to make America a proud, rich land again. You have been scorned. They thought you were the 'lower classes.' They wouldn't give you jobs. They told you to sneak off like bums and get relief. They ordered you into lousy C.C.C. camps. They said you were no good, because you were poor. I tell you that you are, ever since yesterday noon, the highest lords of the land — the aristocracy — the makers of the new America of freedom and justice. Boys! I need you! Help me — help me to help you! Stand fast! Anybody tries to block you — give the swine the point of your bayonet!"

A machine-gunner M.M., who had listened reverently, let loose. The mob began to drop, and into the backs of the wounded as they were staggering away the M.M infantry, running, poked their bayonets. Such a juicy squash it made, and the fugitives looked so amazed, so funny, as they tumbled in grotesque heaps!

The M.M.'s hadn't, in dreary hours of bayonet drill, known this would be such sport. They'd have more of it now — and hadn't the President of the United States himself told each of them, personally, that he needed their aid?

When the remnants of Congress ventured to the Capitol, they found it seeded with M.M.'s, while a regiment of Regulars, under Major General Meinecke, paraded the grounds.

The Speaker of the House, and the Hon. Mr. Perley Beecroft, Vice-President of the United States and Presiding Officer of the Senate, had the power to declare that quorums were present. (If a lot of members chose to dally in the district jail, enjoying themselves instead of attending Congress, whose fault was that?) Both houses passed a resolution declaring Point Fifteen temporarily in effect, during the "crisis" — the legality of the passage was doubtful, but just who was to contest it, even though the members of the Supreme Court had not been placed under protective arrest . . . merely confined each to his own house by a squad of Minute Men!

JEAN TOOMER

A native Washingtonian, Jean Toomer (1894–1967) came from a politically well-connected African American family, the Pinchbacks, of Louisiana. He spent his early years in a mostly white neighborhood north of Meridian Hill and attended a segregated elementary school on U Street in Northwest D.C. He later lived on Florida Avenue with his grandparents and then at 1341 U Street, Northwest, where he wrote most of the stories and poems for the middle or "Washington" section of *Cane* (1923), particularly "Seventh Street," "Avey," and "Theater," portraits capturing conflicts over class, race, and gender early in the twentieth century. Toomer also wrote about Washington both as a journalist, in "Reflections on the Race Riots" (1919), and as a dramatist, in *Natalie Mann* (1922), a play that targets the conventionalism of Washington's mulatto aristocracy and posits an "American" identity that goes beyond race.

Seventh Street
From *Cane*

> Money burns the pocket, pocket hurts,
> Bootleggers in silken shirts,
> Ballooned, zooming Cadillacs,
> Whizzing, whizzing down the street-car tracks.

Seventh Street is a bastard of Prohibition and the War. A crude-boned, soft-skinned wedge of nigger life breathing its loafer air, jazz songs and love, thrusting unconscious rhythms, black reddish blood into the white and whitewashed wood of Washington. Stale soggy wood of Washington. Wedges rust in soggy wood . . . Split it! In two! Again! Shred it! . . the sun. Wedges are brilliant in the sun; ribbons of wet wood dry and blow away. Black reddish blood. Pouring for crude-boned soft-skinned life, who set you flowing? Blood suckers of the War would spin in a frenzy of dizziness if they drank your blood. Prohibition would put a stop to it. Who set you flowing? White and whitewash disappear in blood. Who set you flowing? Flowing down the smooth asphalt of Seventh Street, in shanties, brick office buildings, theaters, drug stores, restaurants, and cabarets? Eddying on the corners? Swirling like a blood-red smoke up where the buzzards fly in heaven? God would not dare to suck black red blood. A Nigger God! He would duck his head in shame and call for the Judgment Day. Who set you flowing?

> Money burns the pocket, pocket hurts,
> Bootleggers in silken shirts,
> Ballooned, zooming Cadillacs,
> Whizzing, whizzing down the street-car tracks.

Avey
From *Cane*

For a long while she was nothing more to me than one of those skirted beings whom boys at a certain age disdain to play with. Just how I came to love her, timidly, and with secret blushes, I do not know. But that I did was brought home to me one night, the first night that Ned wore his long pants. Us fellers were seated on the curb before an apartment house where she had gone in. The young trees had not outgrown their boxes then. V Street was lined with them. When our legs grew cramped and stiff from the cold of the stone, we'd stand around a box and whittle it. I like to think now that there was a hidden purpose in the way we hacked them with our knives. I like to feel that something deep in me responded to the trees, the young trees that whinnied like colts impatient to be let free... On the particular night I have in mind, we were waiting for the top-floor light to go out. We wanted to see Avey leave the flat. This night she stayed longer than usual and gave us a chance to complete the plans of how we were going to stone and beat that feller on the top floor out of town. Ned especially had it in for him. He was about to throw a brick up at the window when at last the room went dark. Some minutes passed. Then Avey, as unconcerned as if she had been paying an old-maid aunt a visit, came out. I dont remember what she had on, and all that sort of thing. But I do know that I turned hot as bare pavements in the summertime at Ned's boast: "Hell, bet I could get her too if you little niggers weren't always spying and crabbing everything." I didnt say a word to him. It wasnt my way then. I just stood there like the others, and something like a fuse burned up inside of me. She never noticed us, but swung along lazy and easy as anything. We sauntered to the corner and watched her till her door banged to. Ned repeated what he'd said. I didnt seem to care. Sitting around old Mush-Head's bread box, the discussion began. "Hang if I can see how she gets away with it," Doc started. Ned knew, of course. There was nothing he didnt know when it came to women. He dilated on the emotional needs of girls. Said they werent much different from men in that respect. And concluded with the solemn avowal: "It does em good." None of us liked Ned much. We all talked dirt; but it was the way he said it. And then too, a couple of the fellers had sisters and had caught Ned playing with them. But there was no disputing the superiority of his smutty wisdom. Bubs Sanborn, whose mother was friendly with Avey's, had overheard the old ladies talking. "Avey's mother's ont her," he said. We thought that only natural and began to guess at what would happen. Some one said she'd marry that feller on the top floor. Ned called that a lie because Avey was going to marry nobody but him. We had our doubts about that, but we did agree that she'd soon leave school and marry some one. The gang broke up, and I went home, picturing myself as married.

NOTHING I DID seemed able to change Avey's indifference to me. I played basket-ball, and when I'd make a long clean shot she'd clap with the others, louder than they, I thought. I'd meet her on the street, and there'd be no difference in the way she said hello. She never took the trouble to call me by my name. On the days for drill, I'd let my voice down a tone and call for a complicated maneuver when I saw her coming. She'd smile appreciation, but it was an impersonal smile, never for me. It was on a summer excursion down to Riverview that she first seemed to take me into account. The day had been spent riding merry-go-rounds, scenic-railways, and shoot-the-chutes. We had been in swimming and we had danced. I was a crack swimmer then. She didnt know how. I held her up and showed her how to kick her legs and draw her arms. Of course she didnt learn in one day, but she thanked me for bothering with her. I was also somewhat of a dancer. And I had already noticed that love can start on a dance floor. We danced. But though I held her tightly in my arms, she was way away. That college feller who lived on the top floor was somewhere making money for the next year. I imagined that she was thinking, wishing for him. Ned was along. He treated her until his money gave out. She went with another feller. Ned got sore. One by one the boys' money gave out. She left them. And they got sore. Every one of them but me got sore. This is the reason, I guess, why I had her to myself on the top deck of the *Jane Mosely* that night as we puffed up the Potomac, coming home. The moon was brilliant. The air was sweet like clover. And every now and then, a salt tang, a stale drift of sea-weed. It was not my mind's fault if it went romancing. I should have taken her in my arms the minute we were stowed in that old lifeboat. I dallied, dreaming. She took me in hers. And I could feel by the touch of it that it wasnt a man-to-woman love. It made me restless. I felt chagrined. I didnt know what it was, but I did know that I couldnt handle it. She ran her fingers through my hair and kissed my forehead. I itched to break through her tenderness to passion. I wanted her to take me in her arms as I knew she had that college feller. I wanted her to love me passionately as she did him. I gave her one burning kiss. Then she laid me in her lap as if I were a child. Helpless. I got sore when she started to hum a lullaby. She wouldnt let me go. I talked. I knew damned well that I could beat her at that. Her eyes were soft and misty, the curves of her lips were wistful, and her smile seemed indulgent of the irrelevance of my remarks. I gave up at last and let her love me, silently, in her own way. The moon was brilliant. The air was sweet like clover, and every now and then, a salt tang, a stale drift of sea-weed...

THE NEXT TIME I came close to her was the following summer at Harpers Ferry. We were sitting on a flat projecting rock they give the name of Lover's Leap. Some one is supposed to have jumped off it. The river is about six hundred feet beneath. A railroad track runs up the valley and curves out of sight where part of the mountain rock had to be blasted away to make room for it. The engines of this valley have a whistle, the echoes of which sound like iterated gasps and sobs. I always think of them as crude music from the soul of Avey. We sat there holding hands. Our palms were soft and warm against each other. Our fingers were not tight. She would not let them be. She would not let me twist them. I wanted to talk. To explain what I meant to her. Avey was as silent as those great trees whose tops we looked down upon. She has always been like that. At least, to me. I had the notion that if I really wanted to, I could do with her just what I pleased. Like one can strip a tree. I did kiss her. I even let my hands cup her breasts. When I was through, she'd seek my hand and hold it till my pulse cooled down. Evening after evening we sat there. I tried to get her to talk about that college feller. She never would. There was no set time to go home. None of my family had come down. And as for hers, she didnt give a hang about them. The general gossips could hardly say more than they had. The boarding-house porch was always deserted when we returned. No one saw us enter, so the time was set conveniently for scandal. This worried me a little, for I thought it might keep Avey from getting an appointment in the schools. She didnt care. She had finished normal school. They could give her a job if they wanted to. As time went on, her indifference to things began to pique me; I was ambitious. I left the Ferry earlier than she did. I was going off to college. The more I thought of it, the more I resented, yes, hell, thats what it was, her downright laziness. Sloppy indolence. There was no excuse for a healthy girl taking life so easy. Hell! she was no better than a cow. I was certain that she was a cow when I felt her udder in a Wisconsin stock-judging class. Among those energetic Swedes, or whatever they are, I decided to forget her. For two years I thought I did. When I'd come home for the summer she'd be away. And before she returned, I'd be gone. We never wrote; she was too damned lazy for that. But what a bluff I put up about forgetting her. The girls up that way, at least the ones I knew, haven't got the stuff: they dont know how to love.

Giving themselves completely was tame beside just the holding of Avey's hand. One day I received a note from her. The writing, I decided, was slovenly. She wrote on a torn bit of note-book paper. The envelope had a faint perfume that I remembered. A single line told me she had lost her school and was going away. I comforted myself with the reflection that shame held no pain for one so indolent as she. Nevertheless, I left Wisconsin that year for good. Washington had seemingly forgotten her. I hunted Ned. Between curses, I caught his opinion of her. She was no better than a whore. I saw her mother on the street. The same old pinch-beck, jerky-gaited creature that I'd always known.

PERHAPS FIVE YEARS PASSED. The business of hunting a job or something or other had bruised my vanity so that I could recognize it. I felt old. Avey and my real relation to her, I thought I came to know. I wanted to see her. I had been told that she was in New York. As I had no money, I hiked and bummed my way there. I got work in a ship-yard and walked the streets at night, hoping to meet her. Failing in this, I saved enough to pay my fare back home. One evening in early June, just at the time when dusk is most lovely on the eastern horizon, I saw Avey, indolent as ever, leaning on the arm of a man, strolling under the recently lit arc-lights of U Street. She had almost passed before she recognized me. She showed no surprise. The puff over her eyes had grown heavier. The eyes themselves were still sleep-large, and beautiful. I had almost concluded — indifferent. "You look older," was what she said. I wanted to convince her that I was, so I asked her to talk with me. The man whom she was with, and whom she never took the trouble to introduce, at a nod from her, hailed a taxi, and drove away. That gave me a notion of what she had been used to. Her dress was of some fine, costly stuff. I suggested the park, and then added that the grass might stain her skirt. Let it get stained, she said, for where it came from there are others.

I HAVE A SPOT in Soldier's Home to which I always go when I want the simple beauty of another's soul. Robins spring about the lawn all day. They leave their footprints on the grass. I imagine that the grass at night smells sweet and fresh because of them. The ground is high. Washington lies below. Its light spreads like a blush against the darkened sky. Against the soft dusk sky of Washington. And when the wind is from the South, soil of my homeland falls like a fertile shower upon the lean streets of the city. Upon my hill in Soldier's Home, I know a policeman who watches the place of nights. When I go there alone, I talk to him. I tell him I come there to find the truth that people bury in their hearts. I tell him that I do not come there with a girl to do the thing he's paid to watch out for. I look deep in his eyes when I say these things, and he believes me. He comes over to see who it is on the grass. I say hello to him. He greets me in the same way and goes off searching for other black splotches upon the lawn. Avey and I went there. A band in one of the buildings a fair distance off was playing a march. I wished they would stop. Their playing was like a tin spoon in one's mouth. I wanted the Howard Glee Club to sing "Deep River," from the road. To sing "Deep River, Deep River," from the road. . . Other than the first comments, Avey had been silent. I started to hum a folk-tune. She slipped her hand in mind. Pillowed her head as best she could upon my arm. Kissed the hand that she was holding and listened, or so I thought, to what I had to say. I traced my development from the early days up to the present time, the phase in which I could understand her. I described her own nature and temperament. Told how they needed a larger life for their expression. How incapable Washington was of understanding that need. How it could not meet it. I pointed out that in lieu of proper channels, her emotions had overflowed into paths that dissipated them. I talked, beautifully I thought, about an art that would be born, an art that would open the way for women the likes of her. I asked her to hope, and build up an inner life against the coming of that day. I recited some of my own things to her. I sang, with a strange quiver in my voice, a promise-song. And then I began to wonder why her hand had not once returned a single pressure. My old-time feeling about her laziness came back. I spoke sharply. My policeman friend passed by. I said hello to him. As he went away, I began to visualize certain possibilities. An immediate and urgent passion swept over me. Then I looked at Avey. Her heavy eyes were closed. Her breathing was as faint and regular as a child's in slumber. My passion died. I was afraid to move lest I disturb her. Hours and hours, I guess it was, she lay there. My body grew numb. I shivered. I coughed. I wanted to get up and whittle at the boxes of young trees. I withdrew my hand. I raised her head to waken her. She did not stir. I got up and walked around. I found my policeman friend and talked to him. We both came up, and bent over her. He said it would be all right for her to stay there just so long as she got away before the workmen came at dawn. A blanket was borrowed from a neighbor house. I sat beside her through the night. I saw the dawn steal over Washington. The Capitol dome looked like a gray ghost ship drifting in from sea. Avey's face was pale, and her eyes were heavy. She did not have the gray crimson-splashed beauty of the dawn. I hated to wake her. Orphan-woman. . .

WILLA CATHER

Willa Cather (1873–1947) made three trips to Washington to visit family and collect material for her work as a journalist. As suggested in the Tom Outland section of *The Professor's House* (1925), she found the city beautiful but overly officious and confused about national priorities and the duty one generation has to the next in any culture. She also found the people too preoccupied with advancing their own careers rather than serving the interests of the country. Surprisingly, her journalism from Washington seems to report on a different city, finding it vibrant and culturally sophisticated — a place of art, music, theater, and festive diplomatic parties.

From *The Professor's House*

I got off the train, just behind the Capitol Building, one cold bright January morning. I stood for a long while watching the white dome against a flashing blue sky, with a very religious feeling. After I had walked about a little and seen the parks, so green though it was winter, and the Treasury building, and the War and Navy, I decided to put off my business for a little and give myself a week to enjoy the city. That was the most sensible thing I did while I was there. For that week I was wonderfully happy.

My sightseeing over, I got to work. First I went to see the Representative from our district, to ask for letters of introduction. He was cordial enough, but he gave me bad advice. He was very positive that I ought to report to the Indian Commission, and gave me a letter to the Commissioner. The Commissioner was out of town, and I wasted three days waiting about his office, being questioned by clerks and secretaries. They were not very busy, and seemed to find me entertaining. I thought they were interested in my mission, and interest was what I wanted to arouse. I didn't know how influential these people might be — they talked as if they had great authority. I had brought along in my telescope bag some good pieces of pottery — not the best, I was afraid of accident, but some that were representative — and all the photographs Blake and I had taken. We had only a small Kodak, and these pictures didn't make much show, — looked, indeed, like grubby little 'dobe ruins such as one can find almost anywhere. They gave no idea of the beauty and vastness of the setting. The clerks at the Indian Commission seemed very curious about everything and made me talk a lot. I was green and didn't know any better. But when one of the fellows there tried to get me to give him my best bowl for his cigarette ashes, I began to suspect the nature of their interest.

At last the Commissioner returned, but he had pressing engagements, and I hung around several days more before he would see me. After questioning me for about half an hour, he told me that his business was with living Indians, not dead ones, and that his office should have informed me of that in the beginning. He advised me to go back to our Congressman and get a letter to the Smithsonian Institution. I packed up my pottery and got out of the place, feeling pretty sore. The head clerk followed me down the corridor and asked me what I'd take for that little bowl he'd taken a fancy to. He said it had no market value, I'd find Washington full of such things; there were cases of them in the cellar at the Smithsonian that they'd never taken the trouble to unpack, hadn't any place to put them.

I went back to my Congressman. This time he wasn't so friendly as before, but he gave me a letter to the Smithsonian. There I went through the same experience. The Director couldn't be seen except by appointment, and his secretary had to be convinced that your business was important before he would give you an appointment with his chief. After the first morning I found it difficult to see even the secretary. He was always engaged. I was told to take a seat and wait, but when he was disengaged he was hurrying off to luncheon. I would sit there all morning with a group of unfortunate people: girls who wanted to get typewriting to do, nice polite old men who wanted to be taken out on surveys and expeditions next summer. The secretary would at last come out with his overcoat on, and would hurry through the waiting-room reading a letter or a report, without looking up.

The office assistants cheered me along, and I kept this up for some days, sitting all morning in that room, studying the patterns of the rugs, and the shoes of the patient waiters who came as regularly as I. One day after the secretary had gone out, his stenographer, a nice little Virginia girl, came and sat down in an empty chair next to mine and began talking to me. She wasn't pretty, but her kind eyes and soft Southern voice took hold of me at once. She wanted to know what I had in my telescope, and why I was there, and where I came from, and all about it. Nearly everyone else had gone out to lunch — that seemed to be the one thing they did regularly in Washington — and we had the waiting-room to ourselves. I talked to her a good deal. Her name was Virginia Ward. She was a tiny little thing, but she had lovely eyes and such gentle ways. She seemed indignant that I had been put off so long after having come so far.

"Now you just let me fix it up for you," she said at last. "Mr. Wagner is bothered by a great many foolish people who waste his time, and he is suspicious. The best way will be for you to invite him to lunch with you. I'll arrange it. I keep a list of his appointments, and I know he is not engaged for luncheon tomorrow. I'll tell him that he is to lunch with a nice boy who has come all the way from New Mexico to inform the Department about an important discov-

ery. I'll tell him to meet you at the Shoreham, at one. That's expensive, but it
would do no good to invite him to a cheap place. And, remember, you must ask
him to order the luncheon. It will maybe cost you ten dollars, but it will get you
somewhere."

I felt grateful to the nice little thing, — she wasn't older than I. I begged her
wouldn't she please come to lunch with me herself to-day, and talk to me. —

"Oh, no!" she said, blushing red as a poppy. "Why, I'm afraid you think — "

I told her I didn't think anything but how nice she was to me, and how lonesome I was. She went with me, but she wouldn't go to any swell place. She told
me a great many useful things.

"If you want to get attention from anybody in Washin'ton," she said, "ask
them to lunch. People here will do almost anything for a good lunch."

"But the Director of the Smithsonian, for instance," I said, "surely you
don't mean that the high-up ones like that — ? Why would he want to bother
with a cow-puncher from New Mexico, when he can lunch with scientists and
ambassadors?"

She had a pretty little fluttery Southern laugh. "You just name a hotel like
the Shoreham to the Director, and try it! There has to be somebody to pay for
a lunch, and the scientists and ambassadors don't do that when they can avoid
it. He'd accept your invitation, and the next time he went to dine with the
Secretary of State he'd make a nice little story of it, and paint you up so pretty
you'd hardly know yourself."

When I asked her whether I'd better take my pottery — it was there under
the table between us — to the Shoreham to show Mr. Wagner, she tittered
again. "I wouldn't bother. If you show him enough of the Shoreham pottery,
that will be more effective."

The next morning, when the secretary arrived at his office, he stopped by my
chair and said he understood he had an engagement with me for one o'clock.
That was a good idea, he added: his mind was freer when he was away from office routine.

I had been in Washington twenty-two days when I took the secretary out
to lunch. It was an excellent lunch. We had a bottle of Château d'Yquem. I'd
never heard of such a wine before, but I remember it because it cost five dollars.
I drank only one glass, and that pleased him too, for he drank the rest. Though
he was friendly and talked a great deal, my heart sank lower, for he wouldn't
let me explain my mission to him at all. He kept telling me that he knew all
about the Southwest. He had been sent by the Smithsonian to conduct parties
of European archaeologists through all the show places, Frijoles and Canyon de
Chelly, and Taos and the Hopi pueblos. When some Austrian Archduke had
gone to hunt in the Pecos range, he had been sent by his chief and the German

ambassador to manage the tour, and he had done it with such success that both he and the Director were given decorations from the Austrian Crown, in recognition of his services. Then I had to listen to a long story about how well he was treated by the Archduke when he went to Vienna with his chief the following summer. I had to hear about balls and receptions, and the names and titles of all the people he had met at the Duke's country estate. I was amazed and ashamed that a man of fifty, a man of the world, a scholar with ever so many degrees, should find it worth his while to show off before a boy, and a boy of such humble pretensions, who didn't know how to eat the *hors d'œvres* any more than if an assortment of cocoanuts had been set before him with no hammer.

Imagine my astonishment when, as he was drinking his liqueur, he said carelessly: "By the way, I was successful in arranging an interview with the Director for you. He will see you at four o'clock on Monday."

That was Thursday. I spent the time between then and Monday trying to find out something more about the kind of people I had come among. I persuaded Virginia Ward to go to the theatre with me, and she told me that it always took a long while to get anything through with the Director, that I mustn't lose heart, and she would always be glad to cheer me up. She lived with her mother, a widow lady, and they had me come to dinner and were very nice to me.

All this time I was living with a young married couple who interested me very much, for they were unlike any people I had ever known. The husband was "in office," as they say there, he had some position in the War Department. How it did use to depress me to see all the hundreds of clerks come pouring out of that big building at sunset! Their lives seemed to me so petty, so slavish. The couple I lived with gave me a prejudice against that kind of life. I couldn't help knowing a good deal about their affairs. They had only a small flat, and rented me one room of it, so I was very much in their confidence and couldn't help overhearing. They asked me not to mention the fact that I paid rent, as they had told their friends I was making them a visit. It was like that in everything; they spent their lives trying to keep up appearances, and to make his salary do more than it could. When they weren't discussing where she should go in the summer, they talked about the promotions in his department; how much the other clerks got and how they spent it, how many new dresses their wives had. And there was always a struggle going on for an invitation to a dinner or a reception, or even a tea-party. When once they got the invitation they had been scheming for, then came the terrible question of what Mrs. Bixby should wear.

The Secretary of War gave a reception; there was to be dancing and a great showing of foreign uniforms. The Bixbys were in painful suspense until they got a card. Then for a week they talked about nothing but what Mrs. Bixby was going to wear. They decided that for such an occasion she must have a new dress. Bixby borrowed twenty-five dollars from me, and took his lunch hour to go shopping with his wife and choose the satin. That seemed to me very strange. In New Mexico the Indian boys sometimes went to a trader's with their wives and bought shawls or calico, and we thought it rather contemptible. On the night of the reception the Bixbys set off gaily in a cab; the dress they considered a great success. But they had bad luck. Somebody spilt claret-cup on Mrs. Bixby's skirt before the evening was half over, and when they got home that night I heard her weeping and reproaching him for having been so upset about it, and looking at nothing but her ruined dress all evening. She said he cried out when it happened. I don't doubt it.

Every cab, every party, was more than they could afford. If he lost an umbrella, it was a real misfortune. He wasn't lazy, he wasn't a fool, and he meant to be honest; but he was intimidated by that miserable sort of departmental life. He didn't know anything else. He thought working in a store or a bank not respectable. Living with the Bixbys gave me a kind of low-spiritedness I had never known before. During my days of waiting for appointments, I used to walk for hours around the fence that shuts in the White House grounds, and watch the Washington monument colour with those beautiful sunsets, until the time when all the clerks streamed out of the Treasury building and the War and Navy. Thousands of them, all more or less like the couple I lived with. They seemed to me like people in slavery, who ought to be free. I remember the city chiefly by those beautiful, hazy, sad sunsets, white columns and green shrubbery, and the monument shaft still pink while the stars were coming out.

I got my interview with the Director of the Smithsonian at last. He gave me his attention, he was interested. He told me to come again in three days and meet Dr. Ripley, who was the authority on prehistoric Indian remains and had excavated a lot of them. Then came an exciting and rather encouraging time for me. Dr. Ripley asked the right sort of questions, and evidently knew his business. He said he'd like to take the first train down to my mesa. But it required money to excavate, and he had none. There was a bill up before Congress for an appropriation. We'd have to wait. I must use my influence with my Representative. He took my pottery to study it. (I never got it back, by the way.) There was a Dr. Fox, connected with the Smithsonian, who was also interested. They told me a good many things I wanted to know, and kept me dangling about the office. Of course they were very kind to take so much trouble with a green boy. But I soon found that the Director and all his staff had one interest which dwarfed every other. There was to be an International Exposition of some sort in Europe the following summer, and they were all pulling strings to get appointed on juries or sent to international congresses — appointments that would pay their expenses abroad, and give them a salary in addition. There was, indeed, a bill before Congress for appropriations for the Smithsonian; but there was also a bill for Exposition appropriations, and that was the one they were really pushing. They kept me hanging on through March and April, but in the end it came to nothing. Dr. Ripley told me he was sorry, but the sum Congress had allowed the Smithsonian wouldn't cover an expedition to the South-west.

Virginia Ward, who had been so kind to me, went out to lunch with me that day, and admitted I had been let down. She was almost as much disappointed as I. She said the only thing Dr. Ripley really cared about was getting a free trip to Europe and acting on a jury, and maybe getting a decoration. "And that's what the Director wants, too," she said. "They don't care much about dead and gone Indians. What they do care about is going to Paris, and getting another ribbon on their coats."

The only other person besides Virginia who was genuinely concerned about my affair was a young Frenchman, a lieutenant attached to the French Embassy, who came to the Smithsonian often on business connected with this same International Exposition. He was nice and polite to Virginia, and she introduced him to me. We used to walk down along the Potomac together. He studied my photographs and asked me such intelligent questions about everything that it was a pleasure to talk to him. He had a fine attitude about it all; he was thoughtful, critical, and respectful. I feel sure he'd have gone back to New Mexico with me if he'd had the money. He was even poorer than I.

I was utterly ashamed to go home to Roddy, dead broke after all the money I'd spent, and without a thing to show for it. I hung on in Washington through May, trying to get a job of some sort, to at least earn my fare home. My letters to Blake had been pretty blue for some time back. If I'd been sensible, I'd have kept my troubles to myself. He was easily discouraged, and I knew that. At last I had to write him for money to go home. It was slow in coming, and I began to telegraph. I left Washington at last, wiser than I came. I had no plans, I wanted nothing but to get back to the mesa and live a free life and breathe free air, and never, never again to see hundreds of little black-coated men pouring out of white buildings. Queer, how much more depressing they are than workmen coming out of a factory.

SAMUEL HOPKINS ADAMS

For many years, Samuel Hopkins Adams (1871–1958) was a muckraking journalist who regularly contributed articles to *McClure's* and *Collier's* magazines and wrote a book about patent medicines, *The Great American Fraud* (1906). His novel of Washington, *Revelry* (1926), was based on the scandals of the

Harding administration, including the misuse of the secret service to spy on the president's "enemies," as in the excerpt reprinted here. This work was followed by a biography of Daniel Webster, *The Godlike Daniel* (1930), and then a biography of Harding, *Incredible Era* (1939).

A Lesson in Politics
From *Revelry*

Braving the season Monsieur Georges Jarry had set a small group of tables on what he was pleased to call his "terrasse." His temerity was justified on this soft-hearted spring noon. Two hardy patrons, arriving at his small, exquisite, and absurdly expensive restaurant at the angle of the pointed corner, had elected to lunch in the open. Everybody who was anybody knew also Edith Westervelt, brief though her inhabitation of Washington had been, but knew little about her. She was unique; that was generally agreed. And her variance from type was comprised mainly in a still indifference, impenetrable, inexorable, and apparent only to those who sought to penetrate beneath the smooth and serene exterior. Whether or not she was beautiful was a popular and often acrimonious topic of debate. She came to Washington, trailing the clouds of a singular European prestige. She had been a silly-season sensation in London and the unimpeachable and quietly disdainful heroine of a duel in Vienna in which near-royal blood might have been shed — if any had been shed. She was the kind of woman who is inevitably discussed and ignores being discussed.

"Just drifting," she was saying in reply to some query of her companion's. "I saw a house that I like so I bought it."

"It's a permanent thing, then."

"Unless I get bored."

"Which you always do, don't you?"

"Don't we all, some time or other? I'm like the man who could resist everything but temptation. I can endure anything but environment. And if you, my oldest friend, disapprove —"

"Disapprove? My dear Edith! Apart from my notorious devotion of years, Washington is flattered and official society enriched by the presence of the young and lovely Comtesse d'Aillys."

"Leave the beautiful language and the title to the society reporters, Peter."

"You have definitely resumed your maiden name?"

"Yes."

"Would it be indiscreet in an old friend to ask —"

"Highly. Therefore I'll tell you before you ask. My husband was too good for me."

"But —"

"No self-respecting woman can endure to live with a man who is too good for her."

"Too good in his own opinion, or in yours?"

"Oh, mine! He considers that I am too good for him — or any man."

"Washington," he observed, "usually means politics."

"For a woman?"

"Politics or society. It can't be the latter for you. You've no more worlds to conquer. But in politics, with your power of influencing men — you won't deny, I suppose, that you have a certain interest for men and that they stay interested?"

"Because they don't understand me."

"Omne ignotum pro magnifica."

"Thanks for changing the gender."

"As I was about to say, you could stir up such a perfectly incredible and delightful mess here."

"Thanks again for the subtle flattery."

He sighed. "You're a hard habit to get over, my dear. I've never been able to, after all these years. I hope you don't mind."

"No. I like it."

"Really? I wonder why."

"I'm a woman, after all."

"It almost requires proof."

"I think I've proved it once," she answered, her voice stilled, her eyes distant.

He nodded gravely as over a confidence renewed.

"Should I prove anything," she added more lightly, "by going into politics?"

"Quite possibly. There is an opportunity here for a woman of brains and charm and breeding to become a real power if she played her cards right."

"Which usually means sex. I don't play that game, Peter. . . . What on earth is that fearful bellowing, up the street?"

Turning in his seat, the Senator took off his glasses to peer at a bow window midway of the block, in which sat a gross, pulpy, jovial, shirt-sleeved figure, his feet cocked up on the sill, his absurdly small mouth distorted around a fat cigar, giving him the appearance of a fish learning to smoke. At frequent intervals a jet of stained saliva shot forth to burst like a miniature bomb and bespatter the pavement: at spaces little less frequent, a greeting to some passing Tim or Phil or Harry smote the air with a clamor startlingly incommensurate with its source.

"That," pronounced Senator Thorne, "is Jeff Sims."

"A person of wide acquaintance, apparently."

"If I passed there you would hear him bellow, 'Hello, Pete! Hear about —' "

"Do you know him so intimately?"

"He knows *me* so intimately. He knows every one so intimately. He is an important person."

"In what possible way?"

"Through being the friend of greatness."

"That loathsome creature? Perhaps his looks belie him."

"Not in the least. He is exactly what he appears; a huge, soft, blustering, good natured, innocent — " He paused, and confirmed his own words —"Yes, innocent moron. I doubt if he realizes even how crooked he is."

"Where does he get his power?"

"From close association with Daniel Lurcock."

She shook her tawny-gleaming head. "That means nothing, either."

"Saints preserve us! Not know of Lurcock? He is the active Attorney-General of the United States of America."

"I thought I knew the Attorney-General. What is his name? Hamline, Hamburg- - -"

"Hambidge. He's a nonentity. A dried leaf, with scarcely enough vitality to rustle. I spoke of Lurcock as the active Attorney-General. I should have said 'actual.' He has his desk at the Department of Justice, though he holds no official position, and gives the orders for the Hon. Morse Hambidge to carry out. And Hambidge carries them out. Oh, yes! He carries them out. Otherwise he would be carried out, himself, on a shutter."

"But I don't see. Where does his authority come from and how is it connected with that dreadful ruffian in the window?"

"As to the latter, because they live together, and are the Damon and Pythias of Federal graft. As to the first item of your question, you may have perhaps heard, for all your justified indifference to your country's politics, of the Hon. Willis Markham, at present gracing an office of some importance."

"Sardonicism isn't becoming to the Senatorial manner," she retorted. "If you mean the President — "

"Precisely. Well, Dan Lurcock invented him."

"Am I supposed to understand that?"

"You're supposed to understand anything that you set your mind to. Some day I'll tell you the story. The general belief in Washington is that Lurcock is the President's mouthpiece. It is not mine."

"What is?"

"Can you keep a treasonable secret?"

"I can keep any secret."

"I know you can, oh, more than woman! My belief is that the President is Lurcock's mouthpiece."

"Is the President such a weakling, then? He wouldn't strike one as being."

"Do you know our Willis?" he asked, surprised.

"I've seen him," she answered evasively.

"It isn't weakness. It's — well, gratitude. Lurcock made him and he gives Lurcock a free hand in the management of things."

"But I thought he had such a strong Cabinet."

"Oh, the official lot. It's a streaky cut of bacon, the Cabinet. They go through their little mechanical processes well enough. But the real core and center of government from a practical standpoint is in that neat little house down there."

Her clearly marked brows went up. "Oh! Is that the house where the poker circle meets? You see I'm not entirely impervious to gossip."

"Then you should know," said he severely, "that in well-posted circles these gatherings are known as 'whist parties.' Yes, at night the Crow's Nest is sacred to the chaste revelry of card and chip. By day, it is severely business. There the real Cabinet meets and does a profitable trade: Secretary of Deals, Secretary of Pardons, Bootlegger General, Secretary of Office Sales, Secretary of Judicial Bargains, Receiver General of Graft, Secretary of Purchasable Contracts, Secretary of Public Health and Private Wealth — he's the worst of the roost — Chief Dispenser of Jobs; you'll find them all there at one time or another. And the actual Attorney-General, Dan Lurcock."

"Does the President stand for all this?"

"They're his friends. Old Bill Markham's friends can do no wrong. If you ever want a quiet job put through and have the price to pay for it, just call up Shoreham 5799."

"Thank you for — what was that number?"

"Shoreham 5799."

"I've already called it up."

Habitude of politics had taught Peter Thorne command of voice and expression. But his surprise was too much for his control. "You? For Heaven's sake, what about?"

"It was rather a queer adventure."

"It would be." The twist of his eyes toward the house was significant.

"Yes. I ran a man down night before last in the alley that I sometimes take as a short cut home. I think he had been drinking."

"Sure to have been."

"What?"

"Nothing. Go on."

"His face was muddied to a mask. But he did not seem to mind. Funny, don't you think?"

"Not so funny, perhaps."

"It seemed so to me. After I got home —"

"Oh! You took him home."

"Yes, my home. I had to take him somewhere and he protested quite violently at the suggestion of the hospital."

"Quite so."

"That is the third time you have commented in that cryptic way of yours."

"Is it cryptic to agree with your very interesting statements?"

"It is. Extremely."

"I beg your pardon, my dear. Go on."

"He asked me to call up Shoreham 5799."

"Whom did you get there?"

"I have no idea. As soon as I got the number, he took the phone and I paid no further attention."

"You wou — I beg your pardon."

"Then some one came for him in a taxi and took him away."

"Did you see the man?"

"Yes."

"A hulky, gruff, fair-haired man with a hard blue eye?"

"Not at all."

"Tall and spare, then? Diaconal suavity?"

"Wrong again. A small man. Quiet. Frightened but calm. Sleeky hair and eyes like a friendly seal."

"Fosgate. Did he say anything in particular?"

"Yes. He said, 'Is he hurt?' Quite anxiously."

"I don't mean Fosgate. I mean the other man."

"He chatted inconsequently. He seemed a restless soul. There was quite fifteen minutes to wait."

"Too long a space for weather talk to cover?"

"We didn't touch on the weather. He tried to explain what he was doing in that rear yard, but it was too blurry for me. Playing the gay Lothario, do you think?"

"A natural suspicion. But didn't it occur to you that he might be indulging a natural taste for solitude?"

"No. I can't say it did. I knew there was something queer about it, so I just chattered away to put him at his ease."

"He must have wondered at his hostess."

"Oh, he did! He hinted about to get a clue to my guilty luxury. He obviously suspected some Senator. What a slur upon your once respectable organization."

"He thought — *you*! Well, I'll — " Peter Thorne laughed, but there was an angry note in his mirth. "He must have been a dreadful ruin when you got through enlightening him."

"But I didn't. I was flattered."

"Flattered at being assigned to the demi-monde?"

"The haute demi-monde at least. The hall-mark of the Senatorial little ladies, I'm told, is their extreme youth. To have so high a market value set on one is surely complimentary to a woman who will never see thirty again."

"Yet you obstinately continue to look ten years younger. It's hardly decent."

"He rather hinted that he would like to call again if he could manage it."

"And you said?"

"Not at three a.m."

"Did that enlighten him?"

"I doubt it."

"You don't intend seeing him again."

"Don't I?"

"If you're asking me — "

"I'm not, I'm asking myself."

"In any case, I doubt if you will."

"A challenge?"

"Heaven forbid! I don't want to drive you to it. Is that the end of your very interesting narrative?"

"Practically. He bade me good night, and left my slandered precincts"— her soft lips quivered a little at the corner —"the best be-fooled man in Washington."

"About you, you mean?"

"About himself."

"You'll have to be more explicit with a failing intellect like mine."

"He never for an instant suspected that I knew who he was all along," she stated with delicate deliberation.

Without his volition, indeed to his disgust, Senator Thorne's hand extended towards his demi-tasse, jerked so sharply that the cup was knocked to the ground and shattered. "Clumsy of me! But it's wholly your fault." He reproached her with a slowly shaken head. "Edith, you're a sad disappointment to me."

"Because of my innocent little coup de theatre?"

"I wanted to be the one to surprise you. And now look at the coffee spots on my newest spring trouserings!"

"I've never seen you startled into a spasm before. I quite liked it."

"There will be no encore, however. Have there been any sequelæ to your adventure?"

"Sequels? What would there be? From the President?"

"More probably from some of those interested in him."

"No. Not that I recall. Wait! What was the name you mentioned? The actual Attorney-General, you called him?"

"Lurcock."

"Yes. A Mr. Lurcock called up yesterday. Several times."

"I don't like that, Edith."

"I didn't answer, of course."

"No, but — "

"But what?"

"I don't want to frighten you."

"Try and do it."

"He can make matters quite unpleasant for you."

"Can he?" she returned disdainfully. "I don't quite see how."

"Have you ever heard of the secret service?"

"It looks after counterfeiters and smugglers, doesn't it?"

"It is the official spy system of Washington. Under this present administration this government is a government by spies. Last week my office was rifled, and my private papers gone over."

"Why?"

"That's quite another story. There are rumors of a Senatorial investigation of certain activities, and though as a good administration man I'm against it, even I am not free from the espionage."

"But you are a United States Senator. I'm a private person."

"Not if the President of the United States comes to see you."

"Peter, you're becoming interesting."

"I don't want to interest you, my dear," said he gravely. "I want to warn you."

"You give me all the thrills of conspiracy. I could even imagine that the man exercising the wolfhound on the sidewalk opposite is a secret service man."

"He is."

"No! Trailing you?"

"Not at all. You."

She laughed. "I'll promise him a chase."

"You'll never get away from them. They've got a network about Washington. Even the President can't escape them."

"They spy on him?" she cried.

"Oh, no! Guard him. He gets dreadfully bored with it and tries to give them the slip once in awhile. He was escaping from them when you ran him down."

"Oh, that was it. Not the Lothario business. I'm glad. But how do you know so much?"

"I have my lines. One must have. However, all Washington is ringing with

the brief nocturnal disappearance of our Bill: but very few of us know where
he was. It is desirable, I think, that no more be informed. You have the gift of
reticence, I know."

"As, for example, today."

"Oh, with me!"

"It's a temptation, though."

"What is?"

"The opportunity to see the inside of politics. Especially if it's as melodramatic as you make it appear."

"I am not exaggerating when I tell you that it may be dangerous."

"Tempting me still further!"

"Edith, I have heard on impeccable authority that you might have exerted a
powerful and intimate — very intimate — influence on the inside diplomacy of
a great European power."

"The price was too high. Intimate, by the way, is the exact word."

"Yes. Well, you cannot take part in this game without paying the price."

"It might almost be worth it."

He threw up his hands. "I give you up. Thank God I still have enough power
to get you out of most forms of trouble. Will you remember that?"

"Yes, Petah, dear."

"By the way, when you get home, go quietly to one of your upper windows
and see if you don't notice a man, or possibly two men, unobtrusively making
the rounds of the circle, always where they can keep your house in sight."

They rose. Down the street the great voice of Jeff Sims fog-horned a message
to a passing acquaintance.

"Hey, Alec! D'ja know that Stickley is out? . . . Sure! Quit for the good of his
health."

The wolfhound leader watched the Senator and his companion pick up a car,
then vanished into a house to telephone.

Three hours later Edith Westervelt called up Thorne.

"The men are there. Two of them."

"Of course. I wouldn't say any more now."

"Why not?"

"Your wires are probably tapped."

"I don't believe it! . . . Well, I'll write."

"Do, remembering always that your letters may be opened and read."

"Isn't there a line somewhere," said Edith Westervelt's voice, "about America
being the land of the free and the home of the brave?"

JOHN DOS PASSOS

The journalist and novelist John Dos Passos (1896–1970) had a deep personal and political connection with Washington through much of his adult life. He reported on the Bonus Expeditionary Force ("Bonus Army") and its march on Washington in 1932 for the *New Republic*; in his series of travel essays, *In All Countries* (1934), he treated the Soviet Union, Mexico, Spain, and the United States. In an attempt to prevent the spread of war, he traveled to Washington in 1937 to try to stop the U.S. arms embargo against Spain. In the brouhaha that followed when he and Hemingway tried to use their collaborative film *The Spanish Earth* for conflicting purposes with Franklin Delano Roosevelt, Dos Passos arguing that life in the hinterland could go on despite the war, and Hemingway emphasizing the deadly fighting and devastating bombing of cities, many thought Dos Passos had changed his political stripes and abandoned the Loyalist cause altogether. Again, *The Adventures of a Young Man* (1939), the first volume in his *District of Columbia* trilogy, alarmed the professional Left, who concluded that Dos Passos was condemning the Communist Party in Spain and becoming a Trotskyite. His politics were changing, but the ruthlessness of the Communists in Spain had much to do with that. *Number One* (1943), the second volume in the trilogy, relates the story of Tyler Spotswood, the alcoholic assistant to Homer "Chuck" Crawford ("Number One"), a corrupt southern politician in the mold of Huey Long, who wins a Senate seat but eventually betrays Spotswood to save his own reputation. As such, it captures Dos Passos's growing disillusionment with U.S. politics and his sense of futility about the future.

From "The State Park Bottoms"
In *Number One* (Volume 2 in *District of Columbia* Trilogy)

The pain went through him like sweet on a hollow tooth. "Oh hell, I'd like a drink right now." His lips formed the words as he pressed his head back into the pillow again. God, he was pooped. As he tried to will himself back to sleep, a cloud of thoughts of what might have been rose and settled stinging like mosquitoes in his head.

Again his ears caught an uneven thump in the sound of the motors. Suppose it was engine trouble. Suppose they crashed. No more threat of indictments. No more hearings. No more lawyers' exceptions. He tried carefully and meticulously to imagine absolute blackness, like passing out but deeper, darker, forever. This bundle of querulous nerve tissue blown out like a match into blackness inevitable and always. He shook his head. He didn't want to die yet. He opened his eyes.

In the groundglass slot above the door in front of him the "NO SMOKING ... ADJUST SAFETY BELTS" sign had flashed on. Suddenly feeling quite cheerful he cupped his eyes with his hands against the window to see if he could look out. Three frail strings of light swept in tremulous diagonals across the darkness of his field of vision; streetlights; then he caught sight of the reassuring glare flooding the runways of an airport blurred in the mist. He let out his breath. A chance to walk around. Stretching his legs a little might make him feel better. As he got his papers together to put them back in the brief case he caught sight of that postal card that had been forwarded from Washington and that had puzzled him so. Written across it in a slanting hand was:

Dear Sir,

For several months I have been most anxious to contact you in connection with a communication from a near relative. At last through the newspapers I am in possession of your esteemed address. Please call me before ten a.m. at Cap 9799. Later I am not in. Accept the sincere consideration of
BENJAMIN BATTISTA, JR.

The plane had landed so smoothly Tyler couldn't tell when the wheels had touched the ground. The cabin shook a little as they taxied in across the grass. The attendant opened the door the moment the plane came to a dead stop. A rush of raw night air poured in.

Tyler shivered as he sat staring at the writing on the post-card. Could it be some detective's bright idea, or some nut who wanted only a few dollars to get him a fortune out of the French Spoliation Claims? If it was a Treasury dick he'd better see him, maybe he'd be able to smell out what the guy was up to. Tyler shoved the card back in with the rest of his papers, took the precaution of locking the briefcase with the little key that hung on his watchchain, and climbed stumbling a little out of the cabin. The raw air cut his wind. Shivering so that his teeth chattered he ran with yanked up coatcollar across the wet cement to the waitingroom. The faces of the other passengers had a bleary look as they stood around, men and women staring sleepily at each other out of their furs and buttonedup overcoats. There was nobody he knew. Their faces had a ghastly haunted look under the reddish halo the mist had given the unshaded light.

When he came out of the toilet he got himself a paper cup of water from the cooler. He'd found in the upper pocket of his vest two of the sedative tablets that doctor at the clinic had given him to take when he felt a craving for a drink. He put them in his mouth and swallowed them. He had to get some sleep.

The tablets gave him confidence. As soon as he'd climbed back on the plane he fluffed up his pillow carefully and settled comfortably into his seat. As the vibration from the climb smoothed out and the plane settled into the easy roar of its northward course again, he found himself drifting amid humming fragments of halfremembered phrases out of the lawyers' briefs, demurrer, plea in abatement, bill of exceptions, helplessly off to sleep.

"Washington, sir, Washington," an attendant was shaking him by the shoulder. He opened his heavy eyes. Faint indigo light was filtering through the cabin window beside him. "Washington, sir," shouted the attendant. "Of course. Thank you," Tyler said in a thick voice. He got shakily to his feet, grabbed his hat and briefcase and stumbled out into the cold gloaming of a drizzly sleety dawn.

The lights of the airport were blurred in his eyes. The man in the big coat was Chuck. "No overcoat . . . you'll catch your death of cold." Chuck's voice rasped harshly. "Say, Toby, you're sober, ain't you? . . . We need to have our dukes up this day, if it's the last thing we do on this earth." Tyler was staring dazedly into Chuck's round gray face that blobbed out of the fur collar of the big overcoat, as full of little wrinkles as a stale apple. His large eyes bulged anxiously into Tyler's out of rings of bruisedlooking violet flesh. Tyler's teeth started to chatter. "I'm all right," he stammered. "A cup of coffee'll wake me up."

"My God, Toby, you're lookin' awful. Here's the car an' the . . ."

A white light flashed in Tyler's eyes. He blinked and drowsily brought his hand up in front of his face.

"Git 'em," Chuck's voice ripped out. "Git those men. Crummit . . . Saunders, smash that camera."

A group of raincoats had rushed out at them from behind the airport building. Flashlight bulbs bloomed against the rainy sky above white faces forming words.

"Use your knee, you sonofabitch . . . Come on. We're gittin' outa here." Before Tyler could see what was happening he was shoved, with Chuck's grip tight on the muscle of his arm, into a long towncar that moved off smoothly with old Sam in uniform at the wheel, and they were speeding across the empty bridge above the shimmer of the old Potomac towards the city. Tyler hardly knew whether he'd really seen Saunders' long arms flailing above a struggling pile of men on the wet pavement or had heard the thud of slugging blows and the light brittle smash of metal and glass on cement.

"Toby, we're in a fight." Chuck spat the words out through panting breaths into his ear. "Ain't no time for lilypads . . . That there tinhorn lawyer who's investigatin' radio stations before the Grand Jury, he's out for blood . . . I ain't fixin' to have my pichur taken with no jailbird . . ." He let loose a kind of grim cackle and leaned forward to speak to old Sam. "Sam, why are you pokin' along like we was mourners at a funeral? You drive, boy . . . You ought to know where the Senate Office Building is by this time . . . Been there every day for the last three years."

Tyler shook his head to get the dense numb cottonwool feeling out of it. "Chuck, you came out of the business down in Horton all right . . . It's Norm Stauch and me got the dirty end of the stick down there."

"If you-all do what I tell you you'll be all right everywhere, every goddam one of you. I ain't never let nobody go to jail yet . . . This here lil chinchbug from the Middle West, this here Mackenzie Turner, a little ignoramus who wants to be Attorney General, he's agoin' to put you on the stand this mornin' an' you're agoin' to sweat . . . Watch out for one thing . . . Like as not he's got a transcript of your testimony down in Horton. Him an' Steve Baskette, that old snappin' turtle, they've had their heads together, both of 'em plannin' to be nabobs of the reignin' empire of St. Vitus' dance. My organization kin buck the gang of 'em, but damn they jumped me before I was ready . . ."

Tyler was looking out at the topheavy manycolumned facades, reduplicated as if in a mirror, late additions still gleaming vaguely through scaffolding, along the edge of Constitution Avenue. The glisten of the wet asphalt on the wide empty streets gave him the feeling the car was a boat skimming across dark ponds and broad canals. He found himself remembering the ominous dark red the bricks used to have on the building of the old Friends' School rainy days and the clopclop of the big white horses of brewery trucks over wet woodblock pavements. Everything he saw brought up recollections. He couldn't seem to bring himself up to date.

"Now, Mister Chuck, you cain't say I didn't git you here quick," said old Sam in a voice like thick chocolate, turning his black face back into the car and showing all his teeth in an indulgent smile as he slowed the car gently to a stop at the inside entrance of the great palegray office building.

"Sam, it was masterly," said Tyler with a vague tinny giggle. "The old hand hasn't lost its cunning."

Sam began to grumble: "This time o' mornin' I ought be in bed or in church, Mister Toby."

Chuck had shot out of the car without a word. Tyler had to run to keep up with him as he crossed the vestibule, skirting a pool of soapy water where two colored men were washing the marble pavements with mops and buckets. They had to ring several times for the elevator. Chuck kept up a low whine of cursing while they waited. "Excuse it, gentlemen," said the elderly night watchman, touching his visored cap as the bronze doors finally slid open. "Good mornin', Senator. Up early this mornin'." Chuck scowled at him as if he were going to haul off and hit him. To smooth over, Tyler rattled off in a chatty tone that sounded silly in his ears, "Early? I haven't been to bed myself. For me it's late."

Chuck hurried on ahead down the corridor and opened the receptionroom door with his own key. Tyler strode after him through the little vestibule into the great office with its big polished desk and its red morocco furniture, with brasstacked bindings and its familiar smell of papers and furniturepolish and stale cigarsmoke. The row of big windows along the wall let in a skyful of steely morning light. Chuck dropped his furlined coat on a chair. His black felt had dropped off his head as he stretched out on his back on the couch across from the desk. "Damned if I been up so early sence I been in Washington," he gasped. "Toby, you're causin' me a whole lot of trouble . . ." "Me?" started Tyler. Chuck interrupted: "For crissake call up that guard downstairs an' see if the boys is come in yet."

Tyler walked sullenly over to the telephone on the desk. When he put the receiver down he looked at Chuck and shook his head. "Don't you make mean eyes at me, you sonofabitch," said Chuck. He took his eyes off Tyler's face and stared at the ceiling. ". . . There's nothin' in my career, sence I was a little shaver totin' those tiedup newspapers too heavy for me down State Line Avenue . . . there's nothin' in my career that can't bear the scrutiny of the most holierthan-thousest sugarsuckin' reformer in this whole mess of crackpots an' visionaries they've got a-cloggin' up the wheels of gover'ment in this town with all this Jew peddler's ragbag of theories and pretenses" . . . Chuck lay on his back talking in a singsong voice. "I'm goin' to say that tonight," he said in a matter-of-fact tone. Then he looked sharply at Tyler. "But no man's reputation is better than the company he keeps."

"Hold your horses, Chuck." Tyler was trying to get a smile out of him. "I thought we were the crackpots."

Chuck didn't answer. Tyler started walking up and down in front of the windows. Across broad stretches of wet asphalt shining in the morning light he could see beyond russet trees the square bulk of the Senate wing with the dome of the Capitol rising against the tinsel-lined clouds behind it. A flight of starlings was blackly circling the cluster of columns that held up the small topmost lantern. His mind still kept skidding off into odd backtracks. He was remembering the peculiar awe he'd felt as a small boy seeing the Capitol dome rise high and rosy into the evening sky at the end of a long treebordered avenue while he was trotting along with a stitch in his side keeping up with his grandfather's fast limping walk, when the old man used to take him out to lecture him on the historic sites of the city. He shook his head to get the fog out of it. But his mind would go slipping off the track like the needle on a wornout phonograph record. To be saying something he muttered vaguely: "This thing's got me worried."

"You better be." Chuck roared scornfully from the couch. "They've got you hoppin' on the griddle, boy . . . I don't know if I kin git you off or not."

The phone rang. Automatically Tyler went over to answer it. "Yes, send 'em right up . . . It's the watchman asking if it's all right for Crummit and Saunders to come up . . . He must be a rookie."

"Thank the Lord . . . If they mixed it up with the cops I'll can the sons-o'bitches."

There was a stamping of feet in the vestibule. Looking pleased with themselves Crummit and Saunders came shambling in. "Well, we're back," they were shouting. "I was jess sayin'," Chuck went on without lifting his head, "that if you two punks had messed with the po-lice I'd let you go back where you came from."

"No, sir," said Saunders, who was patting at a cut on his lip with a handkerchief gray with dirt and covered with little spatters of blood. "Number One, we didn't mess with no po-lice. A patrol car did give us a little chase, but we lost 'em back of the railroad station in Alexandria."

"They got our number all right," Crummit piped up; "but it won't do 'em no good 'cause I had my extry plates."

"We come back in a taxicab . . . Did you see me paste that cameraman, Number One? He won't take no pichurs for some time, no, sir, he won't . . . I had a little bit of somepin' under my glove." His long calf face glowing with workmanlike pride, he brought a set of brass knuckles out of his pocket.

"You git them things out of this office," shouted Chuck, half sitting up. "I didn't tell you to kill the pore fellers."

"That boy was tough," said Crummit. "I had to close in an' give him my lil ole rabbit punch . . . did you see him fold up, Number One?"

"Now one of you grunt and groan artists git the hell outa here an' go to a lunchroom an' git us some breakfast . . . Be sure the coffee's scaldin' . . . Too early to git it here, ain't it, Toby?"

Tyler nodded. "Better send out for it, Number One."

"These here solemn Solons [salons] in Congress assembled, they don't see the light o' day till ten o'clock in the mornin' . . . Lemme tell you boys somethin' . . . When you see a man in this world git up early every mornin', that's the man's a-goin' to git what he's after . . . Allright, what are you standin' around for? Crummit, you go git the breakfast. Let Saunders wash his face . . . I declare," he said to Tyler when they'd left, sitting up in the middle of the couch looking down at the red silk clock on his blue sock as he waggled one foot in an ornate tan oxford over the edge ". . . the way you boys all depend on me it's a wonder I don't have to take down your pants an' set you on the potty."

He lay back again laughing and stretching out his arms over his head. "Chester Bigelow's comin' in a minute an' then the Judge, an' if you'all stop run-nin' around like a chicken with its head cut off, we'll decide how we're goin' to handle this thing . . . I'll git tarred up some, like I said down home . . . we'll all git tarred up some . . . but they can't do me no harm . . . I got the people behind me, don't forgit that."

"Won't do you any good if they break up the organization . . . I don't need to tell you that, Chuck."

"You don't need to tell me nuthin'."

"I'll go an' see what I've got on my desk . . . Call me when you want me," said Tyler huffily.

He went through the communicating door into his own office and sat down at his desk. With a soothing sense of routine he began to look through a mess of papers and clipped-together letters. If only everything would just go on as usual. When he ran his eyes down his appointment pad, Miss Jacoby's little notes swam before his eyes. His swivel chair made a familiar cosy creak as he leaned back in it. He found himself studying the duplicate of the penny postal card he'd found in his briefcase. The same neat laborious handwriting: Dear Sir, for several months I have been most anxious . . . the same phone number. He got up and walked into the outer office to leave a note for Miss Glendinning. *Please call Cap 9799 tell Mr. Battista I can see him here after twelve this noon. T.S.* Tyler found the performance of penciling out the note on a small blue scratch pad habitual and soothing. He settled back at his desk again and started to draw spirals on a piece of legal cap with his fountainpen.

Suddenly Chuck was there standing over his desk. "Toby," he said quietly. "You've always been a drink' man, we mustn't suppress that . . . It's too bad . . . but it's true." His voice grew loud and dramatic. "You ain't got no more head for figures than that birdbrain Saunders. The hookworm ate up that boy's brains so's he kin only count up to the number of his fingers an' toes . . . that is, if you don't hurry him . . . It's notorious that any soak's memory's weak . . . I used to be a drinkin' man myself, so I ought to know . . . I shouldn't wonder if you couldn't remember a goddam thing. The trouble down in Horton was that Sue Ann had the bright idea of keepin' you sobered up. Ain't that like a woman? . . . Now Norm Stauch . . . He's a gambler an' a brothelkeeper an' a lowlife, you know that. What he did was to throw a lot of wild parties an' had you signin' documents you wasn't fit to read . . . You don't remember a goddam thing. You signed 'em by the yard. Tell 'em to ask Stauch why he tried to debauch my private secretary . . . Wouldn't be surprised if the interests put him up to it."

"Norm Stauch's on the level . . ." said Tyler, without lifting his eyes from the spirals he was drawing on the pad.

"He better watch hisself before he messes with me."

"He's a friend of mine." Tyler started slowly getting to his feet. There was a knocking on a door outside somewhere. Tyler saw the corners of Chuck's mouth twitch. "Saunders, see what that is," he shouted in a startled voice.

From the other office came Chester Bigelow's booming "Top of the mornin' to you, my boy . . . Number One in yet? . . . Well, well." He strode in the door with his arms outstretched. "Tyler, I hear Number One got you past the reporters safely . . . We sure were worried for fear you'd get off the plane, having a drop taken . . . and you know . . . let the old tongue rattle." The Reverend Bigelow looked as if he had been up all night too. His aging too boyish face with its broad lips and high cheekbones had a battered unbathed gray look.

"I bet you ain't slept a wink, Reverend," said Chuck teasingly.

"Quit the Reverend when we're among friends; I'm no different from any other man. Whose business is it if I spent the night in watching and . . .?"

"Watchin' some floosie shake her shimmy off, eh Chet?"

"Skip it, Homer . . . This situation has forced me to come to a decision . . ."

"Say, Saunders, has that dope come back yet?"

"Yessir," came two voices in chorus from the other room. Crummit appeared in the door with his arms stiff at his sides; "Number One I set it out for you on a tray on your desk."

"Come an' git it, boys."

As he followed Chuck into the private office, Chester Bigelow went on talking, opening his mouth wide so that his voice rattled the glasses together that stood grouped round a pitcher of icewater on the sidetable. "It is with the greatest pain that I have been forced to repudiate the political doctrines I learned at my mother's knee . . . No thinking man can face the situation in this country today without coming to the conclusion that our democracy is rotten beyond repair. No honest man can forbear to say that force is the only remedy. We are faced with a plot against the supremacy of all the ideals we hold most dear, against our deep faith in our fathers' God, against the sanctity of our beautiful American womanhood, against the existence of the white race itself. . . . That vile conspiracy, that has subverted and degraded that great Christian civilized continent from which our forefathers sprang, has established itself in this country. Its slimy tentacles are twined about the executive and judiciary branches of the government . . ."

Chuck had settled at his desk and drunk off a glass of orange juice. He poured himself out a cup of coffee from a tall carton and snapped his fingers and cursed under his breath at the heat when he put it down. "Better have a cup of coffee, Chet," he said, breaking off a piece of toast to dunk in his cup and stuffing it into his mouth.

"Fortunately, the legislative branch has remained more or less untainted by this plague of isms that darkens the skies of our beloved nation . . . but of what avail is it when they depend for their votes upon an electorate already devitalized and poisoned by the taint of the dark bloods? The great white Anglo-Saxon race was born to empire, Homer Crawford. The time has come for patriotic men to take the law into their own hands. The conspiracy . . ."

"Have a cup of coffee, Chet," Chuck interrupted, talking with his mouth full of toast. "This ain't no time for Lexington and Concord . . . You wait till I'm President sittin' up at my desk down there at 1600 Pennsylvania Avenue . . . We'll start to fix things so's an American kin be proud of his flag . . . You wait."

"Wait? . . . Wait till they murder us in our beds . . . No, Homer, the day has come for the white people of this country to rise in their wrath."

Chuck stopped with a piece of dunked toast halfway to his mouth, letting it drop back into his cup. "What I'm worryin' about is one little federal district attorney that's risen in his wrath an' his wrath ain't worth a pipsqueak . . . All this big colored shirt talk of yours, Chet, might come in handy in a presidential campaign, but now it's the cart before the horse. What we need is to work on that card catalogue." He put the toast in his mouth and pointed to the row of yellow pine cases with ranks of little lettered drawers in them along the wall. "I keep it in here so that nobody won't mess with it. Every man an' woman in that catalogue gits litrachur regular, most of 'em tune in on our programs, an' they'll go to the polls an' vote when I tell 'em to an' they'll stay away when I tell 'em to. An' if I tell 'em to give their chillen castoroil, they'll give 'em castoroil. If I told 'em to go jump in the crick I bet a whole lot of 'em would jump in the crick . . . If the day should come when I was forced to tell 'em to come to Washington an' drive the moneychangers out of the temple, by God, they'd come . . . Wouldn't they, Toby?"

Tyler didn't answer. The oldfashioned mahogany clock on the mantel chimed nine. He wished its sweet tinkle would never stop.

Saunders leaned inquiringly into the room from the vestibule: "Number One . . . hit's Judge Bannin' an Herb Jessup."

"Bring 'em in . . . I didn't tell you to leave 'em out in the rain."

Judge Banning came in first. His face looked almost as white as his hair. The lower lids hung loose and red from his eyes. His whole face had a smudged look. His back was bent and he felt his way carefully with his small shiny pointed feet as if he expected to find the floor uneven before him. His shoes creaked with each step. Right on his heels slouched Herb Jessup's big looselyhung paunchy figure. The pouches of skin under his small eyes were all crumpled up. Under his pouted fish's mouth the flabby chins bulged smoothly over the wing collar. As the two of them came into the room their eyes lit first on Tyler's face. Tyler could feel them apprehensively searching out the lines and contours of his face.

He didn't want to catch their glance. He tried to sit still. With one hand he fished out his cigarettecase and started to fidget with it. He took out a cigarette and put it in his mouth without lighting it. In spite of himself he started to snap his cigarettecase open and shut.

"Hello, Herb." Chuck let out a shout of laughter. "If ever I saw a man with his ass in a sling . . . Ain't nutten to be ascared of, boy . . . Judge, what time did you tell Grossman to pick up Toby?"

"Nine-thirty, Number One."

"That's your lil Jew lawyer, Toby. You didn't think I was goin' to send you down there without a lawyer, did you? What time is he subpoenaed for?"

"Ten o'clock."

Tyler got to his feet to set his empty coffeecup on the corner of the desk. Chuck had started to study some type-written sheets he had picked up from the wire basket in front of him. Tyler lit a cigarette and stood with his back to the window. Judge Banning, Herb Jessup, and Chester Bigelow had settled themselves in a row along the couch. Herb still had his rubbers on. They all had their faces twisted towards him and their eyes screwed up against the light to look in his face.

Miss Jacoby poked her head round the door that led in from the outer office. "Good morning, Senator . . . Good morning, gentlemen. Aren't we all early birds?" she said in her cheerful shriek.

"Any danger of that plane bein' grounded? Weather don't look any too good."

"I'll call right up," said Miss Jacoby. "I've got all the reservations."

"We're goin' to need four seats: Saunders, Crummit, Herb, an' me. It's too late already to make Atlanta by train." Miss Jacoby's head disappeared.

"I hope you lay it on the line, Homer," began the Reverend Bigelow. "We must arouse the people of this country to the dangers . . ."

Chuck had switched on the interoffice dictaphone on his desk. "Miss Jacoby," he called. "Suppose you order us up some more rolls and coffee . . . plenty coffee . . . Some of us are goin' down for the third time." He jumped to his feet and walked to where Tyler stood in front of the window. "Well, Toby . . . ?"

Tyler avoided looking straight in Chuck's face.

"I don't see why I can't say the same thing I said in Horton . . . the profits, at least my share of them . . . were merely placed in my name through loose bookkeeping. Your good friends who had made a killing on a little gamble in leases turned them over to the radio station to promote our political ideas . . . The money was never part of my personal income. That Treasury agent finally admitted we'd paid our corporation taxes all right."

"Son," said Judge Banning smoothly. "It won't do. Too many other names involved. These people are out for blood."

"Stauch got away with saying his was in repayment for a loan . . . which was the truth."

"If they pin him down he can't prove nothin' unless he finds that cancelled note," said Chuck.

Herb laughed. "He won't find that."

"Hell, you've got the transcript of my testimony . . ." said Tyler. "My head's in a whirl . . . I don't remember what I said."

"That's more like it, Toby," said Chuck in a wheedling tone. ". . . You might have been drinkin' right through the trial." The three men on the couch seemed hardly to breathe. The room was so quiet noises of streetcars began to seep in from the street. Sparrows were chirping on the window ledges.

Tyler rammed his clenched fists into his pockets. "You know as well as I do that I haven't had a drink in six months."

Chuck dropped down into the chair back of his desk again and started running his fingers through his curly hair. "Folks kin say I oughtn't to a been associatin' with a hopeless soak, but after all ain't no harm in bein' a little softhearted. I ain't let down an old friend yet."

Tyler backed up against the windowsill. He could hear his own breathing in the intense quiet of the room.

"You sure were hittin' it up last time I saw you," drawled Herb. "Don't you remember the Club Nautilus? That can't have been more'n a couple of months ago."

The buzzer sounded on Chuck's desk. He switched on the dictaphone. It was Miss Glendinning's voice. "Senator, I have a longdistance call for Mr. Spotswood. Will he take it in there?"

Tyler started towards the door. "I'll take it at my own desk," he said.

From "Washington Is the Loneliest City"
In *State of the Nation*

"THE OLD WASHINGTONIAN"

It was a hot June afternoon. I was sitting on a bench in the backyard of one of the houses built on the edge of the low house-crowded ridge that cuts across the northwest section of Washington to form the rim of the shallow bowl in which the downtown city stews. The grass in the sloping yard was very green. The sky over the rooftops in front of us was very blue. A few big tattered white clouds shaded at the base stood motionless in the midst of it.

For the first time in my life I was finding Washington beautiful. When I was a very small child I used to hear my elders talk about the beauty of Washington and never could figure it out. There had been, to my childish mind, a certain cosy dilapidation about Georgetown, vinegrown brick walling in little lives of elderly female relatives sitting in parlors behind drawn shades; there'd been the stately degradation of Alexandria, 'the deserted city,' the colored people used to call it; there'd been Rock Creek and the false feeling of being in the mountains it gave you; and green swampy meadows and the haze over the mudcolored Potomac. My parents used to talk about the beauty of Washington. To me it seemed stifling and hideous. Now I was discovering that I was old enough to find Washington beautiful. Maybe it was the city that had gotten old enough.

The old Washingtonian who was sitting beside me on the bench was working as a checker on the streetcars. He's never done a job of that kind before, but he was enjoying the work. He liked the idea that he was being useful in the war effort. As we looked out at the grassy yard and the ailanthus trees and the nondescript bushes along the fences and the backs of brick buildings, he told me with cheery enthusiasm about his days standing on street corners or in the full weight of the sun on traffic islands, noting the times the cars passed and the number of people on them. Sizing up the number of people in a car at a glance was a trick it took him some time to learn. The work made him feel busy, useful, and in an odd way, free.

He was enjoying the life of the streets, the varieties of people he saw; the change in personnel as the day wore on; the early workers less welldressed, the oldfashioned American mechanics who worked at the Navy Yard or the Bureau of Printing; the floodtide of office workers between eight and nine; the house-wives going shopping; the school kids; the random specimens in the afternoon, fashion plates from embassies, tourists, soldiers and sailors on leave, young women going to the movies in pairs; the great flood of tired heatwilted clerks struggling to get home between five and six; the evening life of the town; people in fresh clothes on the loose, citysized crowds in search of a place to eat, a movie house you could find a seat in, a cocktail bar you could get a table in, a dump to drink beer, aimlessly hopelessly roaming about in what was still a vastly overgrown small Southern town in that stagnant hollow between the Potomac River and Anacostia Creek.

When he came home at night often very late my friend said he'd sit a while on this bench smelling the rankness of wilted leaves the damp brought out from the heattrampled vegetation, listening to neighing voices out of darkened windows, girls' voices making fake dates with men, young men's voices yodeling that they'd be right over. Wartime Washington was essentially a town of lonely people.

We decided to go downtown to eat supper at Hall's to renew a torn fragment of recollection that lingered in my mind of the shadow of foliage against gaslit brick and curlycued gilt mirrors and towboat captains in embroidered suspenders drinking beer in their shirtsleeves against a black walnut bar, and the powdered necks of blowsy women, and of a greataunt of mine, a lame old lady in her seventies who wore a black silk dress with a lace yoke, and who used to like to shock her daughters by saying that her idea of heaven was sitting in Hall's beergarden eating devilled crabs and drinking beer on a Sunday afternoon.

We walked out through the lodginghouse, a big old place that had been a family mansion not so long ago, now partitioned off into small cubicles where lived a pack of young men and women clerks in government offices. The house was clean, but it had the feeling of too many people breathing the same air, of strangers stirring behind flimsy walls, of unseen bedsprings creaking and unseen feet shuffling in cramped space.

Going out the front door it occurred to us that it might be in Washington that the Greenwich Village of this war would come into being. Around the period of the last war it had been in the slums of downtown New York that young Americans, fresh from the uneventful comfort of onefamily homes in small towns, had holed up like greenhorn immigrants in sleazy lodgings to get their first taste of a metropolis. In this war it might be in Washington. Maybe Washington was the new metropolis in the making.

Walking down the densely shaded street I remembered that when an uncle of mine had moved out to a house on this avenue, we had all thought it pretty fine, almost like taking a house in the country. My friend, the old Washingtonian, murmured that it would be all right now if it weren't so near the colored district. There was quite an overflow, especially at night. It was a dark street, he went on, laughing, in more ways than one. At night young negro girls and boys filled up every unlit corner and alarmed the lodginghouse keepers with their obstreperous necking under the trees and on the stoops. Shouted physiological terms flopped in through the open windows to offend the ears of the more respectably lodgers. It was almost as if they did it on purpose.

That started us talking about how people with different colored skins were getting on together in this crowded town. For a while my friend said it had looked as if a bloody race riot were brewing. On the streetcars, in the continual shoving for seats or for a place to stand there was every opportunity for trouble. Some colored people had bad manners. Some white people had bad manners. Everybody was in the habit of giving the colored people the worst end of everything. Remember the moment of painful tension when a car or bus crosses the line into Virginia and the colored people have to move into the back seats. Some of the younger negroes had gotten very uppish. Whites resented it. There were days when he could feel in the background among the crowds on the street a teasing whisper that there was going to be a riot, that there had got to be a riot to teach the niggers a lesson.

Wasn't the streetcar company more or less of a storm centre? Yes, the latest organized negro protest had been against the streetcar company because they wouldn't hire negro conductors and motormen. The company had canvassed its employees and found that if they did, most of them would look for other jobs. He himself, certainly not a man to throw an extra stone at an outcast, had said he would leave if there were colored men hired in his department. Nobody minded having colored men in jobs that could be all colored. It was the mixture the white men resented. They felt that in some jobs there'd be too much rubbing elbows in shelters, at the carbarns in close quarters. It wouldn't be practical.

After all most of the employees were Virginians or old Washingtonians, and old Washingtonians of all Southerners were most set in their ways. My friend said he'd gotten to know them and liked them immensely, found them very nice to work with. They felt they were doing a good job, they were certainly doing their best in a very trying setup. They resented this effort to force them to accept situations they didn't want to accept. As it was, the company was having a hard time getting new motormen. Youngsters who didn't know the routes kept getting their cars on the wrong tracks and snarling things up. Driving a streetcar was a job a man had to learn.

Anyway, the tension seemed to be easing off now. Things had been pretty much touch and go at the time of the mass-meeting in Garfield Park. The town had been full of that sullen sense of a storm brewing. There had been the rumors, the little groups with their heads together, the hysterical individuals suddenly starting to whoop it up for a fight. Luckily the demonstration had turned out to be more of a circus. The parade to the park had been fun. Colored people couldn't help enjoying things like that. The music and the bands had cleared the air. The cops had been ready to quell an insurrection, but they had done nothing to keep one from starting. Somehow the good sense of the majority of people colored and white had staved the riot off. Since then my friend said that hardly a day passed without a colored man's coming up to him at one of his streetcorners and trying to explain to him that the negroes in Washington wanted no trouble with the whites.

While we talked we had been walking eastward. At a corner on U Street we climbed on a streetcar. Sitting in the car my friend started talking about the Civil War. He had been reading Freeman's life of Robert E. Lee. We fell to speculating on the treacherous morass Washington had been during the Civil War, wondering whether there had been less regard for the public interest by officeholders then than now. Looking back on it, it was a miracle that this strange nation of ours had ever held together, the same kind of a miracle the nation was performing right now.

As the car ran east a change was coming over the street. It was losing the vague look of an uptown thoroughfare and becoming a main stem. The color of the population was changing. At every stop white people got off the car and colored people got on. They were as welldressed as the whites and their way of speaking and their manners were about the same. The street was becoming garish with signs, storefronts were taking on the tinselly look of a central city neighborhood. Pavements were crowded. We were riding through the main street of a negro city.

LOUIS J. HALLE

Louis J. Halle (1910–98) was a nature writer who served as a policy-planning expert with the U.S. State Department from 1941 to 1954. His *Spring in Washington* (1947), the product of many early-morning explorations, is now a minor classic. Harvard educated, he became a research professor at the University of Virginia after his tour in the government and later taught at the Graduate Institute of International Studies in Geneva. He authored several books on nature and on foreign policy, including *Birds Against Men* (1938), *Civilization and Foreign Policy* (1955), and *History, Philosophy, and Foreign Relations* (1987).

From *Spring in Washington*

To snatch the passing moment and examine it for signs of eternity is the noblest of occupations. It is Olympian. Therefore I undertook to be monitor of the Washington seasons, when the government was not looking. Though it was only for my own good, that is how the poorest of us may benefit the world. A more ambitious man might seek to improve the President of the United States.

The city of Washington is not so well established a fact as 38°53′ North, 77°2′ West, which came first. The setting preceded the city and will survive it. Before public buildings were erected here to house files and file clerks, our reddish-brown fellow men were doubtless accustomed to observing how the revolution of the seasons manifested itself at the fall line of the Potomac River. To improve my education, I wished to familiarize myself with what they had observed *sub specie aeternitatis*. If I could learn just when spring arrived, in what manner and in what guises, I should have grown in knowledge of reality and established a bond of common experience with my fellow travelers in eternity. My monitoring of the seasons in off hours would thus be more substantial and altogether a more serious matter than anything I could do for the government. I had not had compunctions at interrupting the dictation of an official document to observe, from a government window, a flight of swans moving south overhead; and while I have now forgotten what the official paper was about, I remember the swans. They made me an honorary brother of Audubon then and there, enlarging my experience to include life on the western frontier a century and a half ago.

Another year I shall, perhaps, insert advertisements in the newspapers after New Year's Day, calling attention to the forthcoming arrival of spring in town, proclaiming it the most lavish spectacle on earth, and offering hilltop or valley-bottom seats at a stiff price. You will see how the people flock to buy tickets, though they never thought it worth a free view before. One would like, however, to be honest and announce over the radio to all men: The spring shall make you free, the price of wolfram will enslave you.

The city of Washington has never had the praise it deserves from those of us who do not give ourselves altogether to city life. Unlike New York, it makes room for nature in its midst and seems to welcome it. There is Rock Creek Park, with its forests and fields, which wanders through Washington and remains uncorrupted. The city passes over Rock Creek Valley on bridges a hundred and twenty-five feet above and heeds it not. The muskrat swims and raises its young in the woodland stream beneath Connecticut Avenue, never knowing of the crowded buses and taxis that swarm overhead. Peering down from the railing of the bridge, you overlook what might be a virgin forest with an undiscovered and half-hidden river wandering through it. You may see a hawk circling over the trees, or a kingfisher following the stream. This is as the birds view the world when they fly in their migrations over the forests of the Northwest or the untrodden jungles of Central America. Especially after a cold night in fall, the warm sun rises over a dawn mist curled like a dragon through the length of the valley below. Once in early October, when all else was silent and the first rays of the sun shone from the horizon over the still shrouded valley, from far below the mist came the repeated call of the Carolina wren, *kirtleyou, kirtleyou, kirtleyou, kirtleyou* . . . I could build a house on the bridge and live happily there forever, turning my back to the street. At either end, the valley slopes rise steeply to its level so that, from the railing, you look directly into the top of the forest — its maze of branch and foliage, its leafy green chambers and recesses, the ground far below — and see it from the inside like a bird perched in its upper stories. I should prefer to think that the government built this lofty bridge for a look out, and that it bears traffic incidentally.

Elsewhere in Washington, parks, patches of forest, and trees are common. Squirrels and rabbits can move about a great part of the city at will. Bobwhites are at home in it, and foxes may be found. The roosting ground of the turkey vultures some two and a half miles up Rock Creek, reported by John Burroughs in 1861, is still used by them, though the city has overtaken it. In the late afternoon you may see half a hundred vultures circling over the Kennedy-Warren Hotel, which now dominates the site, or perched on its roof. Tenants of fashionable apartment houses complain that they are kept awake at night by the hooting of barred owls.

I go from my apartment, in the midst of the city, to the countryside of Virginia and Maryland entirely by ways that lead through woods and open green spaces. It is cross-country to Tierra del Fuego or Alaska. From my doorstep through the park to the mouth of Rock Creek, where it empties into the river, is no more than ten minutes by bicycle. Beyond, only a margin of greensward separates the road from the embankment. Across the river the wooded shore of Anolastan Island might in its summer foliage be the forested bank of a tropical river. All through the early spring, after the ice goes out, American mergansers, the drakes showing as sparkles of white at that distance, swim and dive in close to its shore or sun themselves on fallen trees. In summer white egrets hunt there. Once I saw through my binoculars a native, naked except about the loins, hunting with spear or gun along its shore. He vanished into the shrubbery as I watched, and I have never seen any other sign of human habitation on the island.

Anolastan Island (now renamed Theodore Roosevelt Island) stands at the fall line of the Potomac, washed by fresh water above, by tidewater below. The ancient city of Georgetown, long ago incorporated into the city of Washington, confronts it on the left bank, having marked the limit of navigation to generations of river boatmen. Above, the river runs in cataracts between steep banks and through tortuous ways from the Alleghenies. At the head of Anolastan Island its turbulence ends abruptly. Below, it broadens and ceases to flow except with the gentle alternations of the tide. Its expanse bears twinkling sailboats and an occasional river steamer. Colonial mansions, Mount Vernon among them, overlook it; but there are also extensive tidal marshes and marshy inlets. A hundred miles beyond is Chesapeake Bay, and at last the great ocean itself. Washington thus stands at the innermost limit of the coastal plain, mediating between the coast and the interior. This has been forgotten now by those who live in the city, but it was well known at one time, when the river boats dis-

charged their cargo at Georgetown for shipment by canal barge into the North
west Territories, and loaded in turn the cargo brought down by the barges from
the wild interior. It is still known to the red-breasted mergansers, which range
upriver as far as Washington and put in at the Tidal Basin under the Jefferson
Memorial, but stop here because it is the limit of their salt-water habitat, let
other ducks go as far as they please. I do not know how the fishes regard the
matter, but many of them doubtless hold like views, recognizing Washington
as the frontier town it is.

In spring one faces south, which means one looks directly downriver from
Washington. The Arlington Memorial Bridge forms a granite suture between
North and South, connecting President Lincoln's Memorial in Washington
with General Lee's Memorial in Arlington County. At the Arlington end it
opens on grassy fields that, in season, accommodate horned larks, killdeer, and
meadowlarks. The highway runs down the right bank past the Navy and Marine Memorial (bronze gulls scudding over a bronze wave), past the Highway
Bridge, and past Roaches Run. Roaches Run is a marshy lagoon trapped between the National Airport, on one side, and the railway tracks on the other.
Ducks and gulls and herons have remained faithful to it, despite low-roaring
airplanes and smoke-breathing locomotives. They are accustomed to these
dragons and these pterodactyls, regarding them not. The government pays conscience money here, posting the lagoon as a sanctuary and scattering grain, like
Ceres herself, for the wildfowl. At the airport giant transports and little pursuit
planes squat in rows like somnolent dragonflies. The killdeer share the field
with them. At the southern end of the airport, where a trickle of water from
Arlington County forms a wide marshy mouth as it empties into the river, you
look directly down on acres of open water and marsh grass. This, the mouth of
Four Mile Run, is beloved by a variety of river birds and marsh birds. I take it
that the fattest frogs and most succulent waterweeds are found here, amid the
talus of steel drums and other jetsam that has tumbled from the brink of the
airfield above.

MARITA GOLDEN

The recipient of many writing awards, Marita Golden (1950–) was encouraged by her parents from an early age to cultivate her talents as a writer and
storyteller. In her memoir, *Migrations of the Heart* (1983), she tells about growing up in Washington, earning a scholarship to study at American University,
marrying a Nigerian, and living in Africa. Golden has written two novels set
in Washington — *Long Distance Life* (1989), which covers the period from the

Great Migration to the Civil Rights Movement, and *The Edge of Heaven* (1999), which chronicles the breakdown of an African American family following the mother's tragic act of rage. In 1994, she published an informal study, *Saving Our Sons: Raising Black Children in a Turbulent World*, based in part on her experience of raising a son in the nation's capital. She is the cofounder of the African American Writers Guild and the Hurston/Wright Foundation, a national resource center for African American writers. An active teacher who has held appointments at several colleges and universities in the United States and Africa, Golden is currently writer-in-residence at the University of the District of Columbia.

From "Naomi"
In *Long Distance Life*

When I saw Washington, D.C., for the first time in 1926, I thought I'd never seen a prettier place. Down where I come from, Spring Hope, North Carolina, there wasn't nothing, not a single thing, to compare with what I saw here. The big government office buildings, the White House, the Washington Monument . . . and this is where I saw my first streetcar. And the way some colored folks lived! Had colored professors at Howard University and colored folks had houses sometimes just as good as white folks. Some people called it "up South," but it was far enough away from where I come to be North to me.

I'd come to join my cousin Cora, who'd come up the year before to keep house for the son of the family she'd worked for in Raleigh. Their boy had just got a big job as a judge and they let Cora go to come up here and work for him and his family. Cora didn't have husband nor child and she'd lost her mama and daddy back in 1918 when that influenza killed so many people. So when her white folks said they'd buy her ticket North and see to it that their son paid her a few more dollars a month, she just up and went.

Soon as Cora got up here, I started getting letters all about what a good time she was having going to the Howard Theater, how she'd joined a penny-savers' club, and one night on U Street had seen Bessie Smith, who she said was prettier in person than in any of her pictures. And how there was a whole bunch of folks from North Carolina in Washington, how it seemed like damn near every colored person in North Carolina was living in Washington, D.C. She stayed with that judge for a little while, but got sick of "living in," couldn't have no freedom or do what she wanted when she wanted, only had one day off. She wrote in one letter, "Sure they pay me a few dollars more and I got my own room, but the running never stops and they act like I don't never get tired. And his wife like to almost have a stroke if she sees me sitting down. You s'posed to be grateful for the chance to wait on them from six in the morning to whenever at night. They think I come North to work for them. I come North to be free." Then, sooner than you could say Jack Johnson, Cora wrote me saying she had quit her white folks and was working two jobs — at Bergmann's laundry and doing day's work. "I'd be working a third job if I hadn't met me a real nice man from Richmond who I spends my Saturday nights with and who takes me to church on Sunday morning," she said.

Sometimes young people ask why we all left down there. Well, I think folks just got tired. Tired of saying *Yessuh* and being ground down into nothing by crackers or hard work and sometimes both at the same time. And in those days the whites'd lynch you as soon as look at you. It's a shame young folks today don't know nothing about how we were treated then. It's too bad we were so ashamed, we figured it was best to forget and our children not to know. I had a cousin lynched in Florida, a boy — just fourteen years old. He'd been playing with some little po' white trash children and one of the girls said he touched her in her private parts. The white men got together, just rode up to Jimmy's folks' cabin and took him away while his daddy was out in the fields. They lynched Jimmy that night. And his daddy had to cut him down from that tree the next day and bury him. The daddy just went crazy little bit by little bit after that and rode into town one day a coupla months later, walked into the general store and shot the man who'd lynched his boy, then shot himself before they could grab him. Oh, and if you worked hard and made something of yourself, got a little store or some land, the white folks seem like they couldn't sleep nor rest easy till they took that away from you. Maybe they'd burn your store down or run you out of town. Colored folks just got tired. That don't sound like much of a reason, but it's the best one I can think of. . . .

. . . CORA WAS LIVING in a rooming house on Ninth and O streets. Room wasn't no bigger than a minute, but it seemed like a palace to me. She had a Victrola and had cut out pictures of Josephine Baker, Ma Rainey and Louis Armstrong and put them all over her mirror and the walls. Cora was what we used to call a good-time girl. Even down home, she was always the one knew where the fun was and if there was no fun happening she could make some.

First thing I wanted to do was get a job so I could start sending money back home. But Cora wouldn't even let me talk about a job that first week. And all we did was party. The woman that run the rooming house was a big old Black woman named Blue. All you had to do was look at her and you'd know how she got that name. And seemed like the downstairs where Blue lived was always filled with folks coming in all hours of the day and night. And it was always liquor flowing and cardplaying.

We'd go over to the O Street Market and you could get pigs' feet and chitlins and fresh greens as good as down home. And Cora seemed to never run outta money. I figured that had to do with her never running outta men.

We were having a good time, then one night when we were getting ready to go to a party, I noticed Cora putting this cream all over herself. I asked her what it was and she showed it to me. It was bleaching cream. Now, Cora's about the color of half-done toast, so I was confused. "What you using this stuff for?" I asked.

"Everybody uses it, men and women," she told me, snapping her stocking tops into her garter. "Girl, there ain't no such thing as a brown beauty in this here town. You either yellow or you ain't mellow." Cora was just rubbing the cream in her skin, all over her face and arms, as she told me this like she was trying to get it down into her bones.

"Well, I'm gonna take my chances," I told her. "I sure ain't gonna use no mess like this. Besides ain't you heard 'the blacker the berry, the sweeter the juice'?"

But Cora had to have the last word, saying "Naomi, I ain't heard *nobody* say that since I come up here and I'll bet money you won't neither."

Finally I started working. I lived in with a Jewish family for a while, but living in didn't suit my style. The madam worried me to death, all day long talking and complaining 'bout her husband, scared he didn't love her, scared he was running around with somebody else, scared she was getting old. That was 'bout the loneliest woman I ever knew. I could hardly do my work for her bending my ear. But the worst thing was I couldn't go when and where I wanted. Nighttime I'd be so tired, all I wanted to do was go to bed. And so then I started doing day's work, had three or four families I cleaned up for and I got my own room in Blue's house and started sending money home regular like.

Now, day's work wasn't no celebration either. And I had every kinda woman for a madam you could think of — the kind that went behind you checking corners for dust and dirt, the kid that run her fingers over the furniture you just got through dusting, the kind that just got a thrill outta giving orders, the kind that asked more questions 'bout my personal business than anybody got a right to, the kind that tried to cheat me outta some of my pay. But in those days there wasn't much else a colored woman could do. Hell, even some of the college girls — the dinkty, saditty ones — cleaned up for white folks in the summertime.

For the longest time I just worked and saved and worked and saved. Then one evening I come in and Blue was sitting in the dining room. For a change, she was by herself. Seemed like Blue wasn't happy unless there was a crowd of people around her. But this night she was by herself. I'd been having this same dream over and over about somebody named Macon and I figured I might bet a few pennies on the dream's number. So I asked her to look up Macon in her dream book. She looked it up and said the number was 301. "I think I'll put fifteen cents on it," I told her, reaching into my pocketbook. I thought Blue was gonna laugh me right outta that room. "Fifteen cents?" she hollered. "Fifteen cents?" And she commenced to laughing so hard she was shaking all over and tears came into her eyes and start to rolling down her fat old Black cheeks. She wiped her face with a handkerchief and says, "Girl, what you waiting for? I been watching you going out here day after day, cleaning up the white folks' houses. That all you want to do with yourself?"

Now nobody'd ever asked that — what I wanted to do — the whole time I'd been North. Cora was so busy partying and I was so busy struggling I hadn't had time to think further than the day I was in. So I didn't quite know what to say at first. "Well," Blue said, folding her arms in front of her, looking at me like the schoolmarm in that one-room school-house I went to did, when she knew I wasn't ready to give the right answer. And that look in Blue's eyes and her laughing at me made me pull up something I'd been carrying around since I moved in her house. And I just said it all of a sudden. "I want what you got. I want a house. And I want plenty money." And just saying it like that set me trembling so hard I dropped my pocketbook on the floor and my feet kicked over the bag of clothes one of my madams had give me that day instead of my regular pay.

"Well, tell me how you aim to get it? Lessen you got some book education or your folks gonna leave you some money, there ain't no legal way for you to get either one. You gonna have to start gambling with everything you got."

"But I ain't got nothing," I cried.

"You got more than you think. You got dreams, like the one you come to me with just now, and, honey, they worth more than you think. They sho 'nuff worth more than fifteen cents. You got sense and deep-down feelings. Listen to 'em. They'll tell you what to do. You think the Rockefellers got to be Rocke-fellers playing it straight? And if all you gonna put on 301 is fifteen cents, I won't even write it up."

I put a quarter on 301 and it come out the next day. I give Blue a cut and that was how it started.

I got to playing the numbers pretty regular then and soon I was playing every day. To be honest about the thing, though, most folks never won nothing. But seemed like I had some kinda gift. Numbers were about the only thing I paid attention to in that one-room schoolhouse in Spring Hope. That first year I hit two times for small change. Then I played a number that come to me the night one of my madams accused me of stealing. I played that number and hit for enough to start me on the way to saving for a house.

My first house was over on R Street. I rented out the top two floors to decent folks, respectable people who'd come up from the South like me. But where Blue'd let anybody live in her house, I'd only let families or married couples or single folks I thought wouldn't give me no trouble live in my place. Folks who went to church on Sunday and went to bed at night 'cause they had to work the next day. Now, that don't mean I was a saint, but I sure didn't want to live amongst a whole buncha sinners.

I found out I couldn't live in a whole house like I lived in one room. Cora took me downtown and bought me the kinda clothes that said I was a lady and just putting those clothes on made me feel different, made me feel big like Mama and Daddy'd always said I wanted to be. Then Cora told me I couldn't have a house without a car and her and her boyfriend took me to this place where I bought a big black Chevrolet.

When I got settled good in the house, I sent for Mama and Daddy and Jackson and Jesse to come up and spend some time with me. Mama had a time getting Daddy to come, even after I sent them all train fare. But finally they came. And seeing that house through Mama's eyes was like seeing it for the first time. I'd planted a Carolina garden out in the backyard of squash, tomatoes and peas, just like I'd have done back home and Mama sat on the back porch when she saw it, shaking her head and smiling. I'd put a big mirror with gilt framing over the fireplace and seemed like every time I looked up Mama was staring at herself in that mirror, almost like she'd never seen herself before. She took off her shoes in the house and walked barefoot on the carpeting I'd put all on the first floor. And she had me take a bunch of pictures of her sitting in my car. And the big bathtub with running hot water, humph, I thought Mama was gonna live in it, she found a excuse to take a bath three times a day.

But Daddy, seemed like the house just made him mad. Mama was all the time pointing something out to him and he'd just go on out on my porch like he did on the porch back home, and sit there sucking on his pipe and not saying a thing. Daddy and one of my roomers, Mr. Chavis, would sit out there talking about down home. He talked to Mr. Chavis more than he talked to me. And so one night I just went outside and butt into his conversation, told Mr. Chavis I wanted to talk to my daddy. "Now, you ain't said hardly nothing to me since y'all got here," I told him. "Not even Congratulations or Good Job. I worked hard for what I got, Daddy, and I want you to be proud."

He took the pipe outta his mouth and said, "I am proud of you, Naomi. Real proud. But you got to understand. I've worked another man's land for over twenty years and just barely kept my family from starvin'. My daughter comes North and gets so much it puts me to shame. Tell me how I'm s'posed to feel about me. Sure I'm proud of you. So proud I'm damn near ready to bust. But I look at all you done and feel like all my life's been a waste. You a landlord. I'm your daddy and I'm still a tenant." . . .

EDWARD P. JONES

Edward P. Jones (1950–) grew up and attended public schools in Washington, before earning a BA at Holy Cross and an MFA at the University of Virginia. By his own testimony, he knows much of Washington firsthand, having lived in eighteen different neighborhoods by the time he was eighteen years old. In his first book, *Lost in the City* (1992), he collected stories of everyday African Americans, such as the title character of "Marie," who live in the city separated from the corridors of power and who struggle in small but vital ways to make lives of meaning and value. His recent work includes the Pulitzer Prize winning *The Known World* (2003), a novel about the little-known historical phenomenon of free blacks who owned slaves, and another collection of short stories set in Washington, *All Aunt Hagar's Children* (2006). He teaches in the creative writing program at George Washington University in Washington, D.C.

Marie
From *Lost in the City*

Every now and again, as if on a whim, the federal government people would write to Marie Delaveaux Wilson in one of those white, stampless envelopes and tell her to come in to their place so they could take another look at her. They, the Social Security people, wrote to her in a foreign language that she had learned to translate over the years, and for all the years she had been receiving the letter the same man had been signing them. Once, because she had something important to tell him, Marie called the number the man always put at the top of the letters, but a woman answered Mr. Smith's telephone and told Marie he was in an all-day meeting. Another time she called and a man said Mr. Smith was on vacation. And finally one day a woman answered and told Marie that Mr. Smith was deceased. The woman told her to wait and she would get someone new to talk to her about her case, but Marie thought it bad luck to have telephoned a dead man and she hung up.

Now, years after the woman had told her Mr. Smith was no more, the letters were still being signed by John Smith. Come into our office at 21st and M streets, Northwest, the letters said in that foreign language. Come in so we can see if you are still blind in one eye, come in so we can see if you are still old and getting older. Come in so we can see if you still deserve to get Supplemental Security Income payments.

She always obeyed the letters, even if the order now came from a dead man, for she knew people who had been temporarily cut off from SSI for not showing up or even for being late. And once cut off, you had to move heaven and earth to get back on.

So on a not unpleasant day in March, she rose in the dark in the morning, even before the day had any sort of character, to give herself plenty of time to bathe, eat, lay out money for the bus, dress, listen to the spirituals on the radio. She was eighty-six years old, and had learned that life was all chaos and painful and that the only way to get through it was to expect chaos even in the most innocent of moments. Offer a crust of bread to a sick bird and you often drew back a bloody finger.

John Smith's letter had told her to come in at eleven o'clock, his favorite time, and by nine that morning she has had her bath and had eaten. Dressed by nine thirty. The walk from Claridge Towers at 12th and M down to the bus stop at 14th and K took her about ten minutes, more or less. There was a bus at about ten thirty, her schedule told her, but she preferred the one that came a half hour earlier, lest there be trouble with the ten thirty bus. After she dressed, she sat at her dining room table and went over still again what papers and all else she needed to take. Given the nature of life — particularly the questions asked by the Social Security people — she always took more than they might ask for — her birth certificate, her husband's death certificate, doctors' letters.

ONE OF THE LAST things she put in her pocketbook was a seven-inch or so knife that she had, with the use of a small saw borrowed from a neighbor, serrated on both edges. The knife, she was convinced now, had saved her life about two weeks before. Before then she had often been careless about when she took the knife out with her, and she had never taken it out in daylight, but now she never left her apartment without it, even when going down the hall to the trash drop.

She had gone out to buy a simple box of oatmeal, no more, no less. It was about seven in the evening, the streets with enough commuters driving up 13th Street to make her feel safe. Several yards before she reached the store, the young man came from behind her and tried to rip off her coat pocket where he thought she kept her money, for she carried no purse or pocketbook after five o'clock. The money was in the other pocket with the knife, and his hand caught in the empty pocket long enough for her to reach around with the knife and cut his hand as it came out of her pocket.

He screamed and called her a bitch. He took a few steps up 13th Street and stood in front of Emerson's Market, examining the hand and shaking off blood. Except for the cars passing up and down 13th Street, they were alone, and she began to pray.

"You cut me," he said, as if he had only been minding his own business when she cut him. "Just look what you done to my hand," he said and looked around as if for some witness to her crime. There was not a great amount of blood, but there was enough for her to see it dripping to the pavement. He seemed to be about twenty, no more than twenty-five, dressed the way they were all dressed nowadays, as if a blind man had matched up all their colors. It occurred to her to say that she had seven grandchildren his age, that by telling him this he would leave her alone. But the more filth he spoke, the more she wanted him only to come toward her again.

"You done crippled me, you old bitch."

"I sure did," she said, without malice, without triumph, but simply the way she would have told him the time of day had he asked and had she known. She gripped the knife tighter, and as she did, she turned her body ever so slightly so that her good eye lined up with him. Her heart was making an awful racket, wanting to be away from him, wanting to be safe at home. I will not be moved, some organ in the neighborhood of the heart told the heart. "And I got plenty more where that come from."

The last words seemed to bring him down some and, still shaking the blood from his hand, he took a step or two back, which disappointed her. I will not be moved, that other organ kept telling the heart. "You just crazy, thas all," he said. "Just a crazy old hag." Then he turned and lumbered up toward Logan Circle, and several times he looked back over his shoulder as if afraid she might be following. A man came out of Emerson's, then a woman with two little boys. She wanted to grab each of them by the arm and tell them she had come close to losing her life. "I saved myself with this here thing" she would have said. She forgot about the oatmeal and took her raging heart back to the apartment. She told herself that she should, but she never washed the fellow's blood off the knife, and over the next few days it dried and then it began to flake off.

Toward ten o'clock that morning Wilamena Mason knocked and let herself in with a key Marie had given her.

"I see you all ready," Wilamena said.

"With the help of the Lord," Marie said. "Want a spot of coffee?"

"No thanks," Wilamena said, and dropped into a chair at the table. "Been drinkin so much coffee lately, I'm gonna turn into coffee. Was up all night with Calhoun."

"How he doin?"

Wilamena told her Calhoun was better that morning, his first good morning in over a week. Calhoun Lambeth was Wilamena's boyfriend, a seventy-five-year-old man she had taken up with six or so months before, not long after he moved in. He was the best-dressed old man Marie had ever known, but he had always appeared to be sickly, even while strutting about with his gold-tipped cane. And seeing that she could count his days on the fingers of her hands, Marie had avoided getting to know him. She could not understand why Wilamena, who could have had any man in Claridge Towers or any other senior citizen building for that matter, would take such a man into her bed. "True love," Wilamena had explained. "Avoid heartache," Marie had said, trying to be kind.

They left the apartment. Marie sought help from no one, lest she come to depend on a person too much. But since the encounter with the young man, Wilamena had insisted on escorting Marie. Marie, to avoid arguments, allowed Wilamena to walk with her from time to time to the bus stop, but no farther.

Nothing fit Marie's theory about life like the weather in Washington. Two days before the temperature had been in the forties, and yesterday it had dropped to the low twenties then warmed up a bit, with the afternoon bringing snow flurries. Today the weather people on the radio had said it would warm enough to wear just a sweater, but Marie was wearing her coat. And tomorrow, the weather people said, it would be in the thirties, with maybe an inch or so of snow.

Appointments near twelve o'clock were always risky, because the Social Security people often took off for lunch long before noon and returned sometime after one. And except for a few employees who seemed to work through their lunch hours, the place shut down. Marie had never been interviewed by someone willing to work through the lunch hour. Today, though the appointment was for eleven, she waited until one thirty before the woman at the front of the waiting room told her she would have to come back another day, because the woman who handled her case was not in.

"You put my name down when I came in like everything was all right," Marie said after she had been called up to the woman's desk.

"I know," the woman said, "but I thought that Mrs. Brown was in. They told me she was in. I'm sorry." The woman began writing in a log book that rested between her telephone and a triptych of photographs. She handed Marie a slip and told her again she was sorry.

"Why you have me wait so long if she whatn't here?" She did not want to say too much, appear too upset, for the Social Security people could be unforgiving. And though she was used to waiting three and four hours, she found it especially unfair to wait when there was no one for her at all behind those panels the Social Security people use for offices. "I been here since before eleven."

"I know," the woman behind the desk said. "I know. I saw you there, ma'am, but I really didn't know Mrs. Brown wasn't here." There was a nameplate at the front of the woman's desk and it said Vernelle Wise. The name was surrounded by little hearts, the kind a child might have drawn.

Marie said nothing more and left.

THE NEXT APPOINTMENT was two weeks later, eight thirty, a good hour, and the day before a letter signed by John Smith arrived to remind her. She expected to be out at least by twelve. Three times before eleven o'clock, Marie asked Vernelle Wise if the man, Mr. Green, who was handling her case, was in that day, and each time the woman assured her that he was. At twelve, Marie ate one of the two oranges and three of the five slices of cheese she had brought. At one, she asked again if Mr. Green was indeed in that day and politely reminded Vernelle Wise that she had been waiting since about eight that morning. Vernelle was just as polite and told her the wait would soon be over.

At one fifteen, Marie began to watch the clock hands creep around the dial. She had not paid much attention to the people around her, but more and more it seemed that others were being waited on who had arrived long after she had gotten there. After asking about Mr. Green at one, she had taken a seat near the front, and as more time went by, she found herself forced to listen to the conversation that Vernelle was having with the other receptionist next to her.

"I told him . . . I told him . . . I said just get your things and leave," said the other receptionist, who didn't have a nameplate.

"Did he leave?" Vernelle wanted to know.

"Oh, no," the other woman said. "Not at first. But I picked up some of his stuff, that Christian Dior jacket he worships. I picked up my cigarette lighter and that jacket, just like I was gonna do something bad to it, and he started movin then."

Vernelle began laughing. "I wish I was there to see that." She was filing her fingernails. Now and again she would look at her fingernails to inspect her work, and if it was satisfactory, she would blow on the nail and on the file. "He back?" Vernelle asked.

The other receptionist eyed her. "What you think?" and they both laughed.

Along about two o'clock Marie became hungry again, but she did not want to eat the rest of her food because she did not know how much longer she would be there. There was a soda machine in the corner, but all sodas gave her gas.

"You-know-who gonna call you again?" the other receptionist was asking Vernelle.

"I hope so," Vernelle said. "He pretty fly. Seemed decent too. It kinda put me off when he said he was a car mechanic. I kinda like kept tryin to take a peek at his fingernails and everything the whole evening. See if they was dirty or what."

"Well, that mechanic stuff might be good when you get your car back. My cousin's boyfriend used to do that kinda work and he made good money, girl. I mean real good money."

"Hmmmm," Vernelle said. "Anyway, the kids like him, and you know how peculiar they can be."

"Tell me about it. They do the job your mother and father used to do, huh? Only on another level."

"You can say that again," Vernelle said.

Marie went to her and told her how long she had been waiting.

"Listen," Vernelle said, pointing her fingernail file at Marie. "I told you you'll be waited on as soon as possible. This is a busy day. So I think you should just go back to your seat until we call your name." The other receptionist began to giggle.

Marie reached across the desk and slapped Vernelle Wise with all her might. Vernelle dropped the file, which made a cheap tinny sound when it hit the plastic board her chair was on. But no one heard the file because she had began to cry right away. She looked at Marie as if, in the moment of her greatest need, Marie had denied her. "Oh, no," Vernelle Wise said through the tears. "Oh, my dear God . . ."

The other receptionist, in her chair on casters, rolled over to Vernelle and put her arm around her. "Security!" the other receptionist hollered. "We need security here!"

The guard at the front door came quickly around the corner, one hand on his holstered gun and the other pointing accusatorially at the people seated in the waiting area. Marie had sat down and was looking at the two women almost sympathetically, as if a stranger had come in, hit Vernelle Wise, and fled.

"She slapped Vernelle!" the other receptionist said.

"Who did it?" the guard said, reaching for the man sitting beside Marie. But when the other receptionist said it was the old lady in the blue coat, the guard held back for the longest time, as if to grab her would be like arresting his own grandmother. He stood blinking and he would have gone on blinking had Marie not stood up.

SHE WAS TOO FLUSTERED to wait for the bus and so took a cab home. With both chains, she locked herself in the apartment, refusing to answer the door

or the telephone the rest of the day and most of the next. But she knew that if
her family or friends received no answer at the door or on the telephone, they
would think something had happened to her. So the next afternoon, she began
answering the phone and spoke with the chains on, telling Wilamena and
others that she had a toothache.

For days and days after the incident she ate very little, asked God to forgive
her. She was haunted by the way Vernelle's cheek had felt, by what it was like to
invade and actually touch the flesh of another person. And when she thought
too hard, she imagined that she was slicing through the woman's cheek, the way
she had sliced through the young man's hand. But as time went on she began to
remember the man's curses and the purplish color of Vernelle's fingernails, and
all remorse would momentarily take flight. Finally, one morning nearly two
weeks after she slapped the woman, she woke with a phrase she had not used or
heard since her children were small: You whatn't raised that way.

It was the next morning that the thin young man in the suit knocked and
asked through the door chains if he could speak with her. She thought that he
was a Social Security man come to tear up her card and papers and tell her that
they would send her no more checks. Even when he pulled out an identification
card showing that he was a Howard University student, she did not believe.

In the end, she told him she didn't want to buy anything, not magazines, not
candy, not anything.

"No, no," he said. "I just want to talk to you for a bit. About your life and
everything. It's for a project for my folklore course. I'm talking to everyone in
the building who'll let me. Please . . . I won't be a bother. Just a little bit of your
time."

"I don't have anything worth talkin about," she said. "And I don't keep well
these days."

"Oh, ma'am, I'm sorry. But we all got something to say. I promise I won't be
a bother."

After fifteen minutes of his pleas, she opened the door to him because of
his suit and his tie and his tie clip with a bird in flight, and because his long
dark-brown fingers reminded her of delicate twigs. But had he turned out to be
death with a gun or knife or fingers to crush her neck, she would not have been
surprised. "My name's George. George Carter. Like the president." He had the
kind of voice that old people in her young days would have called womanish.
"But I was born right here in D.C. Born, bred, and buttered, my mother used
to say."

He stayed the rest of the day and she fixed him dinner. It scared her to be
able to talk so freely with him, and at first she thought that at long last, as she
had always feared, senility had taken hold of her. A few hours after he left, she

looked his name up in the telephone book, and when a man who sounded like him answered, she hung up immediately. And the next day she did the same thing. He came back at least twice a week for many weeks and would set his cassette recorder on her coffee table. "He's takin down my whole life," she told Wilamena, almost the way a woman might speak in awe of a new boyfriend.

One day he played back for the first time some of what she told the recorder:

> . . . My father would be sitting there readin the paper. He'd say whenever they put in a new president, "Look like he got the chair for four years." And it got so that's what I saw — this poor man sittin in that chair for four long years while the rest of the world went on about its business. I don't know if I thought he ever did anything, the president. I just knew that he had to sit in that chair for four years. Maybe I thought that by his sittin in that chair and doin nothing else for four years be made that country what it was and that without him sittin there the country wouldn't be what it was. Maybe thas what I got from listenin to my father reading and to my mother askin him questions bout what he was reading. They was like that, you see . . .

George stopped the tape and was about to put the other side in when she touched his hand.

"No more, George," she said. "I can't listen to no more. Please . . . please, no more." She had never in her whole life heard her own voice. Nothing had been so stunning in a long, long while, and for a few moments before she found herself, her world turned upside down. There, rising from a machine no bigger than her Bible, was a voice frighteningly familiar and yet unfamiliar, talking about a man whom she knew as well as her husbands and her sons, a man dead and buried sixty years. She reached across to George and he handed her the tape. She turned it over and over as if the mystery of everything could be discerned if she turned it enough times. She began to cry, and with her other hand she lightly touched the buttons of the machine.

BETWEEN THE TIME Marie slapped the woman in the Social Security office and the day she heard her voice for the first time, Calhoun Lambeth, Wilamena's boyfriend, had been in and out the hospital three times. Most evenings when Calhoun's son stayed the night with him, Wilamena would come up to Marie's and spend most of the evening, sitting on the couch that was catty-corner to the easy chair facing the big window. She said very little, which was unlike her, a woman with more friends than hairs on her head and who, at sixty-eight, loved a good party. The most attractive woman Marie knew would only curl her legs up under herself and sip whatever Marie put in her hand. She looked out at the city until she took herself to her apartment or went back down to Calhoun's place. In the beginning, after he returned from the hospital the first time, there was the desire in Marie to remind her friend that she wasn't married to Calhoun, that she should just get up and walk away, something Marie had seen her do with other men she had grown tired of.

Late one night, Wilamena called and asked her to come down to the man's apartment, for the man's son had had to work that night and she was there alone with him and she did not want to be alone with him. "Sit with me a spell," Wilamena said. Marie did not protest, even though she had not said more than ten words to the man in all the time she knew him. She threw on her bathrobe, picked up her keys and serrated knife, and went down to the second floor.

He was propped up on the bed, and he was surprisingly alert and spoke to Marie with an unforced friendliness. She has seen this in other dying people — a kindness and gentleness came over them that was often embarrassing for those around them. Wilamena sat on the side of the bed. Calhoun asked Marie to sit in a chair beside the bed and then he took her hand and held it for the rest of the night. He talked on throughout the night, not always understandable. Wilamena, exhausted, eventually lay across the foot of the bed. Almost everything the man had to say was about a time when he was young and was married for a year or so to a woman in Nicodemus, Kansas, a town where there were only black people. Whether the woman had died or whether he had left her, Marie could not make out. She only knew that the woman and Nicodemus seemed to have marked him for life.

"You should go to Nicodemus," he said at one point, as if the town was only around the corner. "I stumbled into the place by accident. But you should go on purpose. There ain't much to see, but you should go there and spend some time there."

Toward four o'clock that morning, he topped talking and moments later he went home to his God. Marie continued holding the dead man's hand and she said the Lord's prayer over and over until it no longer made sense to her. She did not wake Wilamena. Eventually, the sun came through the man's Venetian blinds and she heard the croaking of the pigeons congregating on the window ledge. When she finally placed his hand on his chest, the dead man expelled a burst of air that sounded to Marie like a sigh. It occurred to her that she, a complete stranger, was the last thing he had known in the world and that now that he was no longer in the world all she knew of him was that Nicodemus place and a lovesick woman asleep at the foot of his bed. She thought that she was hungry and thirsty, but the more she looked at the dead man and the sleeping woman, the more she realized that what she felt was a sense of loss.

TWO DAYS LATER, the Social Security people sent her a letter, again signed by John Smith telling her to come to them one week hence. There was nothing in the letter about the slap, no threat to cut off her SSI payments because of what she had done. Indeed, it was the same sort of letter John Smith usually sent. She called the number at the top of the letter, and the woman who handled her case told her that Mrs. White would be expecting her on the day and the time stated in the letter. Still, she suspected the Social Security people were planning something for her, something at the very least that would be humiliating. And, right up until the day before the appointment, she continued calling to confirm that it was okay to come in. Often, the person she spoke to after the switchboard woman and before the woman handling her case was Vernelle. "Social Security Administration. This is Vernelle Wise. May I help you?" And each time Marie heard the receptionist identify herself she wanted to apologize. "I whatn't raised that way," she wanted to tell the woman.

George Carter came the day she got the letter to present her with a cassette machine and copies of the pages she had made about her life. It took quite some time for him to teach her how to use the machine, and after he was gone, she was certain it took so long because she really did not want to know how to use it. That evening, after dinner she steeled herself and put a tape marked "Parents; Early Childhood" in the machine.

> . . . My mother had this idea that everything could be done in Washington, that a human bein could take all they troubles to Washington and things would be set right. I think that was all wrapped up with her notion of the government, the Supreme Court and the president and the like. "Up there," she would say, "things can be made right." "Up there" was her only words for Washington. All them other cities had names, but words for Washington didn't need a name. It was just called "up there." I was real small and didn't know any better, so somehow I got to thinking since things were on the perfect side in Washington, that maybe God lived there. God and his people . . . When I went back home to visit that first time and told my mother all about my livin in Washington, she fell into such a cry, like maybe I had managed to make it to heaven without dyin. Thas how people was back in those days. . . .

The next morning she looked for Vernelle Wise's name in the telephone book. And for several evenings she would call the number and hang up before the phone had rung three times. Finally, on a Sunday, two days before the appointment, she let it ring and what may have been a little boy answered. She could tell he was very young because he said "Hello" in a too-loud voice, as if he was not used to talking on the telephone.

"Hello," he said "Hello, who this? Granddaddy, that you? Hello. Hello. I can see you."

Marie heard Vernelle tell him to put down the telephone, then another child, perhaps a girl somewhat older than the boy, came on the line. "Hello. Hello. Who is this?" she said with authority. The boy began to cry, apparently because he did not want the girl to talk if he couldn't. "Don't touch it," the girl said. "Leave it alone." The boy cried louder and only stopped when Vernelle came to the telephone.

"Yes?" Vernelle said. "Yes." Then she went off the line to calm the boy who had again begun to cry. "Loretta," she said, "go get his bottle. . . . Well, look for it. What you got eyes for?"

There seemed to be a second boy, because Vernelle told him to help Loretta look for the bottle. "He always losin things," Marie heard the second boy say. "You should tie everything to his arms." "Don't tell me what to do," Vernelle said. "Just look for that damn bottle."

"I don't lose nofin. I don't," the first boy said. "You got snot in your nose."

"Don't say that," Vernelle said before she came back on the line. "I'm sorry," she said to Marie. "Who is this? . . . Don't you dare touch it if you know what's good for you!" she said. "I wanna talk to Granddaddy," the first boy said. "Loretta, get me that bottle!"

Marie hung up. She washed her dinner dishes. She called Wilamena because she had not seen her all day, and Wilamena told her that she would be up later. The cassette tapes were on the coffee table besides the machine, and she began picking them up, one by one. She read the labels. "Husband No. 1." "Working." "Husband No. 2." "Children." "Race Relations." "Early D.C. Experiences." "Husband No. 3." She had not played another tape since the one about her mother's idea of what Washington was like, but she could still hear the voice, her voice. Without reading its label, she put a tape in the machine.

. . . I never planned to live in Washington, had no idea I would ever even step one foot in this city. This white family my mother worked for, they had a son married and gone to live in Baltimore. He wanted a maid, somebody to take care of his children. So he wrote to his mother and she asked my mother and my mother asked me about going to live in Baltimore. Well, I was young, I guess I wanted to see the world, and Baltimore was as good a place to start as anywhere. This man sent me a train ticket and I went off to Baltimore. Hadn't ever been kissed, hadn't ever been anything, but here I was goin farther from home than my mother and father put together. . . . Well, sir, the train stopped in Washington, and I thought I heard the conductor say we would be stopping a bit there, so I got off,

I knew I probably wouldn't see no more than that Union Station, but I wanted to be able to say I'd done that, that I step foot in the capital of the United States. I walked down to the end of the platform and looked around, then I peeked into the station. Then I went in. And when I got back, the train and my suitcase was gone. Everything I had in the world on the way to Baltimore....

...I couldn't calm myself anough to listen to when the redcap said another train would be leavin for Baltimore, I was just that upset. I had a buncha addresses of people we knew all the way from home up to Boston, and I used one precious nickel to call a woman I hadn't seen in years, cause I didn't have the white people in Baltimore number. This woman come and got me, took me to her place. I member like it was yesterday, that we got on this streetcare marked 13th and D NE. The more I rode, the more brighter things got. You ain't lived till you been on a streetcar. The futher we went on that streetcar — dead down in the middle of the street — the more I knowed I could never go live in Baltimore. I knowed I could never live in a place that didn't have that streetcar and them clackety-clack tracks....

She wrapped the tapes in two plastic bags and put them in the dresser drawer that contained all that was valuable to her — birth and death certificates, silver dollars, life insurance policies, pictures of her husband and the children they had given each other, and the grandchildren those children had given her and the great-grands whose names she had trouble remembering. She set the tapes in the back corner of the drawer, away from the things she needed to get her hands on regularly. She knew that however long she lived, she would not ever again listen to them, for in the end, despite all that was on the tapes, she could not stand the sound of her own voice.

THOMAS MALLON

A novelist, essayist, and teacher, Thomas Mallon (1951–) has written more than half a dozen novels, including historical narratives *Henry and Clara*, *Dewey Defeats Truman*, and *Two Moons*, and several nonfiction works. A one-time literary editor at *GQ* magazine, he contributes frequently to the *Atlantic Monthly*, *Harper's*, the *New Yorker*, and the *American Scholar*. *Two Moons* (2000), excerpted here, is a heady love story with unlikely protagonists — a widowed math wiz from New Hampshire and a young Harvard-educated astronomer. It is set mainly at the National Observatory in the 1870s and early 1880s, during the tumultuous Grant and Hayes administrations, which coincided with Asaph Hall's 1877 discovery of the moons of Mars. Mallon recently served as deputy chairman of the National Endowment for the Humanities and currently teaches at George Washington University, where he directs its creative writing program.

From *Two Moons*

The second baseman caught a fly ball. "Only Neptune is missing," said Cynthia.

"Oh, lordy," replied Hugh, pulling his straw hat low against the hot sun. "Another's preacher's Sabbath."

"Well, surely it's occurred to you," said Cynthia, gesturing toward the ball field on the Astoria Grounds. "It all revolves around the pitcher, so he's the Sun, and the infielders are the four small inner planets. Jupiter, Saturn, and Uranus are way out there beyond them."

"Darling, it occurs to every astronomer. That's why they're tiresome company here — and why I thought to bring you along instead of Henry Paul." He put his head on her shoulder and was soon dozing off, even though she was the one most worn out by their recreations of the last two, sweltering weeks: picnics in the Seventh Street park; horse races at Brightwood; shooting contests at the Schuetzen Festival. Hugh acted as if frantic indolence might substitute for meaningful work, or at least distract her from pressing the issue of his idleness at the Observatory. Their traipsing from one amusement to another appealed to her with its appearance of ordinary courtship, but upset her Yankee thrift of money and time.

All the rented velocipedes and bags of butterscotch candy could not really sustain the illusion that they were two young lovers with nothing to do but lark, or that Hugh wasn't in serious trouble with the admiral. She had never learned the details of his meeting with Rodgers, but at the Observatory she's begun to notice shrugging shoulders and pursed lips whenever Hugh Allison's name was mentioned in the industrious presence of someone like Professor Harkness. It was folly to continue this romantic pantomime, so unconvincing even to herself, but she lacked the courage to ask questions that might make him tell her his days in Washington were numbered.

She looked away from his long, sleeping lashes and back to the baseball diamond. In the celestial analogy, what was the batter? And perhaps more to the point, what was the ball? Was it the light Hugh talked about dispatching into the heavens? A loud, sudden crack sent the little sphere disappearing into the late-afternoon light over center field, and for a second she thought of jabbing him in the ribs, of waking him and demanding that he explain, right now and comprehensibly, his preoccupation with those drawings on his wall. But in turning to him, her eyes were caught by the glinting chain of his gold watch. When extracted from his pocket, it showed a quarter to six.

There wasn't time. She would ask him later, or next week.

"Wake up," she whispered, barely able to make herself disturb his nap, let alone hector him over his life's work and purpose. He only murmured, and nestled his head against her breast.

"Get up, you infant. You need to be at work."

"Mmhn," he groaned, rubbing his eyes. "My august responsibilities."

He had been assigned to record, from the Observatory's vantage, the time and position of some flares to be shot later this evening by the Army Signal Service. The Secretary of War and President Hayes, now said to be packing for his New Hampshire vacation, had attended the first round of these demonstrations last night on a road near the Soldiers' Home. Stations inside the District and along the coast were watching for the lights sent up by rocket and mortar. At the Observatory, this vigil could easily be performed by the watchmen making their rounds of the barometers, but the menial task provided Rodgers with another chance to try humiliating Professor Allison into renewed productivity.

Hugh and Cynthia began the long walk back across town in sleepy silence. She wished the Army signals involved some calculations necessitating her presence, or that another collaborative comet were available until he finally came up with some bold but within-the-pale project, one he'd start in order to impress her, but end up truly interested in. She had a fantasy of him rushing to her desk one morning, ablaze with a eureka he'd experienced during his clerical labors over the next year's eclipse, some exciting new scheme for doing those observations that would banish his self-disgust and make him a hero to the admiral.

"Be on the lookout for a red cow," he said, as the two of them crossed Eleventh Street.

She curled her lip against this latest piece of whimsy.

"No, really," he went on. "One's escaped from Gonzaga College. I have this from my barber. It could be anywhere."

She clapped her ears and raced ahead.

"All right," he said, struggling to keep up. "Then be on the lookout for your chariot instead." She was supposed to take the Georgetown horsecar that left from the Treasury building. They would have a late supper at the Union Hotel once the last flares had been launched and he came home from Foggy Bottom. "While you're at it," he added, "see if you can't find me a carriage."

No one could ever keep up with her nervous pace, especially the kind she was setting now, but since leaving the Astoria Grounds she'd noticed that he was a step behind his usual step behind; and now he had stopped altogether.

"Wait here a moment." He veered toward Milburn's drugstore — for a bottle of whiskey, she suspected. She made a face.

"Tomorrow is Sunday," he explained. "We have rather strict laws about such sales in quiet Georgetown."

"Yes," she said. "But today is Saturday."

"Which will be followed by long, lingering, endless Sunday. Don't move."

He came out of Milburn's with a bottle that he asked her to take to his rooms. They parted in front of the Treasury, and as her horsecar made its way up Pennsylvania and then High Street, she tried to look forward to the evening, reminding herself of all the reasons she liked Georgetown more than her own neighborhood near the Capitol. The alley dwellers weren't so thick on the ground, and sitting in the Peabody Library had a way of calming her, of making her feel less like the interloper she always imagined herself in public places. The trees were fuller, too. Alighting from the streetcar, she admired the little colonnade of them leading to Hugh's door, and took note of an advertisement tacked to one maple for a WHITE WOMAN TO DO GENERAL HOUSEWORK.

There was no chance it was Hugh who'd posted this bill. Letting herself in, she saw that his seraglio was even messier than usual, the pillows, cups, and newspapers a whirling agglomeration of debris, just like, he continued to assure her, the average comet.

She couldn't bear sinking into Mrs. Allison's pillows, so she settled into the chair behind the desk, the only hard one in the room, and looked around. Within an hour she could make this lair as orderly and right-angled as her own shabby precinct of Mrs. O'Toole's. But would she? What was the point of prolonging the fancy that she and this young man would soon become respectable dwellers on these leafy heights, with Hugh going contentedly off each day for thirty years to work on a successor to Professor Yarnall's star catalogue? This was not going to happen, and in any case, it wasn't the daydream that had drawn her to him. But what *had* attracted her, besides the eyelashes and mischief? Was it, inscrutably, whatever had made him tack those sketches to the wall?

Or was she drawn to his apparent determination to throw himself away? Did she love this stubborn profligacy, and hope it would drag her worried, frugal self down with him — into some lovely oblivion, where the waters could finally close over her head? She took the bottle from its wrapper and poured herself a glass of whiskey. But a moment later she began straightening up the desktop. No, she was not cut out to be a voluptuary.

And he, poor boy, was not cut out for this. She opened his sunspots notebook, the dull record he was charged with making by himself while young Mr. Todd remained on vacation in New Jersey.

AUGUST	5	10 a.m.	NO SPOTS
	6	6 p.m.	THE SAME
	8	10 a.m.	NO SPOTS
		6 p.m.	THE SAME

The sight of this stupid table caused her to throw back half the whiskey in the unclean glass. But before the sting had left her throat, her eyes widened and her hands began to tremble. He had not even been *near* the Observatory on the 8th, neither at 10 a.m. nor six in the evening. When she'd gone looking for him that morning, Mr. Harrison had said he was nowhere around; and that night they'd had an early supper at the Irving House.

So, she thought, negligence wasn't good enough; he needed actively to disgrace himself. Closing the little notebook, she began to weep, soundlessly, the way she'd taught herself between the thin walls of all her rooming houses. She took a last sip of the whiskey and set the glass down on two unopened envelopes from Hugh's mother — no doubt containing more shrill complaint of debts and darkies. They made her recall the sealed letters, a packet of ten, that John May had written her just before Chickamauga, one to be opened on each of her ensuing birthdays, if he didn't survive. He'd marked the corner of each envelope, 1864 through 1874, and she had read all of them at first light on the day she was supposed to. They became, as the years went by, shorter and somehow less audible, embarrassed by their own repetitions and the ruse they were attempting against fate, until they ceased altogether, John having run out of time to write, or just the ability to imagine her in the world more than ten years later.

In the ones he did write, he had always pictured her in New Hampshire, never here, and certainly not in August. The sun at the ball field had made her tired, she now realized, and as soon as the whiskey muffled her agitation over the sunspots fakery, she gave up the wooden desk chair for one of the couches, kicking away some of the pillows and falling into a dream of Rutherford B. Hayes, with whom she sat on a porch, watching the sun fall into Lake Winnipesaukee.

Hours later, she awoke to see Hugh drinking from the same glass she had used. He smiled as she came to.

"A little fizzle. Barely bigger than D'Arrest's."

She rubbed her eyes and looked at him.

"The Army rockets," he explained.

"Of course," she said, wondering if he'd even gone to the Observatory. Was there room for the sunspots notebook on the agenda of things she couldn't bring herself to ask him about?

At the Union Hotel they were shown to their table at a quarter past ten by Riley Shinn himself, the proprietor who took such pride in the "Pocket Tuileries" he had created on a corner of Bridge Street. They ate their supper, while at the bar several men drunkenly argued the recent railroad strike, each a loud parrot of what he'd read in the papers or heard on the streetcar. "No innocent man ever gets killed in a riot!" declared the loudest of them.

"Hall was there until things fogged over," said Hugh. "Just him and George Anderson. He gave up about an hour ago, and he did the strangest thing before he left."

"What was that?"

"He locked his observer's book in a desk drawer. I've never seen anyone do that before."

Cynthia dismissed the behavior with a shrug, relieved to have at least some evidence that Hugh had actually been on the premises tonight. Lucid with coffee, she was now determined to force him on to another subject: "You have to tell me the exact state of things between you and Admiral Rodgers."

"Things between us are perfectly fine," said Hugh, signaling the waiter for their bill.

"They're obviously not."

"If you don't change the subject, I shall sing. Or order another whiskey."

"Tell me what he — "

"*In the gloaming* . . ." He lilted loudly enough that two of the drunkards at the bar ceased their argument and made ready to join in.

Mortified, she seized his hand. "All right, all right. Fanny Christian had a scandalous letter from a friend who's on her honeymoon."

"That's better," he said, subsiding.

"Now take me out of here."

It was unspoken, not unclear, that they would end up in his rooms, but for a while they walked with no set destination. Two blocks' movement north brought them to Gay Street, and by way of apology, Hugh finally put his arm around her waist. Too weary to refuse the gesture, Cynthia leaned closer to him, and they turned the corner in silence, the whitewashed planting boxes at the foot of the trees helping to guide their steps through the dark.

She was the first to see several people, a whole family, kneeling beneath a cherry tree in the front garden of no. 18. She squeezed Hugh's arm, and the two of them halted, uncertain what to do next, having intruded on a scene that ought to be taking place indoors. Cynthia looked for a light inside, shifting her eyes from the crouched, murmuring figures toward the bay windows. But the house's interior was entirely dark, the people in the garden visible only from a lamp in the hand of Angeline Hall, who was leading her family in prayer. The wavering light flared against the cheekbones of her gaunt face, which looked up at the sky as her free hand urged little Angelo to look up with her. She seemed to be both surveying and beseeching the heavens, as if they were on the verge of revealing something spectacular for the first time. Her husband, Asaph, stole just a single glance upward, concentrating on whatever course of prayer his wife was directing.

"What could have brought them out here?" Cynthia whispered to Hugh. But he was already creeping comically away, his steps as high and stilted as an insect's. With a finger to her lips, she implored him not to make her laugh and give them away. Only after he'd disappeared around the corner, did she start after him, desperate to be away from the Halls' miserable worship, and irrationally frightened that Hugh was somehow gone forever.

She ran through the dark, clutching her reticule, which contained the device Madam Costello had finally procured. She knew that tonight she would not use it, that she would press on the small of his beautiful back and hold him inside her, make him give her a child, as if his sex were the center of the universe and she the god of all creation.

ANDREW HOLLERAN

Andrew Holleran, pen name of Eric Garber (1944–), has written *Dancer from the Dance* (1978), a highly acclaimed gay novel of the post-Stonewall era set in New York City and Fire Island, and two novels focusing on the travails of aging gay men, *Nights in Aruba* (1983) and *The Beauty of Men* (1996). His most recent novel, *Grief* (2006), which won the Stonewall Book Award in 2007, is a meditation on loss and loneliness that ranges over much of Washington history, from Mary Todd Lincoln and Henry Adams to the recent AIDS epidemic, and provides an evocative portrait of contemporary Washington. Holleran teaches creative writing at American University and makes his home in Washington and Florida.

From *Grief*

Across the hall I learned what my landlord had been reading before he went to sleep. Sometimes it was a serious book — on global population problems, the proliferation of nuclear weapons, the problems of the Middle East — other times, just a murder mystery. It was strange that the bedroom doors were never

closed during the day: the room most people keep private. The décor, which
had seemed so cutting-edge in the seventies (chrome and glass, gray walls and
carpet), now looked, incredibly (since we always imagine our era's taste to be
classic), dated. The dark gray comforter that covered the low bed pulled up
neatly to the gray cross-grained pillowcases, the cubelike table beside the bed
under the retractable reading lamp with the book on it, were extremely neat,
almost ascetic; on the other side of the room was something more hedonistic:
a hot tub with mirrored walls and a cluster of bottles with silver caps, a vase
with a single gladiola (the seventies flower), and on the wall some silver-framed
photographs of building cornices with sunlight falling across them in different
patterns.

All of this had been chic thirty years ago but was now just that: the seventies. Still it must have represented his idea of urban refinement. "What are the
people where you grew up like?" I asked him one evening as we were preparing
our dinners.

"Mean and stupid!" he said.

His town, he explained, had a Baptist college from which he'd graduated
before coming to Washington as an intern; everyone there was homophobic.
Like a lot of gay men, he said, he'd come to D.C. for the same reason the slaves
had after the Civil War. "The federal government!" he said. When he was an
intern he had worked in an office that looked right down in to the offices of
another building just like his, where he could see men sitting at their desks
reading the paper. One day he asked his boss what they were doing, and his
boss said, "Drawing salaries." He told his boss that's just what he wanted to do.
At the time he had an office with no windows. Next he asked how you got an
office with a window, and his boss said, "You go to law school." So he went to
law school. "And now I draw a salary in an office with a window — just like the
men I used to see," he said. "You can't imagine how stupid it all is. But they can't
fire me. The whole government, you know is run by gays and Jews." He seemed
to make light of everything he did — till when I pressed him, he admitted he
worked for the Department of Labor on regulations pertaining to safety in coal
mines.

But though he had successfully escaped the small town where everyone was
mean and stupid by becoming a government attorney, there was still something
about his past he could not shake, apparently, because he was still so sensitive
to denunciations of homosexuality. Even the neighbors here concerned him.
When a house on the block changed hands, he seemed relieved that a flight
attendant and his attorney-lover had bought the place, as if he was worried
the neighborhood was becoming too heterosexual. The rest of the world was
even more threatening. He always left *The Washington Post* for me on the din-

ing room table — he was so neat that even though he'd read it, it looked new, though sometimes a story in the paper so upset him he ripped it out and wrote an apology to me in the margin. Then when he came home he would tell me that it was about Jerry Falwell or Pat Robertson. My landlord was, so far as I could tell, like many gay men of a certain age, celibate — because of AIDS, or an inability to attract the partners they wanted, or simply diminishing interest. But he was still angry about the milieu in which he had grown up. Despite his job, his life in the city, his house, there was still something anxious about him — like a man who's entered a witness protection program but thinks even in his new town he may be assassinated. He no longer had sex, but he got all the more angry when anyone challenged his right to do so. One evening he paused on the landing, turned to me, and said: "Did you see what Falwell said in today's paper, that fat pig? He said we're all going to burn in Hell. His daughter has gay friends, I know some of them. But he's still saying that we're going to burn in Hell."

He did not look like someone who would burn in Hell, whatever that look is; like so many men in Northwest Washington, he exuded middle-class propriety. When he set out in the morning in his black overcoat, with cell phone, briefcase, and umbrella, he was one of legions of men who worked in the big faceless office buildings downtown. On the weekends he wore khaki pants and faded flannel shirts that concealed his swelling gut — his efforts at the gym defeated by his habit of eating peanut butter straight from the jar. He loved the arts. He was often out at some cultural event. He had a subscription to the Kennedy Center and two repertory groups; though most of the theater he saw disappointed, and a production of a play about South Africa (Athol Fugard's *The Island*), the night I was sitting in the dining room when he got home, could still plunge him into shock.

"It was unbelievable," he said in a tone of wonderment as he paused on his way upstairs, "the worst thing I've ever seen. But the audience — all white, of course — gave it a standing ovation."

The theater — like homosexuality — was apparently something he still wanted to believe in but which no longer rewarded his original passion; nevertheless, like the Lincolns, he went to at least a play a week. He'd wanted, in fact, to be a stage designer but had thought better of it, he said, his senior year. Now the only set he worked on was his house. I would come downstairs to find he'd used the furniture from a yard sale to transform the living room into a porch in the South Seas — all white wicker — or something Belle Epoque. One morning I walked onto the landing to find a shimmering bolt of blue cloth suspended from the skylight outside my room to the floor two stories below. In the same spirit he lighted his house every night for the benefit of passersby, that anonymous audience that would glance in on a winter evening to see a single spotlight burnishing the *Boy with a Thorn*, or a softer light on the rococo mirror, or a vase of tulips on the dining room table under a pin light. Some nights he sat downstairs on the small sofa, stroking the dog in his lap, and watched people go by, like a playwright watching his audience. Other nights he would bolt when he saw me coming up the stairs outside, and by the time I entered the house, the parlor would be empty. One night he was perched on the sofa laughing when I entered the house. "You wouldn't believe what just happened," he said. "I was sitting here looking out the window, when four gorgeous guys in full leather came to a stop on the sidewalk and began staring up at me — absolutely staring. I couldn't believe it. Then, just as I was about to invite them, Biscuit wagged her tail and I realized it wasn't me they were looking at, it was my dog! It's not easy being an aging actress," he laughed.

"It's not easy being alive," said Frank to me the next day as we say down in Dupont Circle. "Let's face it — like the rest of us, your landlord has no idea, I'm sure, why he's still here — what the others were doing that he was not. That's your landlord's problem, you know."

"What?"

"He's one of thousands of gay men who survived AIDS only to realize they are completely alone and have nothing to live for," he said.

"I asked him the other day how many friends he'd lost to AIDS," I said, "and do you know what he said?"

"What?"

"Three to six hundred. That must be an exaggeration."

"Not in his case," he said. "You don't know what D.C. was like during the eighties. Funerals, funerals, funerals! I got my suntan one summer from just standing in Rock Creek Cemetery. It was a nightmare. I used to think the eighties were like a very nice dinner party with friends, except some of them were taken out and shot while the rest of us were expected to go on eating."

"But then the whole city must remind you of people who aren't here."

"But that's why *you* should live here — you have no memories. You have no past. Here."

He stood up.

"So he did lose a lot of friends."

"Of course," he said.

"But then why is he . . . so cheerful?"

"Cheerful! Cheerful? He's polite!" He lighted a cigarette. "I'm afraid you may be misinterpreting our mutual friend in the light of your own rather desperate wants and needs! What's it like over there, anyways, when you're both home?" he said.

"We live very quietly, like two old bachelors. That's what's so nice. He works in his study balancing his books and I lie upstairs reading the letters of Mrs. Lincoln."

"Not still," he said. "You know, you really have to ask yourself why you're obsessing on this woman."

"Do you know what was written on the inside of her wedding ring?"

"What?"

"*Love Is Eternal*," I said.

"Ah," said Frank. "That's nice. I wonder if I could get the Lug to give me one of those. He wants us to get married, you know."

"Utter devotion to one person," I said.

"Me," he said.

"That's right," I said.

"But that still leaves you. Have you tried speed dating? That thing where they put you in a room with forty other men and you all have three minutes to ask each other questions? Of course that entails a great risk — that no one will want to date you. That's *your* problem, you know."

"What?" I said.

"You want to be needed! But your landlord's not in a nursing home. However, you could help *me* put on my cold cream," he said in an altered voice. "Or sit with me a while until I fall asleep."

"Stop it," I said.

"Is that a no?" he said, retaining the voice. "I'm not surprised. You probably have more important things to do at your age. I just thought maybe you might like to help. I thought perhaps you might even, dare I say, care for me. But I can see that this was an illusion. Oh, look," he said, as someone our age walked into the Circle in tight blue jeans and a baseball cap. "Another case of age-inappropriate fashion! That's one mistake your landlord doesn't make, like these bozos, who make you think it really is all just a case of arrested development," he said as the man our age went by, "as if they still see themselves as twenty-five. No, your landlord dresses very well. He doesn't try to play a role he's far too old for."

The role he played in my opinion came to me quite accidentally one day in the Freer Gallery when I came upon a Chinese scroll painting of a lake hemmed in by steep and snowy mountains, and a little house that contained, when I looked closely, two figures. *On a gloomy winter afternoon*, the text beside the painting said, *a scholar sits in his elegant pavilion as a kneeling servant prepares some warm tea*. That's my landlord, I thought — especially when he closed the doors of his study each evening after work. He seemed to have everything one could want but one — a companion — and the problem there, he said when we were discussing the general issue one day, was that men his age were not attracted to one another. "They're all looking for something younger," he said.

"Just like straight men." So my landlord lived alone, except for his tenant, in a house as still and silent as a pavilion in a winter landscape on a Chinese scroll.

"He *is* his house," was my explanation one day when Frank stopped by to visit, as we sat downstairs waiting for my landlord to put the dog on a leash upstairs so that we could all go to Dupont Circle together. "Look around you," I said. He did, commenting on this and that, till my landlord came down with Biscuit. Though he pulled vigorously at the leash, keeping her close to him, the minute we sat down on a bench in the Circle, she began keening at the sight of another dog passing through the park. "She never does that," my landlord said. The sustained sound was not a bark but something so full of longing and frustrated desire it seemed cruel that she could not pursue her desire for this other dog because she was on a leash, a leash kept firmly in hand by a man no more free to pursue what he wanted than she was, I could not help thinking, though he did not emit a keening sound deep in his throat, he simply said: "I want that," when someone his type (stocky, muscular, broad-chested, dark-haired, about thirty) walked by.

CHAPTER SIX

NATION'S CROSSROADS

Poetry and Politics

[1920–2010]

THE POETRY OF Washington has taken many forms, including intimate portraits of anonymous or nearly anonymous natives by Langston Hughes and Sterling A. Brown; formal pieces honoring public figures, national monuments, or historical sites by Archibald MacLeish; and angry political poems on protest marches and demonstrations during the volatile 1960s and 1970s by Allen Ginsberg and Denise Levertov. There have also been informal, meditative pieces, including poems by U.S. Poet Laureates Allen Tate and Elizabeth Bishop; and sly, humorous pieces or fantasies by Reed Whittemore (another Poet Laureate), May Miller, and E. Ethelbert Miller. These poets have opened fresh vistas on the local landscape, showing us what we may have missed or never otherwise thought on our own.

(OVERLEAF) Lincoln Memorial statue. Courtesy of the Historic American Buildings Survey, Jet T. Lowe, photographer, 1992.

LANGSTON HUGHES

Langston Hughes (1902–67) wrote relatively few poems explicitly about Washington, but several were inspired by the life of the "folk" and the "blues" he discovered along Washington's vibrant Seventh Street, where Jean Toomer also gathered some of his material. After graduating from high school in Cleveland, Ohio, Hughes worked and traveled to Mexico, West Africa, and Europe before heading to Washington to live, for a time, with his mother. There, through a chance encounter with the poet Vachel Lindsay, Hughes gained early fame as the "busboy poet" while working at the Wardman Park hotel. He went on to become one of the most important figures in the Harlem Renaissance — a multitalented poet, fiction writer, playwright, and essayist. Years later, during the Red Scare, Hughes was summoned to Washington to appear before Joseph McCarthy and the Senate Permanent Subcommittee on Investigations to testify about his politics and his associations with known Communists. Careful preparation enabled him to get through this ordeal without harm to his reputation or the reputation of his friends.

Lincoln Monument: Washington
From *The Collected Poems of Langston Hughes*

Let's go see old Abe
Sitting in the marble and the moonlight,
Sitting lonely in the marble and the moonlight,
Quiet for ten thousand centuries, old Abe.
Quiet for a million, million years.

Quiet —

And yet a voice forever
Against the
Timeless walls
Of time —
Old Abe.

Lincoln Theatre
From *The Collected Poems of Langston Hughes*

The head of Lincoln looks down from the wall
White movies echo dramas on the screen.
The head of Lincoln is serenely tall

Above a crowd of black folk, humble, mean.
The movies end. The lights flash gaily on.
The band down in the pit bursts into jazz.
The crowd applauds a plump brown-skin bleached blonde
Who sings the troubles every woman has.
She snaps her fingers, slowly shakes her hips,
And cries, all careless-like from reddened lips!
>   *De man I loves has*
>   *Gone and done me wrong . . .*
While girls who wash rich white folks clothes by day
And sleek-haired boys who deal in love for pay
Press hands together, laughing at her son.

Un-American Investigators
From *The Collected Poems of Langston Hughes*

The committee's fat,
Smug, almost secure
Co-religionists
Shiver with delight
In warm manure
As those investigated —
Too brave to name a name —
Have pseudonyms revealed
In Gentile game
>   Of who,
>   Born Jew,
>   Is who?
Is not your name Lipshitz?
>   Yes.
Did you not change it

For subversive purposes?
>   No.
For nefarious gain?
>   Not so.
Are you sure?
The committee shivers
With delight in
Its manure.

STERLING A. BROWN

Sterling A. Brown (1901–89) was a native Washingtonian who grew up next to Howard University, where his father was head of theology, and after appointments at several black colleges, eventually returned there to teach African American literature. A poet, essayist, and scholar, he was a student of black folklife and black vernacular and the author of groundbreaking studies of black writing—"The Negro Character as Seen by White Authors" (1933), "The American Race Problem as Reflected in American Literature" (1939), and *Negro Poetry and Drama* (1938). He was also editor or coeditor of seminal anthologies of African American writing, especially *Outline for the Study of Poetry of American Negroes* (1931). From 1936 to 1940, he was employed by the federal government as the national editor of Negro affairs for the Federal Writers' Project. In that capacity, he wrote an eye-opening chapter for *Washington: City and Capital* (1937) titled "The Negro in Washington," on the history of African Americans' contributions to the life of the city, which also served as a cool indictment of the majority culture's treatment of blacks in the nation's capital. During the McCarthy era, Brown was investigated by the FBI but managed to hijack the proceedings with his charm and sharp wit. Reprinted here are selected black speech poems of Brown's, which reveal his sophisticated ear and eye.

Sporting Beasley
From *The Collected Poems of Sterling A. Brown*

Good glory, give a look at Sporting Beasley
Strutting, oh my Lord

> Tophat cocked one side his bulldog head,
> Striped four-in-hand, and in his buttonhole
> A red carnation; Prince Albert coat
> Form-fitting, corset like; vest snugly filled,
> Gray morning trousers, spotless and full-flowing,
> White spats and a cane.

Step it, Mr. Beasley, oh step it till the sun goes down.

> Forget the snippy clerks you wait upon,
> Tread clouds of glory above the heads of pointing children,
> Oh, Mr. Peacock, before the drab barnfowl of the world

Forget the laughter when at the concert
You paced down the aisle, your majesty,
Down to Row A, where you pulled out your opera glasses.

Majesty . . .

It's your turn now, Sporting Beasley,
Step it off.

The world is a ragbag; the world
Is full of heathens who haven't seen the light;
Do it, Mr. Missionary.

Great glory, give a look.

Oh Jesus, when his brother's bill falls due,
When he steps off the chariot
And flicks the dust from his patent leathers with his handkerchief,
When he stands in front of the jasper gates, patting his tie,

And then paces in
Cane and knees working like well-oiled slow-timed pistons;

Lord help us, give a *look* at him.

Don't make him dress up in no night gown, Lord.
Don't put no fuss and feathers on his shoulders, Lord.

Let him know it's heaven.

Let him keep his hat, his vest, his elkstooth, and everything.

Let him have his spats and cane
Let him have his spats and cane.

Glory, Glory
From *The Collected Poems of Sterling A. Brown*

When Annie Mae Johnson condescends to take the air,
Give up all your business, make haste to get there,
Glory oh glory, get there, be there.

The last time I saw Annie on the avenue,
She held up traffic for an hour or two.
The green light refused, absolutely, to go off at all;
And the red light and the amber nearly popped the glass,

When Annie walked by, they came on so fast,
Then stayed on together twenty minutes after she went past;
And it took three days for to get them duly timed again.
Even so, they palpitated every now and then.

A driver of a coal truck turned his head around,
Watching her walk and knocked an old man down,
Old man's weak eyes had been dazzled by the gorgeous sight;
Po' man collapsed and he heaved a sigh,
Said, "Lord, I'm willin' at the last to die,
Cause my state is blessed, everything's all right,
Happy, Lord, happy, yes happy am I."

Saw a Rock Creek Bridge car jump off the track,
Do the shim-sham shimmy and come reeling back;
Saw a big steam roller knocked clean off its base,
When it got itself together, the little Austin had its place.

Ambulance came a-clanging, the fire truck banging,
Police patrol a-sailing, the sirens all wailing,
Parked any whichaway and turned their headlights high,
With their engines just a purring, till Annie Mae tipped on by.

Folks gathered from the manors, swarmed in from the alleys,
Deserted their pool-rooms, rushed out of their lodges,
Some took taxis to get them to the place on time;
Way the preachers left their congregations was a holy crime.
Twixt Uncle Ham's sonny boys and Aunt Hagar's daughters
Just like Daddy Moses through the Red Sea Waters,
Annie Johnson made a path, as she laid it on the frazzling line;
The dark waves parted, and then they closed in behind.

Aaanh, Lord, when Annie Mae lays it down,
If you want to take the census proper, better come around.

No More Worlds to Conquer
From *The Collected Poems of Sterling A. Brown*

My boy Alec is a smart bootlegger
He's a race man now and not anybody's Nigger,
And the cars he rides in get bigger and bigger.

He started with a Kettle, and he peddled in a Ford
But now he is reaping his well earned reward,
With a Packard for himself and a Hudson for his broad.

He moves from the slums to the dickty section
And his shrewd advance in the right direction
Makes chances slim for Alexander's detection.

And now he has for customers Senators and such,
He admits his early comrades don't amount to much,
So now he barely speaks to his old boy Dutch.

He forgets the cooncan, and Georgia skin he played,
For the sake of contract contacts he has made,
And his stomps become 'bals' in the Colonade.

He sees a poor drunk on Florida Avenue
And is pierced by nausea through and through
And he wonders what the race is coming to.

MORAL

If we only had the brains that are his,
We too could be great like my boy is
Magnates in the world's great businesses!

ALLEN TATE

Born in Kentucky and educated at Vanderbilt University, Allen Tate (1899–1979) had deep family ties to Washington and nearby Fairfax County, Virginia. Pleasant Hill, the setting for *The Fathers* (1938), his well-known novel of the Civil War, was based on the Fairfax County home of his mother's family. In his memoir, *A Lost Traveller's Dream* (1972), Tate told the story of his childhood discovery of these aging family connections. The neoclassical poem, "Aeneas at Washington" (1933), linking ancient Troy and the American capital, exemplifies the author's strong southern pride and the traditionalism of the "Fugitives," a Vanderbilt-centered group of poets and critics to which Tate belonged. Tate lived in Washington while serving as Consultant in Poetry to the Library of Congress in 1943–44, and then as a Fellow in American Letters, also at the Library of Congress.

Aeneas at Washington
From *Collected Poems, 1919–1976*

I myself saw furious with blood
Neoptolemus, at his side the black Atridae,
Hecuba and the hundred daughters, Priam
Cut down, his filth drenching the holy fires.
In that extremity I bore me well,
A true gentleman, valorous in arms,
Disinterested and honourable. Then fled:
That was a time when civilization
Run by the few fell to the many, and
Crashed to the shout of men, the clang of arms:
Cold victualing I seized, I hoisted up
The old man my father upon my back,
In the smoke made by sea for a new world
Saving little — a mind imperishable
If time is, a love of past things tenuous
As the hesitation of receding love.

(To the reduction of uncitied littorals
We brought chiefly the vigor of prophecy
Our hunger breeding calculation
And fixed triumphs.)

                    The thirsty dove I saw
In the glowing fields of Troy, hemp ripening
And tawny corn, the thickening Blue Grass
All lying rich forever in the green sun.
I see all things apart, the towers that men
Contrive I too contrived long, long ago.
Now I demand little. The singular passion
Abides its object and consumes desire
In the circling shadow of its appetite.
There was a time when the young eyes were slow,
Their flame steady beyond the firstling fire,
I stood in the rain, far from home at nightfall
By the Potomac, the great Dome lit the water,
The city my blood had built I knew no more
While the screech-owl whistled his new delight
Consecutively dark.

Stuck in the wet mire
Four thousand leagues from the ninth buried city
I thought of Troy, what we had built her for.

ARCHIBALD MACLEISH

Archibald MacLeish (1892–1982) was a poet, lawyer, and editor at *Fortune* magazine who came to Washington as Franklin Delano Roosevelt's choice to head the Library of Congress (1939–44). He stayed on to do yeoman work in a variety of other federal offices during World War II: as head of the Office of Facts and Figures (1941–42); assistant director of domestic affairs in the Office of War Information (1942–43); assistant Secretary of State (1944–45); and speechwriter for FDR. Indeed, he became so devoted to public service and government affairs that he almost gave up writing poetry and drama altogether. What he wrote during this time included several poems with Washington settings, such as "At the Lincoln Memorial," which sought strength for the "Union" and national renewal in the image of Lincoln and the nearby Potomac River.

At the Lincoln Memorial
From *Collected Poems, 1917–1982*

*

Slow Potomac, tarnished water
Silent already with the sense of sea
And still the stain upon you of those raging reaches,
Ravaged Shenandoahs and the toppled elm —
Hold us a little in your drifting thought,
O soiled, sad river! We,
We, too, forefeel; we too remember:
Greatness awaits us as it waits for you
Beyond the sea-fall on those shuddering beaches . . .

And the shame pursues.

*

We bring the past down with us as you bring your
Sodden branches,
Froth on your yellow eddies and a few
Blind flowers floating like a dead bird's wing:
All that defiling refuse of old wrong,
Of long injustice, of the mastered man,

Of man (far worse! far worse!) made master —
Hatred, the dry bitter thong
That binds these two together at the last;
Fear that feeds the hatred with its stale imposture;
Spoiled, corrupted tramplings of the grapes of wrath . . .

We bring the past down with us, the shame gathers
And the dream is lost.

                              *

Think of us, river, where your eddies turn
Returning on the purpose of the stream
And the gulls scream!

Think beyond there where the surges burn
Bright on their beaches and the waters live,
Think of us, river!

Is this our destiny — defeated dream?

                              *

A man sits or the image of a man
Staring at stillness on a marble floor.
No drum distracts him nor no trumpet can
Although he hears the trumpet and the drum.
He listens for the time to come.

"As to the policy I 'seem to be pursuing' . . .
I would save the Union . . .
My paramount object in this struggle is to save the Union . . ."

The trumpet's breath,
The drummer's tune —
Can drum and trumpet save the Union?

What made the Union — held it in its origins together?
"I have often inquired of myself
what great principle or idea it was . . .
It was not the mere matter of the separation from the mother-land
but something in the Declaration giving liberty
not alone to the people of this country
but hope to the world . . .
It was that which gave promise
that in due time
the weights should be lifted from the shoulders of all men."

To save the Union:
To renew
That promise and that hope again.

*

Within this door
A man sits or the image of a man
Remembering the time before.
He hears beneath the river in its choking channel
A deeper river rushing on the stone,
Sits there in his doubt alone,
Discerns the Principle,
The guns begin,
Emancipates — but not the slaves,
The Union — not from servitude but shame:
Emancipates the Union from the monstrous name
Whose infamy dishonored
Even the great Founders in their graves . . .

He saves the Union and the dream goes on.

*

Think of us, river, when the sea's enormous
Surges meet you on that morning shore!
Think of our destiny, the place
Named in our covenant where we began —
The rendez-vous of man,
The concourse of our kind, O kindred face!

And you,
Within there, in our love, renew
The rushing of that deeper flood
To scour the hate clean and the rusted blood,
The blind rememberance!
                    O renew once more,
Staring at stillness on that silent floor,
The proud, lost promise of the sea!

Renew the holy dream we were to be!

ELIZABETH BISHOP

Elizabeth Bishop (1911–79) was a highly accomplished poet who won several major poetry prizes. Born in Massachusetts but raised in Canada by her grandparents, she attended Vassar College and then traveled widely before settling in Brazil, where she lived for sixteen years. In 1949–50, she was named Consultant in Poetry to the Library of Congress, and in later years she taught intermittently at several American universities. Unlike her contemporaries, the confessional poets, Bishop turned her eye outward, to nature and the scenes before her, as in "View of the Capitol from the Library of Congress." In "From Trollope's Journal," dated "Winter, 1860," she composed a fantasy based on fact, recapturing the city of Washington as Anthony Trollope found it during the early days of the Civil War.

View of the Capitol from the Library of Congress
From *The Complete Poems, 1927–1979*

Moving from left to left, the light
is heavy on the Dome, and coarse.
One small lunette turns it aside
and blankly stares off to the side
like a big white old wall-eyed horse.

On the east steps the Air Force Band
in uniforms of Air Force blue
is playing hard and loud, but — queer —
the music doesn't quite come through.

It comes in snatches, dim then keen,
then mute, and yet there is no breeze.
The giant trees stand in between.
I think the trees must intervene,
catching the music in their leaves
like gold-dust, till each big leaf sags.
Unceasingly the little flags
feed their limp stripes into the air,
and the band's efforts vanish there.

Great shades, edge over,
give the music room.
The gathered brasses want to go
boom — boom.

From Trollope's Journal

From *The Complete Poems, 1927–1979*

[Winter, 1861]

As far as statues go, so far there's not
much choice: they're either Washingtons
or Indians, a whitewashed, stubby lot,
His country's Father or His foster sons.
The White House in a sad, unhealthy spot
just higher than Potomac's swampy brim,
— they say the present President has got
ague or fever in each backwoods limb.
On Sunday afternoon I wandered — rather,
I floundered — out alone. The air was raw
and dark; the marsh half-ice, half-mud. This weather
is normal now: a frost, and then a thaw,
and then a frost. A hunting man, I found
the Pennsylvania Avenue heavy ground . . .
There all around me in the ugly mud
— hoof-pocked, uncultivated — herds of cattle,
numberless, wond'ring steers and oxen, stood:
beef for the Army, after the next battle.
Their legs were caked the color of dried blood;
their horns were wreathed with fog. Poor, starving, dumb
or lowing creatures, never to chew the cud
or fill their maws again! Th'effluvium
made that damned anthrax on my forehead throb.
I called a surgeon in, a young man, but,
with a sore throat himself, he did his job.
We talked about the War, and as he cut
away, he croaked out, "Sir, I do declare
everyone's sick! The soldiers poison the air."

ALLEN GINSBERG

Allen Ginsberg's (1926–97) deepest connections with Washington came
through the antiwar movement, as seen in "D.C. Mobilization" (1970), retitled
"Anti–Vietnam War Peace Mobilization" in *Collected Poems, 1947–1997* (2006).
He participated in demonstrations in the 1960s and 1970s, in Washington and

other cities, as attested in "Spring 1971 Anti-War Games," and often read his poetry to the crowds, as when he offered the poetic "exorcism" originally called "No Taxation without Representation," used in the 1968 march on the Pentagon. When he despaired at the news of expanded U.S. bombing in Laos, Cambodia, and Vietnam in 1970, Ginsberg began researching the CIA's role in the opium trade in Southeast Asia. Shortly thereafter, he started withholding his income tax payments in a further effort to protest the war in Southeast Asia. A late poem, "Capitol Air" (1980), the last in the 1980 edition of *Collected Poems*, sums up Ginsberg's skepticism and animosity toward all the dehumanizing forces of the modern world, but as the title suggests, the federal government was the locus of much of his wrath.

Anti–Vietnam War Peace Mobilization
From *Collected Poems, 1947–1997*

White sunshine on sweating skulls
Washington's Monument pyramided high granite clouds
over a soul mass, children screaming in their brains on quiet grass
(black man strapped hanging in blue denims from an earth cross) —
Soul brightness under blue sky
Assembled before White House filled with mustached Germans
& police buttons, army telephones, CIA Buzzers, FBI bugs
Secret Service walkie-talkies, Intercom squawkers to Narco
Fuzz & Florida Mafia Real Estate Speculators.
One hundred thousand bodies naked before an Iron Robot
Nixon's brain Presidential cranium case spying thru binoculars
from the Paranoia Smog Factory's East Wing.
                                                        May 9, 1970

Capitol Air
From *Collected Poems, 1947–1997*

I don't like the government where I live
I don't like dictatorship of the Rich
I don't like bureaucrats telling me what to eat
I don't like Police dogs sniffing round my feet

I don't like Communist Censorship of my books
I don't like Marxists complaining about my looks
I don't like Castro insulting members of my sex
Leftists insisting we got the mystic Fix

I don't like Capitalists selling me gasoline Coke
Multinationals burning Amazon trees to smoke
Big Corporation takeover media mind
I don't like the Top-bananas that're robbing Guatemala banks blind

I don't like K.G.B. Gulag concentration camps
I don't like the Maoists' Cambodian Death Dance
15 Million were killed by Stalin Secretary of Terror
He has killed our old Red Revolution for ever

I don't like Anarchists screaming Love Is Free
I don't like the C.I.A. they killed John Kennedy
Paranoiac tanks sit in Prague and Hungary
But I don't like counterrevolution paid for by the C.I.A.

Tyranny in Turkey or Korea Nineteen Eighty
I don't like Right Wing Death Squad Democracy
Police State Iran Nicaragua yesterday
Laissez-faire please Government keep your secret police offa me

I don't like Nationalist Supremacy White or Black
I don't like Narcs & Mafia marketing Smack
The General bullying Congress in his tweed vest
The President building up his Armies in the East & West

I don't like Argentine police Jail torture Truths
Government Terrorist takeover Salvador news
I don't like Zionists acting Nazi Storm Troop
Palestine Liberation cooking Israel into Moslem soup

I don't like the Crown's Official Secrets Act
You can get away with murder in the Government that's a fact
Security cops teargassing radical kids
In Switzerland or Czechoslovakia God Forbids

In America it's Attica in Russia it's Lubianka Wall
In China if you disappear you wouldn't know yourself at all
Arise Arise you citizens of the world use your lungs
Talk back to the Tyrants all they're afraid of is your tongues

Two hundred Billion dollars inflates World War
In United States every year They're asking for more
Russia's got as much in tanks and laser planes
Give or take Fifty Billion we can blow out everybody's brains

School's broke down 'cause History changes every night
Half the Free World nations are Dictatorships of the Right
The only place socialism worked was in Gdansk, Bud
The Communist world's stuck together with prisoners' blood

The Generals say they know something worth fighting for
They never say what till they start an unjust war
Iranian hostage Media Hysteria sucked
The Shah ran away with 9 Billion Iranian bucks

Kermit Roosevelt and his U.S. dollars overthrew Mossadegh
They wanted his oil then they got Ayatollah's dreck
They put in the Shah and they trained his police the Savak
All Iran was our hostage quarter-century That's right Jack

Bishop Romero wrote President Carter to stop
Sending guns to El Salvador's Junta so he got shot
Ambassador White blew the whistle on the White House lies
Reagan called him home cause he looked in the dead nuns' eyes

Half the voters didn't vote they knew it was too late
Newspaper headlines called it a big Mandate
Some people voted for Reagan eyes open wide
3 out of 4 didn't vote for him That's a Landslide

Truth may be hard to find but Falsehood's easy
Read between the lines our Imperialism is sleazy
But if you think the People's State is your Heart's Desire
Jump right back in the frying pan from the fire

The System the System in Russia & China the same
Criticize the System in Budapest lose your name
Coca Cola Pepsi Cola in Russia & China come true
Khrushchev yelled in Hollywood "We will bury You"

America and Russia want to bomb themselves Okay
Everybody dead on both sides Everybody pray
All except the Generals in caves where they can hide
And fuck each other in the ass waiting for the next free ride

No hope Communism no hope Capitalism Yeah
Everybody's lying on both sides Nyeah nyeah nyeah
The bloody iron curtain of American Military Power
Is a mirror image of Russia's red Babel-Tower

Jesus Christ was spotless but was Crucified by the Mob
Law & Order Herod's hired soldiers did the job
Flowerpower's fine but innocence has got no Protection
The man who shot John Lennon had a Hero-worshipper's connection

The moral of this song is that the world is in a horrible place
Scientific Industry devours the human race
Police in every country armed with Tear Gas & TV
Secret Masters everywhere bureaucratize for you & me

Terrorists and police together build a lowerclass Rage
Propaganda murder manipulates the upperclass Stage
Can't tell the difference 'tween a turkey & a provocateur
If you're feeling confused the Government's in there for sure

Aware Aware wherever you are No Fear
Trust your heart Don't ride your Paranoia dear
Breathe together with an ordinary mind
Armed with Humor Feed & Help Enlighten Woe Mankind

                              Frankfurt-New York, December 15, 1980

DENISE LEVERTOV

A poet and essayist, Denise Levertov (1923–97) was deeply committed to the antiwar effort and to other political causes in the 1960s and 1970s — particularly draft resistance and the end of nuclear power — which often took her to Washington to participate in marches and sit-ins. For her, the connections between politics and poetry were natural and inevitable rather than contradictory or forced: "What is in question," she declared in "The Poet in the World" (1973), "is the role of the poet as observer or as participant in the life of his time." The second "Entr'acte," in *To Stay Alive* (1971), datelined "At the Justice Department[,] November 15, 1969," captures the struggle of a group of war protesters, retching and stumbling through a fog of tear gas yet exhilarated in their resistance. "Psalm: People Power at the Die-in," from *Candles in Bablyon* (1982), as Levertov explained in a footnote, "derives directly from events described in prose as 'With the Seabrook Natural Guard in Washington, 1978,'" published in *Light Up the Cave* (1981), describing a three-day sit-in at the Nuclear Regulatory Commission in Washington while commissioners met to consider shutting down the Seabrook nuclear facility.

At the Justice Department, November 15, 1969
From *Poems 1968–1972*

Brown gas-fog, white
beneath the street lamps.
Cut off on three sides, all space filled
with our bodies.
     Bodies that stumble
in brown airlessness, whitened
in light, a mildew glare,
     that stumble
hand in hand, blinded, retching.
Wanting it, wanting
to be here, the body believing it's
dying in its nausea, my head
clear in its despair, a kind of joy,
knowing this is by no means death,
is trivial, an incident, a
fragile instant.   Wanting it, wanting
     with all my hunger this anguish,
     this knowing in the body
the grim odds we're
up against, wanting it real.
Up that bank where gas
curled in the ivy, dragging each other
up, strangers, brothers
and sisters.   Nothing
will do but
to taste the bitter
taste. No life
other, apart from.

Psalm: People Power at the Die-in
From *Candles in Babylon*

Over our scattered tents by night
lightning and thunder called to us.

Fierce rain blessed us,
catholic, all-encompassing.

We walked through blazing morning
into the city of law,

of corrupt order, of invested power.

By day and by night
we sat in the dust,

on the cement pavement we sat down and sang.

In the noon of a long day, sharing the work of the play,
we died together, enacting

the death by which all
shall perish unless we act.

*

Solitaries drew close, releasing
each solitude into its blossoming.

We gave to each other the roses
of our communion —

A culture of gardens, horticulture not agribusiness,
arbors among the lettuce, small terrains.

*

When we tasted the small, ephemeral
harvest of our striving,

great power flowed from us,
luminous, a promise. Yes! . . .

great energy flowed from solitude,
and great power from communion.

MAY MILLER

A native Washingtonian, May Miller (1899–1995) enjoyed several careers — as
a prize-winning playwright of the Harlem Renaissance, a teacher at Baltimore's
Frederick Douglass High School, and a much-published poet. By the 1960s, she
was recognized as a Washington institution, especially in poetry circles. The
daughter of a prominent sociologist, she grew up on the Howard University
campus, where she took her BA. As a child, she often had to give up her room,
she told audiences, for some well-known visitors to the Howard campus —
including W. E. B. Du Bois and Paul Laurence Dunbar. *The Bog Guide* (1925),

an award-winning play, gained recognition for her as a member of the Harlem Renaissance. Several other plays with racial themes followed, and then came several historical plays, including *Harriet Tubman* and *Sojourner Truth*, anthologized in *Negro History in Thirteen Plays* (1935), which Miller coedited with Willis Richardson. From 1959 to 1989, she published nine volumes of poetry, including *Collected Poems* (1989).

The Washingtonian
From *Dust of Uncertain Journey*

Possessed of this city, we are born
Into kinship with its people.
Eyes that looked upon
Cool magnificence of space,
The calm of marble,
And green converging on green
In long distances,
Bear their wonder to refute
Meaningless dimensions,
The Old-World facades.

The city is ours irrevocably
As pain sprouts at the edge of joy,
As grief grows large with our years.
New seeds push hard to topsoil;
Logic is a grafted flower
From roots in a changeless bed.
Skeleton steel may shadow the path,
Broken stone snag the foot,
But we shall walk again
Side by side with others on the street,
Each certain of his way home.

REED WHITTEMORE

Reed Whittemore (1919–) has been writing humorous as well as serious poems of social, political, and personal commentary for more than half a century. Raised in the East, he spent more than two decades as an English professor at Carleton College, in Minnesota. Whittemore has twice served as Consultant in Poetry to the Library of Congress. A longtime observer of national politics, he moved to Washington in the 1970s to become literary editor of the *New Republic*, while also teaching at the University of Maryland. From 1986 to 1991, he held the honorary position of Poet Laureate for the state of Maryland. "The Destruction of Washington" (1981), from *The Feel of Rock: Poems of Three Decades* (1982), imagines a time many years hence when the federal city is an archaeological dig and researchers are trying to ascertain our gods from the rubble of the city's remains.

The Destruction of Washington
From *The Feel of Rock: Poems of Three Decades*

When Washington has been destroyed,
And the pollutants have been silting up for an age,
Then the old town will attract the world's Schliemanns.
What, they will say, a dig! as they uncover
The L'Enfant plan in the saxifrage.

So many plaques, so many figures in marble
With large shoulders and lawman lips
Will have to be pieced together and moved to the new
Smithsonian
That the mere logistics will delight vips.

For how can one pass by a muchness? There will be fund drives
With uplifting glosses.
Teams of researchers will mass with massive machinery
At the Rayburn ruin
To outscoop Athens and Knossos.

Dusty scholars will stumble in, looking nearsightedly
At gray facades
Of pillar and portal,
And at curious acres of asphalt,
For clues to the mystery of that culture's gods.

Money of course they will miss,
Since money is spoke not at all on the plaques there,
Nor will they shovel up evidence
That the occupants of the chambers and cloakrooms
Were strangers in town, protecting their deities elsewhere;

But sanctums they surely will guess at,
Where the real and true pieties were once expressed.

If the Greeks had their Eleusinians,
Surely this tribe on the Potomac had mysteries too?
— Having to do, perhaps, with the "Wild West?"

Like most of us sitting here now beside the Potomac,
They will find the Potomac primitives hard to assess.
Oh, may their ignorance be, than ours,
At least less!

E. ETHELBERT MILLER

E. Ethelbert Miller (1950–) is a Washington institution, known and admired
as a poet, editor, nurturer of new talent, and director of Howard University's
African American Resource Center. For many years, he was also a member and
chair of the D.C. Humanities Council. Born in New York City, he attended
Howard and has made Washington his home ever since. He is the author of
several volumes of poetry, as well as an autobiography, *Fathering Words: The
Making of an African American Writer* (2000). *In Search of Color Everywhere*
(1994), one of several anthologies edited or coedited by Miller, was awarded
the PEN Oakland Josephine Miles Award. Miller appears often on National
Public Radio and for many years hosted "Maiden Voyage," a venue for aspiring
young poets in the Washington area, on WDCU-FM. "Intersections: Crossing
the District Line," from *Season of Hunger/Cry of Rain: Poems, 1975–1980* (1982),
captures in a humorous, allegorical way the alienation and separation from the
white suburbs felt by young blacks growing up in D.C.

Intersections: Crossing the District Line
From *Season of Hunger/Cry of Rain: Poems, 1975–1980*

(for Shirley)

bo willie shirley me
we headin for Maryland
me i'm in the front seat
shirley she mad and fussin
cause she always gotta sit
in the back
i put on a cracker accent
and call her a sassy colored gal
we argue back and forth
bo willie he don't pay us no mind

he thinks we kids
he wears a beard that makes
him look like jesus
and I think to myself
maybe that's why he don't say nothing

         — intersection —

we waitin for the light to change
bo willie looks around for matches
shirley is up front now
my right hip is pressed against
the door handle
it's gonna leave a mark
i know it is
it ain't started to hurt
but I know it's gonna hurt soon
the light changes
and I try to push Shirley over
away from me
me
i've been skinny for a long time
i eat a lot but the food runs out
i usta pass a lot of gas when
i was young
my momma usta yell at me

         "boy
         how come my good food
         smell so bad comin
         out of you?"

shirley she weighs
more than me
she from downsouth
her hips are like yams
big and sweet
you know what I mean?

bo willie he gotta lot
of room
he sittin in the driver's seat

— intersection —

i'm tryin
not to think about the
door in my side
it hurts
but i try not to think about it
i try to think about Shirley
about how good she feels
pressed against my otherside
it ain't true
but my mind is still lookin
for bo willie's matches
so it don't know that i'm lyin

— intersection —

bo willie
turns the radio on
he's singin
shirley she don't like the song
me i'm happy
cause all i need is for her
to jump up and down

i turn my head
from the inside
to the outside

i look out the window
at maryland

i think to myself
damn
the white people here
look whiter then the white people
at d.c.

i'm happy we just drivin thru
somehow my right side
don't hurt too much
somehow all the pain seems outside

i turn and push shirley
over a little
as the light changes again

bo willie he still singin

one hand on the wheel

one hand on his beard

he looks like jesus
drivin on palm sunday

only it be wilderness
his eyes see and not jerusalem

CHAPTER SEVEN

IMPERIAL WASHINGTON

Power, Corruption, Crisis

[1950–2010]

FROM ITS BEGINNING, the federal city provided a model of representative government and democratic principles, with checks and balances to ensure honesty and integrity, shared power, and a steady influx of fresh ideas and leaders. Allen Drury's *Advise and Consent* (1959) is the classic statement of this model, but like a good many other Washington novels, it exposes the corruption of government by public officials, greedy for power, wealth, and other pleasures. Much of the Washington writing after World War II — notably that by Philip Roth, Mary McCarthy, Robert Coover, Joseph Heller, and Kurt Vonnegut — zeroes in on Nixon and the other notorious figures involved in the Watergate scandal and cover-up. Other examples — by Gore Vidal, Norman Mailer, and Joan Didion — take on the great social and political conflicts over presidential prerogatives, McCarthyism, the Vietnam War, and the Clinton scandals. Power, corruption, and crisis are the watchwords of these decades, eliciting writing in the strident tones of satire, ridicule, and dissent — writing that attempts, in no uncertain terms, to speak the truth to power.

(OVERLEAF) Vietnam War protest at the Washington Monument, April 1, 1971. Getty Images/David Fenton, photographer.

ALLEN DRURY

Allen Drury (1918–98) was born in Texas and worked as a reporter in California before traveling East to become a Washington correspondent with the *New York Times* and *Reader's Digest*. Fascinated with the growing power imbalance between the executive and legislative branches of the government after Franklin Delano Roosevelt, Drury turned his attention to fiction and wrote what many regard as the quintessential Washington novel, *Advise and Consent* (1959). This Pulitzer Prize–winning narrative was inspired by a homosexual scandal in a 1954 Senate race, part of the Lavender Scare of the Cold War 1950s. Drury captured the international politics of the Cold War era and its influence on government decision making, including the president's desire to conduct foreign policy and make key appointments without honoring the "advise and consent" clause of the U.S. Constitution. Drury wrote many more novels treating Washington politics, such as *A Shade of Difference* (1962) and *Capable of Honor* (1966), but none were as successful with the public as *Advise and Consent*, which was adapted for the stage (1960) and screen (1962).

From *Advise and Consent*

Like a city in dreams, the great white capital stretches along the placid river from Georgetown on the west to Anacostia on the east. It is a city of temporaries, a city of just-arriveds and only-visitings, built on the shifting sands of politics, filled with people passing through. They may stay fifty years, they may love, marry, settle down, build homes, raise families, and die beside the Potomac, but they usually feel, and frequently they will tell you, that they are just here for a little while. Someday soon they will be going home. They do go home, but it is only for visits, or for a brief span of staying-away; and once the visits or the brief spans are over ("It's so nice to get away from Washington, it's so inbred; so nice to get out in the country and find out what people are really thinking") they hurry back to their lodestone and their star, their self-hypnotized, self-mesmerized, self-enamored, self-propelling, wonderful city they cannot live away from or, once it has claimed them, live without. Washington takes them like a lover and they are lost. Some are big names, some are little, but once they succumb it makes no difference; they always return, spoiled for the Main Streets without which Washington could not live, knowing instinctively that this is the biggest Main Street of them all, the granddaddy and grandchild of Main Streets rolled into one. They come, they stay, they make their mark, writing big or little on their times, in the strange, fantastic, fascinating city that mirrors so faithfully their strange, fantastic, fascinating land in which there are few absolute wrongs or absolute rights, few all-blacks or all-whites, few dead-certain positives that won't be changed tomorrow; their wonderful, mixed-up, blundering, stumbling, hopeful land in which evil men do good things and good men do evil in a way of life and government so complex and delicately balanced that only Americans can understand it and often they are baffled.

In this bloodshot hour, when Bob Munson is assessing anew the endless problems of being Majority Leader and Washington around him is preparing with varying degrees of unenthusiasm to go to work, various things are happening to various people, all of whom sooner or later will be swept up, in ways they may not now suspect, in the political vortex created by the nomination of Robert A. Leffingwell.

At the Sheraton-Park Hotel the Senator himself completes his dressing and starts downstairs to breakfast, stopping on his way at the apartment of Victor Ennis of California to see whether he wants to share a cab later to the Hill. Vic and Hazel Ennis invite him in for coffee, which soon expands to breakfast, and before long Bob Munson has discovered that both Vic and his junior colleague, Raymond Robert Smith, a child of television out of M-G-M who progressed easily from Glamour Boy No. 3 to TV Commentator No. 1 and from there to the House and then to the Senate, will vote for Bob Leffingwell. They have already talked it over, Senator Ennis explains — Ray called from the Coast as soon as he got in last night from the Academy Awards dinner, "and of course you know Hollywood will be behind him, and Ray thinks he'd better be, and so do I." This is entirely aside from the merits of the nominee, but Bob Munson, who knows his two Californians thoroughly, is quite content to accept their votes without quibbling over motives, the first and most valuable lesson he learned in Washington and one he never forgets. Senator Ennis volunteers the information that he called Arly Richardson, just for the hell of it, and the Majority Leader asks quizzically:

"And what did that sardonic son of Arkansas have to say?"

"He said, 'I guess this will make Bobby sweat a little,'" Senator Ennis reports, and Senator Munson laughs.

"I think I'll put him down as doubtful, but probably leaning to Leffingwell," he says, and Victor Ennis nods.

"If you can ever expect Arly to stand hitched," he says, "that's where I'd hitch him."

And as Hazel comes in briskly with the firm intention of diverting the conversation from politics for at least ten minutes, they turn to her excellent meal and start talking baseball.

While the Ennises and the Majority Leader are thus occupied they do not know — although they would hardly be surprised if they did — that at this very moment, out Sixteenth Street in an apartment high in the Woodner, the Honorable Lafe W. Smith, junior Senator from the state of Iowa, is engaged in a most intimate form of activity with a young lady. This is the fourth time in eight hours that this has occurred, and Lafe Smith is getting a little tired of it. The young lady, however, a minor clerk on a House committee and new to the attractions of living in Her Nation's Capital, is still filled with a care-free enthusiasm, and so the Senator, somewhat against his better judgment, is doing his best to oblige. After the standard processes have produced the stan-dard result, the young lady will shower, dress, and amid many tremulous fare-wells and mutual pledges will peek nervously out the door and then hurry away down the corridor, hoping she has not been seen. The Senator, who thinks he knows something the young lady does not know, which is that he will never see her again, will also shower, shave, examine himself critically in the mirror, be amazed as always at how his unlined and engagingly boyish visage manages to stand the gaff, and then will depart by cab for the Hill, where he is scheduled to meet two elderly constituents from Council Bluffs for breakfast. These kindly folk will be suitably impressed by his air of All-American Boy, and they will go away bemused and bedazzled by their meeting, never dreaming that their All-American Boy, like many another All-American Boy is one hell of a man with the old razzmatazz.

As this tender scene, so typical of life in the world's greatest democracy, is unfolding at the Woodner, Walter F. Calloway, the junior Senator from Utah, is also standing before the mirror in the bathroom of his house near Chevy Chase Circle just inside the District-Maryland Line, muttering and whistling through his teeth in his reedy voice just as he does on the floor of the Senate. "It iss my opinion," he is saying (downstairs Emma Calloway, preparing the usual eggs and bacon, hears the faint droning buzz and wonders tiredly what Walter is practicing this time), "that the confirmation of Mr. Leffingwell to this vitally important post would seriously endanger the welfare of the United Statess in thiss most critical time. . ." None of Walter's colleagues would be surprised to hear this, and later in the day, when he issues the statement to the press and takes the time of the Senate to read it into the Congressional Record, they will shrug and look at one another as much as to say, "What did you expect?" They will be convinced then, prematurely as it turns out, that it is not among the Walter Calloways of the Senate that the fate of Robert A. Leffingwell will be decided, and they will promptly dismiss the opinion of the junior Senator from Utah, who is likable as a person, mediocre as a legislator, and generally ineffec-tive as a United States Senator.

Also practicing, although unlike Walter Calloway not on his own superb voice, is Powell Hanson, the junior Senator from North Dakota. Powell is sitting in his study in Georgetown surrounded by Powell, Jr., twelve, Ruth, seven, and Stanley, four, and he is practicing the violin, an instrument he played in high school and hadn't touched since until about six months ago when Powell, Jr., began to play. Now by popular demand of the younger generation, he has resumed it; and since he never manages to get home from the Senate Office Building much before seven or eight, and then only for a brief meal before either going out again socially or locking himself up with legislation, it is only in the half hour before breakfast that he can manage to really see the children. The violin was Powell, Jr.'s own idea, which the Senator feels should be encouraged; under the impetus of their joint scratching Ruth now thinks she may want to start piano, and Stanley bangs a mean drum, purchased for his recent birthday. Elizabeth Hanson, who gave up a promising future as a research chemist to marry the young lawyer in whom she saw the same possibilities he saw in himself, is quite content with the uproar created by the maestro and his crew, even though it makes breakfast a rather catch-as-catch-can meal. The price exacted by public office sometimes seems more to the Hansons than they are willing to pay; but since they know perfectly well that they will go right on paying it just as long as Powell can get re-elected, they are doing what they can to protect their children and their home. As long as the half hour is set aside as a special time, they feel, as long as it comes regularly every day, it forms a small but unbreachable wall around the family; not much, but enough to do the trick.

Also living in Georgetown in houses of varying quaintness and antiquity whose price increases in direct proportion to their degree of charming inconvenience are some twenty-one Senators whom Bob Munson refers to for easy reference in his own mind as the "Georgetown Group." The quietest of these domiciles on this morning of Robert A. Leffingwell's nomination is probably that of the senior Senator from Kansas, Elizabeth Ames Adams, eating breakfast alone overlooking her tiny back garden; the noisiest is probably that of the junior Senator from Wisconsin, Kenneth Hackett, with his hurly-burly seven. Somewhere in between, in terms of decibels and general activity, come such homes as the gracious residence of John Able Winthrop of Massachusetts, the aunt-run menage of Rowlett Clark of Alabama, and the parakeet and fish-filled home of ancient John J. McCafferty of Arkansas and his sole surviving sister, Jane.

Far from the Georgetown Group along their delightfully tree-shaded and quaintly impassable streets, certain other colleagues are also greeting the new day in their separate fashions. Twenty-two Senators are out of town, taking advantage of the lull which has come about during the debate on the pending bill to revise some of the more obscure regulations of the Federal Reserve Board. Some people, like Murfee Andrews of Kentucky, Rhett Jackson of North Carolina, Taylor Ryan of New York, and Julius Welch of Washington, can throw themselves into this sort of abstruse economic discussion with all the passion of Lafe Smith on the trail of a new conquest; but most of the Senate is quite willing to leave such topics to the experts, voting finally on the basis of the advice of whichever of the experts happens to be considered most reliable.

Consequently the experts, aware of their responsibility, are leaving no cliché unturned. All but Taylor Ryan, in fact, are already up and going busily over the economic theories they will hurl triumphantly at one another in a near-empty Senate chamber this afternoon. The small, chunky body of Murfee Andrews is already in imagination swiveling around scornfully as some scathing point sinks home in the unperturbed hide of Rhett Jackson, who in turn is contemplating the delicate sarcasms with which he will show up the ignorance of Murfee Andrews. Julius Welch, who has never gotten over having been a college president, is readying another of his typical fifty-five-minute lectures with the five little jokes and their necessary pauses to permit the conscientious titters to flutter over the classroom. Taylor Ryan, a man who likes his comfort, is still abed, but his mind is busy, and no one need think it isn't. He has no doubts whatever that he will be able to bull his way right through the flypaper arguments of Jay Welch and Murfee Andrews with the sort of "God damn it, let's be sensible about this" approach befitting a man who made his millions on the Stock Exchange and so knows exactly what he's talking about in a way these damned college professors never could.

Among the absentees, there are as many interests on this morning of the Leffingwell nomination as there are geographic locations.

In the great West, Royce Blair of Oregon, that ineffable combination of arrogance, pomposity, intelligence and good humor, is up very early preparing an address to the Portland Kiwanis Club luncheon on the topic, "The Crisis of Our Times." He has selected this title, with his small, private smile-to-himself, as being a sufficient tent to cover all the camels he wants to crowd under it; and the news of the nomination of Robert A. Leffingwell, provoking from him, as it did from the Majority Leader, a startled, "Oh, God damn!" provides the biggest camel of them all. Royce Blair does not like this nomination and Royce Blair, polishing sledge-hammer phrase after sledge-hammer phrase, is going to say so in terms that will take wings from the Portland Kiwanis Club and echo across the nation by nightfall. Already he has tried, in vain, to reach Tom August and tell him what to do, but the chairman of the Foreign Relations Committee, as usual in moments of crisis, is nowhere to be found. . . .

. . . IN ALBUQUERQUE at this moment the first Senator to give a comment to the press has been waylaid by reporters on his way to the plane for Washington. Hugh B. Root of New Mexico, chewing his cellophone-wrapped cigar and giving the whistling, wheezing, mushlike wail that passes for his particular version of the English language, is blurting something that the wire-service reporters hear as, " — mushn't shpend our time on sucsh shtupid — sucsh shtupid — mushn't — I'm opposed — opposed — we shimply mushn't — " which they agree among them must mean, "The Senate must not spend its time and energies on such stupid nominations. I am unalterably opposed to the nomination of Robert A. Leffingwell to be Secretary of State." When they read this back to Hugh Root for confirmation he gestures with his dripping cigar, looks at them with sudden sharpness like an old badger unearthed in the sunlight, nods, waves, and clambers aboard, shaking his head indignantly. Then he takes the wings of the morning and is gone into the cold bright wind of the desert dawn.

In something of the same vein, though more quietly and cogently, the senior Senator from New Jersey, James H. La Rue, bravely fighting the palsy which always afflicts him, says in his quavering voice in St. Louis that "the Senate must and will reject the nomination of Mr. Leffingwell. Mr. Leffingwell's views on world affairs do not agree with those of many patriotic and intelligent Americans. It would not be safe to have him in the office of Secretary of State." It is not an opinion Bob Munson will like to hear about, but Jim La Rue, a good weather vane, has indicated the ground on which the nomination battle will really be fought. It is ground to which Seab Cooley will presently repair along with the rest, and it will make of the matter something much more serious than a thirteen-year grudge. It is ground which is already concerning not only the capital of the United States and its Senate but London, Paris, Moscow, and the whole wide world, which is now beginning to get the news. The fight to confirm Bob Leffingwell is not going to be a simple thing, as Jim La Rue, with customary prescience, foresees.

For seven Senators this fact is brought home with an extra impact, for they are dealing, or have just dealt, with areas where the Leffingwell nomination will create the most lively interest.

High above the Atlantic in a plane bringing home the American delegation to the Inter-Parliamentary Union meeting in Stockholm, the news coming smoothly over the radio brings much the same dismay to John DeWilton of Vermont as it has to Bob Munson and Royce Blair. Turning slowly about in the stately way which is his custom —"Johnny DeWilton," as Stanley Danta once put it, "doesn't bend, he sways" — the silver-topped human edifice which is the senior Senator from the Green Mountain State clears its throat and demands sharply of Alec Chabot, "Now, why in the hell do you suppose — "

The junior Senator from Louisiana shrugs and looks down at his impeccably kept hands and expensive suit, then darts a quick sidelong glance at Leo P. Richardson of Florida.

"Leo probably knows," he says, a trifle spitefully. "Leo knows everything about this Administration."

At this jibe Leo's round and earnest face squinches up in its usual preoccupied expression of intent concentration and he blurts out a short Anglo-Saxon word he does not customarily use. This indication of feeling is not lost on his seatmate, Marshall Seymour, the acerbic old hell raiser from Nebraska, who gives his dry chuckle and asks of nobody in particular, "Did somebody say there's going to be a hell of a fight? Because if nobody did, I will."

The junior Senator from Missouri, Henry H. Lytle, leans forward from the seat in back with the dutifully worried expression he always wears when he is considering matters affecting the fate of mankind and with one of his usual complete non sequiturs blurts out, "But what will the Israelis do?"

"Who gives a good God damn about the Israelis?" Johnny De Wilton snorts brusquely. "What will *I* do is what I'm worrying about." . . .

. . . [I]N THE Washington suburb of Spring Valley, in the comfortable home where the telephone has been ringing incessantly for the past half hour, the senior Senator from Illinois lifts the receiver once more and prepares to give the same answer he has already given to four other newsmen:

"I haven't reached a final decision on this matter and don't expect to until all the facts are in. At the moment, however, I am inclined to oppose the nomination."

But it is not another reporter who is calling Orrin Knox this time, it is the senior Senator from Utah. Brigham Anderson's voice, courteous and kind as always, is troubled and concerned, and Senator Knox can visualize exactly the worried look on his handsome young face.

"Orrin," Brig says in his direct way, "what do you plan to do about Bob Leffingwell?"

"I think I'll oppose him," says Orrin Knox, equally direct, his gray eyes getting their stubborn look and his gray head its argumentative angle. "How about you?"

"I don't know," Brigham Anderson replies, and there is real doubt in his voice. "I just don't know. In some ways I can be for him, but in other ways — well, you know the man."

"Yes," says Orrin Knox, and a tart asperity enters his tone. "I know the man, and I don't like him."

"You and Seab," Brigham Anderson says with a laugh.

"I trust my reasons are more fundamental than that," Orrin replies flatly. "I'm not at all sure he could be as firm as he ought to be in that job. I'm not sure he *wants* to be as firm as he ought to be — not that I'm prepared to say that to everybody yet, but you know what I mean."

"I do," Senator Anderson says. "And there's more to it, as far as I'm concerned. I've had reason to deal with him pretty closely on the Power Commission, you know, and I've never been convinced he's the great public servant the press says he is. I've got plenty of doubts."

"Of course you know what the press is going to do to us if we oppose him," Orrin Knox says.

"I guess we can stand it," Brigham Anderson says calmly, "if we know we're right."

"Which we're not entirely sure we are, at this moment," the Senator from Illinois retorts.

The Senator from Utah chuckles.

"I'll see you on the Hill," he says. . . .

. . . As of that moment similar telephone conversations on the nomination are passing between many other friends in the Senate, and from none of them, Bob Munson would be interested to know, is anything very constructive coming. Right now it is not entirely clear, even to those most astute in judging such things, just how far the fight over Bob Leffingwell is going to extend.

The President; the Senate; some labor and business leaders; the Barres and the Maudulaynes, K.K. and the Indians, Vasily Tashikov in his closely guarded embassy on Sixteenth Street, and all their respective governments; the chairman of the National Committee; the Speaker of the House; that lively, cocktail-partying Associate Justice of the Supreme Court, Thomas Buckmaster Davis; Dolly Harrison with her incessant parties at Vagaries in Rock Creek Park; even a lonely young man nobody but one in the Senate has ever heard of, far away in the Midwest — all will be swept up and drawn into the endless ramifications of the nomination of Robert A. Leffingwell to be Secretary of State.

But mostly, as they well know, it will be the ninety-nine men and one woman who compose the United States Senate who will bear the burden; and each of them on this morning when a Presidential decision becomes a world reality the news has come, is coming, or soon will come, with exactly the same impact. For a brief moment amid the hubbub of morning they are losing their identities to become imperceptibly, inexorably, for a subtle second, institutions instead of people: the Senators of the United States, each with a vote that will be recorded, when the day arrives, to decide the fate of Robert A. Leffingwell and through him, to whatever degree his activities may affect it, the destiny of their land and of the world.

The split-second feeling of overwhelming responsibility strikes them all, then is instantly superseded by thoughts and speculation about "the situation" — how many votes Bob Leffingwell has, how many Seab Cooley can muster, what Orrin Knox thinks, what Bob Munson is planning, who will do what and why, all the web of interlocking interests and desires and ambitions and arrangements that always lies behind the simple, ultimate, final statement, "The Senate voted today —"

Underneath, the feeling of responsibility is still there. It will come back overwhelmingly for them all on the afternoon or evening some weeks hence — will it be two, or four, or twelve, or twenty? None knows; all speculate — when a hush falls on the crowded chamber and the Chair announces that the time has come for the Senate to decide whether it will advise and consent to the nomination of Robert A. Leffingwell.

It is the events between now and then, the bargains to be struck, the deals to be made, the jockeying for power and the maneuvering for position, which occupy them now. From Lafe Smith, staring wryly at his naked body in a mirror at the Woodner, to Hugh B. Root, airborne above the lonely plains and folded hills of Jim Bridger and the mountain men, each is aware that the Senate is about to engage in one of the battles of a lifetime; and each is wondering what it will mean for him in terms of power, reputation, advantage, political fortune, national responsibility, and integrity of soul.

GORE VIDAL

A political activist and dissident writer, Gore Vidal (1925–) is a Washington insider, like Henry Adams. Raised in the home of his grandfather, former U.S. senator Thomas Gore of Tennessee, the young Vidal often accompanied the senator, blind since childhood, to his office on Capitol Hill and served as his personal aide, a story he tells in *Palimpsest* (1995), his memoir. In 1960, Vidal ran for Congress as a Democrat in his home district of upstate New York. In 1982, he contested Jerry Brown in California's Democratic primary for a seat in the Senate. He has written scores of essays and miscellaneous pieces on national politics; has been a keen observer of the presidency, writing portraits of Kennedy, Nixon, and Reagan among others; and has even harbored presidential aspirations. In 1967, he published *Washington, D.C.: A Novel*, now a classic, and the first novel in his ambitious "American Chronicles" series (*Burr, 1876, Lincoln, Empire*, and *Hollywood*). Set mainly during the time of Franklin Delano Roosevelt's administration, it tells of the growing presence of the media in national politics and the corruption of the political process by special interests. In 1998, he published a science fiction novel, *The Smithsonian Institution*, set in the federal city on the eve of World War II.

From *Washington, D.C.: A Novel*

At the Senate Office Building there were a number of Senators and aides. No one quite knew why he was there. After all, war or no war, it was Sunday and there was nothing anyone could do but sit by the radio and wait for the news. But like soldiers assigned to some redoubt that must not fall, certain Senators converged upon Capitol Hill and took up positions, speculating darkly on the fate of a nation so rudely and apparently so successfully challenged.

In response to a journalist in the downstairs corridor, Burden said, "Naturally we are all behind the President. This Sunday there are no isolationists or internationalists. Only . . . Americans." The small hairs at the back of his neck rose. He had thrilled himself. It was a superb if dangerous moment for all of them.

He was stopped by a familiar figure just opposite the door to his office. "Hello, Senator."

"Oh, hello!" He had forgotten the old man's name but he did recall that thirty years earlier he had been a power in the Senate and one of the most awesomely impressive men Burden had ever known. Now, frail and diffident, the old man haunted the Capitol, as though searching for his early self. Like all former Senators, he was allowed the courtesy of the floor and often when the Chamber was nearly empty, he would sit very straight at his old desk, listening solemnly to a dull speech. To Burden's chagrin he still could not recall the other's name, and so he compromised by calling him "Senator," that sonorous title each would carry, in office or out, to the grave.

"I was just in the neighborhood," began the old man.

"Come in, Senator. Happy to see you." Burden, wanting company, any company, led the grateful ghost into the inner office.

"Now whose office was this?" The old man pondered, white brows drawn together, making deep grooves in the pale forehead. Burden was at the telephone, ringing Clay.

"Could it have been Mr. Vardaman, of Mississippi? Yes, I think so. Yes, I'm sure it was his office." He chuckled. "Wore his hair long, all the way to the shoulders, he did. A fine looking man, if you didn't object to the long hair." The old man sank slowly into one of the leather armchairs. He wore the frock coat and striped trousers of an earlier time; on the right lapel, a fragment of dried egg resembled the rosette of a foreign order.

Clay was not at his room in the Wardman Park Hotel. Burden debated whether or not he should telephone Enid. Deciding not to, he telephoned Blaise.

"Well, the bastard's done it! He got us in the war." Blaise's voice sounded thick as though he had been drinking. "I'm looking at the wire now. We've lost the whole Pacific Fleet. There's nothing between Japan and Los Angeles. Nothing! Not a boat, not a gun. Oh, he's a military genius!" Burden asked for other news, alarm growing. Apparently the Japanese were attacking the Philippines, Malaya, Guam, Wake Island and Hong Kong and neither the British nor the Americans seemed able to resist. "We've lost the Pacific. We'll be lucky if we can hold the line at the Rockies. I'll talk to you later." He hung up. Burden's head swam. This could not be true. Then Clay rang to say that he would be right over.

"Very different from 1917," said the old man placidly. "Of course, Mr. Wilson had been conniving for a war too, just like Mr. Roosevelt. Remember the Sunrise Conference or was that before you came here? No, you were here then. Yes, I remember distinctly. That fellow will go far, I said to Senator Lodge, and I'm happy to say I was right. You've certainly stayed the course, and kept the faith."

While Burden tried to telephone the majority leader, the old man talked of the First War and Mr. Wilson's perfidy, as though it was yesterday: then he spoke of the present and how times had changed. "Look at the Senate now and just think what it was then! Aldrich, Jim Reed, the first LaFollette. We had orators then. True debate." The old voice grew suddenly firm, becoming what it must have been in those halcyon days before the public address system when a politician's unaided voice had to be able to fill the largest hall like sounding brass. The majority leader's line was busy.

The door to the inner office opened and Jesse Momberger looked in. "Thought you'd be here. I'm not interrupting, am I?"

"No," said the old man, aware that the moment had come for ghosts to be exorcised. He rose and took Burden's hand in his papery one. "You must come see us soon, Senator. We're at the Congressional Arms, the wife and I. It will be like old times, when we used to discuss monetary reform. Remember? Only now I've really got the problem licked. I've had the time, you see, to think it through. No more fiat money, no paper. Only copper and platinum coinage. *That's* the key to sound finance." Gracefully, he left the living to their turmoil.

"There but for the grace of God," said Momberger, "go I. Or you."

Burden shook his head. "When I leave this place, I'll never come back. Too painful."

"They all say that, and they all come back. If there's a more useless article than a defeated U.S. Senator, I've yet to see it on display. You got the call yet?"

Burden shook his head. "I've been trying to get through to the majority leader. All the lines are busy."

"Nothin' from the White House?"

"No. But I'm standing by. There's a meeting of Congressional leaders at nine tonight. So I am preparing."

"Funny, I never thought this would happen." Momberger rested one hand on the head of what he took to be a poor likeness of his old friend William Jennings Bryan.

"I wonder if *he* did, the President."

"He's a mean cuss but I don't think he'd lose the whole fleet deliberately." At heart Momberger was a New Dealer. As a result, relations were often strained between the two Senators, for the President saw to it that all patronage was funneled through the senior Senator, a situation that would not make easy Burden's fight for re-election in 1944.

"Even Franklin miscalculates on occasion." Burden was neutral. He could afford to be. The President was directly responsible for the greatest defeat inflicted on the United States since the War of 1812. He might yet be impeached. "We must all rally 'round," said Burden.

They sat in silence, with time suspended, as the winter afternoon came to a close and there was nothing anyone could do but wait for the President to lead them into battle.

"How're you feelin', by the way?" Momberger sounded like a concerned friend but Burden knew that he was merely an interested politician.

"Never felt better." This was almost true. "It wasn't really a stroke." This was not true. "But what they call a temporary blockage in the brain, like a spasm." This was euphemistic. "I had difficulty speaking for a week or two, and that was the end of it." The end of it! He still awoke in the middle of the night, panicky lest an artery had burst in the lobes of his brain, depriving him of speech, sight, movement, or, worst of all, creating hell beneath the skull's curve, since he knew now that all the agony and terror of which man is capable can be created simply by a drop of blood seeping into the wrong passage of the brain.

Clay entered with a sudden burst of sound from the corridor behind. "Hello, Senator." He shook hands warmly with Momberger who said, "Howdy, Congressman!" Momberger seemed to like Clay and had already given him tacit support in the special election.

"Not Congressman, *Captain* Overbury, Army of the United States." Clay turned to Burden, as though in apology. "It's all arranged."

"So fast?" was all that Burden could say.

"I've been in touch with the War Department for the last six months, just in case. Well, this is the case."

"Then you're *not* goin' to run?" Momberger was suddenly alert.

Clay shook his head. "How can I, when there's a war?"

"Good boy." Momberger turned to Burden. "We better pass the word on to the Judge."

Burden nodded. "I'll call him tonight."

Momberger crossed to the door. "Tell me what the President says." He was gone and Burden knew that within minutes, national disaster or not, his colleague would be on the telephone to the Judge, proposing his own candidate for the Second District.

"Are you seeing the President?"

"I assume so. According to the radio, all Congressional leaders are to be briefed at the White House tonight. Better get me the Far East file."

Clay put the file on Burden's desk. "Also that memorandum I made right after I talked to Ambassador Kurusu." Burden shook his head with wonder. "Just think, he was in there with Hull, talking, while Pearl Harbor was being bombed. Fantastic people!"

Clay spread papers on the desk as Burden asked, "What are they saying at Laurel House?"

"That it's a plot. What else? Blaise thinks the President blew up the ships himself."

"Maybe he did! Was Enid there?"

Clay frowned. "No. She's at home, as far as I know."

A Senate page appeared at the open door to the inner office. In a rapid sing-song he said, "Senator, majority leader says there'll be joint session Congress tomorrow twelve-thirty. President will speak." The boy was halfway out the office when Burden said, "Come back here, son." The boy stopped. "Is that all the majority leader said?"

"Yes, sir. Same message to all Senators. President speaks tomorrow, twelve-thirty joint session." The boy was gone.

Burden frowned. "Clay, you better check with Senator Barkley's office and find out just when and where we're supposed to meet tonight."

Wanting comfort, Burden telephoned Ed Nillson in New York. But Nillson gave none: he was glad that the United States was at last committed, to which Burden replied, suddenly fervent, "I want no war, of any kind, ever. Nothing is worth a man's life."

Nillson made a dry crackling noise in the receiver. "May I quote you, Senator?"

Burden laughed, too. "No, you may not. But I do mean it."

"But surely Hitler should be discouraged. And how can that be done without war?"

"I don't know the answer. No one has ever known it." Distressed by the resonance of his own unexpected despair, he changed the subject and told of Clay's enlistment.

"A good idea," said Nillson. "He'll make a better candidate if he's been a soldier, with a good record."

"But suppose he's killed?"

Clay returned, unaware that it was his death that was being considered. "Let the future take care of itself." Nillson was cool. "How are you feeling, by the way?"

Burden gave the usual answer and rang off. He looked expectantly at Clay, who said, "I'm afraid you're not on the White House list."

"Not on it?" Burden was astonished. "But Senator Austin is going and I certainly outrank..." He stopped abruptly, refusing to reveal his pain. "Well, that's Franklin's revenge, I suppose."

Clay nodded. "Senator Barkley was apologetic. He said you'd understand that it wasn't his doing."

Burden said good night to Clay and left the Senate Office Building. In the cold twilight, he saw the old anonymous Senator making his slow way toward Union Station and his hotel, where he lived, no doubt, in small rooms filled with piles of yellowing Congressional Records, scrapbooks that smelled of old paste and signed photographs of forgotten celebrities. Depressed, Burden beckoned to Henry who opened the car door with a flourish.

"The White House, Senator?"

"No. Home." As Burden settled back in his seat, he realized that what disturbed him was not so much the President's insult as the fact that he had not anticipated it. One could not survive for long in politics with senses so impaired. Do I begin to fail? he asked himself, and nowhere in his mind could he with much conviction sound the negative.

At Home in Washington, D.C.

Like so many blind people my grandfather was a passionate sightseer, not to mention a compulsive guide. One of my first memories is driving with him to a slum in Southeast Washington. "All this," he said, pointing at the dilapidated red brick buildings, "was once our land." Since I saw only shabby buildings and could not imagine the land beneath, I was not impressed.

Years later I saw a map of how the District of Columbia had looked before the district's invention. Georgetown was a small community on the Potomac. The rest was farmland, owned by nineteen families. I seem to remember that the Gore land was next to that of the Notleys — a name that remains with me since my great-grandfather was called Thomas Notley Gore. (A kind reader tells me that the landowning Notleys were located elsewhere in Maryland.) Most of these families were what we continue to call — mistakenly — Scots-Irish. Actually, the Gores were Anglo-Irish from Donegal. They arrived in North America at the end of the seventeenth century and they tended to intermarry with other Anglo-Irish families — particularly in Virginia and Maryland.

George Washington not only presided over the war of separation from Great Britain (*revolution* is much too strong a word for that confused and confusing operation) but he also invented the federal republic whose original constitution reflected his powerful will to create the sort of government which would see to it that the rights of property will be forever revered. He was then congenial, if not controlling, party to the deal that moved the capital of the new republic from the city of Philadelphia to the wilderness not far from his own Virginia estate.

When a grateful nation saw fit to call the capital-to-be Washington City, the great man made no strenuous demur. Had he not already established his modesty and republican virtue by refusing the crown of the new Atlantic nation on the ground that to replace George III with George I did not sound entirely right? Also, and perhaps more to the point, Washington had no children. There would be no Prince of Virginia, ready to ascend the rustic throne at Washington City when the founder of the dynasty was translated to a higher sphere.

Although Washington himself did not have to sell or give up any of his own land, he did buy a couple of lots as speculation. Then he died a year before the city was occupied by its first president-in-residence, John Adams. The families that had been dispossessed to make way for the capital city did not do too badly. The Gores who remained sold lots, built houses and hotels, and became rich. The Gores who went away — my grandfather's branch — moved to the far west, in those days Mississippi. It was not until my grandfather was elected to the Senate in 1907 that he was able to come home again — never to leave until his death in 1949.

Although foreign diplomats enjoy maintaining that Washington is — or was — a hardship post, the British minister in 1809, one Francis James Jackson, had the good sense to observe: "I have procured two very good saddle horses, and Elizabeth and I have been riding in all directions round the place whenever the weather has been cool enough. The country has a beautifully picturesque appearance, and I have nowhere seen finer scenery than is composed by the Potomac and the woods and hills about it; yet it has a wild and desolated air from being so scantily and rudely cultivated, and from the want of population.... So you see we are not fallen into a wilderness, — so far from it that I am surprised no one should before have mentioned the great beauty of the neighborhood. The natives trouble themselves but little about it; their thoughts are chiefly of tobacco, flour, shingles, and the news of the day." *Plus ça change.*

Twenty years ago, that well-known wit and man-about-town, John F. Kennedy, said, "Washington perfectly combines southern efficiency with northern charm." I think that this was certainly true of the era when he and his knights of the Round Table were establishing Camelot amongst the local chiggers. By then too many glass buildings were going up. Too many old houses were being torn down or allowed to crumble. Too many slums were metastasizing around Capitol Hill. Also, the prewar decision to make an imperial Roman — literally, Roman — capital out of what had been originally a pleasant Frenchified southern city was, in retrospect, a mistake.

When such Roman palaces as the Commerce Department were being built, I can remember how we used to wonder, rather innocently, if these huge buildings could ever be filled up with people. But a city is an organism like any other and an organism knows its own encodement. Long before the American empire was a reality, the city was turning itself into New Rome. While the basilicas and porticoes were going up, one often had the sense that one was living not in a city that was being built but in a set of ruins. It is curious that even in those pre-nuclear days many of us could image the city devastated. Was this, perhaps, some memory of the War of 1812 when the British burned Capitol and White House? Or of the Civil War when southern troops invaded the city, coming down Seventh Street Road?

"At least they will make wonderful ruins," said my grandfather, turning his blind eyes on the Archives Building; he was never a man to spend public money on anything if he could help it. But those Piranesi blocks of marble eventually became real buildings that soon filled up with real bureaucrats, and by the end of the Second World War Washington had a real world empire to go with all those (to my eyes, at least) bogus-Roman sets.

Empires are dangerous possessions, as Pericles was among the first to point out. Since I recall pre-imperial Washington, I am a bit of an old Republican in the Ciceronian mode, given to decrying the corruption of the simpler, saner city of my youth. In the twenties and thirties, Washington was a small town where everyone knew everyone else. When school was out in June, boys took off their shoes and did not put them on again — at least outside the house — until September. The summer heat was — and is — Egyptian. In June, before Congress adjourned, I used to be sent with car and driver to pick up my grandfather at the Capitol and bring him home. In those casual days, there were few guards at the Capitol — and, again, everyone knew everyone else. I would wander on to the floor of the Senate, sit on my grandfather's desk if he wasn't ready to go, experiment with the snuff that was ritually allotted each senator; then I would lead him off the floor. On one occasion, I came down the aisle of the Senate wearing nothing but a bathing suit. This caused a good deal of amusement, to the blind man's bewilderment. Finally, the vice president, Mr. Garner — teeth like tiny black pearls and a breath that was all whisky — came down from the chair and said, "Senator, this boy is nekkid." Afterward I always wore a shirt on the Senate floor — but never shoes.

I date the end of the old republic and the birth of the empire to the invention, in the late thirties, of air-conditioning. Before air-conditioning, Washington was deserted from mid-June to September. The president — always Franklin Roosevelt — headed up the Hudson and all of Congress went home. The gentry withdrew to the northern resorts. Middle-income people flocked to Rehoboth Beach, Delaware or Virginia Beach, which was slightly more racy. But since air-conditioning and the Second World War arrived, more or less at the same time, Congress sits and sits while the presidents and their staffs never stop making mischief at the White House or in "Mr. Mullett's masterpiece," the splendid old State, War and Navy building, now totally absorbed by the minions of President Augustus. The Pentagon — a building everyone hated when it was being built — still gives us no great cause to love either its crude appearance or its function, so like that of a wasp's nest aswarm.

Now our Roman buildings are beginning to darken with time and pigeon droppings while the brutal glass towers of the late twentieth century tend to mask and dwarf them. But here and there in the city one still comes across shaded streets and houses; so many relics of lost time — when men wore white straw hats and suits in summer while huge hats decorated the ladies (hats always got larger just before a war) and one dined at Harvey's Restaurant, where the slow-turning ceiling-fans and tessellated floors made the hottest summer day seem cool even though the air of the street outside was ovenlike and smelled of jasmine and hot tar, while nearby Lafayette Park was a lush tropical jungle where one could see that Civil War hero, Mr. Justice Oliver Wendell Holmes, Jr., stroll, his white moustaches unfurled like fierce battle pennants. At the park's edge our entirely own and perfectly unique Henry Adams held court for decades in a house opposite to that Executive Mansion where grandfather and great-grandfather had reigned over a capital that was little more than a village down whose muddy main street ran a shallow creek that was known to some even then as — what else? — the Tiber.

NORMAN MAILER

Norman Mailer (1923–2007) began his career as a realistic novelist. In the 1960s, he became a highly visible journalist-observer and political antagonist to virtually everything that went on in Washington, particularly in matters of foreign policy regarding Cuba and Vietnam. Early in the decade, he published *The Presidential Papers of Norman Mailer* (1964), ostensibly the work of a court jester or adviser to President Kennedy. By mid-decade, he confessed to what was already self-evident: "[L]ike many another vain, empty, and bullying body of our time, I have been running for president these last ten years in the privacy of my mind." Later in the decade, he assumed a lead (and famously drunken) role in the march on the Pentagon that was intended to shut down the Department of Defense and stop the war in Vietnam, as described in *The Armies of the Night* (1968), a self-promoting tour de force that won both a Pulitzer Prize and a National Book Award.

The Armies of the Dead
From *The Armies of the Night*

Now who would be certain the shades of those Union dead were not ready to come on Lowell and Mailer as they strode through the grass up the long flat breast of hill at the base of Washington Monument and looked down the length of the reflecting pool to Lincoln Memorial perhaps one-half mile away, "then to step off like green Union Army recruits for the first Bull Run, sped by photographers . . ." was what Lowell was to write about events a bit later that day, but although they said hardly a word now, Lowell and Mailer were thinking of the Civil War: it was hard not to.

Walking over together from the hotel this Saturday morning Lowell had again invoked the repetitions of the night before. "Your speech yesterday was awfully good, Norman."

"Yes, Cal, but I thought yours was simply fine."

"Did you really?"

So covering old historic ground, they enjoyed the stroll past the White House, the old State Department — now looking not unlike the largest mansion ever not quite built at Newport — on to the approaches of the Ellipse. Macdonald was following later, they were to meet him at the Washington Monument's end of the reflecting pool in an hour, but for now they were impatient to set out early.

The flat breast of the hill at the foot of the monument had that agreeable curve one finds on an athletic field graded for drainage. Here, the curve was more pronounced, but the effect was similar: the groups and couples walking down from Washington Monument toward the round pool and the long reflecting pool which led to Lincoln Memorial, were revealed by degrees — one saw their hats bobbing on the horizon of the ridge before you saw their faces; perhaps this contributed to a high sense of focus; the eye studied the act of

walking as if one were looking at the gait of a troop of horses; some of the same
pleasure was there: the people seemed to be prancing. It was similar to the way
men and women are caught in the films of very good directors; the eye watching the film knows it has not been properly employed before. These people
were animated; the act of stepping along seemed to loosen little springs in their
joints, the action was rollicking, something was grave. Perhaps this etching of
focus had to do with no more than the physical fact that Mailer, approaching
somewhat lower on the swell of the hill, was therefore watching with his eyes
on a line with those rollicking feet. That could not however be all of it. A thin
high breath of pleasure, like a child's anticipation of the first rocket to be fired
on Fourth of July, hung over the sweet grass of the hill on Washington Monument. They were prancing past this hill, they were streaming to battle. Going
to battle! He realized that he had not taken in precisely this thin high sensuous
breath of pleasure in close to twenty-four years, not since the first time he had
gone into combat, and found to his surprise that the walk toward the fire fight
was one of the more agreeable — if stricken — moments of his life. Later, in
the skirmish itself it was less agreeable — he had perspired so profusely he had
hardly been able to see through his sweat — much later, months later, combat
was disagreeable; it managed to consist of large doses of fatigue, the intestinal
agitations of the tropics, endless promenades through mud, and general apathy
toward whether one lived or not. But the first breath had left a feather on his
memory; it was in the wind now; he realized that an odd, yes, a *zany* part of him
had been expecting quietly and confidently for years, that before he was done,
he would lead an army. (The lives of Leon Trotsky and Ernest Hemingway
had done nothing to dispel this expectation.) No, the sweetness of war came
back. Probably there were very few good wars (good wars being free of excessive
exhaustion, raddled bowels, miserable food, and computerized methods) but
if you were in as good shape for war as for football, there was very little which
was better for the senses. They would be executing Ernest Hemingway in effigy
every ten years for having insisted upon this recognition, they would even be
executing him in Utope City on the moon, but Mailer now sent him a novelist's
blessing (which is to say, well-intended but stingy) because Hemingway after all
had put the key on the table. *If it made you feel good, it was good.* That, and Saint
Thomas Aquinas' "Trust the authority of your senses," were enough to enable
a man to become a good working amateur philosopher, an indispensable voca-
tion for the ambitious novelist since otherwise he is naught but an embittered
entertainer, a story-teller, a John O'Hara! (Born January 31, the same birthday
as Mailer.)

These playful ruminations of high brass on the morning of battle came out
of the intoxication of the day, the place, the event, the troops who were splen-

didly dressed (description later) and the music. As Lowell and Mailer reached
the ridge and took a turn to the right to come down from Washington Monument toward the length of the long reflecting pool which led between two long
groves of trees near the banks to the steps of Lincoln Memorial, out from that
direction came the clear bitter-sweet excitation of a military trumpet resound-
ing in the near distance, one peal which seemed to go all the way back through a
galaxy of bugles to the cries of the Civil War and the first trumpet note to blow
the attack. The ghosts of old battles were wheeling like clouds over Washington
today.

The trumpet sounded again. It was calling the troops. "Come here," it called
from the steps of Lincoln Memorial over the two furlongs of the long reflecting pool, out to the swell of the hill at the base of Washington Monument,
"come here, come here, come here. The rally is on!" And from the north and
the east, from the direction of the White House and the Smithsonian and the
Capitol, from Union Station and the Department of Justice the troops were
coming in, the volunteers were answering the call. They came walking up in
all sizes, a citizens' army not ranked yet by height, an army of both sexes in
numbers almost equal, and of all ages, although most were young. Some were
well-dressed, some were poor, many were conventional in appearance, as often
were not. The hippies were there in great number, perambulating down the hill,
many dressed like the legions of Sgt. Pepper's Band, some were gotten up like
Arab sheiks, or in Park Avenue doormen's greatcoats, others like Rogers and
Clark of the West, Wyatt Earp, Kit Carson, Daniel Boone in buckskin, some
had grown mustaches to look like *Have Gun, Will Travel* — Paladin's surrogate
was here! — and wild Indians with feathers, a hippie gotten up like Batman,
another like Claude Rains in *The Invisible Man* — his face wrapped in a turban
of bandages and he wore a black satin top hat. A host of these troops wore capes,
beat-up khaki capes, slept on, used as blankets, towels, improvised duffel bags;
or fine capes, orange linings, or luminous rose linings, the edges ragged, near
a tatter, the threads ready to feather, but a musketeer's hat on their head. One
hippie may have been dressed like Charles Chaplin; Buster Keaton and W. C.
Fields could have come to the ball; there were Martians and Moon-men and a
knight unhorsed who stalked about in the weight of real armor. There were to
be seen a hundred soldiers in Confederate gray, and maybe there were two or
three hundred hippies in officer's coats of Union dark-blue. They had picked up
their costumes where they could, in surplus stores, and Blow-your-mind shops,
Digger free emporiums, and psychedelic caches of Hindu junk. There were
soldiers in Foreign Legion uniforms, and tropical bush jackets, San Quentin
and Chino, California striped shirt and pants, British copies of Eisenhower
jackets, hippies dressed like Turkish shepherds and Roman senators, gurus, and

samurai in dirty smocks. They were close to being assembled from all the intersections between history and the comic books, between legend and television,
the Biblical archetypes and the movies. The sight of these troops, this army
with a thousand costumes, fulfilled to the hilt our General's oldest idea of war
which is that every man should dress as he pleases if he is going into battle,
for that is his right, and variety never hurts the zest of the hardiest workers in
every battalion (here today by thousands in plaid hunting jackets, corduroys
or dungarees, ready for assault!) if the sight of such masquerade lost its usual
unhappy connotation of masked ladies and starving children outside the ball,
it was not only because of the shabbiness of the costumes (up close half of them
must have been used by hippies for everyday wear) but also because the aesthetic
at last was in the politics — the dress ball was going into battle. Still, there were
nightmares beneath the gaiety of these middle-class runaways, these Crusad-
ers, going out to attack the hard core of technology land with less training than
armies were once offered by a medieval assembly ground. The nightmare was
in the echo of those trips which had fractured their sense of past and present.
If nature was a veil whose tissue had been ripped by static, screams of jet motors, the highway grid of the suburbs, smog, defoliation, pollution of streams,
over-fertilization of earth, anti-fertilization of women, and the radiation of two
decades of near blind atom busting, then perhaps the history of the past was
another tissue, spiritual, no doubt, without physical embodiment, unless its embodiment was in the cuneiform hieroglyphics of the chromosome (so much like
primitive writing!) but that tissue of past history, whether traceable in the flesh,
or merely palpable in the collective underworld of the dream, was nonetheless
being bombed by the use of LSD as outrageously as the atoll of Eniwetok, Hiro-
shima, Nagasaki, and the scorched foliage of Vietnam. The history of the past
was being exploded right into the present: perhaps there were now lacunae in
the firmament of the past, holes where once had been the psychic reality of an
era which was gone. Mailer was haunted by the nightmare that the evils of the
present not only exploited the present, but consumed the past, and gave every
promise of demolishing whole territories of the future. The same villains who,
promiscuously, wantonly, heedlessly, had gorged on LSD and consumed God
knows what essential marrows of history, wearing indeed the history of all eras
on their back as trophies of this gluttony, were now going forth (conscience-
struck!) to make war on those other villains, corporation-land villains, who
were destroying the promise of the present in their self-righteousness and greed
and secret lust (often unknown to themselves) for some sexo-technological variety of neo-fascism.

Mailer's final allegiance, however, was with the villains who were hippies.
They would never have looked to blow their minds and destroy some part of

the past if the authority had not brain-washed the mood of the present until it smelled like deodorant. (To cover the odor of burning flesh in Vietnam?) So he continued to enjoy the play of costumes, but his pleasure was not edged with a hint of the sinister. Not inappropriate for battle. He and Lowell were still in the best of moods. The morning was so splendid — it spoke of a vitality in nature which no number of bombings in space nor inner-space might ever subdue; the rustle of costumes warming up for the war spoke of future redemptions as quickly as they reminded of hog-swillings from the past, and the thin air! wine of Civil War apples in the October air! edge of excitement and awe — how would this day end? No one could know. Incredible spectacle now gathering — tens of thousands traveling hundreds of miles to attend a symbolic battle. In the capital of technology land beat a primitive drum. New drum of the Left! And the Left had been until this year the secret unwitting accomplice of every increase in the power of technicians, bureaucrats, and labor leaders who ran the governmental military-industrial complex of super-technology land.

WARD JUST

Ward Just (1935–) left his native Illinois for Washington in 1961 to work as a reporter for *Newsweek* and the *Washington Post*. Sent by his editor, Ben Bradlee, to cover the war in Vietnam, he was seriously wounded but survived to write *To What End: Report from Vietnam* (1968). Just started writing fiction in the early 1970s, authoring more than a dozen novels and many short stories, several set in Washington. "The Congressman Who Loved Flaubert," the title piece in his first collection, published in 1973, captures the hesitation and uncertainty of a deep-thinking congressman, one with his own legislative agenda, about joining forces with the growing antiwar movement.

The Congressman Who Loved Flaubert

The deputation was there: twelve men in his outer office and he would have to see them. His own fault, if "fault" was the word. They'd called every day for a week, trying to arrange an appointment. Finally his assistant, Annette, put it to him: Please see them. Do it for me. Wein is an old friend, she'd said. It meant a lot to Wein to get his group before a congressman whose name was known, whose words had weight. LaRuth stood and stretched; his long arms reached for the ceiling. He was his statuesque best that day: dark suit, dark tie, white shirt, black beard neatly trimmed. No jewelry of any kind. He rang his secretary and told her to show them in, to give them thirty minutes, and then ring again; the committee meeting was at eleven.

"What do they look like?"

"Scientists," she said. "They look just as you'd expect scientists to look. They're all thin. And none of them are smoking." LaRuth laughed. "They're pretty intense, Lou."

"Well, let's get on with it."

He met them at the door, as they shyly filed in. Wein and his committee were scientists against imperialism. They were physicists, biologists, linguists, and philosophers. They introduced themselves, and LaRuth wondered again what it was that a philosopher did in these times. It had to be a grim year for philosophy. The introductions done, LaRuth leaned back, a long leg hooked over the arm of his chair, and told them to go ahead.

They had prepared a congressional resolution, a sense-of-the-Congress resolution, which they wanted LaRuth to introduce. It was a message denouncing imperialism, and as LaRuth read it he was impressed by its eloquence. They had assembled hard facts: so many tons of bombs dropped in Indochina, so many "facilities" built in Africa, so many American soldiers based in Europe, so many billions in corporate investment in Latin America. It was an excellent statement, not windy as so many of them are. He finished reading it and turned to Wein.

"Congressman, we believe this is a matter of simple morality. Decency, if you will. There are parallels elsewhere, the most compelling being the extermination of American Indians. Try not to look on the war and the bombing from the perspective of a Westerner looking East but of an Easterner facing West." LaRuth nodded. He recognized that it was the war that truly interested them. "The only place the analogy breaks down is that the Communists in Asia appear to be a good deal more resourceful and resilient than the Indians in America. Perhaps that is because there are so many more of them." Wein paused to smile. "But it is genocide either way. It is a stain on the American Congress not to raise a specific voice of protest, not only in Asia but in the other places where American policy is doing violence . . ."

LaRuth wondered if they knew the mechanics of moving a congressional resolution. They probably did; there was no need for a civics lecture. Wein was looking at him, waiting for a response. An intervention. "It's a very fine statement," LaRuth said.

"Everybody says that. And then they tell us to get the signatures and come back. We think this ought to be undertaken from the inside. In that way, when and if the resolution is passed, it will have more force. We think that a member of Congress should get out front on it."

An admirable toughness there, LaRuth thought. If he were Wein, that would be just about the way he'd put it.

"We've all the people you'd expect us to have." Very rapidly, Wein ticked off two dozen names, the regular antiwar contingent on the Democratic left. "What we need to move with this is not the traditional dove, but a more moderate man. A moderate man with a conscience." Wein smiled.

"Yes," LaRuth said.

"Someone like you."

LaRuth was silent a moment, then spoke rapidly. "My position is this. I'm not a member of the Foreign Affairs Committee or the Appropriations Committee or Armed Services or any of the others where . . . war legislation or defense matters are considered. I'm not involved in foreign relations, I'm in education. It's the Education and Labor Committee. No particular reason why those two subjects should be linked, but they are." LaRuth smiled. "That's Congress for you."

"It seems to us, Congressman, that the war — the leading edge of imperialism and violence — is tied to everything. Education is a mess because of the war. So is labor. And so forth. It's all part of the war. Avoid the war and you avoid all the other problems. The damn thing is like the Spanish Inquisition, if you lived in Torquemada's time, fifteenth-century Spain. If you did try to avoid it you were either a coward or a fool. This is meant respectfully."

"Well, it is nicely put. Respectfully"

"But you won't do it."

LaRuth shook his head. "You get more names, and I'll think about cosponsoring. But I won't front for it. I'm trying to pass an education bill right now. I can't get out front on the war, too. Important as it is. Eloquent as you are. There are other men in this House who can do the job better than I can."

"We're disappointed," Wein said.

"I could make you a long, impressive speech." His eyes took in the others, sitting in chilly silence. "I could list all the reasons. But you know what they are, and it wouldn't do either of us any good. I wish you success."

"Spare us any more successes," Wein said. "Everyone wishes us success, but no one helps. We're like the troops in the trenches. The Administration tells them to go out and win the war. You five hundred thousand American boys, you teach the dirty Commies a lesson. Storm the hill, the Administration says. But the Administration is far away from the shooting. We're right behind you, they say. Safe in Washington."

"I don't deny it," LaRuth said mildly.

"I think there are special places in hell reserved for those who see the truth but will not act." LaRuth stiffened, but stayed silent. "These people are worse than the ones who love the war. You are more dangerous than the generals in the Pentagon, who at least are doing what they believe in. It is because of people like you that we are where we are."

Never justify, never explain, LaRuth thought; it was pointless anyway. They were pleased to think of him as a war criminal. A picture of a lurching tumbrel in Pennsylvania Avenue flashed through his mind and was gone, an oddly comical image. LaRuth touched his beard and sat upright. "I'm sorry you feel that way. It isn't true, you know." One more number like that one, he thought suddenly, and he'd throw the lot of them out of his office.

But Wein would not let go. "We're beyond subtle distinctions, Mr. LaRuth. That is one of the delightful perceptions that the war has brought us. We can mumble all day. You can tell me about your responsibilities and your effectiveness, and how you don't want to damage it. You can talk politics and I can talk morals. But I took moral philosophy in college. An interesting academic exercise." LaRuth nodded; Wein was no fool. "Is it true you wrote your Ph.D. thesis on Flaubert?"

"I wrote it at the Sorbonne," LaRuth replied. "But that was almost twenty years ago. Before politics." LaRuth wanted to give them something to hang on to. They would appreciate the irony, and then they could see him as a fallen angel, a victim of the process; it was more interesting than seeing him as a war criminal.

"Well, it figures."

LaRuth was surprised. He turned to Wein. "How does it figure?"

"Flaubert was just as pessimistic and cynical as you are."

LARUTH HAD THIRTY MINUTES to review his presentation to the committee. This was the most important vote in his twelve years in Congress, a measure which, if they could steer it though the House, would release a billion dollars over three years' time to elementary schools throughout the county. The measure was based on a hellishly complicated formula which several legal experts regarded as unconstitutional; but one expert is always opposed by another when a billion dollars is involved. LaRuth had to nurse along the chairman, a volatile personality, a natural skeptic. Today he had to put his presentation in exquisite balance, giving here, taking there, assuring the committee that the Constitution would be observed, and that all regions would share equally.

It was not something that could be understood in a university, but LaRuth's twelve years in the House of Representatives would be justified if he could pass this bill. Twelve years, through three Presidents. He'd avoided philosophy and concentrated on detail, his own time in a third-rate grad school in a southern mill town never far from his mind: that was the reference point. Not often that a man was privileged to witness the methodical destruction of children before the age of thirteen, before they had encountered genuinely soulless and terrible events: the war, for one. His bill would begin the process of revivifying education. It was one billion dollars' worth of life, and he'd see to it that some of the money leaked down to his own school. LaRuth was lucky, an escapee on scholarships, first to Tulane and then to Paris, his world widened beyond measure; Flaubert gave him a taste for politics. *Madame Bovary* and *A Sentimental Education* were political novels, or so he'd argued at the Sorbonne; politics was nothing more or less than an understanding of ambition, and the moral and social conditions that produced it in its various forms. The House of Representatives: *un stade des arrivistes*. And now the press talked him up as a southern liberal, and the northern Democrats came to him for help. Sometimes he gave it, sometimes he didn't. They could not understand the refusals — Lou, you won with sixty-five percent of the vote the last time out. What do you want, a coronation? They were critical that he would not get out front on the war and would not vote against bills vital to southern interests. (Whatever they were, not that the entire region was dominated by industrial combines whose headquarters were in New York or Chicago — and how's that for imperialism, Herr Wein?) They didn't, or couldn't, grasp the paper-thin depth of his support. The Birchers and the segs were everywhere, and each time he voted with the liberals in the House he'd hear from a few of them. *You are being watched*. He preferred a low silhouette. All those big liberals didn't understand that a man with enough money could still buy an election in his district; he told them that LaRuth compromised was better than no LaRuth at all. That line had worked no longer. In these times, caution and realism were the refuge of a scoundrel.

The war, so remote in its details, poisoned everything. He read about it every day, and through a friend on the Foreign Affairs Committee saw some classified material. But he could not truly engage himself in it, because he hadn't seen it firsthand. He did not know it intimately. It was clear enough that it was a bad war, everyone knew that; but knowing it and feeling it were two different things. The year before, he'd worked to promote a junket, a special subcommittee to investigate foreign aid expenditures for education. There was plenty of scandalous rumor to justify the investigation. He tried to promote it in order to get a look at the place firsthand, on the ground. He wanted to look at the faces and the villages, to see the countryside which had been destroyed by the war, to observe the actual manner in which the war was being fought. But the chairman refused, he wanted no part of it; scandal or no scandal, it was not part of the committee's business. So the trip never happened. What the congressman knew about the war he read in newspapers and magazines and saw on television. But that did not help. LaRuth had done time as an infantryman in Korea and knew what killing was about; the box did not make it as horrible as it was. The box romanticized it, cleansed it of pain; one more false detail. Even the blood deceived, coming up pink and pretty on the television set. One night he spent half of Cronkite fiddling with the color knob to get a perfect red, to insist the blood look like *blood*.

More: Early in his congressional career, LaRuth took pains to explain his positions. He wanted his constituents to know what he was doing and why, and two newsletters went out before the leader of his state's delegation took him aside one day in the hall. Huge arms around his shoulders, a whispered conference. Christ, you are going to get killed, the man said. *Don't do that.* Don't get yourself down on paper on every raggedy-ass bill that comes before Congress. It makes you a few friends, who don't remember, and a lot of enemies, who do. Particularly in your district: you are way ahead of those people in a lot of areas, but don't advertise it. You've a fine future here; don't ruin it before you've begun. LaRuth thought the advice was captious and irresponsible and disregarded it. And very nearly lost reelection, after some indiscretions to a newspaperman. *That* son of a bitch, who violated every rule of confidence held sacred in the House of Representatives.

His telephone rang. The secretary said it was Annette.

"How did it go?" Her voice was low, cautious.

"Like a dream," he said. "And thanks lots. I'm up there with the generals as a war criminal. They think I make lampshades in my spare time."

Coolly: "I take it you refused to help them."

"You take it right."

"They're very good people. Bill Wein is one of the most distinguished botanists in the country."

"Yes, he speaks very well. A sincere, intelligent, dedicated provocateur. Got off some very nice lines, at least one reference to Dante. A special place in hell is reserved for people like me, who are worse than army generals."

"Well, that's one point of view."

"You know, I'm tired of arguing about the war. If Wein is so goddamned concerned about the war and the corruption of the American system, then why doesn't he give up the fat government contracts at that think tank he works for —"

"That's unfair, Lou!"

"Why do they think that anyone who deals in the real world is an automatic sellout? Creep. A resolution like that one, *even if passed*, would have no effect. Zero effect. It would not be binding, the thing's too vague. They'd sit up there and everyone would have a good gooey warm feeling, *and nothing would happen*. It's meaningless, except of course for the virtue. Virtue everywhere. Virtue triumphant. So I am supposed to put my neck on the line for something that's meaningless — " LaRuth realized he was near shouting, so he lowered his voice. "Meaningless," he said.

"You're so hostile," she said angrily. "Filled with hate. Contempt. Why do you hate everybody? You should've done what Wein wanted you to do."

He counted to five and was calm now, reasonable. His congressional baritone: "It's always helpful to have your political advice, Annette. Very helpful. I value it. Too bad you're not a politician yourself." She said nothing, he could hear her breathing. "I'll see you later," he said, and hung up.

LARUTH LEFT HIS OFFICE, bound for the committee room. He'd gone off the handle and was not sorry. But sometimes he indulged in just a bit too much introspection and self-justification, endemic diseases in politicians. There were certain basic facts: his constituency supported the war, at the same time permitting him to oppose it so long as he did it quietly and in such a way that "the boys" were supported. Oppose the war, support the troops. A high-wire act — very Flaubertian, that situation; it put him in the absurd position of voting for military appropriations and speaking out against the war. Sorry, Annette; that's the way we think on Capitol Hill. It's a question of what you *vote* for. Forget the fancy words and phrases, it's a question of votes. Up, down, or "present." Vote against the appropriations and sly opponents at home would accuse him of "tying the hands" of American troops and thereby comforting the enemy. Blood on his fingers.

2

LaRuth was forty; he had been in the House since the age of twenty-eight. Some of his colleagues had been there before he was born, moving now around the halls and the committee rooms as if they were extensions of antebellum county courthouses. They smelled of tobacco and whiskey and old wool, their faces dry as parchment. LaRuth was amused to watch them on the floor; they behaved as they would at a board meeting of a family business, attentive if they felt like it, disruptive if their mood was playful. They were forgiven; it was a question of age. The House was filled with old men, and its atmosphere was one of very great age. Deference was a way of life. LaRuth recalled a friend who aspired to a position of leadership. They put him through his paces, and for some reason he did not measure up; the friend was told he'd have to wait, it was not yet time. He'd been there eighteen years and was only fifty-two. Fifty-two! Jack Kennedy was President at forty-three, and Thomas Jefferson had written the preamble when under thirty-five. But then, as one of the senior men put it, this particular fifty-two-year-old man had none of the durable qualities of

Kennedy or Jefferson. That is, he did not have Kennedy's money or Jefferson's brains. Not that money counted for very much in the House of Representatives; plutocrats belonged in the other body.

It was not a place for lost causes. There were too many conflicting interests, too much confusion, too many turns to the labyrinth. Too many *people*: four hundred and thirty-five representatives and about a quarter of them quite bright. Quite bright enough and knowledgeable enough to strangle embarrassing proposals and take revenge as well. Everyone was threatened if the eccentrics got out of hand. The political coloration of the eccentric didn't matter. This was one reason why it was so difficult to build an ideological record in the House. A man with ideology was wise to leave it before reaching a position of influence, because by then he'd mastered the art of compromise, which had nothing to do with dogma or public acts of conscience. It had to do with simple effectiveness, the tact and strength with which a man dealt with legislation, inside committees, behind closed doors. That was where the work got done, and the credit passed around.

LaRuth, at forty, was on a knife's edge. Another two years and he'd be a man of influence, and therefore ineligible for any politics outside the House — or not ineligible, but shopworn, no longer new, no longer fresh. He would be ill-suited, and there were other practical considerations as well, because who wanted to be a servant for twelve or fourteen years and then surrender an opportunity to be master? Not LaRuth. So the time for temporizing was nearly past. If he was going to forsake the House and reach for the Senate (a glamorous possibility), he had to do it soon.

LARUTH'S CLOSEST FRIEND in Congress was a man about his own age from a neighboring state. They'd come to the Hill in the same year, and for a time enjoyed publicity in the national press, where they could least afford it. *Two Young Liberals from the South*, that sort of thing. Winston was then a bachelor, too, and for the first few years they shared a house in Cleveland Park. But it was awkward, there were too many women in and out of the place, and one groggy morning Winston had come upon LaRuth and a friend taking a shower together and that had torn it. They flipped for the house and LaRuth won, and Winston moved to grander quarters in Georgetown. They saw each other frequently and laughed together about the curiosities of the American political system; Winston, a gentleman farmer from the plantation South, was a ranking member of the House Foreign Affairs Committee. The friendship was complicated because they were occasional rivals: who would represent the New South? They took to kidding each other's press notices: LaRuth was the "attractive liberal," Winston the "wealthy liberal." Thus, LaRuth became Liberal Lou and

Winston was Wealthy Warren. To the extent that either of them had a national reputation, they were in the same category: they voted their consciences, but were not incautious.

It was natural for Wein and his committee of scientists to go directly to Winston after leaving LaRuth. The inevitable telephone call came the next day, Winston inviting LaRuth by for a drink around six; "small problem to discuss." Since leaving Cleveland Park, Warren Winston's life had become plump and graceful. Politically secure now, he had sold his big house back home and bought a small jewel of a place on Dumbarton Avenue, three bedrooms and a patio in back, a mirrored bar, and a sauna in the basement. Winston was drinking a gin and tonic by the pool when LaRuth walked in. The place was more elegant than he'd remembered; the patio was now decorated with tiny boxbushes and a magnolia tree was in full cry.

They joked a bit, laughing over the new southern manifesto floating around the floor of the House. They were trying to find a way to spike it without seeming to spike it. Winston mentioned the "small problem" after about thirty minutes of small talk.

"Lou, do you know any guy named Wein?"

"He's a friend of Annette's."

"He was in to see you, then."

"Yeah."

"And?"

"We didn't see eye to eye."

"You're being tight-lipped, Liberal Lou."

"I told him to piss off," LaRuth said. "He called me a war criminal, and then he called me a cynic. A pessimist, a cynic, and a war criminal. All this for some cream-puff resolution that will keep them damp in Cambridge and won't change a goddamed thing."

"You think it's *that* bad."

"Worse, maybe."

"I'm not sure, Not sure at all."

"Warren, *Christ*."

"Look, doesn't it make any sense at all to get the position of the House on record? That can't fail to have some effect downtown, and it can't fail to have an effect in the country. It probably doesn't stand a chance of being passed, but the effort will cause some commotion. The coon'll be treed. Some attention paid. It's a good thing to get on the record, and I can see some points being made."

"What points? Where?"

"The newspapers, the box. Other places. It'd show that at least some of us are not content with things as they are. That we want to change . . ."

LaRuth listened carefully. It was obvious to him that Winston was trying out a speech; like a new suit of clothes, he took it out and tried it on, asking his friends about the color, the fit, the cut of it.

"... the idea that change can come from within the system ..."

"Aaaaaoh," LaRuth groaned.

"No?" Innocently.

"How about, *and so, my fellow Americans, ask not what you can do for Wein, but what Wein can do for you.* That thing is loose as a hound dog's tongue. Now tell me the true gen."

"Bettger's retiring."

"You don't say." LaRuth was surprised. Bettger was the state's senior senator, a living southern legend.

"Cancer. No one knows about it. He'll announce retirement at the end of the month. It's my only chance for the next four years, maybe *ever.* There'll be half a dozen guys in the primary, but my chances are good. If I'm going to go for the Senate, it's got to be now. This thing of Wein's is a possible vehicle. I say possible. One way in. People want a national politician as a senator. It's not enough to've been a good congressman, or even a good governor. You need something more: when people see your face on the box they want to think *senatorial,* somehow. You don't agree?"

LaRuth was careful now. Winston was saying many of the things he himself had said. Of course he was right, a senator needed a national gloss. The old bulls didn't need it, but they were operating from a different tradition, pushing different buttons. But if you were a young man running statewide for the first time, you needed a different base. Out there in television land were all those followers without leaders. People were pulled by different strings now. The point was to identify which strings pulled strongest.

"I think Wein's crowd is a mistake. That resolution is a mistake. They'll kill you at home if you put your name to that thing."

"No, Lou. You do it a different way. With a little rewording, that resolution becomes a whole lot less scary; it becomes something straight out of a Robert A. Taft. You e-*liminate* the fancy words and phrases. You steer *clear* of words like 'corrupt' or 'genocide' or 'violence.' You and I, Lou, we know: our people *like* violence, it's part of our way of life. So you don't talk about violence, you talk about American traditions, like 'the American tradition of independence and individuality. Noninterference!' Now you are saying a couple of *other* things, when you're saying that, Lou. You dig? That's the way you get at imperialism. You don't call it imperialism because that word's got a bad sound. A foreign sound."

LaRuth laughed. Winston had it figured out. He had to get Wein to agree to the changes, but that should present no problem. Wealthy Warren was a persuasive man.

"Point is, I've got to look to people down there like I can make a difference ..."

"I think you've just said the magic words."

"Like it?"

"I think so. Yeah, I think I do."

"*To make the difference. Winston for Senator.* A double line on the billboards, like this." Winston described two lines with his finger and mulled the slogan again. "*To make the difference. Winston for Senator.* See, it doesn't matter what kind of difference. All people know is that they're fed up to the teeth. *Fed up and mad at the way things are.* And they've got to believe that if they vote for you, in some unspecified way things will get better. Now I think the line about interference can do double duty. People are tired of being hassled, in all ways. Indochina, down home." Winston was a gifted mimic, and now he adopted a toothless expression and hooked his thumbs into imaginary galluses. "Ah think Ah'll vote for that-there Winston. Prob'ly won't do any harm. Mot do some good. Mot mek a diff'rence."

"Shit, Warren."

"You give me a little help?"

"Sure."

"Sign the Wein thing?"

LaRuth thought a moment. "No," he said.

"What the hell, Lou? Why not? If it's rearranged the way I said. Look, Wein will be out of it. It'll be strictly a congressional thing."

"Means a whole lot to me."

"Well, that's different. That's political."

"If you went in too, it'd look a safer bet."

"All there'd be out of that is more gold-dust-twins copy. You don't want that."

"No, it'd be made clear that I'm managing it. I'm out front. I make all the statements, you're back in the woodwork. Far from harm's way, Lou." Winston took his glass and refilled it with gin and tonic. He carefully cut a lime and squeezed it into the glass. Winston looked the part, no doubt about that. Athlete's build, big, with sandy hair beginning to thin; he could pass for an astronaut.

"You've got to find some new names for the statement."

"Right on, brother. Too many Jews, too many foreigners. Why are there no scientists named Robert E. Lee or Thomas Jefferson? Talmadge, Bilbo." Winston sighed and answered his own question. "The decline of the WASP. Look, Lou. The statement will be forgotten in six weeks, and that's fine with me. I just need it for a little national coverage at the beginning. Hell, it's not decisive. But it could make a difference."

"You're going to *open* the campaign with the statement?"

"You bet. Considerably revised. It'd be a help, Lou, if you'd go along. It would give them a chance to crank out some updated New South pieces. The networks would be giving that a run just as I announce for the Senate and my campaign begins. See, it's a natural. Bettger is old South, I'm New. But we're friends and neighbors, and that's a fact. It gives them a dozen pegs to hang it on, and those bastards love *you*, with the black suits and the beard and that cracker accent. It's a natural, and it would mean a hell of a lot, a couple of minutes on national right at the beginning. I wouldn't forget it. I'd owe you a favor."

LaRuth was always startled by Winston's extensive knowledge of the press. He spoke of "pieces" and "pegs," a.m. and p.m. cycles, facts "cranked out" or "folded in," who was up and who was down at CBS, who was analyzing Congress for the editorial board of the *Washington Post*. Warren Winston was always accessible, good for a quote, day or night; and he was visible in Georgetown.

"Can you think about it by the end of the week?"

"Sure," LaRuth said.

HE RETURNED TO the Hill, knowing that he thought better in his office. When there was any serious thinking to be done, he did it there, and often stayed late, after midnight. He'd mix a drink at the small bar in his office and work. Sometimes Annette stayed with him, sometimes not. When LaRuth walked into his office she was still there, catching up, she said; but she knew he'd been with Winston.

"He's going to run for the Senate," LaRuth said.

"Warren?"

"That's what he says. He's going to front for Wein as well. That statement of Wein's — Warren's going to sign it. Wants me to sign it, too."

"Why you?"

"United front. It would help him out. No doubt about that. But it's a bad statement. Something tells me not to do it."

"Are you as mad as you look?"

He glanced at her and laughed. "Does it show?"

"To me it shows."

It was true; there was no way to avoid competition in politics. Politics was a matter of measurements, luck, and ambition, and he and Warren had run as an entry for so long that it disconcerted him to think of Senator Winston; Winston up one rung on the ladder. He was irritated that Winston had made the first move and made it effortlessly. It had nothing to do with his own career, but suddenly he felt a shadow on the future. Winston had seized the day all right, and the fact of it depressed him. His friend was clever and self-assured in his movements; he took risks; he relished the public part of politics. Winston was expert at delivering memorable speeches on the floor of the House; they were evidence of passion. For Winston, there was no confusion between the private and the public; it was all one. LaRuth thought that he had broadened and deepened in twelve years in the House, a man of realism, but not really a part of the apparatus. Now Winston had stolen the march, he was a decisive step ahead.

LaRuth may have made a mistake. He liked and understood the legislative process, transactions which were only briefly political. That is, they were not public. If a man kept himself straight at home, he could do what he liked in the House. So LaRuth had become a fixture in his district, announcing election plans every two years from the front porch of his family's small farmhouse, where he was born, where his mother lived still. The house was filled with political memorabilia; the parlor walls resembled huge bulletin boards, with framed photographs, testimonials, parchments, diplomas. His mother was so proud. His life seemed to vindicate her own, his success hers; she'd told him so. His position in the U.S. Congress was precious, and not lightly discarded. The cold age of the place had given him a distrust of anything spectacular or . . . capricious. The House: no place for lost causes.

Annette was looking at him, hands on hips, smiling sardonically. He'd taken off his coat and was now in shirtsleeves. She told him lightly that he shouldn't feel badly, that if *he* ran for the Senate he'd have to shave off his beard. Buy new clothes. Become prolix, and professionally optimistic. But, as a purchase on the future, his signature . . . "Might. Might not," he said.

"Why not?"

"I've never done that here."

"Are you refusing to sign because you don't want to, or because you're piqued at Warren? I mean, Senator Winston."

He looked at her. "A little of both."

"Well, that's foolish. You ought to sort out your motives."

"That can come later. That's my business."

"No. Warren's going to want to know why you're not down the line with him. You're pretty good friends. He's going to want to know *why*."

"It's taken me twelve years to build what credit I've got in this place. I'm trusted. The Speaker trusts me. The chairman trusts me."

"Little children see you on the street. Gloryosky! There goes trustworthy Lou LaRuth —"

"Attractive, liberal," he said, laughing. "Well, it's true. This resolution, if it ever gets that far, is a ball-buster. It could distract the House for a month and revive the whole issue. Because it's been quiet we've been able to get on with our work, I mean the serious business. Not to get pompous about it."

"War's pretty important," she said.

"Well, is it now? You tell me how important it is." He put his drink on the desk blotter and loomed over her. "Better yet, you tell me how this resolution will solve the problem. God forbid there should be any solutions, though. Moral commitments. Statements. Resolutions. They're the great things, aren't they? Fuck solutions." Thoroughly angry now, he turned away and filled the glasses. He put some ice and whiskey in hers and a premixed martini in his own.

"What harm would it do?"

"Divert a lot of energy. Big play to the galleries for a week or two. Until everyone got tired. The statement itself? No harm at all. Good statement, well done. No harm, unless you consider perpetuating an illusion some kind of harm."

"A lot of people live by illusions, *and what's wrong with getting this House on record?*"

"But it won't be gotten on record. That's the point. The thing will be killed. It'll just make everybody nervous and divide the place more than it's divided already."

"I'd think about it," she said.

"Yeah, I will. I'll tell you something. I'll probably end up signing the goddamned thing. It'll do Warren some good. Then I'll do what I can to see that it's buried, although God knows we won't lack for gravediggers. And then go back to my own work on the school bill."

"I think that's better." She smiled. "One call, by the way. The chairman. He wants you to call first thing in the morning."

"What did he say it's about?"

"The school bill, dear."

Oh shit, LaRuth thought.

"There's a snag," she said.

"Did he say what it was?"

"I don't think he wants to vote for it anymore."

3

Winston was after him, trying to force a commitment, but LaRuth was preoccupied with the school bill, which was becoming unstuck. It was one of the unpredictable things that happen; there was no explanation for it. But the atmosphere had subtly changed and support was evaporating. The members wavered, the chairman was suddenly morose and uncertain; he thought it might be better to delay. LaRuth convinced him that was an unwise course and set about repairing damage. This was plumbing, pure and simple; talking with members, speaking to their fears. LaRuth called it negative advocacy, but it often worked. Between conferences a few days later, LaRuth found time to see a high-school history class, students from his alma mater. They were touring Washington and wanted to talk to him about Congress. The teacher, sloe-eyed, stringy-haired, twenty-five, wanted to talk about the war; the students were indifferent. They crowded into his outer office, thirty of them; the secretaries stood aside, amused, as the teacher opened the conversation with a long preface on the role of the House, most of it inaccurate. Then she asked LaRuth about the war. What was the congressional role in the war?

"Not enough," LaRuth replied, and went on in some detail, addressing the students.

"Why not a congressional resolution demanding an end to this terrible, immoral war?" the teacher demanded. "Congressman, why can't the House of Representatives take matters into its own hands?"

"Because" — LaRuth was icy, at once angry, tired, and bored — "because a majority of the members of this House do not want to lose Asia to the Communists. Irrelevant, perhaps. You may think it is a bad argument. I think it is a bad argument. But it is the way the members feel."

"But why can't that be *tested?* In votes."

The students came reluctantly awake and were listening with little flickers of interest. The teacher was obviously a favorite, their mod pedagogue. LaRuth was watching a girl in the back of the room. She resembled the girls he'd known at home, short-haired, light summer dress, full-bodied; it was a body that would soon go heavy. He abruptly steered the conversation to his school bill, winding into it, giving them a stump speech, some flavor of home. He felt the students with him for a minute or two, then they drifted away. In five minutes they were somewhere else altogether. He said good-bye to them then and shook their hands on the way out. The short-haired girl lingered a minute; she was the last one to go.

"It would be good if you could do something about the war," she said.

"Well, I've explained."

"My brother was killed there."

LaRuth closed his eyes for a second and stood without speaking.

"Any gesture at all," she said.

"Gestures." He shook his head sadly. "They never do any good."

"Well," she said. "Thank you for your time." LaRuth thought her very grown-up, a well-spoken girl. She stood in the doorway, very pretty. The others had moved off down the hall; he could hear the teacher's high whine.

"How old was he?"

"Nineteen," she said. "Would've been twenty next birthday."

"Where?"

"They said it was an airplane."

"I'm so sorry."

"You wrote us a letter, don't you remember?"

"I don't know your name," LaRuth said gently.

"Ecker," she said. "My brother's name was Howard."

"I remember," he said. "It was . . . some time ago."

"Late last year," she said, looking at him.

"Yes, that would be just about it. I'm very sorry."

"So am I," she said, smiling brightly. Then she walked off to join the rest of her class. LaRuth stood in the doorway a moment, feeling the eyes of his secretary on his back. It had happened before, the South seemed to bear the brunt of the war. He'd written more than two hundred letters, to the families of poor boys, black and white. The deaths were disproportionate, poor to rich, black to white, South to North. Oh well, he thought. Oh hell. He walked back into his office and called Winston and told him he'd go along. In a limited way. For a limited period.

Later in the day, Winston called him back. He wanted LaRuth to be completely informed, and up-to-date.

"It's rolling," Winston said.

"Have you talked to Wein?"

"I've talked to Wein."

"And what did Wein say?"

"Wein agrees to the revisions."

"Complaining?"

"The contrary. Wein sees himself as the spearhead of a great national movement. He sees scientists moving into political positions, cockpits of influence. His conscience is as clear as rainwater. He is very damp."

LaRuth laughed; it was a private joke.

"Wein is damp in Cambridge, then."

"I think that is a fair statement, Uncle Lou."

"How wonderful for him."

"He was pleased that you are with us. He said he misjudged you. He offers apologies. He fears he was a speck . . . harsh."

"Bully for Wein."

"I told everyone that you would be on board. I knew that when the chips were down you would not fail. I knew that you would examine your conscience and your heart and determine where the truth lay. I knew you would not be cynical or pessimistic. I know you want to see your old friend in the Senate."

They were laughing together. Winston was in one of his dry, mordant moods. He was very salty. He rattled off a dozen names and cited the sources of each member's conscience: money and influence. "But to be fair — always be fair, Liberal Lou — there are a dozen more who are doing it because they want to do it. They think it's *right*."

"*Faute de mieux.*"

"I'm not schooled in the French language, Louis. You are always flinging French at me."

"It means, 'in the absence of anything better.'"

Winston grinned, then shrugged. LaRuth was depressed, the shadow lengthened, became darker.

"I've set up a press conference, a half dozen of us. All moderate men. Men of science, men of government. It'll be out front, doing all the talking. OK?"

"Sure." LaRuth was thinking about his school bill.

"It's going to be jim-dandy."

"Swell. But I want to see the statement beforehand, music man."

Winston smiled broadly and spread his hands wide. Your friendly neighborhood legislator, concealing nothing; merely your average, open, honest fellow trying to do the right thing, trying to do his level best. "But of course," Winston said.

SOME POLITICIANS have it; most don't. Winston has it, a fabulous sense of timing. Everything in politics is timing. For a fortnight, the resolution dominates congressional reportage. "An idea whose time has come," coinciding with a coup in Latin America and a surge of fighting in Indochina. The leadership is agitated, but forced to adopt a conciliatory line; the doves are in war paint. Winston appears regularly on the television evening news. There are hearings before the Foreign Affairs Committee, and these produce pictures and newsprint. Winston, a sober legislator, intones *feet to the fire*. There are flattering articles in the newsmagazines, and editorial support from the major newspapers, including the most influential paper in Winston's state. He and LaRuth are to appear on the cover of *Life*, but the cover is scrapped at the last minute. Amazing to LaRuth, the mail from his district runs about even. An old woman, a woman his mother has known for years, writes to tell him that he should run for President. Incredible, really: the Junior Chamber of Commerce composes a certificate of appreciation, commending his enterprise and spirit, "and example of the indestructible moral fiber of America." When the networks and the newspapers cannot find Winston, they fasten on LaRuth. He becomes something of a celebrity, and wary as a man entering darkness from daylight. He tailors his remarks in such a way as to force questions about his school bill. He finds his words have effect, although this is measurable in no definite way. His older colleagues are amused; they needle him gently about his new blue shirts.

He projects well on television, his appearance is striking; his great height, the black suits, the beard. So low-voiced, modest, diffident; no hysteria or hyperbole (an intuitive reporter would grasp that he has contempt for "the Winston Resolution," but intuition is in short supply). When an interviewer mentions his reticent manner, LaRuth smiles and says that he is not modest or diffident, he is pessimistic. But his mother is ecstatic. His secretary looks on him with new respect. Annette thinks he is one in a million.

No harm done. The resolution is redrafted into harmless form and is permitted to languish. The language incomprehensible, at the end it becomes an umbrella under which anyone could huddle. Wein is disillusioned, the media looks elsewhere for its news, and LaRuth returns to the House Education and Labor Committee. The work is backed up; the school bill has lost its momentum. One month of work lost, and now LaRuth is forced to redouble his energies. He speaks often of challenge and commitment. At length the bill is cleared from committee and forwarded to the floor of the House, where it is passed; many members vote aye as a favor, either to LaRuth or to the chairman. The chairman is quite good about it, burying his reservations, grumbling a little, but going along. The bill has been, in the climactic phrase of the newspapers, watered down. The three years are now five. The billion is reduced to five hundred million. Amendments are written, and they are mostly restrictive. But the bill is better than nothing. The President signs it in formal ceremony, LaRuth at his elbow. The thing is now law.

The congressman, contemplating all of it, is both angry and sad. He has been a legislator too long to draw obvious morals, even if they were there to be drawn. He thinks that everything in his life is meant to end in irony and contradiction. LaRuth, at forty, has no secret answers. Nor any illusions. The House of Representatives is no simple place, neither innocent nor straightforward. Appearances there are as appearances elsewhere: deceptive. One is entitled to remain fastidious as to detail, realistic in approach.

CONGRATULATIONS FOLLOWED. In his hour of maximum triumph, the author of a law, LaRuth resolved to stay inside the belly of the whale, to become neither distracted nor moved. Of the world outside, he was weary and finally unconvinced. He knew who he was. He'd stick with what he had and take comfort from a favorite line, a passage toward the end of *Madame Bovary*. It was a description of a minor character, and the line had stuck with him, lodged in the back of his head. Seductive and attractive, in a pessimistic way. *He grew thin, his figure became taller, his face took on a saddened look that made it nearly interesting.*

MARY MCCARTHY

A popular novelist and memoirist who wrote *The Group* (1963) and *Memories of a Catholic Girlhood* (1957), Mary McCarthy (1912–89) was also an uncompromising essayist who authored three books criticizing the policies of the Johnson administration — *Vietnam* (1967), *Hanoi* (1968), and *Medina* (1972) — and also wrote a group of essays on the Watergate hearings, collected under the title *The Mask of State: Watergate Portraits* (1974). McCarthy was at her best outlining the social, rather than military, costs of America's presence in Vietnam, but she was at her boldest when she was virtually the first to propose that the American military presence there simply had to stop, no matter what. *The Mask of State*, which offers shrewd sketches of most of the key figures in the Watergate scandal, was written from inside Washington, by "a Watergate Resident."

From "Notes of a Watergate Resident"
In *The Mask of State: Watergate Portraits*

JUNE 24, 1973

This has been the week of the so-called Brezhnev recess. Senator Ervin's panel, in order not to embarrass Nixon before his Soviet guest, voted to suspend the Watergate hearings during the state visit. Otherwise we might have had the treat of seeing the First Secretary of the party among the foreign spectators in the Senate Caucus Room, seated in the first row with his translator and his body guards while John Dean testified to whatever he is going to testify — despite leaks, no one yet can be sure. A functionary from the State Department (or maybe General Haig?) could have briefed the Brezhnev party on the curious and to them perhaps Swiftian workings of democracy. Instead, Washington has been waiting irritably for Brezhnev to go home, so that traffic can be restored to normal and Dean can at last be heard. On the personal side, I ought to be grateful for the postponement. For the first time since I have been here, I have leisure to look around at the physical setting of the Watergate break-in and to think a little about the moral setting or "ecology" out of which it emerged.

I get an appreciative chuckle whenever I tell people I am staying at the Watergate Hotel. Even before the break-in, the ten-acre aggregate comprising three co-operatives, the hotel, and two office buildings began to tickle the public fancy because the Mitchells lived here — in the co-operative known as Watergate East — at the time when Martha, looking out of the window of her husband's office downtown at the Justice Department, watched "the very liberal Communists, the worst kind" demonstrating in the street below.

Now the Mitchell tenure here and that of Maurice Stans are only vaguely recalled; what tourists come to look at and be photographed in front of are the office building, where the Democratic National Committee had its headquarters on the sixth floor, and the more plebeian red-roofed Howard Johnson Motor Lodge, opposite, where the listening-post of the wire-tappers was situated. Tourists also roam through the hotel lobby, buy Watergate joke material, including bugs, at the newsstand, and take a peep at the Watergate Terrace Restaurant overlooking the outdoor swimming pool (restricted to co-operative residents; there is an indoor swimming pool, with sauna, for hotel guests), where McCord and his men are supposed to have had a lobster dinner before the break-in.

As the hotel literature puts it, "The Watergate Complex, one of the most distinctive private real estate developments in the nation, offers a way of life that is complete in every respect . . . for you, the visitor, as well as for those who reside and/or work in this pace-setting community." Designed by an Italian architect, the whole complex, with the exception of the office buildings, bristles with rows of stony teeth, which are a sort of coping around the balconies opening off nearly every room. The impression is of an updated medieval fortress, quite extensive, and between Watergate East and Watergate South there is what looks like a Bridge of Sighs, topped by an American flag. Those uniform gray-white teeth projecting from the curious swollen shapes, elliptical, wedge-like, semi-circular, of the building units, suggest a sea animal — a whale, somebody said, but also something sharkish. To assure privacy, balconies are separated from each other by what seem to be cement fins. Maybe the marine imagery is meant to be in harmony with the Potomac setting. The teeth, on close inspection, turn out to be made of tiny stones pressed into cement, giving a scaly effect.

Even though it is summer and not always too hot, almost nobody appears on the balconies, which are the main architectural feature; empty garden furniture stares out from them on the landscaped grounds. Once I saw a single figure, a fat woman in a pink wrapper, wander ghost-like behind her toothy parapet. Yet at some point in time, as the Ervin Committee witnesses express it, somebody must have used my balcony, for when I arrived, ten days ago, two empty beer cans (Budweiser) were lying there; this morning, finally, they were gone — the window-washer had come by. On a few of the co-operative balconies, there are some ill-tended, long-suffering flowering plants. The cells of this "community" are not neighborly; no voices call across the outdoor expanse, and the rooms are effectively sound-proofed.

The sense of being in a high-security castellated fort or series of forts is added to by lower-level passages, known as Malls, which constitute a labyrinth. The whole place, in fact, is a maze, marked here and there by highly misleading signs directing you to "*Les Champs*," "Mall," "Restaurant," "Arcade." When you try to follow them, you either go round in circles or end up against a blank, no-entry wall. It is as if there were a war on, and the red, green, and blue directional arrows had been turned to point the wrong way in order to confuse the enemy expected to invade at sunrise. Every day, so far, I have got lost in this eerie complex, hoping to find an Espresso bar that was rumored to exist somewhere in the vicinity of "*Les Champs*." Once I found myself in "Peacock Alley," and another time standing on the verge of the forbidden swimming pool. Yesterday, though, I reached the goal, following the instructions of a porter: "You just keep goin' around."

This Kafkian quest for the Espresso bar had an economic motive. I was comparison-shopping the breakfasts available. The People's Drugstore, in a "popular" region of the Mall near the hotel, is the cheapest, offering fruit juice, toasted English muffin, grape jelly, and coffee for sixty cents; the Howard Johnson, across from the famed office building, is the best value, giving you the same but with a better muffin and a choice of grape jelly or marmalade for eighty cents; the hotel Terrace Restaurant calls this — with an inferior muffin but more copious marmalade — a Continental breakfast and charges two dollars and fifty cents. The Espresso bar, which doubles as a hot-dog stand, does not serve breakfast, it turns out, but is a fairly good value for a sandwich- or salad-and-coffee lunch. It too has a "popular" clientele, and it was there I heard a young girl, yesterday, say to her friend, "Senator Ervin? I heard him on the radio. He's real sharp."

The main attraction, though, of the Watergate complex was intended, evidently, to be the shopping, ranging from low-cost, lower-level (the People's Drugstore and a Safeway, where Senator Brooke, they say, can be seen with a shopping bag full of groceries), to unarmed robbery in "*Les Champs*." There are Pierre Cardin, Gucci, Yves St. Laurent, Enzo Boutique for men, located in the "exclusive" end, and Saks and more moderate shoe and dress shops along the arcade. But you can buy almost any kind of goods and services, short of guns or a suit of armor, in these labyrinthine ways: wigs, pottery and china, jewelry, antiques, Uruguayan handicrafts, patchwork, Swedish everything, Oriental everything, flowers, liquor (including Watergate brands of scotch and bourbon, now much in demand by souvenir hunters), insurance, air tickets and hotel reservations. In the Mall, there are an optician and a U.S. post office; a bookstore, the Savile, has gone out of business and a cheese shop is moving into the space. On the street level there are a bank and a building-and-loan association. As the hotel flyer indicates, the idea has been to make Watergate as nearly as possible self-sustaining. As though it were under siege.

This, I suppose, is the Watergate mentality, in a more general sense: a compound of money, the isolation or insulation it can buy, and fear. Though conceived as a cosmopolitan center, the result is rather pathetically suburban and middle-American. What it boils down to is not very different from any of the so-called shopping malls along U.S. highways. Except that they can usually support at least a paperback bookstore.

The hotel employment policy seems to be somehow meaningful and to imply a curious notion of classification, like that distinguishing the Malls from the Arcade and "*Les Champs.*" Downstairs, in front, the help is mainly Spanish-speaking — one imagines a staff of brown-uniformed Cuban defectors, potential recruits for CREEP and the CIA. In the Terrace Restaurant, again Spanish-speaking, but in red uniforms and with a few Southeast Asians and East Europeans added — more CIA material? Upstairs, the chambermaids and maintenance men, who constitute the core of the hotel invisible from below, are nearly all black; I think of Ralph Ellison and his invisible man. Probably there is a key to employment policy here that eludes me; maybe it is artistic — a matter of subtle color blends and contrasts, designed to please the eye.

A FRENCH FRIEND, in town for a picture story on the hearings, says he thinks that the Americans are using Watergate to cleanse themselves of guilt for Vietnam. As he says this, a light goes on in my mind. Yes, he is right; if it had not been for Vietnam, the scandal of the break-in might have soon dropped from notice like previous scandals — a tempest in a teapot.

I had assumed it was just luck, a happy coincidence of independent factors — the zeal of the Washington *Post* in tracking down the story, Judge Sirica's determination to be told the truth, the early leaks coming from the Justice Department and the FBI — that had brought about disclosure and led to what is now spoken of as a turning point in the nation's history or at least of Richard Nixon's place in it. None of these factors singly would have sufficed, but all of them converging, plus Senator Ervin, did it, and many editorialists took pride in this as showing that the American system — the judiciary, the press, the Congress — worked to curb the arrogant power of the executive. No doubt this is true (though we have not yet seen the end), but without another factor — Vietnam — the pursuit of truth, I now feel, might have been less vigorous and public interest slight.

Because of Vietnam, the country suddenly wants to be "*clean,*" as my French friend said. Watergate is the scrubbing brush, sometimes painful to the skin, since it is not easy on the national touchiness to have all those cosmetics scrubbed away. Watergate hurts many simple patriots, to the point where they don't want to hear about it. This is understandable when you think of Nixon's "landslide"— the millions of voters who must to some degree have identified themselves with the image he presented on the TV screen. What is surprising is the turnabout: the vast numbers that now watch the rapid erosion of that image without too much complaint. Most of those viewers participated with Richard Nixon and with LBJ before him in the crime of Vietnam.

It is worth examining the fact that those most prominent now in the pursuit of truth about Watergate (i.e., about the character-potentialities of the President; what may he still be capable of?) were not, to say the least, among the leading opponents of the war in Vietnam. I do not know Judge Sirica's voting record but I do not recall seeing his name on any peace manifesto; the same for Archibald Cox. Of the senators on the Ervin Committee I wonder how many took a stand against the war. Well, on the McGovern-Hatfield amendment cutting off funds for Indochina after December 31, 1971 — scarcely the acid test — two, Montoya and Inouye, voted Yes. We know the position of Goldwater, who is now calling for the truth, and I believe he means it. Judge Sirica, most of the senators of the Committee, and Goldwater must be fairly representative of that almost consistent majority that answered "Approve" when asked by pollsters for their opinion of U.S. policy in Vietnam.

The innocent in that crime, if anybody can be considered so, i.e., the liberals and radicals who spoke out and demonstrated, have been taking rather a back seat in the Watergate investigation. As far as the Congress goes, this is being ascribed to a Democratic party strategy of letting the Republicans carry the ball, to avoid giving any appearance of narrow partisanship: let his own party call for Nixon's impeachment or go to him and demand that he resign. No doubt that strategy is operating, but there is something deeper involved that has compelled conservatives of both parties to play leading roles in the investigation and compels ordinary lifelong Republicans to demand the truth almost more loudly than the rest of us — possibly because they had had no suspicion of it before.

One can say that Watergate is a good test to determine who is really a conservative and who just pretends to be: Goldwater passes the test; Senator Ervin passes with honors; Agnew fails; William Buckley gets a D. But are there, then, as many true conservatives in the country as poll results on Watergate (58 per cent think Nixon was in on it, after if not before) by this criterion would seem to show? I wonder, having found it difficult in my private, pre-Watergate experience to meet more than one or two, though I have gone out with a Diogenes lantern.

It might be safer to conclude that 58 per cent of the nation still has some common sense left and can be trusted to serve on a jury. But I will go further and say that a considerable per cent of that per cent (reducing the figure to allow for those who think Nixon guilty but regard it as "just politics," who are in other words a-political and don't care) has a conscience. On which Vietnam has weighed. Despite all rationalization. Napalm, defoliants, area bombing, Lazy Dogs, anti-personnel missiles, these means to achieve an end presumed to be virtuous have cost this country much secret pain.

ROBERT COOVER

Like other postmodern writers, Robert Coover (1932–) works from the premise that all system making is a fiction. In *The Public Burning* (1977), he explores this idea as it applies to the Cold War, when the United States and the Soviet Union considered themselves locked in mortal combat over control of the world, particularly during the three days in June 1953 that preceded the execution of Julius and Ethel Rosenberg. Coover sees the Rosenbergs as the victims of a conception of history in which any number of institutions — the Senate, the judiciary, the president, the press, the FBI — conspired to put them to a ritualistic death. Much of the book is surrealistically narrated by a young senator named Richard Nixon as he bumbles his way through this early, defining crisis in his political career, a strangely sympathetic schlemiel figure.

From "Idle Banter: The Fighting Quaker among Saints and Sinners"
In *The Public Burning*

My old California colleague Bill Knowland was in trouble in his first test as the new Republican floor leader in the Senate, so on the way back to my office Thursday from the emergency meeting of the National Security Council at the White House, I stopped by the Capitol to see if I could be of help. The Hill and Mall were swarming with demonstrators, counterdemonstrators, tourists, cops, dogs, kids, and there were expressions of worry, gloom, apprehension, uncertainty everywhere. There'd been too many setbacks. In the middle of all this, Knowland had decided to pull a fast one: after having told the Minority Leader Lyndon Johnson earlier that there'd be nothing more controversial today than the call of the calendar — which few Senators even bother to show up for — he'd suddenly decided to interrupt the call with an aggressive attempt to ram our new controls bill through and catch the Democrats flatfooted. I wasn't sure Bill was doing the smart thing, but I understood his motives and had to admire them: he'd just taken over from the ailing Bob Taft, and he was trying hard to put his personal stamp on the leadership job, make it his through partisan conflict. It wasn't easy to follow a living legend like Taft, Bill had to do something audacious to signal the change and establish his authority. Of course, he could blow it, too, and the chances were just about fifty-fifty — with Wayne Morse now voting with the Democrats, there were forty-eight votes on each side of the aisle, and my vote was the tie-breaker. I was eager to get back to the Rosenberg case, things were in a mess now, thanks to Douglas, and I didn't know what the hell was going on or what I was supposed to do, but Eisenhower's relationship with Congressional Republicans was so fragile, we couldn't afford to antagonize them in any way — I had no choice but to be on hand and save the day for Knowland if need be. Besides, it was just the kind of political battle I loved: nobody gave a shit about the bill itself, it was a straight-out power struggle, raw and pure, like a move in chess.

On the way in, I saw Bob Taft. The poor bastard, he looked like hell. Mr. Republican. Fighting Bob. The Go-It-Alone Man. He was going it alone now, all right: he was dying, hip cancer apparently, probably wouldn't last the year out. On the side of the angels now. There were some reporters hovering around him, looking very sympathetic, and since sympathy from those sonsabitches was something I rarely enjoyed, I decided Fighting Bob could share a little of it with me, he wasn't going to need it much longer anyway. "Say, Bob," I called out, moving in, "I have news for you!" Taft knew where I'd been that morning, knew about the Korean and German and Rosenberg crises — the whole Capitol was obviously ass-deep in the usual rumors, prophecies, and panic — and so of course he was all ears. He was on crutches and appeared to have lost a lot of weight (which was maybe why he seemed to be "all ears"), but he stretched forward eagerly as though reaching for a cure. The newsguys all turned to me, grabbing for the pencils tucked behind their ears, and photographers snatched up their cameras — I quickly lifted my chin and raised my eyebrows, conscious that my stern Quaker eyes and heavy cheeks often gave me an unfortunate scowly sinister look putting a whole different slant on what I was saying (isn't that a hell of a thing — that the fate of a great country can depend on camera angles?), and said: "I broke a hundred at Burning Tree Sunday, Bob!"

The senator shrank back as though suddenly aged, but he smiled and congratulated me. I bowed acknowledgments, smiling generously, trying to make the best of it, but I was suddenly sorry for him, felt suddenly like a brother, regretted my little joke — hadn't he said when he fell ill that the first thing he'd noticed was a great weariness when he started "whaling golf balls" early last spring? Shit, I was just rubbing it in. I wanted to reach out and embrace him, give him my shoulder to lean on instead of those damned crutches, make him well again, make him President or something.

We went on talking about golf, he seemed cheerful enough, but I felt like hell. I saw that the news reporters had stopped grinning, too, most of them had turned away. I'd been misunderstood again. I'd only wanted to give Taft something to laugh about in these troubled times, I'd meant no harm. He was one of the few guys, after all, who'd stood by me through the Fund Crisis last fall — even if the reason was that he was afraid Bill Knowland would be the guy to take my place. Taft had made a lot of mistakes, but he still might have gone to the White House if he hadn't opposed NATO and collective security in Europe — what the hell, let's fact it, he would have gotten there anyway if a few of us hadn't axed him, he could have won last year, that was clear now. And but a few short weeks ago, he was the most powerful man outside the White House in all America — maybe the most powerful Senator in history. Cut down. Last summer he'd been my enemy. It was I who'd busted up the unity of the California delegation and so assured Eisenhower of the Party's nomination, had beat him out myself for the vice-presidential nomination — but now, looking at him there, shrunken, held up by those crutches, smiling gamely, his belly hanging low in his pants, I thought: Jesus, he's a goddamn saint! I wanted to tell him everything, about the National Security Council meeting, about my talks with Uncle Sam, about the moves soon to be made, about the Rosenberg letters strewn around my office, about my hopes, my fears, the whole works.

I remembered the time he came to my office and asked for my support for the Party's presidential nomination — me, just a green junior Senator from California — and I'd had to put him off. I think in part I objected to the fact he'd asked me. As though he'd demeaned himself. It was too personal, coming to my office like that. It embarrassed me — it flattered me, too, but mostly it made me uneasy, and I didn't want to have anything more to do with him. Besides, with him I had no shot at something bigger myself. It must have been a terribly difficult thing for him to do, I could never do it, I could never walk into some other guy's office and ask him to help make me President, any more than I could fly. I could send somebody else, but I could never do it myself. But now, if he'd come today, I thought, I'd have said yes. Now that it was too late. He smiled feebly but kindly, adjusted his clear horn-rimmed spectacles, said we'd have to get up a game soon, shifted his weight, and hobbled away on his crutches, showing me his bald spot like a kind of halo. Was *he* needling *me* now? I wanted to call out to him, but I didn't.

This often happened to me, this sudden flush of warmth, even love, toward the people I defeat. It worried me, worries me still. It could backfire someday. Back when I was in the Navy, I wrote a note to myself on the subject, I have it still, taped inside my desk drawer: DON'T BECOME OVERGENEROUS ON THE SPUR OF THE MOMENT! But I kept forgetting. It was a weakness. Already some people were complaining I'd made too much of the tragic side of the Alger Hiss case, been too insistent in pointing out his intelligence, sensitivity, idealism, should never have said that I thought he was sincerely dedicated to the concepts of peace and of bettering the lot of the common man, of people generally — I might as well say as much for the goddamn Phantom. But once it was over, once I'd nailed the lying supercilious bastard for good, I couldn't help myself. There's something that makes me want the happy ending. Most conflicts are irresolvable, I know that, someone wins and someone loses, someone's on the right side, someone's on the other side, and what resolutions are possible are got afterwards by way of the emotions. I learned that way back in the seventh grade, first time I beat those girls in the now-famous Insect Debate. I'm no believer in dialectics, material or otherwise, let me be absolutely clear about that, I wouldn't be Vice President of the United States of America if I was, it's either/or as far as I'm concerned and let the best man win so long as it's me. But I want these emotional resolutions when the fights are over.

People misunderstand me. They think it's all vindictiveness. It isn't. Personal hatred is a big waste, it's as simple as that. Issues are everything, even when they're meaningless — these other things like emotions and personalities just blur the picture and make it difficult to operate. But it feels good to indulge in them when it no longer matters. I've often said that the only time to lose your temper in politics is when it's deliberate and useful. I don't always live up to that, I'm human, but I still believe it. I'm a tough sonuvabitch to run against in an election, everyone knows that by now, they say I'm a buzzsaw opponent, ruthless and even unscrupulous, they say I go for the jugular, no holds barred, or as Stevenson put it, "Nixonland is the land of smash and grab and anything to win," and discounting the partisan hyperbole, that's largely true, I guess. You've got to win, or the rest doesn't matter. I believe in fighting it out, in hitting back, giving as good as you get, you've got to be a politician before you can be a statesman, I've said that and it's so. No ruffed-shirt, kid-glove, peanut politics for me. As Uncle Sam once told me: "Politics is the only game played with real blood." I didn't want to believe him at the time, I wanted it to be played with rhetoric and industry, yet down deep I knew that even at its most trivial, politics flirted with murder and mayhem, theft and cannibalism.

But — maybe because I do know that — I've always thought of myself as a healer as well. I was always breaking up fights between my brothers, saving them from Dad's whippings, calming tempers at school, it was I who stopped the ugly brawl between Joe McCarthy and Drew Pearson in the Sulgrave Club washroom two and a half years ago (people thought I was siding with Joe, but actually I was saving Pearson's life: Joe had heard from some Indian that if you kneed a guy hard enough in the nuts, blood would come out of his eyes, and he was eager to test this out), and it was I who bridged the generations in the Republican Party and brought its warring sides together for victory at last this past fall, I who now kept the peace between the President and a truculent Congress. I was Eisenhower's salesman in the Cloakrooms, that was my job, I was the political broker between the patsies and the Neanderthals, I had to cool the barnburners, soften up the hardshells, keep the hunkers and cowboys in line, mollify the soreheads and baby tinhorn egos, I was the flak runner, the wheelhorse, I had to mend the fences and bind up the wounds. Yes, bind up the wounds: I'm a lot like Lincoln, I guess, who was kind and compassionate on the one hand, and strong and competitive on the other. I gave Voorhis no quarter, for example, when I beat him for his seat in Congress in 1946; I called him a puppet of the Communists, hit him with dirty broadsides, anonymous phone calls, the whole lot, and I meant it when I said there was scarcely ever a man with higher ideals than old Jerry Voorhis, even if, like Alger Hiss and a lot of other insolent bums I've run into out there, he did come from Yale.

Probably I got this from my mother. My father was a scrapper, a very competitive man, cantankerous even and aggressive, he loved to argue with anybody about anything, and he always instilled this competitive feeling in all of us, we owed him a lot, my brothers and I, even if sometimes we hated his guts. But my mother was just the opposite, a Quaker, a peacemaker, and she taught us — showed us — charity and tolerance and the need to keep your feelings about people separate from your feelings about moral questions. People were weak, of course they were, but that didn't mean you were supposed to stop loving them, even as you punished them. When my father's Black Irish temper reared up inside him and he went for his strap or rod, she wouldn't interfere, she understood the need for rules and the need for punishment and stood by watching while he laid it on (Jesus! he could really set your ass on fire, he scared the hell out of me early on and I learned how to avoid the beatings, even if I had to lie or throw off on others, but he pounded Don's butt to leather and I used to worry he'd broken poor Harold's health and crushed little Arthur's spirit, I still have nightmares about it), but afterwards she always made him forgive us — some of our best family moments came after the strappings were over and Mother was getting us all together again. I suppose I've got something of both of them in me — "The Fighting Quaker." TIME had called me after my nomination last summer, and that was probably the closest anyone had ever got to summing me up. "Richard M. Nixon: Change Trains for the Future." I liked that touch, it took me back to my childhood in Yorba Linda, and identified me with the westward sweep of Uncle Sam's evangel. Of course, there were the Democrats' inevitable malicious jokes later about "the crash of the Federal Express" after the trainwreck here in Washington. And I wasn't too happy about the anonymous parody I got in the mail shortly after that, titled

"The Farting Quacker," with a picture of me like a train engine chugging butt-backwards — was it my fault I had stomach problems? Some agent of the Phantom, I supposed, like all pornographers and irreligionists. I was used to it by now, I'd been called just about everything as far back as I could remember. When I was in high school, our Latin class put on a play based on Virgil's *Aeneid*, it was maybe the most romantic thing that ever happened to me — I was Aeneas and Ola was Queen Dido and we wore white gowns and fell in love — but even then they started called [sic] me "Anus" and not even Ola could keep from giggling. Years later, when I was in the Navy, I realized we could have called her Queen Dildo, but we were all too green at the time to know about that. It was amazing we knew about anuses.

I stopped in the Chamber but things were dead in there. Bill Langer was reading off a list of aliens who were being let into the country as permanent residents, and George Smathers and silver-headed old Pat McCarran were making wisecracks about all the goofy names. When Langer was done, Smathers got the floor and announced: "I wish to commend the distinguished Senator from North Dakota for his linguistic ability!" The farmers up in the gallery laughed. Smathers waved at me, and I nodded. He was maybe the best friend I had over here, even if he was a Democrat. We were Senate classmates. In the Florida spring primaries, he'd defeated Senator Claude Pepper by calling him Red Pepper and a nigger-lover. I'd studied his techniques and turned them against the Pink Lady in California, a "brilliant campaign," as Herb Brownell said, that laid the groundwork for our Party's national success last fall. Smathers was apparently filling in today as Minority Leader while Lyndon Johnson was out getting his troops formed up for the vote to come — he was showing a lot of promise. Knowland was absent as well, Bob Hendrickson doing the Leader's job for us. Things were quiet yet stirring. Even with the Chamber at low tide, you could smell the impending battle. My own presence here was electrifying in itself.

I let Bill Purtell, the acting pro tem, know I was around, then wandered back to the Republican Cloakroom. Ev Dirksen, another classmate of mine, was in there, and when he saw me he hunched his shoulders and snarled like a lion — with that curly hair, he looked like one, too! I grabbed up a chair as though to fend him off, cracked an imaginary whip. This got a lot of laughs from the old boys standing around (I have a sense of humor like everybody else, I don't know why people doubt this), and Ev shrank back, making a sad face like the Cowardly Lion. He was making fun of course of all the pictures in newspapers and magazines of late showing me in the lion's cage with Sheba, part of my initiation into the Saints & Sinners Club of circus fans. I had suggested through intermediaries that this would be a good year for my old law school at

Duke to give me an honorary doctorate, but for some goddamn reason they'd refused me — me, the Vice President of the United States! Some malicious left-wing Democratic cabal on the faculty, I assumed. The rumor I heard was that it was because of the Dean's Office break-in when I was in my last year there, but that was a lot of sanctimonious bullshit — every student breaks into the Dean's Office to steal exams or find out results, most common prank in the world, it was just an excuse. So hurriedly, since I'd left this gap in my schedule, we'd arranged this initiation into the Saints & Sinners. Just as well. I'd got a lot more publicity out of it. Though not all the photos were flattering: When Sheba took offense — maybe at the smell of Checkers on me — my own reflexes had been pretty quick, and the news-guys had unfortunately caught the moment of panic. Later, they told me she'd only been yawning, but I didn't believe it.

"Hey," Ev rumbled, "I guess you heard about the Rosenbergs taking the Fifth Amendment . . .?"

"Oh yeah?"

We all perked up.

"Yes, they refused to answer on the grounds that it might tend to incinerate them!"

Dirksen grimaced comically and we all responded with groans and laughter.

JOSEPH HELLER

Although his *Catch-22* (1961) is one of the most popular antiwar novels of all time, Joseph Heller (1923–99) was never much of a political activist or one who traded on his celebrity in Washington politics. His one highly charged political play, *We Bombed in New Haven* (1968), was aimed at Johnson and Humphrey for their deceit in promulgating the Vietnam War. He also wrote a novel of Washington politics during the Nixon-Kissinger years, called *Good as Gold* (1979). It blames Richard Nixon, Henry Kissinger, their predecessors, and the corrupt values and political culture of Washington for the profound erosion of civic faith that defined the country's general mood during the 1960s and early 1970s.

From *Good as Gold*

Everything in Ralph Newsome's office in Washington had a bright shine but the seat of his pants. Gold had been greeted at the elevators by a young girl with a pretty face who turned him over to a stunning woman near thirty with straight black hair and a sheer, very expensive dress that clung bewitchingly to her incredibly supple figure, who conducted him at length to Ralph's secretary, a sunny, flirtatious woman of arresting sensual warmth who won his heart instantly with her seductive cordiality and caressing handshake. Everything in view gleamed with a polished intensity that made electric lighting, on these premises, seem superfluous.

Ralph had aged hardly at all. He was tall and straight, with languid movements, freckles, and reddish-brown hair parted on the side. What Gold remembered most clearly about Ralph was that he never needed a haircut or ever looked as though he'd had one. He wore a tapered, monogrammed shirt and his trousers looked freshly pressed. He was still, somehow, the only graduate of Princeton University Gold — or anyone Gold knew — had ever met.

"I hope you had fun last night," Ralph opened innocently. "This town is just bursting with good-looking women who will do almost anything for a good time."

Gold curtly answered, "I was tired when I got in. I wanted a rest."

This was a lie. Rather, he had spent the evening roaming dismally from one public room of his hotel to another, hoping in vain that someone might recognize him and take him somewhere else to girls as lovely as any one of the three who'd just welcomed him.

"Gosh, Bruce, I'm happy to see you again," Ralph said. "It's just like old times again, isn't it?" Gold was silent. It was not at all like old times. "The President will be pleased I'm seeing you today, if he ever finds out. You sure do boggle his mind. He has a framed copy of your review of his *My Year in the White House* under the glass top of his desk in the Oval Office so he can reread it all day long during vital conversations on agriculture, housing, money, starvation, health, education, and welfare, and other matters in which he has no interest." Ralph was in earnest. "I'm told he already has a blowup of your proverb 'Nothing Succeeds as Planned' on a wall of his breakfast room right beside a quotation from Pliny. It's a daily reminder not to attempt to do too much."

Gold was guarded in his reply. "I'm glad," he said and hesitated. "There's still much about his book I don't understand."

"That's one of the things he likes best about your review. He was afraid you might see through him."

"See through him?" Gold shifted his feet uneasily.

"Well, we all knew he really didn't have much to write about his one year in the White House, especially since he was so busy writing about it. He probably wants you here as soon as you can make the necessary arrangements, although he probably doesn't want you making any yet. That much is definite."

"Working as what?" asked Gold.

"As anything you want, Bruce. You can have your choice of anything that's open that we're willing to let you have. At the moment, there's nothing."

"Ralph, you aren't really telling me anything. Realistically, how far can I go?"

"To the top," answered Ralph. "You might even start there. Sometimes we have openings at the top and none at the bottom. I think we can bypass spokesman and senior official and start you higher, unless we can't. You're much too famous to be used anonymously, although not many people know who you are. Got anything else in the works?"

"I'm doing a book on Pomoroy and Lieberman and there's a short piece on education I have in mind."

"How I envy you," Ralph murmured. Gold eyed him with hostility. "What's the book about?"

The question gripped Gold by the throat. "About people in America, Ralph, about Jewish people."

"I gather you're in favor. I would rush that one out while there's still time."

"Still time for what?"

"Still time to risk it. The article on education should help. We'll be organizing another Presidential Commission on education soon and you'll be appointed." Ralph buzzed his intercom. "Dusty, darling, bring in our file on Dr. Gold, will you?"

"Sure thing, honey." The beautiful woman gave Ralph a folder containing a pad on which was written absolutely nothing. "Here you are, sweetheart."

"Thanks, love."

"She's gorgeous," said Gold, when she left. "And Dusty is an exciting nickname."

"That's her real name. Her nickname is Sweets."

"You didn't call her Sweets."

"In a government office?" Ralph chided him benevolently. "Now, let's see where we are." Ralph addressed himself to the blank pad and wrote *spokesman*, *source*, and *senior official*. "We considered beginning you as a press aide, but one of the first things the boys from the press would want to know would be where does someone like you come off being a press aide. Would you like to work as a secretary?"

"It's a far cry from what I had in mind," said Gold stiffly. "I can't type."

"Oh, not *that* kind of secretary," Ralph laughed. "I mean —" he groped — "what do you call it? The Cabinet. You wouldn't have to type or take shorthand. You'd have girls like Dusty and Rusty and Misty to do that for you. Would you like to be in the Cabinet?"

Gold was more than mollified. "Ralph, is that really possible?"

"I don't see why not," was Ralph's reply. "Although you might have to start as an under."

"An under?"

"An under is a little bit over a deputy and assistant, I think, but not yet an associate. Unless it's the other way around. Nobody seems sure any more."

"Could I really begin as an undersecretary?"

"In Washington, Bruce, you rise quickly and can't fall very far. How would you like to be Secretary of Labor?"

Gold, on firmer ground now, hesitated deliberately before evincing repugnance. "I think not."

"I can't say I blame you. How about Secretary of the Interior?"

"That sounds rather dark."

"I believe they work with coal mines. Transportation?"

Gold made a face. "That smacks of labor."

"Commerce?"

"It sounds a little bit like peddling."

"You're showing excellent judgment. What about Ambassador to the U.N.?"

"Don't make me laugh."

"What do you think about Secretary of the Treasury?"

Gold pricked up his ears. "What do you think?"

"It has more tone."

"What would I have to do?"

"I think I could find out. Harris Rosenblatt would know. Most of them are very rich and seem to care about money."

"I care about money."

"But they know about it."

Gold declined with regret. "I'm not sure I'd be comfortable. I'm supposed to be something of a pacifist and a radical reformer."

"But a conservative radical reformer, Bruce," Ralph reminded.

"That's true."

"Imagine what a blessing it might be to have you in the Department of Defense."

Gold had an inspiration. "How about Secretary of Defense?"

"That's good, Bruce. Especially for a pacifist."

"But I'm not a pacifist in times of peace."

"We'll put it down." Ralph added to his list. "And then there's head of the FBI or CIA to consider."

"Would I have to carry a gun?"

Ralph didn't believe so and wrote those down too. "These are all good, Bruce. Someone with your flair for publicity could probably get your name in the newspaper almost as often as the Secretary of State."

"What about Secretary of State?" asked Gold.

"That's a thought," said Ralph.

"Wouldn't I have to know anything?"

"Absolutely not," Ralph answered, and appeared astounded that Gold even should ask. "In government, Bruce, experience doesn't count and knowledge isn't important. If there's one lesson of value to be learned from the past, Bruce, it's to grab what you want when the chance comes to get it."

Gold asked with distress, "Is that good for the world?"

"Nothing's good for the world, Bruce. I thought you knew that. You've more or less said the same in that last piece of yours. Now, Bruce," Ralph continued awkwardly, "I have to be honest. You might have to get a better wife."

"Than Belle?" Gold was elated.

"I'm sorry." Ralph was solemn. "Belle would be okay for Labor or Agriculture. But not for Secretary of State or Defense."

"Belle and I have not been close," Gold confided.

"In that case I'm happy," said Ralph. "Try someone tall this time, Bruce. You're rather short, you know. It would add to your stature if you had a tall wife."

"Wouldn't a tall wife make me look smaller?" inquired Gold.

"No," said Ralph. "You would make *her* look taller. And that would add more to your stature and make her look smaller. Andrea Conover would be perfect."

"I'm seeing her tonight. Is she tall enough?"

"Oh, easily. And her father is a dying career diplomat with tons of money and the best connections. Propose."

"Tonight?" Gold demurred with a laugh. "I haven't seen her for seven years."

"So what?" Ralph laughed back in encouragement. "You can always get a divorce. Andrea's doing a great job with the Oversight Committee on Government Expenditures. She's the reason we can't make personal phone calls any more. You know, Bruce —" Gold rose when Ralph did —"these are really our golden years, that period when men like us are appealing to all classes of women between sixteen and sixty-five. I hope you're making the most of them. A lot of them go for your kind."

"My kind?" Whatever currents of euphoria had been coursing through Gold's veins congealed.

"Yes," said Ralph.

"What do you mean by my kind?" Gold asked Ralph.

"The kind of person you are, Bruce. Why?"

"As opposed to what other kinds, Ralph?"

"The kinds of person you aren't, Bruce. Why do you ask?"

"Oh, never mind," said Gold and then decided to take the inky plunge. "Lieberman thinks you're anti-Semitic."

Ralph was stunned. "Me?" His voice was hurt and astonished. "Bruce, I would feel just awful if I thought I ever did or said a single thing to give you that impression."

Ralph was sincere and Gold was contrite. "You haven't, Ralph. I'm sorry I brought it up."

"Thank you, Bruce." Ralph was placated, and his handsome face fairly shone with grace when he grinned. "Why, I copied your papers at Columbia. You practically put me through graduate school. It's just that I really don't feel Lieberman is an especially nice person."

"He isn't." Gold laughed. "And I've known him all my life."

The strain gone, Ralph said, "Let me take these notes to Dusty and have her type them up. We're really covered a lot of ground today, haven't we?"

Gold was not certain, but never in his lifetime had he felt more sanguine about his prospects. He glanced out the window at official Washington and caught a glimpse of heaven. Through the doorway, the view of the open office space was a soothing pastoral, with vistas of modular desks dozing tranquilly under indirect fluorescent lighting that never flickered; there were shoulder-high partitions of translucent glass, other offices across the way as imposing as Ralph's, and the dreamlike stirrings of contented people at work who were in every respect impeccable. The women all were sunny and chic — not a single one was overweight — the men wore jackets and ties, and every trouser leg was properly creased. If there was a worm at the core in this Garden of Eden, it escaped the cynical inspection of Gold, who could find detritus and incipient decay everywhere. Gold could look through a grapefruit and tell if it was pink.

"You'll like it here, won't you?" said Ralph, reading his mind.

"Is it always like this?"

"Oh, yes," Ralph assured him. "It's always like this when it's this way."

Gold succeeded in speaking without sarcasm. "How is it when it isn't?"

"Isn't what, Bruce?"

"This way."

"Different."

"In what way, Ralph?"

"In different ways, Bruce, unless they're the same, in which case it's this way."

"Ralph," Gold had to ask, "don't people here laugh or smile when you talk that way?"

"What way, Bruce?"

"You seem to qualify or contradict all your statements."

"Do I?" Ralph considered the matter intently. "Maybe I do seem a bit oxymoronic at times. I think everyone here talks that way. Maybe we're all oxymoronic. One time, though, at a high-level meeting, I did say something everyone thought was funny. 'Let's build some death camps,' I said. And everyone laughed. I still can't figure out why. I was being serious."

"I think it's time for me to go," said Gold.

"I'm afraid it is. I'd give just about anything to lunch with you, Bruce, but I can't pass up the chance to eat alone. It's a pity you can't stay through the weekend, although I can't see how that would make any difference. Alma would love to have you out to see her terrarium, but Ellie would be upset."

"Alma?"

"My wife."

"What happened to Kelly?"

"I think you mean Ellie."

"Yes?"

"She got a year older, Bruce. And there was that thin scar from her Caesarean. Ellie would prefer that Alma and I don't start entertaining as a married couple until people first find out I've been divorced." To the blond woman outside his office Ralph said, "Dusty, please tell Rusty and Misty I'll be showing Dr. Gold to the elevator myself. Ask Christy to step inside my office. Tell her I'm horny."

"Sure, love. Bye, sweetheart."

"Who's Christy?" Gold asked.

"The nice-looking one. I don't think you've seen her."

"And what's all this Dr. Gold shit?"

Ralph lowered his voice. "It makes a better impression. Everyone knows professors don't make much money and doctors do. Oooooops — there goes one. Did you see that beautiful ass? Bruce, give my love to Andrea. You might find her a trifle prudish, but she's really as good as gold. It wasn't easy being the only child of Pugh Biddle Conover with all those riches and horses. They ride them, you know." Ralph pronounced this last detail as though describing a tasteless and unhealthy practice. "And give my love to Belle too. How are the children?"

"Fine. One is still at home."

"That's too bad," said Ralph. "Let me give you some good advice, Bruce, from an unofficial opinion of the U.S. Supreme Court. It was seven to one, with the other member abstaining because he was under heavy anesthesia. When you get your divorce, don't fight for custody of the children, or even visitation rights. Make them all ask to come to you. Otherwise they'll think they're doing you a favor by letting you spend time with them, which you will quickly discover they are not."

Nearing the elevators, Gold could contain his curiosity no longer. "Ralph," he said, his fingers clenching nervously, "what do you do here?"

"Work, Bruce. Why?"

"I need some assurance, Ralph, don't I? Before I start making changes, don't you think I ought to find out a few things?"

"I don't see why not."

"What kind of job do you have?"

"A good one, Bruce."

"What do you do?"

"What I'm supposed to."

"Well, what's your position exactly?"

"I'm in the inner circle, Bruce."

"Does that mean you can't talk about it?"

"Oh, no. I can tell you everything. What would you like to know?"

"Well, who do you work for?"

"My superiors."

"Do you have any authority?"

"Oh, yes. A great deal."

"Over who?"

"My subordinates. I can do whatever I want once I get permission from my superiors. I'm my own boss. After all, I'm not really my own boss."

"Well," said Gold, "what are my chances?"

"As good as they ought to be."

"No better?" Gold inquired facetiously.

"Not at this time."

"When should I get in touch with you?"

"When I call you," said Ralph. "Pugh Biddle Conover can help while he's alive," Ralph shouted into the elevator car as the doors were closing.

Gold's mind was shimmering with fantasies of approaching eminence as the car descended. Secretary of State? Head of the CIA? A voice inside cautioned, *Zei nisht naarish.* Where does someone like you come off being Secretary of State? What's so crazy? he answered it brashly. It's happened to bigger *schmucks* than me.

By the time he was outside, only one disquieting thought survived. He'd been fawning.

SUSAN RICHARDS SHREVE

As a young child, Susan Richards Shreve (1939–) moved to the nation's capital with her family. She has written ten novels and many children's books and has edited or coedited several anthologies, including *Outside the Law: Narratives on Justice in America* (1997) and *Skin Deep: Black Women and White Women*

Write about Race (1995; with Marita Golden). She is a founder of the creative writing program at George Mason University, in Fairfax, Virginia, and an original board member and past president of the PEN/Faulkner Foundation in Washington, D.C. Her third novel, *Children of Power* (1979), tells the disturbing story of a feisty high school girl and her politically well-connected family during a tumultuous week at the end of 1954, following the Senate's censure of Senator Joseph McCarthy.

From *Children of Power*

MONDAY, DECEMBER 20, 1954

Natty and Anne Lowry and Paulette sat in the study at Dick Carr's. Dick Carr was there and Peter von Troten; Choo Choo came in late with Sukey, whom she'd met at 30th. Alexander Epps sat on the floor with his eyes closed, drinking a glass of warm bourbon, dreaming of disasters. Al Cox would be there later, Dick said. This meeting was intended to be a gathering of consequence, but they would not wait for Al Cox. Carter Harold brought in pizzas.

"So," Dick Carr began. "We really wanted you here," he said to Natty. Some of the conversation had been prearranged.

"It's for your own good."

Choo Choo spoke up first. "Do you know what McCarthy did?"

"Of course," Natty said.

"I mean really," Choo Choo said. "Do you know what happened to people like my father?"

"Your father got a terrible deal," Natty said. "So did a lot of others."

"He'll never be able to work again," Choo Choo said. "At least as long as there's a blacklist."

"It's sinful," Sukey said. "Innocent people were hurt."

"Listen," Natty said, sensing the unity of the crowd against her and ready instinctively to fight.

"What concerns me, Natty," Carter Harold said with practiced resonance, spreading out on the couch to assume magnified proportions, "are your own convictions and do you have any."

"Of course I have convictions," Natty said angrily. "McCarthy was wrong. Terribly wrong in every way."

"But," Did Carr pointed out, "it's perfectly right for him to be a guest at your house."

"He's not my guest," she said. "He's not a guest at all." And then, her head clearing from the unexpected attack, she said, "McCarthy was wrong and now he's absolutely nothing. He couldn't hurt anyone."

"But he did," Anne Lowry said. "It's immoral," she said, drawing on the word without mercy.

Carter Harold crossed his arms behind his head and stretched.

"It's as though your family accepts the existence of evil as the natural condition of our lives," Sukey said.

"Shut up," Natty said, getting up.

"Supports it even," Sukey added.

"Just a second, Sukey," Carter interrupted. "There're other things to get out in the open tonight, Natty."

"Like what?" she snapped.

"Like Fil DeAngelis."

"What about him?" she said, furious at them all, but not willing to leave without a fight.

"Fil DeAngelis is someone; everyone in the whole town knows him. He's a regular bullshit hero, a kingpin, better known in these parts than Jesus Christ," Dick Carr said.

"It's not a bad deal for a girl like you with liabilities to tie up with Fil DeAngelis," Carter Harold said.

"Basically," Sukey said slowly, "it's insincere."

"What about Will Barnes?" Dick Carr said. "What do you want from a poor sweet guy like that who worships the ground you walk on?"

"You guys," Natty said, "are full of crap."

"It's for your own good, Natty," Carter Harold said. "To see a perfectly decent family like the Taylors fall apart."

"Keeping Joe McCarthy as a house guest."

"And to see what's happening to you," Sukey said.

"You know?" Dick Carr asked.

Natty left the room.

"Proof of the pudding," Dick Carr said without hesitation.

Carter Harold followed her out of the living room. She stopped at the lavatory door and slapped his face.

In the mirror above the sink she did not recognize her own face, as though she had been translated in form to another language. She got up close to the mirror and stuck out her tongue as her mother used to have her do when she was pale as a child. Her tongue was coated gray and thick as oatmeal.

"You've got *something* wrong with you," her mother would say, seeing a tongue like that. "Pretty soon, you'll come down with it and then we'll know what it is."

LATER THEY APOLOGIZED, even Carter Harold, and she practiced cheerleading with Paulette and Anne in the Carrs' recreation room. She did not forget what had happened, but she didn't want to talk about it either.

SAM TAYLOR had called Mrs. Slaughter in Putney, Vermont, once more before he left his office at five.

"No," she said. Still no word from her son, but — she laughed — you know Andrew and his piano.

He didn't know that, Sam said quickly, astonished at this new information. He had only met Andrew once, he said, and that in Washington. This was essentially a business call. Did Andrew play the piano?

"Blues," Mrs. Slaughter said across the wires of New England to the office where Sam Taylor stood. "And jazz," she said. "He's very good, but occasionally he'll begin to play at a pub and just go on and on."

"Well, thank you," Sam said. He gave Mrs. Slaughter his number at home and said her son could call him anytime.

"I'll have him call," she said.

He copied down the number in Putney and put it in his breast coat pocket.

RAMONA'S WAS A BAR behind the *Post* where reporters went, and Sam stopped in now on his way home from work. He had never gone in alone before, and only a few people recognized him. He ordered a double bourbon and drank it straightaway. And then another, which he drank more slowly and felt. Al Cox, standing on the corner of 15th Street, saw him come out, lean against the office building next at hand, rubbing his head, taking off his hat. It was obvious when he walked down 15th Street that he'd had too much to drink.

"I WAS DOWNTOWN," Al Cox now said to the group assembled in Dick Carr's study. "Doing a bunch of things," he was careful to add. "And I saw your father," he said to Natty.

"It must be later than I'd thought," Natty said. "If he's left work."

"He was drunk," Al Cox said, trying to make his voice as kind as possible.

"But he doesn't drink," Natty said. "Only a little, at parties. Not regularly."

"Perhaps," Al said, reaching over to Paulette, taking the cigarette in her mouth and puffing it grandly, "but he's been drinking today."

"Jesus," Natty said. "I wonder if something's the matter," she said. She put on her coat. "I better go home. It must be nearly six."

"Do you want a ride?" Dick Carr asked.

"You're sure about my father?" she asked Al Cox.

"Dead sure," he said. "I'm sorry, Natty. I just thought you'd want to know."

"Jeez," she said again.

On the way home Dick Carr left his hand between their thighs on the front seat. Natty was aware that it was there and didn't move away.

JOE MCCARTHY was not there. Natty had a light-headed sense of his absence when she walked in the front door and checked quickly through the dark downstairs to be certain.

Upstairs she heard her parents arguing. It was after six by the clock in the kitchen, and there was no familiar smell of dinner cooking.

She took off her coat, lit the light in the study and brought out her cello. For a long time she sat in the straight-backed chair with the bow across her knee. She was becoming someone she did not understand — as though her new self divided had stepped out into a cold night without wraps and the familiar warmness of her own body had fallen away like a comforter. Things which had been clear to her since childhood no longer made sense. Above all she wanted friends to think well of her, and they did not. She didn't think well of herself. Something had happened which she could not identify as fact but knew as she knew rottenness in the perfect fruit, soft beneath the skin. It had to do with Joseph McCarthy.

"YOU'VE BEEN drinking," Ellen said, wrapped up on the chaise, a romance folded face down in her lap. "Haven't you?"

"Yes," Sam said. "I have. I was picked up for it. That's why I'm late."

"What do you mean picked up?"

"I was very drunk," he said. "I was arrested on 15th Street and booked for disorderly conduct."

He had swung at the policeman. That he remembered. He'd been resting against a lamp post or a building, something hard which supported him, and a policeman had come up to him, perhaps only noticing he was drunk, inquiring after his well-being, but Sam had swung at him before the officer had a chance to speak. It was entirely a reflexive action.

"How did you get home?" she asked.

"By taxi."

"Will it be in the papers?" she asked, not wanting to press him, not wanting to know.

"It's doubtful. But, of course, as long as I've been booked, I'm fair game for any reporter."

In fact, he was pleased to have been caught, to know there were limits to the recent chaos in his life. He was a public man who had abused the law. His arrest was a warning to him to require laws in his private life as protection against greater chaos.

"You haven't had that much to drink," Ellen said hopefully. She dismissed circumstances out of her control, secreting them away in a bottom drawer under sweaters and old sachets, out of sight. It was only specific emergencies which she could handle, and Sam Taylor's drinking was not one of those. Like termites, eating at the interior of houses, visible too late after the damage is done, Sam Taylor's drinking was a sign of damage beyond her reach. It was not in her temperament to be angry or rail at him for his public exposure, only to pretend he had not been arrested. She tried not to read the papers anyway. She didn't like bad news.

"I feel certain this drinking has to do with Natty," Sam said.

"There's nothing wrong with Natty," Ellen said, "except that Senator McCarthy is breaking up her romance with Fil DeAngelis."

"Nonsense," he said. "Joe McCarthy hasn't the capacity to break up anything any longer."

"Rosa DeAngelis is in Wisconsin —"

"I know." Sam Taylor could not concentrate on the dusky colors of his wife across from him. She was indistinct as an Impressionist painting of flowers.

"I'm terribly sorry, Ellen," he said to her.

"Shh," she said.

"I've had too much to drink to make sense of things."

She put her fingers to her lips.

"Listen," she said.

Natty was playing. For a long time they listened, sitting across from each other in Ellen's room.

"Does she sound off to you?" Sam asked. "Or is it my head?"

"It's off," Ellen said. "She sounds terrible."

SOMETIME IN THE middle of the night Natty heard a crash under her bedroom. She got up and ran to the head of the stairs. The hallway below was dark except for the blue light at the bend of the stairs, the blue light in the living room — sufficient light to recognize the form of Senator Joe McCarthy struggling to his feet.

"What is it?" Ellen Taylor whispered, coming up behind her daughter.

"What do you think?" Natty replied, turning back to her own room.

Ellen looked down the stairwell. Joseph McCarthy was standing now, brushing off his suit. He's thrown his overcoat on the library table in the hall.

"But how did he get in?" Ellen asked.

"He has a key."

"From whom?" she asked.

"From Daddy," Natty replied, "of course." And she shut her bedroom door.

GEORGE P. PELECANOS

A native Washingtonian, George P. Pelecanos (1957–) is an award-winning crime novelist, as well as a journalist, film producer, and screenwriter (whose credits include the popular cable series *The Wire*). His many crime noir novels, all set in and around Washington, have an avid local and national readership. *Nick's Trip* (1993) is a gritty narrative of a tender, tough-guy detective trying to solve the disappearance and murder of the wife of a childhood friend. It reflects something of the rough-and-tumble of Pelecanos's own early life, first as a high school student hanging out in the Washington suburbs around Silver Spring and then as a bartender, construction worker, and salesman in a Washington far removed from national politics.

From *Nick's Trip*

The night Billy Goodrich walked in I was tending bar at a place called the Spot, a bunker of painted cinder block and forty-watt bulbs at the northwest corner of Eighth and G in Southeast. The common wisdom holds that there are no neighborhood joints left in D.C., places where a man can get lost and smoke cigarettes down to the filter and drink beer backed with whiskey. The truth is you have to know where to find them. Where you can find them is down by the river, near the barracks and east of the Hill.

An Arctic wind had dropped into town that evening with the suddenness of a distaff emotion, transforming a chilly December rain into soft, wet snow. At first flake's notice most of my patrons had bolted out of the warped and rotting door of the Spot, and now, as the snow began to freeze and cover the cold black streets, only a few hard drinkers remained.

One of them, a gin-drenched gentleman by the name of Melvin, sat directly in front of me at the bar. Melvin squinted and attempted to read the titles of the cassettes behind my back. I wiped my hands lethargically on a blue rag that hung from the side of my trousers, and waited with great patience for Melvin to choose the evening's next musical selection.

Melvin said, "Put on some Barry."

I nodded and began to fumble through the stack of loose cassettes that were randomly scattered near the lowest row of call. The one I was looking for was close to the bottom, and its plastic casing was stained green with Rose's lime. It was Barry White's first recording, "I've Got So Much to Give," from 1973. The cover art showed the Corpulent One holding three miniaturized women in his cupped hands.

"This the one, Melvin?" I palmed it in front of his face. Mel nodded as I slipped the tape in and touched the PLAY button.

Mel said, "Let me tell you somethin' 'bout my boy Barry. You done been on a bad trip with your girlfriend — you put on Barry. Barry be talkin' real pretty and shit, all of a sudden you sayin', 'I learned, baby. I sweeeear I learned.'" The bass of the Barrance came through the grilleless Realistic speakers, and Mel sensually joined in: "Don't do that. Baby, pleeease don't do that."

Melvin Jeffers had just sunk his fifth rail martini. He had begun to sing and in all probability would continue to sing for the remainder of the night. I eyed my options down the bar.

Buddy and Bubba were in place at the far right corner, seated next to the Redskins schedule that was taped to the wall, the one with the placekicker booting the pigskin through goal-posts shaped suspiciously like long-necked bottles of Bud. Buddy was short and cubically muscular with an angular face and white blond hair. Like many men who took up body building for the wrong reason, he had found to his dismay that having a pumped-up physique did nothing to diminish the huge chip that was on his shoulder. His friend Bubba also considered himself to be an athlete but was simply broad-shouldered and fat. Bubba had the pink, rubbery face that some unlucky alcoholics get and then keep after their thirtieth birthday.

I moved down the bar, picked up Buddy's mug, and with my raised brow asked him if he wanted another. Buddy shook his head and made sure I saw him look me over. I turned my attention to Bubba.

"How 'bout you, Bubber?" I asked in my best whiny, mid-sixties Brando. "You want one?"

Bubba said, "Uh-uh," then looked at his friend inquisitively, something he did every time I addressed him in this manner. In *The Chase*, a film that barely contained one of Marlon Brando's most eccentric performances, the legendary actor continually mispronounced the name of Bubba, Robert Redford's character, as "Bubber." It was a film that the Spot's Bubba had obviously missed.

I left them and, as I passed, avoided eye contact with the only remaining customer, a cop named Boyle. Buddy and Bubba were one thing, rednecks wearing ties, but I was in no mood to open that particularly poisonous, psychotic can of worms named Dan Boyle.

Instead I turned my back on all of them and began to wipe down the bottles on the call rack. I caught a sliver of my reflection in the bar mirror between liters of Captain Morgan's and Bacardi Dark, then looked away.

ALMOST A YEAR had passed since I had taken my first case, a disaster that had ended with a close friend being numbered among the dead. I emerged relatively unscathed but had caught a glimpse of my mortality and, more startling than that, a fairly obvious map for the remainder of the trip. I had three grand in the bank and a District of Columbia private investigator's license in my wallet. In my license photograph I sported a blue-black shiner below my left eye, a trophy I had earned in a Eurotrash disco while on a particularly ugly binge. Clearly I was on my way.

Though my tenure in retail electronics was over (I had made the poor career move of staging a gunfight in my former employer's warehouse), I began the year with energy. I made the yellow pages deadline, listing myself as "Nicholas J. Stefanos, Investigator," even stepping up for the boldfaced type. I bought a used pair of binoculars and a long-lensed Pentax, printed report forms and business cards, and hooked myself up with an answering service. Then I sat back and waited for the cases to roll in.

When they didn't, I began to take long, daily walks through D.C. I visited galleries and museums, spending more than one afternoon studying the large paintings of Jack Dempsey and Joe Louis in the National Portrait Gallery at Eighth and F. Several times on these visits I was followed through the cavernous halls by suspicious security guards, something I attributed to their boredom and to my progressively hangdog appearance. When I had exhausted the museums, I went to the Martin Luther King Jr. Memorial Library and renewed my card, then spent the next week in the Washingtoniana Room on the third floor, mainly in the company of street people who slept silently at the various tables with newspapers wedged in their hands. In that week I read most of the *Washington Star*'s morgue material printed between 1958 and 1961, in an effort to get a feel for those years of my life of which I had no recollection. I then discovered the European reading room at the Library of Congress and read modern history for two weeks in a row, sitting across from an ultrawhite eunuch who wore a bow tie every day and never once looked in my direction. One day I walked the pale yellow tunnel from the Jefferson Building to the Madison Building and stumbled upon the Motion Picture and Television Reading room on the third floor. I spent the month of March in that room, reading everything from scholarly works on the spaghetti western or André Bazin to something called *A Cinema of Loneliness* by a guy named Kolker. Though the room was reserved for professionals, no one questioned my presence or bothered me in any way. In fact, no one spoke to me at all. Spring came and I began to haunt the parks and gardens of the city, returning with frequency to the Bishop's Garden at the National Cathedral. Some days I would walk through cemeteries finding them a curious combination of enigmatic and the starkly real. The Rock Creek Cemetery, with its Adams Monuments, was a particular favorite.

Sometime in May I was suddenly overcome with the natural feeling that it was time to "do" something. The next morning I tied my first Windsor knot in five months and rode the Metro to Gallery Place, where I walked to the offices of Bartell Investigative Services on Eighth at H, located smack in the middle of Chinatown.

I had picked them out of the phone book at random, preferring to work in that section of town, and was surprised upon entering and filling out an application that they would interview me on the spot. But as I stood in a reception area at the front of the office, I studied the other operatives at their desks, beefy guys in tight gray suits with prison haircuts who had the appearance of aging high school linemen, and decided it wasn't for me. I stuffed the application in my breast pocket, thanked the nicotine-throated grandmother type at the desk, and walked out into the street.

I had been all right up to that point, but the experience made me aware of just how irrevocably far from the mainstream I had strayed. I entered the Ruby Restaurant around the corner and had a bowl of hot and sour soup and some sautéed squid. Then I walked to Metro Center and boarded the Orange Line for a short trip to the Eastern Market station. I crossed Pennsylvania and headed down Eighth Street.

On the corner was the bar in which I first met my ex-wife Karen. They had changed both the ownership and the décor, from early eighties new wave to rustic wild West saloon. I looked in the plate-glass window and saw cigarette-smoking Cambodians shooting pool and arguing. One of them had a wad of ones grasped tightly in his fist, his features taut as he shook the bills in his opponent's face. I kept walking.

I passed carryouts and convenience stores and cheap ethnic restaurants. I passed the neighborhood movie theater so hopelessly run down that it was no longer advertised in the *Post*, and a record-and-drug store. I passed two bars that catered to lesbians. I passed a bus stop shielding loud groups of young men wearing L.A. Raiders caps and red jackets, and quiet older folks who could no longer laugh, even in cynicism, at their surroundings. Karen and I had lived in this neighborhood during the early days of our marriage.

Toward the end of the street an MP in full dress was directing traffic near the barracks. I crossed over and headed to a bar whose simple sign had caught my eye: THE SPOT. Other than the rectangular glass in the transom, there were no windows. I pushed on the heavy oak door and stepped in.

There was a room to my right painted dark green, housing a few empty deuces and four-tops. Beer posters were tacked to three of the walls and on the fourth was a dart board.

I stepped down into the main bar, which was to the left and ran the length of the room. There were two hanging conical lamps, which dimly illuminated columnar blocks of smoke. A blue neon Schlitz sign burned over the center of the bar. Billie Holiday was singing in mono through the speakers hung on either side of the room. There were a couple of regulars who didn't glance my way and a redheaded woman behind the bar who did. I had a seat at the stool in front of the area she was wiping down.

"What can I get you?" she asked, seeming mildly interested to see a new face. She was in her twenties but had crossed the line from youthful optimism to drugged resignation.

She pulled a long-neck from the cooler and popped it with a steel opener that looked heavy as a weapon. I waved off a glass as she set down the bottle on a moldy coaster touting Cuervo Gold. After she did that she didn't walk away.

"What's your name?" I asked.

"Sherry," she said.

There was more silence as she stood there, so I pulled a Camel filter from my jacket and lit it. I blew the smoke down, but some of it bounced off the pocked mahogany bar and drifted in her direction. She still didn't move. I thought of something to say, came up blank, then looked up at the cursive neon tubes above my head.

"So," I said lamely, "you sell much Schlitz here, Sherry?"

"We don't sell it at all," she said.

"I thought, you know, with the sign and all . . ."

"We put up whatever the liquor distributors give us," she said, then shrugged and gave me a weak smile. "Fuck it. You know?"

Yeah, I knew. It was my kind of place and I was due. I returned there every day for the next two weeks and drank with clear intent.

In those two weeks I got to know some of the regulars and became a familiar face to the small staff. Sherry was, predictably, looking for other work, as was the other shift bartender, a stout-faced, square-jawed German woman named Mai who had married and then left a young marine as soon as her green card had come through. There was an all-purpose busboy/cleanup man named Ramon, a little Salvadoran with a cocky, gold-toothed smile who didn't understand English except when it had something to do with quiff or his paycheck. The cook, Darnell, worked in a small kitchen to the side of the bar. Mostly I saw his long, skinny arms as he placed food on the platform of the reach-through.

Phil Saylor was the proprietor of the Spot. He came in for a couple of hours in the afternoon and I presumed at closing time to do the book work. Saylor was an unlikely looking — short, soft in the middle, wire-rim spectacles — ex-D.C. cop, originally from South Texas, who had quit the force a couple of years earlier and opened this place. He seemed to make a living at it and to enjoy it. Certainly he enjoyed his abominable bourbon and Diet Cokes, which as owner he inexplicably opted to drink with Mattingly and Moore, the house rotgut.

Saylor's past explained the unusually large percentage of detectives on the D.C. squad who were regulars. Though the Fraternal Order of Police bar in lower Northwest was still popular with D.C.'s finest, this was a place where cops could drink without restraint and in private. And unlike at the FOP, where they were expected to unwind with "a few" after work, they could do their un-scrutinized drinking at the Spot while still on duty. In fact, in my two weeks spent with bent elbows at the bar of the Spot, it became obvious that this was a place where serious drinkers from all across the city came to get tanked in peace, without the presence of coworkers, hanging plants, brass rails, or wait-resses who overfamiliarly (and falsely) addressed them as "gentlemen."

One Monday late in May I watched the bar as Sherry and Saylor retired to the kitchen for a short discussion. I was alone in the place and had gained Saylor's trust to the point where I was allowed to help myself. I reached into the cooler and popped a Bud and nursed it for the next fifteen minutes while I listened to Ma Rainey on the deck.

Sherry emerged from the kitchen and began to gather up what looked to be her things, stuffing a romance paperback into her purse and then picking up a dusty umbrella from the side of the cooler. Her eyes were a little watery as she leaned in and kissed me lightly on the cheek before walking from behind the bar and then out the front door.

Saylor came out of the kitchen a little later and poured himself a straight shot of Mattingly and Moore. He adjusted the wire rims on his nose as if he were going to do something smart, but instead did something stupid and fired back the shot.

When he caught his breath he looked through me and said, "God, I hate that." His face was screwed tight, but I guessed he wasn't talking about the speed-rail bourbon. "I knew she was giving away drinks to jack up her tips — all of 'em do it, even the honest ones — but there was money missing, five, ten a day, all this past month. I had to let her go, man; I didn't have any choice."

"Don't worry about it, Phil." I had pegged Sherry for a gonif the first day I met her but felt I had no duty to inform Saylor. I didn't owe him anything, not yet. "You still got Mai," I said.

He nodded weakly. "Yeah, and she wants more shifts. But she's got a tem-per, man, with me *and* the customers. I don't think I can handle that German wench in here all the time." His hands spread out. "I guess I gotta go through the process of looking for a new girl."

I looked at my beer bottle and saw a thousand more like it on a hundred more dark afternoons. Then I looked into the bar mirror and saw my lips moving. They said, "Hell, I'll bartend for ya, Phil."

He pushed his glasses up again and said, "You kidding?"

"Why not? The cases aren't exactly building up," I said with understatement, then told the biggest lie of the day. "Besides, I've done some bartending in my time."

Saylor thought it over. "I never had a man behind the bar here. Can't say any of these guys would notice the difference." I lit a Camel while he talked himself into it. "I guess I could give you a few shifts, try it out. You start tomorrow?"

"Yeah," I said with the misguided, giddy enthusiasm common in long-term unemployment cases. "Tomorrow."

On the way home I stopped at the MLK Library and borrowed a book on mixology called *Karla's Kocktail Kourse*, then took it back to my apartment in the Shepherd Park area of Northwest. The book was fine (except for those ridiculous *K*'s in the title) and entertaining with its modern fifties, triangularly matted illustrations, complete with hostesses serving drinks in June Cleaver dresses and the author's insistence on displaying cocktails set next to burning cigarettes. I studied into the night; my cat, confused by my diligence, alternately circled and slept on my feet the entire time. When morning came I was ready.

But I was never really put to the test. I found, with some disappointment, that the patrons of the Spot were hardly the type to call for Rob Roys or sidecars, or any of the book's other extravagant concoctions whose ingredients I had memorized. Neither were they, as Saylor had predicted, unhappy (or happy, for that matter) to see me behind the bar. Generally, their nostalgia for the Sherry dynasty faded with my first shift and their first pop of the day. . . .

. . . FOR THE SUMMER I had four shifts a week and accumulated quite a bit of cash in the bottom drawer of my dresser. Ironically, I picked up some investigative work soon after I started at the Spot.

The first was a shadow job on the wife of a greeting-card salesman who suspected her of adultery. The salesman had out-of-town accounts and subsequently was away from home three days a week. I spent a good amount of time sitting in my Dodge at the parking lot of her office building in Rockville, smoking too many cigarettes and listening to what was becoming a decidedly boring, unprogressive WHFS. At noon I'd follow her and a couple of her friends to their lunch destination, then follow her back to the office. It wasn't until her husband left town, however, that she cut loose. On the day of his departure she left work early and drove to some garden apartments off the Pike. Two hours later she was gone and I was reading the name off her lover's mailbox. The next day they met at Romeo's apartment for a lunch boff, and I snapped his picture as he walked out the door to return to work. I gave the photos to the husband and watched his lips twitch as he wrote me a check for seven hundred and fifty dollars. It took the better half of a fifth of Grand-Dad that night to wash his broken face from my mind.

Shortly thereafter, the parents of a high school sophomore in Potomac signed me on to get to the bottom of what they hysterically perceived to be their daughter's growing interest in Satanism. I hooked up with her fairly easily through her mall-rat friends and we had lunch. She seemed bright, though unimaginative, and her devil worship turned out to be no more than hero worship. She was into Jim Morrison and her ambition, man, was to visit his grave in Paris. In the conference with her parents I told them that in my youth I had survived a fling with Black Sabbath and early Blue Oyster Cult without killing a single cat. They didn't smile, so I told them to relax; in six years their daughter would be driving to law school in her VW Cabriolet and listening to Kenny G like her other friends from Churchill High. They liked that better and stroked me a check for two hundred and a half. After that I resolved to be more selective in my cases (my bar shifts were keeping me solvent), but I'll never know if I would have held to it since in any case the phone, for the remainder of the year, neglected to ring.

Summer passed and then the fall. When I wasn't at the bar I spent my time reading, jumping rope, riding my ten-speed and, once a week, sparring with my physician, Rodney White, who in addition to being a reliable general practitioner was a second-degree black belt. Occasionally I kept company and slept with my friend Lee, a senior at American University.

The mayor's arrest on charges of possession was big news, though that event was more significant for the local media's shameful self-congratulatory arrogance and their inability to see the real story: the murder rate was at another record high and the gap was widening between the races, socially and economically, every day. But of course there was no story there, no angle. The colonizer and the colonized, just like the textbooks say.

This was also the year that I was to both lose and make two special friends. The friend I made was Jackie Kahn, a bartender at a woman's club called Athena's, located two doors down from the Spot. . . .

Jackie and I began to spend time together outside of our jobs, going to the movies or having a beer or two at some of the saner places on the Hill. She was an accountant at a Big Eight firm downtown and moonlighted at Athena's for relaxation and to escape the masquerade that was apparently more necessary for gay women than it was for their male counterparts. Occasionally she'd poke her head in the Spot to say hello, and invariably one of my regulars would boast that he could "turn one of those 'rug munchers' around" if he had the chance. This was especially exasperating coming from guys who hadn't even been mercy-fucked by their own wives for years. As our friendship developed I began to pat myself on the back for finally having a close relationship with a woman that didn't involve sex. It had only taken me three and a half decades to learn. What I didn't know then was that Jackie Kahn would have the largest role in the single most important thing that I have ever done.

The friend I lost was William Henry. Henry was a deceptively quiet young man with an offbeat sense of humor who had migrated from the South to take his first job out of college as a reporter for a local alternative weekly. I met him when he sat in on a meeting where his tabloid's sales manager pitched me on buying space when I was advertising director for Nutty Nathan's. Though I didn't step up for any ads, Henry and I discovered from that meeting that we had very similar tastes in music. I hooked up with him downtown a couple of times — once to see Love Tractor at the Snake Pit and on another night to check out a hot D.C. zydeco band, Little Red and the Renegades, at the Knight's Work — but after my career at Nathan's blew up, I heard from him only through the mail. He was that type of friend who, without an explana-tion, would send me headlines from the *New York Post* or buy me unsolicited subscriptions to Australian biker mags, publications with names like *Chrome and TaTas*.

In July, William Henry was found murdered in his condo above Sixteenth and U, just around the corner from the Third District police station. He had been stabbed repeatedly with a serrated knife. A witness had seen a thirtyish man with a medium build leave the building at the time of the murder. The man was light-skinned and wore a blue T-shirt that appeared to have been stained with blood. The Metropolitan Police spokesman said in the *Washing-ton Post* that an arrest was "eminent."

For a few days after that the *Post* ran a daily article on the slaying, returning to their favorite theme of Small-Town Boy Comes to Murder City and Meets his Fate. But when it was clear that the story would not have a pat ending, the articles stopped, and William Henry's killer was never found.

I WAS THINKING of Henry when I stepped up to Boyle that night and gave last call. Buddy and Bubber were gone, as was Melvin. He had left when I put George Jones on the deck. The tape always sent him out the door. Darnell was in the kitchen, cleaning up. I could see his willowy torso in the reach-through and hear the clatter of china, muted by the sound of his cheap radio, as he emptied the dishwasher.

Dan Boyle placed his palm over the top of his shot glass to signal he was done, then drank the rest of the beer from the bottle sitting next to it. I asked if he wanted to put the night on his tab and he nodded, seeming to look both to my right and to my left simultaneously.

Boyle was square-jawed and built like a heavyweight prize-fighter, with stubbornly short, dirty blond, Steve McQueen-style hair, circa *Bullitt*. The age in his bleached blue eyes exceeded his thirty years. He drank methodically, and when he spoke it was through the tight teeth of an angry dog.

Many of the on-duty detectives who frequented the Spot wore their guns in the bar (it was, in fact, a police regulation that they do so), and most of them got tanked up and weaved out into the night without incident. But it wasn't Boyle's weapon (the grip of his Python always showed from beneath his wool jacket where it was holstered) that was disturbing, or the fact that he even carried one. He was clearly on the edge, and he was the last guy in the bar who I ever would have fucked with.

"Hear anything more on the William Henry case?" I asked him carefully. I bent into one of the three sinks and rinsed out the green bar netting.

"You knew him, didn't you?"

"Yeah."

"Haven't heard anything," he said. "But I'll lay you ten to one your friend got burned for drug money. In this town, it all boils down to drugs. Let me tell you what it is. It's" — he glanced around the room —"it's the fuckin' boofers. You know what they ought to do about the drug problem in this city?" I didn't answer, having heard his solution a dozen times. "Take 'em out in the middle of the street and shoot 'em in the head. Public fuckin' executions."

I said, "Check on the Henry case for me, will you, Boyle?" He rose clumsily, nodded, and with a tilted, heavy gait made his way across the room and out the front door. A trace of snow blew through before the door closed. . . .

DIMMING THE LIGHTS . . . I finished wiping down the bar, placing all of the ashtrays but one in the soak sink. Then I slipped Robyn Hitchcock's *Queen Elvis* into the deck and listened to the quiet intro to "Wax Doll" as I poured myself two fingers of Grand-Dad. I brought the shot glass to my lips and with closed eyes tasted sweet velvet.

I opened my eyes to a shock of cold air and a memory fifteen years old. Billy Goodrich glided across the dark room and had a seat at the bar.

"Hey, Greek," he said. "Aren't you gonna' offer me a drink?"

JOAN DIDION

Joan Didion (1934–) was born, raised, and educated in California and continues to be identified with that state, though she now lives in New York. A successful novelist, journalist, and incisive observer of American culture, with a famous deadpan style, she became a nationally known figure with her first collection of essays, *Slouching Towards Bethlehem* (1968), followed by her first big novel, *Play It As It Lays* (1970), and then the best-selling *A Book of Common Prayer* (1977). The excerpt from "Vichy Washington, June 24, 1999" is from *Political Fictions* (2001), a collection of Didion's *New York Review of Books* essays on electoral politics and the growing dominance of political insiders in the nation's governance in the period 1988–2000.

From "Vichy Washington, June 24, 1999"
In *Political Fictions*

On an evening late in April 1999, some 350 survivors of what they saw as a fight for the soul of the republic gathered at the Mayflower Hotel in Washington to honor Representative Henry J. Hyde and the twelve House managers who, under his leadership, had carried the charges of impeachment to the floor of the Senate. C-SPAN caught the distinctive, familial fervor of the event, which was organized to benefit the Independent Women's Forum, an organization funded in part by Richard Mellon Scaife and the "women's group" in the name of which Kenneth Starr volunteered in 1994 to file an amicus curiae brief arguing that *Jones v. Clinton* should go forward. Live from the Mayflower, there on-screen were the familiar faces from the year-long entertainment that had preceded the impeachment, working the room amid the sedate din and the tinkling of glasses. There were the pretty women in country-club dinner dresses, laughing appreciatively at the bon mots of their table partners. There was the black-tie quartet, harmonizing on "Vive la, vive la, vive l'amour" and "Goodbye My Coney Island Baby" as Henry Hyde doggedly continued to spoon up his dessert, chocolate meeting mouth with metronomic regularity, his perseverance undeflected even by Bob Barr, leaning in to make a point.

The word "courage" was repeatedly invoked. Midge Decter, a director of the Independent Women's Forum, praised Henry Hyde's "manliness," and the way in which watching "him and his merry band" on television during the impeachment trial had caused her to recall "whole chunks" of Rudyard Kipling's "If." Robert L. Bartley, the editor of *The Wall Street Journal*, had found similar inspiration in the way in which the managers had "exposed truths to the American people, and they did this in the face of all the polls and focus groups,

and they were obviously doing an unpopular thing, and I think that is why
they deserve our greatest credit." The words of Henry V before the Battle of
Agincourt were recalled by Michael Novak, as they had been by Henry Hyde
in his closing statement during the Senate impeachment trial, but for this occasion adapted to "our Prince Hal, our own King Henry": "He that outlives
this day, and comes safe home, will stand at tiptoe when this day is named. . .
. Then shall our names, familiar in his mouth as household words, Henry the
King, Rogan and Hutchinson, Canady, Cannon, McCollum, Lindsey Graham, Gekas, Chabot, Bryant, Buyer, Barr, and Sensenbrenner."

This evening could have seemed, for those who still misunderstood the Reagan mandate to have been based on what are now called "social" issues, the last
redoubt. Familiar themes were sounded, favorite notes struck. Even the most
glancing reference to the depredations of "the Sixties" (". . . according to Sean
Wilentz, a scholar who exemplifies all the intellectual virtues and glories of
the Sixties . . .") proved a reliable crowd-pleaser. In deference to the man who
had not only sponsored the Hyde Amendment (banning Medicaid payments
for abortions) but who had a year before testified as a character witness for a
defendant accused of illegally blockading abortion clinics ("He's a hero to me,"
Hyde had said. "He has the guts I wish more of us had"), the "unborn" were
characterized as "the stranger, the other, the unwanted, the inconvenient."

Mentions of "Maxine Waters" were cues for derision. "Barney Frank" was a
laugh line that required no explication. The loneliness of the shared position
was assumed, and proudly stressed. Yet the mood of the evening was less elegiac
than triumphal, less rueful than rededicated, as if there in a ballroom at the
Mayflower was the means by which the American political dialogue could be
finally reconfigured: on the sacrificial altar of the failed impeachment, in the
memory of the martyred managers, the message of moral rearmament that has
driven the conservative movement to what had seemed no avail might at last
have met its moment. "As we were coming in," William J. Bennett told the
guests that night, "I said to my friend Dan Oliver, I said 'Good group.' Dan
said, 'Good group? This is it, pal. This is the army. This is all of it.'"

THE NOTION THAT a failed attempt to impeach the president might nonetheless have accomplished exactly what it was meant to accomplish, that the desired phoenix might even then be rising from the ashes of acquittal, might have
seemed to many, in the immediate wake of the November 1998 elections, when
the disinclination of the American people to see the president impeached translated into the loss of five Republican congressional seats, wishful. "It's pretty
clear that impeachment dropped off the public's radar screen," Henry Hyde
said to a *Los Angeles Times* reporter as he realized on election night that he was

losing not only his anticipated mandate but five of his votes. The next morning, in the O'Hare Hilton, he told three aides that his Judiciary Committee inquiry, which party leaders had inexplicably construed as so in tune with public sentiment as to promise a gain of twenty seats, would have to be telescoped, and impeachment delivered out of the House while his lame ducks could still vote.

Over the next several weeks, as they contemplated the unexpected hit they had taken by feeding the greed of their conservative base for impeachment, Republicans would float many fanciful scenarios by which the party could be extricated from its own device. Senator Arlen Specter of Pennsylvania argued on the op-ed pages of *The New York Times* for "abandoning impeachment," in effect handing off this suddenly sticky wicket to the courts, where, since not many lawyers saw a make-able case for perjury, it could conveniently dematerialize. Robert Dole laid out a plan based on the distinctly improbable agreement of the president in his own censure. Even Henry Hyde saw a way for the president to save the day, by resigning: "I think he could be really heroic if he did that. He would be the savior of his party. . . . It would be a way of going out with honor." By mid-December 1998, former Senator Alan K. Simpson was expressing what had become by default the last-ditch position of most Republicans, which was that any hemorrhaging they were suffering outside their conservative base could be contained before 2000 by the putative inability of these less ideological voters to remember that long. "The attention span of Americans," Simpson said, "is 'which movie is coming out next month?' and whether the quarterly report on their stock will change."

THIS CASUAL CONTEMPT for the electorate at large was by then sufficiently general to pass largely unremarked upon. A good deal of what seemed at the time opaque in the firestorm that consumed the attention of the United States from January 1998 until the spring of 1999 has since been illuminated, but what remains novel, and unexplained, was the increasingly histrionic insistence of the political establishment that it stood apart from, and indeed above, the country that had until recently been considered its validation. Under the lights at CNN and MSNBC and the Sunday shows, it became routine to declare oneself remote from "them," or "out there." The rhetorical expression of outrage, or "speaking out," became in itself a moral position, even when the reasons for having spoken out could not be recalled. ". . . Whether or not it happens," Robert H. Bork said to *The Washington Post* in December 1998 about impeachment, which he favored, "I will still think I was right. . . . I just spoke out. I think on a television show, maybe Larry King. I wish I could recall what I was concerned with, but I can't at the moment."

The electorate, as anyone who had turned on a television set since the spring of 1998 had heard repeatedly, was "complicit" in the "corruption" of the president, or of the administration, or of the country itself, which was therefore in need of the "purging" to be effected, as in myth, by the removal of the most visible figure on the landscape. "It would be an enormous emetic — culturally, politically, morally — for us to have an impeachment," the Reverend John Neuhaus, editor of the conservative monthly *First Things*, told Michael Powell of *The Washington Post*. "It would purge us." The reason the public was "complicit," and the country in need of "purging," was that the public was "materialistic," interested only in "the Dow," or, later, "their pension funds." The reason the public was "materialistic" was that the public had, well, no morals. "My wife likes to say they must be polling people coming out of Hooters on Saturday night," Senator Robert C. Smith of New Hampshire said at the time he was announcing his bid for the presidency. "I will not defend the public," William J. Bennett told *The New York Times* in February 1999, after Paul M. Weyrich had written to supporters of his Free Congress Foundation that since the nation was in the grip of an "alien ideology" they should abandon the idea that a moral majority existed and take steps to "quarantine" their families. "Absolutely not. If people want to pander to the public and say they're right they can. But they're not right on this one."

"What's popular isn't always what's right," representative J. C. Watts of Oklahoma said, arguing in the House for impeachment. "Polls would have rejected the Ten Commandments. Polls would have embraced slavery and ridiculed women's rights." On the weekend of January 1999 when the "favorable" rating of the Republican Party dropped to thirty-six percent, the lowest point since Watergate, Senator Phil Gramm said on *Meet the Press* that the people of Texas "didn't elect me to read those polls." Not even when the bumper stickers of the John Birch Society were common road sightings had we been so insistently reminded that this was not a democracy but a republic, or a "representative form of government." For the more inductive strategists in the movement, the next logical step was obvious: since a republic depended by definition on an electorate, and since the electorate at hand had proved itself "complicit," the republic itself could be increasingly viewed as doubtful, open for rethinking. "The Clinton affair and its aftermath will, I think, turn out to be a defining moment that exposed the rot in the institutions of American republican government," Charles Murray wrote in *The Weekly Standard* in February 1999. "Whether the response will be to shore up the structure or abandon it remains an open question."

Residences of Washington Authors Featured in *Literary Capital*

Henry Adams lived at Sixteenth and H streets, NW, on Lafayette Square, current site of the Hay-Adams Hotel.

Elizabeth Bishop lived at 1312 Thirtieth St., NW.

Sterling A. Brown grew up near Howard University and later lived at 1222 Kearney St., NE.

Frances Hodgson Burnett lived on 1215 I St., NW; 1739 K St., NW; and 1770 Massachusetts Ave., NW.*

John Dos Passos lived at 1201 Nineteenth St., NW.

Frederick Douglass lived at 316 A St., NE, and 1411 W St., SE (Cedar Hill, now a National Park Service historic site).

Paul Laurence Dunbar lived at 1934 Fourth St., NW, and 321 U St., NW.*

Langston Hughes lived at 1749 S St., NW, and the YMCA at 1816 Twelfth St., NW.

Sinclair Lewis lived at 1639 Nineteenth St., NW, and 3028 Que St., NW.

Alain Locke lived at 1326 R St., NW.

Archibald MacLeish lived at 1520 Thirty-third St., NW, and 607 Oronoco St., Alexandria.*

May Miller grew up next to Howard University and later lived at 1632 S St., NW.

Jean Toomer resided at 1341 U St., NW, and 1422 Bacon St., NW.

Walt Whitman lived at 1407 L St., NW; 1205 M St., NW; 994 L St., NW; 468 N St., NW; and 535 Fifteenth St., NW.*

Edward Christopher Williams lived at 912 Westminster St., NW.

* From "A Literary Map of Metropolitan Washington, D.C." (2000 Women's National Book Association/Washington Chapter)

Rampersad with David Roessel, associate editor, copyright © 1994 by the Estate of Langston Hughes. Used by permission of Alfred A. Knopf, a division of Random House, Inc.

Langston Hughes, "Lincoln Theatre" (349–50). Reprinted from *The Collected Poems of Langston Hughes* by Langston Hughes, edited by Arnold Rampersad with David Roessel, associate editor, copyright © 1994 by the Estate of Langston Hughes. Used by permission of Alfred A. Knopf, a division of Random House, Inc.

Langston Hughes, "Un-American Investigators" (350). Reprinted from *The Collected Poems of Langston Hughes* by Langston Hughes, edited by Arnold Rampersad with David Roessel, associate editor, copyright © 1994 by the Estate of Langston Hughes. Used by permission of Alfred A. Knopf, a division of Random House, Inc.

Sterling A. Brown, "Sporting Beasley" (351–52). Reprinted from *The Collected Poems of Sterling A. Brown*, selected by Michael S. Harper. Copyright © 1980 by Sterling A. Brown. Reprinted by permission of HarperCollins Publishers.

Sterling A. Brown, "Glory, Glory" (352–53). Reprinted from *The Collected Poems of Sterling A. Brown*, selected by Michael S. Harper. Copyright © 1980 by Sterling A. Brown. Reprinted by permission of HarperCollins Publishers.

Sterling A. Brown, "No More Worlds to Conquer" (353–54). Reprinted from *The Collected Poems of Sterling A. Brown*, selected by Michael S. Harper. Copyright © 1980 by Sterling A. Brown. Reprinted by permission of HarperCollins Publishers.

Allen Tate, "Aeneas at Washington" (355–56). Reprinted by permission of Farrar, Straus and Giroux, LLC, from *Collected Poems, 1919–1976* by Allen Tate. Copyright © 1977 by Allen Tate.

Archibald MacLeish, "At the Lincoln Memorial" (356–58). Reprinted from *Collected Poems, 1917–1982* by Archibald MacLeish. Copyright © 1985 by the Estate of Archibald MacLeish. Reprinted by permission of Houghton Mifflin Harcourt Publishing Company. All rights reserved.

Elizabeth Bishop, "View of the Capital from the Library of Congress" (359). Reprinted by permission of Farrar, Straus and Giroux, LLC, from *The Complete Poems, 1927–1979* by Elizabeth Bishop. Copyright © 1979, 1983 by Alice Helen Methfessel.

Elizabeth Bishop, "From Trollope's Journal" (360). Reprinted by permission of Farrar, Straus and Giroux, LLC, from *The Complete Poems, 1927–1979* by Elizabeth Bishop. Copyright © 1979, 1983 by Alice Helen Methfessel.

Allen Ginsberg, "Anti-Vietnam War Peace Mobilization" (361). Reprinted from *Collected Poems: 1947–1997* by Allen Ginsberg. Copyright © 2006 by the Allen Ginsberg Trust. Reprinted by permission of HarperCollins Publishers.

Allen Ginsberg, "Capitol Air" (361–64). Reprinted from *Collected Poems: 1947–1997* by Allen Ginsberg. Copyright © 2006 by the Allen Ginsberg Trust. Reprinted by permission of HarperCollins Publishers.